THE
HERITAGE
OF
SOUTHERN
COOKING

THE
HERITAGE
OF
SOUTHERN COOKING

CAMILLE GLENN

WORKMAN PUBLISHING, NEW YORK

Library of Congress Cataloging-in-Publication Data
Glenn, Camille.   The heritage of southern cooking.
Includes index.
1. Cookery, American—Southern style. I. Title.
TX715.G5554 1986   641.5975   86-23344
ISBN 0-89480-132-5   ISBN 0-89480-117-1 (pbk.)

Cover design: Charles Kreloff
Cover photograph: William Strode

Workman Publishing Company, Inc.
708 Broadway
New York, NY 10003

Manufactured in the United States of America

First printing October 1986
10   9   8   7   6   5

DEDICATION

◆◆◆

*T*his book is dedicated to my mother, whose sustaining faith and love for her children, and deep aesthetic sensibilities, permeated everything she did. Mother was one of the finest cooks in the South, and hundreds of people who stayed in my parents' little hotel attested to that over and over again. Her repertoire was not extensive, as she had not traveled that much, but she had an innate sense of quality and appropriateness in food. She disliked the spurious and the shabby, and she was a fiend about freshness. Mother's style in cooking was Southern, of course, and she used ham and bacon to season some dishes, but her food was never overloaded with fat, which was revolutionary for that day. Her homemade cakes and breads were divine and her hot rolls as light as feathers. Her pies became the criterion for all pies for the rest of our lives.

Mother cherished the seasons and their bounty—the June apples, the summer vegetables, and the last of the autumn garden, to be made into relishes. Our cook, Lily, and Mother would proudly display the glorious and unbelievable amount of canning they had done—tomatoes, preserves, chutneys, spiced peaches, and green tomato pickles for the winter table. Mother adored to cook game, and we had various kinds, but mostly guinea hens and quail. When the farmers brought rabbits and squirrels to the kitchen door, I knew we would have Brunswick Stew. In the spring we had freshwater fish—bass and crappie. I still dream of them. Childhood memories of flavor touch our psyches in a very special way.

There were always a good many at our family table in a corner of the large hotel dining room—brothers, grandparents, cousins, and friends—and we talked about food most of the time, or so it seemed. We absorbed Mother's enthusiasm by osmosis.

Mother had, above all, a reverence for good food, and she believed it added to the joys of life. She passed that on to me, and I have written this book with the heartfelt wish that I can pass it on to you.

ACKNOWLEDGMENTS

◆◆◆

So many friends and members of my family have helped and encouraged me all through the years with my chosen profession as a food columnist, teacher, and cookbook author that the acknowledgments would fill a small book, so it is with regret that I cannot name them.

For assistance with this book, I feel that I have been fortunate indeed to be associated with all the people at Workman Publishing. I wish to thank Peter Workman and every member of his fine staff. My sincere appreciation and thanks to Paul Hanson, Susan Aronson Stirling, and Barbara Scott-Goodman for the design and final look of this book, and to Rona Beame for finding the photographs. Last, but not least, my deep gratitude goes to my wonderful editor, Suzanne Rafer, and the talented people she worked with: Kathie Ness and Barbara Ottenhoff, and assistant Shannon Ryan.

FOREWORD

◆◆◆

"*A* woman cannot make a good book of cookery!" So thundered Samuel Johnson, in one of the few silly pronouncements he ever made. I usually agree with everything the good doctor said, but here we part company. Possibly there were no inspired female experts on food in eighteenth-century London, though I doubt that. In any case, Johnson obviously never knew the likes of Camille Glenn.

Camille Glenn has already produced cookbooks that challenge the gourmet and inspire the willing amateur. She not only knows fine food, she knows how to describe it in mouth-watering detail. Nothing is neglected—planning, preparation, pleasing presentation.

She is demanding. She suggests no shortcuts, makes no concessions to anything but first-class ingredients. She is indeed an artist, with an artist's respect for her chosen medium of expression. Now she turns her talents to *The Heritage of Southern Cooking*.

The traditional cuisine of the South has long been celebrated, though it also has been debased by inferior practitioners. Walt Whitman expressed his fascination with the region in "Longings for Home" more than a century ago. "O magnet South!" he rhapsodized. "O glistening, perfumed South! My South!" He must have written those lines just after opening the door of a Southern kitchen where the best hot bread was baking in the oven.

Camille Glenn writes as a Southerner, or more precisely, as a denizen of the Upper South that is epitomized in Kentucky. She is not the provincial type of Southerner. This sophisticated traveler and culinary expert goes far beyond the range of the usual Southern hostess.

There are familiar Southern dishes described in this book, but touched with a new seasoning of imagination and a pinch of panache. There are fresh variations on old themes. And there are also new adventures for the enterprising explorer.

The master gastronome Brillat-Savarin was very wise when he said, "The discovery of a new dish does more for human happiness than the discovery of a new star." The road to such a rich reward lies open to those who set out under the skillful guidance of Camille Glenn.

Barry Bingham, Sr.
Former owner and publisher
of *The Courier-Journal* and
The Louisville Times

CONTENTS

❖❖

MY HERITAGE OF SOUTHERN COOKING

◆◆◆

*I*t has for many years been my belief that most of us have a soft spot in our hearts for the foods that we grew up on, especially if that food was delicious. In the case of some memoirs and biographies I have read, the food was not really good but still it evoked memories, pleasant or otherwise. Such was the case of Marcel Proust, the French novelist, writing about his Aunt Léonie's stale madeleines—so stale that she had to dip them in her cup of hot tea to soften them, but the taste evoked a memory Proust recalled with love.

The exchange of letters between Thomas Jefferson and Mary Randolph, his daughter in Virginia, makes luscious reading. They not only wrote of new ideas and recipes in detail, but delineated their concerns about the garden, the orchard, and the vineyard Jefferson planned for Monticello. Even well into old age, Jefferson's writings are filled with memories of good food he had eaten in Europe as our ambassador, in the White House, as well as in Virginia. He was the quintessential gourmet.

Taste memory is a very real thing and it seems to vary greatly in people. Those who have a deep interest in wonderful food and cooking seem to have the most reliable taste memory.

I was reared in a Southern family so "food-minded" that we talked about good food all the time. Many times while we were eating a delicious meal at the family table, we would be reminded of and discuss other dishes that would have been good too, and would recall memorable meals that we had had in foreign countries, in restaurants, or at home.

My parents had a little hotel in Dawson Springs, Kentucky, a so-called health resort or spa. Mother supervised the kitchen and dining room and most every day took a hand in the cooking, she loved it so. I shall never forget her noodle board filled with drying noodles, to be served with Kentucky shoulder of veal roast. It was truly milk-fed veal, almost white and oh, so tender. They had to cook several of these roasts at a time for the hotel, and that was the richest and best gravy on earth—a light golden brown, and so very lightly thickened with flour one would never suspect it was there at all.

I can remember so well the bobwhite quail we had in the winter, sautéed to a perfect glistening brown and served always with hot biscuits and cream gravy. Oh, to taste that quail once more—it was moist and crunchy and beautiful. I think I do taste it—the picture is so clear in my mind it is almost like being there again in that large dining room with the family table in a corner. When Mother cooked something so special for us, like the crappie and bass Daddy had caught in Reelfoot Lake in Tennessee, we had to wait until the guests were gone.

Devil's Rock in Tradewater River, not far from our little town, was a good place to fish when the crappie were biting in the spring. Never shall I forget the day when I, a tiny thirteen-year-old, caught a 1½-pound crappie—and my scream was heard all the way to the old mill. Dozens of fishermen hurried to the rescue. Sorry, folks, my brother said, Camille just caught a fish, that's all. I guess that scream is still in the airwaves around Devil's Rock, and the flavor of that crappie, which Mother cooked that night, will never leave me.

We had the food of the season back then and we cannot improve upon that now. The changing seasons are our best guides still. When the snow was on the ground and the cold air had made us as hungry as all get-out, we would have Beef Brisket with Potatoes on the Half-Shell, and it would soothe our tummies and warm our bones. You couldn't improve on that today. Have this stew next winter, with a warm pudding or Windfall Apple Pie for dessert. Never a frivolous dessert after a hearty meal—the counterpoint of dishes must blend.

The June peas and new potatoes will soon be in and they are worth waiting for. Do have them with Roast Racks of Lamb or a very special treat, Veal Knuckle with Fresh Peas and Asparagus. You could introduce this meal with the most divine Fresh Asparagus Soup and use only the peas with the veal. For a glorious occasion, have Elegant and Easy Strawberry Ice or pineapple sherbet and the Golden Cointreau Cake, the most special cake in this book. The Cointreau Cake seems at its best with strawberries or pineapple, chilled or in sherbet. Ice cream is too rich.

When the large fresh shrimp come into season, do have Jumbo Shrimp and Wild Rice with Tarragon. It is one of the most exquisite shellfish dishes in all the North or the South.

Of all the crabmeat dishes in the South, the most sublime to me is Crabmeat Imperial, and it is as easy as it is elegant. Each year I wait patiently for the fresh crabmeat to come in. Maybe the favorite of most Southerners is Alabama Deviled Crab. Southerners are noted for being partial to highly spiced food. We like peppers of all kinds—chile, paprika, cayenne, pimento—every color and every kind.

Over the years I have cooked every recipe in this book, and hundreds more. I believe that delicious food is an essential part of the good life, and the hours spent in the kitchen are time well spent, and fun.

Build a repertoire of the menus you like best for your family and for parties. Cook the dishes over and over again. Memorize them—make them a part of you. Then you will be at ease with company and can reap the joy of the kitchen.

Camille Glenn
Louisville, Kentucky
September, 1986

CHAPTER ONE

APPETIZERS

BEAUTIFUL BEGINNINGS

◆◆◆

*T*he charm of appetizers and hors d'oeuvres is not only their delicious flavors but also their versatility. Because of the longer summer days in the South, they serve us well for patio parties, outdoor grilling, or for light luncheon dishes. With a touch of improvisation they make exquisite first courses served at the table in any season. Not every appetizer or hors d'oeuvre fills the entire bill, but as you work with them, you will find they are flexible indeed, and in many cases they make superb garnishes for important dinner dishes.

The Sarapico Stuffed Shrimp, for instance, is a delectable "pick-up" appetizer for cocktail parties, but served on Boston or Bibb lettuce with a wedge or two of tomato and several huge black olives, it also makes an exquisite luncheon salad or first course.

Crackers are often perfect accompaniments to serve with appetizers, but they must be bland and crisp. Their function is to lend texture and to blend, not to disturb, the flavors of the appetizers. Crackers that contain malt, powdered garlic or onion, or garlic salt are not suitable.

◆◆◆

OYSTERS ROCKEFELLER

◆◆◆

*I*n looking through my files I found a very old letter from Antoine's restaurant in New Orleans that was written in answer to my inquiry about the true origin of Oysters Rockefeller. The letter was from a descendant of Jules Alciatore, verifying that Jules, the original owner of Antoine's, had indeed created Oysters Rockefeller in 1899. The recipe was not given. Legend has insisted that Alciatore on his deathbed exacted a promise that no one would reveal the exact proportions of the recipe. It has been told, too, that when he first originated the famous oyster dish, he commented that it was as rich as Rockefeller, and the name stuck.

It is believed that watercress was used first instead of spinach, and it is rather certain there was a dash of absinthe; how much we do not know. All through the years, it has remained a classic and favorite way of preparing oysters, which is the greatest test of all—the test of time.

◆

24 oysters on the half-shell (shucked and
*   loosened; see box, page 25)*
6 cups rock salt
1 cup (2 sticks) unsalted butter, at room
*   temperature*
⅓ cup water
⅓ cup minced shallots or scallions (green
*   onions)*
2 cups packed watercress or spinach leaves
⅔ cup finely chopped fresh parsley
⅓ cup finely chopped fresh tarragon
Salt and freshly ground black pepper to taste
Cayenne pepper to taste
¼ cup chopped fennel, if available
4 teaspoons Pernod

◆

1. Place the oysters in their shells on a bed of rock salt (about 1½ inches deep) in one or more baking pans. Set aside. (The rock salt keeps the oysters upright and holds the heat while they are cooking.)

2. Preheat the oven to 450°F.

3. Combine 4 tablespoons of the butter with the water and shallots or scallions in a saucepan, and simmer until they are limp and the water has boiled away, about 5 minutes. The shallots must not brown or sizzle the least bit. Add the watercress or spinach, parsley, and tarragon. Heat only until the watercress has wilted, just a few seconds. It must not actually cook. Add the salt, pepper, and cayenne.

4. Purée the watercress mixture with the fennel, Pernod, and remaining butter in a food processor until it is perfectly smooth, less than a minute. Put a spoonful of the mixture on top of each oyster.

5. Bake the oysters on the middle oven shelf until the sauce is bubbly hot, about 5 minutes. They must not overcook.

   Serves 6

Antoine's has been a landmark restaurant in New Orleans since it opened in 1840.

VARIATION: *Shrimp Rockefeller:* Shell 24 large shrimp but leave the tails intact. Using a small sharp knife, cut along the back of the shrimp, taking care not to cut all the way through. Remove the black vein. Prepare 1½ cups of spinach or watercress exactly as given in Oysters Rockefeller, steps 3 and 4, but omit the fennel and Pernod. Stuff a small spoonful of the mixture in each shrimp cavity and close it with 2 toothpicks. Make 4 foil packets large enough to hold 6 shrimp each. Place the packets in a preheated 425°F oven and bake for 4 to 5 minutes. Put the warm shrimp on a platter and allow guests to help themselves. Accompany with melted butter and lemon wedges. Serves 12 as an appetizer; 6 as a first course.

The Pernod, of course, can be omitted, but it gives the authentic flavor. Licorice-tasting absinthe was the original liqueur used in these oysters, but it was declared against the law in the U.S. years ago, as the wormwood in the true absinthe and its high alcoholic strength—136%—are said to cause deterioration of the brain. Pernod from France (where absinthe is prohibited also) has a definite licorice flavor but is only 80% proof, and no wormwood. Fennel and tarragon have a slight licorice taste also, but fennel is the more assertive.

DELECTABLE SCALLOPS IN SHELLS

*A*ll scallops have a sweet and nutlike flavor no matter where they are found, and they are so tender they can be eaten raw. For this reason they must be cooked a very short time; otherwise, they will be tough and dry. I have used sea scallops in this versatile and superb way of preparing them, but bay scallops do quite well.

1 cup dry white wine
¼ cup water
5 tablespoons butter
1 tablespoon chopped shallots
1 pound sea scallops
½ cup heavy or whipping cream
Salt and freshly ground white pepper to taste
1½ cups fresh bread crumbs
¼ cup chopped fresh parsley
Lemon slices, for garnish

1. Preheat the oven to 375°F.
2. Put the white wine, water, 3 tablespoons of the butter, and the shallots in a heavy skillet over medium heat and cook until the butter melts but does not sizzle or brown the least bit. Add the scallops and cook until they just turn a creamy white, 3 to 4 minutes.
3. Remove the scallops, slice them, and distribute them evenly into large or small scallop shells.
4. Reduce the scallop stock until about ½ cup remains. Add the cream and reduce the sauce a bit. Season with salt and white pepper.
5. Lightly brown the crumbs in the remaining butter. Pour the sauce over the scallops, and cover them well with crumbs. Bake until they are bubbly hot and slightly brown. Sprinkle with parsley and garnish with lemon slices.

Serves 10 to 12 in tiny shells as an hors d'oeuvre, 6 to 8 as a first course, or 4 as an entrée

OYSTER LOAF (LA MEDIATRICE)

*T*here is a culinary tale that claims this oyster loaf is the "famous peacemaker" of old New Orleans. Every husband who needlessly lingered in the French Quarter and felt a bit guilty would stop by the French market on his way home to get an oyster loaf, or *médiatrice* (peacemaker), to pacify his wife. This recipe was adapted from the second edition of the *Picayune Cookbook*. The pages are so brown and crisp with age that I can hardly turn them without their breaking.

1 small loaf French bread
3 tablespoons butter, melted
Perfect Pan-Fried Oysters (see Index)
1 teaspoon chopped fresh parsley
1 teaspoon chopped fresh chervil or tarragon
2 lemon wedges

1. Preheat the oven to 425°F.
2. Take the loaf of French bread and cut off the upper half lengthwise. Dig the soft crumbs out of the center of both halves, leaving the loaf like an open box. Brush the inside of both halves with butter and pop them into the oven to bake until golden brown, about 20 minutes.
3. Fill the hollow of the bottom half with the hot oysters. Sprinkle with the herbs. Replace the top of the loaf, and put the whole thing back in the oven until heated through, about 10 minutes.
4. Cut the loaf in half and serve with lemon. Peace.
Serves 2

DEEP-FRIED FROG LEGS

*V*ery small (the smaller the better) frog legs that are fresh and have not been frozen are a real delicacy. And they are the only frog legs that should be considered. The tiny, flavorful legs when fried in deep fat to a golden, crisp, and crunchy brown make an appealing hot hors d'oeuvre as well as a light supper. Served with a crisp green salad, they make a charming light entrée for a brunch or a summer evening supper party.

36 small frog legs
Juice of 1 lemon
1 clove garlic, peeled (optional)
Salt and freshly ground white pepper to taste
Vegetable oil for deep-fat frying
Delicate Frog-Leg Frying Batter (recipe
   follows)
Tartar sauce or mustard mayonnaise, for
   serving
Watercress, for garnish
Lemon wedges, for garnish

1. Divide each frog leg into 2 pieces.
2. Marinate the frog legs in the lemon juice and garlic, tossing them frequently, for 1 hour.
3. Dry the frog legs well with paper towels. Season with salt and white pepper.
4. In an extra-heavy pan, such as black iron, or in an electric deep-fat fryer, heat 4 inches of oil (not over half the depth of the pan or fryer) to 365°F. (If a cube of bread dropped into the fat sizzles at once and browns in 30 seconds, the fat is ready.)

5. Using a cooking fork, dip the legs one at a time into the batter, holding them over the batter to allow the excess to drip off. Plunge them immediately into the fat, no more than 3 at a time (they must not be crowded). Fry until golden brown on both sides (you may need to turn them). Tiny frog legs will take about 2 minutes. Drain at once on paper towels.

6. Serve immediately on a platter with a bowl of tartar sauce or mustardy mayonnaise in the center. Garnish the dish with watercress and wedges of lemon.

Serves 18 as an hors d'oeuvre, 3 to 4 as a light entrée

VARIATIONS: Butterflied raw shrimp or chicken wings (drumettes) can be prepared and served the same way. Cook the shrimp at 375°F and the chicken at 365°F. Both will need 4 to 5 minutes cooking time. (Drumettes are the pieces of the chicken wing that look like tiny drumsticks.)

🦉 If more than 3 or 4 frog legs are fried at a time, or if the pan is crowded, the temperature of the oil will drop. The legs will absorb unnecessary fat, which prevents the desirable crunchy texture.

DELICATE FROG-LEG FRYING BATTER

◆

¾ cup cold beer or ice water
2 eggs
2 cups sifted all-purpose flour (or cake flour is splendid)
3 tablespoons butter, melted and cooled
1 teaspoon salt or to taste
Cayenne pepper to taste
3 egg whites

◆

1. Place the beer or water in a large mixing bowl or in a food processor. Add the eggs and beat until well mixed. Add the flour and mix very fast either with a whisk, or an electric mixer, or in the processor. (Working fast prevents the gluten in the flour from becoming overworked and rubbery.) Add the butter, salt, and cayenne.

2. Cover the batter and refrigerate it for 1 hour to relax the gluten.

3. Just before using, beat the extra egg whites until they hold a stiff peak. Gently fold them into the batter. The batter should be the consistency of very thick cream; add a small amount of ice water if needed.

BABY HOT BROWNS

◆◆◆

*T*his is a cocktail-size version of the famous Brown Hotel sandwich called "Hot Browns." It is just chicken and a good Mornay (cheese) sauce, of course, but it makes a delectable hot hors d'oeuvre.

◆

20 slices white bread (not too thinly sliced)
1 cup Thick Cheese Sauce (recipe follows)
1½ cups diced cooked chicken or turkey
½ cup freshly grated Parmesan cheese
3 slices bacon, broiled

◆

1. Preheat the oven to 500°F.
2. Cut out 2½- to 3-inch bread rounds and brown them on one side under the broiler.

3. Make the cheese sauce. Mix the sauce with the diced chicken or turkey. There will be 2½ cups of mixture.

4. Spread the untoasted side of the toast rounds with the mixture, about 2 tablespoons on each. Sprinkle each round with Parmesan cheese and garnish with a piece of bacon cut a bit smaller than the toast. Place the rounds on a baking sheet and place them in the oven until the Parmesan cheese begins to melt, only a few seconds. Serve at once.

Makes 20 rounds

THICK CHEESE SAUCE

3 tablespoons butter
3 tablespoons all-purpose flour
½ cup grated sharp Cheddar cheese
1 cup milk
Salt to taste
Cayenne pepper to taste

Melt the butter in a small enameled iron saucepan or a double boiler. Add the flour and blend well. Add the cheese and beat until smooth. Slowly add the milk, stirring constantly; cook until the sauce is thick and perfectly smooth, about 4 minutes. Add the salt and cayenne pepper.

VARIATION: To make grilled Baby Hot Browns, preheat the oven to 450°F and cut 3-inch rounds of bread. Make closed sandwiches of the Baby Hot Brown mixture.

Brown Hotel opened in Louisville in 1923 and remained open until the 1970s. In 1984 it reopened, its original 1920s interior totally restored.

Brush the top and bottom of each sandwich with melted butter. Place them on a baking sheet and put it on the middle shelf of the oven. Grill until golden brown.

Makes 1 cup

CAMEMBERT FRITTERS

*T*hese creamy fritters with their crunchy coating make delightful cocktail fare in any season. Try other cheeses, such as an aged Cheddar or Italian fontina. Wonderful for lunch with a green salad.

3 tablespoons butter
3 tablespoons all-purpose flour
1 cup milk
4 ounces Camembert cheese (without the rind),
*   cubed*
Salt to taste
Cayenne pepper to taste
1 large egg
1 tablespoon water
½ cup fine fresh bread crumbs
Vegetable oil for deep-fat frying

1. Melt the butter in a heavy saucepan over medium heat. Quickly blend in the flour. Add the milk gradually, stirring thoroughly. Bring to a boil, reduce the heat, and cook slowly until the sauce is thickened and smooth, about 4 minutes.

2. Add the cheese to the sauce and stir until it has melted. Add salt and cayenne pepper to taste. Remove from the heat and allow the sauce to cool slightly.

3. Spread the mixture ¾ inch thick on a baking sheet. Cover lightly, place in the refrigerator, and leave until cool and firm, about 2 hours or overnight.

4. Cut the cheese mixture into squares, or use a 1½-inch round cookie cutter. Beat the egg with the water. Roll the cheese pieces in the bread crumbs, then dip them in the egg mixture. Roll them in the crumbs again, and shake off any excess crumbs.

5. Heat the vegetable oil to 375°F in a deep-fat fryer or heavy saucepan. Drop the cheese pieces a few at a time into the oil. Do not crowd the pan. Fry just until they are golden brown, 1 to 2 minutes. Drain on paper towels.

6. Serve hot, as a first course or hors d'oeuvre.

Makes 10 to 12 fritters

ROQUEFORT SQUARES

◆◆◆

Roquefort Squares served piping hot with a crisp green salad and a red wine makes the most charming of luncheons, or they can be served as a first course for a lovely dinner party. These squares can be made days ahead—even weeks—and frozen; bake just before using. The baked squares may also be frozen; simply heat in a preheated 350°F oven and serve. Rather amazing.

◆

1 recipe Cornmeal Puff Paste (see Index)
½ pound Roquefort or blue cheese, softened and mashed until smooth

◆

1. Roll out the puff paste on a lightly floured surface or pastry cloth to a 15 x 12-inch rectangle, ¼ inch thick or as thin as you can roll it. Then cut into 20 pieces 3 x 3 inches each.

2. Put 2 teaspoons of the soft Roquefort or blue cheese in the center of 10 squares. Brush the edges of each square with ice water (so the square will seal together when closed).

3. Place the remaining 10 squares on top and press the outer edges together with the tines of a fork. Trim the edges evenly with a sharp knife. Prick the top of the squares with a fork to form air vents.

4. Place the squares on a pastry sheet that has been sprinkled with cold water. Chill 30 minutes before baking.

5. Preheat the oven to 425°F and bake until golden brown, about 20 minutes. To test for doneness, pick up a square; if it feels very light, the puff paste is done.

Makes 10 appetizer squares

SMOKED BACON TWIRLS
WITH ROSEMARY

◆◆◆

Meals in the dining car of the old Illinois Central Railroad, which ran from Chicago to New Orleans in the early decades of this century, may not have been as glamorous as dining on the Orient Express, but it was high adventure for us. The sparkling crystal, the white linen, the rows of silver at each place setting, and the armada of waiters in starched white coats made us feel like kings. The delicious food that came from that postage-stamp-size kitchen was amazing. We dined on the delicacies of the South—oysters, shrimp, and strawberries in season. For breakfast there were omelets, grits, country ham, hot biscuits, and bacon twirls galore with silver pots of freshly brewed coffee. The bacon twirls were very special. The Henry Mobley family in Mississippi employed a retired Pullman chef as their cook for a while and this is the way he said they did the twirls.

◆

1 pound finest smoked bacon, sliced
1½ tablespoons crushed dried rosemary

◆

1. Preheat the oven to 400°F.
2. Place the bacon slices on a baking sheet. Bake until the bacon is only half done, about 8 minutes. Remove, and sprinkle ¼ teaspoon rosemary on each slice.
3. Allow the bacon to cool slightly, then roll each piece in a tight twirl and spear it with a toothpick to hold it together.
4. When almost ready to serve, preheat the oven again to 400°F. Place the bacon back on the baking sheet and bake until thoroughly done but not overly crisp, about 8 minutes. (If you use thick-sliced bacon, allow 20 minutes, or more, total cooking time.)

Dining aboard the Illinois Central. Keeping one's hat balanced while eating was, no doubt, a challenge.

5. Serve as an hors d'oeuvre, or with scrambled eggs or an omelet for breakfast on a special day.
Serves 4 to 6

VARIATION: The bacon twirls (minus toothpicks) may be served on top of a green salad. Divine.

PIGGIES EN BROCHETTE

◆◆◆

*T*o wrap sausages in bacon may seem an unnecessary fuss, but it isn't. The blend of flavors and the presentation is worth the bother. They are delicious as a hot hors d'oeuvre in the winter and great for a special breakfast with scrambled eggs, hot biscuits, and maybe grits.

◆

1 pound small link pork sausage (piggies)
1 teaspoon crushed dried rosemary
1 pound sliced smoked bacon (very lean)
Round toothpicks

◆

1. Preheat the oven to 400°F.
2. Cut the piggies in half and sprinkle them with rosemary. Wrap each piece of sausage in half a slice of bacon and put them on a baking sheet. Place in the oven and cook until the bacon is done but not too crisp, about 25 minutes.
Makes 30 Piggies

🦉 The piggies may be wrapped in bacon, covered well, and refrigerated for up to 24 hours. Pop into a preheated 400°F oven for 25 to 30 minutes before serving.

HOT AND CRUNCHY EGGPLANT CHIPS

***F**or a large patio party in the summer or a small family group anytime, Eggplant Chips are a favorite appetizer served piping hot with cocktails or cold drinks. The only trouble is they are such a favorite they cannot be fried fast enough. Everybody loves them!*

1 large eggplant (firm, free of any soft, discolored spots)
1 egg
1 cup milk
1½ cups all-purpose flour
3 cups very finely ground fresh bread crumbs
Vegetable oil, shortening, or lard for deep-fat frying
Salt to taste

1. Peel the eggplant and slice it paper thin. Cut each slice into 2-inch-wide fingers.

2. Combine the egg and milk in a roomy bowl and beat them thoroughly with a whisk or rotary beater.

3. Put the flour in a plastic bag. Add the eggplant chips and shake them about until they are completely dusted with flour.

4. Transfer the chips to the egg and milk mixture and stir them about until they are completely covered.

5. Spoon one-quarter of the crumbs into a pie plate. Dip both sides of the eggplant chip into the crumbs. Press hard so the crumbs will adhere to the eggplant. Shake to remove any excess crumbs. As the crumbs become damp, they must be discarded and replenished with dry crumbs. (This process can be done several hours ahead and the chips covered and refrigerated. The cold helps the crumbs to set.)

6. Just before you are ready to serve, fill a deep-fat fryer no more than half full with the chosen fat. Heat to 365°F on a deep-fat thermometer. Add the chips a handful at a time and fry until they turn a golden brown, about 1 minute. Drain on paper towels.

7. Sprinkle the chips with salt and serve them while they are hot. Continue to fry the chips and serve while they are crisp and hot.

Makes enough chips for 8 nibblers

If you are having a large party, it will take one person's full attention to fry the eggplant chips and keep them coming. In any case, an electric fryer will help unbelievably, as the thermostat will prevent the oil from overheating.

REMOULADE ROUGE OF NEW ORLEANS

***T**his is the red rémoulade, spicy, hot, and delicious, that is served in New Orleans over chilled crawfish or shrimp as an appetizer or first course, or on lettuce as a salad with hot crunchy sourdough bread.*

2 cups homemade mayonnaise (see Index)
1½ teaspoons Creole or Dijon mustard
1½ tablespoons capers, drained
2 tablespoons very finely chopped fresh parsley
2 tablespoons very finely chopped fresh tarragon
2 teaspoons Hungarian paprika
1 teaspoon cayenne pepper
Juice of ½ lemon, or to taste
1 clove garlic
1 pound cooked small shrimp or cooked crawfish

1. Combine all the ingredients except the shrimp or crawfish in a bowl and mix well. Cover tightly and refrigerate for 1 to 3 hours. Discard the garlic.

2. Serve over crawfish or small shrimp with hot toasted crackers or French bread.

Serves 4

The first shrimp to be bathed in spicy red sauce was served in this dining room at Arnaud's, New Orleans.

VARIATION: This sauce may be used to serve lobster tails, spiny Florida lobster, or monkfish in the same way.

SARAPICO STUFFED SHRIMP

*T*hese shrimp are as delicous as they are versatile: They can be served on ice as a buffet hors d'oeuvre, they are charming served on a bed of Bibb lettuce and watercress as a first course, and they can also be a luncheon dish. Shrimp and Roquefort blend exquisitely. The amount of stuffing needed will vary with the size of the shrimp.

12 jumbo or large shrimp
3 ounces Roquefort or blue cheese
3 ounces cream cheese
Salt to taste
Cayenne pepper to taste
⅔ cup minced fresh parsley
Watercress or parsley sprigs, for garnish
1½ cups large black olives
6 slivers red bell or pimento pepper

1. Cook the shrimp in a large pot of boiling salted water, or in water seasoned with Shrimp or Crab Boil (see Index), until pink, 2 to 4 minutes. Drain the shrimp, and allow them to cool slightly.

2. Shell the shrimp, but leave the tails intact. Remove the black vein. Cut the shrimp almost all the way through along the length, making a pocket for stuffing.

3. Blend the Roquefort or blue cheese and the cream cheese in a food processor or with an electric mixer. Add salt and cayenne pepper to taste. Stuff a small amount of the cheese mixture into the cavity of each shrimp. (Jumbo shrimp will take about 1 scant tablespoon; large shrimp, about 2 teaspoons.) Dip the stuffed side of the shrimp into the minced parsley.

4. For a cocktail party, serve on a large bed of crushed ice garnished with watercress or parsley, with a mound of huge black olives in the center of the platter. Scatter the slivers of red bell pepper or pimento over the platter. Very beautiful.

Serves 4 to 6

VARIATIONS: The Roquefort and cream cheese can be thinned with cream or milk (cream is best) and used as a dip for shrimp. Fresh dill is a delicious addition to the dip.

As a first course or for a luncheon: Place the stuffed shrimp on a salad plate lined with watercress or Bibb lettuce. (Allow 3 jumbo or 4 to 5 large shrimp per serving.) Sprinkle each shrimp with ½ teaspoon Classic Vinaigrette. Garnish each plate with 2 black olives and a sliver of red bell pepper or pimento. Serve with hot buttered crackers.

The shrimp can be stuffed several hours ahead. Cover with plastic wrap and refrigerate until ready to serve.

OYSTERS ON THE HALF-SHELL

*B*uy oysters in shells that are tightly closed. This indicates freshness and that's what you want.

Oyster shucker piling up the shells in Baltimore, 1935.

18 to 36 oysters (depending on size)
Mignonette Sauce or Caviar Garnish (recipes follow)

Scrub the unopened oyster shells thoroughly with a stiff brush under running water. Shuck the oysters (see box) and drain them. Place the oysters in their shells on a bed of crushed ice and add your choice of garnish.

MIGNONETTE SAUCE

1 cup tarragon vinegar
¼ cup finely chopped shallots, or more to taste
Salt and freshly ground white or black pepper to taste
Lemon wedges

1. Combine the vinegar, shallots, salt, and pepper. Stir well.
2. Garnish the oysters with lemon wedges and serve with a sauceboat of Mignonette Sauce.

Serves 6

There should be a generous amount of pepper—white is traditional, but whichever you use, it must be freshly ground. If you can't find shallots, wait until you can. Onions won't do.

Serves 6

CAVIAR GARNISH

3 to 6 tablespoons black caviar
18 to 36 thin half-slices lemon (2 lemons)
Watercress or parsley sprigs

Place ½ teaspoon caviar on top of each oyster and then add a lemon slice. Garnish the ice between the shells with watercress or parsley.

HOW TO SHUCK AN OYSTER

A strong oyster knife is imperative.

Hold the oyster with the hinge part of the shell in the palm of your hand. Push the blade of a thick oyster knife between the two shells near the hinge and run it around between the shells until you cut the muscle that holds the upper and lower valves together. The lid should pop open.

When the lid pops open, lift up the top shell and sever the muscle attached to it with the point of a sharp paring knife. The liquor around oysters that have been shucked must be clear and the odor pleasing. A bad oyster is easy to detect by its unpleasant odor and milky liquor.

CHICKEN LIVER PATE WITH TARRAGON

*T*his is an easy chicken liver pâté which can be very simple or rather fancy, according to your whim of the day—or who is coming.

4 tablespoons (½ stick) butter
¼ cup minced shallots
¼ cup water
1 pound chicken livers
1½ tablespoons chopped fresh tarragon
*   or ⅓ teaspoon dried (fresh is best)*
1 tablespoon chopped fresh chervil, or
*   additional tarragon*
2 eggs
⅓ cup heavy or whipping cream
1 teaspoon salt
Freshly ground white pepper to taste
1 cup clear beef aspic (optional; recipe follows)
Small black olives, for garnish

1. Preheat the oven to 300°F.
2. Melt the butter in a heavy skillet.
Add the shallots and water and cook over medium heat until the water boils away and the shallots are limp, 4 minutes. Do not allow them to brown. Add the chicken livers and simmer until cooked through.

3. Purée the mixture in a food processor. Add the tarragon, chervil, eggs, cream, salt, and white pepper. Blend well.

4. Spoon the pâté into an oiled terrine or into 2 small round heatproof dishes, or in any oiled molds. Cover tightly with foil and place in a baking pan. Fill the pan halfway with water and bake for 1 hour.

5. Allow the pâté to cool. Remove it from the molds, place it on a dish, cover, and refrigerate. Serve as is or brush with aspic for an elegant presentation. Garnish with olives.

Serves 16

QUICK ASPIC

1 can (10½ ounces) concentrated beef consommé
1 teaspoon unflavored gelatin
1 teaspoon dry sherry, or more to taste

1. Dilute the consommé with an equal amount of water. Measure out 1½ cups into a saucepan. Dissolve the gelatin in the diluted consommé, and bring it to a boil. Remove the pan from the heat at once. Add the sherry, and stir. Allow the aspic to cool.

2. Brush 1 coat of the aspic on the pâté. Refrigerate until the aspic sets, about 5 minutes. Repeat the process 3 times to coat the pâté well.

SPECIAL DRESSED EGGS

Watch the buffet table—the dressed eggs always disappear first.

6 hard-cooked eggs
Dash of cayenne pepper
Dash of freshly ground white pepper
6 anchovy filets
¼ cup oil-packed tuna, drained and flaked
1 teaspoon capers, drained
½ teaspoon Dijon mustard, or to taste
Tarragon vinegar to taste
6 tablespoons mayonnaise, homemade (see Index) or Hellmann's
Black olives, pimento strips, or anchovy filets, for garnish
1 bunch watercress or parsley, for serving

1. Cut the eggs in half lengthwise and remove the yolks. Mash the yolks, or run them through a ricer. Mix until they are smooth. Add a sprinkling of cayenne and white pepper.

2. Lightly crush the anchovy filets, and add them to the yolks. Add the tuna, capers, and mustard. Mix well. Add the vinegar. Blend in mayonnaise just until the mixture is smooth and stiff enough to hold its shape.

3. Fill the egg whites with the yolk mixture. Decorate the top of each with a small sliver of black olive, a pimento strip, or a thin slice of anchovy. Serve on a bed of fresh watercress or parsley, decorated with large black olives.

Serves 6 to 8

VARIATIONS: *With tarragon:* To the yolks of 6 hard-cooked eggs add ½ teaspoon prepared mustard, 1 or 2 tablespoons mayonnaise, tarragon vinegar to taste, 1 teaspoon each chopped fresh parsley and tarragon. Add salt and cayenne pepper to taste.

With crabmeat, cooked shrimp, crawfish, or lobster: To the yolks of 6 hard-cooked eggs add ¼ cup minced seafood, ½ teaspoon Dijon mustard, 1 teaspoon capers, cayenne pepper and lemon juice to taste, and mayonnaise to blend.

With smoked oysters: To the yolks of 6 hard-cooked eggs add tarragon vinegar to taste, chopped fresh tarragon, ½ teaspoon Dijon mustard, cayenne pepper to taste, and mayonnaise to blend. Fill each egg white with a smoked oyster, cover with egg yolk mixture, and garnish with a sliver of black olive.

Women of the Raymond, Georgia, Community Council grading and sorting eggs in 1921.

OLD KENTUCKY BEER CHEESE

◆◆

*I*n the early days of this century there was a German saloon keeper in Frankfort (our state capital) who created this cheese and kept large crocks of it on the counter of his saloon. A nickel glass of beer entitled a customer to ham sandwiches, pickled oysters, potato salad, and cracker after cracker spread with beer cheese—and the saloon keeper was solvent! It boggles our minds today to think that food was so plentiful and so cheap. Anyway, this German beer cheese is still the very best. You must, of course, start with an excellent cheese—as the saloon keeper did.

◆

2 pounds sharp Cheddar cheese, at room
*   temperature*
2 cloves garlic, mashed
3 tablespoons Worcestershire sauce
1 teaspoon dry mustard
Tabasco sauce to taste
½ bottle beer, or more as necessary
1 teaspoon salt, or to taste

◆

The staff at Thompsons Restaurant bar, Louisville, 1933. The sign at the back advertises free baked ham with every beer after 4 P.M.

1. Cut the cheese into cubes and place them in a food processor or electric mixer. Process until perfectly smooth. Add the garlic, Worcestershire, mustard, and Tabasco. Blend well.

2. Add the beer, a little at a time, while continuing to beat the cheese, until the mixture is a good, firm spreading consistency. (Too much beer will make the cheese too fluffy.) Stir in the salt, and refrigerate. (This is a superb keeper.)

3. Serve on small slices of rye or pumpernickel bread, or on crackers. Delicious with cold, cold beer.

Serves 15 to 20

VERY SPECIAL CHEESE STRAWS

◆◆

*T*he most deluxe of all the cheese straws.

◆

1 pound aged sharp Cheddar cheese
8 tablespoons (1 stick) unsalted butter
1 teaspoon cayenne pepper
½ teaspoon salt
2 cups sifted all-purpose flour

◆

1. Grate the cheese by hand or in a food processor. Cut the butter into pieces and blend it with the cheese, in the processor or with an electric mixer, until smooth. Add the cayenne pepper, salt, and flour. Mix well.

2. Chill the dough for at least 1 hour, so it will be easier to handle.

3. You can prepare the straws with a cookie press, using the thin serrated ribbon blade to create 3-inch straws. Or you can form the dough into small balls, then roll them into thin rounds. Use the tines of a fork to etch grooves into the rounds.

4. Preheat the oven to 325°F.

5. Lay the straws on a lightly greased baking sheet and bake until done, about 30 minutes. The straws should have a slight tinge of brown on the bottom but not on the top. If they brown too much, they will toughen.

Makes 90 straws

CRAWFISH, SHRIMP, OR LOBSTER BUTTER

*C*rawfish, shrimp, or lobster butters are delicious served as you would a pâté to be spread on buttered and toasted crackers, French bread, or, best of all, Cornmeal Melba Toast. It makes a fitting appetizer for cocktail parties or a lunch dish when served with a crisp green salad.

½ pound fresh cooked crawfish, shrimp, or lobster
8 tablespoons (1 stick) unsalted butter, cut into 8 pieces
¼ teaspoon Hungarian paprika
Squeeze or two of lemon
Salt and cayenne pepper to taste

1. Put the crawfish, shrimp, or lobster in a food processor and twirl until the seafood is perfectly smooth.

2. Add the butter, paprika, and lemon juice. Twirl until the mixture is smooth. Add salt and cayenne to taste.

3. Spoon into an oiled small pâté mold or a small bowl and chill until firm and ready to serve.

Makes about 1 cup

COUNTRY HAM BUTTER

*T*his favorite country ham pâté, or butter, can be made in 5 minutes in a processor. It is a delightful dish for the hors d'oeuvre table or for a hunt breakfast—or packed in a crock for a picnic basket.

This Maryland party arrived at their picnic destination by steamboat.

8 tablespoons (1 stick) unsalted butter
1 cup minced baked country ham, firmly packed and free of fat

Combine the butter and ham in the bowl of a food processor and process until perfectly smooth. Chill and serve with hot biscuits, buttered toast, or crackers.

Makes 1½ cups

HOT DILLED OLIVES

*H*ave plenty of these on hand—they're irresistible nibbling food and easy to serve when friends drop by unexpectedly.

1½ pints large green olives (pitted)
2 cloves garlic
2 red chile peppers
3 to 4 teaspoons chopped fresh dill or dill seeds
2 bay leaves
5 tablespoons good-quality olive oil

5 tablespoons white wine vinegar

Drain the olives and put them in a clean jar. Add spices, oil, and vinegar. Allow to marinate 2 days. Keep refrigerated.
Makes 3 cups

WASHINGTON WATERFRONT PICKLED SHRIMP

*W*hen we lived in Washington, D.C., before and during World War II, huge glass vats of pickled shrimp lined the walls of the seafood shops on the waterfront. They were plentiful, cheap, and a glorious snack or hors d'oeuvre. That picturesque sight has vanished—pickled shrimp are not plentiful, nor are they cheap, but they are still glorious.

1½ cups distilled white vinegar
½ cup water
3 tablespoons coriander seeds
2 teaspoons mustard seeds
¼ teaspoon dry mustard
1 or 2 blades mace
1 large piece dried ginger
Salt to taste
3 cups cooked medium shrimp, shelled and deveined
½ cup thinly sliced mild onion
1 lemon, thinly sliced and seeded
1 tiny piece red chile pepper
2 bay leaves

A forest of masts surrounds the wharf at the foot of I Street in Washington, D.C.

1. Combine the vinegar, water, coriander seeds, mustard seeds, dry mustard, mace, and ginger in a stainless steel or enamel pan and cook at a medium boil for 10 minutes. Add salt to taste. Remove from the heat and allow to cool.

2. In a quart jar, pack the shrimp, onion, lemon, chile pepper, and bay leaves in layers. Pour in the marinade. Press the contents firmly in the jar until they are completely submerged.

3. Refrigerate for 36 hours. Turn the jar upside down a few times during the first 24 hours so the spices are distributed.

4. Serve ice cold on toothpicks as an hors d'oeuvre, or on a bed of chopped parsley as a first course.

Serves 4 to 6

This is the ultimate marinade for pickled shrimp; it is clear, has a marvelous flavor (coriander seed is the heart of pickled shrimp), and the shrimp stays pinkish-white. The cinnamon, cloves, and allspice found in ready-mixed pickling spices have a tendency to turn the shrimp a little dark. I prefer the clear pink look.

The shrimp must be kept submerged in the marinade and must be kept refrigerated. It will keep for weeks if pickled the day the shrimp is cooked.

PICKLED OYSTERS

❖❖

Serve these oysters in a bowl within a bowl of crushed ice for an hors d'oeuvre, or serve a few as a first course, drained and placed on a bed of chopped parsley or Bibb lettuce, garnished with lemon, with warm toasted and buttered crackers.

A Southern oyster peddler hawks his wares in a Harper's Weekly *illustration from 1889.*

◆

2 cups white wine vinegar (tarragon or plain)
2 cups cold water
5 sprigs fresh parsley or 10 parsley stems
2 ribs celery
1 clove garlic, unpeeled
1 medium onion, sliced or roughly chopped
1 carrot, peeled
1 bay leaf
1 teaspoon dried thyme
1 teaspoon black peppercorns
1 teaspoon coriander seeds
1½ pints large fresh oysters
Salt to taste
Squeeze of lemon juice
¼ cup good-quality olive oil, or more to taste

◆

1. Combine the vinegar and water in a medium stainless steel or enamel pan. Add the parsley, celery, garlic, onion, carrot, bay leaf, thyme, peppercorns, and coriander seeds. Bring to a boil, reduce the heat, and simmer for 30 minutes. Strain the marinade.

2. In a large saucepan, combine the oysters and their juice with the strained marinade. Bring the mixture to a simmer. Remove it quickly from the heat. (The oysters should just begin to curl.) Allow the oysters to cool in the liquid. Then add the salt, lemon juice, and olive oil. Transfer to a

large glass or ceramic bowl, cover, and refrigerate.

   3. Serve with hot toasted and buttered crackers.

   Serves 6 to 8

🦉 The oysters must be kept covered by the marinade. If they are very large, make additional marinade to cover them.

PICKLED MONKFISH

❖❖

*L*ike all pickled dishes, this fish can be prepared days in advance, as it keeps well. It is good most any season, but it is at its best when the fresh tarragon and dill are in. Grouper, striped bass, salmon, mackerel, or jumbo shrimp can be prepared this same way. Serve with dark rye bread, buttered toasted crackers, or good French bread with sweet butter, and cold, cold beer or dry white wine.

◆

2 pounds monkfish steaks, 1 to 1¼ inches thick
3 slices lemon

MARINADE

2 bay leaves
½ teaspoon coriander seeds
3 sprigs parsley
5 sprigs tarragon
7 sprigs dill
3 small sweet white onions, cut into quarters
½ small cucumber, sliced
2 cups distilled white vinegar
2½ cups water
¼ cup vegetable oil
1 tablespoon salt or to taste
8 white peppercorns
1 teaspoon dry mustard
Pinch of sugar or to taste
Several small pieces of red chile pepper, fresh or dried

GARNISHES

Chopped fresh dill
1 small cucumber, peeled, sliced, and marinated in Classic Vinaigrette (see Index)
1 red bell pepper, cored, seeded, and cut into slivers
1 cup colossal black olives
1 cup sour cream blended with 2 tablespoons horseradish

◆

   1. Poach the monkfish (or any of the fish mentioned in the headnote) in simmering salted water to barely cover with the slices of lemon just until it is barely tender. (Ten minutes per inch of thickness is a good rule of thumb; the minute the fish flakes when touched with a fork, it is done. Use one piece as a test.) Allow to cool completely in the poaching liquid.

   2. In the meantime, combine the marinade ingredients in a stainless steel or ceramic bowl or pan. Add the cooled fish steaks and cover them well with the marinade. Cover and marinate at least overnight, under refrigeration, before serving.

   3. Lift the steaks out of the marinade and cut them into squares. Garnish with a generous sprinkling of chopped fresh dill, marinated cucumbers, slices of red bell pepper, huge black olives, and sour cream mixed with horseradish. Serve as an hors d'oeuvre or as a tangy salad.

   Serves 10 as an hors d'oeuvre; serves 6 as a salad

🦉 Monkfish does not flake like other fish; it must be cooked until the center loses its transparency. Ten minutes per 1 inch of thickness is perfect. Monkfish has bits of fat that are easily trimmed off with scissors after poaching.

   All of the steaks for this dish should be cut 1 to 1¼ inches thick.

   If you use this recipe for shrimp, the shrimp can be poached in the shell or out.

FAVORITE PICKLED MUSHROOMS

*M*ushrooms have a natural affinity for thyme and marjoram—they enhance each other. When pickled, mushrooms make a delicious hors d'oeuvre, are wonderful on the relish tray, and glorify beef tenderloin, roasts, chops, or steak.

2½ pounds small or medium mushrooms
⅓ cup good-quality olive oil
1 clove garlic
6 sprigs fresh thyme or 2 teaspoons dried
1 cup white wine vinegar
1⅓ cups water, or as needed
Juice of 1 lemon
Salt and freshly ground white pepper to taste
2 small slivers red chile pepper, dried or fresh

1. Choose firm, tightly closed white mushrooms. Cut off the stems so they are even with the caps. Leave the mushrooms whole or cut them in half.

2. Combine the olive oil, garlic, 4 sprigs of the thyme or 2 teaspoons dried, the vinegar, water, lemon juice, salt, and white pepper in a stainless steel or enamel saucepan. Bring to a boil, reduce the heat, and simmer 3 minutes.

3. Add the mushrooms to the mixture and simmer 2 to 3 minutes, depending upon the size of the mushrooms. (They must stay crisp.) Remove the pan from the heat and set aside to allow the mushrooms to absorb the herby flavors, about 1 hour.

4. Using a slotted spoon, ladle the mushrooms into 2 boiling-hot pint canning jars. Discard the thyme sprigs, if you used them, and the garlic.

5. Strain the liquid through a fine sieve into another saucepan. If the flavor is too acid, add a small amount of water. (It rarely needs it, but this can vary with the vinegar.) Bring the liquid to a boil and pour it over the mushrooms. Place a fresh sprig of thyme and a sliver of chile pepper in each jar. Close the jars, cool, and refrigerate.

Makes 1 quart

The mushrooms will keep indefinitely when refrigerated. To keep them on the shelf, they must be sealed and processed in a boiling-water bath for 5 minutes (see Index).

CHAPTER TWO

SOUPS

THE SONG OF THE SOUP KETTLE

Delicious homemade soups have the culinary grace of being adaptable to everyone's taste and pocketbook. Soup can be a meal in itself, thick and hearty for a cold winter night, or well chilled with a sprinkling of fresh herbs for a hot summer day. Or at least that's the way we've always enjoyed them in the South. Few dishes give us a greater feeling of well-being than a good soup. Few dishes are a greater challenge to the cook than a good soup, with the possible exception of homemade bread. And the two are soul mates.

Making the soup can be timed nicely into a busy person's schedule. For instance, make the stock one day, or in the evening. Refrigerate it overnight and add the vegetables the next day. Leftover cooked vegetables make an inferior soup. Use fresh, crisp vegetables. Blend. Taste and think. Taste and remember the combinations that made your last soup so good.

If the stock is made of chicken, veal, or beef, it must be well seasoned with vegetables and herbs until it is delicious all on its own.

If it is to be a cream soup with character and flavor, whole milk with a judicious amount of heavy cream must be used. Skimmed and 2% milk are for diets, not for wonderful soups. They will curdle when boiled and are flavorless to begin with. Cream has flavor. Cooks find that so-called half-and-half, which is seldom half cream and half milk, as it is reputed to be, also curdles when boiled. Heavy cream when fresh will boil down and thicken without curdling—a good cook's technique for making delicious soups and sauces without the heavy flour-thickened roux of the old cuisine.

BEEF, TOMATO, AND OKRA SOUP

*T*his typical Creole soup is not supposed to be thick and hearty with an overabundance of vegetables, but very flavorful and thinning!

3 pounds beef short ribs
2 quarts cold water
Bouquet garni of 2 bay leaves, several sprigs parsley, and generous pinch of dried thyme, tied in a cheesecloth bag
2 medium onions, peeled and left whole
2 carrots, cut in half
¼ pound small tender string beans
4 ribs celery, chopped
3 ripe large tomatoes, peeled, seeded, and chopped; or canned whole tomatoes, drained and chopped
½ large green bell pepper, cored, seeded, and cut into slivers
¾ pound fresh okra, thickly sliced
⅓ cup raw rice or small pasta
Salt and freshly ground black pepper to taste
⅓ cup chopped fresh parsley
Bouquet of mixed fresh herbs, such as basil, chervil, marjoram, and tarragon

1. Put the meat in a soup kettle or large dutch oven. Add the water and bring to a boil. After boiling 5 or 6 minutes, begin to skim off any scum that rises. Skim often to keep the stock clear.

2. Add the bouquet garni, onions, and carrots. Continue to simmer, uncovered, until the meat is tender, 1 to 1½ hours.

3. Add the beans, celery, tomatoes, and bell pepper. Continue to cook for 25 to 30 minutes.

4. Lift out and set aside the meat. Discard the bouquet garni, carrots, and onions. Add the okra and rice or pasta and continue to simmer until the rice or pasta is done, about 20 minutes. Season with salt and pepper.

5. Five minutes before serving, toss in the chopped parsley and a fresh herb bouquet if available. Serve with slices of the meat, mustard, and French bread—or with thin cucumber sandwiches.

Serves 6

Unless I specifically mention it, do *not* cover your soup pot. A cover causes the vegetables to steam and become mushy.

"CHILLY SPRING" SOUP

*M*arch and April are capricious months in Kentucky. We think we are all set for warm weather one minute—and then the next, snow flurries blow in. That's when we need a pot of hearty soup—"Chilly Spring" soup, they say—to warm our bones and soothe our tummies. It can't be heavy and thick like a February soup. It must be hearty but light. Throw in a handful of escarole—slivered as fine as embroidery floss—and parsley just before the pot comes off the stove. That touch of freshness says "Spring" in spite of the windchill factor. It is sheer magic in a steaming bowl of delicious flavors with a thick piece of homemade bread.

½ pound dried Great Northern or pinto beans
½ pound thick-sliced smoked bacon, or a ham bone or hock, or a small piece of picnic ham
6 quarts cold water
6 sprigs parsley
2 medium onions, peeled and left whole
3 ribs celery
1½ bay leaves
¼ teaspoon dried thyme
¼ teaspoon dried summer savory
4 canned whole tomatoes, drained
¼ cup chopped fresh parsley
1 cup very thinly shredded escarole or romaine lettuce
Salt and freshly ground black pepper to taste

1. Wash the dried beans thoroughly. Discard any stones and blemished beans. Cover with cold water and soak overnight.

2. Drain the beans and put them in a soup pot with the meat. Add the 6 quarts water and the parsley sprigs, onions, celery, bay leaves, thyme, and savory. Bring the mixture to a boil, then reduce to a simmer and cook, uncovered or partially covered, for 2 to 3 hours. Spoon off the surface scum and fat often.

3. When the meat is tender and the stock has developed a good flavor, discard the seasoning vegetables, and using a skimmer, skim off the dried herbs and parsley. Lift out the meat and bones.

4. Chop the tomatoes in a blender or processor and add them to the soup. Cook for 10 to 15 minutes. Add the parsley and lettuce in the last few minutes of cooking, and season with salt and pepper.

5. Serve with warm homemade bread, sliced ham, and relishes.

Serves 6

CHICKEN, HAM, AND SWEET CORN CHOWDER

Chicken, Ham, and Sweet Corn Chowder is as Southern as *Gone with the Wind*, and everyone loves it once they have tasted it. This is a great soup to serve for a summer patio party.

1 chicken, 3 to 3½ pounds
2 tablespoons butter, melted or at room temperature
1 thick slice uncooked ham, or 1 small ham hock (about 1 pound)
4 thick slices lean or slab bacon
3 quarts cold water
3 ribs celery, broken in half
2 small onions, cut in quarters
2 carrots, peeled and cut in half
1 teaspoon dried marjoram
2 bay leaves

8 parsley sprigs, tied with string
8 white peppercorns
½ red bell pepper, cored, seeded, and diced
½ green bell pepper, cored, seeded, and diced
2 cups fresh corn kernels (4 to 6 ears)
6 tiny new potatoes, peeled
Salt and freshly ground black pepper to taste
2 tablespoons chopped fresh parsley

1. Preheat the oven to 400°F.
2. Rinse the chicken well and pat it dry. Brush or rub the chicken all over with

the butter. Place the chicken in a shallow baking pan and bake until it is golden brown, 20 to 30 minutes.

3. While the chicken is browning, put the ham or ham hock, bacon, and cold water in a large soup kettle. Add the celery, onions, carrots, marjoram, bay leaves, parsley sprigs, and peppercorns. Bring to a low boil.

4. When the chicken has browned, add it and all the pan juices to the soup pot. Partially cover the soup pot (so it won't steam) and simmer, uncovered, for 1½ hours.

5. Remove the chicken. Continue to simmer the soup so the flavor will develop and ripen, 25 to 30 minutes. Slip the chicken meat off the bones and put the bones back in the soup kettle. Keep the chicken meat, covered, in the refrigerator.

6. When the soup stock tastes delicious, lift out the ham and set it aside. Discard the chicken bones and bacon. Strain the soup through a fine sieve into a large saucepan. Discard all the seasoning vegetables and herbs. Pour the strained soup stock back into the soup kettle. Add cold water if the stock has boiled too low and the mixture is too thick to be called soup.

7. Add the red and green bell peppers, corn, and potatoes. Cook gently until the potatoes are tender, 20 to 25 minutes.

8. Cut the ham in slivers and return it to the stock. Add the white meat of the chicken, also cut into thick slivers (save the dark meat for another use). Season the

That famous 18-inch waist was not maintained on corn chowder.

soup with salt and pepper to taste. Add the parsley.

9. Ladle the chowder into warm soup plates and serve with homemade bread and butter.

Serves 6 to 8

VARIATIONS: Add 1 cup heavy cream with the corn.

If you would like the stock to have a rosier color, add 1 or 2 ripe tomatoes, peeled and chopped, with the seasoning vegetables.

NORTH CAROLINA CHICKEN, RICE, AND CABBAGE SOUP

◆◆◆

Cabbage of any type should be blanched for 2 minutes in boiling water, then drained well before it is added to soup. This is the expert way of handling strong-flavored vegetables in soups and stews. In the fall, ripe red bell peppers are a beautiful addition in this soup.

6 cups Chicken Stock (see page 57)
2 medium onions, sliced
½ cup rice
½ large head green cabbage, torn into
    medium-size pieces
2 lemon slices
½ pound skinless, boneless chicken, freshly
    cooked and slivered
3 tablespoons chopped fresh parsley
Salt and freshly ground white pepper to taste
Cayenne pepper to taste

1. Put the chicken stock in a large saucepan. Bring to a boil, then add the onions and rice. Reduce the heat and simmer gently, uncovered, until the rice is almost tender, 15 to 20 minutes.

2. In the meantime, boil the cabbage for 2 minutes. Drain. Add the cabbage and lemon slices to the soup. Simmer for 5 to 7 minutes. (The cabbage must not lose its color.)

3. Add the chicken, parsley, and salt, pepper, and cayenne to taste. Simmer until the chicken is heated through. Serve with corn muffins or your favorite cornmeal bread.

Serves 6

Here is the expert way of giving this soup added flavor and color: Butter well half a chicken (1¼ pounds). Place it in a preheated 450°F oven and bake until the chicken is a light golden brown, 20 minutes. Put the chicken in the stock and cook until tender and flavorful, 25 minutes. Remove the chicken from the stock. Allow it to cool, then skin, bone, and cut the meat into slivers. Proceed as directed.

GREEN CABBAGE AND HAM SOUP

*T*he flavors of chicken and ham have a great affinity for cabbage, and this soup is a good example of that counterpoint of flavors. Serve it with sliced tomato salad and Cornmeal Melba Bread or cornmeal muffins, and you will have a delicious country meal that is very sophisticated in its own way.

½ medium head green cabbage
3 medium sweet white onions
3 medium Idaho baking potatoes
2 tablespoons unsalted butter
4 cups Chicken Stock (see page 57), or more as
    needed
2½ cups water
1 cup heavy or whipping cream
¾ cup milk
Salt and freshly ground white pepper to taste
Cayenne pepper to taste
¼ cup chopped fresh parsley
¼ cup chopped chervil, if available
½ cup finely slivered baked ham (Virginia or
    Kentucky country ham or prosciutto)

1. Shred cabbage in rather wide pieces. You should have 5 cups. Set aside.

2. Peel and dice the onions. You should have 1¼ cups.

3. Peel and dice the potatoes. You should have 2 cups.

4. Melt the butter in a heavy soup pot. Add the diced onions and potatoes and sauté over low heat until they have absorbed the butter. (Do not let the butter sizzle or the vegetables brown the least bit.)

5. Add 4 cups chicken stock and 2 cups of the water. Cook, uncovered, over medium heat until the onions and potatoes are tender, 25 minutes. Add the shredded cabbage and continue to cook until the cabbage is just tender—but still a bit crisp and holding its nice green color—3 to 5 minutes. Add more stock if the soup has cooked too low.

6. Purée the soup in a blender or put it through a food mill.

7. Return the puréed soup to the pot and add the cream, milk, and remaining water. This is a rather thick soup; if you wish it to be thinner, add a little more stock or water. Gently reheat the soup and add salt, white pepper, and cayenne to taste.

8. When you are ready to serve the soup, add the parsley and chervil. Ladle the soup into warmed bowls and sprinkle with the ham.

Serves 4 to 6

VARIATION: This is a great soup—have fun with it. Lacking the ham, the soup can be garnished with fresh dill, but the ham is the highlight. The soup can also be garnished with tenderly cooked, but still rather crisp, Brussels sprouts. Slice them crosswise—rather pretty. In the fall you could, if you wish, sprinkle a few tiny flecks of chopped red bell pepper.

A field of Maryland cabbage—picture perfect.

White cabbage will not do for this recipe. Green cabbage is young and fresh. Cabbage turns white as it ages and gets stronger, too! It is very important to retain the fresh colors by not overcooking.

Do not purée the soup in a food processor—it'll make the potatoes gummy.

This can be made several hours ahead, up to step 8. Don't add the herbs until you are ready to heat up the soup.

HEARTY CHICKEN AND HAM GUMBO

❖❖❖

*T*his is an heirloom soup that we love in the fall when the okra is tender and our favorite red bell peppers are on the market.

STOCK

1 stewing hen or capon, about 5 to 5½ pounds
Small piece of ham bone or hock, about ½ pound
4 quarts water
2 medium onions, cut in half
1 carrot, peeled and cut in half
3 ribs celery
2 bay leaves
1 teaspoon dried thyme

SOUP

2 tablespoons butter

1 medium onion, chopped
1 green bell pepper, cored, seeded, and slivered
1 sweet red bell or pimento pepper, cored, seeded, and slivered
¼ cup water
18 to 20 fresh small okra, cut into ¼-inch slices
¼ pound baked ham, cubed
⅓ cup rice
3 ribs celery, diced
3 canned or peeled fresh tomatoes, chopped
Salt to taste
Dash of dried red pepper flakes (optional)

A view of Louisville from the Ohio River in the late 1800s.

1. To make the stock, rinse the hen or capon thoroughly and place it in a large soup pot. Cover the hen and the ham bone with 4 quarts water or more if necessary. Bring to a boil and skim several times before adding the vegetables.

2. Add the onions, carrot, celery, bay leaves, and thyme. Bring to a boil, reduce the heat, and simmer gently, uncovered, until the hen is tender, 1 to 1½ hours. Remove the hen, set it aside, and continue simmering the stock for another 2 to 2½ hours.

3. When the stock is well flavored, strain it through a fine sieve or dampened cheesecloth. Skim off any fat, or refrigerate until the fat solidifies and is easily removed. (This can be done a day ahead.)

4. To make the soup, melt the butter in a heavy saucepan. Add the onion, green and red bell peppers, and water and cook over medium heat until the vegetables are wilted. They must not brown. Add this mixture to the stock. Add the okra, ham, rice, celery, and tomatoes. Taste. Add salt, more thyme if needed, and a sprinkling of dried red pepper if desired. Bring to a boil and simmer, uncovered, for about 45 minutes.

5. Remove the meat from the hen or capon and cut it into cubes. Ten minutes before serving, add it to the soup. Cook over low heat until the soup has thickened sufficiently. Serve in warmed soup plates with corn muffins or homemade bread.

Serves 6 to 8

WILD RICE, BEEF, AND MUSHROOM SOUP

*T*his is one of my finest recipes—just exquisite.

3½ to 4 pounds beef short ribs
5 quarts cold water
2 medium onions
1 pound mushrooms, separated into caps and
    stems
5 ribs celery
3 medium carrots
3 bay leaves
1 large sprig fresh thyme or 1 teaspoon dried
10 parsley stems, tied with string
8 peppercorns
⅓ cup wild rice, well rinsed
2 cups water
¼ teaspoon salt
1 cup chopped fresh parsley

Salt and freshly ground black pepper to taste
Lemon slices, for garnish

1. Put the short ribs and 5 quarts water in a large soup pot. Bring to a low boil. Add the whole onions, mushroom stems, celery, carrots, bay leaves, thyme, parsley stems, and peppercorns. Simmer, uncovered, for 3 to 4 hours, adding cold water as necessary to maintain the original amount. Skim off the scum as it rises to the top.

2. Refrigerate the stock overnight. Cover the mushroom caps and refrigerate overnight.

3. Next day, remove the fat from the stock and discard the seasoning vegetables. Remove the meat from the bones, cut away the fat, and chop the meat into small pieces. Set aside.

4. Place the wild rice and 2 cups water in a heavy saucepan. Add the ¼ teaspoon salt. Bring to a boil, lower the heat, and simmer, partially covered, until the kernels are open but still chewy, about 45 minutes. Drain and set aside.

5. Strain the stock through a fine sieve into a clean pot. Bring to a boil, reduce the heat, and add the mushroom caps. Simmer for 5 minutes, then add the chopped beef, wild rice, and parsley, and season with salt and a generous amount of pepper. Simmer until well heated.

6. Serve piping hot in large soup plates, garnished with lemon slices, and with side dishes of sour pickles, pickled peppers, and pumpernickel or rye bread.

Serves 6

It may be well to add an extra amount of thyme. Mushrooms have an affinity for thyme. Tie the thyme in a cheesecloth bag or a stainless steel bag made for the purpose, for easy removal.

KENTUCKY BURGOO

◆◆◆

Kentucky Burgoo is a thick soup, not a stew. It is at its best in the late summer or early fall when the fresh vegetables are still available, but the goodness of the burgoo at any time depends upon the judgment and talents of the cook.

◆

1 or 2 beef or veal marrow bones, 2½ to 3 pounds
2 pounds beef chuck or lean short ribs
2 pounds breast of lamb
2 pounds breast of veal
1 stewing hen, capon, or roasting chicken, 4 to 5 pounds
1 tender young rabbit, ready to cook
8 to 10 quarts water
2 onions, peeled
1 teaspoon dried thyme
2 bay leaves
4 ribs celery
6 sprigs parsley
4½ cups chopped onions (about 1½ pounds)
4½ cups diced peeled potatoes (about 1½ pounds)
4 carrots, peeled and diced
2 green bell peppers, cored, seeded, and slivered
2 red bell peppers, cored, seeded, and slivered
2 cups fresh lima beans
2 cups fresh corn kernels (4 to 6 ears)
2 cups chopped celery
1½ to 2 quarts canned tomatoes with their liquid, puréed

1 red chile pepper, or more to taste, sliced
Salt to taste
1½ pounds small okra, carefully trimmed
Freshly ground black pepper to taste
Tabasco sauce to taste
Worcestershire sauce to taste
1 cup chopped fresh parsley

◆

General James Tandy Ellis, noted author and humorist, making burgoo for a crowd.

Kentucky Senator Perry Gaines samples the general's burgoo and approves.

1. Put marrow bones, beef, lamb, veal, fowl, and rabbit in a huge pot and cover with cold water. Bring slowly to a boil, then reduce the heat and allow the broth to simmer, skimming often. Add the onions, thyme, bay leaves, celery, and parsley sprigs.

2. Simmer, uncovered, removing the chicken and rabbit after 1½ hours. Continue to cook until the remaining meat is tender enough to fall from the bones, an additional 3 to 4 hours. Cool.

3. Separate the meat, chicken, and rabbit from the bones. Cover and refrigerate. Strain the stock and refrigerate overnight to allow the fat to solidify.

4. The next day, remove most of the fat, but leave a little in the stock for flavor. Add the chopped onions, potatoes, carrots, bell peppers, lima beans, corn, celery, tomatoes, and chile pepper to the stock. Salt slightly. Bring to a boil, reduce the heat, and allow the soup to simmer very quietly, uncovered, until the vegetables are tender and the burgoo has cooked low, 1 to 2 hours. Add the okra with the meat during the last 30 to 40 minutes of cooking. Add water when necessary.

5. Season to taste with salt, freshly ground black pepper, Tabasco, and Worcestershire sauce. Stir in the chopped parsley. Serve with corn muffins, toasted Cornmeal Melba Bread, or any good homemade bread and butter.

Serves 10 to 15

Burgoo must be seasoned after it has reduced in volume, or the seasonings will become too concentrated.

LEEK AND OYSTER SOUP WITH TARRAGON

*T*he compatibility of leeks and oysters is heightened by the addition of tarragon in this unusual and pleasing soup. I believe veal stock blends perfectly and is more delicate than the fish stock.

5 cups Veal or Fish Stock (see pages 58 and 61), or more as needed
1½ tablespoons chopped fresh tarragon or ½ teaspoon dried
4 leeks, white part only
4 tablespoons (½ stick) butter
1¼ pounds Idaho potatoes, peeled and diced
1½ pints oysters with liquor
1 cup heavy or whipping cream
Salt and freshly ground white pepper to taste
Chopped fresh parsley, for garnish
Chopped fresh tarragon, for garnish

1. Season the stock with the tarragon and bring to a boil in a large soup pot. Reduce the heat and simmer to develop the tarragon flavor, about 15 minutes.

2. Meanwhile, rinse the leeks well under running water. Pat them dry and cut them into thin rounds. Melt the butter in a skillet and sauté the leeks over medium heat until they are limp and have absorbed the butter, but do not allow them to brown the least bit, about 1½ minutes.

3. Strain the stock through a fine stainless-steel sieve or through dampened cheesecloth, and return it to the pot. Add the leeks and the potatoes to the stock. Allow the stock and vegetables to boil gently until the potatoes are soft, about 25 minutes.

4. Put the stock mixture in a blender or a food mill (not a processor), and blend until the mixture is smooth. Pour it back into the soup pot and heat. Add more stock if it is needed.

5. Heat the oysters and liquor in a saucepan just until their edges begin to curl (it takes about 1 to 1½ minutes, but it is better to watch the oysters than the clock). Add the cream and gently heat it. Stir the oyster mixture into the soup. Add salt and white pepper to taste, and sprinkle with chopped parsley and fresh tarragon.

6. Serve in warmed soup plates with

Unloading the oyster boat on the Baltimore waterfront, 1925.

rye crisps or Swedish rye crackers, and celery and Roquefort cheese.

Serves 6 to 8

VARIATION: Substitute 2½ pounds mussels for the oysters.

OYSTER AND ARTICHOKE SOUP

❖❖❖

*T*he idea for this soup came to me from New Orleans. It is for the gourmet and worth every effort it takes. The fresh artichokes can be tedious when a number are needed, so why not have a small gathering of your favorite "food-minded" friends and cook it together?

◆

6 large artichokes, freshly cooked (see Index)
4 tablespoons (½ stick) butter
6 shallots, minced
⅓ cup water
2½ tablespoons all-purpose flour
3 cups Veal or Chicken Stock (veal is best; see pages 58 and 57)
⅔ cup oyster liquor
2 bay leaves
3 sprigs fresh thyme or 1 teaspoon dried
Salt and freshly ground white pepper to taste
Cayenne pepper to taste
1 pint oysters
Fresh lemon juice to taste
¼ cup chopped fresh parsley
Thin lemon slices, for garnish

◆

1. Strip (and reserve) the flesh from the end of the artichoke leaves, scoop out the chokes, and cut the artichoke bottoms into cubes. You should have 1½ to 2 cups of artichoke cubes and flesh.

2. Melt the butter in a medium saucepan and add the minced shallots. Add the water (so the shallots will cook without browning) and simmer until the shallots are tender.

3. When the water has boiled away, add the flour and blend it in. Add the stock, oyster liquor, bay leaves, and thyme. Sprinkle lightly with salt and white and cayenne peppers and allow the mixture to simmer about 5 minutes.

4. Stir in the oysters. Add salt, pep-

per, and lemon juice to taste. Stir in the parsley. Heat the soup until piping hot, just to the point when the oysters begin to curl. Garnish with lemon slices and serve at once in heated bouillon cups with Toast Charlotte or French bread.

Serves 4 to 6

🦉 If more liquid is needed, oyster liquor would be the first choice; if you don't have enough, use veal or chicken stock.

SEA ISLAND FISH CHOWDER

◆◆

*G*rouper is a delicious, gelatinous fish for chowder—and it makes a good stock. Any good white fish, such as rockfish, may also be used in this chowder; just be careful not to toughen it by overcooking.

◆

1½ pounds white fish filets (grouper, sole, cod, halibut, haddock, rockfish, or red snapper)
2 cups strained Fish, Veal, or clear Chicken Stock (see pages 61, 58, and 57), or as needed
⅓ teaspoon dried thyme
3 tablespoons butter
½ cup chopped mild white onion
⅓ cup water
2 cups cubed peeled potatoes
½ cup chopped celery
2 cups milk, or more as needed
Salt and freshly ground white pepper to taste
Cayenne pepper to taste
½ cup chopped watercress
2 tablespoons chopped fresh parsley
Chopped fresh dill to taste, if available

◆

1. Cover the fish with 1½ cups stock in a large skillet, add the thyme, and bring it to a low boil. Poach only until the fish flakes when touched with a fork, about 5 minutes. Set aside.
2. Melt the butter in a heavy saucepan and add the onion and water. Cook over medium heat just until the onion is well coated with butter and the water has boiled away. Do not allow the onion to brown. Add the potatoes and celery. Cover with about ⅓ cup stock and cook, uncovered, until the potatoes and celery are tender, about 25 minutes.

3. Add 2 cups milk and heat until piping hot. If you need additional liquid, add more milk. Add the fish. Season with salt, white pepper, and cayenne.

4. Sprinkle with the chopped watercress, parsley, and dill. Heat until almost boiling. Serve with corn muffins or seafood crackers, and tomato and cucumber salad or a fresh vegetable salad.

Serves 4

🦉 A few oysters may be added with the chopped parsley at the last. Cook only until their edges curl.

◆◆

*T*he word "chowder" is believed to have come from the French word *chaudière*, the name of a large cauldron in which the fisherfolk of Brittany cooked their soups and stews.

In our country the earliest chowders came to us via the French and English colonizers. Potatoes were added somewhere along the way and today many chowders include them, except the Southern seacoast gumbos, which are usually served with rice instead. Both are delicious.

CAROLINA SILK SNAPPER CHOWDER

◆◆

A large family of snappers swim from Cape Hatteras to Florida through the Bahamas. The silk snapper and the ever-popular red snapper are much alike in taste and texture. They both look alike in their rosy red coats, but the silk snapper has yellow eyes instead of red. I have always thought the name "silk snapper" came from the Carolina trade with the Far East in the early days of our country.

I much prefer using a veal stock in this chowder, as it never disguises the snapper and shrimp flavor, but "ole salts" usually want the fish stock.

◆

5 cups Fish Stock (see list below and step 1) or
*   Veal Stock (see page 58)*
4 thick slices lean smoked bacon or salt pork
3 onions, peeled and cubed (2 cups)
1 pound Idaho potatoes, peeled and cubed
*   (3 cups)*
Salt to taste
1 silk or red snapper, about 3 pounds, fileted
*   and skinned*
⅓ pound whole small shrimp, shelled (1 cup)
½ cup chopped red bell pepper
Freshly ground white pepper to taste
¼ teaspoon cayenne pepper, or more to taste
Several slices fresh red chile pepper, or pinch
*   dried hot red pepper (optional)*
Juice of ½ lemon
Chopped fresh parsley or chervil, for garnish

◆

FISH STOCK

Head, tail, and bones of 1 silk or red snapper
1 tomato, peeled and chopped, or 1 canned
*   whole tomato, drained and chopped*
1½ teaspoons dried thyme
3 ribs celery, cut in half
¾ cup dry white wine
3 cups cold water

◆

1. Make the fish stock following the directions for the basic Fish Stock (see page 61). Strain through dampened cheesecloth draped over a sieve. You may use the basic Veal Stock as is.

2. Sauté the bacon or salt pork in a heavy enamel or stainless steel pot over medium heat, then lift it out and put it aside (if you used salt pork, discard it). Add the onions and potatoes to the pot. Strain the stock, through dampened cheesecloth or a fine sieve, over the vegetables. Add a touch of salt. Cook, uncovered, over medium-low heat until the onions and potatoes are tender, about 25 minutes.

3. Add the snapper filets to the chowder and continue to simmer gently until the fish flakes with a fork, not over 6 minutes. Add the shrimp and bell pepper and cook 2 to 3 minutes but no longer.

4. While it is cooking, season the chowder to taste with salt, white pepper, cayenne, and chile pepper. Add water if more liquid is needed. Break up the snapper a bit. The chowder must be thick but not so thick one cannot eat it with a spoon. Add the lemon juice, and sprinkle the chowder with parsley or chervil. Use the reserved bacon, crumbled, as a side dish for those who want it. Serve in soup plates with French bread, Cornmeal Melba Toast, or Sour Cream Corn Muffins.

Serves 6 to 8

🦉 You can use 2 pounds snapper filets instead of a whole snapper, if veal stock is used. But the fish must be skinned.

This chowder gains in flavor if set aside to ripen 1 hour or so. But to reheat, set it carefully over hot water and do not allow it to boil, as this will toughen the seafood.

SHRIMP OR CRAWFISH BISQUE

◆◆◆

This is the shrimp or crawfish bisque that is served at the most elegant homes in New Orleans and Charleston. Its presentation in small bouillon cups indicates the first course of a very fashionable dinner. In New Orleans the bisque is peppery. In Charleston it is more delicate. You choose.

The Labranche Buildings in New Orleans's French Quarter were erected in 1840, but the famous cast-iron grillwork wasn't added until after 1850.

◆

1 medium onion, chopped
3 carrots, peeled and chopped
4 ribs celery, chopped
½ cup finely chopped shallots or leeks
2 ripe tomatoes, peeled and puréed
3 tablespoons butter or good-quality olive oil
½ cup cold water
2 pounds small shrimp, or 10 pounds whole crawfish (for 2 pounds crawfish meat)
1 cup dry white wine
1 cup well-cooked rice, kept warm
4 to 5 cups Rich Chicken, Veal, or Fish Stock (see pages 57, 58, and 61)
Salt and freshly ground white pepper to taste
½ teaspoon cayenne pepper
1 teaspoon Hungarian paprika
1 cup heavy or whipping cream
3 tablespoons unsalted butter

◆

1. Combine the vegetables in a heavy enamel or stainless steel pot. Add the butter or olive oil and the water and bring to a boil. Reduce the heat and simmer, stirring, until the vegetables are half-cooked, about 4 minutes. They must not brown.

2. Add the shrimp or crawfish and toss them about until their shells turn a deep pink, 6 to 7 minutes.

3. Add the wine and simmer over low heat about 4 minutes.

4. Carefully lift out the seafood. Shell the shrimp or crawfish, reserving the meat.

5. Toss the shells into a wooden bowl and pound them with a mortar to break them into smaller pieces. Toss the shells back into the pot.

6. Add the warm rice and mix thoroughly.

7. Add 4 cups stock and stir until the mixture is the consistency of a very thick soup. Remove the pot from the heat, cover, and allow the flavors to ripen for 1 hour or more.

8. Put the mixture through a fine sieve. Add more stock if needed, but the soup must be thick. Season to taste with salt, white pepper, cayenne, and paprika. Place the bisque over low heat and add the cream and butter. Stir gently in one direction so the soup will thicken a bit.

9. If the shrimp seem too large, chop them into smaller pieces, then add them to the soup. If you are using crawfish, add them as is. Place the pot over hot water and allow the flavors to ripen again, if desired, no more than 10 minutes.

10. Serve the bisque in small cups with buttered Cornmeal Melba Toast.

Serves 6

CHARLESTON CREAM OF OYSTER SOUP

*I*n Charleston (so we are told) this soup was always served at the St. Cecilia debutante ball. The blades of mace floating with the oysters were the traditional spice. Mace does have a great affinity for oysters—and it has without a doubt a more subtle flavor than nutmeg. This is a rich soup and should be served in bouillon cups, not bowls.

1 pint fresh small oysters
3 tablespoons unsalted butter
3 cups milk, warmed
1 cup heavy or whipping cream, warmed
Salt and freshly ground white pepper to taste
2 blades mace, or sprinkling grated mace

1. Drain the oysters (freeze the liquor for another use). Melt the butter in a large saucepan, add the oysters, and allow them to absorb the butter over gentle heat, ½ minute.

2. Add the milk and cream. Season with salt, white pepper, and mace. Heat the soup slowly, stirring gently, only until the edges of the oysters begin to curl. Do not allow to boil. Taste for salt and white pepper.

3. Set the soup aside in a pan of simmering water, to be served later, or serve at once in small bouillon cups with toasted Cornmeal Melba Bread or hot buttered crackers.

Serves 6 to 8

🦉 Mace is the outer coating of nutmeg. It can be bought ground, of course, but grinding your own is more flavorful.

FABULOUS MUSHROOM SOUP

*T*his is an exquisite light soup for the first course of an important dinner or to serve to friends for lunch with a salad and good cheese. Adding the minced fresh mushrooms at the minute of serving—and no sooner—is what makes this soup unique!

1 quart Brown Soup Stock (see page 55)
2 cups chopped fresh mushrooms (½ pound), or
*   2 to 4 cups mushroom stems and peelings*
*   (see Owl)*
1 medium onion, chopped
Salt to taste
½ cup minced fresh mushrooms (¼ pound)
Freshly ground black pepper to taste

1. Combine the stock, chopped mushrooms or stems and peelings, and onion in a large saucepan. Bring to a boil, then reduce the heat and simmer, uncovered, 1 hour or more.

2. After the soup has simmered long enough to be well flavored, strain it through dampened cheesecloth or a fine-mesh steel strainer. Discard the chopped mushrooms. Add salt to taste.

3. Just before serving, add the minced mushrooms and a generous amount of freshly ground pepper. Correct the seasoning. Serve boiling hot in heavy mugs or bouillon cups with hot, thin rye or buttered white toast.

Serves 4

🦉 If you use mushrooms a great deal, collect the stems and peelings. Put them in plastic bags and freeze until you have a sufficient amount for this delicious soup. Then you will have to buy only ¼ pound of fresh mushrooms to be used for the garnish.

BUFFET SUPPER AT GLENAYRE FARM

Fabulous Mushroom Soup

Beef Tenderloin in Aspic with Fabulous Walnut Butter

Potato, Tarragon, and Fresh Artichoke Salad

Poppy Seed Bowknots

A Very Special Custard

Kentucky Bourbon Truffles

Liqueurs   Coffee

BLACK BEAN SOUP

This hearty black bean soup is beloved in the Deep South, but it is gaining favor everywhere. It keeps well in the refrigerator several days or it can be frozen.

4 cups dried black beans
5 quarts water
8 tablespoons (1 stick) butter
4 ribs celery, chopped
3 medium onions, chopped
2½ tablespoons all-purpose flour
⅓ cup chopped fresh parsley
1 ham bone
3 bay leaves
1 clove garlic, unpeeled
Freshly ground black pepper to taste
Salt to taste
½ cup Madeira or dry sherry
Fresh lemon juice to taste
2 sliced hard-cooked eggs, for garnish
Thin lemon slices, for garnish

1. Rinse and pick over the beans. Place the beans in a saucepan, add water to cover, and bring to a boil. Allow to boil 5 minutes, uncovered, then remove from the heat. Let stand 1 hour.

2. Drain the beans. In a large soup pot, cover the beans with 5 quarts water, bring to a boil, then reduce the heat and simmer, uncovered, for about 1½ hours.

3. Melt the butter in another large kettle. Sauté the celery and onions until they are limp, but do not brown. Blend the flour with the celery, onions, and butter. Add the parsley and beans with their liquid. Add the ham bone, bay leaves, garlic, and pepper to taste. Simmer until the flavor of the soup ripens, 3 to 4 hours.

4. Remove the ham bone, bay leaves, and garlic. Drain the beans, reserving the broth in a saucepan. Purée the beans in a blender or food processor. Combine the purée with the broth and strain into another pot. Add salt and Madeira or sherry. Simmer at least 5 minutes. Add lemon juice to taste. Add more salt if needed, and water if the soup is too thick, as it often is.

5. Ladle into hot soup plates and garnish each with a slice of hard-cooked egg and a slice of lemon.

Serves 6 to 8

VARIATION: In Guatemala, they garnish this soup with slices of avocado.

🦉 Unpeeled garlic is milder than peeled garlic.

CLEAR LEEK AND PARSLEY SOUP

*T*his is a crystal-clear soup that is as tasty as it is beautiful. The flavor depends largely on a delicious homemade stock. In the summer, a combination of fresh herbs—chervil, tarragon, and marjoram—is a glorious addition. As a dinner appetizer, serve the soup with toast points; for a luncheon entrée, serve it with warm French bread and cheese or tiny ham biscuits.

4 leeks, rinsed well and patted dry
2 tablespoons butter
½ cup water
1 pound new waxy potatoes, peeled and diced
*   (3 cups)*
1½ to 2 quarts clear Chicken Stock (see page
*   57)*
Salt and freshly ground white pepper to taste
1 cup chopped fresh parsley

1. Dice the leeks, incorporating a small amount of the green part if they are young and tender. You should have 2 cups.

2. Melt the butter in a large saucepan and add the leeks and water. Simmer until the leeks have softened, 5 to 6 minutes. (The water is needed to prevent the leeks from browning the least bit.)

3. In the meantime, drop the diced potatoes into boiling salted water in another saucepan and cook until they are almost tender, 16 to 17 minutes. The potatoes must not be mushy. Drain, and add to the leeks.

4. Cover the leeks and potatoes with the chicken stock. Bring to a boil and season to taste with salt and white pepper. Add the parsley, stir, and serve piping hot.

Serves 4

This soup must not be overly thick with vegetables. It is a delicate, light soup, and the colors should be shades of yellow and green only. Use new or waxy potatoes because mealy potatoes might prevent the stock from being translucent.

Fresh herbs should be added in the last 3 minutes before serving. This way the full fragrance of the herbs comes through.

HERBS THAT ARE OUTSTANDING IN STOCKS AND SOUPS

Thyme is the indispensable herb in most fine soup stocks. It has an intense flavor but is compatible with other herbs and is usable in a great variety of ways. It's the heart and soul of the bouquet garni. The New Orleans herb, as it is sometimes called, was brought to Louisiana by the French.

French tarragon is the aristocrat of all the herbs. It has great individuality and makes a strong statement. It is especially good with chicken in any guise and is magical in asparagus soup.

Parsley: If we were forced to give up every herb but one, parsley would be the one to keep. It is the most companionable and is truly indispensable on the French cook's table. It is utterly delicious when used in quantity so that its flavor is pronounced.

Summer savory was brought to the Ohio Valley by the German immigrants, along with their chives and dill. Savory is called the bean herb because of its compatibility with all kinds of peas and beans. It is not an indispensable herb but a pleasant and surprising one—for instance, try it with cabbage.

Sweet Marjoram is one of the most amicable of herbs and a delight to good cooks. It is a member of the mint family, as is oregano, but it has a delicacy that is much admired. It is the soul mate of thyme.

Sweet Basil was brought to the U.S. by the Italians, but it was not accepted or well known until the GIs started the fad for pizza after World War II. Now it is a favorite herb—and it's easy to grow too.

Dill is one of the most refreshing of all the herbs—hence the lovely touch it gives as a garnish to summer soups.

ALABAMA SORREL AND POTATO SOUP

*T*his could not be called a fine collection of soups if sorrel soup were omitted. The sorrel that grows wild in our meadows in the spring is called "sour grass." It is easy to grow in your herb garden and when cut often it will provide you generously all summer. This is a versatile soup and the variations are just as delicious—well, almost. Sorrel soup is very special. My favorite way to serve it is in hot weather, well chilled, with crisp Cornmeal Melba Toast, or Sour Cream Corn Muffins. Swing in a hammock in the shade—read a good book until it lulls you to sleep for a long summer nap. You will think you are back in Alabama.

2 quarts water
2 pounds Idaho potatoes, peeled and cubed (6 cups)
6 tablespoons (¾ stick) butter
4 leeks, white part only, rinsed well and thinly sliced (2½ cups)
½ cup cold water
3 cups chopped sorrel leaves
1 to 1½ cups milk
Salt and freshly ground white pepper to taste
Fresh lemon juice to taste
Chopped fresh chervil or parsley, for garnish

1. Bring the water to a boil in a large saucepan and add the potato cubes. Simmer, uncovered, until they are tender, about 25 minutes.

2. In the meantime, melt the butter in a heavy stainless steel or enamel saucepan or soup pot, and add the leeks along with the cold water. Allow the leeks to cook until they are limp and the water has boiled away, 5 minutes. (Do not allow the butter to sizzle or the leeks to get the least bit brown.) Stir in the sorrel leaves and cook until they wilt, 1 minute. (They will turn an odd shade of green, but don't worry.)

3. Add the leeks and sorrel to the cooked potatoes and their liquid. Add the milk as needed, starting with 1 cup. Simmer a few minutes. Purée in a blender (not a processor) or mash and strain through a sieve. If the soup is too thin, simmer it longer to reduce; if too thick, add more milk. Season with salt and white pepper. Add lemon juice to taste.

4. Pour piping hot into a warmed tureen or soup plates. Garnish with a sprinkling of chervil or parsley.

Serves 4 to 6

VARIATIONS: *Potato, Parsley, and Leek Soup:* Follow directions exactly for Alabama Sorrel and Potato Soup, except omit the sorrel and lemon juice, and use ⅔ cup finely chopped parsley leaves instead. (You must use a food processor for this.) Be generous with the white pepper. Garnish each bowl of soup with a small sprig of parsley and a slice of lemon. This is a beautiful soup and just as flavorful as it is beautiful—a wonderful and appetizing shade of green.

Potato and Leek Soup: Follow directions exactly for Alabama Sorrel and Potato Soup, except omit the sorrel and add 1 chopped medium onion with the leeks. Garnish each bowl with a sprig of parsley or a sprinkling of fresh dill. This is a delightful soup served hot or well chilled with your homemade Dark Sourdough Rye Bread or Rolls with Caraway Seeds (see Index).

SOUP OF THE THREE PEPPERS

*T*his is a very old Southern soup which deserves to be better known. It is very delicate and as beautiful as it is delicious. With a blender or food processor, it is a breeze to make. Serve with dainty cucumber sandwiches, or with a cucumber and dill salad and hot toasted crackers.

2 cups fat-free Rich Chicken Stock (see page 57)
1 jar (4 ounces) whole pimentos, drained
¾ cup heavy or whipping cream, or more to
*   taste*
Salt to taste
Tabasco sauce to taste
Hungarian paprika, for garnish

Put 1 cup of the chicken stock in a blender or processor. Add the pimentos and blend until perfectly smooth. Combine with the remaining cup of chicken stock in a saucepan, and add the cream. Heat just to a boil, season with salt and Tabasco to taste, and sprinkle each serving with a dusting of paprika.

    Serves 4

VARIATION: Add 8 to 10 freshly cooked

The tiny incendiary peppers from which Tabasco sauce is made.

small shrimp along with the cream, or purée a few with the pimentos and add the rest whole. You may need to add more stock or cream.

OLD-FASHIONED POTATO SOUP

*T*his is one of the best of family soups. Flavorful, nourishing, and easy for a nervous day. Parsley is essential to delicious potato soup. Don't change the proportions. They are perfect.

4 cups diced peeled potatoes
½ cup chopped celery
½ cup chopped onion
1 quart water
3 cups milk
2 tablespoons butter
8 sprigs parsley, leaves chopped
1¼ teaspoons salt, or more to taste
Freshly ground white pepper to taste

A SOOTHING WINTER SUPPER

Old-Fashioned Potato Soup

Dark Sourdough Rye Rolls

Wilted Slaw with Bacon Dressing

◆

Walnut and Apple Crisp with Coriander

1. Place the potatoes, celery, onion, and water in a large saucepan and bring to a boil. Reduce the heat and simmer until the vegetables are soft but not mushy, about 30 minutes. Drain, or allow the water to reduce until almost gone.

2. Add the milk, butter, parsley stems, salt, and white pepper to taste.

3. Allow the soup to simmer, uncovered, for the flavors to blend, 8 to 10 minutes. Remove the parsley stems; taste for salt. Stir in the chopped parsley leaves.

4. Serve with crisp crackers or one of your best homemade breads.

Serves 6

Potato soup should not be allowed to boil hard after the milk is added, or it will curdle. (Use whole milk, please—not low-fat.)

QUICK TOMATO CONSOMME

An easy cup of warming soup for a wintry night.

1 can (10½ ounces) undiluted beef consommé
1 cup water
2 cups tomato juice
1 bay leaf
1 rib celery
3 slices sweet white onion
3 sprigs parsley
Salt to taste
Chopped fresh parsley, for garnish
4 thin lemon slices, for garnish

Combine all the ingredients except the chopped parsley and lemon in a saucepan. Bring to a boil, reduce the heat, and simmer for 15 to 18 minutes. Strain. Serve with a sprinkling of parsley and a slice of lemon.

Serves 4

SPRING CONSOMME

This is a beautiful clear soup with an exquisite balance of flavors. Add only a tablespoon or so of vegetables to each serving. Just a touch of color in the crystal-clear broth is the most charming. Very small carrots may be scraped and scored deeply with a paring knife, then sliced crosswise very thin to look like daisies—beautiful.

Cut new turnips, carrots, and tiny green beans into little strips, not more than ½ inch long and toothpick thin. Add fresh young peas and cook the vegetables in boiling salted water until just tender, about 2 minutes. Drain and drop into hot consommé. Garnish with finely chopped chervil or parsley just before serving.

FRESH ASPARAGUS SOUP

This is one of the best soups in the whole world—I promise—and a wonderful way to use fresh asparagus. It is worth growing tarragon just for it.

2½ pounds fresh asparagus
2 cups milk
6 tablespoons (¾ stick) butter
¼ cup all-purpose flour
1 cup dry white wine
¼ cup chopped fresh tarragon or

1½ tablespoons dried
Salt and freshly ground white pepper to taste
3 cups fat-free Chicken or Veal Stock (see pages 57 and 58), or as needed
Chopped fresh tarragon, for garnish

1. Wash the asparagus. Remove the tips and drop them into boiling salted water to cook until barely tender, 3 to 4 minutes. Drain and set aside.

2. Remove and discard the tough ends of the asparagus stalks. Peel the stalks and cut each into 2 pieces. Drop the stalks into boiling salted water and cook until just tender but still crisp and bright green, 5 to 7 minutes. Drain. Purée the stalks in the blender with 1 cup of the milk.

3. Melt the butter in a large, heavy dutch oven over low heat. Add the flour and stir until perfectly smooth. Gradually add the remaining cup of milk. Allow the mixture to simmer a bit to rid the flour of its raw flavor, 5 minutes.

4. Add the white wine, asparagus purée, tarragon, and salt and white pepper to taste. Mix well and simmer for the flavors to develop, about 5 minutes or so.

5. Add stock until the soup is the desired thickness. Simmer a few minutes more, but do not allow the soup to boil (the acid in the asparagus will cause it to curdle; see Owl).

6. When the soup is sufficiently flavored with the tarragon, strain it to remove the tarragon, and return the soup to the dutch oven.

7. Drop the asparagus tips into the hot soup and allow them to heat through. Garnish with chopped fresh tarragon—lots of it.

Serves 6 to 8

This soup should have a pronounced tarragon flavor, but go easy with the dried tarragon.

If this soup is allowed to boil after the wine and asparagus purée are added, it is likely to curdle. Reheat the soup over hot water rather than over direct heat.

CREAM OF FRESH PEA SOUP

*S*erved with hot biscuits filled with slices of country ham or with thin buttered toast with Country Ham Butter, this fresh pea soup is one of the great joys of spring dining.

3 cups shelled fresh peas (about 3 pounds in the shell)
6 cups cold water
3 leaves romaine or Boston lettuce
6 slices smoked bacon
1 small white onion, peeled
Pinch of sugar
¾ cup fresh snow peas
2 tablespoons butter
Salt to taste
½ cup heavy or whipping cream

1. In a large saucepan, cover the peas with the cold water. Add the lettuce leaves, bacon, onion, and sugar. Bring to a boil, reduce the heat, and simmer, uncovered,

Peas, like corn, taste their best when picked right before they are cooked.

until the peas are tender, 15 to 20 minutes. (The peas must not lose their color—do not cover the pot!)

2. In the meantime, snip off the ends of the snow peas and string them. Cut the snow peas into thin slivers. Set aside.

3. Remove the bacon, lettuce, and onion from the peas and discard. Purée the peas with the liquid in a blender or food processor. Return the soup to the pan. Add the butter and salt. Add the cream, and heat gently. Do not boil. If the soup is too thick, add water or light chicken stock.

4. Bring a saucepan of salted water to a boil. Drop in the snow peas and blanch no longer than 1 to 2 minutes. Drain. Serve the soup, garnished with slivers of snow peas, in a warmed tureen or soup plates.

Serves 4 to 6

The cream may be omitted and more chicken stock added to your taste, but you will have, of course, a different soup.

FRESH GREEN PEA AND CHICKEN SOUP

◆◆◆

*F*ew soups herald spring with more spirit than this green pea soup, which is a meal in itself.

◆

4 cups shelled fresh peas (about 4 pounds in the
    shell)
6 tablespoons (¾ stick) butter
1 medium onion, chopped
5 sprigs parsley
2 teaspoons sugar
½ teaspoon salt
2 cups water
½ pound fresh spinach, trimmed and rinsed
    well
3 cups Chicken Stock (see page 57)
2 egg yolks
1½ cups light cream
1 whole chicken breast, poached (see Index),
    skinned, boned, and slivered
Salt and freshly ground white pepper to taste
Chopped fresh chervil or tarragon, or carrot
    curls, for garnish

◆

1. Put 3 cups of the peas in a large saucepan. Add the butter, onion, parsley, sugar, salt, and water. Bring to a boil, reduce the heat, and simmer, uncovered, until the peas are tender, 15 to 20 minutes. (The peas must not lose their color—don't cover the pot!)

2. In a separate pan, drop the spinach

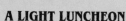

A LIGHT LUNCHEON

Fresh Green Pea and Chicken Soup

Brie or Camembert Cheese

Hot Rolls

◆

Florentine Lemon Cream

Lisa's Butter Leaf Cookies

---

into boiling water. Boil 2 minutes, then drain well and add to the soup.

3. In the meantime, cook the remaining cup of peas until tender in a separate pan of boiling salted water. Drain. Reserve to be used later.

4. Purée the soup in a blender until smooth. Pour it back into the saucepan and add the chicken stock. Simmer 10 to 15 minutes.

5. Stir together the egg yolks and cream, and add this mixture to the soup. Add the chicken. Heat, but do not allow to boil. Season with salt and white pepper.

6. When the soup has been seasoned and is hot enough to serve, add the reserved cooked peas. Heat a few minutes more, and pour into warmed soup bowls. Garnish with chopped fresh chervil, tarragon, or minute carrot curls. Serve with Toast Charlotte.
    Serves 6

VARIATION: Season with 2 tablespoons Madras curry powder or more to taste. Omit the chervil or tarragon. Serve hot or cold.

🦉 1 pound green peas in the shell usually makes 1 cup shelled.

FRESH CORN CHOWDER

◆◆◆

*T*o catch the full flavor of sweet summertime corn, the chowder should be made very simply.

◆

3 thick slices smoked bacon
1 small onion, chopped
5 potatoes, peeled and chopped
5 cups milk
3 cups tender white corn kernels (6 to 8 ears)
1 tablespoon butter, or to taste
Salt and freshly ground white pepper to taste
Chopped fresh parsley, for garnish

◆

1. Sauté the bacon in a skillet over medium heat until done but not overly crisp. Put the bacon aside (see Owl) and add the onion to the skillet. Sauté until the onion is tender and has absorbed the fat, but do not let it brown, 6 to 8 minutes.
    2. Combine the potatoes with the cooked onion in a large saucepan and barely cover with water. Boil until the potatoes are tender and the water has boiled low, 20 to 30 minutes.
    3. Add the milk, corn, and butter. Cook gently until the corn is tender, about

Stirring the kettles for a chowder party in Florida, 1934.

10 minutes. Add salt and white pepper to taste. Serve piping hot, garnished with a sprinkling of parsley.
    Serves 4 to 6

VARIATION: One red or green bell pepper, diced, may be added with the potatoes.

BROWN SOUP STOCK

◆◆◆

A fine brown stock is expensive, as it requires a large amount of meat and bones, but a delicious stock is a challenge to the cook and will be enjoyed by all. The browning of the bones and meat is of utmost importance in Brown Soup Stock. It gives color and flavor to the stock.

*Several pieces meat bones (1 beef shin, cut into
    4 pieces, or 1 veal knuckle, cut into 2
    pieces), or 1 oxtail, cut into 1-inch pieces*
*3 pounds lean beef or veal (brisket, chuck,
    shank, or shoulder), cut in 3-inch pieces,
    or 3 to 4 pounds short ribs*
3 quarts cold water
2 carrots, peeled and cut in half
1 parsnip, peeled and cut in half
4 ribs celery, cut in half
1 large onion stuck with 1 whole clove
6 peppercorns
2 sprigs fresh thyme or ½ teaspoon dried
6 sprigs parsley, tied with string
1 clove garlic
Mushroom stems or peelings, if available
*1 teaspoon tomato paste, or 1 tomato, peeled
    and chopped*
1 bay leaf
Salt to taste

1. Preheat the oven to 400°F.
2. Rinse the bones and pat them dry with paper towels. Place the meat and bones in a shallow pan and bake until the bones and meat have browned on all sides, 30 to 40 minutes.
3. Put the browned bones and meat in a soup pot and cover with the water. Add the remaining ingredients except the salt.
4. Bring the soup slowly to a boil, then reduce to a simmer. Cook slowly, uncovered, for 5 to 6 hours or longer. Skim often to keep the stock clear. As the soup boils away, replenish with cold water.
5. When the stock is rich-tasting, strain it through a fine-mesh strainer or dampened cheesecloth and add salt to taste. (Discard the vegetables and herbs; use the meat for hash.) Allow the stock to cool, then refrigerate overnight.
6. Skim off any fat and taste for salt, pepper, and herbs. If more thyme is needed, add a pinch, cook 6 to 8 minutes, and strain again.
7. Use as desired, or freeze.
Makes about 2 quarts

Stock is the basic liquid obtained by long cooking of meat, poultry, or fish with vegetables.

Stock and broth are used interchangeably. The word broth is usually used when a plain soup is made from chicken or beef and served as is. No one says, "Have a cup of stock."

Bouillon is a cooking term derived from the French that is used to describe the strained and clear liquid from the stockpot.

Consommé is made from the bouillon of the soup kettle. If the stock in the kettle is made correctly and not allowed to boil hard, it is often not necessary for the home cook to clarify the stock to make bouillon or consommé clear and limpid. Consommé in American cooking terminology usually means that gelatin has been added so the consommé will gel when chilled.

WHITE SOUP STOCK

This stock is excellent for all vegetable soups. It may be strained, cooled, and frozen until needed.

*1 veal knuckle, cut into 2 pieces, or 3 pounds
    neckbones*
*2 pounds lean beef or veal or a mixture (shins,
    brisket, chuck, shoulder, neck, or short
    ribs)*
3 quarts water
2 carrots, peeled and cut in half
1 large onion stuck with 1 whole clove
6 ribs celery, cut in half
8 parsley sprigs
2 bay leaves
12 peppercorns
Salt to taste

1. Rinse the bones well. Put the bones and meat in a large soup pot. Add the water and bring slowly to a boil. Reduce the heat to keep the stock at a bare simmer and skim off any scum that has risen to the top. Cook for at least 1 hour, uncovered, skimming frequently, until the scum has ceased rising. Do not stir the stock at any time; stirring makes a cloudy stock.

2. Add the vegetables and seasonings, except for the salt. Continue to cook, uncovered or partially covered to cook somewhat faster, until all the flavor has been extracted from the meat, at least 4 to 5 hours or as long as all day (always keeping the broth simmering, not boiling hard). Add water as needed to maintain the level, but do not stir.

3. When the stock is full-flavored, strain, and add salt to taste. Allow the stock to cool, then place it in the refrigerator for several hours or overnight. Remove most of the solidified fat. Some fat left in the stock will add flavor.

Makes about 2 quarts

Soup stock is not salted until the end, since it might become too salty as the stock is reduced.

Adding water to the soup stock must be left to the wisdom of the cook. If the stock boils too rapidly, the water evaporates before it is seasoned. If cooked insufficiently, the stock will not derive enough flavor from the meat and herbs.

CHICKEN STOCK

❖❖❖

Chicken stock is one of the true essentials in a good cook's larder. Poach the chicken, make sandwiches or salad with the meat, and freeze the stock. You will have at your command the basic stock for dozens of dishes.

◆

1 chicken, 2½ to 3 pounds (see Owl)
Several extra wings and backs
1 medium onion stuck with 1 whole clove
4 ribs celery, cut in half
2 or 3 sprigs fresh thyme or about ½ teaspoon
    dried
1 bay leaf
3 quarts water
Salt to taste

◆

1. Rinse the chicken well and place it with the extra pieces in a soup pot with the onion, celery, thyme, bay leaf, and water. Add salt sparingly. Bring to a boil, lower the heat, and simmer, uncovered, for 1½ hours, skimming off any scum that rises to the top.

2. When the chicken is tender and the broth well flavored, remove the chicken and pieces. Reserve the meat for salad or sandwiches. Strain the broth and allow it to cool. Then refrigerate for several hours or overnight.

3. Skim off the solidified fat when you are ready to use the stock or before you freeze it.

4. Just before using, taste the stock for salt. If the stock is not rich enough in flavor, simmer over medium heat until it reduces a bit. If it is too rich or has cooked too low, add water.

Makes about 1½ quarts

VARIATION: *Rich Chicken Stock:* In a soup pot, barely cover a chicken with half cold Chicken Stock and half cold water, about 3 quarts liquid. Add 1 onion and 3 ribs celery. Bring to a boil, reduce the heat, and simmer, uncovered, until the chicken is just tender, about 1 hour. Taste for salt. Allow the mixture to cool. Then remove the chicken from the stock. Use the meat for chicken curry, salad, à la king, hash, or any favorite dish calling for precooked chicken. (It is important that the chicken not be overcooked and the flesh retain some firmness.)

as an extra-flavorful stock for basic cream soups, chicken consommé, and special sauces.

Makes about 1½ quarts

🦉 Cooked chicken and chicken stock must not be refrigerated until they have cooled. A cover also must not be placed on hot chicken dishes or stock until they have cooled, as they are likely to spoil.

Cut the chicken into 6 to 8 pieces to ensure a richer stock. If the chicken itself is of utmost importance, cut the bird in half only.

Strain the stock and refrigerate. Remove the solidified fat. Taste for salt. Use

A QUICK LIGHT STOCK

A good choice for sauces, ragouts, and light vegetable soups.

3 or 4 veal marrow bones
2 pounds bony pieces chicken, such as wings
4 quarts cold water
2 small onions
2 carrots, peeled and cut in half
1 cup mushroom stems and peelings (see Index)
1 cup tomato peelings
½ cup cucumber peelings
Bouquet of fresh herbs, such as thyme, parsley,
    marjoram, and tarragon, or 2 teaspoons
    mixed dried herbs
Salt to taste

1. Rinse the bones well. Place the bones, chicken, water, vegetables, and seasonings, except the salt, in a large soup pot. Bring to a boil, then reduce the heat and simmer, uncovered, 1 hour or more. Add water as needed to maintain the level. Salt very lightly.
2. Strain the stock, and allow it to cool. Refrigerate several hours or overnight, then skim off the solidified fat. This stock freezes well.

Makes about 3 quarts

VEAL STOCK

*T*he great value of veal stock is its versatility. It will serve well in any recipe that calls for a light chicken or beef stock, and it can be used instead of a fish stock in almost every case.

3 pounds veal shoulder bones
1½ pounds veal meat
6 quarts water

OPTIONAL SEASONINGS

1 medium onion stuck with 1 whole clove

4 ribs celery, cut in half
2 or 3 sprigs fresh thyme
1 bay leaf

1. Rinse the bones well and place the

bones and meat in a large soup pot. Add all the optional seasonings, if desired (the plain veal stock is wonderful, especially for seafood soups). Cover with the water and bring to a boil. Reduce to a simmer and cook, uncovered, until well flavored, 2 to 4 hours.

2. Strain the stock and allow it to cool.

Refrigerate several hours or overnight. Skim off any solidified fat. You may freeze this stock for future use.

Makes about 3 quarts

Instead of shoulder bones and meat, you can use veal shanks cut into rounds.

HAM-BONE STOCK

A good ham stock is the heart and soul of many Southern country dishes. To be truly delicious, the stock must be prepared with a knowing hand.

1 small uncooked smoked ham hock, or a
    leftover ham bone
¼ pound thick-sliced smoked bacon
2 quarts cold water
2 carrots, peeled and cut in half
1 small onion stuck with 1 whole clove
2 ribs celery, cut in half
4 sprigs parsley
2 small potatoes, peeled

1. Place the ham hock or bone and bacon in a large pot, and cover with the water. Add the remaining ingredients and bring to a boil. Reduce the heat and simmer, uncovered, until the stock has devel-

oped a pleasing flavor, 1½ to 2 hours.

2. Strain the stock and allow it to cool.

Makes about 5 cups

The stock is very flavorful as is, but it may be refrigerated overnight and the fat skimmed off. However, the richness and fine flavor of the stock will suffer if every particle of fat is removed. Use soon after making as this stock doesn't freeze well.

This is the traditional Southern stock for cooking green beans, cabbage, and bean soup. This amount is enough for 2 pounds green beans or 1 pound dried navy or pinto beans.

A SIMPLE HAM AND BACON STOCK

T his is a basic, uncluttered way of preparing a flavorful stock for cooking beans—shellouts, green, dried beans of all types—and for making bean soups. Using leftover fat from the breakfast bacon is the poorest way of seasoning beans or soup—the flavor has been spent.

½ pound thick-sliced lean smoked bacon, or
    smoked slab bacon cut in 1½-inch cubes
¼ pound uncooked smoked country ham or

hock, or small piece of any good smoked
    ham or hock
2 quarts cold water

A farmer's wife tends the stockpot in Green Springs, Virginia, 1947.

1. Place the bacon, ham, and water in a large pot. Bring to a boil, reduce the heat, and simmer, uncovered, 30 minutes to 1 hour.

2. Strain the stock and allow it to cool. If desired, the stock may be refrigerated and some of the fat skimmed off. Use soon after making as this stock doesn't freeze well.

Makes about 1½ quarts

🦉 In making hearty country soups and stews, the flavor of the bacon and ham fat is often the keynote. If you must have it completely fat-free, cook another dish.

HOW TO CLARIFY STOCK FOR ASPIC JELLY AND BOUILLON OR CONSOMME

◆◆◆

*T*his technique may seem tedious, but if you want a truly fine, sparkling aspic, this is how it is made. If the stock is to be used for soup, sauces, or plain bouillon, omit the gelatin. This makes a fine consommé.

◆

6 cups well-flavored Brown, Veal, or Rich Chicken Stock (see pages 55, 58, and 57)
3 egg whites, beaten until stiff
1 tablespoon tomato paste, or 2 ripe tomatoes, chopped
¼ cup dry Spanish sherry or Madeira
1 tablespoon white wine tarragon vinegar
1½ tablespoons unflavored gelatin (for aspic)
⅓ cup water (for aspic)

◆

1. Put the stock (which must be completely fat-free) and the beaten egg whites, tomato paste or tomatoes, sherry or Madeira, and tarragon vinegar in a large stainless steel or enamel pan or stockpot. Mix well and bring to a boil. Remove from the heat and allow to stand for 10 minutes. Strain the stock through dampened cheesecloth in a large sieve, or through a fine-mesh sieve.

2. If you are making an aspic, blend the gelatin and cold water in a heatproof measuring cup and place the cup in a pan of boiling water. Heat until the gelatin has dissolved and the liquid is clear. Stir the gelatin into the hot stock.

Makes 3½ to 4 cups clarified stock

🦉 A certain amount of stock is lost when it is clarified with egg whites and strained through damp cheesecloth. The cooked egg white is a foamy mass that attracts all of the undesirable substances in the stock, such as pepper, and all residues from the meat. This mass reduces the amount of liquid when it is strained. Also, a certain amount of liquid is lost when it is absorbed by the cheesecloth. The cheesecloth must not be squeezed, which would force the unwanted particles back into the soup. So if your recipe calls for a certain amount of clarified stock, always be sure to start out with more than enough.

CHICKEN CONSOMME WITH ZUCCHINI AND HAM

*T*o 6 to 8 cups of well-flavored chicken consommé, add 1½ cups zucchini cut into matchstick slivers and 1 cup slivers of lean baked ham. Bring to a boil and simmer 4 to 5 minutes.

Just before serving, add 2 tablespoons each chopped fresh parsley and basil. Add salt if needed. Serve piping hot and pass a dish of freshly grated Parmesan cheese if desired.

Serves 6

FISH STOCK

*U*se this for fish soups, bouillabaisse, seafood bisques, and fish sauce.

1½ pounds fresh fish bones
1 fresh small fish, cleaned and gutted (1½ pounds)
4 quarts cold water
1 carrot, peeled and cut in half
2 onions
2 ribs celery, cut in half
½ cup dry white wine
1 clove garlic
10 white peppercorns
½ teaspoon dried tarragon
¼ teaspoon dried thyme
¼ teaspoon dried marjoram
1 bay leaf
3 sprigs parsley
Salt to taste

1. Put the fish bones and fish in a stainless steel or enamel stockpot. Cover with the water. Add the vegetables, wine, and seasonings except for the salt. Bring to a boil, reduce the heat, and simmer, uncovered, for 1 to 2 hours. (If the stock is flavorful after 1 hour, it has cooked enough.) Skim the scum off carefully when the stock starts to boil and keep skimming as needed.

Whiling away an afternoon in Pensacola, Florida.

2. Strain through dampened cheesecloth draped over a large sieve. Add salt to taste. Cool and refrigerate. Freezes well for a short time.

Makes about 2½ quarts

If fresh herbs are available, use a few sprigs of each in place of the dried.

LAMB STOCK

*L*amb stock is not used in soups, but it is used instead of water to make a fuller-bodied broth for braising lamb dishes.

Can there be a flavorful stock made without onions? Well maybe, but I wouldn't want to chance it very often.

2½ *pounds lamb bones*
1 *rib celery*
1 *small onion*
1 *bay leaf*
1 *sprig parsley*
2 *quarts water*

Combine all the ingredients in a large pot and bring to a boil. Reduce the heat and simmer for at least 1 hour. Strain, and reserve for use in lamb stews or sauces.

Makes 1 quart

CHAPTER THREE

SALADS AND SALAD DRESSINGS

DRESSED AND READY

*T*here are two main categories of salads, the composed salad and the green salad. The composed salad's proper place is usually as the main course of a light and informal meal. These salads are enticing to the eye and refreshing to the palate but they are rather substantial, and little else is needed to round out the menu but a good bread, a glass of wine perhaps, and a delicious dessert. Our top favorites in the South, I believe, are made from chicken, shrimp, or crabmeat tossed in homemade mayonnaise, with celery hearts—more often than not—for crunch and texture.

The joy of any green salad is its talent to refresh, to lend texture and beauty to your menu as well as to lighten it. A mixture of different lettuces, for a variety of texture and taste, dressed with a vinaigrette is superb. But I confess that I have a prejudiced palate: I often serve Bibb lettuce alone as a simple salad with an important meat or as a separate course. It is crisp, with a lovely flavor, and it is beautiful. Bibb is a world traveler now, but it was born in Kentucky and named for Judge Jack Bibb, who propagated it around 1865 in his hobby greenhouse in Frankfort. It was called limestone lettuce at first, as the alkaline limestone soil of central Kentucky was credited with helping to produce a superior lettuce. The heads of true Bibb lettuce are compact and exquisitely small—one head is a perfect single serving. The vibrant tones of strong greens and soft yellows are as beautiful as the lettuce is crisp, and its crunchiness never fails to amaze gardeners. But how did Judge Bibb compose and control the size? What strains of lettuce did he cross to achieve these dainty heads of perfect balance in flavor and texture? No one knows. No one has been able to break the code.

SHADY LANE SALAD

◆◆◆

*I*n the heart of the bluegrass country there is an old curvy road, seldom traveled now, that goes from Frankfort to Lexington. There are vine-covered stone fences on either side of this road, built long ago by slave labor and still strong and beautiful. Large trees bend over the road, forming a canopy of protection from the sun. We take this narrow old road very slowly so we can drink in the beauty of the rolling land and farm pastures where the Thoroughbred horses romp. Many times, if we stop, the high-spirited mares come up to peep over the fence to see what's going on. When they decide that all is well, they toss their gorgeous heads and fly away. What elegance.

I never intended to let a spring blend into summer without a day's outing to drive along Shady Lane to Lexington. I haven't missed many.

◆

4 heads Bibb, or 1 to 2 heads Boston, or other leaf lettuce
1 center slice country ham
4 hard-cooked eggs, sliced
1½ tablespoons capers, drained
⅓ cup chopped chives or tender scallion (green onion) tops
Chopped fresh marjoram, chervil, and tarragon, for garnish

VINAIGRETTE

⅓ cup good-quality olive or vegetable oil
1½ tablespoons white or red wine vinegar
Salt and freshly ground black pepper to taste

◆

1. Separate the lettuce, rinse it, and dry in a spinner.

2. Cut the ham into slivers. Grease an iron skillet well with a piece of ham or bacon fat. Sauté the ham quickly.

3. In the meantime, put the lettuce in a salad bowl. Scatter the eggs and capers about. Put the hot ham slivers in the center. Add the chives or scallions and the fresh herbs.

4. Blend the vinaigrette ingredients together with a whisk.

5. Present the salad, then add the dressing, toss, and serve.

Serves 4

🦉 Delicious with bread, corn muffins, biscuits, or hot rolls for luncheon, or with tender ears of corn dripping with butter for a light supper on the patio.

Stone fences line a straight, tree-sheltered stretch of memorable Shady Lane.

SALAD GREENS

Leaf lettuce is an early spring favorite that comes along in country gardens with the radishes and scallions. This famous trilogy tossed in a bowl with crisp smoked bacon and a touch of vinegar is dear to the heart of every Southerner. The ruffled, sweet leaves are highly perishable and should be used the day the lettuce is gathered or purchased. It is a poor choice for a garnish. Red leaf lettuce is a member of the same family.

Boston, a soft, flavorful lettuce, is one of the best of all the lettuces if it is to be used alone for a salad. It also combines well, however, with crisp romaine and endive. Only the beautiful yellow inside leaves (or heart) are useful in garnishing.

Romaine, or Cos, has long, slim, crisp leaves that are almost plumelike. Because of its crunchy texture and fresh grassy flavor, it is a great favorite for mixed salad bowls. It makes a lovely cream soup and an outstanding soufflé. Choose small heads, as the dark green outside leaves are somewhat tough. It's easy to wash.

Curly chicory is a kind of endive. The beautiful shades of light green and yellow make chicory a lovely garnishing lettuce. Its bitter tang and curly leaves are invaluable in a mixed green salad and are especially attractive when combined with Belgian endive. It is of little value when not properly pale, as the dark green leaves are bitter.

Beautiful Red Vernone, Red Treviso, and Castelfranco are all chicories and are all called *radicchio.* Treviso has a long, tapered leaf; Castelfranco is variegated and has a fairly firm globe-shaped heart. These are wonderful lettuces. Keep asking for them so the produce merchants will bring them in from California. Better still, plant them in your garden.

Escarole grows in a sprawling head with irregular light-yellow inner leaves. It is nice in mixed green salads with mustardy dressings and is superb cooked as a green vegetable to accompany roast lamb.

Spinach, a great favorite for the winter salad bowl, may be used alone with a generous dose of fruity olive oil and Dijon mustard, or with sliced, crisp white mushrooms. Tender young spinach leaves blend well in mixed green salads and they are almost as good as leaf lettuce with hot crisp bacon, vinegar, and hard-cooked egg. The Italians blanch spinach about 3 minutes, drain it well, and serve it chilled with olive oil and lemon as a side dish with veal roast and chops—delicious. Spinach is tedious to clean, but it is one of our most valuable greens.

Belgian or French endive, sometimes called witloof, comes in small, oval, tightly closed heads of satin-white leaves that shade into yellow. It is the aristocrat of all the lettuces and is considered to be the epicure's favorite. It has a pleasing tangy flavor and a lovely crisp texture, which make it perfect for a mixed salad or for use alone. It remains expensive, as it is tedious to grow and to harvest. The French hold a dish of braised endive and mushrooms to be the ultimate of all vegetable cookery, but it is used more often to grace the salad bowl.

Watercress is another favorite green of the gourmet. First of all, it is highly flavored, and second, it is most attractive and appetizing looking. It has a peppery, stimulating taste that combines well with most meats and has a much more aristocratic presence than parsley when used as a garnish. Watercress is frail, however, and does not keep well even in the refrigerator. It wilts quickly on a platter, but no other green has quite its quality or charm as a garnish.

Sorrel, the tart, lemony perennial that is grown in all French gardens, is a relative of our sour grass that comes up wild in the spring. A tiny bit of it is enlivening to a green salad, but it is more notable in soup or an omelet—and divine as a stuffing for black bass. Plant a small row and it will greet you happily year after year.

Iceberg lettuce is the most inexpensive of the salad greens. It is short on flavor, but it is crunchy. It comes in tight heads that are easy to wash and that stay crisp forever, so it is the most commonly used in the U.S. When buying, choose the dark green heads that are not so compact.

Arugula, also called rocket (roquette in seed catalogues), is one of the salad greens in fashion today. All of the so-called "rocket clan" are members of the large mustard family, hence their pungent but pleasing flavor. And true to any of the mustard family, it is best when picked young. Arugula is the beloved green of the Mediterranean countries, especially Italy. It is delicious used alone, but it can be mixed with other greens.

French dandelion looks very much like arugula but it has a milder flavor. It adds a zesty bite to a green salad. This green can be planted from seed, or you can stalk it in the wild. Like other members of the mustard family, it must be picked and eaten while very young and tender. By the time the yellow blossoms mature, the leaves are too strong-tasting for salad.

BLACK-SEEDED SIMPSON SALAD

*B*lack-Seeded Simpson is special, but any variety of leaf lettuce is fine for this salad. The red-leaf is pretty but it wilts very fast.

2 large heads leaf, butter, or romaine lettuce, or mixed as desired
4 scallions (green onions), chopped
8 slices smoked bacon, fried and crumbled
3 tablespoons fresh bacon drippings
2 tablespoons sugar
½ teaspoon salt
¾ cup cider vinegar
¼ cup water (see Owl)

1. Wash and dry the lettuce, tear it into bite-size pieces, and put it in a wooden bowl. Add the scallions and bacon.

2. Combine the remaining ingredients in a small saucepan and bring to a boil. Taste for seasoning. Pour over the lettuce and toss. Serve immediately.

Serves 4

VARIATION: Chopped hard-cooked eggs may be added as a garnish if desired.

If you are using a strong-flavored vinegar, increase the water to ½ cup.

SALAD OF LAMB AND LIMESTONE LETTUCE

*L*eftover lamb needs assertive seasonings such as curry powder, chutney, or anchovies. The combination given here is flavorful and appetizing in a salad. Lamb, of course, has a great affinity for chutney in any guise—they are the best of friends.

2½ cups slivered leftover roast lamb, leg or shoulder, at room temperature
1 cup freshly cooked small green beans, trimmed
2 shallots or white part of 2 scallions (green onions), chopped fine
2 sprigs fresh tarragon
1 tablespoon capers, drained
10 colossal black olives, sliced
5 anchovy filets, rinsed well, dried, and coarsely chopped
Freshly ground black pepper to taste
3 tablespoons tarragon vinegar
Salt to taste
6 tablespoons good-quality olive or vegetable oil
4 heads Bibb lettuce
Chopped fresh parsley, for garnish
Aunt Nettie's Major Grey Mango
Chutney (see Index)

1. Combine the lamb, beans, shallots or scallions, tarragon, capers, olives, and anchovies in a large bowl. Sprinkle with a few grinds of pepper.

2. Mix the tarragon vinegar, a pinch of salt, and the oil in a small bowl. Toss the salad with the dressing, using just enough dressing to coat the ingredients. Taste for salt.

3. Line a salad bowl or deep platter generously with lettuce. Spoon the salad into the center, and sprinkle with chopped parsley. Serve with mango chutney.

Serves 4

WATERCRESS AND WALNUT SALAD

One of the best wintertime salads.

1 large bunch watercress, stems trimmed
⅓ cup coarsely chopped walnuts
¼ cup Classic Vinaigrette (see page 87)

Toss the watercress with the walnuts. Serve the salad, and pass the dressing in a sauceboat.

Serves 4

Watercress turns dark and limp faster than almost any other green when dressing is added. It is best to toss the salad at the table or allow each guest to add the dressing.

COUNTRY THICK BACON, CHEVRE, AND WALNUT SALAD

On a small farm named "Woodside" in Subtle, Kentucky, the Peter Shafers are making a delicious *chèvre* (goat cheese) called Kentucky Jubilee. A few years ago we thought only the French could make *chèvre*. I, for one, was very incredulous but now I am a believer. Kentucky *chèvre* can be used in any of the traditional—or new—ways, but it is at its most charming served simply with green salad and crisp, thin Cornmeal Melba Toast or in the delicious salad below. Cover the cheese while it is very fresh with good-quality olive oil and a sprig or two of thyme, and it will keep a week or more in the refrigerator to use at will.

8 thick slices smoked bacon
6 cups lettuce—a mixture of leaf, Bibb,
*   romaine, red leaf, and curly chicory*
¼ cup red wine vinegar
½ cup good-quality olive oil or to taste, or
*   ¼ cup imported French walnut oil and*
*   ¼ cup vegetable oil*
½ teaspoon Dijon mustard
Salt to taste
Fresh lemon juice if needed
5 ounces chèvre, trimmed of rind and cubed
½ cup coarsely chopped walnuts

1. Preheat the oven to 425°F.
2. Bake the slices of bacon until done but not overly crisp. Drain, cut into 1-inch pieces, and keep warm.
3. Wash and dry the lettuces. Put them in a salad bowl.
4. In a small bowl, blend the vinegar with the oil, mustard, salt, and a squeeze of lemon juice.
5. At the moment of serving, pour the dressing over the lettuce. Sprinkle with the cheese and bacon. Sprinkle walnuts over the top of the salad.

Serves 6

A sprinkling of fresh thyme, tarragon, and marjoram would be a glorious added touch.

GOAT CHEESE IN OIL AND HERBS

*T*his is an exquisite cheese to serve with hot French bread, Italian Fettunta, or Toast Charlotte to accompany salads or soups.

1 pound chèvre *(goat cheese)*
Good-quality olive oil to cover cheese
6 coriander seeds
3 bay leaves
1 teaspoon crushed dried rosemary
1 tablespoon chopped fresh thyme or
*   ⅔ teaspoon dried*
10 black peppercorns, crushed

1. Put the pieces of cheese in a large wide-mouthed jar. Pour olive oil in to cover. Add the herbs and spices. Store in a cool place, not the refrigerator, for 3 days.
2. When ready to serve, remove the cheese and cut into attractive individual servings. Sprinkle the cheese with additional fresh or dried thyme and some coarsely crushed black pepper.
Serves 16

 Do not allow the cheese to marinate more than a week.

TOAST CHARLOTTE

*T*his is a delectable way of serving a crisp, warm toast. It is the low temperature that does the trick. At 325°F the bread toasts from the inside out—and it stays crisp a long time.

Use white homemade-type bread, or Cornmeal Melba Bread, sliced thin. Cut each piece in half. Lay the pieces on a baking sheet. Brush the tops lightly with melted butter, covering the entire surface. Sprinkle with poppy seeds, if desired. Bake in a preheated 325°F oven until golden brown, about 25 to 30 minutes. Serve warm with cheese, pâtés, soups, and salads.

WARM BROCCOLI AND RED BELL PEPPER SALAD

*S*erve this gorgeous Southern salad with veal chops or roast, broiled chicken, or steak. If you wish to make it an entrée, just before serving sprinkle the salad with hot chopped, broiled bacon, hot slivers of fried country ham, or thin slivers of chicken breast or steak sautéed quickly in butter.

1 bunch broccoli
2 red bell peppers, cored and seeded
1 sweet yellow banana pepper, cored and
*   seeded*
½ cup homemade mayonnaise (see page 93)
½ cup sour cream
2 ounces Roquefort or Danish blue cheese, at
*   room temperature*

Salt to taste
½ cup black olives (Niçoise type is best here),
*   or 1½ tablespoons capers, well drained*
4 hard-cooked eggs, quartered
Chopped fresh parsley, chervil, or tarragon, for
*   garnish*
⅓ cup Classic Vinaigrette (see page 87)

1. Peel the stems of the broccoli. Divide the head into serving pieces. Set aside.

2. Cut the red and yellow peppers into thin slivers. Set aside.

3. Blend the mayonnaise, sour cream, and Roquefort in a small bowl. Add salt if needed.

4. Drop the broccoli into boiling salted water to cover. Cook until tender but still crisp and green, 8 to 10 minutes, depending on the freshness of the broccoli. Drain well. Transfer to a warmed shallow platter, making a pleasing design. Sprinkle the pepper slivers over the broccoli. Place the black olives in a mound in the center of the platter, if you are using them. Arrange the eggs around the platter, and sprinkle them with chopped parsley, chervil, or tarragon, salt, and capers, if you are using them.

5. Spoon the vinaigrette over the warm broccoli. Serve with a sauceboat of the mayonnaise mixture.

Serves 4 to 6

VARIATIONS: If you like anchovies, 3 or 4 may be chopped and added to the vinaigrette dressing, or they can be passed separately in a small bowl.

Warm Broccoli, Pasta, and Red Bell Pepper Salad: Cut the broccoli in smaller pieces, make the salad, and add warm, freshly cooked small shell pasta. Toss all together with the vinaigrette dressing. Sprinkle with chopped parsley or a bouquet of herbs such as fresh tarragon and chervil.

HERBS THAT ARE DELICIOUS IN SALADS

French Tarragon—Few herbs lend their flavor and fragrance to summer salads more readily than tarragon. And what would we do without tarragon vinegar all year long?

Sweet Basil—There are several types of basil, but sweet basil is by far the most pleasant in salads. It is an assertive herb.

Chives are a member of the onion family, and a soft-spoken one. They are most pleasant used in salads and sandwiches where just a hint of the onion flavor is needed.

Chervil is always included in a list of the "fine herbs." It is a beautiful herb but very delicate. It is delicious in all egg dishes, salads, and sandwiches.

Parsley is the stalwart character of the group of "fine herbs." Its value is unlimited. It has a worthy place in almost every salad.

Sweet Marjoram's freshness and flavor is appreciated in the summer salad, in pasta, hot or cold, and in green salad of all kinds.

Rosemary—One of the important things to remember about rosemary is that it has an affinity for fruit—not so much in the fruit as by its side as a garnish.

Thyme—Fresh thyme does not blend with every salad, as it is often too intense, but a touch of thyme is special in meat salads.

Dill—To use dill just in pickles is to miss one of the great herbs for salad. Fresh dill leaves have a tang that is the perfect partner for cucumbers, tomatoes, potatoes, and cream and cottage cheese.

WARM ASPARAGUS SALAD WITH MUSTARD DRESSING

*T*his salad of warm asparagus can be an exquisite first course, or you can serve it with the entrée. The sauce is so delicious and easy that you will enjoy serving it with many dishes instead of hollandaise.

2 pounds asparagus, stems trimmed and peeled
1 hard-cooked egg yolk
1 raw egg yolk
1½ teaspoons light yellow Dijon mustard
1½ tablespoons tarragon vinegar

½ teaspoon salt, or to taste
Cayenne pepper to taste
½ cup good-quality olive or vegetable oil
1 red bell pepper, cored, seeded, and slivered

1. Drop the asparagus into boiling salted water to cover and cook until tender but still crisp, 5 to 7 minutes. Drain and keep warm.

2. In the meantime, put the hard-cooked egg yolk in a blender or small bowl along with the raw yolk. Add the mustard, vinegar, salt, and cayenne pepper. Gradually add the oil to the blender as it is running, or beat in briskly but gradually with a whisk, until the dressing is smooth and looks like thin mayonnaise.

3. Divide the asparagus among 4 salad plates. Spoon the dressing over the asparagus and garnish with the red pepper strips.

Serves 6

This dressing may be made with tepid melted butter instead of the oil, if you desire.

Save the hard-cooked egg white for a tossed salad.

GREEN BEAN AND SMOKY BACON SALAD

This is delicious with grilled or broiled chicken.

2 pounds tiny green beans, or half green and half wax beans
⅓ pound sliced lean smoked bacon
3 scallions (green onions), chopped
¼ cup chopped fresh parsley
2½ tablespoons sherry vinegar or good white wine vinegar
1 teaspoon light yellow Dijon mustard
Vegetable or olive oil to taste
Salt and freshly ground white pepper to taste

1. Prepare the beans by trimming off the ends and stringing or trimming off the side seams to make them very tender. Drop the beans into boiling salted water and cook until tender but still crisp and green, about 5 minutes. Drain at once.

2. Put the bacon in a skillet and fry until golden brown but not overly crisp. Remove the bacon, saving the fat, and chop. Add the bacon to the warm beans. Add the scallions and parsley.

3. In a small bowl, combine the warm bacon fat, vinegar, mustard, and oil to make ½ cup vinaigrette. Mix thoroughly with salt and white pepper to taste. Taste—does it need more vinegar? It is your say.

4. Pour the dressing over the beans. Toss, and taste for salt.

Serves 4 to 6

Trimming off the stringy side seams of green beans is better than "frenching," which sometimes causes them to lose flavor and be watery.

FRESH LIMA AND GREEN BEAN SALAD

For really tender green beans, select the ones that are pencil thin and brittle. Check to see if they "snap" when they are bent; if they don't, they are not fresh. Instead of stringing beans or cutting them through the middle, slice off the side seams and the ends very judiciously. This leaves the tender portion intact. So-

called "frenching" makes green beans watery. If beans have developed inside the pod, it has grown beyond the salad or quick-cooking stage and should be prepared in other ways.

———————◆———————

2 cups fresh lima beans
¼ pound small tender green or yellow wax
    beans
5 slices lean smoked bacon
¼ cup chopped red bell pepper
2 tablespoons chopped fresh tarragon
2 tablespoons chopped fresh parsley
¾ cup Tangy Mustard Vinaigrette (see page 88)

———————◆———————

1. Preheat the oven to 425°F.
2. Cook the lima beans in boiling salted water to cover until tender but not mushy, 20 to 25 minutes. Drain thoroughly.
3. With a sharp knife, trim stringy edges and ends off the green or wax beans. (This ensures their tenderness.) Cook in boiling salted water to cover until tender but still somewhat crisp, 7 to 10 minutes.

Drain the beans thoroughly.
4. In the meantime, cook the bacon on a baking sheet in the oven for 10 to 12 minutes. Do not allow it to get overly crisp. Drain on paper towels, then chop.
5. Blanch the red bell pepper in ½ cup boiling water for 1 to 2 minutes. Drain.
6. Combine the beans, bell pepper, tarragon, and parsley.
7. Toss the salad with the dressing and the bacon just before serving so the tarragon and parsley will remain fresh and green and the bacon will not become limp.

Serves 4

🦉 The salad may be presented on a large platter, surrounded by sliced tomatoes, and accompanied with corn muffins or your favorite homemade bread.

ZUCCHINI AND PARSLEY SALAD

———◆◆◆———

*P*arsley salads are fabulous for summer patio and barbecue parties with grilled meats of all kinds and are also delicious for a family dinner in the kitchen with hamburgers. The simplicity of this salad is its virtue. The fresh basil is a very important additional flavor.

———————◆———————

5 or 6 very small firm zucchini
6 to 8 cherry tomatoes
1 cup chopped Italian (flat-leaf) parsley
1 cup chopped curly parsley
Classic Vinaigrette to taste (see page 87)
Salt to taste
¼ cup chopped fresh basil leaves, or more to
    taste

———————◆———————

Slice the zucchini into julienne pieces not larger than matchsticks. You should have 1½ cups. Cut the tomatoes in half. Toss the zucchini and tomatoes gently with all the parsley. Season with the dressing and sprinkle with salt. (No pepper should be added when using basil.) Toss gently. Sprinkle with fresh basil leaves.

Serves 6

A NOTABLE VARIATION: Combine matchstick-slivered zucchini with lots of fresh basil (added at the last minute), and toss with vinaigrette. Serve on a bed of chopped parsley or on a layer of sliced garden tomatoes.

AVOCADO, APPLE, AND GRAPEFRUIT SALAD

*A*delicious winter salad when these fruits are the best available. Notable with lamb. If you wish, try it sometime with The Breakers Sunshine Dressing below.

2 avocados, peeled and sliced
1 apple (Red or Golden Delicious), peeled and sliced
2 navel oranges, peeled and cut into sections
1 grapefruit, peeled and cut into sections
12 to 18 leaves Bibb or Boston lettuce or endive
6 tablespoons olive or vegetable oil
1 teaspoon Dijon mustard
2 tablespoons fresh grapefruit juice
1 tablespoon white wine vinegar, or to taste
Salt to taste

Place the avocado and apple slices and the orange and grapefruit sections on a bed of lettuce. Mix the remaining ingredients in a small bowl and pour over the fruit when ready to serve.
Serves 6

THE BREAKERS SUNSHINE DRESSING

*H*ere's another dressing that goes well on Avocado, Apple, and Grapefruit Salad.

The dining room at one of America's glamorous old resorts, The Breakers, Palm Beach.

½ cup fresh lemon juice
½ cup good-quality vegetable oil
2 tablespoons sugar
¼ teaspoon salt

Beat all ingredients thoroughly with a whisk and serve on fruit salads.
Makes about 1 cup

AVOCADO AND BROCCOLI SALAD

*B*roccoli, in my estimation, is one of our most valuable winter vegetables, as its strong flavor is so compatible with the season's heartier dishes. Serve with steak, rib roast, scaloppine, pork roast, or sautéed or broiled fish.

1 large bunch broccoli
2 large ripe avocados
2 teaspoons light yellow Dijon mustard
6 tablespoons good-quality olive oil
2 tablespoons fresh lemon juice, or to taste
Salt and freshly ground black pepper to taste

Large black olives, for garnish
Pimento strips, for garnish

1. Strip the broccoli of all leaves. Peel the stems. Discard the woody part of the

stems. Cut the broccoli into individual serving pieces with not too much stem.

2. Drop the broccoli into boiling salted water and cook uncovered until tender but still crisp, 7 to 10 minutes. The timing depends upon the freshness and size of the broccoli, and it must retain its crispness. A limp salad is an abomination! Drain and chill the broccoli.

3. When ready to assemble the salad, peel and slice the avocados.

4. In a small bowl mix the mustard, olive oil, lemon juice, and salt and pepper.

5. Arrange the broccoli and avocado on an attractive platter. Season with the dressing, and garnish with black olives and strips of pimentos.

Serves 6

VARIATION: If avocados are not available, coarsely chopped hard-cooked egg may be used instead.

GREEN SALAD WITH AVOCADO AND BACON

Smoked premium-quality bacon is one of the finest appetizers that we have. It is always amazing to see what it does to a dish. Serve this salad with steak, chops, or grilled chicken for an informal supper.

Teddy Roosevelt (second from the right) sits down to an informal dinner, possibly in South Carolina.

6 cups lettuce—a mixture of Bibb, romaine, chicory, Boston
½ bunch watercress

3 slices smoked bacon
1 Florida avocado
1 tablespoon capers, drained
2 ounces Roquefort cheese
Chopped fresh parsley, for garnish
Chopped chives, for garnish
⅓ cup Classic Vinaigrette (see page 87)

1. Wash the greens carefully, and drain well. Wrap in paper towels and refrigerate until ready to serve (no more than 2 hours).

2. Fry the bacon (or cook it in a 425°F oven) until done but not overly crisp. Drain it on paper towels and keep warm.

3. Place the salad greens in a glass bowl, and just before serving, dress with slices of avocado, the capers, crumbled Roquefort, and pieces of crumbled hot bacon. Sprinkle with fresh parsley and chives if desired.

4. Bring the salad bowl to the table and toss the salad with the dressing.

Serves 4

WALNUT, APPLE, AND CHICORY SALAD

*T*his fruit and nut salad with chicory makes a beautiful winter luncheon salad with toasted crackers and *chèvre* (goat cheese), Roquefort, or natural cream cheese (available at cheese stores), or it can be served as dessert after an entrée of lamb, ham, or chicken—not beef or veal.

WALNUT OIL MAYONNAISE

1 egg
1 egg yolk
¼ teaspoon salt
2 tablespoons raspberry vinegar, sherry vinegar, or lemon juice
⅓ cup walnut oil
¾ cup flavorless vegetable oil

SALAD

3 heads Belgian endive or Bibb lettuce
3 tart apples (Granny Smith or McIntosh), peeled and sliced
½ cup buttered freshly toasted walnuts
Salt to taste
Pinch of sugar (optional)
1 head light-green curly chicory
Walnut halves, for garnish

1. In a small bowl or a blender, combine the mayonnaise ingredients and blend well. (See page 93 for mayonnaise instructions.) Cover and refrigerate.

2. Core out the bottom cone from each head of endive. Sliver the endive leaves.

3. Toss the apple slices, walnuts, and slivered endive together with the mayonnaise. Add a pinch of salt and sugar, if needed.

4. Line 4 salad plates with yellow curly chicory. (Use only the pale yellow center of the curly chicory or use Bibb or the yellow inside leaves of Boston lettuce). Spoon the salad into the center. Garnish with a few walnut halves tucked into the chicory at the side.

Serves 4 to 6

VARIATION: Juicy hard winter country pears or Anjou or Bosc pears (not too soft) may be sliced and added to the apple for a nice contrast of flavors.

The well-bleached curly chicory is not only delicious and enlivening in salads, it is very beautiful and appetizing looking as well.

A GLORIOUS POTATO SALAD

*T*his is the potato salad I learned to make when I was a young cook, and I have taught it for many years. It will win many friends for you, as it has for me. One time a reader told me that all of her furniture and belongings had been lost or damaged in transit to another city. She said, "I didn't mind losing the furniture the way I did the potato salad recipe!" Here it is.

2 pounds Idaho potatoes
¼ cup chopped onion
½ cup chopped shallots or white part of
   scallions (green onions)
2 tablespoons chopped chives or tender tops of
   scallions (green onions)
½ small clove garlic, crushed (optional)
2 tablespoons chopped fresh parsley

VINAIGRETTE

⅓ cup good-quality olive oil
1½ tablespoons cider vinegar, or more to taste
⅛ teaspoon dry mustard
Salt and freshly ground white pepper to taste

1. Peel the potatoes and drop them in a large pot of boiling water. Cook until tender but not mushy, 30 minutes.
2. Meanwhile, prepare the vinaigrette, blending the ingredients well in a small bowl.
3. Drain and slice the potatoes. Pour the vinaigrette over them while they are still warm. (Warm potatoes absorb the dressing readily.) Add the onion, shallots or scallion bulbs, chives or scallion tops, and garlic. Taste for salt, white pepper, and vinegar and correct as necessary. Sprinkle with the parsley.
4. Allow to ripen for 1 hour, if possible.

   Serves 6

VARIATION: *French Potato Salad:* Omit the onions and garlic, and dress with Classic Vinaigrette. Serve warm, garnished with parsley and tarragon or a mixture of fresh herbs.

POTATO SALADS

I like to use new, or waxy, potatoes when the recipe calls for a mayonnaise dressing.

When the dressing is a vinaigrette or a warm dressing, mealy potatoes, such as Idaho potatoes, are best because they absorb the dressing better.

POTATO SALAD WITH OLIVES

*T*he simplicity of this potato salad belies its wonderful flavor. Don't add a thing—but the mayonnaise must be homemade and delectable. Serve this with hot or cold fried chicken, steak, hamburgers, thin veal chops, or sautéed ham.

2 pounds new potatoes
½ cup chopped white celery hearts
½ cup chopped sweet white onion
1 cup sliced pimento-stuffed olives
Salt and freshly ground white pepper to taste
Cayenne pepper to taste
1 cup homemade mayonnaise (see page 93), or
   more as needed

1. Peel the potatoes and drop them in boiling salted water to cover. Cook until fork-tender, about 30 minutes. Drain at once and cool completely before slicing (so they will not crumble).
2. Add the celery, onion, and olives to the sliced potatoes. Sprinkle with salt and white and cayenne peppers. Add the mayonnaise and toss lightly with a fork. Taste for seasoning.
3. Allow to ripen a few hours if possible. Taste again and correct seasoning if necessary.

   Serves 6

POTATO, TARRAGON, AND ARTICHOKE SALAD

◆◆◆

*T*his is one of the most delightful of potato salads.

---

*2½ pounds Idaho potatoes, peeled, boiled, and
      cooled*
5 fresh artichoke hearts, cooked (see Index)
¾ cup Golden Hills Salad Dressing (see page 90)
3 tablespoons chopped fresh tarragon
Watercress or Bibb lettuce, for garnish
Large black olives, for garnish
3 firm ripe tomatoes, quartered, for garnish

1. Slice the potatoes and artichoke hearts into separate bowls. Season both vegetables with dressing. Sprinkle fresh tarragon over the artichokes.
2. Mound the potatoes in the center of a round platter. Surround with sliced artichokes. Garnish with watercress or Bibb lettuce, black olives, and tomatoes.

Serves 6

ARUGULA, BACON, AND POTATO SALAD

◆◆◆

*A*rugula is listed in seed catalogues as "roquette." It has a delectable tangy flavor that gives salads a delightful appetizing quality.

¼ cup puréed tomato pulp (see Owl)
*1½ tablespoons white wine or cider vinegar, or
      to taste*
Salt to taste
*½ cup good-quality olive oil, or ¼ cup fresh
      warm bacon drippings and ¼ cup olive oil*
1½ pounds tiny potatoes, peeled
5 thick slices lean smoked bacon
Freshly ground black pepper to taste
*4 cups arugula leaves, or 3 cups arugula leaves
      and 1 cup curly chicory or escarole*
8 to 10 cherry tomatoes
*Bouquet of chopped fresh herbs, such as
      marjoram, parsley, tarragon, chervil, and
      basil, for garnish*

The potato crop is in at the farmers' market in Louisville.

1. Pour the tomato purée into a small bowl. Add the vinegar, and salt to taste, and blend thoroughly. Add the oil (if you are using the bacon fat, see step 2). Keep warm.
2. Boil the potatoes in salted water to cover until tender, about 30 minutes. Drain at once. While the potatoes are boiling, fry the bacon (or bake it in a 425°F oven) until done but not overly crisp. Drain, chop, and set aside. (If you are using bacon fat in the dressing, keep ¼ cup warm.)
3. Slice the potatoes while still warm and toss them with the dressing. Sprinkle

on salt and pepper to taste.

4. Line a salad bowl or deep platter with arugula and pale green chicory leaves (torn into comfortable eating pieces). Spoon the salad into the bowl or platter. Garnish with bacon, tomatoes, and herbs.

Bring to the table and toss.

Serves 4 to 6

For perfect tomato purée, peel and seed 2 or 3 ripe tomatoes and purée the pulp in a blender or processor.

NEW POTATO SALAD WITH ASPARAGUS AND CHICORY

◆◆◆

The divine combination of new potatoes and fresh asparagus is a gastronome's delight. To give it the place of honor it deserves, use it as an entrée for a light Sunday night supper or a luncheon. It is delicious also with a slice of baked country ham, broiled chicken, or a rare steak.

◆

2½ pounds new potatoes, peeled, boiled, and
    cooled
¾ cup homemade mayonnaise (see Index) made
    with tarragon vinegar
12 spears fresh green asparagus, cooked
2 tablespoons Classic Vinaigrette (see page 87)
    made with lemon juice
Pale chicory or Bibb lettuce, for garnish
6 hard-cooked eggs, quartered, for garnish
2 tablespoons chopped fresh tarragon
Salt and freshly ground white pepper to taste

1. Slice the potatoes and toss them with the mayonnaise.

2. In a separate bowl, season the asparagus with the Classic Vinaigrette.

3. Mound the potatoes in the center of a round platter. Surround with asparagus spears. Garnish the platter with lettuce and the hard-cooked eggs. Sprinkle the entire salad with fresh tarragon and salt and white pepper to taste.

Serves 6

WILD RICE SALAD

◆◆◆

Connoisseurs place our native wild rice among the great foods of the world. It is not a rice at all, but a grain that grows wild around the lakes of Wisconsin and Minnesota. It is still harvested there as Indians did of old, by men gliding along in canoes. They bend the tall stalks and thrash them in such a way that the ripe grains fall into the boat. This is an expensive process, but wild rice is divine food even if it is luxurious. The Indians called it *manomin,* "the good berry." Indeed it is. Serve this salad with steak, rare rib or sirloin roast, lamb chops, leg of lamb, or veal in any guise.

1 ½ cups wild rice, uncooked
½ pound fresh crisp mushrooms, cleaned and
    slivered
3 tablespoons chopped fresh marjoram
½ cup chopped fresh parsley (Italian if
    possible)
2 tablespoons chopped chives or tender scallion
    (green onion) tops
⅔ cup Tangy Mustard Vinaigrette (see page 88)
    made with red wine vinegar, or more taste
Salt and freshly ground black pepper to taste
Sprigs of marjoram, parsley, or watercress, for
    garnish

1. Wash the wild rice thoroughly, rinsing it 6 to 8 times. Drop it into boiling salted water and boil until "al dente," or firm to the bite, 30 to 40 minutes. Drain at once. Cool.

2. A short while before serving, toss the rice with the mushrooms, marjoram, parsley, chives or scallion tops, and enough vinaigrette to moisten it well. Taste. Add salt and pepper if needed.

3. Place in a salad bowl and garnish with sprigs of watercress, parsley, or, best of all, marjoram.

Serves 6

A SUPERB VARIATION: Combine 1 ¼ cups wild rice, 5 or 6 chopped anchovy filets, ½ pound slivered crisp fresh mushrooms, 1 clove garlic mashed and marinated in ⅔ cup vinaigrette (sieve out the garlic before using the dressing), 3 tablespoons chopped fresh parsley, 2 tablespoons chopped fresh marjoram leaves, and ½ cup pitted Niçoise or Greek black olives. My favorite. Delicious with veal roast, scaloppine, steak, or rare rib or sirloin roast.

COUNTRY GARDEN SLAW

You can choreograph this salad to your taste. Green cabbage, cauliflower, and an assortment of herbs may also be used.

5 carrots, peeled
6 small firm zucchini
1 cucumber, sliced thin and slivered
4 celery hearts, sliced thin
1 green bell pepper, cored, seeded, and chopped
1 red bell pepper or 1 sweet yellow banana
    pepper, cored, seeded, and slivered
Salt to taste
½ cup chopped fresh parsley
¼ cup chopped fresh basil, or more to taste
¾ cup (approximately) Classic or Rich
    Vinaigrette or Golden Hills Dressing
    (see pages 87, 88, and 90)

Cut the carrots and zucchini into matchsticks. Mix with the cucumber, celery, and peppers, and add salt to taste. Add the parsley and basil. Toss with the dressing and serve.

Serves 6

When fresh basil is out of season, use a basil wine vinegar or add a generous amount of French Dijon mustard.

Fresh basil is sufficiently peppery without adding black pepper.

When fresh herbs are out of season, use a large handful of chopped parsley. Green is in.

Green peppers are a Southern gardener's favorite.

WILTED SLAW WITH BACON DRESSING

*T*his is a true country salad of the deep South that is right in tune with our old-fashioned vegetables and meats—but quite out of tune with today's "count your calories" cooking. But oh, how delicious these old-fashioned dishes can be! Delicious and heart-warming. I think I shall have this salad tonight.

6 thick slices very lean bacon
½ small head tender green cabbage
3½ tablespoons cider vinegar
2 tablespoons water
1½ tablespoons sugar, or more to taste
Salt and freshly ground black pepper to taste

1. Preheat the oven to 425°F.
2. Cook the bacon in the oven until cooked through but not brittle, 15 to 18 minutes (or sauté in a heavy skillet).
3. In the meantime, shred the cabbage and chop it rather fine. You should have 6 cups.
4. Remove the bacon, reserving the fat, and chop. Set aside.
5. Combine the bacon fat, vinegar, water, and sugar in a small saucepan. Heat, and add salt to taste.
6. When you are ready to serve the salad, pour the warm dressing over the shredded cabbage. Toss with the chopped bacon and add pepper to taste.

Serves 4

The German people in Louisville (and there are many) like to sprinkle celery seed on this salad. If bacon is tossed into salads too soon, it becomes soggy and limp.

ONION SALAD

*T*hinly sliced onions are delicious with hamburgers or grilled steak or chops.

1 large red onion
1 large Spanish onion
½ cup vegetable oil

AN INFORMAL SUPPER AT BRENNAN HOUSE

Grilled Butterflied Leg of Lamb

Onion Salad

Fresh Lima and Green Bean Salad

Sliced Tomatoes

Sour Cream Corn Muffins

♦

Summertime Peach Ice Cream

2 tablespoons white wine vinegar, or more to taste
1 teaspoon fresh lemon juice
Salt and freshly ground black pepper to taste
2 tablespoons chopped fresh parsley
2 tablespoons chopped fresh chives

1. Peel the onions and cut into thin slices. Lay the slices in a dish in an attractive design.
2. Mix together the oil, vinegar, lemon juice, and salt and pepper. Taste and correct the seasoning as needed. Pour the dressing over the onions and sprinkle them with parsley and chives.

Serves 6

CHICKEN SALAD WITH COUNTRY HAM

*F*or a luncheon in the bluegrass country of Kentucky. Serve the salad on Bibb lettuce with a relish dish of watermelon pickle, brandied peaches, honeydew pickle, and a basket of hot rolls.

3 freshly poached whole chicken breasts, cubed (see Index)
1 cup peeled and slivered celery root or chopped white hearts of celery
1½ cups slivered baked country ham
⅔ cup Classic Vinaigrette (see page 87)
1 cup homemade mayonnaise (see page 93)
½ cup heavy or whipping cream, slightly whipped
2 tablespoons imported Bocquet French Mustard Sauce or another mild mustard sauce (see Owl)
Salt to taste
Cayenne pepper to taste
Bibb lettuce, for garnish
Chopped fresh tarragon, for garnish

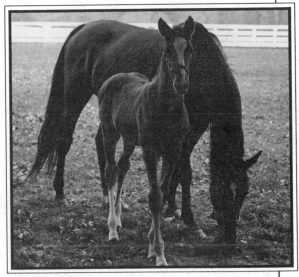

A mare and foal on one of the more than 350 Thoroughbred horse farms in Kentucky.

1. Combine the chicken, celery root or celery, and country ham. Toss with the vinaigrette.

2. Blend the mayonnaise and cream with the mustard sauce. Add salt and cayenne pepper to taste and fold into the chicken mixture. Serve any leftover sauce in a small bowl.

3. Line 6 salad plates with Bibb lettuce. Spoon the salad onto the lettuce and garnish with a sprinkling of fresh tarragon. (If tarragon is unavailable, garnish each serving with 2 black olives.)

Serves 6

VARIATION: The chicken, celery, and ham can be mixed with the mayonnaise, omitting the vinaigrette.

Bocquet French Mustard Sauce is found in specialty food shops. If mustard sauce is unavailable, season the mayonnaise with light yellow Dijon mustard.

CURRIED SOUTH CAROLINA CHICKEN SALAD

*C*runchy, delicious, and beautiful—a great favorite for a luncheon, a light summer supper, or a gourmet picnic. Curry is traditional in South Carolina, an echo of its English heritage.

2 cups slivered freshly poached chicken breasts
    (see Index)
½ cup slivered tender snow peas (stems and
    strings removed)
½ cup sliced water chestnuts, fresh or canned
⅓ cup slivered white celery heart
2 tablespoons imported Madras curry powder,
    or more to taste
2 tablespoons boiling water
1 cup homemade mayonnaise (see page 93)
2 medium heads Bibb lettuce
1 red bell pepper, cored, seeded, and thinly
    sliced
Watercress sprigs, for garnish

1. Combine the chicken with the snow peas, water chestnuts, and celery heart in a medium bowl.

2. Measure the curry powder into a small bowl. Add the boiling water and blend (this is to soften the raw flavor). Add the mayonnaise and blend well. Fold into the chicken mixture.

3. Serve in a bowl or on salad plates lined with Bibb lettuce. Garnish with tiny strips of red bell pepper and sprigs of watercress.

Serves 4

VARIATION: Blend 1 cup cooked rice with some of the curried mayonnaise, and spoon a small portion onto each plate of lettuce before covering with the chicken salad.

BREAST OF CHICKEN IN TARRAGON ASPIC

Served with a delectable, freshly made mayonnaise, baked country ham, and hot rolls, this salad can be a glorious thing.

A gourmet picnic in Charleston, at a time when picnic dress was hardly casual.

3 whole chicken breasts, skinned
1 onion, quartered
1 carrot, peeled and cut in half
4 ribs celery, cut in half
1 bay leaf
Salt to taste
1 tablespoon unflavored gelatin
4 cups clarified Rich Chicken Stock, chilled (see
    Index)

3 tablespoons fresh tarragon leaves or 1
    tablespoon crushed dried (fresh is best)
½ teaspoon white peppercorns
1 large head Boston lettuce, or 1 bunch
    watercress
1 can (16 ounces) black olives, largest size,
    unpitted
4 hard-cooked eggs, quartered, for garnish
Caper Mayonnaise (recipe follows)

1. Cut each chicken breast in half. Place the chicken in a large pot and cover with water (or for a better flavor, half water and half chicken broth). Add the onion, carrot, celery, bay leaf, and salt to taste. Bring to a simmer. Cover the pot loosely and poach the chicken until it is tender, 20 to 25 minutes.

2. Remove the cover and allow the chicken breasts to cool slightly in the broth.

Strain the broth; cool, and refrigerate or freeze for another use.

3. Remove the breast meat from the bones while the chicken is warm. Cut it into thick julienne strips, cover, and set aside.

4. Soften the gelatin in 1 cup of the chilled clarified chicken stock.

5. In the meantime, simmer the remaining clarified stock with the tarragon, peppercorns, and salt to taste, for 10 minutes. Strain, and add the dissolved gelatin while the stock is hot. Cool a bit.

6. Rinse two 6-cup ring molds in cold water. Pour in ½ inch of the gelatin mixture. Chill until set, about 2 hours in the refrigerator or 30 minutes in the freezer.

7. When the aspic has set, add the slivers of chicken, pressing them down in order to fill the molds generously with chicken. Pour in gelatin mixture to cover, and chill again until set.

8. To unmold, dip the molds in hot water for a few seconds. Then run a thin, sharp knife around the sides of the aspic. Place round platters on the molds and invert.

9. Garnish the platters with the tender inside leaves of Boston lettuce or with watercress. Fill the center of the rings with the black olives. Place the hard-cooked eggs on the lettuce or watercress. Serve with a sauceboat of Caper Mayonnaise.

Serves 6

This may be put in individual baba molds, or 6- to 8-cup charlotte molds may be used instead of ring molds.

This elegant salad can be made a day ahead. It can also be placed in the freezer to set quickly when time is of the essence—just keep an eye on it.

CAPER MAYONNAISE

2 cups homemade mayonnaise (see page 93)
½ cup sour cream
3 tablespoons capers, well drained
1½ tablespoons fresh lemon juice, or to taste

Stir together all the ingredients in a medium bowl, and refrigerate, covered well, until ready to use.

WARM TARRAGON CHICKEN WITH SWEETBREAD SALAD

*T*his is an entrée that is served as the main course for a luncheon, or Sunday night supper, or after the theater. It is so versatile that it is a joy for the cook. Sweetbreads are dear, but they have such a mellifluous texture and flavor, do treat yourself to them. Glorious dining.

2 whole chicken breasts
1 "heart" sweetbread (see box)
1 tablespoon tarragon vinegar
6 tablespoons (¾ stick) unsalted butter
2 sprigs thyme
1 tablespoon chopped fresh tarragon or ⅓ teaspoon dried
⅓ cup Rich Chicken or Veal Stock (see Index), or dry white wine
Salt and freshly ground white pepper to taste

24 fresh asparagus spears, peeled and tied in bundles of 6
1 head Boston lettuce
2 to 3 heads Bibb lettuce
1 Belgian endive, slivered
Classic Vinaigrette (see page 87), made with walnut or olive oil
Chopped fresh tarragon, chervil, and parsley, for garnish

1. Split the chicken breasts, and dry them well so they will brown nicely.

2. Put the sweetbread in simmering water to cover along with the vinegar and simmer 15 to 18 minutes. Drain.

3. Melt 4 tablespoons of the butter in a heavy skillet. Add the sprigs of thyme and swish them around. When the butter is good and hot, remove the thyme and add the chicken breasts, skin side down. Sauté over medium heat until golden brown, but don't overcook. Turn to the other side and cook until attractively browned, about 18 to 20 minutes in all. Test for tenderness with a skewer. Add the fresh or dried tarragon and the stock to the pan juices and swirl about and over the chicken. Keep warm.

4. Heat the remaining 2 tablespoons butter in another skillet. Sauté the sweetbread on both sides over medium heat until it becomes a light brown, about 5 minutes. Sprinkle with salt and pepper to taste. Keep warm.

5. In the meantime, drop the prepared asparagus in boiling salted water to cover and simmer just until tender, 6 to 7 minutes, depending on the size and freshness of the asparagus. Drain at once.

6. Slice the chicken off the bone. Slice the sweetbread.

7. Shred the lettuce and toss it with endive in the vinaigrette.

8. Line 4 salad plates with the lettuce and lay the slices of chicken and sweetbread on top. Heat the pan juices from the chicken and sweetbread and spoon them over the slices. Garnish each plate with asparagus. Spoon a little vinaigrette over the asparagus. Sprinkle a bouquet of chopped tarragon, chervil, and parsley over each salad.

Serves 4

PREPARING SWEETBREADS

A sweetbread is the thymus gland of a calf. Each sweetbread consists of two parts, the round and solid "heart," which is the choice piece, and the "throat," which is in broken pieces usually. Sweetbreads must be rinsed several times with cold water, then allowed to soak in cold water 1 to 1½ hours. Always pull off any filament which covers sweetbreads without tearing the flesh. Sweetbreads should always be parboiled in water with a touch of vinegar.

CRAB NORFOLK SALAD

*I*n Virginia and Maryland, Crab Norfolk has long been a great favorite—one of our best dishes and thoroughly indigenous to native American cuisine. Crabmeat Norfolk teams so well with rice that I make an entrée salad with the combination, or you can create a chic and delectable salad using orzo (small pasta shaped like rice). Both are pleasing served cold or warm, and they are excellent as a first course.

1 pound fresh backfin lump crabmeat
1 cup long-grain rice
5 tablespoons unsalted butter
3 thin slices baked country ham, slivered
½ cup heavy or whipping cream, or as needed
2 tablespoons chopped fresh tarragon
Salt if needed

Cayenne pepper to taste
2 bunches watercress, 3 heads Bibb lettuce, or
      1 large head Boston lettuce
Chopped fresh tarragon, chervil, and parsley,
      for garnish
1 lemon, cut into wedges

1. Pick over the crabmeat well, discarding any cartilage. Leave the pieces as large as possible.

2. Cook the rice until tender but still "al dente," or firm to the bite. Keep warm.

3. Melt 3 tablespoons of the butter in a heavy enamel or stainless steel skillet. Add the crabmeat and toss it lightly in the butter. Add the ham and mix well. Add just enough cream to make a small amount of sauce. (It should bind the crabmeat and ham lightly. When served, the sauce should not drown the rice or run over the plate.)

4. When ready to serve, toss the warm rice with the remaining butter and the tarragon. Add salt if desired (the ham is salty) and cayenne pepper.

5. Line 4 salad plates with watercress or lettuce. Spoon the warm tarragon rice

Sailboats in Norfolk harbor.

onto the lettuce. Make a small well in the center of the rice and fill it with the crabmeat and ham mixture. Sprinkle chopped fresh herbs over the entire dish. Garnish each plate with a wedge of lemon (to squeeze over lettuce as well as crabmeat).

Serves 4

VARIATION: Omit the ham and season the rice with imported Madras curry powder. Sprinkle with a few buttered toasted slivered almonds or toasted pine nuts. Sprinkle chopped fresh coriander over the crabmeat just before serving.

A true Crab Norfolk is never seasoned with garlic or onions, nor is the sauce thickened with flour or egg yolks, which rob it of its lightness.

A LUNCHEON IN WILLIAMSBURG

Crab Norfolk Salad

Monticello Rolls

Green Olives

Chilled White Wine

◆

Cold Chocolate Soufflé

Coffee

AN ELEGANT STUFFED TOMATO

◆◆◆

Fresh tarragon may be used if dill is unavailable. Dill is, however, especially delightful when combined with cucumber.

◆

½ pound cooked small shrimp
1 cup Classic Vinaigrette (see page 87)
Fresh lemon juice to taste
1 cucumber
1 avocado
¼ cup chopped fresh dill or 1½ teaspoons dry dill weed (fresh is far superior)
⅓ red bell pepper, cored, seeded, and slivered

⅓ green bell pepper, cored, seeded and slivered
4 firm ripe large tomatoes
Salt to taste
2 bunches watercress, or 2 heads Bibb lettuce
8 colossal black olives
Homemade mayonnaise (see page 93)

◆

1. Marinate the shrimp in ⅓ cup of the dressing with extra lemon juice to taste for 1 hour before assembling the salad.

2. Peel the cucumber and cut it in half lengthwise. Scoop out the seeds with a teaspoon and discard. Slice the cucumber in ¼-inch slices. Set aside.

3. Peel and cube the avocado.

4. Toss the cucumber slices, avocado cubes, shrimp, dill, and peppers with the remaining dressing.

5. Remove the core from each tomato. Cut the tomatoes partly into quarters, but do not cut them all the way through the bottom. Season the tomatoes with salt. Place each tomato on a bed of watercress or Bibb. Fill the center of the tomato attractively with the shrimp mixture. Garnish each plate with 2 black olives. Pass a sauceboat of homemade mayonnaise, if desired.

Serves 4

TOMATOES STUFFED WITH SEAFOOD AND RICE

A very old and delicious salad comes back—but as with all fashions, with a few small changes.

A wagonload of baskets newly arrived in the fields.

1 pound cooked small shelled shrimp, crabmeat, crawfish, or lobster
1 cup cooked long-grain rice or small pasta (orzo)
2 tablespoons chopped fresh pimento or red bell pepper
2 cups homemade mayonnaise (see page 93)
1½ teaspoons dry mustard
2 teaspoons chopped fresh tarragon
2 tablespoons chopped fresh parsley
2 tablespoons capers, drained
Salt to taste
Cayenne pepper to taste
Freshly ground white pepper to taste
Fresh lemon juice to taste
4 firm ripe large tomatoes
Leaf lettuce or watercress, for garnish
Chopped fresh tarragon and parsley, or dill and parsley, for garnish

1. Combine the cooked shrimp, crabmeat, crawfish, or lobster, with the rice or pasta and pimentos or red bell pepper.

2. Mix 1½ cups of the mayonnaise with the mustard, tarragon, parsley, and capers. Add salt, cayenne pepper, and white pepper. Fold the seafood mixture into the mayonnaise. Add lemon juice to taste.

3. Remove the cores from the tomatoes. Cut them into thick vertical slices, but do not cut all the way to the bottom. Place each tomato on a bed of lettuce or watercress. Open up each slice and fill with the seafood mixture. Put a generous spoonful of the remaining plain mayonnaise on top of each stuffed tomato. Sprinkle with a bouquet of fresh chopped herbs.

Serves 4

◆◆ THE DRESSINGS FOR SALADS

*T*he dressings for salads are very simple, really. Most salads require a vinaigrette dressing, which combines an excellent oil (the most flavorful is Italian or French olive oil, or an imported nut oil, such as walnut or hazelnut) with an acid which complements the ingredients of the salad and adds a zest and spark to the oil. The nature and flavors of these oils and acids vary and should blend with the chosen salad. A salad of delicate lettuce leaves should have a mild dressing, for instance; a hearty salad with beef or ham calls for an assertive mustardy dressing. All of these things you learn through trial and triumph, or through trial and error, remembering the next time what you did to make the previous salad so great, or what you think led the salad astray.

The traditional dressings for salads besides vinaigrette are cream dressings, and mayonnaise. With a little practice, you will get the hang of all three and will then always make your own. Bottled vinaigrette is more expensive than homemade and an anathema to a good cook. Your own will be so very much better.

CLASSIC VINAIGRETTE

◆◆

*I*n making all vinaigrettes, the vinegar or lemon juice, salt, pepper, and any other seasoning must be combined before adding the oil. All vinaigrettes are at their best when made just before serving.

◆◆

VINAIGRETTE PLUS

Garlic Vinaigrette: Allow 1 clove garlic to marinate in 1 cup Classic Vinaigrette from 12 to 24 hours. Remove the garlic.

Warm Vinaigrette: To 1 cup Classic Vinaigrette, add 2 chopped hard-cooked eggs, 1 tablespoon each chopped fresh parsley and chives, and 1 teaspoon dry mustard. Serve hot over broccoli, fresh green asparagus, or hot potato salad.

Roquefort Vinaigrette: To 1 cup Classic Vinaigrette, add ⅓ cup crumbled Roquefort or blue cheese. Serve with green salad.

Chutney Vinaigrette: To 1 cup Classic Vinaigrette, add 3 tablespoons finely chopped mango chutney, 1 chopped pickled walnut or 3 tablespoons walnut ketchup, and 1 teaspoon finely chopped fresh parsley. Use on green or sliced chicken salad.

Bell Pepper Vinaigrette: To 1 cup Classic Vinaigrette, add 1 tablespoon each chopped red bell pepper, green bell pepper, shallots or chives, and chopped fresh parsley. Serve over vegetable or green salad.

Dill Vinaigrette: To 1 cup Classic Vinaigrette, add 3 tablespoons chopped fresh dill or 1 tablespoon dry dill weed and 3 tablespoons chopped fresh parsley. Serve over cucumbers, tomatoes, or green salad.

◆

¼ cup good-quality vinegar (see Owl) or fresh lemon juice
Salt and freshly ground black pepper to taste
¾ cup good-quality olive or vegetable oil, or more to taste

◆

Combine the vinegar or lemon juice, salt, and pepper in a small bowl. Gradually whisk in the oil to taste.

Makes 1 cup

Many types of vinegar can be used: white wine, red wine, or any of the herb-flavored wines such as tarragon.

Cucumbers, onions, and impressive braids of garlic in a New Orleans market.

RICH VINAIGRETTE

◆◆

*T*his is a popular variation on the Classic Vinaigrette and can be made in a blender. The herbs should complement the menu—use tarragon with veal, chicken, or fish, and sweet basil with beef. Parsley and chervil are pleasant with all dishes.

◆

1 egg yolk
2 tablespoons white wine vinegar
1 tablespoon Dijon mustard
¾ cup good-quality olive or vegetable oil
Salt and freshly ground white pepper to taste
Fresh lemon juice, if needed
Bouquet of mixed chopped fresh herbs,

2 tablespoons each (see headnote)

Combine the egg yolk, vinegar, mustard, oil, salt, and white pepper in a blender. Mix well. Taste, and add more salt and a squeeze of lemon juice if needed. Add herbs to taste.

Makes 1 cup

*F*TANGY MUSTARD VINAIGRETTE

◆◆

*F*or artichokes, asparagus, and all salads that need the flavorful blessings of a good mustard.

◆

⅓ cup white wine vinegar
⅔ cup good-quality olive oil, or ⅓ cup olive oil and ⅓ cup vegetable oil
1½ teaspoons light yellow Dijon mustard, or

more to taste
⅔ teaspoon salt, or more to taste

◆

◆◆ OILS

*F*lavorless vegetable oils, such as Wesson oil, are used in many dressings, as they are lighter than the olive or the nut oils and are especially good in mayonnaise for that reason. These could be called background oils, as they impart no flavor of their own, but allow the flavors of the other ingredients in vinaigrette to predominate, which is as it should be.

Olive oil is the time-honored oil for flavor and finesse, with no contender in the field. Walnut and hazelnut oils from France are indeed delicious and are much appreciated in certain salads. These nut oils are expensive and do not keep well, so we find from day to day we depend upon olive and vegetable oils.

The finest olive oils in the world come from Italy and France. As a rule the best of the Italian oils have a more robust nature than those from France, but there are exceptions, of course. If at any time you have a rich olive oil that is lustier than you like, dilute it with a flavorless vegetable oil. Many times in using walnut oil, which has a rich nutty flavor, you may find it more appealing and lighter if it is diluted. The vegetable oil used must be flavorless, however, and American corn or peanut oil certainly are not.

If you are trying to develop your palate or have had no experience with olive oils, please don't start with the cheapest ones. As in wine, the price is indicative of quality when sold by a trustworthy merchant. When I see some of the oils that are for sale, I realize why people do not admire olive oil. Supermarket olive oil is usually terrible. You don't have to have a Val di Pesa extra virgin oil to enjoy olive oil, but it has to be decent. California presses some good olive oils, but they are not in wide distribution yet. If they are available in your area, by all means try them.

Combine the ingredients in a blender and mix well. If using a whisk, combine all the ingredients except the oil in a small bowl.

Gradually add the oil, whisking briskly.
Makes 1 cup

BARBECUE VINAIGRETTE DRESSING

◆◆

*T*his all-American dressing came from Mary Frost Mabon, the daughter of Robert Frost. The small amount of ketchup and Worcestershire sauce is rather perfect for many tossed salads, especially those with avocado.

◆

1 tablespoon ketchup
1 teaspoon Worcestershire sauce
¼ cup red or white wine vinegar, or more to taste
⅔ teaspoon salt, or to taste
¾ cup vegetable oil
1 clove garlic
Fresh lemon juice to taste

◆

Measure the ketchup, Worcestershire sauce, and vinegar into a bowl. Add the salt and beat with a whisk. Continue to beat while adding the oil rather slowly. When all the oil is incorporated, taste for salt and vinegar. Add more of both if needed, then add the garlic and the important squeeze of lemon juice. Discard the garlic after marinating it for several hours in the dressing.
Makes 1 cup

◆◆
VINEGARS

Herb Vinegars: Vinegars with an infusion of fresh herbs are easy to make, but many home-made concoctions are travesties of fine flavor. In the first place, the vinegar chosen must be fine enough to be used alone. White distilled vinegar is for pickling, not for salads. Malt vinegar has no place in a good kitchen.

Tarragon Vinegar is the star. It is an essential in a great kitchen. It speaks up, so do not use it where the tarragon flavor is not compatible.

Parsley, dill, rosemary, mint, and sweet basil (not purple basil, please) are the other herbs that make fair vinegars. They are made exactly like the tarragon vinegar.

Chinese and Japanese Rice Vinegars: These are the most delicate vinegars of all and have found great favor with the gourmet. They are especially valuable when an acidic but unasser-tive note is needed, as in seafood salads, and for those who do not especially favor the tang of vinegar. One especially worthy use of these

mild vinegars is in salads when good wines are on the menu.

Sherry Vinegar is fairly new on our market. It is a very robust vinegar—very rich tasting. In most cases it is best to dilute it a bit with white wine vinegar. It is largely a matter of taste and what your salads should say. Can salads speak up? I think so. Hit a wrong note and you will taste it.

Wine Vinegars: The wine vinegars, both red and white, are essential for salad making, and excellent ones are made in California. One should choose which vinegar to use very much as one chooses either red or white wine for a menu. The red wine vinegar is usually best with hearty salads of meats and zestful lettuces and herbs and flavorful mustards. White wine vine-gar is usually best in more delicate salads.

Raspberry Vinegar is a great deceiver. Its very name suggests salads with fruit, but it is far more versatile than that. It is very mild and is compatible in many salads. Surprises await you.

GOLDEN HILLS DRESSING

*T*he mustards, both black and white, are wild herbs with pretty yellow blooms that grow in our fields and whose seeds are cultivated to make all kinds of condiments. The black seeds are used to make brown mustard, and the white seeds, light yellow mustard. The young plants of white mustard can be raised in your garden to be added to green salad—one of my grandfather's specialties.

This is one of my favorite dressings, and it is so delicious on a variety of vegetables, such as zucchini, celery, cauliflower, broccoli, red, yellow, and green bell peppers with a bouquet of fresh herbs, and all kinds of crisp fresh letuce. You will love it, especially if you are the "mustard type" as I am.

Judge John Bibb's well-known legacy.

⅓ cup Dijon mustard (grainy or smooth)
⅓ cup boiling water
1 cup good-quality olive oil, or ½ cup olive oil
    and ½ cup vegetable oil
3 tablespoons fresh lemon juice or white wine
    vinegar, or more to taste
Salt and freshly ground white pepper to taste

Put the mustard in a small bowl and whisk in the boiling water. Add the olive oil in a light stream, whisking briskly, then the lemon juice or vinegar and salt and white pepper. (Or, after adding the boiling water to the mustard, spoon all the ingredients into a blender or processor and blend.)
Makes 1¾ cups

FRENCH CREAM DRESSING

*O*ne tablespoon of heavy sweet cream has exactly the same number of calories as the same amount of vegetable oil, so it is not as "deadly" as some might have you think. This cream dressing is perfection for many salads, especially those with cucumbers. It blends vegetables, herbs, and seafoods in a most harmonious way.

1 teaspoon salt
3 tablespoons fresh lemon juice, or more to taste
1 cup heavy or whipping cream
Cayenne pepper to taste

Measure the salt and lemon juice into a small bowl. Add the cream slowly, beating with a whisk until the dressing has thickened like mayonnaise. Taste for lemon juice. Add more if needed, and cayenne to taste.
Makes 1¼ cups

🦉 If the lemon juice is too mild for you, use a touch of white wine vinegar.

BUTTERMILK-ROQUEFORT DRESSING

A thinning salad—assorted lettuces, sliced cucumbers, or sliced tomatoes, and this dressing. The wee touch of Roquefort gives the dressing a nice tang.

1 tablespoon Roquefort or blue cheese, or more
*   to taste*
1 cup buttermilk
2 teaspoons white wine vinegar
1½ teaspoons chopped fresh parsley
Salt and freshly ground white pepper to taste

Mash the Roquefort or blue cheese in a small bowl. Add the buttermilk, vinegar, parsley, salt, and pepper and whisk briskly until well blended.
   Makes 1¼ cups

TARRAGON-EGG DRESSING

T his is one of the best egg dressings imaginable—a great favorite for green salads, especially when served with shrimp, crabmeat, fried fish, fish croquettes, or broiled country ham.

6 hard-cooked eggs
¾ cup heavy or whipping cream
1 teaspoon light yellow Dijon mustard
3 tablespoons tarragon white wine vinegar, or
*   to taste*
Salt and freshly ground white pepper to taste
¼ cup chopped fresh tarragon
3 tablespoons chopped fresh parsley
2 tablespoons chopped fresh chervil

Mash the egg yolks well in a small bowl. Chop the whites and set them aside. Add the cream, mustard, vinegar, salt, and white pepper to the yolks. Blend well with a whisk. Pour the dressing over chilled and dried greens. Sprinkle with the egg whites, tarragon, parsley, and chervil.
   Makes 1½ cups

🦉 Eggs, tarragon, and watercress are particularly compatible.

DRESSING FOR SOUTHERN WILTED LETTUCE

T his is an old-fashioned dressing for potato salad, green salad, or slaw. It soothes and quiets our Southern sweet tooth. The German immigrants who settled in the Ohio Valley added the sugar to a deep South version that was just vinegar, water, bacon drippings, and salt. We like it and still add the sugar no matter if sugar has become a "demon."

Serve it over leaf lettuce or Bibb with chopped scallions (green onions) and bacon. It is also delicious over thickly sliced, freshly cooked potatoes. With potatoes the dressing should be hot, so the potatoes absorb as much as possible.

◆

¼ cup sugar
½ cup cider vinegar
½ cup water
½ cup fresh bacon drippings, hot
Salt to taste

◆

Mix the sugar, vinegar, and water in a small saucepan. Bring to a boil and simmer until the sugar has dissolved, about 1 minute. Add the hot, fresh bacon drippings and salt to taste, and stir well.

Makes 1¾ cups

See Black-Seeded Simpson Salad and Wilted Slaw with Bacon Dressing for other "wilted" salads (see pages 67 and 80).

HERB VINEGAR

1 cup fresh tarragon or other herb leaves, packed
2 cups white wine vinegar or Oriental rice vinegar

Wash the herb leaves thoroughly in cold water, and dry them with a clean cloth towel. Pack them into a sterile canning jar. Measure the vinegar into a stainless steel or enamel pan. Heat the vinegar only to a simmer (not boiling hard), then pour it over the herb. Cover the jar and allow the vinegar to ripen up to 10 days. Strain the vinegar into a clean jar through several thicknesses of cheesecloth. Discard the herb.

BUTTERMILK, CUCUMBER, AND FRESH DILL DRESSING

◆◆◆

*T*his is a marvelous low-calorie dressing. Serve it over tomatoes, cucumbers, cottage cheese, and assorted lettuces.

A quiet moment at the French Market in New Orleans, around 1900.

◆

1 cup buttermilk
1 tablespoon sour cream
1 teaspoon white wine vinegar, or to taste
1 cup chopped peeled cucumber
2 teaspoons chopped fresh dill
Salt and freshly ground white pepper to taste

◆

Combine all the ingredients in a small bowl, and whisk briskly until well blended. Chill before serving.

Makes 2¼ cups

Yogurt can be used instead of buttermilk.

THE QUINTESSENTIAL BOILED DRESSING

◆◆◆

*T*his dear old-timer is one of the best dressings in our Southern cuisine. Maybe it did go out of fashion, but good recipes, like old soldiers, never die. Use it for potato or egg salad or over assorted lettuces.

1 teaspoon salt
2 tablespoons sugar
1 tablespoon all-purpose flour
Pinch of cayenne pepper
½ cup cider vinegar
¼ cup water
4 egg yolks
4 tablespoons (½ stick) butter
½ cup heavy or whipping cream, or more to
*   taste, or 1 cup sour cream*

1. Put the salt, sugar, flour, and cayenne in the top of a double boiler. Add the vinegar and water and mix well.
2. Beat the yolks and add them to the mixture. Add the butter and cook over hot water, stirring constantly, until thickened about 2 minutes.

On the Ashley River, a flatboat laden with vegetables makes its way to Charleston.

3. Put the dressing in the refrigerator to chill 1 hour. When it is cold, add the heavy or sour cream.
Makes 1¾ cups

MAYONNAISE

◆◆◆

*T*his is the classic way to make mayonnaise. A whisk can be used instead of a mixer. Wine vinegar can be substituted for lemon juice, but the dressing will not be as delicate. Note: no sugar.

2 egg yolks, at room temperature
½ teaspoon salt, or taste
1 tablespoon fresh lemon juice, or more to taste
½ teaspoon dry mustard
2 cups good-quality vegetable oil, at room
*   temperature*
2 tablespoons boiling water
Dash of cayenne pepper

1. Put the egg yolks, salt, lemon juice, and mustard in the small bowl of an electric mixer, or use a bowl for a hand mixer. Beat until slightly thickened, about 5 minutes.
2. Start adding the oil, 1 teaspoon at a time, beating continuously. Watch closely and do not add more oil until the last addition has been absorbed.
3. After 1 cup oil has been added and you have a thick emulsion, the oil may be added a bit faster, such as a tablespoon or two at a time, until all the oil has been incorporated. Add the boiling water, still beating continuously.

4. Taste the mayonnaise for lemon juice and salt. Add more if desired, and a dash of cayenne.

Makes 2¼ cups

🦉 If the oil is added to the yolks too fast at any time, the emulsion will be broken and the mayonnaise will curdle. Keep a small pan of boiling water on the stove during the whole process of making mayonnaise. Watch the mayonnaise closely. If it starts to separate or curdle, add a tablespoon or so of boiling water, beating fast.

If the emulsion separates completely, you will have to start over: Put the curdled mixture in a glass measuring pitcher or bowl. Add oil to make 2 cups; mix well. Put 1 egg yolk (room temperature) in a clean, dry bowl. Add a tiny bit of salt and lemon juice. Beat until the yolk thickens a bit. Then start adding the curdled mixture, 1 teaspoon at a time, beating continuously. Slowly—slowly. Gradually an emulsion will be formed. Add all of the curdled mixture, then complete the mayonnaise by adding 2 tablespoons boiling water. This will be a richer mayonnaise with the extra yolk, but it will be good. As you become more experienced, you can add ½ cup extra oil to cut the richness of the extra yolk.

GREEN MAYONNAISE

3 tablespoons chopped fresh parsley
1 tablespoon chopped chives
1½ tablespoons chopped fresh tarragon
2 cups homemade mayonnaise (see page 93)
Fresh lemon juice to taste

Fold the herbs into the mayonnaise and season with lemon juice to taste. Allow to stand an hour or so in the refrigerator to ripen before using. Serve with cold salmon, hard-cooked eggs, and a variety of seafood hors d'oeuvres.

VARIATION: Chopped fresh dill may be used instead of tarragon—especially good when the entrée is fish or shellfish.

BLENDER MAYONNAISE

*T*he electric blender is still one of our best gadgets in the kitchen. In many cases it is better than a processor, as in making a small amount of mayonnaise. The method given here makes a delightful mayonnaise and it is the quickest of all.

1 whole egg, at room temperature
1 egg yolk, at room temperature
1 cup good-quality flavorless vegetable oil (or use part olive oil if you wish), at room temperature
½ teaspoon (scant) salt
½ teaspoon dry mustard (Colman's is excellent)
2 tablespoons fresh lemon juice, or to taste
Cayenne pepper to taste

1. Put the whole egg, egg yolk, ¼ cup of the oil, the salt, mustard, and lemon juice in a blender. Turn the motor on. After a minute, start pouring in the remaining oil in a thin stream.

2. After using about half of the oil, stop the blender, remove the cover, and stir the mayonnaise with a long-handled spoon. Turn it on again and continue to add the oil slowly. If at any time a puddle of oil accumulates at the top of the mayonnaise, shut off the blender and stir the mayonnaise well with the long-handled spoon.

3. Taste the mayonnaise for salt and lemon juice, and correct if necessary. Add cayenne pepper to taste.

Makes 1½ cups

The purpose of making mayonnaise in small amounts is to always use freshly made mayonnaise, which is far superior.

If the mayonnaise is too thick for your taste, add a tablespoon of boiling water just before finishing it up.

A small amount of white wine vinegar may be used with or instead of the lemon juice. Generally, lemon juice is the best acid for mayonnaise, but tarragon vinegar can be delicious in mayonaise for chicken or seafood salad.

SMOOTH AND CREAMY DRESSING FOR SLAW AND GREEN SALADS

◆◆

*T*his salad dressing is a cross between a vinaigrette and a mayonnaise. It can be made quickly in a blender, but the consistency is better when it is beaten with a whisk—and no dressing could be easier. It is a favorite, served with Bibb lettuce and a sprinkling of chopped pimentos, or with a salad of half shredded green cabbage and half lettuce, or with shredded lettuce and celery cabbage and a few pimentos. There's plenty here for two to three salads.

◆

2 egg yolks, at room temperature
2 teaspoons dry mustard
1 scant teaspoon sugar
2 teaspoons white wine or cider vinegar
½ teaspoon salt
¼ teaspoon Hungarian paprika
Cayenne pepper to taste
1 cup vegetable oil, at room temperature
2 tablespoons fresh lemon juice
¼ cup heavy or whipping cream

◆

1. Combine the egg yolks, mustard, sugar, vinegar, salt, paprika, and cayenne in a bowl. Beat hard with a whisk, then add the oil a little at a time while continuing to beat constantly. The mixture will look like a thin mayonnaise.

2. Add the lemon juice and cream, and beat thoroughly. Taste for salt. Spoon the dressing into a jar, cover, and refrigerate. It will keep for several days.

Makes 1¼ cups

It was in the backyard greenhouse of his home that John B. Bibb first developed his special lettuce.

VARIATIONS: The sugar can be omitted or reduced or increased according to your taste and the kind of salad you are making.

Two or 3 tablespoons Dijon mustard (the light yellow type) can be substituted for the dry mustard. The dressing will be delicious and will have more zing.

🦉 The oil and the egg yolks must be the same temperature. If they are lifted straight from the refrigerator, bring them to room temperature by placing the bottle of oil in a pan of warm water and the egg in a glass of warm water.

If the oil is added 3 tablespoons or so at a time to the egg yolk, rather fast in other words, you will have a homogenized salad dressing. If the oil is added 1 teaspoon at a time, the mixture will thicken rapidly and become more like mayonnaise.

SAUCE LOUIS

◆◆◆

Sauce Louis is a classic dressing for crabmeat, shrimp, or spiny lobster served on lettuce and garnished with huge black olives. Best to use homemade mayonnaise in this.

◆

1 cup homemade mayonnaise (see page 93)
½ cup heavy or whipping cream
¼ cup bottled chili sauce
¼ cup chopped red or green bell pepper
¼ cup chopped scallions (green onions) or
    chives
Salt to taste
Fresh lemon juice to taste

Cayenne pepper or Tabasco sauce (optional)

◆

Mix the mayonnaise, cream, chili sauce, bell pepper, and scallions or chives in a bowl. Add salt if needed, and stir in a generous amount of lemon juice. Add a dash of cayenne or Tabasco if desired.
    Makes 2¼ cups

THOUSAND ISLAND DRESSING

◆◆◆

This is the Southern gentleman's kind of dressing, especially with the egg added to it. The dressing went out of fashion for a few years but it was too beloved to die.

◆

3 to 4 tablespoons bottled chili sauce (no more)
1 cup finely chopped celery
1 cup chopped stuffed green olives
¼ cup finely chopped sweet pickles
1 chopped pimento, or more to taste
1 teaspoon onion juice (see Owl)
2 cups homemade mayonnaise (see page 93) or
    Hellmann's mayonnaise

◆

Combine all the ingredients with the mayonnaise in a large bowl and stir well. Allow the dressing to ripen in the refrigerator for about 1 hour for the flavors to blend.
    Makes 4½ cups

VARIATION: A chopped hard-cooked egg may be added, but the dressing should not be kept over 1 day if the egg is added.

🦉 To make the juice, grate an onion and strain it through cheesecloth to extract the liquid. Or add 1 medium onion cut in quarters to the sauce. Bruise it with a wooden spoon in the sauce to extract the juice. Remove the pieces of onion after the dressing has ripened for an hour or so.

CHAPTER FOUR

MEATS

ALL MANNER OF MEN
LOVE MEAT

*I*n my long years of cooking, I have never doubted for a minute that fine food enhances the quality of life. And one of the favorite foods of the great family of man is the pleasing taste of good meat. Although meat is very expensive now, you do not have to have it every day. But when you do have it, cook it with care.

Successful meat cookery begins in the market, and the key to it is recognizing good-quality meat when you see it or finding a knowledgeable butcher who will help you. If you find one, you are fortunate; remain loyal to his shop.

Different cuts of meat vary in the ways they should be prepared. Cuts that respond to grilling, broiling, or sautéing are the choice for Old Seelbach House Tenderloin Chunks, Veal Chops with Pine Nuts and Vermouth, and A Rack of Spring Lamb. Cuts that take longer cooking are delicious in Beef Brisket with Potatoes on the Half-Shell and Casserole of Braised Stuffed Lamb Steaks.

In choosing which meat to buy, the most important decision of all is the menu. The vegetable, salad, bread, and dessert must be compatible with that meat. They must taste good together. It is as simple as that.

BEEF TENDERLOIN IN ASPIC
WITH WALNUT BUTTER

◆◆◆

*P*repare this the day ahead for an elegant summer buffet.

◆

2 beef tenderloins, 3 to 4 pounds each
3 tablespoons good-quality olive oil
Salt and freshly ground black pepper to taste
1 tablespoon unflavored gelatin
¼ cup cold water
3 cups Brown Soup Stock (see Index)
¼ cup sherry, or to taste
Watercress, for garnish
Pickled walnuts, for garnish (see Owl)
French tarragon mustard
Fabulous Walnut Butter (see page 106)

◆

1. *The day before serving:* Preheat the oven to 450°F.

2. Trim the tenderloins and rub them with the olive oil. Season with salt and pepper. Place in the oven on a rack set in a roasting pan and roast until the meat registers 125°F on a meat thermometer for rare, 30 to 35 minutes. (If desired, one tenderloin may be roasted longer for those who do not appreciate rare meat.) Allow the beef to cool thoroughly.

3. Soften the gelatin in the cold water.

4. Bring the stock to a boil. Add the sherry and continue to boil a minute or so more. Add the softened gelatin, mix well, and set aside to cool.

5. Slice the tenderloin very thin, being careful to keep the slices in place as much as possible. The tenderloins should be reassembled to look whole. Use skewers to hold the tenderloins together.

6. Season the sliced meat again with salt and pepper. Brush the tenderloins well with some of the gelatin mixture. Chill. After the aspic on the meat has set, brush the meat again with the liquid, then chill to set again. Repeat the process until you have about ¼ inch of jellied aspic covering the meat. If at any time the unused aspic stiffens too much, warm it up a bit, then allow it to cool, and continue.

7. Place the glazed tenderloins in the refrigerator. Pour the remaining aspic in a shallow pan. Refrigerate.

8. *To serve:* Place the glazed tenderloins on a platter. Remove the skewers. Cut the aspic from the shallow pan into cubes. Use it to garnish the beef, along with the watercress and pickled walnuts. Serve with a pot of French tarragon mustard and a sauceboat of Fabulous Walnut Butter.

Serves 8 to 10

🦉 Tarragon mustard and pickled walnuts are found in gourmet departments and food specialty stores.

GRILLED BEEF TENDERLOIN
WITH ROQUEFORT AND
RED PEPPER BUTTER

◆◆◆

A galaxy of divine flavors—hot tenderloin steak with butter, Roquefort, slivers of red pepper, and the freshness of tangy watercress. Serve with buttered toasted French bread that has had the lightest brushing of cut garlic.

A good old-fashioned outdoor pit barbecue in Baxley, Georgia, 1919.

3 pounds beef tenderloin
Roquefort and Red Pepper Butter (recipe
    follows)
5 tablespoons butter
Salt and freshly ground black pepper to taste
2 tablespoons chopped fresh tarragon or
    1 teaspoon dried
2 tablespoons chopped fresh parsley
Watercress or fresh spinach, for garnish

1. Have every particle of fat trimmed from the tenderloin. Let it stand, lightly covered, at room temperature for several hours before cooking.

2. Meanwhile, prepare the Roquefort and Red Pepper Butter.

3. When you are ready to cook, melt 4 tablespoons of the butter. Brush the meat well with butter and season with salt.

4. Barbecue the meat on a spit or on the grill (place an oiled rack 4 to 6 inches above medium-hot coals). In either case, it will take about 30 minutes for the tenderloin to cook to rare. (If cooking on a grill, turn it every 10 minutes.) It should register 125°F on a meat thermometer for rare.

5. When the meat is done, remove it to a carving board and let it stand for 8 minutes. Sprinkle generously with salt, pepper, and fresh tarragon and parsley.

6. Carve the tenderloin into medium-thick slices and serve on warm plates garnished with watercress or fresh crisp spinach and several slices of Roquefort and Red Pepper Butter. Quickly spoon the juice that was released from carving the steak into a small pan. Heat it quickly with the remaining butter and add a touch of salt. Pour it over the steaks or serve in a sauceboat.

Serves 6

VARIATION: *Grilled Tenderloin Chunks*: Cut the steak into 3-inch pieces, skewer, and grill or sauté in butter. Slide the chunks of steak off the skewers. With a sharp knife cut down through the chunks, across the grain, into thin slices. Present as described above.

ROQUEFORT AND RED PEPPER BUTTER

1 small red bell pepper, or 1 red sweet banana
    pepper
5 ounces Roquefort cheese
1 cup (2 sticks) unsalted butter, at room
    temperature
Salt to taste
Cayenne pepper or Tabasco to taste
Hungarian paprika

1. Wash, core, and seed the red pepper. Cut it into wire-thin slivers.

2. Cream the cheese and butter together in a processor or with an electric mixer. Add the red pepper and blend. Season with salt and cayenne or Tabasco to taste.

3. Form the mixture into 2 balls and rotate them in paprika sprinkled on a piece of foil. Refrigerate to chill.

Makes two ½-cup balls

*I*n the South, the word "barbecue" brings to mind the taste of ketchup, Worcestershire sauce, onions, cayenne pepper, and Tabasco, because that is the way the meat has traditionally been seasoned. A barbecue, however, really means any meat, fish, or fowl that is cooked over the coals or on a spit—not necessarily basted with a highly seasoned sauce.

COOKING BEEF

*T*here is a different cut of beef appropriate to every meal of the day and for most occasions, from Southern country stews and pot roasts to tenderloin for elegant dinners. The many different ways to cook beef make it a joy to eat as well as interesting to cook.

A premium beef will be well marbled, with tiny veins of fat running through it, and the fat on the outside will be creamy white and very firm. Yellow fat indicates poor-quality beef. Rib roasts, tenderloin, and steaks are the luxurious cuts and are cooked more quickly. The tender-ness in stews and pot roasts does not come from using expensive cuts. It is best to use the cheaper cuts of meat, as premium beef would overcook before the meat has absorbed the flavors of the vegetables and herbs. Brisket, short ribs, and rump are the most delicious cuts for stews and pot roasts.

There is, of course, a time and place for each cut. But don't forget to have before long Old Seelbach House Tenderloin Chunks, or Marinated Short Ribs of Beef, or a Beef Brisket with Potatoes on the Half-Shell. Mighty good!

OLD SEELBACH HOUSE TENDERLOIN CHUNKS

*T*his is a herb-filled tomato steak sauce for all seasons. Delightful with tenderloin, delicious with hamburgers. Grill the beef in the summer—sauté it in a skillet in the winter. Serve with french-fried potatoes, baked potatoes, scalloped potatoes, or Potatoes Anna—and parsley and red cabbage slaw. Eat...eat...eat! Live...live ...live!

⅓ pound beef kidney suet
2 pounds beef tenderloin or sirloin, cut into
    1½- to 2-inch cubes
Salt and freshly ground black pepper to taste
Old Seelbach House Steak Sauce (recipe
    follows), heated
Chopped fresh parsley, for garnish

1. Put the suet in a very hot black iron skillet. Add the meat and sauté it quickly over high heat, about 3 to 4 minutes. Turn the pieces to brown on all sides but keep them rare. Season with salt and pepper.

2. Put several spoonfuls of piping hot sauce in the center of each warm dinner plate and lay chunks of steak in the center of the sauce. Sprinkle with parsley. Work fast to serve everything very hot.

Serves 4 to 6

OLD SEELBACH HOUSE STEAK SAUCE

4 cups good-quality canned tomatoes, or
    2 pounds firm ripe tomatoes, peeled
3 shallots, or 4 scallions (green onions), white
    part only
1 small clove garlic
1 cup dry red wine
1 cup red wine vinegar
2 tablespoons chopped fresh marjoram leaves or
    1½ teaspoons dried
1 tablespoon fresh thyme leaves or 1 teaspoon
    dried
3 tablespoons chopped fresh parlsey
1 bay leaf
¼ cup water
¼ cup sugar
Salt and freshly ground black pepper to taste
¼ pound mushrooms, sliced or chopped
3 tablespoons unsalted butter

1. Combine the tomatoes and shallots or scallions in a blender or processor and blend well. Pour into a large stainless steel or enamel saucepan and simmer over medium heat until a thick sauce has formed, about 30 to 40 minutes.

2. In the meantime, combine the garlic, wine, vinegar, marjoram, thyme, parsley, and bay leaf in a stainless steel or enamel saucepan and simmer until the ingredients have reduced to ⅓ cup, 30 to 40 minutes. Strain into a bowl and set aside.

3. Combine the water and sugar in a heavy pan or skillet and cook over low heat until a medium-brown caramel is formed, 2 to 3 minutes. Do not allow it to become the least bit burned or the sauce will be bitter.

4. Add the wine and herb infusion to the caramel. Stir to blend and add to the tomato sauce. Add salt and pepper to taste and allow the flavors to ripen an hour or so before using; or the sauce can be made several days ahead and refrigerated. Before serving, sauté the mushrooms in the butter and fold them into the sauce.

Makes about 2½ cups

OYSTERS AND TENDERLOIN EN BROCHETTE

◆◆◆

*W*e have dozens of ways to prepare oysters in the South, but there are no skewered dishes more elegant than oysters and tenderloin. They make a very charming hot hors d'oeuvre for a special outdoor party when the late summer evenings are a bit cool, and they are delectable served as a first course or as a light supper entrée. For formal parties, serve them accompanied by the Mustard and Tarragon Hollandaise and white wine. For informal parties, serve them with Old Seelbach House Steak Sauce and cold beer.

16 fresh large oysters (allow 4 per person),
*   shucked (see Index)*
8 slices smoked bacon, cut in half
4 to 5 tablespoons unsalted butter, melted
Salt to taste

1 tablespoon chopped fresh marjoram leaves or
*   1 teaspoon dried*
16 large mushroom caps (allow 1 per oyster)
1 pound beef tenderloin, cut into 1-inch chunks
Freshly ground black pepper to taste
2 cups chopped fresh parsley, or as needed
Mustard and Tarragon Hollandaise (recipe
*   follows), Old Seelbach House Steak Sauce*
*   (see page 101), or lemon wedges*

◆

1. Preheat the oven to 450°F.

2. Drain the oysters. (Reserve the liquor, which can be frozen for later use.) Lay the oysters on paper towels or a clean cloth, to absorb the excess moisture. Wrap each oyster in a piece of bacon. Secure with a toothpick.

3. Season the melted butter with salt and marjoram, and dip the mushroom caps in the butter mixture. Thread the buttered mushrooms alternating with the bacon-

covered oysters on thin short skewers. Thread the tenderloin chunks on identical skewers.

4. Place the oyster-and-mushroom-filled skewers in a shallow pan in the oven and cook until the bacon has cooked through but is not overly crisp, about 20 to 25 minutes. After the oysters have cooked for 10 to 15 minutes, brush the tenderloin-filled skewers with some of the butter and place them in a separate pan in the oven. (The tenderloin must stay rare and it cooks faster than the bacon.)

5. When the tenderloin-filled skewers have cooked for 6 to 8 minutes, turn them so they will cook evenly. When the beef is done but still pink, remove all the skewers from the oven, not over 3 minutes more. Season with salt and freshly ground pepper.

6. Serve a skewer of tenderloin chunks and a skewer of oysters and mushrooms on a bed of chopped parsley on each warm plate. Pass a sauceboat of Mustard and Tarragon Hollandaise, old Seelbach House Steak Sauce, or, if desired, wedges of lemon.

Serves 4

If you prefer, the tenderloin on skewers may be sautéed in butter in a black iron skillet while the oysters are cooking in the oven.

MUSTARD AND TARRAGON HOLLANDAISE

2 hard-cooked egg yolks, mashed
2 raw egg yolks
2 teaspoons light yellow Dijon mustard, or more to taste
3 tablespoons tarragon vinegar
1 teaspoon salt, or to taste
1¼ cups good-quality olive oil, vegetable oil, or hot, melted unsalted butter
Cayenne pepper to taste

Put the hard-cooked egg yolks in a blender, processor, or a roomy bowl. Add the raw egg yolks, mustard, vinegar, and salt. With the machine running, or while beating, gradually blend in the oil or melted butter. Taste for salt. Add cayenne to taste.

Makes 1½ cups

VARIATION: Lemon juice may be used instead of vinegar, or use half vinegar and half lemon juice. Lemon juice is milder than vinegar, and for this reason some people prefer it.

If the mixture should start to curdle, add 1 tablespoon boiling water, or quickly heat it in a pan over simmering water, and beat with a whisk.

The salt and acid are always added to the egg yolks before the oil or butter in making mayonnaise or hollandaise.

Chopped fresh tarragon is delicious folded into this hollandaise.

This hollandaise may be served on broccoli, asparagus, or new potatoes.

RIB-EYE STEAKS WITH RED WINE AND TARRAGON SAUCE

To broil or grill a steak usually means to cook it over an open fire, under a broiler, or in a heavy skillet. Pan-broiling in a black iron skillet is one of the best ways of cooking small steaks. The old black iron skillet is as important in the South for our beloved outdoor steak suppers as it is for frying chicken. The skillet will tolerate intense heat—and it will hold the heat well and cook the steaks quickly, which helps produce a tender steak—but you must, of course, start with good beef.

Rib-eye steaks are an economical cut, but they are flavorful and delicious prepared this way.

⅔ cup dry red wine
1 tablespoon dried tarragon
3 tablespoons unsalted butter
Salt to taste
Small piece beef suet or fat
4 rib-eye steaks (6 ounces each)
Freshly ground black pepper to taste

1. Combine the red wine with the tarragon and allow the mixture to sit for 1 hour if possible. Simmer the wine and tarragon a few minutes, until the wine loses its raw flavor. Add the butter, and salt to taste. When the butter melts and a sauce is formed, strain out the tarragon, and the sauce is ready for the steaks. (This can be done way ahead.)

2. When you are ready to serve the steaks, place a large black iron skillet or 2 small iron skillets over medium heat. When the pan is hot, grease it with the beef suet.

3. Raise the heat and place the steaks in the pan without crowding. The steaks should sizzle right away. Brown them on one side for 2 to 3 minutes, then turn and brown the second side about 3 minutes (about 6 minutes in all for rare, thinly cut steaks). Season with salt and a generous amount of freshly ground pepper.

4. Remove the steaks to warm plates and pour the Red Wine and Tarragon Sauce in the skillet to blend quickly with the meat juices, then pour it over the steaks.

Serves 4

KENTUCKY BOURBON GRILLED STEAK

*A*n interesting thing about a fine, aged Kentucky bourbon is that it tastes very much like some brandies and very often it can be substituted for brandy in cooking. It must, however, be an excellent bourbon and an old one.

A flank steak will profit in flavor if marinated in either the Kentucky Bourbon Marinade or the Wine and Soy Marinade before grilling. Flank steak must be premium quality or it is likely to be tough. Marinating helps to tenderize it, but the steak must be grilled quickly and sliced very thin on the bias—this is mandatory, and so is a sharp knife.

1 premium flank steak, 2 to 2½ pounds
Good-quality vegetable or olive oil

KENTUCKY BOURBON MARINADE

1 clove garlic, cut in half
1½ tablespoons Kentucky bourbon
1 tablespoon vegetable oil
1 tablespoon soy sauce
1 or 2 small slivers fresh ginger or piece of dried
*   ginger*

WINE AND SOY MARINADE

¾ cup dry white wine
½ cup soy sauce
2 small slivers fresh ginger or piece of dried
*   ginger*
3 or 4 scallions (green onions), chopped, or 1
*   clove garlic, cut in half*
3 sprigs parsley

1. Remove all the excess fat and the tough membrane from the outside of the flank steak, or have the butcher do it for you.

2. Combine the ingredients for the chosen marinade in a glass, enamel, or stainless steel pan or bowl. Place the steak in the marinade, coating it well on both sides. Allow the steak to marinate in the refrigerator for 12 to 24 hours—the longer the better. Turn the steak several times to distribute the flavors.

3. When you are ready to cook the steak, remove it from the marinade. Brush off the herbs and dry it well with paper towels.

4. Brush the steak with vegetable or olive oil. (The soy sauce in the marinade usually provides sufficient salt.) Broil or grill 4 inches from the heat for about 5 minutes on each side for rare steak. After the steak has been seared, brush it again with the marinade while it is cooking, if desired.

Serves 4 to 6

RED WINE STEAK SAUCE

For all beef steaks or venison steaks, or grilled hamburgers.

2 tablespoons butter
1 tablespoon chopped shallots
1 tablespoon water
1 cup dry red wine
1 clove garlic, mashed
1 teaspoon tomato paste
Salt to taste
1 tablespoon Madeira, or more to taste

1. Melt the butter in a skillet, and add the shallots and water. Cook gently until the water boils away and the shallots are tender, 2 minutes. Do not allow them to brown.

2. Add the wine and simmer for a few seconds. Then add the garlic, tomato paste, salt, and Madeira, and simmer 30 minutes.

3. Serve at the table in a sauceboat.
Makes 1 cup

KENTUCKY SPICED BEEF

*T*his superb and beautiful roast lends itself to many elegant occasions. You don't have to pickle the garnishing mushrooms, of course, but if you do you will love them. Stuffed with black walnuts, pickled mushrooms are stunning tucked among the sprays of watercress, and with the amber aspic they make quite a show. All of these little amenities blend in a litany of wonderful flavors. As a rule, beef is cooked in red wine, but beef in white wine is a very different thing—not as robust, perhaps, but fascinating to one's tastebuds, and the flavor is lovely.

Clod of premium beef shoulder or face of rump,
  5 to 6 pounds (see step 1 and Owl)
2 cloves garlic
1 pound mushrooms, sliced
8 shallots, minced (do not substitute onions)
1 cup chopped fresh parsley
Salt and freshly ground black pepper to taste
½ pound sliced lean smoked bacon
2 tablespoons butter if needed
2 cups dry white wine
1½ teaspoons dried thyme
2 ribs celery, cut in half

1 whole tomato, fresh or canned
Several sprigs parsley
2 carrots, peeled and cut in half
1 onion, peeled and left whole
Brown Soup Stock (see Index) or water
2 teaspoons unflavored gelatin
3 tablespoons cold water
Watercress, for garnish
Pickled Mushrooms (see Index), for garnish
Pickled walnuts, for garnish
Fabulous Walnut Butter (recipe follows)

1. Have your butcher cut across the clod of shoulder twice horizontally, making 1½- to 2-inch layers of beef, but leaving the meat slightly hinged on one side by not cutting the layers all the way through. (This makes the roast easier to handle.) The roast will be in 3 thick layers.

2. Preheat the oven to 450°F.

3. Rub each layer of meat with a cut clove of garlic.

4. Mix together the mushrooms, shallots, and chopped parsley. Season each layer of the meat with salt and pepper. Cover the top of the bottom and middle layers with slices of bacon and the mushroom mixture, filling one layer at a time. Close the layers and press down rather hard. (Some stuffing will ooze out. Add it with the stock or water in step 7.)

5. Tie the roast securely with twine. Salt and pepper the outside of the roast. Brush the top with the butter or lay 3 strips of bacon over the top.

6. Put the roast in a heavy dutch oven (not black iron) and cook in the oven until well browned, about 35 minutes. Reduce the heat to 325°F.

7. Add the white wine, thyme, celery, tomato, parsley sprigs, carrots, onion, and beef stock or water to cover the roast two-thirds of the way. Cover and cook until the meat is perfectly tender, another 1½ to 2 hours . The time will vary with the quality of the meat.

8. Remove the meat from the stock and allow it to cool. Cover with foil and refrigerate.

9. Remove the seasoning vegetables from the stock. Strain the stock through cheesecloth or a very fine sieve. Cool and refrigerate, or if pressed for time, place in the freezer.

10. Remove the fat from the stock. Clarify the stock if desired (see Index). Dissolve the gelatin in 3 tablespoons water. Heat the stock, and add the gelatin.

11. Remove the strings from the roast. Place the roast in a snug round mixing bowl. Cover it with the stock. Return it to the refrigerator and leave it until the aspic has set, overnight if desired.

12. When ready to serve, unmold the

◆◆◆
AN ELEGANT DINNER AT DERBY TIME

Cream of Fresh Pea Soup

◆

Kentucky Spiced Beef

Fabulous Walnut Butter

New Potato Salad with Asparagus and Chicory

◆

Roquefort   Brie

Cornmeal Melba Toast

◆

Strawberry Sherbet

Camille's Golden Cointreau Cake

Coffee   Tea

---

roast and place it round side up on a beautiful round platter. Some of the aspic may fall off—just place it around the roast. Garnish with watercress and large pickled mushrooms, stemmed side up. Place a pickled walnut in each mushroom. Accompany with a sauceboat of Fabulous Walnut Butter. When serving, carve the roast straight down through the layers. The meat alternating with the stuffing is very attractive.

Serves 8 to 10

There are 3 large muscles in a beef shoulder. The center muscle is the best and it is called the clod. It usually weighs from 5 to 7 pounds and is the choice shoulder cut for this roast as it is one large piece of meat.

◆
FABULOUS WALNUT BUTTER
◆

1 cup Major Grey's mango chutney (homemade or imported Madras chutney)
1 cup English pickled walnuts, drained

◆

Combine the chutney and the pickled walnuts, including their juice, in a blender or a food processor and blend until perfectly smooth.

Makes 1½ cups

BEEF BRISKET WITH POTATOES ON THE HALF-SHELL

*T*his heirloom recipe will be one of your family's favorites. Serve it with Sour Cream–Horseradish Sauce.

4 to 4½ pounds whole brisket
Salt and freshly ground black pepper to taste
2 cups water, or as needed
3 sprigs fresh thyme or 1 teaspoon dried
2 bay leaves
6 to 8 Idaho potatoes, uniform size (1 per
   person)
Watercress or parsley, for garnish
Sour Cream–Horseradish Sauce (recipe follows)

1. Preheat the oven to 450°F.
2. Wipe the brisket with a clean, damp cloth and season it with salt. Roast it in a deep roasting pan until golden brown, 30 to 35 minutes.
3. Add about 2 cups of water to the pan, or just enough to keep the roast from sticking and burning on the bottom. Sprinkle the roast with freshly ground pepper. Add the thyme and bay leaves. Cover, and reduce the heat to 325°F. Cook until the meat is tender, another 2 to 2½ hours (this will vary with the size and grade of the brisket).
4. Meanwhile, scrub the potatoes and cut them in half lengthwise.
5. About 35 to 40 minutes before the meat is done, lay the potatoes skin side up, cut side down, around the brisket. Taste the meat juices for salt. Add salt to the potatoes if needed. Allow the potatoes to cook in the meat drippings in the roasting pan. About 15 minutes before they are done, raise the heat to 425°F. Remove the cover and baste the potatoes thoroughly with the pan juices. The cut side will absorb the juices from the meat, get brown, and be delicious. Test the meat for tenderness with a thin skewer.
6. Place the brisket, whole, on a

Dinner on the "Henry M. Stanley," a steamboat built in West Virginia in 1907. The pilot and crew are seated at the table.

warmed platter. Surround it with the potatoes and garnish with watercress or parsley. Slice the meat only as it is served, as brisket dries out quickly. Serve with sauceboats of skimmed pan juices and Sour Cream-Horseradish Sauce.

Serves 6 to 8

SOUR CREAM–HORSERADISH SAUCE

1 cup sour cream
3 tablespoons prepared horseradish
Salt to taste

Combine the ingredients in a small bowl. Transfer to a sauceboat and serve.

A WINTER NIGHT'S HEARTY SUPPER

Beef Brisket with Potatoes on the Half-Shell

Sour Cream–Horseradish Sauce

Spinach Salad with Tangy Mustard Vinaigrette

◆

Windfall Apple Pie

Coffee

GEORGETOWN'S OLD-FASHIONED POT ROAST

*B*raising pot roasts is a procedure that requires time and care, but nothing else quite takes their place. These pot roasts have that Old World flavor all of us love, and the leftovers—sandwiches and hash—are greeted with just as warm a welcome. The roast may be cooked with or without the vegetables.

4 to 5 pounds beef rump or chuck roast or brisket (choose well-marbled beef; see step 1)
¼ cup melted beef suet or vegetable oil
Salt and freshly ground black pepper to taste
2 small onions
3 ribs celery, cut in half
2 bay leaves
1 teaspoon dried thyme or 2 or 3 sprigs fresh
2 or 3 sprigs parsley
1½ to 2 cups cold water or clarified Brown Soup Stock (see Index)
2 tablespoons butter, at room temperature, if needed
1 tablespoon all-purpose flour, if needed

VEGETABLES

6 to 8 fresh small carrots, peeled
6 small onions, peeled
6 ribs celery, cut into 2-inch pieces
6 fresh small turnips, peeled (optional)
6 to 8 mealy potatoes, peeled (allow ½ pound per person)

1. Have your butcher bone and tie the roast.
2. Preheat the oven to 325°F.
3. Heat the fat (rendered suet is best) in a black iron skillet or heavy flameproof casserole. Sear the roast on all sides until golden brown. Skim off all but 3 tablespoons of fat or transfer it to a casserole or a dutch oven if the roast was browned in a skillet. Sprinkle well with salt and pepper.
4. Add the onions, celery, bay leaves, thyme, parsley, and enough water or beef bouillon to cover the lower half of roast. Bring to a boil.
5. Place the casserole in the oven and cook, covered, skimming off the fat and basting the meat from time to time. Allow the stock around the roast to cook rather low and to take on a good, rich, beefy flavor. If the stock has cooked too low, add a little water. After about 1½ hours, when the meat begins to seem tender and the sauce is a golden brown, discard the seasoning vegetables. If the sauce does not have enough body, cream together the butter and flour and whisk it into the stock, stirring well.
6. Lightly sprinkle the vegetables with salt and scatter them around the meat. The broth should not cover the vegetables completely, only about halfway. Baste the vegetables thoroughly with the broth. Cover the pan and continue to cook until the vegetables are tender, another 30 minutes. Continue to baste the vegetables so they will absorb the meat flavor.
7. If the vegetables need browning a bit at the end, remove the cover and step up the heat to 450°F for 10 to 15 minutes. Taste for salt.
8. Remove the roast from the oven and allow it to rest in the pan for 15 minutes before carving. Serve the roast garnished with the vegetables.

Serves 6 to 8

This is a roast of the old-fashioned method—cooked very, very tender. The length of time that it takes depends upon the quality of the meat.

Carve the roast with a very sharp knife. An Old World braised pot roast that has developed lots of flavorful stock will not slice well, but it has exquisite flavor. Leftovers may be sliced and served with Sour Cream–Horseradish Sauce (see page 107).

NEW ORLEANS DAUBE OF BEEF

◆◆◆

*I*n New Orleans they call this a "daube," and it is a charming way of preparing beef that they inherited from their French ancestors. It is a large piece of braised beef or veal that is served cold in its own aspic. The pig's feet are used for the natural gelatin they supply as well as for their enriching flavor.

◆

1 whole brisket or beef rump roast, 4 to 5
*   pounds*
Salt and freshly ground black pepper to taste
2 cups dry white wine or water
2 pig's feet, ready to cook
6 sprigs parsley, plus several additional stems
2 onions, each stuck with 1 clove
2 carrots, peeled and cut in half
2 tomatoes (canned or fresh)
2 ribs celery, cut in half
1 clove garlic, unpeeled
2 bay leaves
1½ teaspoons dried thyme
2 cups Brown Soup Stock (see Index) or
*   bouillon, or as needed*
1½ teaspoons unflavored gelatin
Watercress or parsley, for garnish

◆

1. Preheat the oven to 450°F.

2. Season the roast with salt and pepper. Place it in a casserole or dutch oven and roast until it is golden brown, about 35 minutes.

3. Pour in enough wine or water to only half cover the roast. Add the pig's feet, parsley, onions, carrots, tomatoes, celery, garlic, bay leaves, and thyme. Add ½ teaspoon salt. Reduce the heat to 325°F, cover, and cook until the meat is tender, 2½ to 3 hours. The time will vary with the meat, but do not overcook or the meat will be dry.

4. Lift the roast and pig's feet from the broth and refrigerate them. The pig's feet can be used for another meal.

5. Use a slotted spoon to remove the seasoning herbs and vegetables from the stock. Strain the stock through a fine stainless steel sieve or doubled cheesecloth into a large bowl. Refrigerate, so the fat will solidify, 8 hours or overnight. (If you wish to speed up the process, place in the freezer in a shallow pan for 30 to 40 minutes.)

6. Skim off the fat. If the stock is clear you can use it as is, or it can be clarified (see Owl). You will need 4 cups stock. Add enough extra beef stock or bouillon to make this amount. Taste and correct the seasoning if needed.

7. Pour a few tablespoons of the stock into a saucer and chill it in the refrigerator for 5 minutes. If it does not jell, you will need to heat the stock and add the gelatin

◆◆

CHECK POINTS FOR BRAISING MEATS

*M*eat for braising can be lightly dusted with flour before searing it in fat, but this often results in a heavy, floury sauce. This was the old way of cooking. Browning the meat in the oven or searing it without flour gives a clearer, brighter sauce with a fresher meat flavor.

If overbrowned (which means the natural sugar in the meat was overcaramelized), the meat or its juices will taste bitter.

Baste the meat often so the top will stay moist and the flavors of the meat and liquids can blend.

Skim the fat from the meat each time before you baste.

The fat will rise easily to the surface of braising meats unless too much flour was used or the meat is cooking too rapidly. An excess of flour (used either to dust the meat before browning or in a mixture of butter and flour to thicken the sauce) will hold the fat in the liquid and a fatty sauce will result. Slow cooking releases the natural fat and allows it to float to the top.

A little butter worked into flour for the thickening prevents the flour from lumping.

to it. Then allow the stock to cool but not jell.

8. Put the roast in a close-fitting bowl or pan. Pour the aspic over it. Refrigerate so the aspic will jell, 8 hours or overnight.

9. When you are ready to serve it, transfer the daube to a platter and garnish it with chopped extra aspic and parsley or watercress. Slice and serve as is or with Dijon mustard, relishes, and sour pickles.

　　　　　　Serves 6 to 8

🦉 To clarify stock, add 1 tablespoon white wine vinegar, 2 tablespoons medium-dry sherry, and 2 slightly beaten egg whites to the cold, fat-free stock. Simmer gently for 10 minutes. Allow it to rest and settle for 5 to 10 minutes. (The egg whites will look awful, but underneath there will be a clear lake.) Skim off the egg whites and strain the stock through a dampened double thickness of cheesecloth.

THE FALLS CITY CARBONNADE

◆◆

*I*n the late nineteenth century and the early decades of our own time, many German families settled in the Ohio Valley around Louisville, and they brought their food and brewery talents with them. In many ways our food preferences reflect this influence. Most of our food today is lighter and fresher, but the old flavors linger on—one of which is this beef cooked in beer. Cook it ahead, heat it up, prepare some noodles and broccoli or kohlrabi—it works like a charm.

Back in the old days, the Rathskellar in the Seelbach Hotel served good German-style food. Mr. Carter, the manager, was one of my father's best friends.

◆

1 beef rump roast, 3 to 3½ pounds (see step 1)
4 to 5 tablespoons beef suet or vegetable oil
Salt and freshly ground black pepper to taste
2 tablespoons butter

4 onions, sliced
¼ cup water
2 tablespoons cider vinegar
1 teaspoon sugar
1¼ cups beer
3 cups Brown Soup Stock (see Index) or
　　bouillon
2 ribs celery, cut in half
2 carrots, peeled and cut in half
2 or 3 sprigs parsley
2 bay leaves
1 teaspoon dried thyme
2 tablespoons butter, at room temperature
2 tablespoons all-purpose flour

◆

1. Have your butcher slice the roast into 12 to 14 slices.

2. Melt the suet, if using, in a 400°F oven while you flatten the slices of beef a bit with the flat side of a mallet. Then reduce the heat to 325°F.

3. Heat the suet or vegetable oil in a large iron skillet over medium heat. Sauté the slices of meat, a few at a time, in the fat until they have browned lightly on both sides. Be careful not to burn the fat. Season the meat with salt and pepper. Transfer the slices of meat as they brown to another pan to keep warm.

4. Add 2 tablespoons butter to the skillet and blend it with the brown crustiness from the beef. Add the onions and water. Cook until the onions absorb the butter and meat juices somewhat. Season with salt.

5. Layer the meat and onions in a casserole or dutch oven, ending with a top layer of meat.

6. Combine the vinegar, sugar, and beer in the skillet and deglaze over medium heat. Stir well and pour over the meat and onions.

7. Add enough beef stock or bouillon to cover the meat well. If there is not enough, add some water. Add the celery, carrots, parsley, bay leaves, and thyme.

8. Cover, and cook in the oven for 1½ hours. Then blend together the softened butter and flour and whisk it into the meat juices. Season with salt and pepper to taste.

A WINTERTIME FAMILY SUPPER

The Falls City Carbonnade

Buttered Noodles

Warm Broccoli and Red Bell Pepper Salad

Dark Sourdough Rye Rolls

♦

Cam's Prune and Walnut Cake

Coffee   Tea

Cover and continue to cook until the meat is exquisitely tender and the juices have thickened. This may take another 30 minutes, depending upon the quality of the meat. Discard the seasoning vegetables and herbs.

Serves 6 to 8

VARIATION: *Pot Roast of Beef Carbonnade*: Sear a 2½- to 3-pound whole rump roast in suet or vegetable oil in an iron skillet until browned on all sides. Then follow the directions as in Falls City Carbonnade, seasoning it exactly the same way.

MARINATED SHORT RIBS OF BEEF

*F*or a family supper serve this with mashed potatoes or spoonbread and a green or vegetable salad with a mustardy dressing.

4 pounds beef short ribs (see step 1)
2 teaspoons Dijon mustard
1 teaspoon dried thyme
6 tablespoons vegetable oil
1 clove garlic, unpeeled
1½ tablespoons red or white wine vinegar or
    lemon juice
Salt and freshly ground black pepper to taste
½ to 1 cup water
2 medium onions, peeled and left whole
2 carrots, peeled and cut in half
2 bay leaves
3 sprigs parsley

1. Select lean short ribs and have your butcher cut them into 2½- to 3-inch pieces.

2. Make a marinade combining the mustard, thyme, oil, garlic, and vinegar or lemon juice. Pour the marinade over the meat in a non-aluminum bowl. Leave it, covered, in the refrigerator for 6 to 24 hours before cooking. Turn the ribs occasionally to distribute the seasoning.

3. Preheat the oven to 425°F.

4. Remove the ribs from the marinade, reserving the marinade. Dry them well with paper towels, and season with salt and pepper.

Barbecue was a crowd-pleaser at the Tampa Fair in 1924. It probably still is.

5. Cook the ribs in a large shallow roasting pan, uncovered, until the meat is golden brown, about 30 minutes.

6. Strain the marinade and pour it over the ribs along with enough water to cover the bottom third of the ribs. Add the onions, carrots, bay leaves, and parsley. Reduce the heat to 325°F. Cover the pan and cook the ribs until they are tender, another 1 to 1½ hours. If necessary, remove the cover so the meat can brown more at the end. Discard the vegetables.

Serves 4 to 6

If you would like more sauce or a gravy, 1 to 1½ cups beef stock can be added with the onions and carrots (thickened, if you desire, with 1 tablespoon soft butter blended with 1 tablespoon flour).

HERBS THAT ARE OUTSTANDING IN STEWS

Parsley is of time-honored importance to the good cook. It lends a needed freshness to winter stews, and it is the greatest companion of all to the potato.

Rosemary is a beautiful name and a charming herb. It does wonders for all kinds of stews—lamb, chicken, and especially pork. Its fragrance is stronger when fresh than when dried.

Sweet Marjoram: A sprig of fresh marjoram is a delight to our sense of smell. It almost tells you where to use it. Chicken and pasta, lamb dishes, veal dishes, and the herb bouquet. I never seem to plant enough.

Tarragon: It is said that tarragon is the herb of the gourmet. It does have a style all its own. Tarragon seems to elevate each dish it flavors. It is not a country herb—far from it. Tarragon is not as indispensable as thyme, but used in the appropriate dish, such as chicken or veal, it is exquisitely pleasing.

Thyme and Bay Leaf are two herbs that enhance each other and work their magic in meat and seafood stews. Make a fine stew without them? It can't be done. But use the dried imported bay leaf as the American bay leaves do not have the authentic flavor.

VIRGINIA STEAK AND KIDNEY PIE

◆◆

I once lived in Virginia, and with each return visit I am reminded of how alive the influence of the early English settlers remains. They brought with them the idea of baking savory pies in a crust. They used leftover roasted meats or game, veal, ham, seafood, lamb, or steak—all wonderful ideas, too wonderful to be forgotten. Suet crust is the traditional pastry for these pies, but Cornmeal Puff Paste is the ultimate. Flaky Butter Pastry is superb and not difficult, but a Cream Cheese Pastry is probably the easiest to make. You choose.

♦

½ recipe Suet Pastry (recipe follows)
2½ pounds prime round steak or sirloin
¼ pound beef kidney suet or fat trimmed from
   the steak
All-purpose flour for dusting beef
Salt and freshly ground black pepper to taste
1 teaspoon dried thyme
1 bay leaf
1 large onion, finely chopped
Brown Soup Stock (see Index) or bouillon to
   cover meat
8 lamb kidneys, skinned and cleaned (see
   page 114)
2 tablespoons butter
1 egg yolk
1 teaspoon water

♦

1. Make the suet pastry, freezing half for another use. Cover and refrigerate.

2. Cut the steak into strips 2½ to 3 inches long and 1 inch wide, or into 1½- to 2-inch cubes.

3. Melt the beef suet or fat in a heavy skillet over medium heat or in a 400°F oven (the oven process is easier).

4. While the suet is melting, dust the steak pieces lightly with flour and season them with salt. Brown the steak quickly in several tablespoons of hot melted fat in a heavy skillet (such as black iron), a few pieces at a time. Do not crowd the pan or the meat will stew and not brown. As they brown, toss the steak pieces into a casserole or pot that has a cover.

5. Season the browned steak with pepper. Add the thyme, bay leaf, and onion. Add the beef stock or bouillon, covering the meat well. Cover the pot and simmer until the meat is perfectly tender, 1 to 1¼ hours. Discard the bay leaf. Allow the steak and broth to cool.

6. Slice the kidneys thin. Sauté them in the butter, quickly or they will toughen. Sprinkle with salt and set aside to cool. (If the filling isn't cooled before assembling the pie, it will cause the crust to get sodden.)

7. When you are ready to bake the pie, roll out the pastry large enough to cover the top of a shallow baking dish (about 1½ quarts).

8. Preheat the oven to 425°F.

9. Arrange the steak and kidneys in layers in the dish. Add stock or bouillon as necessary to bring it to 1 inch below the top of the dish. Nestle a small custard cup upside down in the center of the dish to keep the crust from sinking in the center and to gather in the meat juices so they will not boil over while baking. Cover the dish with the pastry, pressing the edges down firmly. Make several gashes in the pastry to allow the steam to escape. Mix the egg yolk and water and brush it over the pastry. Bake on the middle shelf of the oven for 15 to 18 minutes. Reduce the heat to 375°F and bake until the crust is golden brown, another 30 to 35 minutes.

10. Serve at once. Spoon out the steak and kidney pie. If you wish, remove the custard cup, but it won't interfere with the presentation.

🦉 If the edges of the pie crust brown too soon or to excess, cover them with thin strips of aluminum foil.

♦

SUET PASTRY

♦

*T*he suet from around the kidney is much preferred, as it is white and crumbly and has fewer tendons or fibrous tissue. It is definitely worth going to a good butcher to find it.

♦

2 cups sifted all-purpose flour
1 teaspoon salt
1 cup finely chopped beef kidney suet
1 egg yolk
Ice water as needed

♦

1. Place the flour in a roomy bowl. Add the salt and toss it with the flour using a pastry blender. Blend in the suet until it resembles very coarse meal or grits.

2. Put the egg yolk into a ⅓-cup measure and add enough ice water to fill the cup. Pour the contents into a larger bowl and mix it thoroughly.

3. Add the yolk mixture to the flour mixture and work it in fast with a pastry blender. Add a few tablespoons of ice water if it is needed to make a pliable dough.

(This step is done best with your hands, as you can get the feel of the pastry.)

4. Divide the dough evenly into 2 balls and roll out as directed.

🦉 The ice water is an immeasurable help, as it keeps the dough cold, which prevents the fat from being absorbed by the flour, which would in turn toughen the crust. This pastry, when carefully made and not overworked, is easier to roll out as soon as it is made. But it can be formed into a ball, wrapped and refrigerated if desired.

TO CLEAN KIDNEYS

Lamb kidneys are the most superior and delicate in flavor of all edible kidneys. Veal kidneys are second best, but they must be from very young calves. Slice off the fat from the center of the kidney and discard. Peel off the thin filament surrounding the kidneys. All kidneys must be very fresh and not have the slightest ammonia-like odor. Kidneys must be cooked very quickly or they will be as tough as leather.

HOW TO MAKE YOUR OWN CORNED BEEF OR TONGUE

Corned beef, although not as versatile as ham, does have a worthy place in our family menus.

Beef in the early days was preserved by a method called "dry salting." The fresh meat was embedded in coarse salt the size of corn kernels for a certain length of time, hence the name "corned beef." Brining or pickling ultimately took the place of salting, but the name stuck.

It is difficult to achieve a juicy, succulent piece of corned beef if it weighs less than 4 to 5 pounds. This, of course, is true of all roasts. Small pieces of meat dry out quickly.

Corned beef is easy to cook if you start it in cold water and never let the water boil hard. Slow, even heat, as in cooking all cured meat, is the answer.

The vegetables that are best with corned beef are cabbage, carrots, and potatoes. The old way (and the wrong way) was to cook these vegetables in the broth surrounding the corned beef. This produced an off-flavored corruption of good food. The vegetables should be cooked separately. This way they retain their own delicious flavors and, at the same time, are compatible with the corned beef.

TO CORN THE MEAT

1 whole brisket or 1 beef tongue, 4 to 5 pounds, or 2 small calf tongues, 4 to 5 pounds total
1 gallon cold water, or more if needed
1½ cups uniodized coarse salt
2 tablespoons light brown sugar
2 teaspoons (½ ounce) saltpeter (sodium nitrate)
8 bay leaves
5 cloves garlic

2 tablespoons coriander seed
2 dried red chile peppers
2 tablespoons mustard seed
1 teaspoon whole cloves
1 teaspoon whole allspice

TO COOK THE CORNED MEAT

1 bay leaf
3 or 4 whole allspice, depending on size of meat
1 clove garlic, unpeeled

1. *To corn the meat:* Place the brisket or tongue in a large non-aluminum pan, crock, or jar. Cover completely with the water. Add the remaining ingredients and mix well. Weigh the meat down with a heavy plate so it will remain under the liquid. Refrigerate for 2 to 3 weeks, turning the meat every 2 or 3 days to distribute the flavors.

2. *To cook the corned meat:* Discard the marinade and its seasonings from the cured corned beef. Rinse the meat thoroughly under cool water.

3. Place the meat in a deep roasting pan. Add the bay leaf, allspice, and garlic. Cover the meat with cold water. Cover the pan and place it in an unheated oven. Set the oven at 325°F and simmer until the meat is tender, 3½ to 4 hours.

4. Allow the meat to cool in the broth if possible. Discard the seasonings.

5. Serve warm corned beef or tongue with a variety of mustards, Sour Cream–Horseradish Sauce (see page 107), or Louisville's Famous Mustard Sauce (right). Serve cold corned beef or tongue with a variety of mustards or Sour Cream–Horseradish Sauce.

Serves 6 to 8

🦉 Store-bought corned beef comes now in a packet of seasoning that has too much powdered garlic. I suggest rinsing the store-bought corned beef and discarding the spices it comes with. Cook the beef using the spices in the list above.

LOUISVILLE'S FAMOUS MUSTARD SAUCE

This is a superb example of a true sweet-and-sour German mustard sauce. A cook at Mr. Seelbach's restaurant gave me the recipe. It is best served warm on warm or hot meats, especially ham, smoked tongue, or ham loaf. It is not a cold mustard dressing.

6 tablespoons dry mustard
1⅔ cups water
4½ tablespoons all-purpose flour
¾ cup sugar
1 cup plus 1 tablespoon cider vinegar
6 tablespoons (¾ stick) butter
1½ teaspoons salt, or to taste

1. In a heavy stainless steel or enamel saucepan, or in the top of a double boiler, combine the mustard and the water and allow the mixture to stand a few minutes to lose its sting.

2. Mix together the flour and sugar. Add the vinegar and the flour mixture to the mustard, and stir well. Simmer over low heat, or over hot water, 15 to 20 minutes. Add the butter and salt, and keep warm.

Makes 1¼ cups

🦉 Be sure to let mustard ripen a few minutes in the water before cooking. This expels the mustard gas, which otherwise would give it a bitter twang made in this quantity.

CHARLOTTESVILLE SHEPHERD'S PIE

*T*his is a favorite Virginia recipe that came straight from the English colonizers—and is a wonderful way to use leftover pot roast and stews.

2½ to 3 cups plain mashed potatoes
3 tablespoons butter
¼ to ⅓ cup milk
Salt to taste
2 eggs
2 cups finely minced leftover beef

or lamb (see page 116)
½ to ⅔ cup gravy or drippings from the leftover roast or stew
2 tablespoons chopped fresh parsley
White pepper to taste

1. Preheat the oven to 375°F.

2. Mix the mashed potatoes with 1 tablespoon of the butter, ¼ cup milk, and salt to taste. Add more milk if the potatoes seem too dry. Add the eggs and beat thoroughly (but not in a processor). Taste for salt.

3. Spread 1 cup of the potatoes on the bottom of a buttered casserole or baking dish. Cover the layer of potatoes with the meat. Add the sauce to cover well and sprinkle with the parsley. Spread the remaining potatoes on top of the meat and sauce, and dot with the remaining butter.

4. Bake, uncovered, until the potatoes are well puffed and golden brown, 25 to 30 minutes.

Serves 4

PERFECT LEFTOVERS TO USE IN SHEPHERD'S PIE

Beef Brisket with Potatoes on the Half-Shell

Georgetown's Old-Fashioned Pot Roast

The Falls City Carbonnade

Marinated Short Ribs of Beef

All lamb roasts

To make ahead: Shepherd's Pie may be completely assembled in the morning, then refrigerated until a couple of hours before the final baking. If you take the casserole directly from the refrigerator to the oven, allow extra time for baking.

PERFECT BEEF HASH

The secret to a wonderful hash is well-seasoned meat and stock. Never stir a hash—shake the pan instead. The Idaho potato thickens the sauce beautifully without using any flour.

3 cups cooked beef roast, cubed
2 cups Brown Soup Stock (see Index) or sauce from the roast, or more as needed
1 bay leaf
1 medium Idaho potato, peeled and cut in half
1 cup chopped onions
1 cup chopped celery
2 cups diced potatoes
Salt and freshly ground black pepper to taste
2 teaspoons chopped fresh parsley

1. Put the meat in a deep skillet or flameproof casserole. Cover with the stock or sauce and add the bay leaf.

2. Cook the Idaho potato in boiling water until tender. Place it in a small bowl and mash it with a fork. Add it to the meat and gently distribute it throughout the broth.

3. In a saucepan, cook the onions, celery, and the diced potatoes in water just to cover until tender but not mushy. Drain at once.

4. Put the vegetables on top of the meat. Do not stir. Shake the pan to distribute the broth through the vegetables. Taste for seasoning. Add salt and pepper if needed. Add more broth if necessary. (There should be enough broth to make a very moist hash.) Cook over low heat, shaking the pan every few minutes. Keep the heat low and do not allow the hash to overcook. It is done when the hash has heated through.

5. Sprinkle with the parsley and serve.
Serves 4

NOTABLE VARIATIONS: Omit the potatoes. Add 1 to 2 cups of sautéed mushrooms. Or soak ¼ to ½ cup dried mushrooms (see page 119) in water to cover for a few hours.

Drain, grind or mince in a processor, and add to the hash. (Dried mushrooms give a very rich, earthy flavor.)

About ¼ cup cubed ham, substituted for an equal amount of cubed beef, is especially good.

Do not mash the ingredients by stirring. The cubes of meat and vegetables should absorb the broth but remain intact. The meat must not overcook, or it will toughen and shred.

◆◆ A LATE SATURDAY BRUNCH

Perfect Beef Hash

◆

Spinach, Romaine, or Watercress Salad with Mushrooms

French Cream Dressing

◆

Strawberries

Coffee

AUNT NETTIE'S EL PASO CHILI

◆◆

*A*unt Nettie was a Kentuckian but she lived in Texas for many years. Wear rubber gloves when you prepare these peppers, she warned me, and don't touch your face or eyes! This is a hot chili, but the heat can be controlled by reducing the chile pepper and cumin to your taste. Authentic chili is not cooked with beans, but the uninhibited Texans usually use them.

◆

2 cups dried red or pinto beans
¼ cup chopped or ground beef suet
1½ pounds lean beef, cut into ½-inch cubes
2 medium onions, chopped
3 cups canned whole tomatoes
1 cup Brown Soup Stock (see Index) or bouillon
1 clove garlic, finely chopped (optional)
2 or 3 dried ancho chile peppers, soaked for 6
*   hours or overnight, then peeled, seeded,*
*   deveined, and ground, or 3 tablespoons*
*   chili powder or to taste*
¾ teaspoon ground cumin
Salt to taste

◆

1. Rinse and pick over the dried beans thoroughly. Cover with cold water, bring to a boil, and simmer for 5 minutes. Remove from the heat and allow the beans to rest, covered, 1 hour.

2. Rinse the beans again. Cover with fresh cold water and cook over medium heat until the beans are almost tender, about 1 hour. They must retain their shape.

A butcher's sign from 1889 showing the tools of the trade.

3. In the meantime, melt the suet in a heavy dutch oven over medium heat, then add the beef. Brown the beef to seal in the juices and to take on a little color. Add the onions and toss about with the beef. Allow it to absorb the beef juices but not to fry.

4. Drain the tomatoes and reserve the juice. Purée the tomatoes in a blender or processor and add to the beef and onions. Add the stock or bouillon, garlic (if desired), the ground chiles or chili powder, cumin, and about 1 teaspoon salt. Bring to a boil and simmer for 1 to 1½ hours. Add a little of the reserved tomato juice from time to time as the chili cooks down. If more liquid is needed, add water. The chili must be succulent but not soupy.

5. Add the beans and simmer until they are perfectly tender, but do not allow them to get mushy. Taste for salt.

6. Remove from the heat. Allow the chili to ripen several hours before serving.
Serves 4

VARIATIONS: If you prefer a richer tomato flavor, add 1 to 2 teaspoons tomato paste. Or use canned plum tomatoes.

The ancho chiles may be soaked and peeled but added whole instead of ground to the chili. Discard them before serving. This chili will not be quite as hot.

The seeds and spines of all chiles are the hottest parts.

ESPECIALLY GOOD MEAT LOAF

◆◆◆

*I*n the South a flavorful blend for meat loaf usually includes beef, pork, and veal. The pork is added for moistness and the veal for delicacy. The smoked ham is added here for flavor. If I do not have a flavorful ham, I use only beef, veal, and pork, increasing the pork to ½ pound.

◆

1 pound ground beef
½ pound ground veal
¼ pound ground pork
¼ pound ground baked smoked ham (¾ cup)
1 medium onion, finely chopped
2½ teaspoons fresh thyme leaves, or 1½ teaspoons dried
⅔ cup soft bread crumbs
2 eggs
1½ teaspoons salt, or to taste
Freshly ground black pepper to taste
6 slices lean smoked bacon, cut in half

◆

1. Preheat the oven to 350°F.
2. In a large bowl, combine the meats with the onion, thyme, bread crumbs, eggs, salt, and pepper and mix well with a fork (not your hands; the heat of your hands toughens freshly ground meat). Form the mixture into 1 or 2 loaves.
3. Put 2 or 3 pieces of bacon on the bottom of a baking dish. Lay the meat loaf on top of the bacon. Cover the top of the

meat loaf with bacon. (The bacon adds flavor and helps keep the loaf moist.)
4. Bake until the outside of the loaf is golden brown, the juices run clear when the loaf is poked with a skewer, and it feels firm to the touch, about 1 hour for a small loaf, 1½ hours for a large loaf. Discard all the bacon. Serve hot as is or with a good tomato sauce, or serve cold for sandwiches with chili sauce.
Serves 4 to 6

◆◆◆

A FAMILY SUPPER IN MARYLAND

Especially Good Meat Loaf

Scalloped Potatoes with Marjoram

Zucchini and Parsley Salad

◆

Bishop Woodforde's Pudding

Coffee

VARIATION: *Meat Loaf with Dried Mushrooms:* Mix the meats with the onion, thyme, bread crumbs, eggs, salt, and pepper. Measure out ½ cup dried mushrooms (see box), plump them in water, then drain, and grind. Or use 1 cup coarsely chopped fresh mushrooms that have been sautéed in butter. Add the mushrooms to the meat mixture.

The flavor of the dried mushrooms is very different—very earthy. I like to add a pinch of marjoram with the thyme when using mushrooms, and a generous amount of black pepper. Use the bacon as described; the juices from the meat will blend with the bacon flavor and, skimmed of excess fat, you will have a delicious sauce.

If you are baking 2 loaves in the oven at the same time, they must not touch. A good circulation of air is needed for the loaves to brown nicely. If they touch, they will stew instead.

TO DRY MUSHROOMS

If the mushroms are fresh and crisp, wash them quickly under running water. Pat dry on paper towels. Do not allow them to soak up any water. Remove the stems and use them for another purpose.

If the mushrooms are several days old, remove the stems and peel the caps.

Slice the mushrooms. Lay them on a rack that you have covered with a piece of clean cheesecloth. Set them in a warm, dry place or in a slow (150°F) oven for about 12 hours, turning them once in a while.

The mushrooms should then be kept in a cool, dry place for about 12 hours longer. All of the mushrooms must be brittle before they are stored in airtight containers.

Sliced cleaned mushrooms may be dried in a microwave oven on very low power in about 3 hours.

One pound fresh mushrooms equals about 1 ounce dried. They will keep indefinitely.

BEEF AND BASIL MEATBALLS

*T*hese beef and basil meatballs can be made two days ahead and refrigerated, or they can be frozen for a week or more. Wonderful for teenage parties.

1 ½ slices white homemade-style bread
⅓ cup milk, or Brown Soup or Chicken Stock (see Index)
1 pound finely ground beef chuck
¼ pound ground baked ham or prosciutto
1 tablespoon finely chopped onion
2 tablespoons chopped fresh parsley
½ teaspoon dried marjoram
1 egg
Salt and freshly ground black pepper to taste
¼ cup olive oil or vegetable oil, or more if needed
2 cups canned whole plum or regular tomatoes
1 clove garlic, chopped
1 tablespoon chopped fresh basil, or 1 ½ teaspoons dried

Freshly grated Parmesan cheese

1. Soak the bread in the milk or stock until soft. Mash the bread with a fork.

2. In a large bowl, combine the bread, beef, ham, onion, parsley, marjoram, egg, and salt and pepper to taste. Mix thoroughly with a fork or large spoon. Shape into balls about the size of a golf ball—or make them tiny if you are using them as an hors d'oeuvre.

3. Heat ¼ inch of oil in a heavy skillet over medium heat and sauté the meatballs a few at a time. Do not crowd. Allow the meatballs to brown but be careful not to

Wm. P. Schlachter's window displays the 1928 Grand Champion of the Fat Cattle Show.

burn the fat. Lift the meatballs out as they brown and add more until all the meatballs are cooked.

4. Discard all but 1 tablespoon of fat from the skillet. Add the tomatoes and garlic to the skillet. (If the fat and brown crusty bits in the skillet have burned the least bit, discard them and wash the skillet, then add the garlic and tomatoes and 1 tablespoon olive oil.) Cook the tomatoes over medium heat until they begin to thicken, 10 to 15 minutes.

5. Gently put the meatballs in the tomato sauce, add the basil, and simmer until the sauce is sufficiently thick. Season with salt and add more basil if desired.

6. Serve plain or over spaghetti, as desired, and pass the Parmesan cheese.

VARIATION: Add 3 to 4 tablespoons freshly grated Parmesan cheese to the raw meat with the parsley.

The garlic must not be browned ever as it then would take on an acrid taste. Garlic is a valuable herb that must be handled with care.

◆◆
VEGETABLES THAT ARE GOOD WITH BEEF

Artichokes	Leeks
Broccoli	Lima beans
Brussels sprouts	Mushrooms
Carrots	Onions
Cauliflower	Peas
Celeriac	Tomatoes
Celery	Turnip greens
Eggplant	White potatoes
Green beans	Yellow squash
Kale	Zucchini

◆◆
COOKING VEAL

*V*eal, like chicken, lends itself to a great variety of preparations. However, veal is not as easy to cook as chicken—or beef, for that matter. It is a lean meat, not protected by layers of fat to help make it tender and succulent. To be delicious, veal must be top-quality, entirely milk-fed, between 5 and 12 weeks old with flesh that is firm and fine grained with just a tinge of pink, not the least bit red.

Premium cuts of veal such as the loin, tenderloin, or thin slices from the leg can be sautéed or grilled very quickly over high heat and be tender and delicious; this is one of the truly great ways to prepare it. But veal will toughen if it lingers in the skillet or while grilling. When this happens, your only alternative is to add a little moisture, cover, and cook very slowly in a 325°F oven or on top of the stove until the veal becomes tender. This changes the flavor, of course, and you have a braised meat; but once the veal becomes tough, this is the best technique to use. Braising veal (as in cooking stews and pot roasts), however, is an especially good technique to use when the dish must be cooked ahead. The braising liquid prevents the meat from drying out and the veal, when cooked slowly, has time to absorb the flavors from the vegetables and herbs.

Veal responds to the same herbs as chicken. It is compatible with tarragon, thyme, and sweet marjoram—and parsley and chervil, of course. It accepts the accents of wines both white and red, and all in all it is a most companionable meat—delectable to eat and inspirational to cook.

COUNTRY ESTATE MEATBALLS

◆◆

*T*his is one of the most pleasant and delicate of meatballs—rather typical of the way Southerners use ham. The charm of the dish is that the meatballs, potatoes, and onions are all the same size, all quite small. Tiny onions are available but some carving will have to be done on the potatoes.

◆

1 pound ground veal
½ pound ground pork
½ pound ground baked ham
2 small onions, very finely chopped
5 slices fresh white bread, soaked in ½ cup
    milk and mashed with a fork
3 egg yolks
1½ teaspoons salt, or more to taste
Freshly ground black pepper to taste
½ to ¾ cup dry white wine
½ cup all-purpose flour
3 tablespoons unsalted butter
2½ cups Rich Chicken or Veal Stock (see Index)
3 sprigs fresh thyme or ½ teaspoon dried
1 bay leaf
1 rib celery, cut in half
12 tiny round sweet onions
15 tiny round potatoes
Chopped fresh parsley, for garnish

Mr. Quaack's meat counter in Louisville, 1926.

◆

1. In a large bowl, mix the veal, pork, ham, chopped onions, bread, egg yolks, salt, pepper, and ½ cup of the wine. Blend the ingredients well and roll into small round balls the size of golf balls. Dust with flour. Melt the butter in a skillet over medium-high heat. Add the meatballs and sauté until very lightly browned on all sides.

2. Transfer the sautéed meatballs to a heavy pot or dutch oven. Add enough stock to reach the top of the meatballs. Add the herbs, celery, onions, and potatoes. If desired, add ¼ cup white wine to the stock. Cover. Simmer over low heat (or in a 325°F oven) until the meat and vegetables are tender, about 1 hour. I prefer the oven, but watch it. This must cook slowly.

3. Discard the celery, bay leaf, and thyme sprigs if you used them. Sprinkle with parsley and serve with a salad.

Serves 6

🦉 In general, Americans are not devoted to meats that are not browned. That is why I cover these meatballs with parsley to serve. No matter, the parsley is awfully good here.

WINTERTIME VEAL LOAF

◆◆

A meat loaf served cold is what the French call a pâté. But the name couldn't matter less—we enjoy a delicious meat loaf, and we adore sandwiches made with the leftover loaf garnished with chili sauce.

1½ pounds ground veal
½ pound ground lean pork
1 medium onion, finely chopped
1¼ teaspoons dried marjoram
½ teaspoon dried thyme
1 cup fresh bread crumbs
2 eggs
1½ teaspoons salt
Freshly ground black pepper to taste
3 slices bacon
Chopped fresh parsley, for garnish
Elegant and Easy Tomato Sauce (recipe
    follows)

1. Preheat the oven to 350°F.
2. Combine all the ingredients, except the bacon, parsley, and tomato sauce, in a large mixing bowl. Mix thoroughly with a large fork or spoon. (To test your seasoning, make a tiny meatball and fry it lightly. Taste and correct, if necessary.) Shape the meat like a long, fat loaf of bread and place it in a heavy baking pan. Place the bacon strips on top of the meat. Put the loaf in the oven and bake for about 1½ hours.
3. Check after 45 minutes and remove the bacon strips when they are crisp. Set them aside. (If the top seems to be browning too rapidly or too much before the loaf is done, cover it loosely with foil.)
4. When the loaf is done, garnish it with the bacon slices and sprinkle with the parsley. Serve in thick slices with a piece of bacon. Pass the tomato sauce.
Serves 4 to 6

The warmth of your hand toughens ground meat so mix it with a metal or wooden utensil and never overmix.

ELEGANT AND EASY TOMATO SAUCE

1 large can (28 ounces) whole tomatoes
3 tablespoons good-quality olive oil
2 tablespoons butter
1 clove garlic, unpeeled
Salt and freshly ground black pepper to taste
¼ cup chopped fresh parsley

Combine the tomatoes, olive oil, butter, and garlic in a saucepan. Bring to a boil, reduce the heat, and simmer until the sauce is thick, 30 to 35 minutes. Discard the garlic. Add salt and pepper to taste, and stir in the parsley. Taste. If the sauce is a bit acid, add more butter and simmer a few minutes longer. No sugar, certainly.
Makes about 4 cups

CALVES' LIVER WITH TARRAGON AND BACON

*T*here is a world of difference between the flavor and tenderness of calves' liver and that of young beef. Calves' liver is now a luxurious meat, but it is wonderful with grits for a late, hearty, and leisurely breakfast or as a delicious supper dish with a baked Idaho potato.

3 tablespoons unsalted butter
2 teaspoons vegetable oil
3 to 4 very thin slices calves' liver, about 1¼
    pounds (not over ¼ inch thick)
⅓ cup all-purpose flour
Salt and freshly ground black pepper to taste

1½ tablespoons chopped fresh tarragon leaves
    or 1 tablespoon dried
Lemon juice
2 tablespoons chopped fresh parsley
5 slices lean smoked bacon, broiled or sautéed

1. Heat the butter and oil in a heavy skillet. Dust the liver lightly with the flour, add it to the skillet, and sauté it over fairly high heat. When the first side has browned, turn the liver over and season with salt, pepper, and tarragon. Brown the second side.

2. Season with a squeeze of lemon juice and a sprinkling of parsley. Serve piping hot, garnished with the bacon.

Serves 2 to 4

Liver must be sautéed. It toughens when broiled or grilled.

VEAL FRICASSEE

For ease of preparation and exquisite flavor, this fricassee is outstanding—a great favorite of my students. Serve it with noodles or mashed potatoes, and fresh peas, snow peas, or asparagus.

2 pounds thin veal cutlet
4 tablespoons (½ stick) butter
2 shallots, finely chopped
1½ teaspoons all-purpose flour
1 cup dry white wine
1 cup Chicken or Veal Stock (see Index)
½ cup heavy or whipping cream
Salt and freshly ground black pepper to taste
2 tablespoons chopped fresh parsley

1. Pound the veal with the flat side of a heavy knife or with a mallet until it is very thin. Cut it into 1- to 1½-inch wide strips with a sharp knife or scissors. Discard any fat and gristle.

2. In a heavy saucepan or skillet (not iron or aluminum), melt the butter. Add the veal and sauté over medium heat until it is lightly browned on both sides.

3. Add the shallots and cook a few minutes, but do not allow them to brown. Tip the skillet so the juices run to one side, and add the flour to them, blending it in well.

4. Add the white wine and stock. Simmer until the sauce is well blended and has thickened, 5 minutes.

5. Add the cream and blend. Simmer 3 minutes, then season with salt and pepper (season only after the sauce has reduced as much as desired). Sprinkle with the parsley and serve.

Serves 4

VARIATIONS: Increase the chicken stock by 1 cup and omit the white wine. The shallots may be omitted, but they are a delicious addition. Don't substitute onions.

Sauté ½ pound sliced mushrooms and add to the fricassee with the cream. Or garnish with whole sautéed mushrooms and serve broiled tomatoes alongside.

If the sauce reduces too much, add more chicken stock, not wine.

ELEGANT VEAL BIRDS WITH TARRAGON

Veal Birds are delicious with rice or noodles and a green vegetable—broccoli, green beans, peas, or asparagus. A very compatible meat.

16 veal scallops (3 pounds), cut very thin
½ pound well-seasoned pork sausage meat
1 cup fresh bread crumbs
2 eggs, beaten
2 tablespoons chopped fresh parsley
2 tablespoons chopped fresh tarragon or 1½
     teaspoons dried
Salt and freshly ground black pepper to taste
5 tablespoons butter, at room temperature
2 tablespoons all-purpose flour
1½ cups Veal or Chicken Stock (see Index)
½ cup dry white wine
Watercress or parsley, for garnish
16 large mushrooms, sliced and sautéed in
     butter, for garnish (optional)

1. Have your butcher cut the veal scallops as thin as possible, then pound them even thinner with the flat side of a mallet.

2. Preheat the oven to 325°F.

3. In a medium bowl, mix together the sausage, bread crumbs, eggs, parsley, tarragon, and salt and pepper to taste. Spread a little of this mixture on each scallop. Roll the scallop up in a small tight bundle and secure it with toothpicks or tie with butcher's twine. Season the "birds" with salt and pepper.

4. Melt 4 tablespoons of the butter in a heavy ovenproof skillet or enameled iron casserole. When the butter is hot, add the veal and sauté over medium heat until golden brown on all sides.

5. Meanwhile, blend together the remaining butter and the flour. When the veal is browned, add this to the pan, add the veal or chicken stock and wine, and stir to blend well.

6. Cover the pan, place it in the oven, and bake until the veal is tender and the sauce has good flavor, about 45 minutes.

7. Serve the veal birds with the sauce. Garnish with watercress or parsley, and mushrooms if desired.

Serves 6

VEAL CHOPS WITH PINE NUTS AND VERMOUTH

*A*n exquisitely delicious and easy veal dish. I leave the bones on the chops as they always lend flavor. Serve with buttered wild, brown, or white rice and asparagus, broccoli, or spinach. The pine nuts and the vermouth are the happiest of flavors with veal—subtle but charming.

7 tablespoons unsalted butter
½ cup pine nuts
6 veal loin chops, cut thin
Salt and freshly ground black pepper to taste
1 cup French dry vermouth
6 lemon wedges
Watercress or parsley, for garnish

1. Melt 1 tablespoon of the butter in a small skillet. Add the pine nuts and sauté over low heat, stirring continually, until the nuts turn a very pale brown, 1½ minutes. Set aside.

2. Pound the veal chops very thin with the smooth side of a mallet.

3. Melt the remaining butter in a heavy stainless steel or enamel skillet. Add the chops (do not crowd them in the skillet), and sauté them quickly until brown on both sides, turning them only once. Season with salt and pepper.

4. Add the vermouth and simmer until only a small amount of sauce is left, about 12 minutes.

5. Sprinkle with the pine nuts and serve, garnished with lemon wedges and watercress or parsley.

Serves 6

THE HUNTER'S VEAL STEW

I was reared in the country where we had wonderful milk-fed veal—it is still my favorite meat. Thoughts of Mother's veal roasts are warm and wonderful memories. She always made noodles to go with these veal dishes.

2 tablespoons vegetable oil
5 tablespoons butter
2 pounds veal cutlet, cut in 1½-inch-long
   julienne strips (or use veal shoulder; see
   Owl)
Salt and freshly ground black pepper to taste
1½ tablespoons finely chopped shallots
2 cups Chicken or Veal Stock, approximately
   (see Index)
1 tablespoon tomato paste, or 1 ripe tomato,
   peeled, seeded, and chopped
2 sprigs fresh thyme or ½ teaspoon dried
1 bay leaf
1½ teaspoons chopped fresh marjoram or ½
   teaspoon dried
½ pound mushrooms, sliced
⅓ cup chopped fresh parsley

1. Preheat the oven to 325°F.
2. Heat the vegetable oil and 2 tablespoons of the butter in a heavy skillet. Add the veal and sauté over high heat until it is lightly browned on both sides. Season with salt and pepper. Remove the meat to a casserole with a tight-fitting cover.
3. Add the shallots to the skillet with ½ cup stock or water and cook until they are limp and the liquid has evaporated. Add the remaining stock and the tomato paste or tomato and bring to a boil. Pour this over the veal and season with the thyme, bay leaf, marjoram, and salt and pepper to taste. Cover the casserole tightly and place it in the oven. Cook for 15 minutes.
4. Meanwhile, melt the remaining butter in a medium-size skillet. Add the mushrooms and sauté them quickly over medium-high heat. Add them to the veal with their juices. Cover, and bake 20 to 25 minutes longer. Sprinkle with the parsley and serve with fresh egg noodles.
Serves 4

Ready for the hunt in Tallahassee.

VARIATION: *Veal Stew with Wild Rice:* Add 1 to 1½ cups cooked wild rice to the stew with the sautéed mushrooms. (Additional stock may be needed—the stew must not be dry.)

The shoulder of veal may be used instead of the cutlet, but remove all ligaments, sinews, and excess fat. Cut it into cubes. The shoulder meat will have to be cooked about 1¼ hours longer or until very tender, but the flavor is excellent.

SUNDAY NIGHT SUPPER

The Hunter's Veal Stew

Homemade Noodles

Bibb Lettuce Salad

Upside-Down Fruit Pudding

Sparkling Apple Cider

VEAL KNUCKLE WITH GREEN PEAS AND ASPARAGUS

*T*his is one of the best veal stews in the whole world, and the veal knuckles are inexpensive compared to other cuts. It is a cut of meat rich in gelatin and utterly delicious.

Serve this in a beautiful deep platter, sprinkled with fresh chervil, parsley, or tarragon, or a combination of herbs. Any small pasta, egg noodles, or new or mashed potatoes will be delicious with this stew.

A familiar-looking dining room in Frankfort, Kentucky, around 1910, is complete with sideboard, china cabinet, and simply set table ready for good food.

6 pieces (6 pounds) veal knuckle, sliced 2½
     inches thick
Salt to taste
3 tablespoons unsalted butter
⅔ cup dry white wine
1 cup Veal or Chicken Stock, or more as needed
     (see Index)
2 medium onions, peeled and left whole
1 clove
2 pounds green peas (2 cups shelled)
½ teaspoon sugar
Several sprigs summer savory or chervil or 1
     teaspoon dried
18 stalks fresh asparagus

1. Preheat the oven to 325°F.
2. Season the meat with salt to taste. Melt the butter in a heavy flameproof casserole, add the meat, and sauté over medium heat until it is brown on both sides, 12 to 15 minutes.
3. Pour the wine over the veal and simmer until it has reduced almost completely. Add the stock (it should half cover the meat) and 1 onion stuck with the clove. Cover the casserole, place it in the oven, and cook until the meat is deliciously tender, about 2 hours. Baste the meat often to keep it moist. If the sauce boils too low, add more stock or water, not wine. If the liquid around the meat has not thickened into a sauce, step up the oven heat to 425°F or place the pan on a burner over medium heat and allow the stock to reduce to a sauce, basting the meat constantly.
4. In the meantime, cook the peas in boiling salted water to cover with the remaining onion, the sugar, the summer savory or chervil, about 8 minutes. When the peas are tender, drain them and discard the onion and herb sprigs, if used. Set aside.
5. Peel the stalks of the asparagus and cut them on the diagonal into 1½-inch pieces. Drop the asparagus into boiling salted water to cover and cook just until tender, 2 to 3 minutes. Drain and set aside.
6. When you are ready to serve the veal, add the peas and asparagus to the casserole and coat them gently with the sauce. Allow the vegetables to heat through.
Serves 6

VARIATIONS: Parboil 18 or so tiny white onions and add them to the veal about 15 minutes before it is done.

A peeled, seeded, and chopped tomato may be added to the veal about 1 hour before it is done. This gives the stew a lovely color.

The asparagus may be omitted, or you

can use it as a salad with a vinaigrette.

Breast of Veal with Spring Peas: Cook 2 veal breasts exactly as you do the veal knuckle, but in step 2, brush the veal breasts (a breast averages 3 pounds) with butter and brown it in a preheated 450°F oven. The breasts may be cut into several pieces or 2 pieces. This makes an inexpensive but delicious family dish. The bones of the breast meat are very gelatinous and make a good, syrupy stew. If you omit the wine, substitute water or stock.

VEGETABLES THAT ARE GOOD WITH VEAL

Artichokes	Green bell peppers
Asparagus	Lima beans
Broccoli	Mushrooms
Carrots	Onions
Cauliflower	Peas
Celeriac	Tomatoes
Celery	White potatoes
Eggplant	Zucchini
Green beans	

VEAL ROAST WITH PICKLED MUSHROOMS

I created this intriguing dish one day when I was pickling mushrooms and cooking a veal roast for dinner, with white wine and tarragon. (The counterpoint of flavors is what cooking is all about anyway.) The pickled mushroom idea worked like magic. This roast, sliced and served hot, is a marvelous hot hors d'oeuvre—or serve it on larger rolls for an informal party or as the entrée with new potatoes or noodles and asparagus. You can, of course, buy pickled mushrooms, but then you may need to add thyme.

1 veal shoulder roast, 4 to 5 pounds, boned
2 tablespoons butter, at room temperature
Salt and freshly ground black pepper to taste
1½ cups dry white wine
1 to 2 cups light Chicken or Veal Stock (see Index)
2 teaspoons dried tarragon, or more to taste
1 pint Pickled Mushrooms (recipe follows)

1. Preheat the oven to 425°F.
2. Remove the cartilage and gristle from the veal. Roll and tie the roast securely with butcher's twine or string. Rub the roast with the butter and season with salt and pepper to taste.
3. Place the veal in a roasting pan or casserole that has a cover. Put it in the oven, uncovered, and cook until golden brown, 35 to 40 minutes.
4. Add the white wine and 1 cup stock. Sprinkle with the tarragon. Cover

"George Booth as a Young Man," attributed to William Dering of Virginia, 1740s. Dressed for the hunt perhaps?

454ня

the pan, reduce the heat to 325°F, and cook another 30 to 40 minutes.

5. Add the pickled mushrooms, juice and all, and continue to cook until the roast is tender, about another 40 minutes, basting it several times. Taste the pan juices and add salt and more tarragon if needed. If the veal needs more liquid at any time, add part or all of the remaining stock.

6. When the veal is done, remove it to a warm platter. Reduce the pan juices if necessary. There should be a sufficient amount to serve in a sauceboat. Remove the trussing strings from the roast, carve, and serve.

Serves 6

PICKLED MUSHROOMS

2 pounds white button mushrooms, firm and tightly closed
⅓ cup good-quality olive oil
1 clove garlic
2 teaspoons dried thyme
1 cup white wine vinegar
1⅓ cups cold water, or more to taste
Juice of 1 lemon, or more to taste
Salt and freshly ground white pepper to taste

1. Clean the mushrooms and remove the stems.

2. Put the mushrooms in a stainless steel or enamel saucepan. Add the olive oil, garlic, thyme, vinegar, water, lemon juice, and salt and white pepper. Taste. Add more water or more lemon juice if needed. Bring to a boil and simmer 2 to 3 minutes, no more. Set the mixture aside to cool.

3. Discard the garlic and taste for salt. Ladle the mixture into sterilized glass jars (see Index), cover, and refrigerate.

Makes 1 quart

VARIATION: You may use dry white wine instead of vinegar, but then cut down on the amount of water. The proportions should be two-thirds wine to one-third cold water.

Mushrooms for pickling must be white and firm. They are at their best when pickled the day they are harvested.

The mushrooms also may be sliced or quartered.

MOTHER'S KENTUCKY VEAL ROAST

*M*eat is one food that profits greatly by being cooked in quantity, as it develops a deeper and more intense concentration of the juices. Larger pieces of meat retain their succulence and moistness, whereas small amounts simply dry out and toughen. When I was growing up, Mother cooked several roasts of veal at a time for our little hotel, the Hamby Hotel, so the sauce was always rich and flavorful all on its own. In cooking a single veal roast, the veal or chicken stock is added for enrichment.

This is delicious with scalloped potatoes, noodles, tiny green beans, fresh spinach, turnips, or cauliflower.

1 small veal shoulder, about 5 to 6 pounds (see step 1)
4 tablespoons (½ stick) butter, at room temperature
Salt and freshly ground black pepper to taste
2 cups Veal or Chicken Stock (veal is best; see Index)
1 onion, quartered
2 bay leaves

1. Have the butcher bone, roll, and tie the shoulder, or leave it as is. The boned roast will be easier to carve but not as flavorful.

2. Preheat the oven to 425°F.

3. Brush the top of the roast with the butter. Season well with salt and pepper. Place it in a roasting pan or large casserole with a cover and roast, uncovered, until a beautiful glistening brown, about 35 to 40 minutes.

4. Add the stock, onion, and bay leaves. Cover the pan, reduce the heat to 325°F, and cook until the roast is tender, about 1 hour 20 minutes longer. Baste often and add stock if necessary. You want plenty of sauce.

5. When the meat is tender, remove it to a platter and keep warm. Taste the sauce for salt. Heat and strain it into a sauceboat. Serve the sauce alongside the roast.

Serves 6 to 8

Hotel Hamby, in Dawson Springs, Kentucky, is the hotel of my youth, where Mother oversaw one of the finest kitchens in the South.

The veal is buttered before roasting to enrich the flavor by browning the roast. Margarine would burn and add no flavor whatsoever.

CLASSIC LAMB STEW WITH VEGETABLES

◆◆◆

*T*his classic lamb stew can be varied with different meats, but adhere to this technique and you will have a number of glorious dishes to add to your collection.

◆

2 or 3 tablespoons solid vegetable shortening
3 pounds boneless lamb shoulder, neck, or
     breast, cut into 1-inch pieces
Salt and freshly ground black pepper to taste
2 tablespoons all-purpose flour
2 tablespoons chopped shallots or onion
1 clove garlic
½ cup drained canned tomatoes or 2 fresh
     tomatoes, peeled
Bouquet garni: 2 ribs celery, 1 bay leaf, 1 sprig
     parsley, 1 carrot, 1 pinch dried thyme

     or 1 sprig fresh
2 tablespoons butter
12 small whole onions
5 carrots, peeled and sliced
3 small turnips, cut in half
8 to 10 small potatoes
1 cup cooked peas or tender green beans
     (optional)
Chopped fresh parsley, for garnish

◆

1. Preheat the oven to 325°F.

2. Melt the shortening in a heavy iron pot. Add the meat in small batches and sauté over medium-high heat until brown on all sides, 6 to 7 minutes for each batch. Sprinkle with salt and pepper.

3. Drain off the fat, reserving 1 tablespoon. In one corner of the pan blend the flour with the reserved fat. Cook until it takes on color. Return the meat to the pot. Add the chopped shallots or onion, garlic, tomatoes, bouquet garni, and enough water to barely cover the meat.

4. Cover the pot and put it in the oven, or, if you prefer, over a very low flame. Cook until the meat begins to get tender, about 45 minutes.

5. In the meantime, in a skillet melt the butter and cook the whole onions, allowing them to brown a wee bit.

6. Remove the pot from the oven and, using a slotted spoon, remove the meat. Then strain the broth and discard the seasonings. Return the meat to the pan. Lay the onions, carrots, turnips, and potatoes on top of the meat cubes. Pour the strained broth over all. Taste, and correct the seasoning if necessary. Return the pot to the oven and cook until the vegetables are thoroughly tender, 25 minutes. Add 1 cup of peas or beans and heat through. Remove the garlic and garnish the stew with parsley.

Serves 6

VARIATIONS: The following combinations make entirely new dishes out of an old standby. They are deliciously interesting flavor changes and the kind of thing that makes cooking fun. Instead of all lamb try: 1 pound each of lamb, pork, and beef; 1 pound each of veal, pork, and beef; or 1½ pounds each of veal and beef.

COOKING LAMB

Genuine milk-fed lamb is usually 3 to 4 months old, with fat that is almost white and flesh that is a pale red. It can be grilled, roasted, or broiled. Older lamb, 5 to 8 months old, should be roasted or slowly braised with compatible vegetables and a discreet amount of liquid. It is browned, then very slowly cooked in a covered casserole or roaster until it is exquisitely tender. This is one of our favorite ways of preparing lamb in the South.

It is as important for lamb to be well aged as it is for fine beef. Slow cooking or braising meat does take time and may seem old-fashioned, but the flavors are inimitable. Many of the new ways of cooking are good, of course, but we must not throw away the wisdom of the ages.

AN ELEGANT LAMB STEW

The virtue of lamb is its delicious, unique flavor, and the versatility of the different cuts. No meat requires more expert handling and aging than lamb, but it pays off in tenderness and succulence. Lamb is receptive to many spices and herbs when judiciously handled. This stew is too delicious to be called a stew. This makes an elegant dish when served with pasta, rice, or potatoes. It is one of the treasures of the world's so-called casserole dishes or stews.

½ cup olive oil

4 tablespoons (½ stick) butter or vegetable oil

3 pounds lamb, leg or shoulder, cut into 1½-inch pieces

3 medium onions, chopped

3 to 4 sprigs fresh rosemary or good pinch of dried

1½ cups dry white wine

1 pound ripe tomatoes, peeled and seeded, or 1 can (16 ounces) whole tomatoes

Salt and freshly ground black pepper to taste

1½ pounds tiny new potatoes

Chopped fresh parsley, for garnish

You could drive up to Hall's Wayside Market near Savannah in 1940.

1. Heat the olive oil and the butter or vegetable oil in a heavy flameproof casserole over medium-high heat. Add the lamb and sauté until brown. (Do not crowd the skillet or the lamb will stew and not brown.) Remove the meat to another pan as it is sautéed. Once all the pieces are browned, return the meat to the casserole.

2. Add the onions to the lamb and cook a bit, 5 minutes. Add the rosemary and white wine. Lower the heat and simmer, uncovered, until the wine has almost boiled away, 8 to 10 minutes. Add the tomatoes and salt and pepper to taste. Continue cooking until the tomatoes are soft and fully cooked, 30 to 35 minutes.

3. Preheat the oven to 350°F.

4. Add the potatoes, cover, and transfer the casserole to the oven. Check the stew after 30 minutes, and mix it carefully. When the potatoes and meat have cooked low and are tender, another 10 to 20 minutes, sprinkle with parsley and serve.

Serves 6

VARIATIONS: Add quartered artichoke hearts with the potatoes.

Omit the potatoes and serve with rice or noodles.

BRAISED SHOULDER OF LAMB ROSEMARY

A luscious and easy way to cook a lamb shoulder. With the leftover meat you can make a lamb curry to serve with rice and your best homemade chutney.

Serve this lamb with cooked dried beans (white or cranberry), green beans, ratatouille, broccoli, cauliflower, baked tomatoes stuffed with mushrooms, scalloped potatoes, or carrots.

1 shoulder of lamb, 3 to 4 pounds (see step 1)

2 teaspoons dried rosemary

Salt and freshly ground black pepper to taste

⅔ cup dry white wine or water

1. Have the butcher bone and roll the lamb, or leave it as is.
2. Preheat the oven to 425°F.
3. Wipe the meat with a clean damp cloth and cut several gashes in it. Fill the gashes with dried rosemary that you have crushed a bit in your hand. Season the meat thoroughly with salt and pepper.
4. Place the meat in a roasting pan with a lid, uncovered, in the oven and roast until golden brown, about 30 minutes.
5. Add the white wine or water. Cover the pan, reduce the heat to 325°F, and cook until a meat thermometer reads 165° to 170°F, about 1 hour longer. Baste often to distribute the flavors throughout the meat. A shoulder of lamb must be cooked until well done, as it is not sufficiently tender to be served rare like the leg.

LAMB SHOULDER WITH POTATOES AND ESCAROLE

*T*his is a favorite way of cooking a lamb shoulder. Since it is a tougher cut of meat than the leg, it responds to slower cooking, which makes it sweet and flavorful. The potatoes and onions absorb the juices from the lamb and become a delicious brown. If you can find the escarole, do use it. In the early days, many of our little country town "cafes," as they were called in the South, were run by Greeks and they always had lamb. I serve this dish with wedges of lemon, a relish, and corn muffins.

1 lamb shoulder, 4 to 5 pounds, boned if desired
½ lemon
Salt and freshly ground black pepper to taste
½ cup Lamb Stock (see Index) or water
4 large Idaho potatoes, peeled and sliced
3 medium onions, thickly sliced
1 large head escarole, cut into quarters and well rinsed
Chopped fresh parsley, for garnish

1. Preheat the oven to 450°F.
2. Rub the lamb well with the lemon, salt, and pepper. Place the lamb in a heavy casserole and cook until golden brown, about 35 minutes. Turn the oven heat down to 350°F and add the stock or water to the pan. Cover the pan and cook until the lamb is tender, another 50 to 60 minutes.
3. Lift the lamb out of the pan. Place the sliced potatoes in the pan juices. Cover the potatoes with the onions. Sprinkle with salt to taste. Place the lamb on top of the vegetables, cover the pan, and return to the oven. Cook until the vegetables are tender, 40 minutes.
4. Place the escarole in the juices alongside the meat. Cook until the escarole has wilted, 10 to 15 minutes longer. Season with salt and pepper if needed.
5. Carve the meat and serve with the vegetables, sprinkled with parsley.
Serves 6

VEGETABLES THAT ARE GOOD WITH LAMB

Artichokes	Mushrooms
Asparagus	Onions
Carrots	Peas
Dried white beans	Tomatoes
Eggplant	White potatoes
Green beans	Zucchini
Lima beans	

CASSEROLE OF BRAISED STUFFED LAMB STEAKS

*O*ne can often find lamb steaks that are more economical than a roast. Braised with vegetables, they make a hearty family meal, and, with a fresh green salad, a garden relish or chutney, and a good cookie for dessert, what more could you ask!

6 lamb steaks, each ¾ to 1 inch thick
3 tablespoons chopped fresh parsley
1½ teaspoons dried rosemary or tarragon
¼ pound baked ham, prosciutto, or lean
    bacon, minced
2 shallots or 1 small onion, finely chopped
1 tablespoon fresh lemon juice
Salt to taste
1 tablespoon unsalted butter
1 tablespoon vegetable oil or solid vegetable
    shortening
1½ to 2½ cups Lamb, Veal, or light Chicken
    Stock (see Index)
6 potatoes, sliced
3 ribs celery, cut on the diagonal into 1-inch
    slices
4 carrots, peeled and cut on the diagonal into
    1-inch slices
Freshly ground black pepper to taste
2 bay leaves
Lemon wedges, for garnish

For the very lazy—a drive-through supermarket! Kentucky was way ahead of its time in 1928.

1. Cut a small pocket in the side of each steak, or have your butcher do this. It requires a sharp knife.

2. Preheat the oven to 325°F.

3. Mix the parsley, rosemary or tarragon, ham or bacon, shallots or onion, and lemon juice in a small bowl. Stuff the pocket of each steak with this mixture. Secure with a skewer or toothpick and season with salt.

4. Heat the butter and oil or shortening in a large skillet. Add the steaks in batches and sauté over medium-high heat until they are light brown on both sides. Return all the steaks to the skillet, cover with 1½ cups of the stock, cover the skillet, and allow to simmer a few minutes.

5. Make a layer of the potatoes on the bottom of a casserole or ovenproof dish. Cover with a layer of the celery and then the carrots. Sprinkle each layer lightly with salt. Place the steaks on top of the vegetables. Pour in the stock from the skillet. The stock should reach almost to the top of the lamb. (If you boiled the stock too rapidly you may need more.) Sprinkle the chops with pepper and add the bay leaves.

6. Cover the casserole and cook in the oven until the meat is very tender, 1 hour. Serve with lemon wedges.

Serves 6

VARIATION: Breast of lamb may be stuffed with this mixture by adding 1 cup cooked rice. Browning the breast in a preheated 425°F oven is easier than searing it.

A RACK OF SPRING LAMB

*T*he rib section of a lamb is called a rack when the ends of the bones are trimmed by cutting away the meat and fat, leaving the top of the bones exposed. This technique is called "frenching." The ends of the rib bones are usually covered with paper frills before serving—an attractive presentation. Serve with buttered rice or noodles.

1 rack of lamb (about 8 ribs), trimmed,
  2 pounds (see step 1)
1 small onion, chopped
2 ribs celery, chopped
2 small carrots, peeled and chopped
2 tablespoons unsalted butter, cut into small
  pieces
Salt and freshly ground black pepper to taste
½ cup bread crumbs, buttered and lightly
  toasted (see Index)
1 teaspoon grated lemon peel
¼ cup finely chopped fresh parsley
Watercress, for garnish
Lemon wedges, for garnish

1. Ask your butcher to remove the blade and the chine bone from the lamb. (Reserve the bones.) "French" the ends of the rib bones (see headnote) and cover them with small pieces of foil to keep them from burning.

2. Preheat the oven to 400°F.

3. Spread the onion, celery, and carrots in the bottom of a baking dish. Dot with butter and season with salt. Lay the blade and chine bones on top of the vegetables.

4. Place the baking dish in the oven and cook until the vegetables are somewhat browned, about 15 minutes. If they seem to be sticking, add a few tablespoons of water.

5. Raise the oven heat to 450°F. Stand the rack of lamb (bone ends up) over the bones and vegetables. Roast for about 15 minutes, then turn the heat down to 400°F and roast 10 minutes longer.

6. Remove the lamb from the oven and sprinkle with pepper to taste. Combine the bread crumbs, lemon peel, and parsley in a small bowl and spread over the lamb. Return the lamb to the oven. The dressing should brown a bit as the lamb finishes roasting, another 5 minutes.

7. Remove the lamb to a warm platter or a carving board. Serve 2 ribs per person, garnished with watercress and a wedge of lemon—and a small spoonful of the aromatic vegetables at the side if you like.

Serves 2

This lamb is not usually covered, so the heat must be regulated properly or the vegetables could burn. A lid would steam the lamb and overcook it.

LAMB CHOPS WITH ARTICHOKES

*I*t would be difficult to imagine a more elegant combination than small tender lamb chops with artichokes. Serve with rice or tiny new potatoes.

8 artichokes
1 lemon, quartered
¼ cup vinegar or lemon juice
4 tablespoons (½ stick) butter
¼ cup good-quality olive oil
8 small rib or loin lamb chops
1 clove garlic, crushed
1 small onion, minced
3 sprigs fresh marjoram or 1 teaspoon dried
Salt and freshly ground black pepper to taste
1 cup dry white wine
1 cup water
2 teaspoons tomato paste

1. Break off the stems of the artichokes and remove the first 2 layers of tough leaves at their base. Using a sharp paring knife, trim the leaves off the artichokes down to the bottoms (the heart with the tender base of the leaves). Rub the artichokes with a piece of lemon as needed to keep them from darkening; drop the finished bottoms into a bowl of cold water containing the vinegar or lemon juice. When all of the artichokes are trimmed, cut them into quarters and remove the choke.

2. Using a slotted spoon, remove the artichoke pieces and put them in a pot of boiling salted water to cover. Boil until tender but still crisp, about 15 to 20 minutes. Drain, return to the pot, and set aside, covered, to keep warm.

3. Heat the butter and olive oil in a large heavy skillet. Sauté the lamb chops until golden brown on both sides. Add the garlic, onion, and marjoram. Season with salt and pepper. Add the white wine and simmer, allowing the flavors to marry, until the wine has almost evaporated. Remove the chops and set them aside, but keep them warm.

4. Combine the water and tomato paste and add this to the skillet. Cover tightly and allow to simmer about 20 minutes. Add the artichokes and the lamb chops. Simmer a minute or so. Taste the sauce and adjust the seasoning as necessary.

Serves 4

VARIATION: Sautéed whole mushrooms may be used to garnish the chops, or chopped Italian (flat-leaf) parsley may be sprinkled over them.

 Be sure to keep the chops medium rare.

DINNER ON CHEROKEE ROAD

Lamb Chops with Artichokes

Buttered Brown Rice

Watercress and Walnut Salad

Tidewater Feather Rolls

Dry Red Wine

♦

Frozen Cointreau Soufflé

GRILLED BUTTERFLIED LEG OF LAMB

1 leg of lamb, 5 to 6 pounds, boned
¼ cup vegetable oil
¼ cup lemon juice
1 tablespoon crushed dried rosemary or
    marjoram
1 clove garlic, mashed (optional)
Salt and freshly ground black pepper to taste

1. Cut all extra fat off the lamb. Mix the remaining ingredients and rub them well into the lamb. Place the lamb in a large bowl or heavy polyethylene bag, pour the marinade over, and cover or seal. Allow the meat to marinate in the refrigerator overnight or for 24 hours, turning it several

times so it will absorb the flavor of the marinade evenly.

2. Prepare the grill. Remove the lamb from the marinade and dry it with paper towels. Place 2 long skewers through the meat at right angles so it will lie flat. Salt and pepper the meat well, and place it 6 to 8 inches above medium-hot coals. Grill 30 to 40 minutes, turning once. If you like pink lamb, shorten the cooking time.

3. Slice the lamb on the diagonal very thin.

Serves 6

Take care to thoroughly dry the lamb, or any meat, before grilling.

Serve with a good peach or mango chutney (see Index).

BARBECUED BONED LEG OF LAMB

*T*o many gourmets, the tender meat of young lamb has no peer in outdoor cooking. The choice cuts of lamb come from the hindquarter—the leg and both the large and small loin.

Actually, any cut of meat that can be roasted successfully (roasted is cooking with dry heat) can be barbecued, and lamb lends itself most graciously to many sauces and combinations of food.

Even at the turn of the century, men were kings of the barbecue.

¼ cup dry red wine
2 tablespoons good-quality olive or salad oil
1 tablespoon crushed dried rosemary or
    marjoram
½ onion, sliced
Juice of 1 lemon
1 leg of lamb, 6 to 7 pounds, boned
3 slices smoked bacon
Salt and freshly ground black pepper to taste
Kentucky Heirloom Barbecue Sauce (recipe
    follows) or Kentucky Bluegrass Barbecue
    Baste (see Index)

1. In a small bowl, combine the wine, oil, rosemary or marjoram, onion, and lemon juice.

2. Cut 3 deep incisions in the thickest part of the meat. Dip each piece of bacon into the marinade and then roll it up and insert it deep into one of the incisions.

3. Place the lamb in a large bowl or heavy polyethylene bag, pour the marinade

DINNER ON OSAGE ROAD

Fresh Asparagus Soup

Barbecued Boned Leg of Lamb

Aunt Nettie's Major Grey Mango Chutney

Corn on the Cob

Fresh Garden Tomatoes with Basil

Red Jug Wine   *Iced Tea*

Fresh Strawberries

Coffee

over it, and cover the bowl or tie the bag. Marinate the meat in the refrigerator overnight or for 24 hours.

4. Next day, prepare the grill.

5. Lift the lamb from the marinade and dry it with paper towels. Salt and pepper it well, and fold the meat into a compact shape, tucking in the ends. Skewer the meat together with long metal or wooden skewers, sliding one in lengthwise and one in crosswise.

6. Place the lamb on the grill or on a rotisserie, either one at least 18 inches above the coals. Allow the meat to cook until almost done, then baste it with the barbecue sauce.

Serves 8 to 10 generously

It is necessary to have the meat 18 inches above the coals when using a basting sauce containing ketchup or brown sugar, as it will burn otherwise.

KENTUCKY HEIRLOOM BARBECUE SAUCE

*I*n my family's little country hotel, this was the special barbecue sauce for lamb and pork roasts—especially lamb, with which it is exquisitely compatible. In the summer a lamb barbecue with fresh corn and lima beans is pretty close to heaven.

¾ cup cider vinegar
⅔ cup good-quality tomato ketchup
3 tablespoons light brown sugar
½ cup coarsely chopped onion
1 clove garlic, cut in half and cored
½ teaspoon ground ginger
2 thin lemon slices
1½ cups water
Salt and freshly ground black pepper to taste
1 tablespoon Worcestershire sauce
Tabasco sauce to taste
4 tablespoons (½ stick) unsalted butter

1. Combine the vinegar, ketchup, brown sugar, onion, garlic, ginger, lemon, and water in a stainless steel or enamel saucepan. Bring to a boil, lower the heat, and simmer for about 25 minutes, adding a little more water if the sauce cooks too low.

2. Strain the sauce, discarding the onion, garlic, and lemon slices. Add the salt, pepper, Worcestershire, Tabasco, and butter to the strained sauce and stir well. Simmer about 5 minutes longer.

3. Set aside to ripen for 1 hour, or more if possible, before using. Keeps well under refrigeration, but freezing weakens the spices.

Makes 1¼ cups

COOKING PORK AND HAM

A great deal of our native Southern cuisine has been built on the glories of the pig. We enjoy pork in every fashion—from crown roasts to spareribs and sausages spiced with plenty of pepper, sage, or rosemary. But when asked to name the South's most illustrious meat dish, our country hams quickly come to mind. They are reputed to be unique in the world of smoked meat, with a very special flavor. The men who process the finest of them are as proud of their craft and art as the vintage wine makers, and they guard their methods well.

The old-fashioned dry-cured hams that have been leisurely smoked with hickory wood are still to be found in Kentucky and Virginia (although they are no longer plentiful nor easy to find). A 6-month-old ham is more in demand today, as it is milder than the older hams. Do not allow a Kentucky or Virginia ham to age more than 1½ to 2 years. A 2-year-old ham has a delicious flavor, but it is often salty and a bit dry. It is, however, still delectable sliced thin and served on a small, hot biscuit for cocktails, brunch, for lunch with friends, or just for yourself when you are feeling blue.

BARBECUED SPARERIBS

*B*arbecued spareribs should be braised first in the oven. They will grill more quickly, will be tender and juicy, and the sauce will not burn.

Yet another original barbecue sauce in the works.

2 sides small, tender, meaty pork spareribs,
   3 pounds each
2 cups cold water
1 small onion, sliced
1 bay leaf
½ teaspoon dried thyme or several sprigs fresh
2 tablespoons butter, at room temperature, or
   ¼ cup vegetable oil
Salt and freshly ground black pepper to taste
Barbecue sauce (see step 5)

1. Preheat the oven to 350°F.
2. Place the ribs in a roasting pan with the water, onion, bay leaf, and thyme. Cover and cook in the oven until the meat is tender, 35 to 40 minutes.
3. Meanwhile, prepare the grill by placing an oiled rack 4 to 6 inches over hot mesquite or hickory chips.
4. Remove the ribs from the pan juices. Brush thoroughly with the butter and season with salt and pepper. Grill briskly until crisp but still juicy, 6 to 7 minutes total. Serve with a barbecue sauce on the side.
5. *Or* brush the ribs with vegetable oil and place them over a brisk fire. As soon as they begin to brown, baste them with

Talmadge Farm Barbecue Sauce or Kentucky Heirloom Barbecue Sauce. Baste them quickly on both sides and do not allow the sauce to char, 3 to 4 minutes total.

Serves 6

TALMADGE FARM BARBECUE SAUCE

*T*his is a true Georgia barbecue sauce from the famous Talmadge Ham Farm in Georgia. It is the quintessential barbecue sauce of the Deep South. If that's where you grew up and you have wandered away to the North, one taste will bring nostalgic tears to your eyes. I promise. Old-fashioned pit barbecues... roadside stands...summer sun beaming down! The old swimming hole saved our young lives.

1 cup cider or red wine vinegar
1 tablespoon grated fresh ginger (about 2 ounces
   peeled)
2 tablespoons dry mustard
1¼ cups good-quality ketchup
5 tablespoons Worcestershire sauce
1 clove garlic, cut in half and cored, or more to
   taste
1 cup light brown sugar, loosely packed
1 lemon, thinly sliced and seeded
3 tablespoons unsalted butter
Salt to taste
Lemon juice to taste

Combine the vinegar, grated ginger, mustard, ketchup, Worcestershire, garlic, brown sugar, and lemon slices in a stainless steel or enamel saucepan. Bring to a boil, reduce the heat, and simmer 15 minutes. Add the butter, and simmer 2 minutes longer. Stir in the salt and lemon juice. Set the sauce aside to ripen for several hours or overnight. (The sauce may be used as soon as it is made, but ripening improves it.) Then strain, and store it in a covered jar in the refrigerator. This will keep for several weeks, but it doesn't freeze well.

Makes 4 cups

STUFFED PORK CHOPS

◆◆◆

*E*very cut of fresh pork, even chops, prospers by slow, even, moist cooking—exuding its own flavors and mingling with herbs in a pleasing broth.

◆

Flavorful Pork Stuffing (recipe follows)
6 double-thick pork loin chops
Salt to taste
¼ cup all-purpose flour
4 tablespoons (½ stick) butter
Freshly ground black pepper to taste
⅔ cup Chicken Stock (see Index)
Stuffed Poached Apples (recipe follows)
Chopped fresh parsley, for garnish

◆

1. Preheat the oven to 325°F.
2. Prepare the stuffing.
3. Make a pocket in each pork chop with a sharp knife.
4. Stuff the pockets of the pork chops. Close each chop with toothpicks. Season with salt, and dust with flour on both sides.
5. Melt the butter in a heavy oven-proof skillet over medium-high heat. Add the chops and sauté until both sides are golden brown. Do not cook them any further. Season with pepper, add the chicken stock, and cover the skillet with a lid or foil.
6. Place the skillet in the oven and bake until the chops are extremely tender, 30 to 40 minutes.
7. Serve with Stuffed Poached Apples and garnish with parsley.

Serves 6

◆

FLAVORFUL PORK STUFFING

1½ cups fresh bread crumbs
4 tablespoons (½ stick) butter, melted
¾ cup finely chopped celery
1 tablespoon chopped fresh parsley
1 teaspoon crushed dried rosemary or marjoram
¼ cup Chicken Stock to moisten, or more if needed
Salt and freshly ground black pepper to taste

◆

Brown the bread crumbs lightly in 1 tablespoon of the melted butter in a large skillet.

Mix them with the remaining melted butter, celery, parsley, and rosemary or marjoram. Moisten with just enough chicken stock to hold the crumbs together. Season with salt and pepper to taste.

◆

STUFFED POACHED APPLES

6 large apples (Golden Delicious, Granny Smith, or Rome Beauty)
1½ cups water
2 thin slices lemon
1 small slice fresh ginger or small piece dried ginger (optional)
¾ cup sugar, approximately
1 cup boiling water
6 dried prunes or apricots

◆

1. Peel and core the apples. Trim a thin slice off of the bottoms so the apples will sit steady.
2. Combine the water, lemon slices, ginger, and sugar in a fairly deep heavy pan and bring to a simmer. Place the apples in the seasoned water and simmer, basting almost constantly, until the apples become transparent, about 30 minutes in all. (After 15 minutes, the bottom half of the apples should begin to be transparent. Turn them over gently and continue to simmer and baste with the hot syrup.) Do not let the syrup boil or the apples will overcook in spots and not hold their shape. Transfer the apples to a shallow dish and allow them to cool. Reserve the syrup.
3. Pour the boiling water over the dried fruit and let it soak until plump, 15 minutes.
4. Gently stuff the center of each apple with a prune or apricot. Before serving, reheat the apples in a preheated 300°F oven. Heat the syrup and spoon some over the apples to make them shine.

CROWN ROAST OF PORK

◆◆◆

A crown roast of pork is a glorious thing—it is the epitome of charm and flavor during the holidays or for any festive winter occasion. The crown may be stuffed with any number of delicious fillings, but an aromatic dressing brimming with herbs and chestnuts is the most traditional. It has nostalgia for the old and is beguiling to the young. Serve with a tray of relishes and chutneys.

A Christmas dinner in 1930 — even the moose looks festive.

◆

Center cuts of 2 pork loins, 7 to 8 pounds total
Salt and freshly ground white pepper to taste
2 teaspoons dried marjoram or crushed
*   rosemary*
Apple, Raisin, and Rosemary Dressing, or
*   Chestnut Dressing (recipes follow)*
Watercress or parsley, for garnish

◆

1. Have the butcher make a crown roast by tying the center cuts of 2 loins together. Cover the ends of the bones with foil so they will not burn.
2. Preheat the oven to 325°F.
3. Rub the meat thoroughly with salt, white pepper, and marjoram or rosemary. Put it in a roasting pan and cook, uncovered, basting often with the pan juices, 3½ to 4 hours (30 minutes per pound).
4. About 40 minutes before the roast is done, stuff the center of the crown loosely with the dressing. Continue to cook until the roast registers 170°F on a meat thermometer. If necessary, turn the oven up to 400°F for a few minutes to lightly brown the top of the stuffing.

5. Remove the foil from the ribs. Place the roast and stuffing on a warm platter and garnish it with watercress or parsley.
Serves 10 to 12

VARIATION: Buttered, cooked Brussels sprouts and chestnuts may be used to fill the cavity of the crown just before serving.

◆

APPLE, RAISIN, AND ROSEMARY DRESSING

◆

*T*his amount of stuffing can be used to stuff a crown roast of pork. The apples should be a tart variety, such as Granny Smith.

◆

2 cups fresh bread crumbs
4 tablespoons (½ stick) butter
3 tablespoons water
⅔ cup chopped celery
½ cup chopped onions
1½ cups chopped peeled apples (about 2)
¼ cup golden raisins
½ teaspoon baking powder
1 teaspoon dried rosemary
2 tablespoons dry Madeira or 1 tablespoon
*   brandy*
Salt and freshly ground black pepper to taste

◆

1. Preheat the oven to 225°F.
2. Spread the crumbs on a baking sheet and dry and toast them in the oven, 5 to 10 minutes.
3. Melt the butter in the water in a large skillet. Add the celery and onions, and sauté until the onions have absorbed the butter and are limp. Do not allow them to brown the least bit.
4. Add the apples, raisins, bread crumbs, baking powder, rosemary, and Ma-

deira or brandy. Season with salt and pepper to taste, and toss well with a fork to keep the stuffing loose.

Makes about 2½ cups

🦉 If the stuffing seems overly dry, add an egg or a little chicken stock. The stuffing will not pick up much moisture from the pork.

◆

CHESTNUT DRESSING
◆

*T*his makes quite a bit of dressing, certainly more than enough for a crown roast or turkey. Any leftover dressing can be baked in a casserole alongside the meat. It's so good everyone will want more.

◆

10 cups coarse fresh bread crumbs
2 pounds chestnuts
1½ cups (3 sticks) butter
2 cups finely chopped onions
2 cups chopped celery
1 teaspoon dried thyme
1 teaspoon dried marjoram
¼ cup chopped fresh parsley
Salt and freshly ground black pepper to taste

◆

1. Preheat the oven to 225°F.
2. Spread the bread crumbs on 1 or 2 baking sheets and dry and toast them in the oven, 5 to 10 minutes. Set aside and raise the oven temperature to 450°F.
3. With a sharp knife, cut a cross or 2 gashes in the flat side of each chestnut. Place the chestnuts in a baking pan and cook for 10 minutes. Allow them to cool slightly, then remove the shells and the inner brown skin.

4. Drop the chestnuts into boiling water to barely cover and boil until pleasantly tender but not soft, 6 to 8 minutes. Drain and set aside to cool. Cut into halves or chop coarsely.
5. Melt the butter in a large skillet or saucepan. Add the onions and celery and sauté over medium heat until well saturated with butter and limp, but do not allow to brown, 2 minutes. Add the bread crumbs, chestnuts, thyme, marjoram, and parsley. Mix well. Add salt to taste and season generously with black pepper.
6. Stuff a pork roast or turkey. Put any leftover dressing in a casserole and bake, uncovered, until browned, 25 minutes.

Makes 6 to 8 cups

🦉 If the stuffing seems too dry for your taste, add 1 or 2 eggs or moisten with chicken stock. Remember, the stuffing will not pick up much moisture from the meat.

THANKSGIVING DINNER
Washington Waterfront Pickled Shrimp
◆
Crown Roast of Pork
Chestnut Dressing
October Pickled Seckel Pears
Brussels Sprouts
Walnut, Apple, and Chicory Salad
Southern Heritage Potato Rolls
◆
Old-Fashioned Brandied Pumpkin Pie
Champagne Truffles

SWEET AND TENDER PORK ROAST

◆◆◆

*T*o cover this pork roast with milk might surprise you, but it is a delectable dish. Serve it with Swiss Chard Almondine or any of the following: creamed celery, green cabbage, or scallions (green onions—tops and all).

*1 pork loin roast, 2½ to 3 pounds (about 7
    inches long; see step 1)*
Salt and freshly ground white pepper to taste
1 quart milk, or more as needed
1 carrot, peeled and cut in half
2 potatoes, cut in half
1 medium onion, cut in half
2 ribs celery, each cut in 4 pieces
½ teaspoon dried thyme or 2 sprigs fresh
1 bay leaf
4 sprigs parsley
1 clove garlic, unpeeled
½ cup chopped fresh parsley, for garnish
Grated peel of ½ lemon, for garnish
*Sweet and Tender Pork Cream Sauce (recipe
    follows)*

1. Have the butcher remove the chine bone, or have the roast completely boned.
2. Preheat the oven to 450°F.
3. Remove all but a ⅛-inch layer of outside fat from the roast. Rub the pork well with salt and white pepper, set it in a shallow baking pan, and roast until the meat is golden brown, 30 to 35 minutes. Remove the roast and reduce the oven heat to 325°F.
4. Place the roast in a dutch oven or deep casserole. The pork should fit in the pan snugly, but allow room for the seasoning vegetables and milk. Pour in milk to cover, then add the carrot, potatoes, onion, celery, thyme, bay leaf, parsley sprigs, garlic, and salt and white pepper to taste.
5. Cover the casserole, put it in the oven, and cook until the pork is tender and registers 170°F on a meat thermometer,

about 1½ hours longer.
6. Lift the roast out of the milk and discard the vegetables and seasonings. With a paper towel, brush the curds of milk from the roast. Toss together the chopped parsley and lemon peel, and use this to garnish the roast. Serve with the cream sauce.

Serves 6 to 8

SWEET AND TENDER PORK CREAM SAUCE

*1½ cups milk used to cook the pork, plus
    additional fresh milk, if needed*
2 tablespoons butter
2½ tablespoons flour
½ cup heavy or whipping cream
Salt and freshly ground white pepper to taste
*1 tablespoon chopped fresh parsley or fresh
    tarragon*

1. Strain the milk through a very-fine-mesh sieve. Discard the vegetable and herb seasoning. If you don't have 1½ cups milk, add enough fresh milk to make up the difference.
2. Melt the butter in a heavy saucepan over medium-low heat. Blend in the flour. Slowly whisk in the milk and cream. Simmer until the sauce is thickened and smooth and has lost its raw flavor, about 8 minutes.
3. Add the salt carefully, as the milk from the roast will be salty. Grind in plenty of white pepper. Just before serving, add the parsley or tarragon.

Makes about 2 cups

PORK TENDERLOIN WITH DRIED FRUIT

*T*his wintertime dish is lightened by serving it with a very simply prepared fresh green vegetable such as broccoli or spinach. The mashed potatoes are almost a must with this flavorful sauce. Which bread? Hot biscuits.

6 pork tenderloin filets or boned loin chops (6 to
    8 ounces each)
Salt and freshly ground white pepper to taste
6 dried pears
12 dried prunes
12 dried apricots
2 tablespoons butter
1 tablespoon vegetable oil
3 finely chopped shallots or white part of 4
    scallions (green onions)
½ cup Chicken or Veal Stock (see Index)
1½ tablespoons brandy or Calvados
1 cup heavy or whipping cream
1 tablespoon lemon juice, or to taste
Watercress, for garnish

1. Season the pork with salt and white pepper.

2. Preheat the oven to 325°F.

3. Put the dried fruits in separate saucepans. Cover each with cold water, bring to a boil, and simmer until tender, 5 to 10 minutes. This will vary with the quality of the fruit. (Some dried fruits on the market now need only to be simmered a few minutes.) When they are plump, drain and set aside (keep warm).

4. In the meantime, heat the butter and the oil in a heavy ovenproof skillet. Sauté the chops slowly until they are golden brown, about 15 minutes on each side. Add the shallots or scallions and the stock. Cover the skillet and put it in the oven. Bake until the chops are perfectly tender, 30 to 35 minutes.

5. Remove the chops to a platter or another pan. Keep warm.

6. Skim off the excess fat from the skillet. Add the brandy or Calvados and the cream. Simmer a few minutes for the brandy to lose its raw flavor and to allow the sauce to reduce and thicken if desired. Add the lemon juice and taste to check the seasoning. Strain the sauce.

7. Arrange the chops on a warm large platter. Garnish attractively with the plumped fruit and watercress. Serve the sauce in a sauceboat.

Serves 6

PORK TENDERLOIN HAZELET

*A*ll the flavors in this dish blend so beautifully, and it is an easy dish for a buffet—no carving. This makes Pork Tenderloin Hazelet fabulous for a dinner party.

6 pork tenderloin filets (6 to 7 ounces each)
Salt and freshly ground black pepper to taste
2 tablespoons butter or vegetable oil
1 large Spanish onion, sliced
3 large tomatoes, sliced
12 slices smoked bacon

1 teaspoon dried marjoram
1 cup Chicken Stock (see Index)
3 tablespoons heavy or whipping cream
Watercress or parsley, for garnish

1. Flatten the tenderloins a bit with the flat side of a mallet. Season with salt and pepper to taste.

2. Preheat the oven to 400°F.

3. Heat the butter or oil in a heavy skillet and brown the filets quickly over medium-high heat. Do not allow them to cook through.

4. Place the filets in a shallow casserole or a baking pan and cover each one with a slice of onion and a slice of tomato. Sprinkle the tomato with salt to taste. Cover each tomato slice with 2 strips of bacon laid crisscross over the top. Secure with toothpicks. Cook uncovered in the oven until the bacon is done, 20 to 25 minutes. Remove the bacon and set it aside. Discard the toothpicks. Reduce the oven heat to 325°F.

5. Sprinkle the filets with the marjoram, and add the stock. Return the pan to the oven and bake until the meat is tender, basting often to keep it moist.

6. When the filets are tender, place the meat on a warmed platter. Stir the cream into the sauce and pour over the filets. Garnish with the bacon and watercress or parsley.

Serves 6

VARIATIONS: Thick pork chops may be prepared this way for a family supper.

Sautéed whole mushrooms may be added as an elegant garnish.

VEGETABLES THAT ARE GOOD WITH PORK

Broccoli	Lima beans
Brussels sprouts	Mushrooms
Braised red and	Glazed onions
white cabbage	Mashed potatoes
Celery (au gratin or	Roast potatoes
almondine)	Tomatoes
Green beans	Turnips
Leeks	

LOIN OF PORK AND MUSHROOM STEW

Southerners love pork in almost any form, and you will love this stew redolent of mushrooms and white wine. Serve with broccoli or asparagus, a simple green salad, and spoonbread or hot biscuits. The spoonbread is especially good with the wonderful sauce from the stew.

A Southerner's dream—pork in all its many variations.

1 pork loin roast, 2½ to 3 pounds (reserve the bones)
2 tablespoons vegetable oil
4 tablespoons (½ stick) butter
2 small onions, finely chopped
3 tablespoons water
Salt and freshly ground black pepper to taste
1 pig's foot, ready to cook
1 clove garlic, unpeeled
1 cup dry white wine
3 cups fat-free Veal or Chicken Stock, or more as needed (see Index)
1 pound mushrooms, stems removed (see Owl)
3 tablespoons all-purpose flour
8 ounces uncooked smoked ham, cut into cubes
1 teaspoon dried marjoram or 1½ tablespoons chopped fresh
½ teaspoon dried thyme or 3 or 4 sprigs fresh
3 tablespoons chopped fresh parsley, for garnish

1. Preheat the oven to 450°F.

2. Put the reserved pork bones in a shallow pan and roast them until they are deep brown, 30 to 35 minutes. Set aside. Reduce the oven heat to 325°F.

3. Trim the fat from the pork and cut the meat into 1½-inch cubes. Heat 1 tablespoon of the vegetable oil and 1½ tablespoons of the butter in a heavy skillet over medium heat. Sauté the pork cubes a few at a time until golden brown, adding the remaining oil and 1½ tablespoons more butter as needed. Place the browned pork in a large dutch oven.

4. Pour the excess fat from the skillet. Add the onions to the skillet along with 2 tablespoons of the water. Stir the onions around over medium heat so they will take on some color (but they must not brown). When the water has boiled away, add the onions to the pork. Deglaze the skillet with the remaining water, loosen the brown bits (unless they were burned), and add them to the pork. Season the pork with pepper, but go easy on the salt because the ham you will be adding will be salty. Add the browned bones and the pig's foot. Add the garlic, wine, and enough stock to barely cover the meat.

5. Place the stew over medium heat and bring it to a low boil. Immediately cover the pan, place it in the oven, and bake for 1 hour. Check the stew after 30 minutes. If it is boiling too hard, cut down the heat. (A stew must simmer, not boil.)

6. In the meantime, sauté the mushrooms in the remaining 1 tablespoon butter until they have absorbed the butter, about 3 minutes. Do not brown. Set aside.

7. When the hour is up, remove the stew from the oven. Tip the pan so the fat runs to the side. Degrease by spooning off as much fat as possible. Reserve the fat.

8. Blend 2 tablespoons of the fat with the flour and whisk this into the stew. Add the mushrooms, juice and all, the ham cubes, marjoram, and thyme. Cover and return the pan to the oven. Continue to cook for another hour.

9. Remove the bones, pig's foot, and garlic. Degrease the stew again. Return the pan to the oven and simmer until the meat is exceedingly tender, another 30 minutes to 1 hour. The sauce should have a little body but not be thick like gravy.

10. Spoon the stew into a warm serving bowl. Sprinkle with the chopped parsley.

Serves 4 to 6

VARIATION: *Pork, Mushroom, and Chestnut Stew* (a delightful Christmas holiday stew): Follow directions for Loin of Pork and Mushroom Stew but add 1 to 1½ pounds cooked fresh chestnuts for the last 20 minutes of cooking. The amount of ham can be reduced or it can be omitted.

The mushroom stems can be made into a broth to use as part of the liquid in the stew. Cover the stems or stems and mushroom peelings with a generous amount of cold water. Bring it to a boil and cook about 5 minutes. Strain the broth and discard the stems. Use the broth as directed.

HOW TO COOK A COUNTRY HAM

◆◆◆

A cooked country smoked ham keeps under refrigeration much better than most any meat, but it does not freeze well. There are dozens of recipes, but a really good country ham only needs to be cooked in water. No fancy recipe will make a good ham out of a bad one. Note that you'll need to begin preparing the ham two days before you get a bite of it.

Seessel's Market opened in 1858 in Memphis and is still operating in that city, with a chain of seven supermarkets.

◆

1 whole smoked country ham, about 15 pounds
2 teaspoons ground cloves
⅔ cup light brown sugar
Medium-dry to dry sherry or red wine or cider vinegar (see step 8)

◆

1. Scrub the ham thoroughly with a stiff brush.

2. Place the ham in a large pot or pan or even in a picnic cooler and cover it completely with water. Allow it to soak for 12 to 24 hours. Discard the water.

3. Preheat the oven to 325°F.

4. Put the ham in a large roaster, fat side up, and again cover completely with water. Place in the oven on the lowest rack and bake for 2 hours. Do not allow the water to exceed a gentle simmer at any time. If necessary, lower the oven heat.

5. At the end of the 2 hours, turn the ham on its other side and cook another 2 hours, so it will cook evenly throughout. It takes 4 to 4½ hours in all, or 15 to 18 minutes per pound for a tender ham. An instant-reading thermometer inserted in the meaty part should read 170°F when the ham is done.

6. Remove the ham from the oven but leave it in the water overnight (not refrigerated). (This procedure is important to help ensure a moist ham.)

7. The next day, preheat the oven to 425°F.

8. Remove and discard the ham skin. Sprinkle the fat with the ground cloves. Combine the light brown sugar with just enough sherry or vinegar to make a paste, and brush this mixture over the top of the ham.

9. Bake the ham until it has a beautiful golden glaze, 20 to 30 minutes. Allow the ham to rest for 1 hour or more, then slice it very, very thin.

Serves 25 to 30

🦉 After baking, a properly smoked country ham will keep well under refrigeration for 4 to 5 weeks. After that time, place the ham, or what is left of it, back in a 325°F oven and heat thoroughly for 1 to 1½ hours. The ham will then keep for another 4 to 5 weeks under refrigeration.

◆◆

A LIGHT BREAKFAST BUFFET

Southern Buttermilk Biscuits with Country Ham

St. Petersburg Orange and Apricot Bread

Stuffed Prunes in Sherry

◆

Carolina Figs and Raspberries

Crackly-Top Spice Cookies

PIQUANT HAM WITH JUNIPER BERRIES

◆◆◆

*P*iquant ham with juniper berries, fresh asparagus and new potatoes, hot rolls and strawberry shortcake—this is a menu that Thomas Jefferson would have loved, a touch of France and Old Virginia.

4 tablespoons (½ stick) butter, at room
  temperature
2 slices baked ham cut from the butt or center,
  ½ inch thick
4 shallots, chopped
10 juniper berries
6 tablespoons white or red wine vinegar
1 tablespoon all-purpose flour
½ cup dry white or red wine
1½ cups Chicken or Veal Stock (see Index)
1 cup heavy or whipping cream
Freshly ground white pepper to taste
4 mushrooms, stems removed, for garnish
Watercress sprigs or chopped parsley, for
  garnish

This unusual portrait was taken at Cliff Owens's dairy farm in Louisville around 1900.

1. Melt 1 tablespoon of the butter in a stainless steel or enamel skillet over low heat. Add the ham slices and gently heat on both sides. Do not allow the ham to brown.

2. Meanwhile, put the chopped shallots, juniper berries, and vinegar in a saucepan and cook over medium-high heat until the vinegar has almost evaporated, 5 minutes.

3. Mix 2 tablespoons of the butter with the flour and blend until smooth. Add this to the shallot mixture. Add the wine and stock, and cook until the raw taste of the flour is gone, at least 5 minutes. Add the cream and white pepper. Simmer until the sauce has reduced sufficiently and thickened, 10 to 12 minutes.

4. Melt the remaining 1 tablespoon butter in a small skillet and sauté the mushrooms over medium-high heat until they have absorbed some of the butter but are still somewhat crisp. (They must not brown.)

5. Put the ham on a warm platter and strain the sauce over it. Garnish with the sautéed mushrooms and clusters of watercress or a sprinkling of chopped parsley.

Serves 6 to 8

You can use fresh juniper berries, or dried ones are obtainable in the spice department of gourmet markets.

KENTUCKY-STYLE HAM IN CREAM

*H*am in cream—one of Kentucky's and Virginia's favorite flavors. Delicious with Grits Soufflé or served with rice or grilled toast, in crêpes or omelets. Cook, cover, and refrigerate if made a day ahead.

5 tablespoons butter
½ pound mushrooms, sliced if large
3 tablespoons all-purpose flour
2 cups milk

½ cup heavy or whipping cream
2 cups cubed baked ham
Salt and freshly ground white pepper to taste

1. Melt 2 tablespoons of the butter in a medium skillet. Add the mushrooms and sauté over medium-high heat until they absorb the butter but are still somewhat crisp. (They must not brown.) Set them aside.

2. Melt the remaining butter in a heavy saucepan or skillet over medium heat. Add the flour and mix with a whisk until smooth. Whisk in the milk gradually. Cook until the sauce thickens and is smooth, 3 minutes.

3. Add the cream, ham, and mushrooms. Season with salt and white pepper to taste. (Watch the salt because of the ham.) Heat thoroughly, and serve immediately.

Serves 6

🦉 This is also delicious accompanied by poached apples that have been cut in

---

◆◆◆
BRUNCH ON A JUNE SUNDAY

Kentucky-Style Ham in Cream

Casserole of Grits

Fresh Asparagus

The Ultimate Extra-Flaky Biscuits

Homemade Preserves

◆

Fresh Strawberries and Pineapple

Charleston Shortbread Cookies

Hot Coffee   Amber Iced Tea

---

half and dolloped in the center with a teaspoon of currant jelly. (For poaching apples, see page 139.)

HAM AND MUSHROOM PIE

◆◆◆

A Derby breakfast to remember: Ham and Mushroom Pie, Bibb lettuce, Warm Asparagus Salad, The Ultimate Vanilla Ice Cream, Chocolate Whispers.

◆

2 pounds mushrooms
6 tablespoons (¾ stick) butter
Salt and freshly ground black pepper to taste
2 cups cubed baked ham
3 tablespoons all-purpose flour
1½ cups Chicken Stock (see Index)
⅓ cup dry Madeira or Spanish sherry
½ cup heavy or whipping cream
Cream Cheese Pastry (recipe follows) or Flaky
*   Butter Pastry (see Index)*

◆

1. Clean the mushrooms and remove their stems. Reserve the stems for another purpose. Slice the mushrooms, not overly thin.

2. Melt 4 tablespoons of the butter in a heavy skillet (but not black iron). Add the mushrooms a few at a time and sauté them over medium-high heat until they absorb the butter but are still somewhat crisp, 5 to 6 minutes. (They must not brown.) Season

with salt and pepper.

3. Using a slotted spoon, transfer the mushrooms to a 1½-quart shallow baking dish or pie pan. Cover them with the ham.

4. Add the remaining 2 tablespoons butter to the juices in the skillet. Stir in the flour and blend until smooth. Add the chicken stock gradually and cook the sauce over medium heat, stirring constantly, until it has thickened and is smooth, about 5 minutes.

5. Stir in the Madeira or sherry and the cream. Season with salt and pepper if needed. (Remember, the ham will be salty.) Pour the sauce over the ham and mushrooms.

6. Preheat the oven to 425°F.

7. Roll out the pastry for a top crust large enough to extend 1 inch beyond the edge of the baking dish or pie pan. Lay it over the pie. Fold the edges of the pastry under and press the pastry to the edge of the pan with the prongs of a fork. Make several slits in the crust for the steam to escape. Bake the pie until the pastry is golden brown, about 30 minutes.

Serves 6

🦉 The ingredients for the pie may be prepared ahead. The pie may be covered with the pastry and held in the refrigerator a few hours, but not overnight.

◆

CREAM CHEESE PASTRY

8 tablespoons (1 stick) butter, at room
temperature
1 package (3 ounces) cream cheese, at room
temperature
1 cup sifted all-purpose flour

◆

1. Cream the butter and cream cheese together with an electric mixer, in a processor, or by hand until well blended.

2. Add the flour and mix well. Form into a ball. Cover with foil and refrigerate until the dough has chilled and will roll easily, at least 30 minutes.

🦉 Mixing the pastry with your fingers makes a flakier crust, and bringing the butter and cheese to room temperature makes it very easy to blend by hand.

◆◆

A VERY SPECIAL SUPPER

Ham and Mushroom Pie

Spinach Salad with Rich Vinaigrette

Bibb Lettuce with Wedges of Roquefort

◆

Apricot Ice Cream

Classic Chocolate Butter Cake

Coffee

WOODLAND MUSHROOMS, HAM, AND OLIVES

◆◆

*A*nother delectable combination with a variety of uses. Especially charming served as a garnish for veal or pork roast, or for broiled chicken. Or, use it as a hot hors d'oeuvre, served from a chafing dish, to be put on small toast points. Finally, it is lovely as a filling for an omelet or as a stuffing for zucchini or baked tomatoes.

◆

1 pound small mushrooms
½ pound baked ham
3 tablespoons butter
1 large red bell pepper, cored, seeded, and
slivered
½ cup chopped fresh parsley
12 pitted small green olives
Freshly ground black pepper to taste

◆

1. Clean the mushrooms and trim the stems. Cut the ham into julienne slivers.

2. Melt the butter in a heavy skillet. Add the mushrooms and bell pepper and sauté over medium-high heat until the mushrooms have heated thoroughly but re-

The Schotts were early advocates of punning in advertising, even though bird-hunting had nothing to do with what they were selling.

main crisp. (They must not brown.) Stir in the ham. Add the parsley and olives. Season with pepper to taste. (Usually no salt is needed.)

Serves 4

VARIATION: A small clove of garlic may be tossed with the mushrooms but remove it before serving. A few leaves of fresh marjoram may be added with the parsley.

OLD SEELBACH HOUSE HOT HAM MOUSSE

*T*his Old World dish must be made with a good country ham. Commercial hams today are cured with water and will not work.

The meat counter at the A & P in Louisville, 1928. Definitely a different era.

1 pound baked country ham, ground fine in a
   food processor
4 egg whites, chilled but not whipped
2⅛ cups heavy or whipping cream
½ teaspoon dry mustard
2 tablespoons Spanish sherry or dry Madeira
Salt, if needed
2 hard-cooked eggs, coarsely chopped
Watercress, for garnish

1. Preheat the oven to 325°F.
2. Blend the ham and egg whites with a wooden spoon. When well mixed, add the cream and dry mustard and then the sherry or Madeira. Taste. Add salt if needed.
3. Pour the mixture into an oiled 6-cup mold and cover the top with foil. Set the mold in a baking pan and pour in enough warm water to reach halfway up the mold. Bake it in the oven until the mousse is firm, about 30 minutes.
4. Remove the mousse from the oven and allow it to sit for about 3 minutes. Then loosen the edges with a sharp knife, and unmold it onto a beautiful round platter. Garnish with the chopped eggs and watercress sprigs.

Serves 6 to 8

VARIATION: For a touch of the elegant Old South, bake the mousse in a ring mold and fill the center with hot, buttered fresh spinach, or creamed sweetbreads or mushrooms.

VEGETABLES THAT ARE GOOD WITH HAM

Artichokes	Onions or leeks in
Asparagus	cream
Dried beans (all	Parsnips
types)	Peas
Cabbage (au	Sweet potatoes
gratin)	Mashed white
Celeriac	potatoes
Celery (almondine)	Spinach
Corn	Tomatoes
Green beans	Turnips
Kale	Turnip greens
Lima beans	Zucchini
Mushrooms	

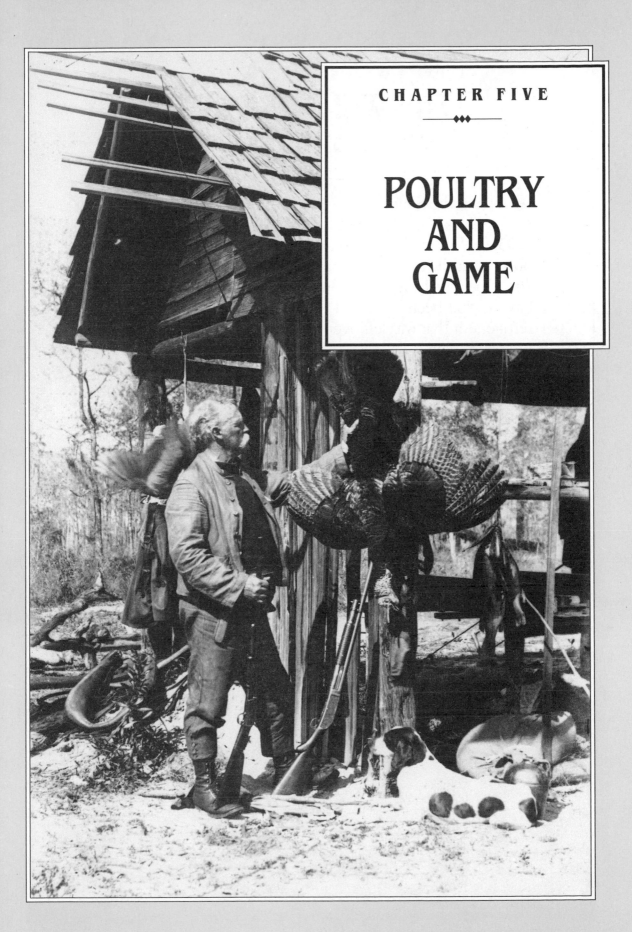

CHAPTER FIVE

POULTRY AND GAME

THE WELL-DRESSED BIRDS

◆◆◆

*I*f we in the South had to choose only one meat for the rest of our lives, I believe the overwhelming vote would go to chicken. We can cook chicken a hundred ways and never be bored, but the topmost favorite, I think, is fried. Properly fried chicken is delicious, no doubt about it. On a restless night haven't you been delighted to find some fried chicken in the refrigerator that was left over from supper? That flavor stays in my taste memory.

If you wish to learn to cook game birds, cook chicken, lots of chicken, in various ways. Learn the difference between sautéing and frying and the change it makes with the menu. Roast, poach, and braise chickens, using the different herbs. Cook and taste—taste and think.

Then transfer what you've learned from chicken to game birds, or any "wild thing" that you are fortunate enough to have often. The intricacies of the different flavors in all wild birds make them endlessly fascinating. But don't let them throw you. Remember, everything was wild at one time, even the turkey. Now so plentiful, he takes his rightful place upon the throne on Thanksgiving Day, roasted to a gleaming, golden brown and dressed to the nines with oysters or chestnuts. No other meat or bird can take his place. He looks important, and the taste is right. Turkey and dressing, sweet potatoes, cranberry sauce, hot rolls, celery and olives, and pumpkin pie. Who would dare to change this menu? Certainly not I.

◆◆◆

HOW TO ROAST A PERFECT CHICKEN

◆◆◆

*A*glistening, golden brown roasted chicken that is succulent and moist is a thing of beauty and flavor—well worth your tender, loving care. Baste with pure butter and keep basting! This prevents the skin from drying out and seals in the natural juices. When a meat thermometer inserted into the thigh registers 180°F, the chicken is done. A meat thermometer is a valuable tool to a good cook.

Serve roast chicken with boiled new or small potatoes with fresh herbs when available, and stuffed zucchini.

◆

1 fresh roasting chicken, 4 to 4½ pounds
1 lemon, cut in half
Salt and freshly ground white pepper to taste
8 tablespoons (1 stick) butter, or more as
*   needed, at room temperature*
1 cup Rich Chicken Stock (see Index)
1 tablespoon chopped fresh parsley
Watercress or parsley, for garnish

◆

1. Preheat the oven to 425°F.

2. Rinse and clean the chicken well, removing any innards that cling to the cavity. Pat dry with paper towels, then rub the cavity of the chicken with the lemon and sprinkle with salt.

3. Blend the butter with salt and white pepper to taste, and rub it well all over the chicken.

4. Put the chicken, breast side up, on a rack in a fairly shallow pan and roast until golden brown, 30 minutes.

5. Turn the chicken on one side and baste with pan drippings and some of the remaining butter. Lower the heat to 325°F and cook the chicken until the exposed skin is golden brown, about 20 minutes. Baste the bird several times. Sprinkle with pepper if desired.

6. Turn the chicken onto the other side. Brush well with butter. Continue to cook until the second side is golden brown, another 20 minutes. Sprinkle with pepper if desired, and baste with the pan drippings several times.

7. Lay the chicken on its back. If you own a meat thermometer, use it to test for doneness (see headnote) or plunge a skewer into the thick part of a thigh. If the juices run perfectly clear, the chicken is done. Place the chicken on a hot platter and keep warm. Allow the chicken to rest 15 minutes for easier carving.

8. Meanwhile, drain off all the fat from the pan and add the stock, scraping the browned bits and glaze from the bottom of the pan. Allow the stock to boil a few minutes. Season with parsley, and salt if needed.

9. Serve the sauce in a sauceboat alongside the chicken. Garnish the platter with bouquets of watercress or parsley.

Serves 4

VARIATIONS: *Roast Chicken with Herbs:* Put 1 tablespoon dried tarragon or rosemary in the cavity of the chicken before roasting.

Creamy Chicken Gravy: Skim off as much fat as possible from the pan juices. Add 1 cup chicken stock and cook until the sauce is smooth, stirring constantly. Add ¾ cup cream and allow the sauce to reduce until it thickens a bit. Taste for seasoning. Correct with salt and white pepper if needed. Serve in a sauceboat with chicken and buttered rice—white, brown, or wild.

The chicken is turned on its side so the juices will run down to the breast and keep it moist and succulent. If the chicken is not perfectly browned at the end of 1¼ hours, the oven is not quite hot enough. Turn the oven temperature higher, baste with butter, and roast until the chicken is a golden, shiny brown.

SOUTHERN FRIED CHICKEN

◆◆◆

Correctly fried Southern chicken is simplicity itself—and one of the best ways to cook chicken in all the world. It is never tenderized in any way before frying, nor is it steamed or braised in the oven after frying. It is not dipped in milk, crumbs, or batter—just in a generous coating of flour. Season with salt and pepper. Use fresh fat and an iron skillet. Lard makes the crispest chicken, but vegetable shortening is fine. No bacon drippings. Serve hot or cold. Never do we have a picnic without fried chicken.

◆

1 frying chicken, 3 to 3½ pounds
1 teaspoon salt, plus more to taste
Freshly ground pepper to taste
1 cup all-purpose flour
Lard or solid vegetable shortening for frying

◆

1. Cut the chicken into comfortable serving pieces (breast cut in half, thigh and leg separated). Rinse the pieces and dry them well with paper towels. Season the chicken with salt and pepper to taste.

2. Mix 1 teaspoon salt into the flour and coat the chicken by rolling the pieces firmly in the flour or by tossing them in the flour in a plastic bag. Before frying, shake the pieces to rid them of any excess flour.

3. Heat enough lard or shortening to come to a depth of 1½ inches in a heavy black iron pan. When the fat is piping hot but not smoking, add the largest pieces first. Do not crowd. Cover the pan and fry over medium-high heat for 8 minutes.

4. After the chicken has browned on one side, turn it to brown the other side. Keep the fat at a medium-high temperature but remove the cover. (You will have to watch the chicken as it cooks.) The total cooking time for tender chicken will be about 20 minutes. Drain on paper towels.

Serves 4

◆

FRIED CHICKEN GRAVY

◆

2 tablespoons drippings from fried chicken
3 tablespoons all-purpose flour
1½ cups milk
Salt and freshly ground white pepper to taste

◆

Pour off all the fat from the pan except about 2 tablespoons, leaving the golden brown crunchy bits. Add the flour and blend over rather low heat. Add the milk and cook, stirring constantly, until the gravy has thickened. Add salt and lots of pepper to taste. Serve over hot biscuits.

BALTIMORE BARBECUE CHICKEN

◆◆◆

This is Maryland's way of basting chicken for the oven or grill. It is tart and spicy, but at the same time, it has a delicacy unlike the tomato-rich, earthy country barbecues of the deep South.

4 shallots or scallions (green onions; white bulb
     only), finely chopped
⅓ cup water
1 teaspoon dry mustard
2 tablespoons tarragon white wine vinegar
2 tablespoons good-quality ketchup
2 tablespoons lemon juice
8 tablespoons (1 stick) butter, cut into pieces
     and chilled
½ teaspoon Tabasco sauce, or to taste
Cayenne pepper to taste
Salt to taste
2 frying chickens, 2½ to 3 pounds each, split
6 tablespoons (¾ stick) unsalted butter, at
     room temperature

1. Combine the shallots or scallions with the water in a small stainless steel or enamel saucepan, and simmer until the shallots are soft, 1½ to 2 minutes. Don't allow them to sizzle or boil dry.

2. Add the mustard, vinegar, ketchup, and lemon juice to the shallots and cook over low heat, 5 to 6 minutes. Remove from the heat and allow the flavors to ripen about 30 minutes.

3. Preheat the oven to 450°F.

4. Reheat the sauce over low heat until just warm, no hotter. Beat in the chilled butter 1 piece at a time. Add the Tabasco, cayenne, and salt. Set aside.

5. Rinse the chicken halves and dry them well with paper towels. Lay them bone side down in a large roasting pan. Season with salt, then brush with 3 tablespoons of the unsalted butter and place in the oven. Cook the chicken, basting several times with the pan drippings and the remaining butter, for 25 minutes. Allow the birds to become golden and crisp. Continue to cook, brushing the birds with the barbecue sauce several times, 6 minutes. Be careful not to let the sauce burn.

Serves 4

Baltimore Barbecue Chicken is easy to prepare outdoors on the grill. Just follow the grilling directions in steps 1 and 3 of Rosemary Grilled Chicken, page 156.

Grazing in Kentucky's lush bluegrass.

KENTUCKY BLUEGRASS BARBECUE BASE

*T*his is a far more delicate barbecue baste and sauce than the usual Southern pit barbecues. It has much more tang and is not overly sweet. Best of all, it does not overpower the meat or fish on which it is used. Using a thin coating of the sauce is the trick. It is delectable on chicken.

½ cup cider vinegar
1 teaspoon ground ginger, or 1 small piece
     (1 ounce) fresh ginger, grated or chopped
     (see Owl)
1 tablespoon dry mustard
2 tablespoons Worcestershire sauce
¾ cup good-quality ketchup
6 tablespoons medium-dry sherry
1 bay leaf
1 clove garlic, or more to taste, cut in half and
     cored
2 thin lemon slices
2 tablespoons flavorless vegetable oil
6 tablespoons (¾ stick) unsalted butter
Salt to taste
Tabasco sauce to taste

1. In a stainless steel or enamel saucepan combine the ingredients through the oil.

2. Set aside to mellow for 1 hour, or more if possible.

3. Strain the sauce and discard the ginger (if using fresh), garlic, bay leaf, and lemon slices. Add the butter, salt, and Tabasco, and simmer for 3 minutes.

Makes 4 cups

You can grate the fresh ginger by hand, or slice it and combine it with the vinegar in a food processor. Process just a few seconds. The ground ginger works quite well in this recipe, however.

ROSEMARY GRILLED CHICKEN

◆◆◆

Cooking over charcoal is one of our favorite outdoor sports in the South. Sometimes it seems that summers are just not long enough. Be sure to accompany this chicken with Carolina Buttered Okra, Grilled Corn, garden fresh tomatoes, and warm homemade bread.

2 broiling chickens, 3 pounds each, split and
　　backbones removed
¼ cup vegetable oil
8 tablespoons (1 stick) butter, melted
½ cup dry white wine, or ⅓ cup lemon juice
2 teaspoons crushed dried rosemary
½ clove garlic (optional)
1 teaspoon salt
Freshly ground black pepper to taste

1. Prepare the grill by placing an oiled rack 4 to 6 inches over medium-hot coals.

2. Combine the oil, butter, wine or lemon juice, rosemary, garlic (if desired), and salt. Brush the chicken halves inside and out with ¼ cup of the seasoned butter.

3. Place the chickens bone side down on the grill. Baste them frequently with the remaining seasoned butter and turn the pieces every 10 minutes for a total of 30 to 40 minutes in all. Sprinkle well with pepper and serve.

Serves 4

CHICKEN AND RED PEPPER STEW

◆◆◆

This is one of those deliciously flavored chicken dishes that makes a meal in itself. All you need with it is a very simple green salad—crisp Bibb or romaine, or both—more would be too much.

1 frying chicken, 3 to 3½ pounds
1 clove garlic, cut in half
1 tablespoon vegetable oil
2 tablespoons good-quality olive oil or butter
Salt to taste
2 medium onions, chopped
8 ripe but firm tomatoes, peeled, seeded, and
　　chopped
½ teaspoon dried thyme
2 large red bell peppers, cored, seeded, and cut
　　into thin strips
1 large green bell pepper, cored, seeded, and
　　cut into thin strips
6 ounces uncooked ham, cut into cubes
½ cup dry white wine
½ cup Chicken or Veal Stock (see Index),
　　or as needed
1½ cups rice
½ pound small mushrooms, stems removed
2 tablespoons butter
Freshly ground black pepper to taste
Black olives, for garnish
Chopped fresh parsley, for garnish

1. Cut the chicken into comfortable serving pieces (breast cut in half, thigh and leg separated). Rinse the pieces and dry them well with paper towels. Rub each piece of chicken with the cut side of the garlic.

A PATIO PARTY IN THE GARDEN DISTRICT OF NEW ORLEANS

Rémoulade Rouge of New Orleans

•

Rosemary Grilled Chicken

Corn on the Cob

Bibb, Romaine, and Watercress Salad with French Cream Dressing

•

Honeydew Wedges with Lime

The Palm Beach Cooler

2. Heat the vegetable oil and the olive oil or butter in a heavy dutch oven or flameproof casserole. Sprinkle the chicken with salt and brown it evenly over medium-high heat without burning the fat the least bit.

3. Add the onions, tomatoes, thyme, peppers, and ham. Add the white wine and ½ cup of the stock. Cover the pot and simmer over very low heat, or place in a preheated 325°F oven, for about 20 minutes.

4. While the chicken is simmering, cook the rice and keep it warm.

5. Sauté the mushroom caps in the butter over medium-high heat for 2 to 3 minutes (do not let them brown) and add them to the stew. Simmer until the chicken is tender, 10 to 15 minutes longer. Add salt and pepper to taste. (If the chicken is done but the sauce has not developed enough flavor, remove the chicken pieces and reduce the sauce. Then return the chicken to the sauce.)

6. Serve the chicken and sauce over the rice. Sprinkle with black olives and chopped parsley.

Serves 4

VARIATION: *Pork, Mushroom, and Red Pepper Stew:* Substitute 4 pork loin or rib chops and prepare exactly the same way as Chicken and Red Pepper Stew.

If this tomato sauce is too tart (so much depends upon the flavor of the tomatoes), caramelize 2 teaspoons of sugar in 2 tablespoons of water in a small skillet and add it to the stew. This lends a softer flavor than adding plain sugar.

CHICKEN WITH HAM IN RED WINE

*O*f all the chicken dishes that hold their own when cooked ahead, this one is among the best. It is not a new dish, but the affinity of flavors—the ham and the herbs with the chicken—is so delicious, and it is charming served with Lexington Spoonbread.

2 frying chickens, 3½ pounds each
Salt and freshly ground black pepper to taste
½ cup diced salt pork
6 tablespoons (¾ stick) butter, at room temperature
15 small onions
15 mushrooms, cut in half
¾ pound smoked baked ham, cubed
3 shallots, coarsely chopped
1 clove garlic, unpeeled

2 ribs celery
1 bay leaf
3 parsley sprigs
½ teaspoon dried thyme
2 tablespoons all-purpose flour
2 cups dry red wine (Burgundy type)
1 cup Chicken Stock (see Index) or water, or more as needed

Preparing whole chickens in 1926.

1. Cut the chickens into comfortable serving pieces (breast cut in half, thigh and leg separated). Rinse the pieces and dry them well with paper towels. Season with salt and pepper.

2. Parboil the salt pork for 1 minute. Drain and dry completely on paper towels.

3. Preheat the oven to 325°F.

4. Melt 4 tablespoons of the butter in a heavy flameproof casserole or dutch oven and sauté the salt pork over medium heat. When it has browned, set it aside or discard.

5. Add the chicken pieces a few at a time and brown quickly on both sides—do not cook through. Set the browned pieces aside until all are done. Then return all the pieces to the pot and add the onions. Allow them to take on a little color but do not fry them. Lift the onions out of the pan and set aside.

6. Add the mushrooms, ham, shallots, garlic, celery, bay leaf, parsley, and thyme to the chicken. Blend the flour with the remaining 2 tablespoons butter until smooth, and add it to the chicken. Add the wine and stock or water to almost cover the chicken.

7. Cover the casserole, place it in the oven, and bake until the chicken begins to be tender, about 25 minutes. Then add the onions. Continue to cook until the chicken and onions are tender and the sauce has ripened and is fully flavored, another 15 to 25 minutes. (If the chicken has not browned sufficiently, remove the cover and increase the heat to 375°F. Watch carefully or the sauce might boil away. Add a little chicken stock or water if needed, but never wine at this point.) Remove the celery, bay leaf, parsley sprigs, and garlic.

Serves 6 to 8

A heavy-bodied red wine, domestic or imported, is best for this dish—certainly not a Beaujolais.

THE CATHEDRAL HERB GARDEN CHICKEN

◆◆◆

*W*hen I lived in Washington, D.C., before World War II, Leonie de Sounin, who wrote *Magic with Herbs,* was teaching cooking and overseeing an herb farm which was the inspiration for the Cathedral Herb Garden. Ms. de Sounin was my mentor, and I spent a great deal of time with her learning about herbs, which I adore to this day. This recipe is adapted from one of her lessons.

◆

2 small broiling chickens, about 2½ pounds each
1 lemon, cut in half
2 teaspoons chopped fresh rosemary or 1 teaspoon crushed dried, or more to taste
8 tablespoons (1 stick) butter, at room temperature

1 teaspoon finely chopped fresh ginger or ¼ teaspoon ground
6 slices lean smoked bacon
Salt and freshly ground black pepper to taste

◆

1. Preheat the oven to 425°F.

2. Rinse and clean the chickens well, removing any innards that cling to the cavities. Pat dry with paper towels, then rub the cavities with the lemon.

3. Blend the rosemary with the butter and ginger. Spread some of the butter under the skin of the breasts and thighs.

4. Place the chickens on their sides in a roasting pan, cover with strips of bacon, and bake about 20 minutes. Turn the chickens to their other sides, rearrange the partially cooked bacon on top of the chickens, and bake for another 15 to 20 minutes. (If the bacon becomes overly brown, discard it.)

5. Turn the chickens breast up, reduce the heat to 375°F, and baste often with the remaining butter and the pan drippings. The time will vary with the size and tenderness of the chickens, but the chickens are done when the juices run perfectly clear when a skewer is inserted into the thigh, about another 25 minutes.

Serves 4

VARIATION: These chickens may be split, if desired, and roasted in the same fashion.

🦉 If at any time the chickens seem to be browning too fast, cover them loosely with foil.

MOTHER'S CHICKEN TREILLAGE

◆◆◆

*T*his is my favorite chicken recipe in all the world. Mother called it chicken pie—I think because she used pie crust for the lattice. Cream Cheese Pastry or Cornmeal Puff Paste, either one, is perfect used this way, as they both absorb the flavor of the chicken and its browned buttery skin but remain very crisp. Cream Cheese Pastry, especially, is perfection here. It melts in your mouth, I promise.

◆

1 frying chicken, 3 to 3½ pounds
4 to 6 tablespoons butter, at room temperature
Salt and freshly ground white pepper to taste
Cream Cheese Pastry or Cornmeal Puff Paste
    (see Index)

◆

1. Preheat the oven to 450°F.

2. Cut the chicken into comfortable serving pieces (breast cut in half, thigh and leg separated). Rinse the pieces and dry them well with paper towels. Brush both sides of the chicken pieces with butter. Season with salt and white pepper.

3. Place the chicken pieces bone side down in a shallow baking dish and put it on the middle shelf of the oven. After 5 minutes, brush the chicken well with the butter from the bottom of the pan. Continue to baste the chicken often. When the chicken is golden brown and tender, remove the dish from the oven; it should take about 25 minutes. Reduce the oven heat to 425°F.

4. Roll out the pastry into a rectangle, 10 x 6 inches and ¼ inch thick. Cut the pastry into six 10-inch strips.

5. Cover each piece of chicken with strips of pastry, interweaving them to form a lattice. Fold the edges of the pastry under the chicken. Return the chicken to the oven just long enough for the pastry to brown, about 8 to 10 minutes. Serve at once.

6. If more sauce is desired, deglaze the pan with a bit of chicken broth.

Serves 4

A NOTABLE VARIATION: Thin slices of baked country ham may be placed under the chicken after the pastry is baked. This is sufficient to heat the ham.

COLONIAL CHICKEN CURRY

*T*he Southerners' love of spices shows in their fondness for curry. It is not difficult to master and it must be made ahead, which makes it a fabulous large-party dish. Do not forget the Indian River Hot Mango Slices—very special indeed.

Rushing both live and prepared chickens to market, 1930s style.

¾ cup (1½ sticks) butter, at room temperature
2 medium onions, finely chopped
⅓ cup water
2 tart, juicy apples (Granny Smith, Winesap, or Rome Beauty), cut in eighths
3 ribs celery
2 bay leaves
½ teaspoon finely chopped fresh ginger, or more to taste
3 cups Chicken Stock (see Index), or more as needed
¼ cup all-purpose flour
1 cup heavy or whipping cream
2 tablespoons imported Madras curry powder, or more to taste
Salt and freshly ground white pepper to taste
Cayenne pepper to taste
3 cups cubed freshly poached chicken breasts (see box)
4 cups cooked rice
Mango chutney, for garnish

1. Melt 8 tablespoons of the butter in a heavy saucepan or dutch oven. Add the onions and water. Cook over medium heat until the onions are limp and the water has boiled away. Do not let the onions sizzle or brown the least bit.

2. Add the apples, celery, bay leaves, ginger, and stock. Blend the remaining 4 tablespoons butter with the flour until smooth, and add this to the pot. Allow to simmer, adding more stock if needed, 30 to 35 minutes. Remove from the heat.

3. Skim out the apples and celery. Add the cream and curry powder. Season with salt, white pepper, and cayenne pepper to taste. Add the cubed chicken and shake to blend. Do not stir. Allow the dish to rest for 1 hour or more so the flavors will ripen. Taste, and correct the seasoning if necessary.

4. When you are ready to serve the curry, heat the mixture in the top of a

HOW TO POACH CHICKEN BREASTS

1. Rinse 3 whole chicken breasts and dry them well with paper towels. Cut the breasts in half. Remove the wing tip, if the wing is attached, but not the wing bone.

2. Put the breasts in a tight-fitting kettle or enamel dutch oven. Cover with fresh, cold, fat-free chicken stock or water, using as much chicken stock as you can spare, but at least half. Add 2 ribs of celery cut into pieces, 1 medium onion, 1 bay leaf, and a pinch of dried thyme. Taste the broth for salt, then add salt accordingly. Breasts must cook in lightly salted stock.

3. Bring the liquid to a boil, reduce the heat, cover loosely, and simmer only until the breasts are tender, about 20 minutes. Overcooking makes the meat dry.

4. Uncover the pot and let the chicken cool in the stock. Remove the meat from the bones. Use for salad, hash, curry, and sandwiches.

double boiler over hot water. Serve with boiled white rice and mango chutney.

Serves 4

VARIATION: This sauce may be used for curried shrimp or lobster, but add ½ cup dry white wine to the sauce before the cream is added. Serve with rice, mango chutney, and almonds.

Condiments to accompany curry, if desired: Slivered almonds, buttered and toasted; moist canned, packaged, or freshly grated coconut; Indian River Hot Mango Slices; small cubes of fresh pineapple; sliced bananas; cubes of tart apples marinated in pineapple juice; and chopped crisp bacon.

CHICKEN NEWBURG

*A*n old Maryland recipe for Sunday night company. Crabmeat may be used instead of chicken. Sinfully rich, deliciously good, and very easy.

5 tablespoons butter
½ cup sliced mushrooms, or more to taste
1½ tablespoons all-purpose flour
1½ cups fat-free Rich Chicken Stock (see Index)
½ cup heavy or whipping cream
3 cups cubed poached chicken breasts (see page 160)
3 egg yolks, at room temperature
3 tablespoons medium-dry sherry or Madeira, or more to taste
Salt to taste
Cayenne pepper to taste

1. Melt 2 tablespoons of the butter in a small skillet. Add the mushrooms and sauté over medium heat until just tender, 2 to 3 minutes. Set them aside.
2. Melt the remaining butter in a heavy stainless steel or enamel saucepan.

Add the flour and blend it in with a whisk until smooth. Add the stock and cook until smooth, 2 to 3 minutes. Add the cream, the chicken, and the mushrooms.

3. In a small bowl, beat the yolks and then add a little of the hot liquid to them. Add the yolks and sherry or Madeira to the chicken.

4. Simmer a few minutes, but do not allow the mixture to boil or it will curdle. Season with salt and cayenne. Serve with rice, over toast points, or as a filling for crêpes.

Serves 4

If the chicken mixture is to be made ahead, add the egg yolks and sherry just before serving. The yolks are used to enrich as well as to thicken. To reheat, use a double boiler. Care must be taken that the mixture does not boil.

OLD SEELBACH HOUSE PERFECT CHICKEN HASH

*T*he technique for achieving a delicious hash is the same with all meats and fowl. The stock must be rich and flavorful, and the ingredients must not be mashed in cooking. Shake the pan. Don't ever stir a hash.

1 cup diced potatoes
¼ cup chopped onion
3 ribs celery, chopped
4 cups Rich Chicken Stock (see Index)
3 tablespoons butter, at room temperature
3 tablespoons all-purpose flour
4 cups cubed poached chicken (see pages 160
    and 166)
Salt and freshly ground white pepper to taste
¼ chopped fresh parsley

1. Bring a large saucepan of salted water to a boil and drop in the potatoes, onion, and celery. Cook, uncovered, just until the potatoes are tender but not mushy, 15 to 20 minutes. Drain well.

2. Pour the stock into a heavy saucepan. Gently heat the stock. Blend the butter with the flour until smooth, and add this to the stock. Simmer until thickened.

3. Place the cubed chicken in the bottom of a heavy skillet or pot. Put the cooked potatoes, onion, and celery on top, and pour the rich stock over the vegetables. Simmer until it has thickened slightly. Season with salt and white pepper. (Be generous with the pepper.) Shake the pan—do not stir. Allow to ripen 1 hour if possible.

4. When you are ready to serve the hash, check the seasonings again. Heat, gently over hot water, sprinkle with parsley, and serve on grilled toast or with corncakes or hot biscuits.

Serves 4

VARIATIONS: One-half cup of dried mushrooms soaked in water for 1 hour or so, then drained, ground, and simmered in the stock before it is thickened makes a superb, if not traditional, chicken hash. Dried mushrooms have a rich, earthy taste completely in keeping with the homey quality of hash.

Make Chicken Almond Hash by omitting the onion and potatoes and adding more celery and buttered, toasted slivered almonds. This makes more of a creamed hash.

THE HERMITAGE CHICKEN CORNBREAD SANDWICH

The Hermitage Hotel in Nashville, Tennessee, so named for the beautiful home of Andrew Jackson, served this very Southern dish for Sunday brunch. It is actually a delicious chicken hash made without potatoes. The cornbread is at its best oven fresh, of course, but it can be made ahead and frozen, and the chicken hash holds better than when it is made with potatoes. The cornbread can be baked and cut into squares, or it can be made into muffins, then split and filled. Serve with your best garden relish—chow chow, green tomato, or red and green pepper relish.

Hot Tennessee Sour Cream Cornbread (recipe
    follows), or use Sour Cream Corn Muffin
    recipe (see Index)
2 tablespoons butter, at room temperature
3 tablespoons all-purpose flour
5 cups Rich Chicken Stock (see Index), not quite
    fat-free, or more as needed
4 cups cubed freshly poached chicken (see pages
    160 and 166)
¼ cup chopped onion
2 cups chopped pale celery or celery hearts
Salt and freshly ground white pepper to taste
Cayenne pepper to taste
Parsley sprigs, for garnish

1. Prepare the cornbread and keep it warm.

2. Blend the butter with the flour in a

saucepan. Add 1 cup of the stock and cook over medium-low heat, stirring constantly with a whisk, until thickened and smooth, about 5 to 6 minutes. Add the chicken and shake the pan to blend.

3. Simmer the onion and celery in 4 cups stock in a large heavy pan until they are tender but retain some texture. Spoon the chicken mixture on top of the vegetables. Shake the pan to distribute the chicken lightly through the vegetables. Don't stir.

4. Add, if needed, just enough additional stock to make a pleasing amount of sauce for spooning the hash over the cornbread. Season with salt, white pepper, and cayenne.

5. Spoon the piping hot chicken hash over the lower half of each cornbread square, allowing some to run over the sides. Cover with the top piece of cornbread. Garnish with a sprig of parsley and serve at once.

Serves 6

VARIATION: *September Red Bell Pepper and Chicken Cornbread Sandwich:* Follow the directions for The Hermitage Chicken Cornbread Sandwich but cook 1 or 1½ large red bell peppers or 2 or 3 fresh pimento peppers, cored, seeded, and finely slivered, with the onion and celery. In the fall when the red bell peppers and pimentos are ripe, they make the best chicken hash of all.

CHECK POINTS FOR POULTRY

3 pounds of dressed poultry yields approximately 1 pound cooked meat

A 4½- to 5-pound hen yields 1¼ pounds meat

1 pound of cooked poultry meat yields 3 cups cubed

Poultry for salad or hash should be poached, not baked

Allow freshly cooked fowl or broth to cool to room temperature before refrigerating

Never cover hot fowl or stock

Chicken stock freezes well for a long period

Chervil, parsley, marjoram, and tarragon are herbs that are compatible with poultry

The Hermitage, as it appeared in 1917.

TENNESSEE SOUR CREAM CORNBREAD

⅞ cup fine white cornmeal
1 cup sour cream
2 tablespoons milk
2 eggs
¾ teaspoon salt
1 teaspoon sugar
⅛ teaspoon baking soda
1½ teaspoons baking powder
4 tablespoons (½ stick) butter, melted

1. Preheat the oven to 425°F. Butter a 7- or 8-inch square glass or metal cake pan.

2. Measure the cornmeal into a roomy bowl. Add the sour cream, milk, and eggs and beat thoroughly with a whisk. Add the salt, sugar, baking soda, baking powder, and melted butter. Mix thoroughly and fast. Spoon into the prepared cake pan.

3. Place the pan on the middle shelf in the oven and bake until the cornbread is golden brown, about 25 minutes. The center of the bread should be fairly firm to the touch.

4. Cut the bread into squares. Split each square horizontally, as for a sandwich. Keep warm.

POACHED CAPON WITH LEMON, CHIVE, AND TARRAGON SAUCE

*T*his is an old love of a recipe—very delicate—exquisitely so—and lovely in the early summer when the new potatoes are on the market and your herbs are flourishing.

1 capon, 5 to 6 pounds
Salt and freshly ground white pepper to taste
2 medium onions
3 ribs celery
4 cups Chicken Stock (see Index)
3 sprigs parsley
1 bay leaf
½ teaspoon dried thyme
2 bunches watercress
Lemon, Chive, and Tarragon Sauce (recipe follows)

1. Rinse the capon and dry it well with paper towels. Sprinkle inside and out with salt and white pepper. Place 1 of the onions and 1 rib of celery, cut in half, in the cavity of the capon. Truss the bird by closing the cavity with skewers or by sewing it with string and tie the legs together.

2. Place the capon breast side down in a large kettle. Add the stock and enough cold water to cover the capon well. Slowly bring to a simmer. Skim off any scum that rises to the surface. Add the remaining onion and celery, the parsley, bay leaf, and thyme. Cover and simmer until the bird is tender but not falling off the bone, 1½ to 2 hours. Remove the bird from the poaching liquid. Set aside but keep warm.

3. Place the kettle back over high heat and reduce the liquid until there are about 5 cups of concentrated stock left, about 35 minutes. Strain the stock through dampened cheesecloth. Use as needed to prepare the sauce. Cool and freeze the rest for other uses.

4. Carve the capon. Arrange the slices on a warm platter with clusters of watercress. Spoon over the Lemon, Chive, and Tarragon Sauce. Serve any extra sauce in a warm sauceboat.

Serves 4

LEMON, CHIVE, AND TARRAGON SAUCE

1 cup (2 sticks) unsalted butter
Juice of 1 lemon or to taste
2 tablespoons chopped chives or tiny slivers of scallion (green onion) tops
2 teaspoons chopped fresh parsley
1 tablespoon chopped fresh tarragon or 1 teaspoon dried
½ cup strained fat-free capon stock
Salt and freshly ground white pepper to taste

Melt the butter in a small heavy saucepan over low heat. Add the lemon juice, chives or scallion tops, parsley, and tarragon. Add the stock and the salt and white pepper to taste. Whisk and taste. For a more pungent sauce, add more lemon juice.

A JUNE LUNCHEON IN THE BLUEGRASS

Poached Capon with Lemon, Chive, and Tarragon Sauce

Fresh Green Peas

New Potatoes

Romaine and Bibb Salad with Classic Vinaigrette

Rich Chocolate Ice Cream

Lisa's Butter Leaf Cookies

Coffee

STUFFED CORNISH GAME HENS

*A*ny recipe for Rock Cornish Game Hens can also be used for pheasant, partridge, chicken, or quail, but the timing will vary. Birds that have been frozen profit from a stuffing, which helps keep them moist. Baste and baste.

6 Cornish hens, ready to cook
Herb or Almond Stuffing (recipes follow)
Salt and freshly ground black pepper to taste
4 tablespoons (½ stick) butter, at room
    temperature
½ cup plus 3 tablespoons Chicken Stock (see
    Index)
¼ cup dry white wine
1½ teaspoons all-purpose flour
2 tablespoons medium-dry Spanish sherry
Watercress or parsley sprigs, for garnish

James P. Sams, manager of the River Valley Club in Louisville, was a great hunter, as can be attested to by his success with bobwhite quail.

1. Preheat the oven to 450°F.
2. Rinse the game hens thoroughly and dry them well with paper towels. Fill the cavities of the game hens loosely with stuffing and truss the birds lightly. Season the hens with salt and pepper, and rub them well with the butter.
3. Place the hens in a flameproof baking pan, put them in the oven, and cook, basting frequently, until they are a light golden brown, 15 to 20 minutes.
4. Lower the temperature to 350°F and continue to roast the birds until they are tender, another 30 to 40 minutes.
5. Remove the birds to a platter and keep warm. Add the ½ cup of stock and the white wine to the pan juices, stirring to loosen all the brown bits. Blend the flour in 3 tablespoons of stock, add it to the pan, and cook until the sauce is smooth and thickened.
6. Season the sauce with Madeira or sherry, and allow it to cook a few minutes to lose the raw flavor of the wine. Pour it over the birds or serve in a sauceboat. Serve the birds garnished with watercress or parsley.

Serves 6

HERB STUFFING

3 tablespoons butter
4 shallots, minced
3 slices smoked bacon, diced
2 cups finely ground fresh bread crumbs
2 to 3 tablespoons chopped fresh parsley
1 teaspoon dried tarragon
½ cup Chicken Stock (see Index), or as needed
Salt to taste

1. Melt the butter in a large skillet over medium heat. Add the shallots and sauté until they are limp but not brown. Add the bacon and continue to cook until it has browned.
2. Add the bread crumbs, parsley, and tarragon. Toss well with a fork.
3. Add just enough chicken stock to make a barely moist dressing, and season with salt to taste if needed.

Makes about 2 cups

ALMOND STUFFING

4 tablespoons (½ stick) butter
4 to 5 shallots, finely chopped
1 cup minced baked ham (¼ pound)
2 tablespoons chopped fresh parsley
½ teaspoon dried thyme
2 cups buttered toasted bread crumbs (see Index)
1 egg
2 tablespoons dry Madeira or Spanish sherry
⅓ cup slivered almonds
Salt and freshly ground black pepper to taste
½ cup Chicken Stock (see Index), or as needed

1. Melt the butter in a large skillet over medium heat. Add the shallots and sauté until they are limp but not brown.

2. Add the ham, parsley, thyme, and bread crumbs. Mix well. Add the egg, Madeira or sherry, and almonds.

3. Mix thoroughly and taste for seasoning. Add just enough chicken broth to make a moist dressing.

Makes about 3 cups

Almond Stuffing may be made a day ahead. It is delicious with chicken or pheasant, too.

HOW TO POACH A WHOLE CHICKEN OR CAPON

1. Rinse and clean the chicken well, giving special attention to the cavity.

2. Place the chicken in a kettle or an enamel dutch oven that is not overly large. The chicken should fit snugly. Cover the bird with part cold water and, for a richer stock and bird, part cold, fat-free chicken stock using as much stock as you can spare. Add 2 ribs of celery cut into pieces, 1 small onion, 1 bay leaf, several sprigs of parsley, a pinch of dried thyme, and plenty of freshly ground white pepper. Taste the stock for salt, then add salt accordingly. It must be salted very lightly.

3. Cover the kettle, leaving the lid a bit ajar, and bring the liquid to a boil. Reduce the heat and simmer until the chicken is tender. The cooking time will vary with the size of the chicken, but it should take about 35 to 40 minutes. Do not overcook (this makes the chicken dry).

4. Uncover the chicken and leave it in the stock until it cools. Then remove the meat from the carcass. Cover well and refrigerate until ready to use. Strain the stock, cool it, discard the fat, and store it in the refrigerator or freezer.

HOW TO ROAST A PERFECT TURKEY

*O*ur national harvest day, as every schoolchild knows, was first consecrated in the autumn of 1621 by the Pilgrim fathers at Plymouth, Massachusetts.

The Pilgrim historians did not leave us a menu of that first feast of Thanksgiving, but the writings indicate that the provisions were plentiful. "Turkey abounds," wrote one naturalist. There was game of many sorts—venison, quail, partridge; foods from the sea in unimaginable quantities; but the turkey was crowned king of their bounty. It remains so to this day.

The bronze bird with chestnut tail bands is a native of our own North America. Thanksgiving is our day. It is a time set aside for rest, feasting, and fellowship. It belongs to all of us—north, south, east, and west. It is American Heritage Day.

1 fresh turkey hen, 12 to 14 pounds
½ lemon
¾ cup (1½ sticks) unsalted butter, at room temperature
2 teaspoons salt
1 teaspoon freshly ground white pepper
1½ tablespoons all-purpose flour
3 cups Chicken Stock (see Index)
1 teaspoon chopped fresh chervil
Salt and freshly ground white pepper to taste

1. Preheat the oven to 425°F.

2. Rinse and clean the turkey well. Dry with paper towels and rub the entire cavity with the lemon.

3. Blend 6 tablespoons of the butter with the salt and pepper. Rub the outside of the turkey thoroughly with the butter.

4. Place the turkey, breast side up, on a rack in a fairly shallow flameproof roasting pan. Place it in the oven and roast until golden brown, 30 to 35 minutes. Baste the turkey again with the pan juices and rub on 2 tablespoons butter.

5. Turn the turkey gently onto one side. Brush again with butter. Lower the heat to 325°F. Continue to cook the turkey for 1 hour, basting it thoroughly again with the pan juices and butter after 30 minutes.

6. When the one side of the turkey has browned, turn it gently onto the other side and brush with butter. Continue to cook, basting it thoroughly after 30 minutes, until golden brown, 1 hour.

7. When the second side has browned, turn the turkey onto its back, breast side up. The turkey will have cooked 2½ hours and should be tested for doneness. If a quick-reading meat thermometer registers 180°F when inserted into the fleshy part of the leg, the turkey is done. You can also test for doneness by inserting a skewer into the leg. If the juices run clear, the bird should be cooked. To make sure, twist one of the turkey legs. If it moves easily in its socket, the turkey is done. If the turkey isn't fully cooked, continue roasting and basting breast side up and check again in 20 minutes.

8. Remove the turkey from the pan to a carving board and allow it to rest before carving, 15 to 20 minutes.

9. Meanwhile, prepare the gravy: Discard all but ¼ cup fat from the pan. Place the pan over low heat, add the flour, and blend thoroughly. Gradually stir in the stock. Continue to stir as the gravy comes to a simmer and thickens. Be sure to scrape up the crusty bits from the bottom of the pan. Season with the chervil, and salt and white pepper to taste. Continue simmering for 10 minutes. Pour the gravy into a sauceboat and keep warm while you carve the turkey.

Serves 6 to 8

PERFECT ROAST TURKEY WITH DRESSING

Stuffed turkey takes slightly longer to cook than unstuffed. Allow at least 3 hours for a 12- to 14-pound bird.

Chesapeake Oyster or Kentucky Cornbread Dressing (recipes follow)
1 fresh turkey hen, 12 to 14 pounds
½ lemon
¾ cup (1½ sticks) unsalted butter, at room temperature

2 teaspoons salt
1 teaspoon freshly ground white pepper
1½ tablespoons all-purpose flour
3 cups Chicken Stock (see Index)
1 teaspoon chopped fresh chervil
Salt and freshly ground white pepper to taste

1. Preheat the oven to 350°F.

2. Prepare your choice of dressing and set aside.

3. Rinse and clean the turkey well. Dry with paper towels and rub the cavity with the lemon.

4. Stuff the bird lightly with the prepared stuffing. (The stuffing must remain loose, as it expands in baking.) Truss the opening of the turkey closed with skewers or by sewing it with twine. Tie the legs firmly together.

5. Blend 6 tablespoons of the butter with the salt and white pepper. Rub the turkey thoroughly with the butter.

6. Set the turkey breast side down on a rack in a shallow flameproof roasting pan and roast for 1 hour.

7. Remove the pan from the oven, turn the turkey on one side, and rub the exposed side with 2 tablespoons of the butter. Return the turkey to the oven and baste often with the pan juices for 1 hour more.

8. When one side has browned, carefully turn it onto the other side and brush with 2 more tablespoons butter. Cook, basting often, for 1 hour.

9. Remove the turkey from the oven. Turn it on its back. Rub the breast with the last 2 tablespoons butter. Continue to roast the turkey, another 15 minutes, then test for doneness. If a quick-reading meat thermometer registers 180°F when inserted into the fleshy part of the leg, the turkey is done. You can also test for doneness by inserting a skewer into the leg. If the juices run clear, the bird should be cooked. To make sure, twist one of the turkey legs. If it moves easily in its socket, the turkey is done. If the turkey isn't fully cooked, continue roasting and basting breast side up. Check again in 20 minutes.

10. Remove the turkey from the pan to a carving board to rest 15 minutes before carving.

11. Meanwhile, make the gravy with the remaining ingredients (see How to Roast a Perfect Turkey, step 9, page 167).

Serves 8 to 10

CHESAPEAKE OYSTER DRESSING

*T*his is a favorite dressing for the Thanksgiving turkey in Virginia, Maryland, and Washington, D.C. The bountiful board is often laid with a turkey on one end and a Smithfield ham on the other! Bountiful and delicious indeed!

---

1 pound white homemade-style bread,
*   approximately (see step 1)*
1 cup (2 sticks) unsalted butter, melted
1 cup chopped onions
1 cup chopped celery
1 dozen large oysters or 1 pint small oysters
1 cup fine fresh bread crumbs
2 tablespoons chopped fresh parsley
1 teaspoon dried thyme
Salt and freshly ground black pepper to taste

---

1. Make 7 cups dried bread cubes: Cut the bread into cubes or tear it into small pieces. Put the bread on a baking sheet and allow it to dry out overnight, or dry it in a 225°F oven for 1 hour. Preheat the oven to 325°F and lightly brown the bread cubes, 15 to 20 minutes.

2. Melt half the butter in a large heavy saucepan or skillet. Add the onions and celery and sauté over medium heat until tender, 20 minutes. Do not allow them to get too soft or brown.

3. Drain the oysters. Add the remaining butter to the bread crumbs, blend well, and roll the oysters individually in the crumbs.

4. Add the bread cubes to the onion and celery. Add the parsley, thyme, and oysters and toss lightly with a fork. Season to taste with salt and pepper and stuff the turkey.

Makes about 8 cups

VARIATIONS: Roll the oysters in the crumbs and sauté them in 2 tablespoons butter until light brown, then add them to the dressing. This makes a richer dressing than if the oysters are added without sautéing.

In Step 4, add 1 or 2 eggs, 1 teaspoon baking powder, and ¼ cup Chicken Stock (see Index), and bake in a casserole in a preheated 375°F oven until golden brown, 20 to 25 minutes. Serve alongside the turkey.

🦉 Rolling the oysters in crumbs keeps the stuffing from getting sodden and heavy, as it can when plain oysters are added.

KENTUCKY CORNBREAD DRESSING

*T*his is a traditional dressing for turkey and chicken in Kentucky and all the South. In days gone by, crumbled sage was used—and there are many who use it still—but marjoram and thyme are more delicious in my opinion. A good dressing depends largely on the judgment of the cook—it is like playing a musical score.

CORNBREAD

2½ cups white cornmeal
1¼ teaspoons salt
1 teaspoon sugar
3 eggs
1¼ cups milk or buttermilk, at room
  temperature
4 teaspoons baking powder
4 tablespoons (½ stick) butter, melted

STUFFING

8 tablespoons (1 stick) butter, melted
⅓ cup water
1 cup chopped onions
1½ cups chopped celery
1 cup toasted bread crumbs
1½ teaspoons dried marjoram
½ teaspoon dried thyme
1½ teaspoons baking powder
5 or 6 eggs
Salt and freshly ground black pepper to taste
Rich Chicken Stock, if needed (see Index)

---

1. Make the cornbread: Preheat the oven to 425°F.
2. Measure the cornmeal into a large bowl. Add the salt, sugar, eggs, and milk or buttermilk, and beat thoroughly by hand.

Add the baking powder and melted butter and beat again.
3. Pour the mixture into a greased shallow baking dish (1½-quart size) or large skillet, and bake until golden brown, 30 to 35 minutes. Cool, and crumble rather fine.
4. Make the stuffing: Heat 4 tablespoons of the butter and the water in a large skillet, add the onions and celery, and sauté over medium heat until the vegetables have absorbed the butter and the water has

---

CHECK POINTS FOR ROASTING AND KEEPING A PERFECT TURKEY

- Turkeys and other fowl must be cooked in one continuous cooking period or the meat will toughen.
- The turkey is roasted on its side so the juices will flow to the breast. The turkey could be turned breast side down after browning, but the bird will not be as beautiful. The skin becomes moist and is likely to break. The most delicious turkey is basted with butter and by you—not self-basting.
- Dipping a clean piece of cheesecloth into the pan juices or melted butter and laying it over the turkey is also very helpful in achieving a moist bird. When the cloth dries out, simply dip it again into the pan juices or butter, then lay it over the turkey, or use a basting bulb. Repeat this several times.
- A turkey roasted with stuffing will not keep as well as a turkey roasted without stuffing. (But stuffing seems to help ensure a more moist bird.) Removing the remaining stuffing after the turkey has been served does not help. Small particles of the dressing are left in the cavity, and they have a tendency to sour quickly. Do not keep a turkey that was cooked with stuffing over 2 to 3 days in the refrigerator. Freeze it whole or in slices or chunks.
- It is possible to roast a turkey in a tent of foil with plenty of air pockets, but any bird cooked in such a tight enclosure will have a steam-table flavor. Who wants that? To allow the turkey to cool in the foil is to court spoilage. Only use foil if the turkey is browning too quickly.
- Allow any fowl or broth to cool before placing it in the refrigerator. Never, never cover warm fowl, broth, or gravy before it has cooled.

boiled away. Do not allow the vegetables to brown the least bit.

   5. Combine the crumbled cornbread and the bread crumbs with the vegetables. Add the remaining butter and the marjoram, thyme, and baking powder. Mix well with a fork (not a spoon, to help keep the stuffing loose).

   6. Add 5 eggs, and salt and pepper to taste. Mix thoroughly again with a fork. If the stuffing is too dry, add a sixth egg or some chicken stock.

   7. Spoon the dressing loosely into the cavity of a small turkey or a hen or capon, and roast. If there is dressing left over, moisten it with some chicken stock and bake, uncovered, in a shallow baking dish in a 425°F oven until golden brown.

   Makes 5 cups

VARIATIONS: Add 1 pound cooked chestnuts or ½ pound crumbled cooked sausage just before dressing the bird.

   Roll ½ to 1 pint well-drained oysters in toasted bread crumbs and add them to the dressing.

   The cornbread can be made ahead and frozen if necessary.

   The dressing should not be overly moist as it will pick up succulence from the bird.

   The baking powder is added to the dressing to make it lighter in texture. A superb dressing is never sodden or heavy.

SLICED BREAST OF TURKEY WITH ASPARAGUS AND RED BELL PEPPER

*I*f I lived in France, I would slice a luscious black truffle into this dish—but living in the southern U.S., we use the red bell peppers in the fall and pimentos in the winter. Simple enough, but good.

   Serve with an avocado and tomato salad or a very simple green salad with vinaigrette.

2 cups freshly cooked rice, seasoned with 2 teaspoons butter, and salt and cayenne pepper to taste
2½ pounds cooked turkey breast, thinly sliced
1½ pounds freshly cooked asparagus
2 medium red bell peppers, cored, seeded, and slivered, or 1 jar (4 ounces) pimentos, slivered
4 tablespoons (½ stick) unsalted butter
3 tablespoons all-purpose flour
2 cups Rich Chicken Stock (see Index)
1 cup heavy or whipping cream
Salt to taste
Cayenne pepper to taste
1 cup freshly grated aged Swiss, imported Gruyère, or Parmesan cheese

   1. Line the bottom of a shallow baking dish, or 6 individual ramekins, with the rice. Lay the slices of turkey over the rice, then cover the turkey with the asparagus. Sprinkle with the slices of red bell pepper or pimento.

   2. Melt the butter in a heavy saucepan over medium-low heat. Add the flour and blend well. Stir until smooth and then gradually whisk in the stock. Simmer until the raw flavor of the flour is gone and the sauce has thickened, 5 minutes. Add the cream, and salt and cayenne to taste. Blend in half of the cheese.

   3. Spoon the sauce over the turkey and vegetables. (This can be done hours ahead; cover, and refrigerate.)

4. About 30 minutes before serving, preheat the oven to 375°F.

5. Sprinkle the remaining cheese over the sauce. Place the dish in the oven and bake until it is bubbly hot and lightly browned.

Serves 6

🦉 In the winter broccoli can be used instead of asparagus. Broccoli is not delicate and tastes better in winter.

The Thanksgiving gathering—the traditional meal and the traditional pose before feasting.

PONTCHARTRAIN TURKEY WITH OYSTERS AND MUSHROOMS

*T*his is an excellent way to use the dark meat of the turkey. Very delicious and appealing with the oysters and mushrooms. Serve on wild rice, on grilled Cornmeal Melba Toast, on split and toasted Cornmeal Croissants garnished with watercress, or serve in shallow ramekins sprinkled with chopped fresh parsley. Accompany with pickled walnuts or Fabulous Walnut Butter.

½ pint oysters
5 tablespoons butter
1 ½ cups sliced mushrooms
1 ½ tablespoons all-purpose flour
¼ cup Chicken Stock (see Index), or as needed
½ cup heavy or whipping cream
1 ½ cups cubed cooked dark meat of turkey (see Owl)
Salt and freshly ground black pepper to taste

1. Drain the oysters and reserve the liquor. Melt 1 tablespoon of the butter in a small saucepan. Add the oysters and cook just until the edges begin to curl, 2 minutes. Set aside.

2. Melt 1 ½ tablespoons of the butter in a medium skillet over medium-high heat. Add the mushrooms and sauté until they absorb some of the butter, but are still crisp, 2 to 3 minutes. (They must not brown.) Set aside.

3. Melt the remaining butter in a saucepan. Add the flour and blend, stirring until it is smooth. Combine the oyster liquor and enough chicken stock to make ½ cup. Whisk it into the butter mixture. Whisk in the cream and simmer until the sauce thickens, 2 to 3 minutes.

VEGETABLES THAT ARE GOOD WITH POULTRY

Artichokes	Lima beans
Asparagus	Mushrooms
Broccoli	Onions
Carrots	Peas
Cauliflower	Potatoes, white
Celeriac	and sweet
Celery	Tomatoes
Eggplant	Yellow squash
Green beans	Zucchini

A woodcut depicting a fussy cook choosing just the right turkey, from Frank Leslie's Illustrated Newspaper, *1885.*

4. Add the oysters, turkey, and mushrooms to the sauce. Season with salt and pepper to taste. Simmer until heated through, 5 minutes.

Serves 3 to 4

VARIATIONS: It is delicious and most appealing to add 3 dried black Chinese mushrooms that have been revived in water, slivered, and cooked with the sauce. That touch of black! And the flavor!

It is not amiss to add 1 tablespoon of medium dry sherry or Madeira to the sauce and allow it to cook a minute or so to mellow.

One pound of cooked turkey removed from the bone equals 3 cups cubed.

ABOUT GAME

The great charm of game is its exquisite natural flavor. Wild game and birds are very delicious roasted or braised quite plainly, as they often are in the country. I have heard huntsmen grow lyrical when they retell the stories of grilling their birds at dusk by a campfire. There are natural embellishments, however, that have a worthy place in cooking game—wines and herbs, for instance.

Thyme, parsley, and red wine blend with the more assertive flavors of duck and venison. White wine lends a more delicate touch and is better used with the milder birds. Rosemary is a valuable herb with most game, and it is especially good when fruit is involved. When fruit is used with the stuffing, the menu as a whole should be in harmony and not confuse the palate with strange combinations. "Be simple" is the best advice I know.

QUAIL IN GRAPE LEAVES

The fruit trees and the hawthorne in my backyard have been a gathering place for quail lately. I catch them pecking around near my herb garden. I think they, too, like the fragrance of the herbs. Who can blame them? The birds are beguiling, but I cannot help but think how delicious they would be roasted with butter and served on toast. A cook's mind....

12 grape leaves (packed in brine)
12 quail, ready to cook
10 tablespoons (1 ¼ sticks) butter, at room
    temperature
Salt and freshly ground black pepper to taste
36 dried juniper berries
12 thin slices smoked bacon
1 cup dry white wine
1 cup halved seedless green grapes
12 slices toast

1. Preheat the oven to 400°F.

2. Rinse the grape leaves and pat them dry with paper towels.

3. Rinse the quail thoroughly and dry them well with paper towels. Rub the quail well with the butter, and sprinkle with salt and pepper to taste. Put 3 juniper berries in the cavity of each quail. Place a slice of bacon over each quail, and wrap the bird in a grape leaf. Secure the leaf with string.

4. Place the quail in a shallow flame-proof baking pan and cook in the oven for 25 to 30 minutes. Reduce the heat to 325°F. Cover and continue to cook and baste until the birds are tender, 15 minutes more. Do not overcook.

5. When the birds are tender, remove them to a hot platter. Remove the string and keep warm. Skim the fat from the pan juices and add the wine. Cook for 5 minutes over high heat, then reduce the heat, add the grapes, and just heat them through.

6. Serve the quail wrapped in their grape leaves on grilled toast, and pour the sauce over the quail. Serve with wild rice.

Serves 6

Quail, drawn by the 18th-century naturalist Mark Catesby.

Grape leaves may be found in groceries that specialize in gourmet products. They come packed in brine in glass bottles.

To test for doneness, insert a skewer into the leg of just one bird, rather than sticking all the birds, which will cause them to become dry. If the juices run clear, the bird is done.

ROAST QUAIL WITH COUNTRY HAM

*I*f you are searching for one of the South's most elegant and traditional winter dishes, go no further.

Big brother returns from the hunt, in an 18th-century painting attributed to Payne Limner.

◆

8 quail, ready to cook
Salt and freshly ground black pepper to taste
16 slices salt pork or bacon
8 pieces toast
8 thin slices baked country ham
Watercress sprigs, for garnish

◆

1. Preheat the oven to 375°F.
2. Rinse the quail thoroughly and dry them well with paper towels. Sprinkle them with salt and pepper to taste. Lay the birds in a baking pan, and cover each one with salt pork or bacon.
3. Place the pan in the oven and bake until tender, 25 to 30 minutes. A few minutes before the birds are done, remove the salt pork so the breasts will brown.
4. Place a slice of ham on each piece of toast, then put a quail on each slice of ham. Serve garnished with watercress.
   Serves 4

◆◆

DINNER AT
603 BLANKENBAKER LANE

Charleston Cream of Oyster Soup

Chilled White Wine

◆

Roast Quail with Country Ham

Fabulous Spiced Green Seedless Grapes

Carolina Grits Soufflé

Monticello Rolls

◆

Bibb Lettuce Salad

◆

Frozen Lemon Soufflé

Coffee

MISSISSIPPI FLYWAY DUCK

◆◆

*T*he duck is a web-footed water bird of many varieties, of which the mallard is undoubtedly one of the best for eating. The wild mallard feeds on seeds and marsh plants, which gives it a clear flavor—gamey, of course, but delicious. When the October winds grow cold in Canada, the ducks fly south to the Mississippi Valley to get warm. The hunters are in paradise—and the good cooks can hardly wait. Roasted on a spit, over mesquite, or in a hot oven, and stuffed with apples, rice, and such good things, it is the greatest kind of fun. You'll see.

◆

4 wild canvasback or mallard ducks, 2½ to 3 pounds each, ready to cook
2 lemons, cut in half
Salt and freshly ground black pepper to taste
1 teaspoon dried thyme
2 tablespoons chopped fresh parsley
3 ribs celery, coarsely chopped

2 onions, coarsely chopped
4 large tart apples, cut into eighths, cored
6 tablespoons butter (¾ stick), at room temperature
½ cup Chicken or Veal Stock (see Index)

◆

1. Preheat the oven to 350°F.

2. Rinse the ducks thoroughly and dry them well with paper towels. Rub the cavities with the lemon and sprinkle them with salt and pepper, thyme, and parsley.

3. Toss together the celery, onions, and apples in a large bowl. Stuff the mixture loosely into the cavities of the ducks. Truss the ducks by closing the opening in each with skewers or sewing with string.

4. Rub the ducks thoroughly with the butter and place them on their sides, with space between them, in a low-sided flameproof baking pan. Cook for 20 minutes, then baste them and turn them to the other side. Baste often and continue to cook, turning the birds, for another 20 minutes.

5. Lay the ducks on their backs (to brown the breasts) and continue to cook, basting but not turning, for 30 minutes. The ducks should be tender in 1 to 1½ hours for well-done duck. (Test for doneness by inserting a skewer in the duck's thigh. If the juices run clear, it is done.)

6. Remove the ducks from the pan, discard the strings and skewers, and keep warm.

7. Skim off all the fat from the pan

Man and dog, quietly looking out for duck in South Carolina.

juices. Add the stock and scrape to loosen the brown crusty bits from the bottom of the pan. Reduce over medium-high heat to make a pan gravy. Season with salt and pepper if needed.

8. Remove the dressing from the ducks and serve alongside with a sauceboat of pan gravy.

Serves 8

VARIATION: *Wine-Basted Flyway Duck:* Follow the directions for Mississippi Flyway Duck, but baste the ducks with 1 cup of a full-bodied red wine along with the butter. Just before serving, flame the hot ducks with ⅓ cup brandy or cognac. This creates a crisper skin, which is most delicious.

BRAISED FLORIDA BLUE-WINGED TEAL

*W*hen the air in the far north gets frosty in late August and September, the blue-winged teal ducks head for Florida and Louisiana. The teals—the bluewing and its cousin the greenwing—are smaller than mallards, but are truly delicious. They have a great affinity for oranges, and good cooks have a great affinity for duck.

3 wild blue-winged teal, ready to cook
1 lemon, cut in half
3 navel oranges or tangelos
Salt and freshly ground black pepper to taste
8 tablespoons (1 stick) butter, at room temperature
1 cup dry white wine
2 cups Stock (recipe follows)
⅓ cup sugar

3 tablespoons water
¼ cup Cointreau, Grand Marnier, brandy, cognac, or Curaçao
3 whole cloves
2 tablespoons cornstarch
⅓ cup cold water or dry white wine
Watercress sprigs, for garnish

1. Preheat the oven to 450°F.

2. Rinse the ducks thoroughly, and dry them well with paper towels. Leave the ducks whole or cut them in half. Rub the cavities with the lemon. Cut three ½-inch slivers of peel (no white pith) from one of the oranges and place one in each cavity (or cut the slivers in half and place them under the halves when you put them in the pan). Season the ducks with salt and pepper, and brush them thoroughly with 4 tablespoons of the butter.

3. Place the ducks in a heavy shallow roasting pan and roast until golden brown, about 25 minutes. Reduce the heat to 350°F.

4. Pour the white wine over the ducks, add the stock, and cover loosely with foil. Cook, basting often, for another 45 minutes or so. (The time varies with the birds; halves will cook more quickly than whole birds.)

5. While the ducks braise, make the caramel: Combine the sugar and water in a skillet and allow it to cook over medium heat to a golden brown, not overly brown, 2 minutes. (If it turns black, start over.) Remove from the heat and add the liqueur. Set aside.

6. Remove the remaining peel (without any of the white) from the oranges and slice it into toothpick-size slivers. Drop them into boiling water and cook no more than 1½ minutes. Drain, and set aside.

7. With a sharp knife, remove all the white pith from the oranges, and cut the fruit into sections. Set aside.

8. Remove the ducks from the pan. Reduce the oven heat to 300°F. Strain the pan juices into a saucepan. Put the ducks back into the pan, cover loosely with the foil, and return to the oven to keep warm.

9. Skim the fat from the pan juices. Add the cloves and reduce over high heat, about 8 minutes. Add the caramel.

10. Mix the cornstarch with ⅓ cup cold water or wine and add it to the sauce. Add the orange peel and cook over medium heat until the sauce thickens. Taste for seasoning, and add salt if needed. Blend in the remaining butter. Skim out the cloves.

11. Ring a warmed deep platter with the orange sections. Place the ducks in the center, and spoon the boiling sauce over the ducks. Garnish with clusters of watercress tucked under the orange sections.

Serves 2

Mallard, canvasback, green-winged teal, or domesticated duck or duckling can be cooked this same way.

STOCK

*T*his stock should be made ahead of time.

---

2 pounds bony chicken pieces, such as backs and wings, or veal bones
8 cups water
2 onions, roughly sliced
3 ribs celery, roughly broken
2 carrots, roughly sliced
1 parsnip, peeled and sliced
1 bay leaf
2 or 3 sprigs parsley
2 whole cloves
½ teaspoon dried thyme
6 white peppercorns
Salt

Cover the meat and bones with the water in a large saucepan. Add the onions, celery, carrots, parsnip, bay leaf, parsley, cloves, thyme, and peppercorns. Bring to a boil, reduce the heat, and simmer, uncovered, until the liquid is reduced to about 2½ cups, about 1 hour. Add salt to taste. Strain, cool, and refrigerate.

A HUNT DINNER PARTY AT IDLEWILD

Fabulous Mushroom Soup

◆

Roast Green-Winged Teal with Wild Rice Dressing

◆

Watercress and Walnut Salad

◆

Frozen Cointreau Soufflé

ROAST GREEN-WINGED TEAL WITH WILD RICE

*T*here are no ducks more delicious than the blue- and green-winged teal, but they are small, so the seasonings and stuffings must be proportioned to the size of the game on hand.

2 wild green-winged teal, ready to cook
1 lemon, cut in half
Wild Rice Dressing (recipe follows)
Salt and freshly ground black pepper to taste
1½ cups Chicken Stock (see Index)
1 pinch dried thyme

1. Preheat the oven to 375°F.
2. Rinse the ducks thoroughly and dry them well with paper towels. Rub the cavities with the lemon, and stuff loosely with Wild Rice Dressing. Truss the ducks by closing the opening in each with skewers or sewing with string. Season with salt and pepper.
3. Place the ducks on a rack in a shallow flameproof baking pan and cook for 50 to 60 minutes for well-done duck. Reduce the oven to 300°F.
4. Remove the ducks to a hot platter, cover loosely with foil, and return to the oven to keep warm. Add the stock and thyme to the pan and place over medium-high heat. Loosen the brown crusty bits from the bottom and reduce until the sauce is well seasoned, 2 minutes. Strain, and serve over slices of the duck with the stuffing. You'll have plenty of additional stuffing to serve on the side.

Serves 2

This recipe is also good with mallards, canvasbacks, and domestic ducks. Mallards are often large, so you will have to proportion the amount of stuffing to the bird.

WILD RICE DRESSING

*W*ild rice dressing is especially compatible with most all wild game, including duck, rabbit, and guinea hen, but try it as a side dish for chicken and other poultry, too.

1 cup wild rice
Salt and freshly ground black pepper to taste
2 tablespoons water
6 tablespoons unsalted butter
3 shallots or 1 medium onion, chopped
1 pound mushrooms, sliced

1. Rinse the rice thoroughly under running water. Bring a large pot of salted water to the boil, add the rice, and boil until tender but still a little chewy, about 45 minutes. Drain at once, and keep warm.
2. In the meantime, heat 2 tablespoons water and 2 tablespoons of the butter in a skillet, add the shallots or onion, and sauté until the shallots are limp. Do not allow them to brown or sizzle. Add the mushrooms and 3 tablespoons of the butter, and simmer until the mushrooms give off their juice, 2 to 3 minutes.
3. Add the mushroom mixture to the wild rice. Season with salt and pepper, add the remaining butter, and toss well with a fork.

Makes about 5 cups

VARIATION: Dust ¼ pound chicken livers with flour and a pinch of thyme, then sauté them in butter until well done. Coarsely chop the livers and toss them into the cooked wild rice.

GRILLED DUCK WITH KUMQUATS

*T*his is not an old method of cooking duck, to my knowledge, but one that has evolved from the interest in the Chinese way of using fruit. Preserved kumquats are available in gourmet shops, but I have made my own and they are best.

Duck hunting off Fox's Island, Virginia, as the sun begins to rise.

1 cup Preserved Kumquats, homemade (see Index) or purchased
2 teaspoons chopped fresh ginger
1½ teaspoons green peppercorns (dried or in brine, drained)
2 tablespoons soy sauce
2 domestic ducks, 2½ to 3 pounds each, ready to cook, split
1 lemon, cut in half
Salt to taste
Watercress sprigs, for garnish

1. Prepare the grill with an oiled rack placed 6 inches above medium-hot hickory chips.

2. Prepare the kumquats: Strain the syrup into a small saucepan, add the ginger, and cook over medium heat to reduce, 3 to 5 minutes. Add the peppercorns and soy sauce. Set aside. Meanwhile, heat the kumquats in a separate pan over very low heat. Cover and set aside to keep warm.

3. Rub the cavities of the ducks with the lemon and sprinkle with salt. Grill the ducks, turning every 10 minutes, for about 1 hour for medium-rare, 1 to 1½ hours for well done. Prick the skin often so the fat will run out and the skin will become crisp. Glaze the duck skin with the kumquat syrup a few minutes before you remove them from the grill.

4. Remove the ducks to a warm platter. Garnish the platter with the kumquats and clusters of watercress. If any syrup is left, spoon it over the ducks.

Serves 4

You can also prepare these ducks in a preheated 375°F oven. Roast on a rack set in a roasting pan. They will cook in the same amount of time as when prepared on the grill. Turn up the heat to 400°F a few minutes before removing them from the oven. This will help crisp up the skin.

DOVE OR PARTRIDGE WITH ORANGES AND GRAPES

*T*his is a very old classical way of preparing partridge or dove. The dish is especially delicious and beautiful with small red seedless grapes. When the grapes are unavailable, I just use the oranges. The vegetables are added to lend moistness to the birds and to help make a delicious sauce. Serve with wild or brown rice and a green salad.

4 partridges or 8 doves, ready to cook
Salt and freshly ground black pepper to taste
1 carrot, peeled and coarsely chopped
2 ribs celery, coarsely chopped
2 onions, coarsely chopped
4 sprigs parsley
¾ cup (1½ sticks) butter, at room temperature
1 teaspoon dried thyme
8 slices smoked bacon (country cured if possible)
½ cup plus 4 tablespoons orange juice
½ cup fat-free Rich Chicken Stock (see Index)
2 tablespoons brandy or Grand Marnier
4 navel oranges, sectioned, for garnish
2 cups halved seedless red or green grapes, for
    garnish
Watercress sprigs, for garnish

The Commercial Café in Richmond, Virginia, advertised the day's offerings.

1. Preheat the oven to 425°F.

2. Rinse the birds thoroughly. Dry well with paper towels, and season inside and out with salt and pepper.

3. Scatter the chopped vegetables and the parsley over the bottom of a dutch oven or shallow flameproof casserole. Lay the birds on top of the vegetables. Brush them generously with the butter, and sprinkle them with the thyme. Lay the bacon over the breasts.

4. Place the casserole in the oven and bake, uncovered, until the bacon has browned lightly, 15 to 20 minutes. Reduce the heat to 350°F, cover loosely with foil, and continue to cook until the birds are tender when pierced with a skewer, 40 to 45 minutes in all. (If at any time the vegetables are cooking too dry, add a tablespoon or so of stock to prevent their burning.)

5. Remove the birds from the casserole and keep warm. Save the bacon for garnish, or discard it. Lift the vegetables from the pan with a slotted spoon and discard them.

6. Add ½ cup of orange juice, the stock, and brandy to the pan juices. Boil a few minutes over medium-high heat and season to taste with salt and pepper.

7. Put the orange sections in a small saucepan with 2 tablespoons of the orange juice and barely heat them. In a separate pan, barely heat the grapes in the remaining 2 tablespoons of orange juice. (The fruit must not be actually cooked, but it should not be cold.)

8. Place the birds on a warm platter. Place the orange sections at one end and the grapes at the other. Tuck sprigs of watercress under the fruit. Pour some of the hot sauce over the birds, and pass any additional sauce in a sauceboat. Serve at once.

Serves 4

BRAISED GUINEA HEN
WITH SAUSAGE DRESSING

❖❖❖

*G*uinea hens are well suited to several dressings, including Chestnut Dressing at holiday time. This classic sausage dressing is especially welcome in cold weather. We are very partial to smoked ham and bacon in the South, but salt pork can be used—and game does need barding to help keep it moist.

6 slices homemade-type white bread
2 guinea hens, about 2 pounds each, ready to
   cook
½ pound bulk pork sausage
1 egg
2 tablespoons chopped fresh parsley
¼ teaspoon dried thyme
¼ teaspoon dried marjoram
Salt and freshly ground black pepper to taste
6 slices smoked bacon or salt pork
2 carrots, peeled and chopped
1 rib celery, chopped
1 small onion, chopped
1½ cups Chicken Stock (see Index)
3 tablespoons butter, at room temperature

AN OCTOBER DINNER AT FOX HARBOR

Chicken Liver Pâté with Tarragon

◆

Braised Guinea Hen with Sausage Stuffing

Brussels Sprouts

◆

Bibb Lettuce Salad

◆

Walnut and Apple Crisp with Coriander

Coffee   Tea

1. Preheat the oven to 300°F.

2. Cube or crumble the bread with your hands and place it on a baking sheet. Bake it in the oven until very dry and lightly toasted, 20 to 30 minutes. Remove the baking sheet and increase the heat to 375°F. Set the bread aside.

3. Rinse the hens thoroughly and dry them well with paper towels. Set aside.

4. Sauté the sausage in a heavy skillet over medium-high heat until thoroughly cooked and light brown, 10 minutes. Break it into bits with a fork as it cooks.

5. In a large bowl, toss the bread cubes, sausage, egg, parsley, thyme, marjoram, and salt and pepper to taste. Mix carefully with a fork.

6. Stuff the hens loosely, close them with skewers, and tie the legs and wings with string. Place them in a shallow flame-proof baking pan, breast side up. Cover them with the bacon or salt pork. Add the carrots, celery, and onion to the pan along with 1 cup of the chicken stock.

7. Place the pan in the oven and bake for 30 to 35 minutes. Remove the bacon or salt pork from the hens and brush the breasts with the butter. Continue basting the birds often for another 20 to 25 minutes. When a skewer goes into the thighs easily and the juices run clear, the birds are done.

8. Remove the hens to a hot platter and keep warm. Add the remaining stock to the pan and stir well. Place over medium-high heat and reduce for 6 to 8 minutes. Strain the sauce, discard the vegetables, and season to taste. Remove the strings and skewers from the birds.

9. Serve the hens with the dressing and sauce alongside.

Serves 4 to 6

MOTHER'S KENTUCKY PHEASANT

*W*ild pheasant and quail are two of the most delicate and delicious morsels on earth. If you have a huntsman in the family, lucky you, because the unique flavor of the birds that feed on nature's larder in the fields and woods is far superior to that of the cultivated birds. The preparations, however, are the same. Just don't overcook.

2 plump pheasant hens, 2½ pounds each,
    ready to cook
Salt and freshly ground black pepper to taste
1 cup plus 2 tablespoons all-purpose flour
1 teaspoon salt
3 tablespoons butter, at room temperature
Vegetable oil, solid vegetable shortening, or lard
    (see step 3)
1 cup milk
½ cup heavy or whipping cream

1. Cut the pheasants into comfortable eating pieces. Rinse them thoroughly, dry well with paper towels, and sprinkle with salt and pepper.

2. Stir 1 teaspoon salt into 1 cup flour. Roll the pieces of pheasant in the seasoned flour or toss them with the flour in a plastic bag. Before cooking, shake the pieces well to rid them of any excess flour.

3. Heat the butter and the oil, shortening, or lard in a heavy iron skillet. The fat should be about ¾ inch deep. Add the pieces of pheasant, but do not crowd them in the skillet. Cover the pan and allow the pheasant to brown on one side over medium-high heat for 8 to 10 minutes. Shake the pan often so the pieces will sizzle and brown evenly. (Do not allow the fat to smoke.)

4. Uncover the pan, turn the pieces to brown on the other side, and leave the pan uncovered. The pheasant should cook in 18 to 20 minutes, but this varies. Watch the pan closely and regulate the heat so neither the fat nor the birds burn.

5. When the pheasant is golden brown all over and is tender when pierced with a skewer, turn the heat up for a minute or two to make the skin rather crunchy. Then remove the pieces from the skillet and keep warm.

6. Pour off all but 2 to 3 tablespoons of the fat from the skillet. Add 2 tablespoons flour, and stir well to loosen the golden brown bits in the skillet. Add the milk and cream and simmer until the gravy thickens sufficiently, about 4 minutes. Season to taste with salt, and be generous with the pepper.

7. Serve the pheasant with the gravy in a sauceboat.

Serves 4 to 6

This country-style pheasant is cooked very much like chicken, except it is sautéed, which is a gentler technique than frying. Butter is used because it enhances the natural flavor of the birds. The vegetable oil or shortening is added only to reduce the low burning point of the butter. Lard adds good flavor but it cannot be compared to butter in sautéing.

KENTUCKY PHEASANT WITH COUNTRY CURED BACON

If natural country-smoked thick bacon is not available, hold this recipe until it is. The flavor of the bacon is just as important as the pheasant. Chicken, rabbit, quail, and partridge can be prepared this same way. Serve the pheasant just as soon as it is done—it dries out quickly. Quail holds a little better and is wonderful when you eat it cold next day.

A female ring-necked pheasant.

◆

2 plump young pheasants, 2½ pounds each,
    ready to cook
1 cup all-purpose flour
1 teaspoon salt
8 to 10 thick slices country smoked bacon
Solid vegetable shortening or lard (see step 4)
Freshly ground black pepper to taste
Stuffed Poached Apples (see Index), warm

◆

1. Preheat the oven to 425°F.
2. Cut each pheasant into 4 pieces.
Rinse them thoroughly and dry well with
paper towels. Stir the flour and salt together
and dredge the pheasant pieces with the
seasoned flour. Set aside.
3. Lay the slices of bacon in a baking
pan and bake in the oven until fairly crisp,
10 minutes. Drain the bacon on paper
towels.
4. Pour the bacon fat into a large black
iron skillet. Add enough vegetable shortening or lard to bring the depth to about ¾
inch and heat.
5. Shake any excess flour off the
pheasant pieces and sauté, covered, over
medium-high heat for 8 minutes.
6. Remove the cover and continue to
cook until the pieces are golden brown all
over and tender when pierced with a
skewer, about 12 minutes longer. Sprinkle
well with pepper (you probably will not
need extra salt because of the bacon fat).
7. Drain the pheasant on paper towels. Crumble the bacon and use it to garnish
the pheasant. Serve with poached apples.
   Serves 4 to 6

◆◆

A HUNTSMAN'S DINNER PARTY

Charleston Cream of Oyster Soup

◆

Mother's Kentucky Pheasant

Brown Rice

Chopped Buttered Broccoli

◆

Watercress and Walnut Salad

◆

Chocolate Floating Island

ROAST PHEASANT WITH APPLES AND CHESTNUTS

◆◆

*A*gorgeous and festive bird for the holidays or to celebrate the hunter's bag.

◆

2 pounds large chestnuts
2⅔ cups Veal or Chicken Stock (see Index)
Salt to taste
½ cup plus 1 tablespoon sugar
4 tablespoons (½ stick) butter, or more as
    needed
1 large young pheasant, 3 pounds, ready to
    cook
Freshly ground black pepper to taste
9 tart apples, such as Winesap

1 rib celery, broken in half
¼ small onion
½ teaspoon crushed dried rosemary
2 slices salt pork or smoked bacon
⅓ cup dry Madeira or Spanish sherry
Juice of 1 lemon
¾ cup water
Watercress sprigs, for garnish

◆

1. Preheat the oven to 425°F.

2. With a sharp knife, cut a cross or 2 gashes in the flat side of each chestnut. Put the nuts in a baking pan and roast in the oven for 10 minutes. Remove the pan and reduce the heat to 375°F.

3. Cool the chestnuts, then remove the shells and inner brown skin. Put the peeled chestnuts in a saucepan with 2 cups of the stock. Add a pinch of salt, the 1 tablespoon of sugar, and 2 tablespoons of the butter. Cover, bring to a boil, and simmer until tender, 10 to 15 minutes. Drain and set aside.

4. Rinse the pheasant thoroughly and dry it well with paper towels. Season the cavity with salt and pepper. Peel 1 apple and put it and the celery, onion, and rosemary in the cavity. Sew the opening closed and cover the pheasant with the salt pork or bacon. Secure the legs and wings with string.

5. Place the pheasant in a flameproof roasting pan and cook in the oven, basting the bird often with the remaining butter, 30 minutes. Pour the Madeira or sherry into the pan and continue to baste until the pheasant is tender, about 15 minutes more.

6. While the bird is roasting, prepare the apples: Peel and core the remaining apples, and put them in a flameproof baking dish. Combine the lemon juice and water, and pour this over the apples. Cook on top of the stove over low heat or in the 375°F oven, basting the apples often with the lemon water. Add the ½ cup sugar as needed if the apples are too tart. Continue basting until the apples are transparent and tender but not mushy. Sprinkle the tops of the apples with a little sugar and run them under the broiler to glaze a bit. Set aside and keep warm.

7. Remove the pheasant to a warm platter. Discard the salt pork or bacon.

8. Add the remaining stock to the pan and loosen the brown crusty bits from the bottom of the pan over medium-high heat. Taste, and correct the seasonings if needed. Pour the hot sauce over the pheasant, surround it with the chestnuts and apples, and garnish with watercress.

Serves 4

SAUTEED PHEASANT WITH RASPBERRY VINEGAR

◆◆◆

*I*t is well documented that raspberry vinegar was used in colonial Virginia, but it did have sugar added, and I have not been able to find that it was used in salads and with poultry as we use it today. Raspberry vinegar will fool you—and in a glorious way. It sounds as if it would be delicious only with fruits. Not so! If you can't find pheasant, this recipe is excellent with chicken.

1 large plump pheasant hen, 3 pounds, ready to cook
Salt and freshly ground white pepper to taste
10 tablespoons (1¼ sticks) unsalted butter
3 shallots, chopped
¾ cup Raspberry Vinegar (recipe follows)
¼ cup chopped fresh parsley
4 pieces freshly grilled toast
Watercress sprigs, for garnish

1. Cut the pheasant into comfortable eating pieces. Rinse them thoroughly and dry well with paper towels. Season with salt and white pepper.

2. Melt 6 tablespoons of the butter in a heavy skillet. Sauté the pheasant in the butter over medium-low heat until very light gold on both sides, regulating the heat so the butter does not burn, and adding fresh butter as needed. Turn the heat quite

low if necessary. When the pheasant is tender, remove the pieces to a hot platter and keep warm, 25 minutes.

3. Add the shallots and the vinegar to the pan juices, and simmer until the shallots are limp and the vinegar has reduced by half, 5 minutes.

4. Add the remaining butter. Taste for salt—the sauce should be mellow and utterly delicious. Add the chopped parsley and spoon over the pheasant. Serve on grilled toast with clusters of watercress.

Serves 4

RASPBERRY VINEGAR

*R*aspberry vinegar can be found in gourmet shops, but, when raspberries are in season, make your own.

1 pint fresh raspberries
3 cups good-quality red wine vinegar

Steep the raspberries in the vinegar at room temperature for 4 weeks. Strain through dampened cheesecloth. Discard the raspberries. Refrigerate the vinegar for up to 3 weeks.

BRUNSWICK STEW

*W*hen the farmers or hunters brought squirrel and rabbits to our hotel kitchen door, we knew we would have Brunswick Stew next day, and we loved it. Brunswick Stew is a hearty, thick game and vegetable dish, somewhere between a soup and a stew, and eaten with a spoon. It has a touch of red pepper but no Worcestershire sauce. It is not a burgoo. It is believed to have been created first in Brunswick County, Virginia, but it is well known all through the good ham country of the South. The vegetables in a traditional Brunswick stew are tomatoes, onions, celery, carrots, potatoes, lima beans, and corn, with the emphasis on the lima beans and corn. Any delicate game such as squab or pheasant or dove is admissible, but the ham bone is a necessity. If you can only get chicken and ham, you can still have a delicious Brunswick stew. Serve with corn muffins.

1 baked ham bone, from a Virginia or other good-quality country-cured ham if possible
6 quarts water, or as needed
1 stewing hen or 2 fryer chickens, 5 pounds total, split
1 young rabbit, 2½ pounds, ready to cook and cut into 4 pieces
1 small young squirrel, 1½ pounds, ready to cook, cut into 4 pieces
2 bay leaves
1 teaspoon dried thyme or several sprigs fresh
4 sprigs parsley
2 ribs celery, cut in half
2 small onions
Several black peppercorns
4 cups tomatoes, fresh or canned, peeled and chopped
1½ cups chopped peeled carrots

2 cups chopped celery
1½ cups chopped onions
3 large or 4 small mealy potatoes (Idaho or russet), cubed
2 cups lima beans, fresh if possible, or home frozen
3 cups corn, fresh if possible, or frozen
½ crushed dried red chile pepper, or 1 fresh chile pepper, chopped
Salt and freshly ground black pepper to taste

1. Put the ham bone in a large kettle with the water, bring to a boil, reduce the heat, and simmer 1 hour. Let the stock cool down a bit.

2. Rinse the hen or chickens, the rabbit, and the squirrel thoroughly and dry

them well with paper towels. Add the hen or chickens to the kettle. (Use the giblets for another purpose or discard them.) Add the rabbit, squirrel, bay leaves, thyme, parsley, halved celery ribs, whole onions, and the peppercorns. Simmer, uncovered, until the chickens, squirrel, and rabbit are thoroughly tender, 1¾ hours.

3. Remove the ham bone, chickens, squirrel, and rabbit. Cover the meat and set it aside. Strain the stock and discard the seasoning vegetables and herbs. Skim some of the fat from the stock.

4. Add the tomatoes, carrots, chopped celery and onions, the potatoes, lima beans, corn, and red chile pepper. Simmer, uncovered, until all the vegetables are tender, 45 minutes.

5. Bone the chicken, rabbit, and squirrel, and remove any pieces of ham (free of fat) from the ham bone. Return the meat to the kettle. Add more water if needed to

Father, son, hunting dog, and their bounty in Florida around 1900.

make a thick soup. Simmer for 10 to 15 minutes to let the flavors ripen and season with salt and freshly ground pepper.

Serves 15 to 18

🦉 You can, if you wish, refrigerate the stew until the next day. Remove most of the solidified fat, but not all of it. The fat has flavor.

BAKED RABBIT STUFFED WITH KALE OR SPINACH

*T*he goodness of any rabbit dish depends to a great extent upon the rabbit being young and tender and cooked until well done. A rabbit stuffed with kale or spinach is especially good. Either green cooked this way makes a delicious vegetable dish all on its own. Serve baked rabbit with mashed or baked potatoes, Carolina Grits Soufflé, or Lexington Spoonbread.

1 young rabbit, about 2½ pounds, ready to
    cook
½ lemon
Salt and freshly ground black pepper to taste
5 tablespoons butter, or as needed, at room
    temperature
2 tablespoons water
4 shallots or 2 scallions (green onions), chopped
4 slices smoked bacon, chopped
½ pound mushrooms, sliced
½ pound fresh kale or spinach leaves, chopped
1 tablespoon Dijon mustard
2 cups full-bodied dry red wine
½ teaspoon dried thyme or 2 sprigs fresh

1 bay leaf

1. Preheat the oven to 450°F.
2. Rinse the rabbit thoroughly and dry it well with paper towels. Rub the cavity with the lemon. Season the rabbit with salt and pepper inside and out and set it aside.
3. Heat 1½ tablespoons of the butter and 2 tablespoons water in a small saucepan, and sauté half the shallots or all the scallions over medium heat until limp, but do not brown the least bit. Toss into a mixing bowl.

This rabbit hunter from Jefferson County, Florida, has plenty of fine eating ahead of him (1931).

4. Sauté the bacon over medium-high heat until done but not overly crisp. (Reserve the fat.) Drain the bacon on paper towels and then add it to the shallots.

5. Sauté the mushrooms over medium heat in not more than 2 tablespoons of the bacon fat for 2 minutes. Add the mushrooms to the shallots and bacon and toss together with the spinach. Add salt and pepper to taste.

6. Fill the cavity of the rabbit loosely with the stuffing and sew it closed with a needle and thread. Put the rabbit in a shallow, close-fitting baking dish. Blend the remaining butter and the mustard. Brush it thoroughly on all sides of the rabbit.

7. Place the rabbit in the oven. Cook, basting it several times with the pan drippings, and more butter if needed, until it is golden brown, 10 to 15 minutes. Reduce the heat to 375°F.

8. Add the wine, thyme, bay leaf, and the remaining shallots to the pan. Cover, and bake until the rabbit is tender, depending upon the age and size of the rabbit, another 45 minutes to 1 hour. When a skewer slips into the thigh easily, the rabbit is done. A meat thermometer should register 170°F.

9. Remove the rabbit from the sauce and taste the sauce for salt and pepper. Reduce it over high heat if needed, and add a little butter if the flavor is too sharp. Discard the bay leaf.

10. Carve the rabbit and serve it on warm plates with some of the stuffing. Pass the sauce.

Serves 4

RABBIT SIMMERED IN RED WINE AND THYME

*R*abbit cooked in red wine, thyme, and garlic is an earthy, delectable dish— one for a cold autumn or winter night. If you like a heavy fragrance of garlic, then the garlic can be peeled. Serve this dish with new potatoes and crunchy French or Italian bread.

*2 young rabbits, 2 to 2½ pounds each, ready to
    cook*
Salt and freshly ground black pepper to taste
¼ cup good-quality olive oil or unsalted butter
1 cup full-bodied dry red wine
3 sprigs fresh thyme or 1 teaspoon dried
2 cloves garlic, unpeeled

*3 firm ripe small tomatoes, peeled and
    chopped, or 2 whole canned tomatoes,
    puréed*
1 cup pitted black olives, drained
Chopped fresh parsley, for garnish

1. Rinse the rabbits thoroughly and dry them well with paper towels. Cut the rabbits into comfortable eating pieces and season with salt and pepper.

2. Heat the olive oil or butter in a heavy stainless steel or enamel skillet or flameproof casserole. Sauté the pieces of rabbit over medium-high heat (do not crowd in the pan) until golden brown on both sides but not thoroughly tender.

3. Add the wine, thyme, garlic, and tomatoes. Cover, and reduce the heat. Simmer until the rabbit is tender, about 10 to 15 minutes longer (this varies with the age and size of the rabbits). Discard the garlic and thyme sprigs if used.

4. If the sauce has not mellowed enough, remove the rabbit pieces, raise the heat, and reduce it slightly. Taste for salt and pepper.

VEGETABLES THAT ARE GOOD WITH GAME

Carrots	Onions
Celeriac	Rice, wild and brown
Chestnuts	Spinach
Frenched green beans	Turnips (for duck)
	Watercress
Lentils	White potatoes
Mushrooms	

5. Combine the rabbit and sauce, add the olives, and sprinkle with chopped parsley.

Serves 4 to 6

Chicken or squab can be cooked this same way.

COLONEL HAMBY'S BARBECUED HAUNCH OF VENISON

My brother, Colonel Henry Gordon Hamby, of Williamsburg, Virginia, a real gourmet who has eaten all over the world, says that he doesn't cook a haunch of venison every day but when he does, this is the way he cooks it. A haunch of venison consists of the leg (without the shank), the rump, and the loin—a colossal piece of meat—but a smaller roast can be prepared by this same method.

Top-Secret Barbecue Sauce (recipe follows)
1 small haunch of young deer (10 to 12 pounds), ready to cook
Salt to taste

1. Make the barbecue sauce and set it aside.

2. Preheat the oven to 425°F.

3. Place the venison on a rack in a roasting pan and season it with salt. Roast the meat in the oven until golden brown, about 30 to 35 minutes.

4. Reduce the heat to 350°F and

Despite its name, the New York Restaurant made its home in Richmond, Virginia. The proud proprietor stands on the left.

A Florida huntsmen's club, around 1910: hats on, guns in hand. They're ready for sport.

baste the meat thoroughly with the barbecue sauce. Continue to baste often as the venison cooks. The roasting time is the same as beef and can be calculated the same way; on a quick-reading meat thermometer inserted in the thickest part, it should register 125°F for rare or 140°F for well done.

5. Allow the roast to rest for 15 to 20 minutes before carving. Brush the roast again with the sauce just before carving.

Serves 3 people per pound

VARIATION: *Spit-Roasted Barbecued Venison:* Spit the roast and cook over medium-hot coals until golden brown. Then baste with the barbecue sauce often and continue to roast over low but constant coals until it reaches the desired temperature on a quick-reading meat thermometer.

TOP-SECRET BARBECUE SAUCE

◆◆◆

*T*his unusual barbecue sauce contains no tomato. An old soldier gave this recipe to my brother during World War II. He was sworn to secrecy, but after all these years, we think it should be shared.

This basting sauce is at its best with lamb or a haunch of venison. Work with it yourself and discover its hidden magic and the ways you like to use it.

◆

½ cup cider vinegar
1½ cups water
1 teaspoon dry mustard
¼ teaspoon cayenne pepper, or more to taste
1 teaspoon Hungarian paprika
2 tablespoons sugar
2 teaspoons salt
1 tablespoon Worcestershire sauce
1 tablespoon Tabasco sauce
1 tablespoon chili powder
1 tablespoon freshly ground black pepper
Juice of ½ lemon
1 medium onion, coarsely chopped
1 clove garlic, crushed or sliced, or more to taste
8 tablespoons (1 stick) unsalted butter

◆

1. Combine all the ingredients except the butter in a stainless steel or enamel pan. Bring to a boil, reduce the heat, and simmer 15 minutes. Remove the pan from heat, and allow the flavors to ripen 30 minutes.

2. Strain the sauce into another pan and add the butter. Bring to a simmer again and cook until the butter melts. Mix well, and remove from the heat. This sauce keeps well under refrigeration, but don't freeze it.

Watch the sauce carefully so it does not burn. If at any time it begins to cook too low, add a small amount of water.

CHAPTER SIX

FISH
AND
SHELLFISH

A FINE KETTLE OF FISH

***

*T*ake a quick glance at a map of the United States, following the Chesapeake Bay in Maryland to the Florida Keys, and you will see why Southerners have an embarrassment of riches in fish and seafood. The waters adjoining the land provide crabmeat, crawfish, shrimp, oysters, scallops, clams, the great family of snappers, pompano, and redfish— the list goes on and on, with all the mollusks, crustaceans, and fish one's heart could desire.

Another glance at our inland states, such as Kentucky and Tennessee, shows the blue of lakes and rivers that deliver a bountiful larder of freshwater fish—bass, crappie, walleyed pike, catfish, bluegills, and salmon trout. This list, too, goes on and on.

In the pages that follow you will find my favorite fish and seafood recipes gleaned from 50 years of cooking, tasting— and loving it. Give me a fresh fish with some butter, salt and pepper, and lemon juice, a few boiled new potatoes with a bouquet of herbs from the garden, a little green salad, some good bread, and chilled white wine, and we shall dine tonight.

***

CRABMEAT-STUFFED FLOUNDER

◆◆◆

*C*rabmeat makes an exquisite stuffing for almost any delicate fish. This dish can be prepared a few hours before cooking, if that would help. Rockfish, trout, bass, or any white fish may be stuffed the same way.

◆

6 tablespoons (¾ stick) butter
⅓ cup water
2 tablespoons chopped red or green bell pepper
3 shallots, chopped
1 tablespoon chopped fresh parsley
½ pound lump backfin crabmeat
Salt and freshly ground white pepper to taste
Juice of 2 lemons, or to taste
4 small to medium whole flounder, about 1¼
*   pounds each, cleaned, gutted, and split for*
*   stuffing*
Lemon wedges, for garnish
Parsley or watercress sprigs, for garnish

◆

1. Preheat the oven to 425°F.
2. Melt 3 tablespoons of the butter in the water in a saucepan. Add the chopped pepper, shallots, and parsley and cook over medium heat until the water has evaporated and the shallots have absorbed the butter, about 2 minutes. Remove from the heat.
3. Stir in the crabmeat. Add salt, white pepper, and lemon juice to taste.
4. Season the inside of the fish with lemon juice and salt to taste. Stuff each fish with some of the crabmeat mixture, and fasten it together with skewers.
5. Melt the remaining 3 tablespoons butter. Lay the fish on a buttered baking dish, and brush it with the melted butter, lemon juice and salt to taste.

Mending nets—a fisherman has work to do ashore as well.

6. Oven-broil the fish on the middle shelf of the oven until they are golden brown and flake easily when touched with a fork.
7. Using a wide spatula, remove the fish to a heated platter. Garnish with quarters of lemon and sprigs of parsley or watercress.

Serves 4

🦉 Do not substitute onions for shallots; just omit them.

FRENCH-FRIED FINGERS OF FLOUNDER

◆◆◆

*I*n New Orleans these small pieces of fried flounder are called "goujonettes." A goujon is a coupling bolt or a link-pin on a bicycle, and these small, curly pieces of fish are shaped somewhat like one. Hot, crunchy goujonettes—and french-fried potatoes. I think I shall make homemade mayonnaise for the tartar sauce—it will be simply delicious with the fresh dill I found at the market today.

2¼ pounds flounder filets
Salt to taste
1 cup all-purpose flour
2 eggs
⅓ cup milk
3 cups fresh bread crumbs
Solid vegetable shortening or oil for deep-frying
    (see Index)
Freshly ground black pepper to taste
Sprigs of watercress or parsley, for garnish
Lemon wedges, for garnish
Tartar Sauce with Dill (recipe follows)

1. Dry the filets well and cut them into diagonal strips about ½ inch wide. Season with salt. Roll each piece of fish in flour.

2. Beat the eggs and milk in a bowl until well mixed. Shake off any excess flour, and dip the fish fingers into the egg mixture, then roll them in the crumbs, pressing hard so the crumbs will stick. (This can be done a few hours ahead if desired.)

3. Add shortening or oil, 3 inches deep or more, to a heavy deep skillet or pan, and heat to 370°F on a deep-fat thermometer. The shortening or oil will ripple in the pan when ready. Do not allow it to smoke or the fish will cook so fast on the outside the inside won't have a chance to get done.

4. Drop the fish fingers into the hot fat a few at a time and fry only until golden brown, about 2 to 3 minutes. Drain at once on paper towels. Sprinkle with salt and pepper and serve garnished with watercress or parsley and lemon wedges and tartar sauce on the side.

Serves 4

Accompany the fish with french-fried potatoes and Country Garden Slaw.

TARTAR SAUCE WITH DILL

To serve with fried fish or shellfish.

3 tablespoons fresh onion juice (see step 1)
1 cup Blender Mayonnaise (see Index)
2 tablespoons finely chopped dill pickle
2 teaspoons fresh lemon juice
1½ tablespoons chopped fresh dill

1. Prepare the onion juice by straining a grated onion through cheesecloth to extract the liquid.

2. Combine and blend all the ingredients. Place in a closed jar and refrigerate.

Makes about 1¼ cups

VARIATION: Tartar Sauce with Capers: Omit the dill pickle and fresh dill. Add 2 tablespoons drained capers and 3 tablespoons chopped fresh parsley.

One onion peeled and cut in half can be marinated in the sauce for several hours, then discarded. Omit the onion juice.

SOUTHERN FLOUNDER WITH WOODLAND MUSHROOMS

The mushrooms that grow in the woods in the spring or in the fall heighten the flavor of any dish, but lacking these, cultivated mushrooms are good. This is a notable low-calorie dish, but rich in food value. If fresh herbs are unavailable, cook a pinch of dried marjoram along with the mushrooms.

♦

6 flounder filets, 6 ounces each
8 tablespoons (1 stick) butter
Salt and freshly ground white pepper to taste
½ pound wild or cultivated mushrooms, sliced
3 shallots, finely chopped
½ cup dry white wine, or more as needed
Juice of 1 lemon
3 tablespoons chopped fresh parsley
Bouquet of mixed, chopped fresh herbs, such as tarragon, marjoram, and dill (about 1 teaspoon each)

♦

1. Preheat the oven to 350°F.
2. Lay the filets flat, not overlapping, in a buttered shallow flameproof baking dish or skillet. Dot with 5 tablespoons of the butter, sprinkle with salt and white pepper, and set aside.
3. Melt the remaining butter in a skillet. Add the mushrooms and shallots and sauté over medium heat until they have absorbed the butter, no more than 2 minutes. Sprinkle them over the fish.
4. Pour in the white wine and lemon juice, to barely cover the fish. Loosely cover with foil.
5. Bake until the fish flakes when touched with a fork, 15 to 20 minutes.
6. Lift the filets and mushrooms onto a warm platter. Reduce the pan juices by half by simmering over medium heat. Pour the juices over the fish, and sprinkle with parsley and the fresh herbs. Serve at once.

Serves 6

FLORIDA SOLE AND SCALLOPS WITH SAFFRON

◆◆

*T*he Spanish left a notable trademark in Florida cookery with their saffron. It is a luxurious spice now—but still unique, delicious, and beautiful. Splurge.

♦

4 tablespoons (½ stick) butter
2 tablespoons all-purpose flour
1¾ cups well-flavored Fish or Veal Stock (see Index)
Few threads of Florida saffron or ½ teaspoon powdered saffron
½ cup heavy or whipping cream
Salt and freshly ground white pepper to taste
Cayenne pepper to taste
½ pound scallops
1 pound lemon sole filets
Chopped fresh parsley, for garnish

♦

1. Preheat the oven to 375°F.
2. Melt 2 tablespoons of the butter in a heavy saucepan or in a double boiler over simmering water. Add the flour and blend well. Stir until smooth, about 1 minute.
(Do not allow the flour to brown.)
3. Gradually add 1¼ cups of the stock and the saffron. Beat well with a whisk until the sauce has thickened and has turned a

Elegant dining under the palms of the Flamingo Hotel in Miami, 1923.

lovely shade of yellow.

4. Add the cream, season with salt, white pepper, and cayenne, and cook over medium-low heat for a few minutes to thicken. Set aside but keep warm.

5. Cut the scallops in half if they are large. Put the sole and scallops in a shallow baking dish. Season with salt. Pour the remaining stock over the seafood, and cover lightly with foil.

6. Bake in the oven until the sole flakes easily with a fork, 5 to 6 minutes.

7. Gently pour off the liquid. Pour the saffron cream sauce over the sole and scallops. Dot with the remaining butter. Return to the oven to heat only until bubbly and just beginning to brown, 2 minutes. Sprinkle with parsley and serve immediately.

Serves 4

Any fresh sole, northern or southern, as well as any kind of scallops can be used in this dish.

POMPANO EN PAPILLOTE

*T*he most highly esteemed fish that swims from the Carolinas to Florida is the silver pompano—fine-grained, delicate, and delectable, but fragile. It must be eaten very fresh from the water. Pompano ages rapidly; it does not withstand shipping or idling too long in your refrigerator. I used to meet the boats in Florida as they came in late in the afternoon—and then sauté, broil, or bake the fish for supper. For company, it's fun to do Pompano en Papillote—elegant but easy.

8 whole small pompano (as uniform in size as possible), ¾ to 1 pound each (see step 2)
Juice of 2 lemons, or more as needed
Salt to taste
8 tablespoons (1 stick) butter, or more as needed, at room temperature
3 shallots, minced
½ pound mushrooms, chopped
2 slices canned pimento, chopped
Freshly ground white pepper to taste
Chopped fresh parsley, or a mixture of parsley

and tarragon, for garnish
Watercress sprigs, for garnish
Lemon wedges, for garnish

1. Cut aluminum foil or cooking parchment into 8 heart-shaped pieces large enough to enclose the fish.

2. Clean and gut each fish, leaving the head and tail intact (or discard the head if you wish). Dry them well with paper towels. Season the cavity of each fish with lemon juice and salt. Set aside.

3. Melt 4 tablespoons of the butter in a skillet and gently sauté the shallots and mushrooms, so that the shallots cook in the juice of the mushrooms and do not sizzle. Add the chopped pimento and a little lemon juice (this enhances the flavor of the mushrooms). Set aside to cool.

4. Preheat the oven to 425°F.

5. Spread the fish generously with the remaining butter and season with salt and white pepper. Lay the fish on one side of each piece of foil. Put a tablespoon or so of the mushroom filling on top of each fish, followed by a sprinkling of parsley or herb

A fishing smack in Pensacola, Florida, in the 1930s, being readied for the next day's sail.

mixture. Fold the foil over the fish and crimp the edges together.

6. Arrange the fish packets on a pastry sheet and place them in the oven. Bake 5 to 6 minutes plus 10 minutes per inch of thickness of the fish. Use one fish (yours) as a test—if it flakes easily when touched with a fork, it's done.

7. Serve each pompano in its packet, opened a bit and steaming hot, with a cluster of watercress and a wedge of lemon by its side.

Serves 8

TROUT A LA MARGUERY

*T*his is a very old and famous dish of New Orleans, but it was created at Marguery's restaurant in Paris in the late nineteenth century. In the New Orleans restaurants they usually make a hollandaise sauce and let it go at that, but the original Trout Marguery was made the way it is given here. It is a rich dish, but that can be balanced nicely with a light menu, so it need not be overpowering.

1 pound white-fleshed fish, such as grouper or sole
¾ to 1 pound extra fish bones
2 carrots, peeled and sliced
1 medium onion, cut into quarters
4 sprigs parsley
8 peppercorns
1 bay leaf
3 slices lemon
2 quarts water
6 small trout, about 6 ounces each, cleaned and gutted
5 tablespoons butter, melted
Salt to taste
Cayenne pepper to taste
⅓ cup dry white wine
8 tablespoons (1 stick) butter, chilled
3 egg yolks, at room temperature
Squeeze of lemon juice, or to taste
24 small shrimp, shelled and deveined
25 shucked small oysters
Lemon wedges, for garnish
Fresh parsley or watercress sprigs, for garnish

1. Put the white-fleshed fish and bones in a large saucepan. Add the carrots, onion, parsley, peppercorns, bay leaf, lemon slices, and water. Bring to a boil and cook until the liquid is reduced to 2 cups, 15 to 25 minutes depending on the pan's

A favorite fishing spot has always been a well-treasured secret.

shape. Strain through a fine sieve into another saucepan, and discard the bones and fish. Reduce the strained stock to ⅓ cup, 8 minutes.

2. Dry the trout with paper towels.

3. Lay the trout in a generously buttered baking dish. Brush them well with the melted butter, and season with salt and cayenne pepper.

4. Preheat the oven to 375°F. Uncover the trout and bake it until the fish flakes easily when touched with a fork, 15 to 18 minutes. (Allow about 10 minutes per inch of thickness of the fish.)

5. While the fish is cooking, put the reduced stock and the white wine in a double boiler over simmering water. Add

the chilled butter a little at a time, beating it in until the sauce thickens. Don't allow the sauce to get too hot or it will not thicken. Beat in the egg yolks slowly. Do not allow the sauce to become too hot or the yolks will harden. Season to taste with salt, cayenne, and lemon juice.

6. Add the shrimp and oysters to the hot butter sauce around the trout. Return the pan to the oven just long enough to cook the seafood (the edges of the oysters will curl).

7. Lift the trout onto a warmed ovenproof platter, and raise the oven heat to 500°F. Place the shrimp and oysters around the trout. Spoon the sauce over the shrimp and oysters. Add some of the liquid from the trout if there isn't enough sauce to cover. This dish must not be dry.

8. Place the platter in the oven (or run it under the broiler) just long enough for the dish to heat thoroughly, about 1 minute. Watch it carefully or the sauce will curdle.

9. Garnish with wedges of lemon and clusters of parsley or watercress.

Serves 6

🦉 Grouper and sole are especially good for making fish stock, as they are rich in gelatin. The fish stock can be made ahead and strained (step 1) and then refrigerated, if desired.

SPRING SHAD STUFFED WITH SPINACH AND SORREL

◆◆◆

*T*he early spring shad on the Eastern Seaboard around Washington, D.C., and Maryland is a rare treat, especially when stuffed with spinach and sorrel—but red snapper, striped bass, and the red drumfish of the Carolinas and Louisiana respond just as well to this lemony stuffing. Sorrel turns an unappetizing color when cooked, but when added to spinach, it makes this an appealing and attractive dish. Serve with buttered small new potatoes and Green Mayonnaise.

◆

1 whole shad, 2½ to 3 pounds, cleaned and gutted
Juice of 1 small lemon
Salt to taste
8 tablespoons (1 stick) butter, or as needed, at room temperature
⅓ cup water
3 shallots or scallion (green onion) bulbs, minced
1 quart fresh sorrel leaves, washed
3 cups fresh spinach leaves, washed
Freshly ground white pepper to taste
2 medium onions or leeks, cleaned and chopped
4 carrots, peeled and chopped
3 ribs celery, chopped
¼ cup chopped fresh parsley
3 tablespoons mixed chopped fresh herbs, such
as tarragon, chervil, and thyme, or tarragon only
2 cups Veal, Chicken, or Fish Stock (see Index), or dry white wine
Lemon wedges, for garnish

◆

1. Preheat the oven to 350°F.

2. Season the cavity of the fish with lemon juice and salt and set the fish aside.

3. Melt 3 tablespoons of the butter in the water in a heavy saucepan. Add the shallots or scallion bulbs and simmer over medium-low heat until the shallots or scallions have wilted, 2 minutes. Do not allow them to sizzle or brown in the butter.

4. Add the sorrel and spinach and sim-

mer until they have wilted, 2 minutes. Season with salt and white pepper.

5. Stuff the fish with the seasoned sorrel and spinach. Secure with toothpicks or sew together with a trussing needle. Spread the remaining butter on the fish, and season with salt and white pepper.

6. Cover the bottom of a shallow baking dish with the onions or leeks, carrots, celery, parsley, and half the mixed herbs. Lay the fish on top. Pour the stock or white wine over the vegetables.

7. Place the dish on the lower shelf of the oven and bake 10 minutes per inch of thickness of the fish, 35 to 40 minutes. Baste and baste—often. This helps to distribute the flavors. When the shad has developed a lovely golden hue and flakes easily when touched with a fork, it is done.

It took many hands to pull in a net full of fish from the waters of the Chesapeake.

8. Serve pieces of the fish with some of the vegetables. Sprinkle each serving with the remaining mixed herbs and serve with wedges of lemon.

Serves 4

POACHED GROUPER WITH SHRIMP SAUCE

*T*his dish may be made with grouper, rockfish (striped bass), monkfish, or any firm fish. It is also a pleasing way to prepare salmon. Grouper has a very tough skin that has to be removed by the fishmonger. It is not edible, but the fish itself is delicious and delicate.

4 grouper or rockfish steaks, 1 inch thick
2 shallots, coarsely chopped
2 large sprigs parsley
2 bay leaves
2 cups Veal or light Chicken Stock (veal is best; see Index)
2 cups dry white wine
1 to 1½ cups cold water
20 small shrimp in the shell, rinsed well
1¼ cups rice
Salt and freshly ground white pepper to taste
Cayenne pepper to taste
2 tablespoons butter, at room temperature
2 tablespoons all-purpose flour
1 cup heavy or whipping cream
1 red bell pepper or fresh pimento pepper, cored, seeded, and slivered
1½ tablespoons fresh lemon juice, or to taste

Hungarian paprika, for garnish
Watercress sprigs, for garnish
Large black olives, for garnish

1. Clean the fish well and set aside.

2. In a large saucepan, combine the shallots, parsley sprigs, bay leaves, stock, white wine, and enough water to cover the fish. Bring to a boil and simmer 6 to 8 minutes. Add up to 1 cup of cold water if the liquid evaporates too much.

3. Add the shrimp to the simmering bouillon. Cook 1 to 2 minutes, then remove the pan from the heat. Allow the shrimp to finish cooking in the hot bouillon. They are done when they just turn pink.

4. Sieve out the shrimp from the

bouillon. When they are cool enough to handle, remove the shells and toss the shells back into the bouillon. Devein the shrimp, and set them aside. Simmer the bouillon with the shrimp shells for 3 to 4 minutes, then set the bouillon aside.

5. In the meantime, steam the rice (see Index).

6. About 30 to 35 minutes before serving, strain the bouillon into a shallow, heavy flameproof pan. Place the fish steaks in the pan. If the bouillon does not completely cover the steaks, add broth or water to barely cover.

7. Season the bouillon with salt, white pepper, and cayenne to taste. Place the pan over medium-low heat, and allow the fish to poach in the simmering (no hotter) bouillon until it flakes easily when touched with a fork, 5 to 7 minutes. Remove from the heat but hold in the warm bouillon until ready to serve.

8. Strain 2 cups of the bouillon through dampened cheesecloth or a fine sieve into a saucepan.

9. Blend the butter and flour until smooth. Whip this into the bouillon with a whisk. Add the cream and pepper slivers and boil until the sauce has reduced and thickened somewhat. Add the shrimp and cook until barely heated. Taste for seasoning. Add lemon juice to taste.

10. Heat the fish in the remaining bouillon over very low heat for just a few seconds. Place a mound of buttered hot rice in the center of each warm plate. Place a serving of fish on each mound of rice. Nap the fish generously with the shrimp sauce. Sprinkle discreetly with Hungarian paprika, and add a sprig of watercress and a huge black olive.

Serves 4

BAKED STUFFED ROCKFISH

*I*n Maryland striped bass is called rockfish; it is one of the finest fish that swim in American waters. Any large bass or shad can be stuffed in this typical Southern way. I often lay two or three slices of well-seasoned bacon over the top of the fish as it bakes. Mighty good.

1 large rockfish, about 5 pounds (see step 1)
Juice of 1 lemon
8 tablespoons (1 stick) butter, at room temperature
¾ cup dry white wine or Chicken Stock (see Index), or more as needed
6 shallots or scallions (green onions), finely chopped
3 ribs celery, finely chopped
3 tablespoons chopped fresh parsley
Bouquet of mixed chopped fresh herbs, such as tarragon, thyme, and chervil
4 slices lean smoked bacon, broiled and finely chopped
Salt and freshly ground white pepper to taste
Chopped fresh parsley, for garnish
Lemon wedges, for garnish

1. Have the fish cleaned, gutted, and split, but leave the halves attached. Sprinkle the lemon juice over the inside of the fish.

2. Preheat the oven to 350°F.

3. Melt 2 tablespoons of the butter in 3 tablespoons of the white wine or water (not stock) in a skillet, and add the shallots or scallions, celery, parsley, mixed herbs, and bacon. Cook gently over low heat until the mixture blends, 1 minute. When the liquid has boiled away, season with salt and white pepper and set aside.

4. Season the inside of the fish with

salt and white pepper. Cover the inside of one half with the filling. Fold the other half over and lay the fish in a well-buttered shallow baking dish. Pour the remaining wine or the stock over the fish. Spread the top of the fish with the remaining butter and sprinkle with salt and white pepper.

5. Place the dish in the oven, uncovered, and bake until the fish flakes when touched with a fork, about 35 minutes, basting often with the pan juices. (The cooking time will vary with the size of the fish.) Add butter if needed to make a smooth and delicious sauce.

6. Sprinkle the fish with chopped parsley, garnish with lemon wedges, and serve at once.

Serves 4

PAN-FRIED CRAPPIE IN CORNMEAL

❖❖

*O*f all the freshwater fish in the South, crappie and bass (small- and large-mouth) are the finest—at least, the finest to fry coated in cornmeal. They are the fisherman's kind of fish—fresh, moist, and tender on the inside, and hot, crunchy, and crisp on the outside. Beat it if you can . . . but you can't. Serve with corn muffins and a crisp, fresh slaw.

◆

4 crappie or bass, about 1 pound each, cleaned
and gutted
Salt to taste
1½ cups white cornmeal (not water-ground)
Lard or solid vegetable shortening
Freshly ground black pepper to taste
Lemon wedges, for garnish

◆

1. Dry the fish well on paper towels. Discard the heads but not the tails—the tails have a delightful crisp, nutty flavor when prepared this way.

2. Sprinkle the fish with salt and dip lightly (don't dredge) in cornmeal. Their flesh is so delicate in flavor, a heavy dredging would rob them of their very special sweetness.

3. Melt lard or shortening to a depth of 1½ inches in an iron skillet and allow it to get quite hot but not smoking.

4. Lay the fish in the skillet without crowding and fry until golden brown on both sides, turning the fish only once. (Turning the fish several times makes it absorb unnecessary fat; it will be greasy.)

5. If desired, drain the fish on paper towels, but quickly. Sprinkle with pepper and serve with wedges of lemon as soon as possible after frying. From skillet to plate is the best possible method. This dish will not wait.

Serves 4

VARIATION: *Pan-Fried Catfish:* If you insist upon eating catfish, pan-fry it this way, but you need to skin it first.

🦉 Lard is the preferred fat for frying these fish, as it produces a very crisp coating.

Fishing off a houseboat on the Kentucky River, near Frankfort, around 1910.

TO POACH FISH

❖❖❖

*P*oaching, as opposed to boiling, means to simmer gently in a seasoned or compatible liquid. Fish cooked this way is delicious served hot with a sauce, or it may be served cold as an entrée in summer, or used in salad.

To poach a fish steak, filet, or small chunk of fish, you will need cheesecloth and a pan large enough to immerse the pieces in simmering liquid.

◆

2 quarts water, or as needed
1 medium onion
5 or 6 white peppercorns
3 whole allspice
5 tablespoons fresh lemon juice or white wine
    vinegar
1½ bay leaves
1 teaspoon salt
½ cup dry white wine (optional but excellent)

◆

1. Preheat the oven to 400°F (unless you plan to use a burner).

2. Combine all the ingredients in a large saucepan. You will need enough liquid to just cover the fish pieces (the amount of water will vary).

3. Wipe the fish with a damp cloth, wrap the fish in cheesecloth, and arrange it comfortably in a baking pan.

4. Bring the poaching liquid almost to a boil and pour it over the fish in the baking pan; or lower the cheesecloth-wrapped fish into the simmering (not boiling) liquid.

5. Cover the pan and put it in the oven. Reduce the heat to 325°F. Or simmer the fish on top of the stove. Allow 10 minutes per inch of thickness; start testing serving-size pieces of fish after 6 minutes.

6. Lift the cooked fish from the liquid with a wide spatula and with the support of the cheesecloth. Drain well. Use as directed in recipes calling for poached fish.

Makes enough poaching liquid for up to 4 pounds of fish

❖❖❖

FISH THAT ARE GOOD FOR GRILLING AND BROILING

Bass	Pompano
Black striped bass (rockfish)	Porgy
Cod	Redfish
Crappie	Red snapper
Flounder	Scrod
Freshwater bass	Sole
Grouper	Salmon trout
Mackerel	Swordfish
	Trout

DEEP-FRY BATTER FOR FISH AND SHELLFISH

❖❖❖

*E*ven though you have a processor, don't store your blender in the basement or give it away. It is marvelous for mixing many things, such as fritter batters like this one—excellent for shrimp but *not* for mushrooms and other fresh vegetables.

1 cup sifted all-purpose flour, or ½ cup sifted
    flour and ½ cup sifted cornstarch
¾ teaspoon baking powder
1 tablespoon vegetable oil
¾ cup ice water, or more as needed

1. Combine all the ingredients in a blender or beat by hand with a whisk (which is more arduous but does give a lighter texture).

2. When the batter is perfectly smooth and well mixed, transfer to a bowl, cover, and refrigerate until ready to use.

3. The batter will thicken up as it stands. Thin as desired by adding a little extra ice water.

Makes about 2 cups

There are other pleasures in fishing, in addition to catching the evening meal.

The batter is harder to mix thoroughly when using cornstarch, but cornstarch gives a glossier coating than flour.

TO GRILL FISH

Grilling over an open fire was man's first method of cooking fish (and meat), and flavorwise, we haven't gone many steps beyond that—in spite of our fabulous modern ovens.

Food cooked in the open air loses its moisture rapidly, so it browns more quickly and more effectively. The process of browning, when controlled, is one of the great flavor enhancers, as it adds a light but exceedingly pleasing touch of natural caramel to all foods.

The process may be further enhanced by grilling over natural woods, or mesquite or hickory chips. Controlling the coals and evaluating the distance from the heat are the ticklish parts. If the fish is allowed to brown too rapidly or to form a thick outside crust that the heat cannot penetrate, the inside flesh will remain raw. If the outside is burned the least bit, it will taste bitter. Thick fish steaks (1 to 1½ inches) should be placed at least 6 inches from the coals. Those thinner than 1 inch can be placed 4 inches from the coals.

In grilling fish, 10 minutes per inch of thickness is almost perfect timing. Use one fish (yours) as a test. When the fish flakes easily with a fork, it is done. Serve at once.

Thin, tender filets such as flounder, perch, or trout should be cooked in packets of foil and not directly on the oiled grids.

Swordfish, tuna, and monkfish are sturdy, lean "fish steaks" that respond well to grilling, but they must be sliced not less than 1 inch thick, and they must be basted constantly.

Shrimp threaded on skewers and grilled over mesquite is everybody's favorite. The presentation is charming and the menu can be very simple—a crisp salad, a good bread, and dessert—easy does it.

Our freshwater fish—bass, crappie, and Jax salmon (walleyed perch)—are delectable grilled whole if they don't exceed 1¼ pounds. Larger fish should be scaled, cleaned, and split in half with the skin intact, then grilled in a hinged basket to facilitate turning.

Score the sides of fish weighing up to 1½ pounds that are to be grilled whole. Fish weighing over 1½ pounds to be cooked whole should be baked or poached, not grilled. Don't attempt to grill any fish over 2 inches in thickness.

The freshness of fish is the most important element of all. Butter, oil, and lemon as seasonings come next. The herbs—tarragon, chervil, parsley, and dill—have a close affinity for all fish; and tomatoes, shallots, or a touch of onion blends in very well. The flavors of Jax salmon, crappie, and bass are far too unique and delicate to mask with heady seasonings.

Grilling out-of-doors is admittedly not the easiest way to cook fish, but it is an absolutely delicious way, and to the food-minded, nothing is more fun.

DEEP-FRY ALL-PURPOSE BATTER

◆◆

*A*n excellent batter for fish, seafood, or vegetables.

Recorded proof that this young fisherman had at least one day when no fish escaped his bait and hook.

◆

1 cup ice water, or more as needed
1 tablespoon vegetable oil
1 egg yolk
1 cup sifted all-purpose flour
1 tablespoon cornstarch
1 teaspoon baking powder
1 teaspoon salt

◆

1. Combine all the ingredients in a blender or electric mixer. Or mix thoroughly in a large bowl with a whisk, combining the water, oil, and egg yolk first, then whipping in the dry ingredients.

2. Allow to stand 30 to 60 minutes, covered, in the refrigerator before using.

3. If the batter is too thick for your taste or purpose, add a few more spoonfuls of ice water.

Makes about 2 cups

CHOOSING FRESH FISH

*T*he best fish of all is the fish you catch yourself and cook on the spot. That freshness is a glorious thing. But most of us must find a good market and buy our fish.

Every species of seafood and fish smells sweet, with no strong odor whatsoever, when it is fresh. The liquid around oysters is clear, and if there is any odor at all it is an appetizing one.

The eyes of fresh fish are clear and full. As the fish ages, the eyes become milky, sunken, and dull. Press the flesh of a fish with your fingers; if it is fresh it will feel firm and your fingers will not leave an indentation. The gills of fresh fish will be red, and the skin color will be clear and unblemished around the ventral or abdominal area.

Filets, fish steaks, and scallops will have a firm, moist texture, almost shiny, when they are fresh.

Never buy fish that is dry looking and that has traces of browning around the edges.

Fresh does not mean freshly thawed, but fish that has been correctly frozen will smell sweet and clear as soon as it is thawed.

Every kind of fish and seafood is delicate fare, and every kind of fish and seafood must not be overcooked. It must be cooked quickly or it will toughen. When fish flakes easily with a fork, it is done. Remove it from the heat at once. Overcooked shrimp will taste rubbery.

Fresh lemon juice is the great enhancer of all fish and seafood. It brings out their individual flavors. It is one of the best friends a seafood cook can have. Always have plenty on hand.

CLASSIC BREAD AND HERB DRESSING

◆◆◆

*D*ressings for fish and shellfish are great fun for the cook and, needless to say, for the diners. They help keep the fish moist, and in some menus no other starch is needed. Fish goes with fish, and the dressings with oysters, crabmeat, and shrimp make a good counterpoint in flavor. The amount of dressing needed will vary with the size of the fish—usually ⅓ to ½ cup dressing per pound of fish is a safe guess.

◆

1 cup soft white bread crumbs (see step 1)
4 tablespoons (½ stick) unsalted butter, at
*   room temperature*
¼ cup water
5 shallots or scallion (green onion) bulbs, finely
*   chopped*
⅓ cup chopped fresh parsley
½ teaspoon dried thyme, or 1 teaspoon chopped
*   fresh thyme, or 2 teaspoons chopped fresh*
*   tarragon*
1 large egg
Salt and freshly ground white pepper to taste

◆

1. Make the crumbs in a blender or food processor, using homemade-type bread (1 slice makes about ⅓ cup). Set aside.

2. Melt 2 tablespoons of the butter in the water in a skillet. Add the shallots or scallions and simmer over medium heat until the water has boiled away. The onions must not sizzle or brown the least bit.

3. Add the remaining butter, the parsley, thyme or tarragon, and the reserved bread crumbs. Blend in the egg, mixing the stuffing with a fork to keep it loose. Add salt and white pepper to taste.

Makes about 1½ cups

VARIATIONS: *Bread and Almond Dressing:* Add ½ cup sliced or slivered blanched almonds.

Mushroom Dressing: Add ½ to 1 cup sliced and sautéed mushrooms. Use fresh or dried marjoram instead of thyme or tarragon. Especially good with red snapper.

AUTUMN CATCH DRESSING

◆◆◆

A wonderful dressing for redfish and bass.

◆

3 tablespoons unsalted butter
3 tablespoons water
⅓ cup finely chopped shallots, onions, or
*   scallion (green onion) bulbs*
1 large red or green bell pepper or fresh pimento
*   (the red peppers are best here), cored,*
*   seeded, and chopped*

4 firm ripe tomatoes, peeled, seeded, and
*   chopped*
¼ cup chopped fresh parsley
Salt and freshly ground white pepper to taste
Cayenne pepper to taste

◆

Does this Maryland fisherman's jug contain a secret brew for keeping warm while ice-fishing?

1. Melt the butter in the water in a large skillet or saucepan, and add the shallots, onions, or scallions. Simmer over medium heat until the shallots have absorbed the butter and are limp (this is where shallots are best) and the water has boiled away, 2 minutes. The shallots must not sizzle or brown the least bit. Add the red or green pepper and a spoonful or so of the juice from the tomatoes. Simmer the mixture a few seconds longer.

2. Add the tomatoes and parsley, and mix thoroughly. Season to taste with salt, white pepper, and cayenne.

Makes about 1½ cups

VARIATION: *With Fresh Basil:* Add 2 to 3 tablespoons chopped fresh basil leaves with the tomatoes.

MARYLAND SHORE OYSTER DRESSING

*G*ood to stuff pompano, all of the snappers, rockfish, bass, or trout.

1 cup oysters (½ pint)
⅓ cup water
4 tablespoons (½ stick) unsalted butter, at
*   room temperature*
⅓ cup minced celery hearts
4 shallots or 3 scallion (green onion) bulbs,
*   minced*
¼ cup finely chopped red or green bell pepper
*   or fresh pimento*
⅓ cup chopped fresh parsley
1 teaspoon dried tarragon or thyme, or 1
*   tablespoon fresh thyme or chopped tarragon*
*   leaves*
1⅔ cups fresh bread crumbs
Salt and freshly ground white pepper to taste
Cayenne pepper to taste

1. Drain the oysters and reserve the liquor. If the oysters are large, cut them in half with sharp scissors. Set aside.

2. Heat the water and 2 tablespoons of the butter in a heavy saucepan and add the

VEGETABLES THAT ARE GOOD WITH FISH	
Asparagus	Potatoes
Green beans	Spinach
Mushrooms	Tomatoes
Onions (in tartar sauce)	

celery, shallots or scallions, and chopped pepper. Simmer over medium heat until the shallots are limp and the vegetables have absorbed the butter. They must not sizzle or brown the least bit.

3. Add the remaining butter, the parsley, thyme or tarragon, bread crumbs, and oysters. Cook over medium heat, mixing lightly with a fork, only until the oysters curl. Add the oyster liquor as needed; the dressing should be moist but not wet.

4. Season with salt, white pepper, and cayenne.

Makes about 3 cups

PONTCHARTRAIN CRABMEAT OR SHRIMP DRESSING

*F*or pompano, snapper, redfish, jumbo shrimp, trout, or flounder.

1½ cups fresh lump crabmeat or minced cooked shrimp
⅓ cup water
5 tablespoons unsalted butter, at room temperature
¼ cup minced shallots or scallion (green onion) bulbs
⅓ cup minced celery hearts
¼ cup minced red or green bell pepper or fresh pimento
1 teaspoon dry mustard
¼ cup chopped fresh parsley
1 cup fresh bread crumbs
Salt to taste
Cayenne pepper to taste
Tabasco sauce to taste
Juice of ½ lemon

1. Pick over the crabmeat well, removing all the cartilage. Set aside.

2. In a large skillet, melt 2 tablespoons of the butter in the water. Add the shallots or scallions, celery, bell pepper or pimento, and mustard. Simmer over medium heat until the shallots are limp and the vegetables have absorbed the butter. Do not allow them to sizzle or brown the least bit.

3. Add the remaining butter, the parsley, bread crumbs, and crabmeat or shrimp. Mix with a fork—gently, to keep the dressing light and porous. Season to taste with salt and cayenne. Add Tabasco and the lemon juice.

Makes about 3 cups

VARIATION: *Pontchartrain Dressing with Capers:* Omit the shallots or scallions and the bell or pimento pepper. Substitute 2 to 3 tablespoons drained capers and 2 chopped canned pimentos. Use less Tabasco, but still add the same amount of lemon juice.

DINNER IN BALTIMORE

Oysters on the Half-Shell

Mignonette Sauce

◆

Crabmeat-Stuffed Redfish

Spring Asparagus

Monticello Rolls

Chilled Dry White Wine

◆

Coffee and Cognac Ice Cream

TO FREEZE FISH

*W*ater freezing—Although you can freeze fish in freezer paper or foil, water freezing keeps it much, much better. Clean fish thoroughly—scale, gut, remove fins and heads. Wash in cold water. Freeze small fish whole, immersed in cold water. Large clean milk cartons are excellent for this. Large fish may be frozen whole or cut into steaks or filets.

To Ice Glaze—Large whole fish should be cleaned, scaled, and gutted. Remove fins and heads. Place the fish on a tray in the freezer. As soon as the fish is frozen, dip it in near-freezing ice water. Place the fish back in the freezer to harden the glaze. Repeat this procedure until you have a ⅛-inch-thick ice glaze on the fish. Wrap well in freezer paper or foil.

Frozen Fish—A whole fish can be thawed more quickly by placing it in a pan under cold running water. Filets and small fish should be thawed in the refrigerator, not at room temperature. Use frozen and thawed fish at once. It does not keep well.

CRAWFISH ETOUFFEE

◆◆◆

*C*rayfish, or crawfish as they are called in Louisiana, are fresh-water crustaceans, and so delicate and sweet, hundreds of gastronomes have made the journey to New Orleans just to eat them. Etouffée means "smothered" in French, and it became a Creole term for crawfish smothered in their own juices and butter, and seasoned with red peppers—cayenne, red bell pepper, and paprika. The great charm of a good Crawfish Etouffée is that the unique flavor of the fish is honored and is not disguised by an armada of ersatz powders and nonessential seasonings.

Traditionally, Etouffée was served with rice but it is never mixed with rice. Now it is often served around pasta.

◆◆◆

SHELLFISH PREPARATION

1. *For crawfish:* To 4 quarts of cold water add 3 slices of lemon and salt to taste. Bring to a boil.

2. In the meantime, wash the crawfish thoroughly. Remove the intestinal tract by inserting the tip of a small, sharp knife under the intestine in the middle of the tail and pulling the intestine out gently.

3. Plunge all of the crawfish as quickly as possible into the boiling water. Cook 1 to 2 minutes. Remove the pan from the heat so the crawfish will not overcook. Strain out the crawfish but reserve the bouillon.

4. To remove the meat: Separate the body of the crawfish from the tail. Remove the meat from the tails and the claws.

5. Put the shells back into the bouillon and boil it hard to strengthen the flavor, 10 to 15 minutes. Strain the bouillon.

◆

1. *For shrimp:* Rinse shrimp thoroughly. To 4 quarts of cold water add 3 slices of lemon, 1 slice of onion, and salt to taste. Bring to a boil.

2. For large shrimp: Add the shrimp, and the minute the water returns to a boil, remove the pan from the heat. Allow the shrimp to stay in the bouillon until the water has cooled, 10 minutes. Peel and devein the shrimp, cover, and set aside. Return the shrimp shells to the bouillon and boil 10 to 15 minutes longer. Strain.

For very small shrimp: Follow directions for large shrimp, but remove the pan from the heat as soon as you plunge the shrimp into the boiling bouillon. Allow them to remain in the bouillon only 1 to 2 minutes. Very small shrimp need only to be shelled.

◆

3 cups peeled cooked crawfish tails (see box)
½ cup finely chopped onions
½ cup finely chopped scallions (green onions) or shallots
¼ cup finely chopped green bell pepper
¾ cup finely chopped red bell pepper
¾ cup (1 ½ sticks) unsalted butter, chilled
1 cup crawfish bouillon (see box) or Fish Stock (see Index) or water
1 ripe firm large tomato, peeled, seeded and chopped
1 teaspoon Hungarian paprika
½ teaspoon cayenne pepper or to taste
½ teaspoon salt, or to taste
4 cups freshly cooked white rice or pasta, such as thin linguine (see Index)
Watercress, for garnish
8 cooked whole crawfish tails, for garnish

◆

1. Prepare the crawfish and set aside.

2. Combine the onions, scallions or shallots, green and red bell peppers, 2 tablespoons of the butter, and ¼ cup of the bouillon, stock, or water in a large non-aluminum skillet or saucepan. Simmer over medium heat until the onions are limp and the stock has boiled away, about 5 minutes. Do not allow the onions to sizzle or brown the least bit.

3. Add the tomato and remaining ¾ cup bouillon, stock, or water. Continue simmering until the peppers, onions, and tomato are soft, about 20 minutes. Do not allow this to boil. Add the paprika, cayenne, and about ½ teaspoon salt. Stir to blend.

4. Add the remaining butter, 1 tablespoon at a time, keeping the pan over low heat, and stirring constantly with a wooden spoon. Always stir in one direction so the sauce will become homogenized and thicken.

5. When all the butter has been added, toss in the crawfish. Continue to stir in the same direction, allowing the crawfish to blend with the sauce, but do not overcook. (The sauce should look as if heavy cream has been added.) Taste for salt and cayenne, and add more if desired.

6. Mound hot rice or pasta on warmed plates. Surround with the blushing pink crawfish in its delectable sauce.

7. Place a few sprigs of watercress on each plate and a cooked red crawfish tail on either side of the watercress.

Serves 4

VARIATION: *Shrimp Etouffée:* Follow the directions exactly for Crawfish Etouffée except increase the red bell pepper to 1 cup (the flavor of shrimp is much more assertive than crawfish). Two cups of large cooked and cubed shrimp makes 4 servings. If small river shrimp or tiny shrimp are used whole, measure about the same amount as for crawfish.

A small clove of freshly peeled garlic can be tossed about in the sauce when you add the tomato to either étouffée, but discard it before serving. (Never use garlic that has been chopped and bottled. Powdered garlic and garlic salt are abominations.)

JUMBO SHRIMP AND WILD RICE WITH TARRAGON

Not long ago a call came from a friend in Florida: "Please send the recipe for your favorite shrimp dish by return mail." Here it is—my very favorite. Figure four to five shrimp per person. The more shrimp you cook, the better the dish will be, as you will have a more concentrated seafood flavor.

1½ cups wild rice
8 tablespoons (1 stick) butter, or more if needed
24 to 30 enormous shrimp, shelled and
  deveined
3 shallots, or 1 clove garlic, finely chopped
1 cup dry white wine, or more if needed
½ cup Fish, Veal, or Chicken Stock (see Index),
  or more if needed
1 tablespoon dried tarragon (see Owl)
Salt and freshly ground black pepper to taste
Chopped fresh parsley, for garnish

1. Wash the rice thoroughly, and cook it in boiling salted water until tender, but not mushy, about 45 minutes. Drain, and set aside.

2. About 30 minutes before serving, melt the butter in a large skillet. Add the shrimp and the shallots or garlic and cook

A Louisiana shrimp boat, the "Capt. Atles," ready for a big haul.

over medium heat for 6 to 8 minutes (depending on the size of the shrimp), turning the shrimp once. Cover the pan for a few seconds but do not overcook. Remove the shrimp to another pan and keep warm.

3. Add the wine, stock, and tarragon to the pan juices left from the shrimp. Reduce the stock by about half, and add salt and pepper to taste. You must have enough liquid to make the rice quite moist and to have some left to pour over the shrimp as you serve it. If you need more wine and stock, be sure to allow it to reduce until it has lost its raw flavor before pouring it on the rice. Taste it; you may need to add more tarragon. This dish should be well perfumed with tarragon.

4. Pour some of the sauce over the wild rice until it is quite moist. Taste it; add more butter if necessary (it usually is).

5. Heat the rice and the shrimp separately over very low flames, stirring constantly, until piping hot. Spoon the hot rice into a large shallow bowl or deep platter.

A FAVORITE SEAFOOD MENU

Camembert Fritters

♦

Jumbo Shrimp and Wild Rice with Tarragon

Warm Asparagus Salad with Mustard Dressing

Chilled White Wine

♦

Raspberry Sherbet

Chocolate Whispers

Coffee   Tea

Put the hot shrimp on top of the rice. Pour the remaining sauce over the shrimp, sprinkle with parsley, and serve.

Serves 6

Even if fresh tarragon is available, use dried tarragon, as its more concentrated flavor is needed with this dish.

SHRIMP WITH FRESH TARRAGON OR DILL

*T*his is such a gloriously easy shrimp dish to prepare—and gloriously good with either of these fresh herbs. Serve it with buttered white rice and peas or asparagus.

⅔ cup unsalted butter, or more as needed
3 tablespoons water
2 pounds shrimp, shelled and deveined
3 tablespoons chopped fresh tarragon leaves, or
   ¼ cup chopped fresh dill
3 tablespoons fresh lemon juice
Salt to taste
Cayenne pepper to taste
Scant sprinkling of Hungarian paprika

1. Combine the butter and water in a saucepan and place over medium-low heat. When the butter has melted, add the shrimp. Toss them about in the butter for about 3 minutes for medium shrimp, not over 5 minutes for jumbo shrimp. Do not allow the butter to brown or sizzle the least bit. (For the very large shrimp, you may need more butter, as it should form a nice sauce.)

2. When the shrimp have turned pink, add the tarragon or dill and the lemon juice. Shake the pan to distribute the flavorings. Season with salt and cayenne, and sprinkle with a touch of paprika. Serve immediately.

Serves 3 to 4

When a skewer goes into the shrimp easily, it is done. Watch carefully for shrimp cook quickly. Overcooking toughens all seafood.

SHRIMP FLORENTINE

◆◆

*T*his is one of the favorite so-called casserole dishes of my students. Served with broiled tomatoes, rice, and French bread, it makes a beautiful company meal. The spinach is barely wilted as it must be a fresh, vibrant green.

◆

8 tablespoons (1 stick) butter
⅓ cup all-purpose flour
2¾ cups milk
½ cup heavy or whipping cream
Salt to taste
Cayenne pepper to taste
¼ cup water
2 tablespoons minced shallots
½ cup dry white wine
3 cups freshly cooked spinach (3 pounds raw)
3 cups shrimp, cooked and deveined
    (1½ pounds)
Juice of ½ lemon, or to taste
6 tablespoons freshly grated Parmesan or aged
    Swiss cheese
¼ cup buttered and toasted bread crumbs (see
    Index)

◆

1. Preheat the oven to 375°F.
2. Melt 6 tablespoons of the butter in a heavy saucepan or in a double boiler over hot water. Add the flour and blend, stirring constantly, until it has cooked a bit and is smooth, about 1½ minutes. Add the milk, stirring all the while, until it thickens, another 4 minutes. Add the cream, and salt and cayenne to taste. Set aside.
3. Melt the remaining butter in the water in a small skillet. Add the shallots and sauté over medium heat until the butter is absorbed and the water has evaporated. Add the wine and cook until the liquid has almost evaporated. Add this to the cream sauce, and blend. Add ½ cup of the sauce to the spinach. Stir. Taste and correct the seasoning if necessary.
4. Spread half the spinach in a shallow casserole. Cover with the shrimp, and season with lemon juice. Cover the shrimp with the remaining spinach. Pour on the remaining sauce. Stir together the cheese and bread crumbs, and sprinkle this over the sauce. Bake until the sauce begins to brown and is bubbly hot, 5 to 6 minutes.

Serves 6 to 8

SHRIMP SALAD WITH TOMATO MAYONNAISE

◆◆

*T*his salad is elegant in its simplicity, and the varieties of ways it can be done are fun for the cook. You can substitute 1 pound of crabmeat for the shrimp in the main recipe and its variations. Serve on lettuce or in scallop shells as an entrée salad or as a first course.

◆

3 ribs white celery hearts
1 pound cooked small shrimp
Juice of ½ lemon, or to taste
2 ripe firm tomatoes, peeled, seeded, and cut
    into cubes
1½ cups Blender Mayonnaise (see Index)

1 tablespoon chopped fresh parsley
Salt to taste
Cayenne pepper to taste
Watercress sprigs, for garnish
Large black olives, for garnish

1. Trim the celery and cut it into matchstick slivers ½ inch long. You should have ½ cup. Toss the shrimp with the lemon juice and celery.

2. Add the tomato cubes to the mayonnaise, blending gently. Fold the mayonnaise with the parsley into the shrimp and celery. Add salt and cayenne to taste.

3. Serve garnished with watercress and black olives.

Serves 4 as an entrée

VARIATIONS: *Shrimp Salad with Cucumber and Dill:* Omit the celery, and add peeled and cubed cucumber and a bouquet of fresh dill. Use a vinaigrette dressing instead of the tomato mayonnaise. Garnish with tomatoes, fresh dill, and slivered black olives.

Shrimp Salad with Peas: Add 1 cup of blanched fresh, tender young peas and ½ cup slivered water chestnuts. Blend with curried mayonnaise, or blender mayonnaise, omitting the tomatoes.

JAMBALAYA

◆◆

Jambalaya originated with the Spanish when they came to Louisiana in the late 1700s. It is a direct descendant of their paella, but in the new world it became known as a Creole dish—and a delicious one indeed. For a dinner party what could be better than Jambalaya, a crisp green salad with vinaigrette dressing, French bread, and praline ice cream. You will think you are dining in the French Quarter.

A contestant at work during the World Champion Jambalaya Chef Contest in Gonzales, Louisiana—where they take their food seriously!

◆

2 tablespoons lard or solid vegetable shortening
6 ounces unbaked country smoked ham or any good smoked ham, cut into ½-inch slivers
3 slices smoked bacon
½ cup chopped onion
1 large can (28 ounces) tomatoes, or 3½ cups peeled fresh ripe tomatoes plus 1 cup fresh tomato juice
2 ribs celery, cut in half
2 bay leaves
4 sprigs thyme or 1 teaspoon dried
4 large sprigs parsley
1 fresh small red chile pepper, sliced, or ½ dried, crumbled, or to taste
¼ teaspoon ground cumin or to taste
1 clove garlic, unpeeled
Salt to taste
1 cup long-grain rice
3 cups Chicken or Veal Stock (see Index) or more as needed
1½ pounds small shrimp, shelled, deveined, and refrigerated
Chopped fresh parsley, for garnish

◆

1. Heat the lard or shortening in a large heavy pan or dutch oven. Add the ham and sauté lightly, but do not fry or allow it to become brown.

2. Add the bacon, onion, tomatoes with their juice, celery, bay leaves, thyme, parsley, chile pepper, and cumin. Stick the garlic with a toothpick (for easy removal) and add it. Bring to a boil, reduce the heat, and simmer for about 1 hour. If the sauce boils too low, add a little of the stock. Season with salt.

3. When the sauce has developed a good flavor, add the rice and 3 cups stock. Toss thoroughly with a fork. Cover the pan and simmer over low heat (or bake in a 350°F oven) until the rice is almost tender, about 1 hour, adding more stock if the mixture becomes too dry. It must remain moist and almost creamy. You may have to place it over a "flame-tamer" to prevent it from sticking.

4. Five minutes before the dish is done, remove the bacon, celery, bay leaves, sprigs of thyme, parsley, and garlic. Season with salt if needed. Add the shrimp and toss them through the rice with a fork. Add a little stock if it is needed. Simmer just long enough for the shrimp to cook, 3 to 4 minutes. (The time depends upon the size of the shrimp; they will toughen if overcooked.) Sprinkle with chopped parsley and serve.

Serves 4

VARIATION: *Jambalaya Sauce with Pasta:* This flavorful sauce, especially when made with country ham, is delightful served over hot noodles. Follow directions for Jambalaya, but omit the rice and shrimp. It is not traditional, but 1 slivered red bell pepper is a good addition.

SHRIMP OR CRAB BOIL

*I*mported bay leaves should be used in this mixture. For each pound of shrimp or blue crab, use 3 tablespoons of seasoning, plus 2 slices lemon, to 1 quart of cold water.

¼ cup coriander seed
⅓ cup yellow mustard seed
1 dried red pepper, crushed (about 1 tablespoon)
2 imported bay leaves, crumbled
3 whole cloves
8 whole allspice
1¼ tablespoons coarse (kosher) salt

1. Combine all the ingredients and mix well. If stored in a tightly covered, clean jar in a dry, cool place, it will keep for 6 months.

2. To use, tie the seasoning mixture in a cheesecloth bag. Drop it into the water in a stainless steel or enamel saucepan along with the lemon slices, bring to a boil, and simmer 10 minutes.

3. Add the shrimp (in the shell) or hard-shell crabs and boil gently, uncovered, 1 to 3 minutes for shrimp (depending upon the size), 20 minutes for crabs.

4. Drain, and use as directed.
Makes ⅔ cup

Separating the shrimp from the fish in the day's catch off the Louisiana coast.

ALABAMA DEVILED CRABMEAT

*W*hen Southerners call a dish "deviled," expect it to contain mustard, Worcestershire sauce, Tabasco, and peppers galore—four of their favorite things.

1 pound fresh lump crabmeat
3 tablespoons butter
2 tablespoons all-purpose flour
1 cup heavy or whipping cream
3 tablespoons finely chopped scallions (green onions)
3 tablespoons chopped fresh parsley
½ large green bell pepper, chopped
½ large red bell or fresh pimento pepper, chopped
2 teaspoons Worcestershire sauce
½ teaspoon dry mustard
Juice of ½ lemon, or to taste
Tabasco to taste
Salt to taste
Cayenne pepper to taste
1 cup buttered and very lightly toasted bread crumbs (see Index)

1. Preheat the oven to 375°F.
2. Pick over the crabmeat well, discarding any cartilage. Set aside.
3. Melt the butter in a heavy saucepan. Add the flour and blend until smooth over medium heat. Slowly add the cream and then the scallions. Cook, stirring the sauce constantly, over medium heat until the scallions have cooked somewhat and are limp and the sauce has lost its raw flavor, 3 minutes. Remove from the heat.
4. Stir the crabmeat, parsley, and bell peppers into the sauce. Add the Worcestershire sauce, mustard, a squeeze or two of lemon juice, Tabasco, salt, and cayenne. Blend thoroughly.
5. Spoon the mixture into a lightly buttered baking dish or scallop shells, and cover with the toasted crumbs. Bake until the crabmeat is bubbly hot and the crumbs are golden brown. Serve at once.
Serves 4

CRABMEAT IMPERIAL

*O*f the many crabmeat dishes I have taught, this remains my favorite. It is worthy of the freshest and best lump backfin crabmeat you can buy.

1 pound fresh lump crabmeat
3 tablespoons butter
1½ tablespoons all-purpose flour
1 cup heavy or whipping cream
2 egg yolks
2 tablespoons medium-dry Spanish sherry or Madeira
3 tablespoons chopped fresh parsley
3 tablespoons capers, or more to taste, drained
Salt to taste

Cayenne pepper to taste
¾ cup buttered and toasted bread crumbs (see Index)
Lemon slices, for garnish
Parsley sprigs, for garnish

1. Preheat the oven to 400°F.
2. Pick over the crabmeat well, discarding any cartilage, but do not shred it.

The lumps should remain intact.

3. Melt the butter in a heavy saucepan, add the flour, and stir until smooth. Add the cream and whisk over medium-low heat until the sauce thickens, 3 minutes. Turn the heat down to allow the sauce to cool a bit.

4. Blend in the egg yolks and sherry or Madeira. Do not allow the mixture to boil but stir it gently until it thickens. Add the parsley, capers, salt, and cayenne. Place over hot water or very low heat and cook until the sherry loses its raw flavor, about 2 minutes.

5. Add the crabmeat and blend. Allow the mixture to ripen over hot water at least 30 minutes.

6. Spoon the mixture into 4 scallop shells or shallow ramekins, and sprinkle the tops generously with the toasted crumbs. Put the shells or ramekins on a pastry sheet, and bake until the mixture is bubbly hot, 2 to 3 minutes.

The ladies of North Carolina dressed elegantly, even while crab-fishing, around 1900.

7. Place a slice of lemon on each dish of crabmeat and garnish with a small sprig of parsley. Serve at once.

Serves 4

VARIATIONS: Three-quarters cup slivered fresh mushrooms, sautéed in butter and seasoned with fresh lemon juice to taste, may be added to the crabmeat instead of the capers.

If you wish to serve 6 people with 1 pound crabmeat, add ½ cup cooked white rice along with the crabmeat.

Capers were always packed in tarragon vinegar before the inflation days. The vinegar enhanced their flavor. The vinegar from present-day capers can be discarded and replaced with tarragon white wine vinegar, then allowed to ripen a few days in the refrigerator before using.

LUNCHEON FOR SPECIAL FRIENDS

Crabmeat Imperial in Scallop Shells

Cornmeal Croissants

Boston Lettuce with Rich Vinaigrette

◆

Luscious Chocolate Cake with Whipped Cream

Coffee

SAUTEED SOFT-SHELL CRABS

*T*he simplest way of all is the best way to cook soft-shell crabs. Their flavor is that delicate and that evanescent. Don't even dip them in beaten egg—that too masks their flavor. Dust them with flour, then sauté in butter and season with salt, freshly ground white pepper, and lemon juice. Serve with new potatoes, tiny green beans, peas, or asparagus with a light hollandaise. Add homemade hot rolls and frozen chocolate soufflé. Live.

6 small soft-shell crabs, dressed
Salt to taste
6 tablespoons all-purpose flour, or as needed
8 tablespoons (1 stick) unsalted butter
Freshly ground white pepper to taste
Fresh lemon juice to taste
Watercress sprigs, for garnish
Lemon wedges, for garnish

1. Dry the crabs well, sprinkle them with salt, and dust lightly with the flour. Do not dredge or coat the crabs too heavily.

2. Melt the butter in a heavy skillet over medium-high heat. (I am partial to my heavy copper skillet, but black iron is fine.) Sauté the crabs (do not crowd them) in the foaming butter until golden brown on one side, then turn to brown the other side. Turn them only once, about 3 to 5 minutes on each side. The crabs, like almost all fish and shellfish, should be cooked fast, but the butter must not burn nor turn very dark.

3. Sprinkle the crabs again with a little salt, and season with white pepper and a squeeze or two of lemon juice. Spoon the lovely golden butter in the skillet over the crabs, and serve garnished with watercress and lemon wedges.

Serves 3

VARIATIONS: Add 1½ teaspoons buttered and toasted sliced or slivered almonds per crab at serving time.

Add a sprinkling of chopped fresh herbs, such as dill and parsley, or tarragon and parsley, or chervil and parsley. Chervil possibly is the best.

A few capers that have been marinated in tarragon vinegar are delicious when added with the sprinkling of lemon juice.

HOW TO DRESS SOFT-SHELL CRABS

Cook soft-shell crabs as soon as possible after they have been dressed. If you have to buy the crabs the day before using, have the fishmonger pack them alive in seaweed or grass. Refrigerate them, then dress shortly before using.

1. Select crabs that are alive and "wiggling."

2. Snip off the eyes with scissors. This brings instant and painless death.

3. Turn the crab on its back and remove the apron. Lift up the flaps at each end and pull out the spongy gill tissue.

4. Press above the legs and pull out the bile sac. Clean the crabs well under cold running water.

5. Pat the crabs dry with paper towels.

NORFOLK NOODLES WITH CRABMEAT AND HAM

Delicious with snow peas, asparagus, fresh green peas, or tiny tender green beans.

½ pound crabmeat
½ pound fresh noodles, such as thin fettuccine
3 tablespoons unsalted butter
1¼ cups heavy or whipping cream
6 ounces baked Virginia or Smithfield ham, prosciutto, or any good baked ham, cut into julienne strips
Salt and freshly ground white pepper to taste

Cayenne pepper to taste
Bouquet of mixed chopped fresh herbs, such as parsley, chervil, and tarragon

1. Pick over the crabmeat well, discarding any cartilage.

2. Plunge the noodles into a pot of boiling salted water and cook until tender.

(Tasting is the best test.) Drain at once and return to the pot. Add 1 tablespoon of the butter, toss to coat the noodles—this will prevent them from sticking—and cover to keep warm.

3. In the meantime, boil the cream to reduce and thicken it a bit, 1½ minutes. Add the crabmeat, ham, and remaining butter. Blend, and season with salt, white pepper, and cayenne to taste. Sprinkle with herbs.

4. Divide the noodles among 4 plates and spoon some of the crabmeat sauce over each. Serve at once.

Serves 4

It's tedious work, shelling crabs—but oh, that delicious fresh crabmeat!

MARYLAND CRAB CAKES

*C*rab cakes are one of the most famous dishes of the Eastern Shore. The recipes vary a little but not much. They must be sautéed in butter, and I think they scream for capers. These Maryland crab cakes are considered to be very fine. They do not have onions or shallots as many do. If you wish, the extra flavor of lemon or onion juice, no pulp, can be added to the mayonnaise.

1 pound fresh lump crabmeat
Juice of ½ lemon
2 tablespoons butter
2 tablespoons all-purpose flour
½ cup milk
¼ teaspoon dry mustard
2 egg yolks, at room temperature
1 tablespoon capers, or more to taste, drained
Salt and freshly ground white pepper to taste
Cayenne pepper to taste
6 tablespoons (¾ stick) unsalted butter
2 tablespoons vegetable oil
Lemon wedges, for garnish
Homemade mayonnaise (see Index), for garnish

COATING

1¼ cups fresh bread crumbs (see step 4)
½ cup all-purpose flour
1 egg
⅓ cup milk

1. Pick over the crabmeat well, removing any cartilage. Mash it lightly, add the lemon juice, and mix.

2. Melt the butter in a heavy saucepan. Add the flour and blend until smooth. Add the milk slowly, beating with a whisk. Cook over medium-low heat until the sauce is smooth and has lost its raw flavor, 2 minutes. Blend in the mustard and remove from the heat. Beat in the egg yolks. Add

*C*ontrary to the belief of many, the blue crab and the so-called soft-shelled crab are the same species (*Callinectes sapidus*). This sapidus crab (*sapidus* means savory and tasteful) is found in the U.S. from the Delaware Bay down to Florida and the Gulf states. They shed their hard coats many times before maturity. In the season for shedding, the fishermen call these beautiful swimmers "peelers." The meat that we buy fresh by the pound, however, is from the crabs with the hard shell. All crabmeat is perfect summer fare—very *sapidus*.

the crabmeat, capers, salt, white pepper, and cayenne. (Seafood is especially compatible with cayenne as well as capers.)

3. Refrigerate the crabmeat mixture to allow it to firm up, at least 1 hour.

4. Prepare the coating: Make the bread crumbs in a processor (quicker and easier than a blender), using homemade-type white bread, and set aside in a bowl. Put the flour in a bowl, and beat together the egg and milk in another bowl.

5. Form the crabmeat mixture into 8 patties. Dip each patty in flour, then in the egg and milk mixture, and then coat well with bread crumbs. Refrigerate for 1 hour or so for the crab cakes to set.

6. Heat the butter and oil in a heavy skillet and sauté the crab cakes until they are golden brown on both sides, 5 to 6 minutes. Serve with wedges of lemon and homemade mayonnaise.

Serves 4

VARIATION: A few tablespoons of finely slivered Smithfield ham added to the crab is delicious.

NEW ORLEANS FROG LEGS

Sautéed small fresh frog legs have a delicate, almost fleeting flavor that is very bland when cooked in vegetable oil only. Butter enhances their flavor, as does lemon juice. The garlic is added to the nut-brown butter that is poured over the frog legs after they are sautéed—not during the cooking.

12 small frog legs, ready to cook
½ cup all-purpose flour
6 tablespoons (¾ stick) unsalted butter, or more as needed
1 tablespoon vegetable oil
Salt and freshly ground white pepper to taste
Cayenne pepper to taste
1 or 2 squeezes lemon juice
1 clove garlic, cut in half
Chopped fresh parsley, for garnish
Lemon wedges, for garnish

1. Roll the frog legs in the flour, pressing them firmly to make the flour stick. Shake to remove any excess flour.

2. Melt 4 tablespoons of the butter in a heavy skillet and add the vegetable oil. Sauté the frog legs over medium-high heat until golden brown on both sides, turning them only once. Season with salt, white pepper, cayenne, and lemon juice. Transfer the frog legs to a warm platter.

3. In a clean skillet, melt the remaining butter over low heat and add the garlic. Toss the garlic around in the skillet until the butter has taken on a little color and has absorbed the flavor of the garlic, about 30 seconds. Discard the garlic and pour the butter over the frog legs.

4. Sprinkle with parsley, and serve with lemon wedges alongside.

Serves 4

You will notice how carefully I handle garlic. These frog legs, correctly cooked, have only a slight hint of garlic, and the clove isn't added until after the frog legs are removed from the pan. Why have fresh, wonderful food if it is smothered in garlic. Amen!

Frog legs have always been a delicacy. They are at their best when fresh and very small. Only the legs of the frog are eaten. If you are preparing them yourself, cut off the hind legs only close to the body. Wash the legs in cold water, and strip off the skin as you would pull off a glove. Chop off the feet and soak the legs in cold water for at least 2 hours, changing the water often.

OYSTER PAN ROAST

*F*or the true Chesapeake oyster lover, this is *the* dish.

Shallot and White Wine Sauce (recipe follows)
   or lemon wedges
4 to 6 slices piping hot Grilled Buttered Toast
   (recipe follows)
8 tablespoons (1 stick) unsalted butter
1 pint shucked fresh oysters, well drained
Salt and freshly ground black pepper to taste
Juice of 1 lemon
Tabasco sauce to taste (optional)
Several sprigs watercress, or chopped parsley,
   for garnish

1. Prepare the Shallot and White Wine Sauce, if using, and set aside.

2. Grill the toast.

3. In the meantime, melt the butter in a large heavy skillet. Place the oysters in the butter and cook over low heat just until the oysters have plumped and begun to curl. Quickly sprinkle with salt and pepper and the lemon juice.

4. Immediately place the hot oysters on the hot grilled toast. Sprinkle with the Tabasco, if desired. Garnish with watercress or chopped parsley, and serve with Shallot and White Wine Sauce or lemon wedges. Don't forget the chilled dry white wine or cold, cold beer.

Serves 4 to 6

SHALLOT AND WHITE WINE SAUCE

4 tablespoons (½ stick) unsalted butter, or more
   as needed
¼ cup water
⅓ cup chopped shallots (do not substitute
   onions)
¼ cup chopped red or green bell pepper (red is
   best)
½ cup dry white wine
Salt and freshly ground black pepper to taste

1. Melt the butter in the water in a heavy stainless steel or enamel skillet. Add the shallots and chopped bell pepper. Simmer until the water has boiled away, 2 minutes.

2. Add the wine and simmer until it has lost its raw flavor, about 5 minutes. Add more butter if needed for the sauce to be smooth and creamy. Add salt and pepper to taste. Set aside.

3. Bring again to a simmer before pouring over the oysters on grilled toast.

Makes about 1 cup

GRILLED BUTTERED TOAST

1. Preheat the oven to 450°F.

2. Spread pieces of homemade-style white bread with butter on both sides. Put on a pastry sheet and place in the oven to grill. This will take from 8 to 10 minutes.

CHESAPEAKE BAY OYSTER STEW

*O*yster stew is really not a stew, as it is barely cooked. The oysters are heated only until the edges start to curl. Treated this way, the full delicate flavor of the oysters is retained, and they do not toughen the least bit.

1 cup milk
1 cup light cream
1 cup shucked fresh oysters
2 tablespoons butter
Salt to taste
Cayenne pepper to taste
Tabasco sauce, for garnish

1. Heat the milk and cream together in a saucepan until very hot, but do not allow to boil. Add the oysters, butter, and salt.

2. When the butter has melted, remove the stew from the direct heat. Place the saucepan over or in a larger pan of hot water. Allow the stew to ripen a few minutes, stirring it gently. Taste for salt, and add cayenne to taste.

3. Pass the Tabasco and fresh, crisp oyster crackers or French bread.

Serves 2 to 4

PERFECT PAN-FRIED OYSTERS

*F*or perfect pan-fried oysters, choose large ones and keep the coating dry so it will stick. Don't use a lightweight or stainless steel skillet—it won't work.

Oysters—mountains of oysters! A cook's dream.

12 to 18 large oysters, shucked (see Index)
1 cup all-purpose flour, or as needed
2 whole eggs
1 tablespoon water or milk
3 cups fresh bread crumbs or very fine matzoh
    cracker crumbs, or more as needed
6 tablespoons (¾ stick) butter
3 tablespoons vegetable oil
Salt to taste
Lemon wedges, for garnish
Mustard and Tarragon Hollandaise, or
    homemade mayonnaise (see Index) flavored
    with horseradish or chili sauce

1. Drain the oysters. (Reserve the liquor and freeze it for later use, if desired.) Lay the oysters on paper towels or a clean cloth that will absorb any extra moisture.

2. Put the flour in a shallow pan. Whisk the eggs with the water or milk in a small bowl. Put 1 cup of the crumbs in a shallow pan.

3. Dust each oyster in flour, then dip in the beaten egg, then in the crumbs. Add fresh crumbs to the pan as needed (if all the crumbs are placed in the pan at once, they will become damp and compact).

4. Lay the oysters on a paper-towel-lined pastry sheet after breading. Refrigerate for 1 hour for the crumbs to set.

5. Place a black iron skillet over medium-high heat. Add 2 tablespoons of the butter and 1 tablespoon of the vegetable oil and heat until melted and hot but not smoking. Add the oysters, a few at a time, to the pan. Sauté until golden brown on both sides, then sprinkle with salt. Drain the oysters on paper towels, and keep warm. Repeat until all the oysters are done, adding butter and oil as needed.

6. Serve the oysters piping hot, with wedges of lemon and one of the sauces. The choice is yours.

Serves 2 to 3

🦉 Matzoh cracker crumbs make a crisp, crisp crust, as they contain no fat, but they must be ground fine in a processor.

If at any time the crumbs on the oysters burn, stop, wash the skillet, and start over. The butter is used for a delicious flavor; the oil is added to help prevent the butter from burning.

NEW ORLEANS OYSTERS AND ARTICHOKES

◆◆◆

*T*his is beyond a doubt one of the finest dishes from New Orleans. It is usually served as a first course, but it can also be a light entrée. It is, in any case, among the great dishes of the South.

◆

6 large artichokes
2 lemons
8 tablespoons (1 stick) butter
3 tablespoons all-purpose flour
½ cup finely chopped shallots
½ chopped fresh parsley
Pinch dried thyme
2 cups oyster liquor or Veal Stock (see Index)
Salt to taste
Cayenne pepper to taste
1½ pints shucked fresh oysters
1½ cups buttered and toasted bread crumbs
   (see Index)
Thin lemon slices, for garnish

◆

Martina's is one of a number of companies that deliver fresh oysters to the restaurants in New Orleans.

1. Remove and discard the stems of the artichokes. Drop the artichokes into a large pot of boiling salted water. Squeeze in the juice of 1 lemon. Cook until tender, 25 to 35 minutes, depending on their size and tenderness. Test at 25 minutes. Do not overcook. Drain, and set aside to cool.

2. Scrape and reserve the pulp from the bottom of the artichoke leaves. Remove and discard the chokes. Cut the artichoke hearts into thin slices, and set the slices aside with the pulp.

3. Preheat the oven to 375°F.

4. Melt the butter in a heavy saucepan. Add the flour, and stir constantly until the mixture is smooth and the flour has lost its raw flavor, about 1 minute. Add the shallots, parsley, thyme, oyster liquor or veal stock, and salt and cayenne to taste. Bring to a boil, reduce the heat, and simmer

about 15 minutes. Taste. Add juice from the remaining lemon, to taste.

5. Add the oysters, and heat just until their edges begin to curl, not more than 1 minute. Remove from the heat and keep warm.

6. Divide the artichoke slices and pulp evenly among 6 ramekins. Spoon the oysters and sauce over the artichokes, and sprinkle generously with the toasted crumbs. Place 2 thin slices of lemon, over-lapping, on top of the bread crumbs in each ramekin.

7. Bake only until bubbly hot. In shallow ramekins it will take only a few minutes. If prepared ahead and refrigerated, bring to room temperature so the oysters will not overcook and toughen. Serve at once with French bread and a dry white wine.

Serves 6

CLAM AND OYSTER FRITTERS

*T*his is an excellent basic seafood fritter that can be made with all oysters, or all clams, or a mixture of oysters, clams, and mussels—according to your whim of the day. The quickest and easiest way to chop oysters or clams in the home kitchen is with scissors. Barber shears are my favorite. This batter holds very well for 24 hours. It may thicken up even a bit more on standing.

TO CLEAN AND STEAM MUSSELS OR CLAMS

Scrub the shells with a stiff brush, or scrape off the dirt with a paring knife. Pull out the beard, or cord, on mussels just before they are to be used; otherwise they will die. This is their life-sustaining cord.

Some mussels are open slightly but this does not always indicate that they are bad. Touch the inside and edge with the point of a sharp knife. If the mussel is alive, the shell will close at once; if it doesn't, discard it. Spoiled mussels or clams have a strong, unpleasant odor. The live ones smell only of the sea and iodine.

Toss the mussels in a large pan of cold water with a handful of salt and leave for 1 hour. They will throw off most of the sand that remained after the first washing. Clams should not be soaked.

Place the mussels or clams in a kettle with ½ inch salted water and steam only until the shells open, about 6 minutes. Discard any that do not open.

½ cup clam juice or oyster liquor
½ cup milk
2 eggs
¾ cup sifted all-purpose flour
⅔ cup cracker crumbs (saltines or matzoh crackers)
1¼ teaspoons baking powder
1 tablespoon chopped fresh parsley
1 cup shucked fresh clams, chopped
1 cup shucked fresh oysters, chopped
1 teaspoon salt, or to taste
Freshly ground black pepper to taste
Cayenne pepper to taste
Peanut or vegetable oil for deep-frying (see Index)
Lemon wedges, for garnish
Tartar sauce with capers (see page 192)

1. Combine the clam juice or oyster liquor, milk, and eggs in a roomy bowl and beat thoroughly with a whisk.

2. Add the flour and beat until smooth

and free of lumps. Add the cracker crumbs, baking powder, and parsley. Mix well.

3. Stir in the clams and oysters. Add the salt, and black pepper and cayenne to taste. Allow the mixture to rest and thicken for 15 to 20 minutes before frying.

4. Heat the oil in a deep saucepan to 365°F on a deep-fat thermometer. Drop the fritters by spoonfuls into the oil, and fry until light golden brown. When the fritters have browned on one side, turn them gently to brown on the other.

5. Drain on paper towels, and serve at once with lemon wedges and tartar sauce.

Serves 4 to 6

Taking a break at the Maryland docks for the freshest shellfish of all.

MARYLAND OYSTERS AND SCALLOPS

*T*his is one of the most subtle of all the seafood dishes I know and have taught. No amount of praise would be extravagant, but the recipe must be followed to the letter. Each ingredient plays its part as in an orchestra—the bacon, the herbs, and the counterpoint of oysters and scallops is near perfection.

1 pound scallops
1 pint shucked fresh oysters
4 slices smoked bacon or salt pork
3 tablespoons finely chopped red or green bell pepper
3 shallots, peeled and chopped
1 bay leaf
2 sprigs each thyme and tarragon, or ⅓ teaspoon each dried
1 cup dry white wine
½ cup Fish or Veal Stock (see Index) or oyster liquor
Salt to taste
⅔ cup heavy or whipping cream
2 egg yolks, at room temperature
Freshly ground white pepper to taste
Cayenne pepper to taste
1 cup buttered and toasted bread crumbs (see Index)
Lemon slices, for garnish
Parsley sprigs, for garnish

1. Preheat the oven to 450°F.

2. Rinse the scallops thoroughly in a colander under running water to rid them of sand. Drain well. If you are using large sea scallops, cut them in half. Set aside. Drain the oysters but reserve the liquor.

SPRING CANDLELIGHT DINNER

Very Special Cheese Straws

◆

Maryland Oysters and Scallops in Ramekins

Green Rice

Fiddlehead and Mushroom Salad

Chilled White Wine

◆

Yellow Sponge Cake Roll

Coffee

3. Sauté the bacon or salt pork in a heavy saucepan. Lift it out (use the bacon for another purpose), and add the bell pepper, shallots, bay leaf, thyme, and tarragon to the fat. Cover, and cook slowly for the flavors to blend.

4. Add the scallops, wine, and stock or oyster liquor. Simmer 3 to 5 minutes, no longer. Add salt to taste. Lift out the scallops with a slotted spoon. Set aside.

5. Strain the sauce into another saucepan, and discard the seasonings. Add the cream, and simmer until the sauce has thickened and reduced so that it is not thin or runny, about 1½ minutes.

6. Lower the heat and cook for a few seconds. Add the egg yolks to the sauce, and blend them in quickly with a whisk.

7. Add the scallops and oysters, and simmer only until the edges of the oysters begin to curl, 3 minutes. Season with white pepper, cayenne, and salt to taste.

8. Divide the mixture among 6 small shallow ramekins or scallop shells. Cover with the toasted crumbs. Heat thoroughly in the oven, not over 4 minutes. Do not allow the seafood to cook further.

9. Garnish each ramekin with a slice of lemon and a tiny sprig of parsley. Serve at once.

Serves 6

CLASSIC SCALLOPS IN SHELLS (COQUILLES ST. JACQUES)

W hen Aphrodite, the goddess of love and beauty rose from the sea, she skimmed the waves in a scallop shell. Thus scallops are the only bivalve with a "patron saint." Scallops are just as delicious as the shells are beautiful, but great care must be taken in cooking them or they will be dry and tough—not over 3 minutes total cooking time for the bay scallops and 4 to 5 minutes for the sea scallops.

¾ pound scallops
1 cup dry white wine
¼ cup water
2 shallots, finely chopped
1½ cups heavy or whipping cream
Salt and freshly ground white pepper to taste
Cayenne pepper to taste
Juice of ½ lemon
1¼ cups buttered (use 2½ tablespoons butter)
    and lightly toasted bread crumbs (see
    Index)
Chopped fresh parsley, for garnish

1. Rinse the scallops thoroughly in a colander under running water to rid them of sand. Drain well.

2. Preheat the oven to 375°F.

3. Combine the wine, water, and shallots in a heavy stainless steel or enamel saucepan. Bring to a simmer, add the scallops, and cook only until they lose their transparency, about 3 to 4 minutes for large sea scallops, less for small scallops.

4. Remove the scallops with a slotted spoon. If you are using large sea scallops, slice them in half. Distribute the scallops evenly among scallop shells or shallow ramekins.

5. Reduce the scallop stock over medium-high heat until only about ½ cup remains, 2 to 3 minutes. Add the cream, and cook to reduce the sauce until it has thickened and is rich and creamy, another 2 to 3 minutes. Season to taste with salt,

white pepper, cayenne, and a squeeze or two of lemon juice.

6. Spoon the sauce over the scallops, and cover with the toasted crumbs. Bake only until the crumbs are lightly browned and bubbly hot, 2 to 3 minutes. Do not allow the scallops to cook further or they will toughen. Garnish with parsley, and serve at once.

Serves 4 as an entrée

The cooked scallops may be combined with the sauce a few hours ahead, then popped into the shells before heating. Allow the mixture to come to room temperature before placing them in the oven.

This recipe is sufficient for 6 to 8 as a first course. To serve as a hot hors d'oeuvre, 2 scallops per person is sufficient.

Scallop shells are considered by artists to be one of the most beautiful designs in nature, and the scallop is most certainly one of our most delicious seafoods.

In France scallops are always called Coquilles Saint-Jacques, or St. James shells, a name that goes back to the Middle Ages. According to legend, Saint James the Great, after his martyrdom in Judea, was set adrift at sea but was safely guided by the angels to the shores of Padrón, in Spain.

In the twelfth century a cathedral was erected over St. James's grave at Santiago de Compostela, and this soon became a shrine for French pilgrims, who crossed the Pyrenees into Spain. Souvenirs of these pilgrimages were the beautiful shells of St. James from the beaches of Padrón.

SCALLOPS IN SHELLS WITH MUSHROOMS

The sauce for these scallops may seem thin, but the bread crumbs will thicken it up at the end more deliciously than additional flour. Serve this dish accompanied by buttered fresh spinach and a garden tomato salad with fresh basil or tarragon.

1 pound large sea scallops
1 cup dry white wine
2 sprigs thyme or ¼ teaspoon dried thyme
1 bay leaf
2 sprigs parsley
6 tablespoons (¾ stick) unsalted butter
¼ pound mushrooms, sliced
3 small shallots, finely chopped
Fresh lemon juice to taste
3 tablespoons all-purpose flour
¼ cup heavy or whipping cream
2 egg yolks, at room temperature
Salt to taste
Cayenne pepper to taste
1¼ cups buttered and toasted bread crumbs (see Index)

1. Rinse the scallops thoroughly in a colander under running water to rid them of sand. Drain well and set aside.

2. Preheat the oven to 400°F.

3. Bring the wine, thyme, bay leaf, and parsley to a boil in a large saucepan. Add the scallops, and simmer (do not allow them to boil) 3 to 5 minutes, depending upon the size. Remove the scallops as soon as they look opaque, reserving the liquid. Slice the scallops and set them aside in a large bowl.

4. Melt 3 tablespoons of the butter in a small skillet and lightly sauté the mushrooms and shallots over medium heat. Add a squeeze or two of lemon juice and combine with the scallops.

5. Melt the remaining butter in a heavy saucepan. Add the flour and stir until smooth. Add the scallop stock and cream. Cook over low heat until the sauce has thickened and is smooth, 2 to 3 minutes. Stir a spoonful of the hot sauce into the egg yolks, then add the yolks, and salt and cayenne to taste, to the sauce. Blend with the scallops and mushrooms.

6. Spoon the mixture into scallop shells and cover with the toasted crumbs. Bake just until bubbly hot, 2 to 3 minutes. Serve at once.

Serves 4

🦉 The egg yolks are added for richness and a slight thickening as well as flavor, but they can be omitted.

SCALLOPS WITH SNOW PEAS AND MUSHROOMS

◆◆◆

*A*nother elegant and easy dish—delicious with the Florida calico scallops, or use sea scallops sliced in half.

◆

1 to 1¼ pounds scallops
½ pound fresh, tender snow peas
5 tablespoons butter
1½ cups slivered mushrooms
Salt and freshly ground white pepper to taste
2 cups heavy or whipping cream
Cayenne pepper to taste
Fresh lemon juice to taste
⅓ cup chopped mixed herbs, such as fresh
*   parsley, chervil, and tarragon, for garnish*

◆

1. Rinse the scallops thoroughly in a colander under running water to rid them of sand. Drain well and set aside.

2. String the snow peas. Cut the tips off both ends. Rinse, and drain well. Sliver the snow peas into 2 to 3 pieces lengthwise. (This is easily done with sharp thin scissors such as barber shears.)

3. Melt 2 tablespoons of the butter in a heavy saucepan over medium heat. Add the snow peas and mushrooms, and toss until the vegetables are well coated with the butter and are partially cooked but still crisp, 1 minute. Add salt and white pepper to taste, and set aside. Keep the vegetables warm by placing them over a pan of hot water.

4. In another pan, combine the cream and 1 tablespoon of the butter. Boil (heavy cream will not curdle when boiled) until the sauce has reduced by one-third and is rich and creamy, 1 to 2 minutes. Set aside and keep warm.

5. Melt the remaining 2 tablespoons butter in a heavy saucepan. Add the scallops. Cook quickly over rather high heat, tossing the scallops in the butter. The scallops will give off a flavorful broth that will blend with the butter to make a lovely sauce. Cook the scallops 3 to 5 minutes, depending upon their size. As soon as they turn white all the way through, they are done. Taste one to test it. They must stay as tender as butter. Add salt, cayenne, and a squeeze or two of lemon juice. Stir, then drain the broth into the cream sauce.

6. Add the vegetables to the cream sauce. Cook over low heat only a few seconds for the flavors to blend. Taste for seasoning and correct as necessary.

7. Divide the vegetables and sauce evenly among 4 warm plates. Spoon the scallops out of the pan and place them in the center of the sauce. Sprinkle with the herbs and serve at once.

Serves 4

CHAPTER SEVEN

VEGETABLES

THE GARDENER'S PRIDE

◆◆◆

*I*n planning which vegetables to have with certain menus, the season is our best guideline. The early Southern spring and sun-laden summers bring us green peas, asparagus, tender green beans, new potatoes, and corn, all of which are especially delicious with our lighter meals of fish, seafood, veal, and lamb. In the winter, the vibrant vegetables such as acorn squash, cauliflower, cabbage, broccoli, and dried beans are more compatible with the heartier meats such as fresh pork, beef, and game; and there are almost no vegetables in the South that are incompatible with ham and chicken.

A steadfast rule that weathers all fads and fashions is that the vegetables must taste of what they are. It would be a shame to take great pains to grow fresh vegetables in the garden or to shop tirelessly for them in the market and then disguise their exquisite natural flavors by overcooking or overseasoning.

Freshness is at the heart of all fine vegetable cookery, and that freshness must be guarded jealously.

◆◆◆

FRESH ARTICHOKE BOTTOMS STUFFED WITH ASPARAGUS

*T*he beauty and form of the artichoke have made it a great favorite of artists. A friend of Matisse, the French painter, is said to have asked one day, "And what is your greatest happiness, Henri?" "To watch the sunlight and shadows on my artichokes," replied Matisse.

The flavor is subtle and rather difficult to describe, but it is utterly delicious. I am sure that all vegetables would be artichokes if they could.

1 cup Rich Vinaigrette (see Index)
6 extra-large artichoke bottoms, cooked and
    chilled (see box, page 228)
18 fresh asparagus spears, cooked and diced
3 hard-cooked eggs, sliced
2 pitted colossal black olives, sliced

1. Put about 1½ teaspoons of Rich Vinaigrette in the cavity of each artichoke bottom. Fill the cavities with the asparagus. Sprinkle with more vinaigrette. Lay a slice of egg over the asparagus, and put a slice of black olive in the middle of the egg.

2. Serve with a sauceboat of vinaigrette, as a first course for dinner or luncheon or as a light entrée.

Serves 6 as a first course

If the artichoke bottoms are not extra large, place them on a leaf or two of Bibb lettuce or on a layer of chopped fresh parsley and herbs.

My daughter and I chanced upon some artichokes in a garden once and it was an exciting moment. They do have dramatic presence. They are as beautiful as flowers.

TO COOK WHOLE ARTICHOKES

*W*ash the artichokes by holding them under cold running water. Break off the stem even with the base. Trim off the prickly top of each leaf with scissors.

Drop the artichokes into a large amount of boiling salted water (1½ teaspoons salt per quart of water). Add a slice of lemon or a little lemon juice.

Simmer until a cooking fork goes through the stem end easily, from 30 to 40 minutes, depending upon the artichoke. Remove from the water at once, and drain well.

Serve hot, one to each person, with melted lemon butter or hollandaise; or remove the choke with ice tongs and serve the artichoke cold with vinaigrette.

ARTICHOKES BARIGOULE

*B*arigoule is the old Provençal word for thyme. This recipe came from Mapie Lautrec, an in-law of the famous artist Toulouse-Lautrec, who, by the way, was a very good cook himself. Of all the stuffed artichokes I have met, this is the masterpiece—and it is marvelous with thin, thin crisp hoe cakes. If you don't believe me, try it for lunch soon.

◆

4 artichokes
Salt and freshly ground black pepper to taste
2 shallots, chopped
¼ cup chopped fresh parsley
1 teaspoon thyme (dried or fresh)
4 slices smoked bacon, diced
6 tablespoons good-quality olive oil, or more as needed
6 tablespoons white wine, or more as needed
1 clove garlic

◆

1. Bring a large pot of salted water to a rolling boil.

2. Break off and discard the stem and cut off the top third of the artichokes. With scissors, trim off the thorny tips of the remaining leaves. Drop the artichokes into the water, season with salt and pepper, and cook at a low simmer until barely tender, 25 to 30 minutes. Turn the artichokes upside down in a colander to drain, and discard the cooking water.

3. Remove the chokes (see box), and place the artichokes back in the pot.

4. Combine the shallots, parsley, thyme, and bacon in a small bowl. Divide this mixture among the artichokes, placing a spoonful in the cavity of each one. Pour 1 tablespoon olive oil and 1 tablespoon wine into the cavity of each artichoke, and add the remaining 2 tablespoons each of oil and wine to the pot, around the artichokes. Place the garlic clove in the pot.

5. Cover the pot, and cook over low heat for 35 to 40 minutes, adding more oil and wine to the pot if it becomes dry—you want to have some sauce.

6. Spoon the sauce over the artichokes and serve.

Serves 4

VARIATIONS: Use 1 tablespoon slivered baked ham instead of the bacon.

Place 1 slice of peeled tomato in the cavity of each artichoke with the bacon or ham mixture.

TO PREPARE ARTICHOKE BOTTOMS

*B*reak off the artichoke stems. (This permits any fibrous strings to be pulled out. If the stems are sliced off, the strings remain in the bottom.) Tear off all the tough outer leaves, pulling each backward, then down toward the base.

Using a small, well-sharpened stainless steel (not carbon steel) knife, neatly pare the bottom where the stem has been torn off.

The pared surface of an artichoke darkens rapidly in contact with the air, so it is best to rub it with the cut surface of half a lemon several times during the process. Don't worry about the chokes at this point.

Plunge the pared artichokes into a stainless steel or enamel saucepan of boiling water (to each quart add the juice of half a lemon and a pinch each of thyme and salt). Cook at a simmer until the flesh no longer resists a sharp knife or the tines of a cooking fork, 10 to 30 minutes, depending on the quality and age of the artichokes. They should remain firm. Cool them in the liquid and keep them well submerged, the receptacle covered and refrigerated, until ready to use. Before using them, carefully remove the chokes, using a teaspoon or small ice tongs to gently pry them loose. Wipe the artichoke bottoms with a towel.

ASPARAGUS HOLLANDAISE

◆◆◆

*H*ollandaise is one of the greatest of the sauces and will never go out of fashion, but it is highly caloric, so we use it as a special treat. In France it is made with just a touch of lemon, but in the U.S. we make hollandaise with a strong accent of lemon.

◆

1 pound fresh asparagus
Classic Hollandaise (recipe follows)

◆

1. Wash the asparagus. Bend each spear in half until it breaks. This divides the tender stalk from the tough end. Discard the ends.

2. Remove the scales with a sharp paring knife or vegetable peeler, and peel the asparagus almost to the bud end. Cut on the diagonal into 1- to 1½-inch pieces, or tie the stalks in bundles of 6 with string.

3. Drop into boiling water and cook not more than 2 to 3 minutes. Test. The stalk should be just tender when pierced with a cooking fork. Do not overcook. Drain at once, then untie, and serve with Classic Hollandaise.

Serves 3 to 4

◆

CLASSIC HOLLANDAISE

◆

3 large egg yolks, at room temperature
2 tablespoons fresh lemon juice, or to taste
½ teaspoon salt, or to taste
8 tablespoons (1 stick) unsalted butter
Cayenne pepper to taste

◆

1. Put the egg yolks in the top of a heavy stainless steel or enamel double boiler over simmering water. Add 1 tablespoon of the lemon juice and the salt at once, and beat with a whisk until the yolks have thickened a bit, less than 1 minute.

2. Start adding the butter, a small piece at a time. Don't add more butter until the last piece has been absorbed by the yolks.

3. When all the butter has been added and the sauce is smooth, taste for tartness.

Add more lemon juice if desired, then add the cayenne. Remove from the heat but keep warm until ready to use.

Makes ¾ cup

VARIATIONS: *Tarragon Hollandaise:* When the hollandaise is ready to be removed from the heat, add 2 tablespoons chopped fresh tarragon. Especially good with broiled fish and seafood.

Dill and Cucumber Hollandaise: Peel and seed a firm small cucumber. Cut it into small thin slices or cubes. Add ⅓ cup cucumber to the hollandaise when it is removed from the heat. Fold in 1 tablespoon chopped fresh dill. Also delicious with fish and seafood.

Keep a small pan of boiling water on the stove while you are making the hollandaise. If the sauce starts to curdle, add a tablespoon of boiling water and beat hard.

A little lemon added to the hollandaise sauce after it is made gives a more refreshing flavor than adding all the lemon juice at the beginning.

◆◆

BLENDER HOLLANDAISE

*T*o make hollandaise in a blender, use the same ingredients but melt the butter and keep it warm. Rinse the blender jar with boiling water to heat it. Dry the jar, and add the egg yolks, lemon juice, and salt. Turn the blender to a high speed. Blend the yolks, then immediately start pouring in butter in a thin stream. Stop the motor after a few seconds and stir the mixture with a long thin spoon. Start the blender again, and add the remaining melted butter. Add the cayenne pepper, and more salt if needed. To keep the sauce warm, place the blender jar in a pan of hot water.

ASPARAGUS WITH HAM AND EGGS

2 pounds fresh asparagus
4 thin slices baked ham (about 1 pound)
Juice of 1 lemon
4 tablespoons (½ stick) butter, melted
1 to 2 tablespoons butter
4 eggs

ASPARAGUS

*W*hen we see the graceful, lacy branches of asparagus waving in the air, we know that summer is here. The beautiful fernlike plant which borders the roadside and hedgerows is exactly the same species as the one that grows in our gardens.

Asparagus lends itself to many different occasions. It can be important or it can be humble. It is delicious in an omelet, in a soufflé or quiche, or served rather plain. It makes one of the truly great salads, served with a vinaigrette. It is unsurpassed as a dainty sandwich for weddings or as a cold hors d'oeuvre covered with a lemony mayonnaise and rolled in thin fresh bread.

New peas and asparagus, two of our best summer vegetables, are great companions. They like being served together, and we like them that way, too.

Salt to taste
¾ cup grated Swiss or Parmesan cheese
¾ cup chopped fresh parsley
Cayenne pepper or paprika to taste
Freshly ground black pepper to taste

1. Break or cut off and discard the tough stem ends of the asparagus. Peel the asparagus stems with a thin sharp knife or vegetable peeler. Divide the asparagus into bundles of 6 to 8 and tie with string.

2. Drop the asparagus bundles into a large pot of boiling salted water and cook only until the stem end is easily pierced with a cooking fork, 2 to 3 minutes. Lift out of the water at once, and drain on paper towels, then untie the bundles.

3. Line the bottom of a shallow flame-proof casserole with the ham. Cover the ham with the asparagus. Season the asparagus with the lemon juice and melted butter. Set the casserole in a warm place.

4. Melt enough butter in a heavy skillet to keep the eggs from sticking. Add the eggs and sauté, covered, over medium heat until they are just set. Lift the eggs out with a broad spatula and place them on top of the asparagus. Salt the eggs.

5. Sprinkle the cheese over the eggs, and place the dish under the broiler (6 inches from the heat source) for just a few minutes for the cheese to melt and become a bit brown.

6. Remove the casserole from the broiler, fill in the sides of the dish with the parsley, and season with a quick dash of cayenne or paprika. Serve, and pass the black pepper.

Serves 4

VARIATIONS: This dish may be served in individual ramekins.

The eggs can be shirred in the oven instead of sautéed.

ASPARAGUS AND TARRAGON SOUFFLE

◆◆

*W*ait to make this soufflé when the fresh tarragon is in, as it complements the asparagus and the cheese so knowingly.

◆

1 pound fresh asparagus
3 tablespoons butter
3 tablespoons all-purpose flour
1 cup milk
¼ cup freshly grated Parmesan or Swiss cheese
3 egg yolks
1 tablespoon chopped fresh tarragon
Salt to taste
Cayenne pepper to taste
4 egg whites

◆

1. Preheat the oven to 375°F.
2. Break or cut off and discard the tough stem ends of the asparagus. Peel the stems with a thin sharp knife or vegetable peeler, and cut the asparagus into 2-inch pieces. Drop into a pot of boiling salted water and cook only 2 to 3 minutes. The asparagus must remain crisp. Drain well.
3. Melt the butter in a heavy saucepan (enameled iron is good) or in a double boiler. Add the flour and stir with a whisk until smooth. Add the milk slowly, whisking constantly; cook over medium-low heat until the sauce has thickened, 2 minutes. Add the cheese, and blend. Stir in the egg yolks, tarragon, salt, and cayenne. Keep warm.
4. Put the asparagus in a buttered 4-cup shallow baking dish (see Owl).
5. Beat the egg whites with a pinch of salt until they are stiff but not dry and grainy. Fold a bit of the egg white into the yolk and cheese mixture to lighten it, then add the mixture to the remaining egg whites, folding it in gently with a rubber spatula. Leave a few specks of egg white showing for greater volume. Spoon the mixture over the asparagus.
6. Place the dish on the middle or lower shelf of the oven, and bake until the soufflé is well puffed and golden brown, 25 to 30 minutes. It should feel fairly firm to the touch. Serve immediately remembering to scoop up the asparagus from the bottom.

   Serves 4

🦉 An oval baking dish is best for this soufflé, as it gives more even distribution of asparagus.

◆◆

CLASSIC ASPARAGUS

Asparagus Polonaise: To 8 tablespoons melted butter in a small skillet, add 2 or 3 tablespoons bread crumbs. Brown slightly, and sprinkle over hot cooked asparagus.

Flemish Asparagus: Mash the yolks of 2 or 3 hard-cooked eggs. Add 8 to 12 tablespoons melted butter to the yolks, making a sauce. Salt to taste. Serve in a sauceboat or over hot cooked asparagus. Sprinkle the asparagus with the chopped or sieved egg whites.

Asparagus au Gratin: Cover hot cooked asparagus with a Mornay sauce (1 cup cream sauce heated with ¼ cup grated Swiss, Gruyère, or Parmesan cheese). Run the dish under the broiler for a few seconds, only until the cheese takes on a little color. Or pour 7 tablespoons heavy cream over the asparagus tips, and sprinkle generously with grated sharp Cheddar or Swiss, or a combination. Run under the broiler for a few seconds.

Asparagus Tarragon: Put freshly cooked and drained warm asparagus on lettuce. Cover with vinaigrette made with tarragon vinegar. Garnish with fresh tarragon if available.

Asparagus Mousseline: Blend ½ cup whipped cream into 1½ cups hollandaise. Pour over hot cooked asparagus or serve in a sauceboat.

AWFULLY GOOD BEANS

❖❖

*F*resh tomatoes are best here, as they can be cooked a shorter time. With hot corn muffins, this is a meal in itself. Or serve with lamb or veal.

◆

2 cups dried white navy beans
6 tablespoons (¾ stick) butter
5 tablespoons good-quality olive oil
1½ teaspoons dried marjoram or summer
*   savory*
¾ cup chopped, seeded, peeled fresh tomatoes
*   or chopped, drained canned Italian plum*
*   tomatoes*
Salt and freshly ground white pepper to taste

◆

1. Pick over the beans, and rinse them well. Cover with water, bring to a boil, and boil 5 minutes. Allow to stand in the water, uncovered, for 1 hour.

2. Drain the beans, and place them in a saucepan with water to cover. Simmer, partially covered, until the beans are tender but not mushy, about 45 minutes.

3. Heat the butter and olive oil in a heavy saucepan. Add the beans, marjoram or savory, tomatoes, and salt and white pepper. Cook 5 to 8 minutes. The beans should taste "awfully good" and be soft but not mushy.

Serves 4

FRESH KENTUCKY WONDER SHELLOUTS OR CRANBERRY BEANS

❖❖

◆

3 pounds fresh Kentucky Wonder or cranberry
*   beans (in the pods)*
6 tablespoons (¾ stick) butter
Salt and freshly ground black pepper to taste
2 tablespoons chopped fresh parsley

◆

1. Shell the beans and drop them into a large pot of boiling salted water. Simmer, partially covered, until the beans are tender. The time will vary with the beans, but about 25 to 30 minutes is usually sufficient.

2. Drain the beans, toss them with the butter, and season to taste with salt and pepper. Sprinkle with parsley and serve.

Serves 6

VARIATIONS: *Shellouts or Cranberry Beans*

with Ham or Bacon: Before adding the beans, cook ¼ pound smoked ham hock or bacon in the water for at least 30 minutes. Cook the beans until tender. Discard the ham or bacon. Season to taste with salt if needed, and pepper. Omit the butter, but sprinkle with the parsley.

❖❖

SOME BEAN WEIGHTS

1 pound fresh green beans equals about 4
    cups (3 to 4 servings)
1 pound large lima beans equals about 2 cups
    shelled (2 servings)
1 pound fresh cranberry beans equals about
    1½ cups shelled (2 servings)

CRANBERRY BEANS WITH CRISP SMOKED BACON

6 slices smoked bacon
3 pounds fresh cranberry beans (in the pods)
Salt and freshly ground black pepper to taste
3 scallions, chopped
2 tablespoons chopped fresh parsley

1. Preheat the oven to 425°F.
2. Oven-broil the bacon until crisp, 10 minutes. Drain it well on paper towels. Reserve the fat, and keep it warm. Crumble the bacon and keep it warm also.

2. Shell the beans and drop them into a large pot of boiling salted water. Simmer, partially covered, until the beans are tender, 25 to 30 minutes. Drain them well.

3. Toss the beans with the reserved bacon fat, and season to taste with salt and pepper. Sprinkle with the bacon, scallions, and parsley.

Serves 6

DOUBLE BROCCOLI SOUFFLE

Delicious with beef tenderloin, rare roast beef, broiled chicken, or veal.

1½ pounds fresh broccoli
3 tablespoons butter
3 tablespoons all-purpose flour
¾ cup milk
1 teaspoon dry mustard
3 tablespoons freshly grated Parmesan cheese
3 egg yolks
Salt to taste
Cayenne pepper to taste
4 egg whites
Pinch of cream of tartar

1. Butter a 4-cup soufflé or 1½-quart shallow baking dish, and set it aside.
2. Preheat the oven to 375°F.
3. Wash the broccoli well and cut off the tough stem ends. Peel the stems with a sharp paring knife, and cut them in half lengthwise.
4. Drop the stems into a pot of boiling salted water and cook before adding the tops for 5 to 6 minutes. Cook the broccoli until stems and tops are tender. Drain it thoroughly, and with a sieve or in a processor, purée enough broccoli (flowerets and

BROCCOLI

Freshness is the key to really fine vegetable dishes, as only through freshness are the distinctive flavors and textures retained. A variety of textures makes food interesting to our palates, but overcooking, which happens all too often, robs vegetables of this great attribute. The crispness, for instance, of properly prepared broccoli, our choice green winter vegetable, is as important as its flavor.

Broccoli has an assertive flavor. It never fades into the background. It has grown in favor with Americans because it is companionable with steak, roast beef, chicken, ham, and fish—and it is easy to prepare.

In selecting broccoli at the market, look for the bunches that have slender stems and tight, dark green flower buds. If the flower buds are the least bit yellow, the broccoli is past its prime. Don't buy it.

tender stems) to make 1 cup of purée.

5. Coarsely chop enough of the remaining broccoli (flowerets and tender stems) to make about 1 cup. Sprinkle this in the bottom of the buttered soufflé dish.

6. Put a collar around the soufflé dish (see box and Owl), and set it aside.

7. Melt the butter in a heavy saucepan, and then add the flour, mixing it well with a whisk until smooth. Add the milk gradually, whisking constantly; cook over medium-low heat until the sauce has thickened and is perfectly smooth, 2 minutes. Add the mustard and Parmesan cheese. Mix thoroughly.

8. Add the egg yolks, broccoli purée, salt, and cayenne. Cook just a few minutes longer, stirring well. Remove from the heat but keep warm.

9. Beat the egg whites with the cream of tartar until they are stiff but not dry and grainy. Gently fold some of the egg whites into the broccoli mixture to lighten it. Then fold the broccoli mixture gently into the remaining egg whites, leaving a few flecks of whites showing. Pour into the soufflé dish over the chopped broccoli.

10. Place the dish in a shallow pan.

◆◆◆
TO MAKE A SOUFFLE COLLAR

1. Cut a sheet of foil that will encircle the soufflé dish with the ends overlapping about 1 inch, and that will extend from the bottom of the dish to 3 inches above the top when folded in half lengthwise.

2. Fold the foil strip in half lengthwise, and brush the top 4 inches of the foil on one side with soft butter.

3. Wrap the collar, with the buttered foil facing in, around the outside of the soufflé dish. Fasten the ends tightly with freezer tape or paper clips, or tie a string around the dish to hold the collar on. The foil must fit snugly so the soufflé will extend securely above the top of the dish.

Fill the pan three-quarters full with hot water, put it on the middle shelf of the oven, and bake until the center feels very firm to the touch, 30 to 40 minutes. Serve immediately, remembering to scoop up the broccoli from the bottom.

Serves 4

🦉 This soufflé can be baked in a shallow baking dish, which makes a nice presentation. No collar is needed.

CASSEROLE OF CHOPPED BROCCOLI

◆◆◆

*B*roccoli should be allowed to cook until it is tender but still retains its bright green color. Watch it carefully, and drain it at once. Children often prefer chopped broccoli over the larger branches.

◆

---

1 bunch broccoli (about 1 pound)
4 tablespoons (½ stick) butter
4 tablespoons heavy or whipping cream
Salt and freshly ground black pepper to taste
½ cup buttered and toasted bread crumbs or as needed (see page 251)

◆

---

1. Preheat the oven to 375°F.
2. Wash the broccoli well and cut off the tough stem ends. Peel the stems with a sharp paring knife, and cut them in half lengthwise.

3. Drop the stems into a pot of boiling salted water and cook before adding the tops for 5 to 6 minutes. Cook the broccoli until stems and tops are tender. Drain thoroughly, and chop fine.

4. Return the broccoli to the empty pot and allow it to cook over a low flame for a few minutes to thoroughly rid it of water,

stirring constantly. Remove from the heat, and add the butter, cream, and salt and pepper to taste.

5. Pour the broccoli mixture into a shallow casserole and cover it with the crumbs. Bake until bubbly hot and a golden, even brown, 10 to 12 minutes.

Serves 4

🦉 This broccoli can be prepared a few hours ahead: Cover it with the crumbs and leave at room temperature until you are ready to heat it just before serving.

WHEN PREPARING BROCCOLI

*T*he most important thing in preparing broccoli is to peel the stems from right under the flower bud to the end of the stem, plucking off and discarding all the leaves. Cook only until barely tender but still somewhat crisp— not raw, certainly, but cooked to the point of a pleasing texture. There is a difference.

GREEN CABBAGE AU GRATIN

*T*his cabbage dish will fool you—it is mild-flavored, and delicious with pork roast, broiled chicken, or ham. Cabbage does not store well—it grows stronger even in your refrigerator. To be mild, cabbage must be green and fresh—then and only then will you find it to be delicate. Celery, Savoy cabbage, cauliflower, and Swiss chard are also delicious prepared au gratin.

---

4 cups coarsely shredded fresh green cabbage
2 cups Cheese Sauce (recipe follows)
½ cup grated aged Swiss cheese, or half Swiss and half Cheddar
¾ cup lightly buttered and toasted bread crumbs (see page 251)

---

1. Preheat the oven to 375°F.
2. Drop the cabbage into a large pot of boiling salted water. Cook until just tender, no more than 7 minutes. Drain well.
3. Spread the cooked cabbage in a shallow 1½-quart casserole. Spoon the sauce over the cabbage. Mix the cheese and bread crumbs and sprinkle over the top.
4. Bake until heated through and the crumbs are light brown, 20 to 30 minutes.

Serves 6

VARIATION: *Cauliflower and Cabbage au Gratin:* Follow the directions for Green Cabbage au Gratin, but use half cauliflower and half cabbage. Delightful.

🦉 Always buy tight firm heads of cabbage. When preparing cabbage, discard the tough outer leaves, then split the head in two through the core. Cut out the core from both halves. Don't shred the cabbage overly fine; it should retain some crispness after it is parboiled (if the cabbage is not parboiled, the casserole will be watery).

CHEESE SAUCE

4 tablespoons (½ stick) butter
3 tablespoons all-purpose flour
2 cups milk
½ cup grated aged Swiss cheese, or half Swiss and half Cheddar
½ teaspoon salt, or to taste
Freshly ground white pepper to taste
Cayenne pepper to taste

Melt the butter in a heavy saucepan. Add the flour and beat well with a whisk until smooth. Add the milk gradually, and beat constantly over medium-low heat until the sauce has thickened sufficiently and lost its raw flavor, 2 minutes. Add the cheese and stir continuously until it is completely melted. Add salt, white pepper, and cayenne to taste.

Makes 2 cups

WONDROUS CARROTS

◆◆◆

*T*hese are very special carrots—I teach them wherever I go and have done so for years. They are delectable with lamb roasts, especially the rack or saddle, or with chops. They are compatible with chicken or ham, but not with beef, veal, or highly seasoned meats. In fact, these carrots are so special they should be savored alone.

Selling carrots, even freshly pulled ones, may require great patience, or a good book.

◆

2 cups sliced fresh carrots
3 tablespoons unsalted butter
1½ teaspoons sugar, or to taste

2 tablespoons cognac or brandy, or more to
    taste
Salt to taste (very little)
Chopped fresh parsley, for garnish

◆

1. Drop the carrots into boiling water to barely cover. Don't add salt. Simmer, uncovered, until just tender, 15 to 17 minutes. The carrots should not get too soft, but they should lose a measure of their crispness.

2. Drain the carrots if the water has not boiled away. Add the butter, sugar, and cognac or brandy. Toss over low heat just a few seconds for the cognac to mellow. Add very little salt, if any, and garnish with parsley.

   Serves 2

Never add salt to any pot of carrots until they have finished cooking. Carrots hate salt—but love sugar, and contain a great deal of natural sugar.

CAULIFLOWER AND GREEN CABBAGE

◆◆◆

*W*hen the cauliflower and cabbage is really fresh and green, this is one of the most delightful winter vegetable dishes I know. It is delicate, which might fool you a bit as cabbage does not have that reputation, but the secret lies in the freshness of the vegetables and in proper cooking. This changes the whole flavor.

◆

2 cups coarsely chopped cauliflower
2 cups coarsely slivered fresh green cabbage
2 tablespoons unsalted butter, at room
    temperature

½ cup heavy or whipping cream, or more as
    needed
Salt and freshly ground black pepper to taste
Chopped fresh parsley, for garnish

◆

1. Drop the cauliflower into a large pot of boiling salted water and cook for 3 to 4 minutes. Add the cabbage, and cook until both cauliflower and cabbage are tender but still somewhat crisp, 3 to 4 minutes longer. Drain thoroughly and return to the pot.

2. Add the butter and enough cream to cover the vegetables with a good sauce. Simmer gently to melt the butter and blend the flavors. (If you happen to have more sauce than you like, allow it to boil down a bit to reduce and thicken.) Season with salt, pepper, and a sprinkling of parsley.

Serves 4

Heavy cream will boil down and thicken without curdling. Half-and-half will curdle.

GRILLED CORN

◆◆◆

1. Select tender, perfect corn. Do not remove any shuck to see the corn. The corn must be protected in order to steam.

2. Carefully pull the shucks away from the corn just enough to remove the silk. Be sure to leave the shucks attached to the ear. Brush the silk from the ears. Pull the shucks back over the corn, and tie them with strings made of corn shucks or with floral wire. Soak in cold water (no salt) for 30 minutes.

3. Prepare the grill by placing an oiled rack 4 to 6 inches over hot gray coals. Lay the corn on the rack or thread them on a spit. Turn the corn 3 or 4 times as it cooks so that all sides will be exposed to the heat. It will cook in 15 to 20 minutes.

4. When the corn is ready to serve, have a large oval platter containing plenty of salted melted butter nearby. Each guest shucks the corn and rolls his own in butter.

To help keep the corn moist, lay a wet burlap sack over the corn as it cooks. Leave for about 5 minutes. Remove the burlap, dampen it again, turn the corn, replace the burlap, and grill about 5 minutes longer.

◆◆◆

One of the glories of summer—and there are many—is fresh corn, boiled on the cob, cooked in a soup, stewed or baked with fresh tomatoes, combined with lima beans in succotash, baked in corn pudding, or grilled over coals. One word of warning: Don't add salt to grilled, boiled, or stewed corn until it is tender. Salt toughens fresh corn. And don't overcook corn dishes. They will toughen if you do.

CORN ON THE COB WITH RED PEPPER BUTTER

◆◆◆

It is not an old wives' tale that one should put the water on to boil, then run to the garden to gather the corn! Corn does have an abundance of sugar that starts turning to starch the minute it is cut free from the stalk. It is then at its peak of sweetness. But not all of us have gardens, so we must shop around—farmers' markets, produce markets, wayside vegetable stands—because the fresher the better.

¼ cup milk
9 tablespoons butter
¼ cup water
1 red bell pepper, cored, seeded, and chopped
6 to 8 ears tender fresh corn, unshucked
Salt and freshly ground black pepper to taste

1. Bring a large kettle of cold water to which you've added the milk and 1 or 2 pieces of corn shuck to a boil.

2. Meanwhile, make the red pepper butter. Melt 3 tablespoons of the butter in the water in a small saucepan. Add the red bell pepper and sauté over medium heat until the water has boiled away, 3 minutes. Do not allow the pepper to sizzle the least bit. Add the remaining butter to the pan. Allow it to melt and blend with the red pepper, then set aside.

3. When the kettle of water comes to a rolling boil, shuck the corn. Add the corn to the kettle and boil 4 minutes. Cut off the heat. The corn will keep hot for a while in the large amount of hot water.

4. When ready to serve, drain the corn and serve with a sauceboat of red pepper butter, salt, and pepper.

Serves 6 to 8

HOW TO ROAST AND PEEL BELL PEPPERS

The green peppers are available in our markets most of the time and they are excellent in many recipes, especially for stuffing, but they are not as sweet nor as delicious as the ripe, red bell peppers. The red bell pepper is a ripened green bell pepper as they are the same species.

1. Preheat the broiler.

2. Choose perfect peppers that have no dark or soft spots. Wash thoroughly and dry with paper towels.

3. Place the whole peppers in a baking or broiler pan about 4 inches from the heat. Turn the peppers often until they have charred black all over, about 5 minutes.

4. Wrap the peppers in dampened paper towels to steam or place them in a closed paper bag to cool for about 10 minutes. This helps to loosen the skin.

5. When the peppers have cooled, cut them in half. Discard the seeds, membranes, and stem. Peel off the loosened skin with a sharp pointed paring knife.

Bell peppers also can be charred by holding them on a long cooking fork over a gas flame and turning them frequently until the skins are black. Follow the directions for steaming and peeling in the above recipe.

EARLY SUMMER FRESH CORN PUDDING

For those who like more corn than custard in their pudding, use 3 cups of corn, which should be about 9 ears.

Some of summer's most elegant vegetables.

6 ears tender fresh corn
3 eggs, beaten
1 cup heavy or whipping cream
⅓ cup milk
1 teaspoon salt
1 tablespoon sugar

1. Preheat the oven to 350°F.
2. Cut the corn from the cob and

scrape the cobs well to extract the milk. You should have 2 cups of corn.

3. In a large bowl, mix the eggs, cream, and milk. Add the salt, sugar, and corn.

4. Pour the mixture into a buttered shallow casserole or heatproof glass dish. Place in a shallow pan of warm water and bake until a knife inserted in the center comes out clean, about 1 hour.

Serves 6

VARIATION: *Corn and Red Bell Pepper Pudding:* Add ¼ to ⅓ cup finely chopped red bell pepper with the corn, or use the sweet red pimento pepper that ripens in the fall.

TENDER CORN PUDDING SOUFFLE

*T*his soufflé version of the corn pudding is delicious with beef—especially beef tenderloin—as it contains no sugar. The soufflé bakes better in a shallow casserole, where it will cook more quickly than in a deep soufflé dish.

6 to 9 ears tender fresh corn (see Owl)
1 cup heavy or whipping cream
2 tablespoons butter, melted
3 large eggs, separated
Salt and freshly ground white pepper to taste

1. Preheat the oven to 350°F.
2. Cut the corn from the cobs, and scrape the cobs well to extract the milk.

(This adds extra starch to help thicken the pudding.) You should have 2 to 3 cups.

3. In a large bowl, combine the corn, cream, melted butter, egg yolks, and salt and pepper. Mix thoroughly.

4. Beat the egg whites in a separate bowl until stiff but not dry and grainy. Fold them into the corn.

5. Spoon the mixture into a shallow buttered casserole. Place it in a pan of hot water and bake until firm, 30 to 35 minutes. A knife blade inserted in the center should come out fairly clean when the soufflé is done. Serve immediately.

Serves 6

If you use 2 cups of corn you will have a lighter, fluffier dish; 3 cups makes the dish more like a pudding instead of a soufflé. You choose.

*C*orn puddings whey, or curdle, from prolonged or intense heat. They should be cooked in shallow baking dishes (the shallow 1½-quart heatproof glass ones are excellent). The typical American casseroles or soufflé dishes are too deep for corn pudding. By the time the heat has penetrated to the center of the pudding, the custard has curdled. A great deal of flour was used in the older recipes to overcome this. Few seemed to blame the depth of the dish.

Tender corn puddings are made with little, if any, flour. The eggs and the starch from the corn are sufficient thickening agents.

DELICATE CORN FRITTERS

*T*here may be a finer corn fritter somewhere, but I rather doubt it. Corn fritters are one of the South's finest and most typical dishes. We adore them with fried chicken, lima beans, garden tomatoes, and hot rolls. Then just serve up a slice of Rhubarb Cream Pie or Windfall Apple Pie....

2 ears tender fresh corn
⅓ cup sifted all-purpose flour
½ teaspoon baking powder
2 eggs, separated

½ teaspoon salt, or to taste
Cayenne pepper to taste
Oil for deep-frying

1. Cut the corn from the cobs and scrape the cobs well to extract the milk. You should have ½ cup of corn.

2. Sift the flour with the baking powder and mix it with the corn and the egg yolks. Add salt and cayenne pepper.

3. Beat the egg whites until stiff but not dry and grainy. Fold them into the corn mixture.

4. Drop the batter by tablespoonfuls into deep, hot, fresh oil, about 375°F. Cook the fritters until they have browned on one side, about 2 minutes. Turn, and when both sides are golden brown, remove with a slotted spoon and drain on paper towels. Serve at once.

Serves 4

Don't attempt to make delicate fritters with large-kerneled corn. They will turn out tough.

A WELCOME HOME DINNER

Southern Fried Chicken

Delicate Corn Fritters

Creole Okra and Tomato Stew

Pickled Zucchini with Peppers and Dill

Potato Yeast Biscuits

◆

Maryland Chess and Apple Tart

Amber Iced Tea

OLD STONE INN CORN FRITTERS

◆◆◆

*T*his makes a round ball-type fritter—delicious but sturdier than the Delicate Corn Fritter.

◆

6 ears tender fresh corn
3 eggs, separated
⅞ cup sifted all-purpose flour
1 teaspoon salt
1 teaspoon sugar
Cayenne pepper to taste
2 teaspoons baking powder
Oil for deep-frying

◆

1. Cut the corn from the cobs, and scrape the cobs well to extract the milk. You should have 1½ to 2 cups of corn. Mash ¼ cup of the corn pulp with a potato masher or in a blender or processor. (This helps to distribute the corn flavor and extract some starch.) Return it to the rest of the corn.

2. Mix the egg yolks with the corn. Sift together the flour, salt, sugar, cayenne, and baking powder. Add to the corn and mix well.

3. Beat the egg whites until stiff but not dry and grainy, and fold them into the corn mixture.

4. Heat fresh oil in a deep-fat fryer to about 375°F. Drop the batter by tablespoonfuls into the fat, and cook the fritters until browned on one side, about 2 minutes. Turn, and when both sides are golden brown, remove with a slotted spoon and drain on paper towels. Serve at once with fried chicken or broiled country ham.

Serves 4 to 6

The Old Stone Inn of Simpsonville, Kentucky, started attracting diners in 1779.

BAKED CORN AND TOMATOES

◆◆◆

When the fresh corn and tomatoes are in, try this "old time" favorite Southern way of cooking them. The flavor of the smoked bacon drifts through the entire dish in a delicate and delectable way.

◆

9 ears tender fresh corn
3 ripe tomatoes
1 tablespoon grated onion
1 small green bell pepper, cored, seeded, and
    chopped
Salt and freshly ground black pepper to taste
2 tablespoons butter
4 slices lean smoked bacon, diced
Chopped fresh parsley, for garnish

◆

1. Preheat the oven to 350°F.
2. Cut the corn from the cobs, and scrape the cobs well to extract the milk. You should have about 3 cups. Put half the corn in a layer in the bottom of a buttered 1½-quart casserole. Peel and slice the tomatoes, and put half the slices in a layer over the corn. Add a little of the onion and green pepper. Season with salt and pepper, and dot with 1 tablespoon of the butter.
3. Add another layer of corn, cover it with the remaining tomatoes, and add the rest of the onion, green pepper, and butter. Season lightly with salt and heavily with pepper. Sprinkle the bacon over the top.
4. Bake until the bacon is cooked, about 30 minutes. Sprinkle lavishly with parsley.

Serves 4 to 6

SUCCOTASH STEW

◆◆◆

This is a traditional Southern combination of fresh lima beans and corn. You simply cannot achieve a delicious succotash with commercially frozen vegetables. Especially delicious with fried chicken, garden tomatoes, and hot rolls or biscuits.

◆

2 cups fresh lima beans
2 cups tender fresh corn kernels (6 ears)
1½ cups water, or more as needed
6 tablespoons (¾ stick) butter
Salt to taste
Freshly ground white pepper to taste, or a
    sprinkling of cayenne

◆

1. Drop the lima beans into a pot of boiling salted water to cover, and cook at a low boil until almost tender, 18 to 20 minutes. Tasting is the best test. Drain.

2. Combine the corn, lima beans, and 1½ cups water in a saucepan. Bring to a boil and cook, uncovered, over medium heat, shaking the pan often, until the corn is tender and the water has almost evaporated, 3 minutes. (If the water boils away before the vegetables are tender, add a little more and cook until the vegetables test done.) Drain, add the butter, and allow it to melt over the vegetables. The succotash should be creamy. Season with salt and white pepper or cayenne.

Serves 6

GEORGIA FIDDLEHEADS

◆◆◆

*I*n the damp woods and the swampy land of Georgia and Louisiana, the fiddlehead ferns pop up in the spring looking for all the world like the end of a green, edible violin—and edible and delicious they are. They are there free for the picking, and as I said—delicious! The fiddleheads must be picked when the ostrich ferns first poke their heads out of the ground and before they unfurl their feathery fronds; otherwise, it is too late.

The produce market is the source for the freshest vegetables—after the garden, of course.

◆

½ pound ostrich fern fiddleheads
3 tablespoons unsalted butter or good-quality
peanut oil
Salt to taste

◆

1. Rinse the fiddleheads carefully and allow them to dry on paper towels.
2. Heat the butter or oil in a wok or skillet, and stir-fry or sauté the fiddleheads for 1 to 2 minutes. They must remain crisp. Season with salt to taste.
3. Serve with broiled chicken, rabbit, quail, pheasant or veal, or use in stir-fried dishes, especially rice.

Serves 4

FIDDLEHEADS AND WILD MUSHROOMS

◆◆◆

◆

½ pound ostrich fern fiddleheads
1 pound fresh morels or other edible woodland
mushrooms, or cultivated mushrooms,
sliced
3 tablespoons unsalted butter or good-quality
vegetable oil
Salt, or soy sauce and fresh lemon juice, to taste

◆

1. Rinse the fiddleheads carefully and allow them to dry on paper towels.
2. Heat the butter or oil in a wok or skillet and stir-fry or sauté the fiddleheads

and mushrooms for only 2 to 3 minutes. They must remain crisp. Season with salt, or soy sauce and lemon juice.

Serves 4

◆◆◆

FIDDLEHEAD AND MUSHROOM SALAD

*S*team the fiddleheads for just a few minutes; they must retain their fresh green color and taste. Set aside to cool. Combine with sliced raw crisp mushrooms, and serve on Bibb lettuce with Classic Vinaigrette, but no garlic. Don't you want to taste the fiddleheads?

OLD-FASHIONED GREENS

*W*hen you are offered old-fashioned greens cooked with slab bacon or ham hock, and corn muffins, you know you are south of the Mason-Dixon line. The greens all have different flavors, so the choice is up to the cook. Always pass the vinegar to be sprinkled on the greens.

2 pounds greens, such as turnip greens, mustard greens, collard greens, or kale, or mixed as desired
½ pound slab smoked bacon, or 1 pound piece smoked ham hock
3 quarts water
½ small pod dried or fresh chile pepper or to taste, slivered
Salt to taste

1. Select fresh tender greens with no yellow leaves. Remove and discard the stems. Set aside.
2. Add the bacon or ham hock to 3 quarts of water in a large stainless steel or enamel pot, and allow to boil, uncovered, for 30 to 40 minutes. The water should be reduced by half.
3. In the meantime, wash the greens in at least 3 changes of water, swishing them about to rid them of sand. Lift the greens out of the water each time. Drain.
4. Add the greens to the pot. Add the chile pepper and allow the greens to simmer long and slowly until they are really tender, 1 hour. The greens should be simmered no more than ½ inch below the stock line. Strain off any extra stock and add it to the pot only if needed as the greens cook. Taste for salt when the greens are almost done; as the bacon and ham hock are salty, it may be unnecessary to add any. Discard the bacon or ham hock, drain the greens, if necessary, and serve.

Serves 6

A delicious pot of greens is never made with bacon fat or "drippings." The best flavor comes from the uncooked smoked bacon or ham hock, never salt pork. It is not worth the trouble to clean the greens if bacon drippings are to be used. All you are getting is grease.

FRENCH MARKET KALE STEW

*T*he flavor of this dish is glorious and, with good bread, it is a meal in itself. Three thick slices smoked bacon may be substituted for the ham, but remove them before serving.

2 pounds kale, stems removed
2 cups fat-free light Veal, Brown Soup, or Chicken Stock (see Index)
1 medium onion, chopped
4 mushrooms, sliced
¼ cup chopped baked ham
2 tomatoes, peeled and quartered
Salt and freshly ground black pepper to taste

Bouquet of mixed chopped fresh herbs, such as parsley, marjoram, and summer savory

1. Wash the kale in at least 3 changes of water, swishing them about to rid them of sand and dirt. Lift the greens out of the water each time. Drop the kale into boiling

A display of vegetables often seems too beautiful to disrupt. Never you mind—dig in and cook them up quickly. You'll be glad you did!

salted water and cook until tender, 15 minutes. Drain, and return to the pot.

2. Add the stock, onion, mushrooms, and ham to the kale. Cook slowly, stirring frequently, for 10 to 15 minutes. Add the tomatoes, and cook until the liquid has reduced and thickened and the stew is well flavored, 5 minutes. Season with salt and pepper.

3. Serve sprinkled with the fresh herbs.

Serves 4

VARIATION: You may substitute 8 sticks salsify for the kale. If you do, add the juice of ½ lemon to the boiling salted water in step 1. (Salsify is often called oyster plant, as some think it tastes like oysters. It is hard to find on the market, but when you do stumble upon it, grab it, as it is one of our best rare vegetables.)

SAVORY MUSHROOM PIE

W onderful with steak, rare roast beef, and veal chops or roasts.

Flaky Butter Pastry or Cornmeal Puff Paste (see Index) for a 1-crust pie
1½ pounds mushrooms
4 tablespoons (½ stick) butter
2 tablespoons minced shallots (do not substitute onions)
¼ cup all-purpose flour
1 cup well-flavored fat-free Brown Soup, Veal, or Rich Chicken Stock (see Index)
1 cup plus 1 tablespoon heavy or whipping cream
1 tablespoon chopped fresh parsley
Salt and freshly ground black pepper to taste

1. Make the pastry. Gather into a ball, cover well, and refrigerate until ready to use.

2. Clean and slice the mushrooms, not too thin.

3. Melt the butter in a heavy stainless steel or enamel pan or skillet (not black iron), and sauté the mushrooms and shallots over medium heat until the mushrooms give off some of their juice but are still crisp, 2 to 3 minutes.

4. Tip the pan slightly, and stir in the flour, blending until it is smooth.

5. Add the stock, simmer a few minutes, and then add 1 cup cream and the parsley. Season with salt and pepper. Spoon into a 9-inch baking dish and allow the mixture to cool.

6. Preheat the oven to 400°F.

7. Roll out the pastry to ⅛ inch, or thinner if possible. Cover the mushrooms with the pastry, crimping the edges of the pastry to the rim of the dish. Cut some slashes in the pastry for steam vents. Brush the pastry with 1 tablespoon cream, and bake until it is golden brown, 25 to 30 minutes.

Serves 6

MUSHROOMS

*D*o you happen to know where there is an old apple orchard? A deserted one is best. That's where the mushrooms pop up—thick as hops—in the spring. Windfall apples sink into the soil as compost. This is nature's perfect incubation for morels, the early mushrooms.

I have a friend who knows where there is such an orchard, but she won't tell. And who could blame her? Not I. But I do keep looking for it.

My friend says that morels are the easiest of all wild mushrooms to identify—that anyone can learn if they try. And I've seen her come home from a day's pleasure in the country with her basket just brimming. She must know.

There are hundreds of species of wild mushrooms. A few types grow in every park or meadow in the temperate zone. Some are called chanterelles, some cèpes, and some morels—all have lyrical names. The Italians call all mushrooms *funghi,* and it sounds like a tone in music.

The white mushrooms that grow in our fields like clusters of tiny parasols are called the "meadow pink," and they are identical to the one that lends itself to cultivation. The wild ones always have more aroma. Their delicate, yet earthy flavor does, indeed, smell and taste of the woods and April rain, and they enhance many wonderful dishes.

Experts say it is easy to tell the edible variety of fungi from the "death caps," but unless you are an expert, don't dare try. The novice should walk in the woods and enjoy the charm and colors of the mushrooms but cook with those that come from the market.

The kitchen at Monticello, as it must have looked in Thomas Jefferson's day.

AN ELEGANT WINTER DINNER

Clear Leek and Parsley Soup

◆

Oysters and Tenderloin en Brochette

Savory Mushroom Pie

◆

Belgian Endive with Classic Vinaigrette

◆

New Orleans Burnt Cream

CAROLINA BUTTERED OKRA

*O*kra is a late-season, highly nutritious summer vegetable and as Southern as Robert E. Lee. We adore it, but Northerners have never liked it, and I don't think they ever will. It still divides the Blue and the Gray.

To be delicious, okra must be (and I emphasize "must be") freshly picked and small; the tiny okra is the best. Okra bruises easily, even in a grocery sack, and the spines turn black. If it grows large, it is scratchy, hard, and fibrous. The stem ends must not be cut so close that the okra pod is severed. If this happens the okra stuffing oozes out, and that's when the trouble begins.

A clever way to keep your hands free when making a sale.

1 pound freshly picked small okra
6 tablespoons (¾ stick) unsalted butter, melted
Salt and freshly ground white pepper to taste
1 or 2 squeezes fresh lemon juice, to taste
Chopped fresh dill or parsley, for garnish

1. Trim the stem ends off the okra—carefully, so as not to cut into the pod itself.
2. Drop the okra into boiling salted water to cover well, and simmer until tender. Okra shouldn't be overly crisp; 5 to 10 minutes usually does it. Taste it. Drain at once and toss in the butter.
3. Season with salt, white pepper, and lemon juice, and add a sprinkling of dill or parsley.

Serves 3 to 4

CREOLE OKRA AND TOMATO STEW

*E*ven those who are not okra fans seem to like it cooked as they do in New Orleans.

1½ pounds freshly picked small okra
Juice of ½ lemon
4 tablespoons butter
¼ cup cold water
2 medium onions, chopped
5 ripe medium tomatoes, peeled and chopped
½ bay leaf
1 or 2 sprigs fresh thyme or ¼ teaspoon dried (fresh is best)
Salt and freshly ground black pepper to taste

1. Trim the stem ends off the okra—carefully, so as not to cut into the pod itself.
2. Drop the okra into boiling salted water to cover well. Add the lemon juice and simmer until just tender, 5 to 6 minutes. Drain at once, and set aside.
3. Melt the butter in a heavy skillet, and add the water and onions. Cook over medium-low heat until the onions are limp and have absorbed the butter, and the water has boiled away. Do not allow the onions to sizzle or brown. Add the tomatoes, bay leaf, thyme, and salt and pepper. Raise the heat slightly and cook until the tomatoes have cooked rather low, 20 to 30 minutes.
4. Add the okra, lower the heat again, and simmer gently for about 5 minutes longer. Taste and adjust the salt and pepper if necessary. Serve with fried chicken, pork, veal, lamb, or beef.

Serves 4

VIDALIA ONION PIE

◆◆◆

*F*rom a luncheon in Savannah: Vidalia Onion Pie, green salad, garden tomatoes, Yellow Sponge Cake Roll, coffee.

◆

3 tablespoons butter
5 medium Vidalia onions, thinly sliced
1 partially baked 9-inch Standard Pastry crust (see Index)
1 cup grated aged Swiss cheese
2 whole eggs
2 egg yolks
1 cup milk
½ cup heavy or whipping cream
1 teaspoon salt
Cayenne pepper to taste

◆

1. Preheat the oven to 350°F.
2. Melt the butter in a heavy sauce-pan. Add the onions and cook over medium-low heat until they are limp but not the least bit brown.
3. Drain the onions and arrange them in the pastry shell. Cover the onions with the grated cheese.
4. Beat the eggs, egg yolks, milk, and cream together. Season with salt and cayenne pepper, and pour over the cheese.
5. Place the pie pan on the lower shelf of the oven and bake until the pie has puffed in the middle and is golden brown all over, 35 to 40 minutes.

Serves 6

SOUTHERN GREEN PEAS AND POTATOES

◆◆

*B*eautifully cooked fresh peas are worthy of being served as the highlight of the menu. They accompany ham, lamb, beef, veal, or fowl, or can be delicious all on their own.

◆

3 cups fresh green peas (3 pounds in the pod)
3 slices smoked bacon
1 teaspoon sugar, or to taste
3 tablespoons butter
Salt and freshly ground black pepper to taste
2 tablespoons chopped fresh parsley
1½ pounds small new potatoes, freshly cooked, peeled, and kept warm

◆

1. Drop the peas into boiling water to cover, along with the bacon and sugar. Cook, uncovered, until the peas are tender, 15 to 25 minutes, depending upon the size and freshness of the peas. Taste for doneness; the peas should retain their bright green color. Drain, and discard the bacon.

2. Add the butter, salt, pepper, parsley, and potatoes. Toss well. Serve piping hot.

Serves 4 to 6

◆◆

GREEN PEAS

*G*reen peas are the most beloved and delicate of our early summer vegetables. They came originally from the lands around the Nile. Dried peas have been found in ancient Egyptian tombs, and they were so generally known in England during the Middle Ages that the word "porridge" became synonymous with them. Remember the nursery rhyme, "Peas porridge hot, Peas porridge cold"? It sings of green peas—not at all of a gummy, hot cereal as some have thought.

FRESH GREEN PEA PIE

*I*f I were asked to name the greatest fresh vegetable dish in the whole wide world, I believe it would have to be Fresh Green Pea Pie, a combination of buttery fresh peas and crisp crust. It has succulence, flavor, freshness, elegance, and charm—and one doesn't meet it every day.

EARLY JUNE PEAS

*Flaky Butter Pastry or Standard Pastry for
   9-inch 2-crust pie (see Index)
3 cups fresh green peas (3 pounds in the pod)
1 teaspoon sugar
8 tablespoons (1 stick) butter
2 tablespoons chopped fresh parsley
Salt and freshly ground white pepper to taste
¼ cup Chicken Stock (see Index), if needed
1 tablespoon heavy or whipping cream*

1. Make the pastry. Gather into a ball, cover well, and refrigerate until ready to use.

2. Drop the peas into a deep pot of boiling salted water (it should cover the peas by 3 or 4 inches). Add the sugar, and allow the peas to cook, uncovered, until tender, 15 to 25 minutes depending upon the size and freshness of the peas. Taste for doneness; the peas should retain their bright green color. Drain the peas and pour them back into the saucepan.

3. Add the butter, parsley, salt and white pepper, and toss over low heat, so the peas will absorb most of the butter. The peas should be moist, with a bit of butter sauce. If the peas are dry, add more butter or a few tablespoons of chicken stock. Allow the peas to cool.

4. Preheat the oven to 425°F.

5. To assemble the pie, remove the dough from the refrigerator and divide it in half. Roll the first half out on a lightly floured surface or pastry cloth to ⅛ inch thickness. Lift the dough carefully and lay it on a 9-inch pie pan. Press it lightly into the bottom. Do not stretch the dough tightly—give it some play so it will not shrink in cooking.

6. Fill the pie shell with the cooled peas, taking care that there is a bit of sauce; otherwise, the pie will cook dry.

7. Roll out the remaining dough to ⅛ inch thickness and lay it over the top. Brush the underneath edge of the top crust with water and press the edges firmly together. Trim off excess dough with scissors. Crimp the rim with a fork. Make a few slits with a sharp knife in the top crust, or cut a small hole in the center of the pie and insert a small funnel or a large metal tip of a pastry decorator in the center, to allow the steam to escape.

8. Brush the top crust of the pie with the cream. Place it on the bottom rack of the oven and bake until both bottom and top crusts are golden brown, 40 to 60 minutes. (If the top crust seems to be browning too much, cover it loosely with foil.)

9. Allow the pie to settle for about 5 minutes before slicing.

Serves 6 to 8

❖❖ HOW TO PREPARE SPINACH

*C*hoose young, tender spinach with dark green crisp-looking leaves. Bunches of spinach with wilted or yellow leaves should be avoided. One pound of uncooked trimmed and cleaned spinach equals 1 cup cooked.

Remove the stems at the base of each leaf. (If the stems are really tender and crisp, they are good in green salads.)

Plunge the spinach leaves in a large bowl or pan of water and swish them around to rid them of sand and dirt. Lift the spinach out of the water and transfer to a colander. Discard the water with the sand and rinse the pan. Repeat the process not less than 3 times for thoroughly clean spinach that will be free of grit. For salads, dry well with paper towels.

To prepare spinach for special dishes or to eat as is, it may be cooked in three different ways:

Method #1: Cook the spinach in a large wide-mouthed pan (a stainless steel wok is excellent) with a very small amount of boiling water (about ¼ cup) over fairly high heat. Turn it constantly until it is thoroughly wilted and slightly cooked but retains some texture and its bright green color. Discard the water that remains in the pan and toss the spinach about with a fork over low heat to dry it out. This spinach is ready to be seasoned as desired or to be used for special dishes requiring cooked spinach.

Method #2: Drop the spinach in a large amount of salted boiling water. As soon as the water returns to a boil, the spinach should be almost sufficiently cooked, but retain some of its crispness and bright color, which takes about 3 minutes. Drain the spinach thoroughly in a colander and press down firmly to extract as much water as possible. Spinach is fresh and flavorful with this method but is not as dry as in Method #1. In soufflés, for instance, this spinach would be too wet.

Method #3: This is the Chinese stir-fry method of cooking spinach, and delicious it is. Clean the spinach thoroughly and spin-dry in a salad spinner or dry it with paper towels. Put 2 tablespoons of good-quality peanut or vegetable oil in a wok. Heat the oil, and add 1 pound of spinach a little at a time, tossing it well, until the spinach is cooked but retains much of its crispness and color. Season with soy, salt, or as desired.

🦉 Do not cook spinach in iron or aluminum. It will pick up an astringent taste, and aluminum turns spinach dark.

Peanut oil varies greatly in quality. The best is almost taste-free.

SPINACH AND MUSHROOMS AU GRATIN

———❖❖❖———

*T*his is a hearty but pleasing spinach dish, and, as it is rather filling, it goes best with a very light meat. Keeping some texture and the bright green color of the spinach is the secret—and using good cheese.

———◆———

2 pounds fresh spinach
Salt to taste
Freshly grated nutmeg to taste
4 tablespoons (½ stick) butter, or more to taste
½ pound mushrooms, sliced
1 cup Cream Sauce (recipe follows), or heavy or whipping cream
1 cup grated aged Swiss, imported Gruyère, or Parmesan cheese (or a combination of the 3)

⅓ cup buttered and toasted bread crumbs (see page 251)

———◆———

1. Preheat the oven to 350°F.
2. Clean the spinach well and cook it in boiling salted water for 3 minutes. Drain well, and chop fine. Season the spinach with salt and nutmeg to taste and 1 tablespoon of the butter or more to taste. Set aside.

3. Melt the remaining butter in a medium skillet and sauté the mushrooms over medium-low heat until they absorb some of the butter, 2 to 3 minutes. They must not brown or sizzle the least bit. Season with salt to taste, and stir into the Cream Sauce or heavy cream.

4. Cover the bottom of a shallow casserole with the mushroom mixture. Cover the mushrooms with the spinach, sprinkle with the cheese, and top with the bread crumbs.

5. Bake until the spinach is bubbly hot and the cheese is a delicate golden brown, about 20 minutes.

Serves 6

VARIATION: Add a few slivers of baked ham to the spinach for a heartier dish.

This casserole may be assembled, covered, and stored in the refrigerator 24 hours ahead of the final cooking. Be sure to bring the dish to room temperature before reheating so the spinach will not overcook.

CREAM SAUCE

2 tablespoons butter
2 tablespoons all-purpose flour
1 cup milk
Salt and freshly ground white pepper to taste

Melt the butter in a small heavy saucepan. Add the flour and blend with a whisk until smooth over medium-low heat. Gradually add the milk, whisking constantly; cook until the mixture is thickened and smooth, 2 to 3 minutes. Season with salt and white pepper to taste.

Makes 1 cup

SWISS CHARD ALMONDINE

*T*he textured crispness of almonds is exquisitely pleasing with the creaminess of this Swiss Chard Almondine. Delightful with pork roast, broiled chicken, capon, quail, or rare roast beef.

4 cups chopped Swiss chard
1 onion, halved
1 carrot, peeled and halved
3 tablespoons butter, at room temperature
3 tablespoons all-purpose flour
2 cups vegetable cooking broth, Chicken Stock (see Index), or milk
½ cup heavy or whipping cream
Salt and freshly ground white pepper to taste
Cayenne pepper to taste
⅔ cup buttered and lightly toasted bread crumbs (see box)
½ cup lightly toasted slivered almonds (see Index)

1. Combine the Swiss chard, onion, and carrot in a heavy saucepan. Cover with water (or light chicken stock or a mixture of both). Bring to a boil, then lower the heat and simmer, uncovered, until the chard is not quite tender, about 15 minutes.

2. Preheat the oven to 375°F.

3. Drain the Swiss chard into another pan. Save the vegetable cooking broth if desired. Discard the carrot and onion.

4. Without washing the pan, add the butter and allow it to melt over low heat. Add the flour. Mix well with a whisk until it is smooth. Add the vegetable cooking broth, chicken stock, or milk. Beat well and cook over medium heat, stirring constantly, until the sauce is smooth, 2 minutes.

5. Stir in the cream. Add the drained Swiss chard. Season to taste with salt, white pepper, and cayenne.

6. Pour into a shallow casserole and cover with the crumbs and almonds. Bake until the vegetable is bubbly hot and the crumbs are a very light brown, 20 to 30 minutes.

Serves 6

VARIATION: *Carolina Artichoke Almondine:* Follow the directions for Swiss Chard Almondine, but use thickly sliced, peeled Jerusalem artichokes, parboiled only about 2 minutes.

BUTTERED AND TOASTED BREAD CRUMBS

*M*elt 1 tablespoon butter per 1 cup of crumbs in a skillet over low heat. Toss the crumbs until lightly browned.

BAKED STUFFED TOMATOES

6 ripe but firm large tomatoes
Salt to taste

1. Preheat the oven to 375°F.
2. Slice off the top of each tomato. Scoop out the flesh with a small spoon, leaving a firm outer wall of tomato so it will hold the filling without breaking. Season with salt.
3. Fill as directed below and place in a lightly oiled shallow baking pan. Bake 20 to 25 minutes.

Baked Stuffed Tomatoes with Zucchini: Combine the pulp removed from the tomatoes with about 1½ cups slivered tender zucchini in a saucepan. Season with olive oil or butter, and chopped fresh basil and salt to taste. Simmer until the zucchini is tender, 3 to 4 minutes. Fill tomato shells with the mixture and bake as directed. Sprinkle with chopped fresh parsley and serve.

Baked Stuffed Tomatoes with Corn: Put 2 cups of freshly cut corn in a saucepan and add water to cover. Cook gently until the corn is tender, 4 minutes. Drain thoroughly and season with butter, salt, and white pepper. Fill the tomato shells with the corn. Bake as directed, loosely covered with foil so the corn will not become crusty on top. Before serving, sprinkle the tops with buttered toasted bread crumbs or chopped fresh parsley. Serve with a Southern menu: fried chicken, broiled ham, or roast beef.

Baked Stuffed Tomatoes with Spinach and Mushrooms: Cook 1½ pounds fresh spinach

Ripening on the vine—the only way to get that sun-drenched flavor.

in boiling salted water for 3 minutes. Drain thoroughly, and chop. Sauté ½ pound sliced fresh mushrooms in butter only until the mushrooms absorb the butter and give off their juice. Sprinkle with salt. Combine the spinach, mushrooms, and 3 tablespoons heavy cream. Simmer only a few minutes. Add 3 to 4 tablespoons butter, and salt and freshly ground black pepper to taste. Fill the tomato shells, cover loosely with foil, and bake as directed. Be careful not to overbake or the spinach will turn dark. Sprinkle the tomatoes with chopped fresh parsley. Serve with beef, seafood, veal, or chicken.
Serves 6

When they are covered with foil to prevent an unappetizing crust from forming on the filling, the filled tomatoes are covered only loosely. If they were covered tightly, the tomatoes would steam and break down.

PERFECT BAKED TOMATOES

◆◆◆

8 ripe but very firm perfect tomatoes (of equal size)
Salt to taste
1 clove garlic, cored and mashed (see Owl)
⅓ cup chopped fresh basil leaves or 2 teaspoons dried
½ cup good-quality olive oil
¼ cup chopped fresh parsley

---

1. Preheat the oven to 425°F.
2. Remove the core of each tomato. Cut the tomatoes in half, and lay the halves, cut side up, in a lightly oiled baking pan. Season with salt.
3. Blend the garlic and basil with the olive oil and sprinkle the mixture over the tomatoes.
4. Bake for 15 minutes. Remove the tomatoes from the oven and lightly press them with a spoon. If they feel softer, they are almost done. Sprinkle with parsley and return to the oven for about 5 minutes. (The time will vary with their size, but 20 minutes is usually perfect for a medium tomato.) The tomatoes must stay firm enough for the skin to remain unbroken.
5. Serve at once. If the tomatoes have to wait, they will wilt. Use to garnish a pork, veal, or lamb roast, or meat loaf.
   Serves 8

A NOTABLE VARIATION: Sprinkle a mixture of buttered and toasted bread crumbs and toasted pine nuts over the tomatoes.

To core a clove of garlic, cut a peeled clove in half with a small sharp knife. Remove the core, which is usually a creamy greenish yellow, from the center of each clove. The garlic will be milder and more digestible.

SOUTHERN FRIED GREEN TOMATOES OF AUTUMN

◆◆◆

*W*hen the crickets and the katydids are singing their hearts out under the porch or in the garden, and ham is cooking on the stove to be eaten with the last of the fresh corn and fried green tomatoes—green tomatoes coated with a crisp cornmeal crust—one knows that another summer has gone, but autumn has blessed our table and life is good. Green tomatoes dipped in cornmeal, you ask? Of course. Dipped in flour would be blasphemy. Where are you from, my friend?

---

2 pounds green tomatoes
1½ cups finely ground white cornmeal
Oil or solid vegetable shortening for frying (see step 2)
Salt and freshly ground black pepper to taste

---

1. Slice the tomatoes ¼ inch thick. Dredge both sides of the tomatoes in cornmeal, pressing the slices firmly into the meal so it will make a good coating. Shake off any excess meal.
2. Put enough oil or shortening in an

iron skillet to come to a depth of about ¼ inch, and place the skillet over medium heat. Add the tomatoes to the hot oil a few at a time, without crowding, and fry until golden brown, about 2 minutes. Turn, and when both sides are golden brown, drain on paper towels and sprinkle with salt and pepper. Serve piping hot.

Serves 4

A SUMMER'S-END PATIO SUPPER

Country Ham

Southern Fried Green Tomatoes

Corn on the Cob with Red Pepper Butter

The Ultimate Extra-Flaky Biscuit

◆

Poached Peaches and Raspberries

Iced Coffee

HAM WITH ZUCCHINI

*E*xquisitely easy and just that delicious. Serve this with veal roast, veal scallopini, or broiled chicken, or use it as the entrée dish for a light meal.

4 firm small zucchini
2 tablespoons butter, or more as needed
½ pound baked ham, slivered
¼ cup chopped fresh basil, or ½ teaspoon dried
Salt and freshly ground black pepper to taste
¼ cup chopped fresh parsley

1. Wash and dry the zucchini, trim off the ends, and cut into slivers.
2. Melt the butter in a large heavy skillet and sauté the zucchini over medium-low heat until almost tender, 3 to 4 minutes.
3. Add the ham and toss lightly. Cook until the zucchini is tender but still crisp, adding more butter, if needed, 1 minute. Add the basil. Season with salt and pepper, sprinkle with the parsley, and serve.

Serves 4 as a light lunch; 6 as a side dish

🦉 The slivers of ham and zucchini should be uniform, and the zucchini must remain crisp for this to be the delicious dish that it should be.

ZUCCHINI PARMESAN SOUFFLE

*O*f all the vegetable soufflés—or may I say of all fancy vegetable dishes—this is the most superb.

◆

1¼ *pounds small firm zucchini (3 to 4)*
2 tablespoons butter
2 tablespoons all-purpose flour
½ *cup milk*
6 tablespoons freshly grated Parmesan or Swiss
    cheese
3 egg yolks
Salt to taste
Cayenne pepper to taste
3 egg whites
10 thin slivers of Parmesan or Swiss cheese, or
    ½ *cup grated Parmesan*

◆

1. Preheat the oven to 375°F.
2. Wash and dry the zucchini, trim off the ends, and slice. Drop the slices into boiling salted water to cover. Boil until just tender, 5 to 7 minutes. Drain at once in a colander, pressing down hard with a wooden spoon to extract all the water. Chop fine. You should have 1¼ cups.
3. Melt the butter in a heavy sauce-pan, add the flour, and mix with a whisk over medium-low heat until blended. Add the milk, and whisk until the sauce is thick and smooth, 2 minutes. Stir in the grated cheese, then the egg yolks, and blend. Season with salt and cayenne to taste. Remove from the heat.
4. Gently stir the zucchini into the egg mixture. Taste, and correct the seasoning if necessary.
5. Beat the egg whites with a pinch of salt until stiff but not dry and grainy. Fold them gently into the zucchini mixture, allowing some particles of egg white to show. Pour the mixture into a buttered 3-cup soufflé dish, shallow 3-cup casserole, or gratin dish. Top with the slivers of cheese, and bake until the soufflé is golden brown, well puffed, and fairly firm to the touch, 30 to 40 minutes. Serve at once.

Serves 4

🦉 The cooking time depends upon the size and kind of baking dish used.

CHAPTER EIGHT

POTATOES,
RICE,
AND
NOODLES

THE MIGHTY POTATO
AND THE
MAGNIFICENT
GRAINS

◆◆◆

*I*n spite of our casual acceptance of the white potato, this life-sustaining root vegetable is one of our favorites. Originally kept in the flower garden as a novelty, it was thought to be poisonous long before it was accepted and admired as a food. Is there one among us who isn't fond of potatoes, mashed to perfection and seasoned well with "oodles" of butter? Not one.

The sweet potato is as native to the Southern states as corn is. It was known in the colonial days as the potato of Virginia, and although not as useful as the white potato, it takes its natural place with ham and the Thanksgiving turkey.

One of our favorite of the grains is hominy, or grits, made from the South's native corn. We love grits cooked almost any way. When you are served them hot for breakfast along with your eggs and bacon or sausage—without even ordering them—then you know you are deep inside Dixie.

Rice, the most venerable of all the grains, has deep roots in the South. Texas and Louisiana produce the largest volume of rice today, and South Carolina was the first among the early colonies to grow rice. It is well documented that Thomas Jefferson, ever the agronomist, in 1787 smuggled a small bag of rice out of Italy when he was on a diplomatic mission there. It was this rice that provided the seed to revive the stricken Carolina rice industry after the Revolutionary War.

◆◆◆

SPRING MEADOW POTATOES

*T*here is a fresh and incomparable flavor in new potatoes. I mean the ones that are fresh from the earth in which they grew—not those that have been dyed red to fool us! These potatoes, when cooked with ham and served with a green vegetable, a salad of cottage cheese on lettuce with a dollop of sour cream, and Hoe Cake, make a beautiful Southern meal.

2 pounds tiny new potatoes
Water or Chicken, Veal, or White Soup Stock
  (see Index and step 2)
¼ cup slivered baked smoked ham
3 tablespoons butter, at room temperature
Salt, if needed
Freshly ground white pepper to taste
3 tablespoons chopped fresh chives
3 tablespoons chopped fresh parsley

1. Select small, firm new potatoes. Cut out any blemishes and peel away a ribbon of skin around the center of each potato. (There is lots of good flavor in fresh new potato skins.)
2. Bring the water or stock to a boil and drop in the potatoes. There should be enough stock to cover the potatoes by 3 inches. Add the ham, and cook until the potatoes are tender, 30 minutes.
3. Drain, and toss the potatoes with the butter, and salt and white pepper to

Taking produce to market in 1910, before the day of the refrigerated truck.

taste. Sprinkle with the chives and parsley, and serve.
  Serves 6

VARIATION: If you have some extra good smoked bacon, it can be partially broiled and used instead of the ham. The bacon must not be crisp as that changes the flavor of the entire dish.

PLANTATION POTATOES WITH LEMON, CHIVES, AND PARSLEY

*P*otatoes fresh from the garden are one of Mother Nature's most delicious creations. Old potatoes are good, but freshly dug potatoes are sublime—and perfumed with lemon, chives, and parsley, they are unforgettable.

2 pounds tiny new potatoes
4 tablespoons (½ stick) butter
3 tablespoons good-quality olive oil
Juice and grated peel of 1 lemon

Salt and freshly ground white pepper to taste
2 tablespoons minced fresh chives
1 tablespoon chopped fresh parsley

1. Peel away a ribbon of skin around the center of each potato. Drop them into a large pot of boiling salted water to cover well, and cook until tender, 30 minutes.

2. While the potatoes are cooking, melt the butter in a small saucepan. Add the olive oil, lemon juice and lemon peel, and stir. Keep warm.

3. Drain the potatoes well and pour the butter mixture over them. Taste a little piece of potato for salt. Sprinkle with white pepper, chives, and parsley. Serve at once.

ALFRED LUNT'S POTATOES

*L*eftover baked potatoes, if the skin is not broken, develop a "nutty" flavor. The actor Alfred Lunt, who gave some cooking lessons for the U.S.O. in Washington, D.C. during World War II, taught me this. You'll love them. Everyone does.

6 baked Idaho potatoes, chilled with their skin on
8 tablespoons (1 stick) butter
1 teaspoon salt, or to taste
2 tablespoons chopped fresh dill
1 tablespoon chopped fresh parsley

1. Preheat the oven to 400°F.
2. Slice the potatoes very thin and lay them in a buttered baking pan, each slice slightly overlapping the one next to it. Dot with the butter and sprinkle with salt.
3. Bake until golden brown and crunchy, 25 to 30 minutes.

4. Sprinkle with the chopped dill and parsley.
Serves 6

VARIATION: Chopped fresh chives may be used instead of fresh dill.

These potatoes really are a bit better when they are made from leftover baked potatoes that have been refrigerated uncovered. They lose moisture this way, so they become crunchier and have a rather nutlike flavor. Delicious with steak or hamburgers.

SCALLOPED POTATOES WITH MARJORAM

*M*ealy potatoes such as Idahos are best for scalloping. They cook more quickly and they absorb the flavorings, which gives them a creamy goodness. Serve these with steak, veal scallopini, broiled chicken, or as an entrée with a green salad.

2 pounds potatoes
6 tablespoons (¾ stick) butter
1½ teaspoons dried marjoram or 1½ tablespoons fresh
1 tablespoon all-purpose flour (optional)
Salt and freshly ground white pepper to taste

½ cup heavy or whipping cream, plus milk as needed (see Owl)

1. Preheat the oven to 350°F.
2. Peel the potatoes and slice them as

thin and evenly as possible.

3. Butter a shallow 1½-quart glass or ceramic baking dish. Put one layer of potatoes in the dish. Dot them with some of the butter, and sprinkle with some of the marjoram, flour, salt, and white pepper. Repeat layering the potatoes with all the ingredients except the cream and milk. Reserve 1 tablespoon of the butter.

4. Pour the cream over the potatoes. Add milk if necessary to just barely cover. Dot the top with the remaining butter, and sprinkle with salt and white pepper. Cover loosely with foil.

5. Bake until the potatoes are tender, about 1¼ to 1½ hours. Remove the cover, raise the heat to 375° or 400°F, and bake until the potatoes brown, another 15 minutes. The total cooking time will vary with the potatoes.

Serves 6

In the Florida Keys, around the turn of the century, produce was often delivered by boat.

VARIATION: Add ½ pound sliced fresh mushrooms. Mushrooms, like potatoes, have an affinity for marjoram.

All milk will curdle on scalloped potatoes; so will half-and-half. Use at least two-thirds heavy or whipping cream to one-third milk.

POTATO PANCAKES

*T*hese are wonderfully delicious pancakes, but the cook has to work fast. They are so good with steaks or roasts, they are well worth the hurry.

½ cup finely shredded aged Swiss cheese
1 tablespoon chopped fresh parsley
1 large egg
¼ cup sifted all-purpose flour
4 medium Idaho potatoes, peeled and very finely shredded
Salt and freshly ground white pepper to taste
Cayenne pepper to taste
2 to 3 tablespoons heavy or whipping cream
6 tablespoons (¾ stick) unsalted butter
6 tablespoons vegetable oil

1. Preheat the oven to 400°F.
2. Combine the cheese and the parsley in a small bowl and set aside.
3. In a large bowl, beat the egg thoroughly with a whisk. Add the flour and beat until there are no lumps. (This can be done with a mixer or in a processor.)
4. Stir the cheese mixture into the egg mixture, and then add the shredded potatoes. Season with salt, white pepper, and cayenne. Add just enough cream to form a moist, but not runny, batter.

5. Melt ½ tablespoon of the butter in ½ tablespoon of the oil on a griddle. When they sizzle, begin frying the pancakes. Spoon on 3 to 4 tablespoons of batter for each and cook over very high heat until they are a glowing golden brown, 2 to 3 minutes. Turn, and when both sides are golden brown, place the pancakes on a baking sheet on the middle shelf of the oven and bake for 4 to 5 minutes to finish cooking.

6. Add more butter and oil to the griddle and continue cooking the pancakes. Serve hot.

Serves 4

VARIATION: Add 1 tablespoon finely chopped chives or scallion (green onion) tops to the shredded potatoes.

MASHED OR PUREED POTATOES

❖❖❖

*T*he perfect potato for a hundred menus, and beloved by all.

◆

4 medium Idaho potatoes
2 tablespoons butter, or more to taste
¼ to ½ cup milk or heavy or whipping cream,
*   as needed, heated*
Salt and freshly ground white pepper to taste

◆

1. Peel the potatoes and drop them into salted cold water to cover. Bring the water to a boil, and cook the potatoes until tender, 30 to 35 minutes. Drain at once.
2. Put the potatoes in the bowl of an electric mixer (not in a processor) while still hot. Beat until well mashed. If any lumps remain, put the potatoes through a ricer. Add the butter and ¼ cup of the warm milk or cream. Beat well. The potatoes should be moist but not runny. Add more milk or cream if needed. Season with salt and white pepper to taste.
   Serves 3 to 4

🦉 If you make a mistake and add too much milk or cream, rest the pan over low heat and beat the potatoes hard. This will dry them out. Easy though, don't burn them.

◆◆

THURSDAY NIGHT DINNER

Wintertime Veal Loaf

Mashed or Puréed Potatoes

Buttered Carrots, Peas, and Tiny Onions

◆

Winter Apple Cookies

Fresh Fruit

OLD-FASHIONED HOME-FRIED POTATOES

❖❖❖

*S*erve with steak, ground steak patties, or veal chops. Notable with scrambled eggs or as a filling for an omelet.

◆

3 tablespoons fresh bacon fat
5 Idaho potatoes, thinly sliced
3 slices bacon, diced
1 sweet onion, thinly sliced
Salt and freshly ground black pepper to taste
Chopped fresh parsley, for garnish

◆

1. Heat the bacon fat in a heavy iron skillet. Add the potatoes, bacon, and onion and cook, covered, over medium heat 10 to 15 minutes. Shake the pan while the pota- toes are cooking so the bacon and onion will not burn (you can place the bacon and onion on top of the potatoes, to help pre- vent their burning). Turn the potatoes from time to time with a spatula and try to keep the onion on top.
2. Remove the cover, and continue cooking until the potatoes are golden brown and crunchy, 10 to 12 minutes. Sprinkle with salt, pepper, and parsley.
   Serves 6

SCRUMPTIOUS BAKED POTATOES

*I*f you like cheese, this potato is for you. Rich and creamy, they are a meal in themselves with a green salad and a bite of dessert.

6 large Idaho potatoes
6 tablespoons (¾ stick) butter
2 tablespoons all-purpose flour
1⅔ cups milk, or as needed, heated
½ cup loosely packed grated Swiss cheese
Salt to taste
Cayenne pepper to taste
1 cup freshly grated Parmesan cheese

1. Preheat the oven to 375°F.
2. Scrub and dry the potatoes (do not grease them). Place them on a baking sheet and bake until they are done, 1 hour. Reduce the heat to 350°F.
3. While the potatoes are cooling, make the cheese sauce: Melt 2 tablespoons of the butter in a small saucepan over medium-low heat. Add the flour, and blend well with a whisk. Slowly pour in 1 cup of the milk, stirring with a whisk; cook until the mixture is thickened and smooth, 2 minutes. Add the Swiss cheese, salt, and cayenne pepper. Whisk until smooth, 4 to 5 minutes. Set aside.
4. When the potatoes are cool enough to handle, cut them in half lengthwise and scoop out the pulp. (Leave a fairly firm shell or it will collapse when refilled.) Rice the potato pulp while it is still warm (otherwise it will be lumpy) into a large mixing

Market day in Baltimore, around 1925.

bowl. Add the remaining butter and milk. (Add the milk a little at a time—the potatoes must be moist but not runny.) Season with salt and cayenne to taste. Beat with an electric mixer until fluffy.
5. Fill the potato shells with the seasoned whipped potatoes. Make a rather deep trench lengthwise in the top of the potato mixture, and fill the trench with the cheese sauce. Place the potatoes on a baking sheet, and sprinkle the tops generously with Parmesan cheese.
6. Bake the potatoes for 20 minutes. Then increase the heat to 400°F and cook until the cheese sauce is light golden brown, 10 minutes. Serve at once.

Serves 6

MY FAVORITE SAVORY PIE

*T*his is an entrée pie I learned at French cooking school years ago and have taught ever since. Once it is tasted, it never fails to win a friend. If I were asked to name one dish as my final request, I think it just might be this savory pie! Serve it with a green salad for a special lunch for very special people. It is good with any well-made crust, but divine with puff paste.

5 large Idaho potatoes
Pastry for a 10-inch 2-crust pie: Standard,
*   Flaky Butter, French, or Cornmeal Puff*
*   Paste (see Index)*
¼ cup chopped fresh parsley
3 tablespoons chopped fresh marjoram or 1½
*   tablespoons dried*
Salt and freshly ground white pepper to taste
6 tablespoons (¾ stick) butter
½ cup light cream (or ¼ cup milk and ¼ cup
*   heavy or whipping cream)*
⅓ cup heavy or whipping cream
1 egg yolk

1. Peel the potatoes and slice them paper-thin. Drop them into salted boiling water and blanch 3 minutes. Drain at once, and refrigerate.

2. Preheat the oven to 425°F.

3. While the potatoes are cooling, line a 10-inch pie pan with pastry ⅛ inch thick, with a 1½-inch overhang around the rim.

4. Put a layer of cooled potatoes in the bottom of the pastry-lined pan. Sprinkle it with some of the parsley, marjoram, and salt and pepper. Dot with part of the butter. Repeat until all the potatoes, seasonings, and butter are used up. Pour the light cream carefully over the potatoes.

5. Roll the top crust very thin. Place it over the pie, and cut a small round hole in the center of the crust.

6. Brush the edges of the bottom crust with water. Crimp the two crusts together with the tines of a fork. With a sharp knife, trim the crust even with the rim of the pan. Brush the top with a little heavy cream.

7. Place the pie on the bottom shelf of the oven and bake for 50 minutes. (If the edges of the crust brown too quickly, cover them with strips of foil. If the top crust browns too fast, lower the heat to 375°F and cover the pie loosely with foil.) When the bottom of the pie is golden brown, remove the pie from the oven.

8. Mix the egg yolk with the remaining heavy cream. Pour it very slowly and carefully through the center hole in the crust, using a small kitchen funnel. It may not take all of the mixture, but use as much as you can. Place the pie back in the oven for 5 minutes. The cream and egg yolk will form a lovely custard.

9. Slice, and serve the pie hot.
Serves 6 to 8

VARIATIONS: Add one or more of the following to the potatoes: Very thinly sliced onions (alternate layers of potatoes and onions), sautéed sliced mushrooms, and julienne slivers of ham.

Supermarket half-and-half is very seldom half cream and half milk, and like a low-fat milk, it will curdle when used in scalloped potato dishes or this pie. Fresh cream will boil down and thicken without curdling, and it adds flavor.

DEEP-FRIED SWEET POTATOES

*Y*ou will find that fried sweet potatoes or yams are more delicious if they have been boiled first—it brings out their flavor. In Florida they sprinkle them with sugar. Your sweet tooth or lack of one will guide you. I have a sweet tooth. Serve with broiled ham, warm baked ham, or broiled or fried chicken.

2 pounds sweet potatoes or yams
Oil for deep-frying
Salt or sugar (optional)

1. Drop the sweet potatoes in boiling salted water to cover by 3 to 4 inches. Remove them before they are thoroughly cooked, 20 to 25 minutes. Cool the pota-

toes, then peel them, and cut them into pieces about 2 inches long and ½ inch thick.

2. Heat the oil in a deep-fat fryer to 375°F.

3. Plunge the potato sticks into the oil a few at a time and cook only until light brown. Remove, drain on paper towels, and sprinkle with salt or sugar. Keep warm while you fry the rest.

Serves 6

SWEET POTATO SOUFFLE

*T*his is a good holiday sweet potato dish, perfumed with brandy and grated lemon peel. If you wish, or if time is of the essence, beat the whole eggs together and fold them into the potato purée, then bake. The dish won't rise as high but it will be flavorful—that is, if you don't forget the brandy.

2 cups mashed cooked sweet potatoes (about 1 pound)
4 tablespoons (½ stick) butter, at room temperature
½ cup milk, heated
½ teaspoon salt, or to taste
1 teaspoon grated lemon peel
¼ cup brandy
4 eggs, separated

1. Preheat the oven to 400°F.

2. With a whisk or an electric mixer (do not use a food processor), whip the potatoes well in a large bowl. Add the butter, milk, salt, lemon peel, and brandy, and stir. Add the egg yolks, and mix well.

3. In another bowl, beat the egg whites until they are stiff but not dry and grainy. Fold them into the potato mixture, then pour the mixture into a buttered 4-cup soufflé dish or shallow 1½-quart casserole.

4. Bake until the soufflé is well puffed and has begun to brown, 25 to 30 minutes. Serve at once.

Serves 4

HOME FOR THE HOLIDAYS

Hot Dilled Olives

Washington Waterfront Pickled Shrimp

◆

Roast Chicken with Herbs

Sweet Potato Soufflé

Fresh Lima and Green Bean Salad

Potato Yeast Biscuits

◆

The Jewel Box Cake

A holiday gathering in the 1890s gives proof that even the most elegant included the family dog.

ALABAMA YAMS WITH ORANGES

*T*his is the Deep South way with yams or sweet potatoes. It seems to always show up with the Thanksgiving turkey, but it is just as compatible with a good ham or chicken. Do not peel either the potatoes or the orange. If you don't have a luscious rich sauce, you have been too cautious with the butter.

2 tablespoons fresh lemon juice, or more to taste

1. Preheat the oven to 375°F.
2. Peel and slice the sweet potatoes very thin and place one layer in a shallow buttered baking dish. Top with a layer of orange slices. Dot generously with butter and sprinkle with sugar. Continue layering. You should have 3 layers, ending with a layer of potatoes, butter, and sugar.
3. Mix the orange juice with the lemon juice, and pour it over the potatoes.
4. Bake until a pleasant syrup has formed and the top is tinged with brown, 1½ hours.

Serves 6 to 8

VARIATION: *Yams or Sweet Potatoes with Lemon:* Omit the sliced oranges and orange juice. Season the layers of potatoes with the grated peel of 1½ lemons, the sugar, and the juice of 2 lemons combined with ⅓ cup water. Use the full ¾ cup of butter. A favorite that's nice with duck.

6 yams or sweet potatoes, fully cooked and
    cooled
3 navel oranges, thinly sliced
½ to ¾ cup (1 to 1½ sticks) butter
¾ cup sugar
1 cup fresh orange juice

MASHED SWEET POTATOES

*S*weet potatoes are lighter in color than the darker Alabama yams, but they are prepared the same way. The yams usually have a richer flavor. At Thanksgiving these potatoes are rather highly seasoned.

6 large sweet potatoes or yams
¼ cup sugar
8 tablespoons (1 stick) butter
⅔ cup milk or heavy or whipping cream,
    heated

¼ cup Madeira or medium-dry sherry, or more
    to taste, or 2 tablespoons brandy
Salt to taste

1. Scrub the sweet potatoes and drop them into a large pot of boiling salted water to cover by 3 to 4 inches. Cook until they are fork-tender, 30 minutes. Drain, and allow to cool slightly.

2. Preheat the oven to 350°F.

3. When the potatoes are cool enough to handle, peel them and put them in a large mixing bowl. Mash the potatoes, using a ricer or an electric mixer (do not use a food processor), and then stir in the sugar, butter, milk or cream, and wine or brandy. Blend well, and add salt to taste.

4. Spoon the potato mixture into a well-buttered casserole and bake until bubbly, 25 to 30 minutes.

Serves 6 to 8

FLORIDA'S YELLOW RICE

*S*affron rice was brought to Florida by the Spanish, who were seeking gold, high adventure, and the fountain of youth. They left us a great legacy of rice dishes. The one given here is the most delicious of all the many varieties. You can use either the threads or powdered saffron, but the powdered is best.

1 cup medium-grain top-quality rice, such as Carolina
4 tablespoons (½ stick) butter
3 cups Rich Chicken Stock (see Index), heated
1 medium onion, cut in half
1 teaspoon ground saffron or 6 to 8 threads, crushed
½ cup dry white wine
½ cup freshly grated Parmesan cheese or to taste
Salt if needed
Freshly grated Parmesan cheese, for garnish

1. Combine the rice and 2 tablespoons of the butter in a heavy saucepan (enameled iron is excellent). Stir over medium heat until the grains of rice are coated with the butter. Add 1 cup of the stock, and stir well. Add the onion and simmer, adding more stock as the rice dries out, stirring constantly with a wooden spoon and always touching the bottom of the pan so the rice doesn't stick. (It would be well to use an asbestos pad to help keep the rice from sticking.)

2. Dissolve the saffron in ¼ cup of the remaining stock, and add it and the white wine to the rice. Continue to stir, adding the remaining stock a little at a time.

3. Stir constantly until the rice is cooked, 20 to 25 minutes.

4. When the rice is tender, discard the onion, and stir in the remaining butter and the Parmesan cheese with a fork. Add salt if needed. Serve with a side dish of grated Parmesan cheese.

Serves 4 to 6

VARIATION: The white wine can be omitted, but it gives the rice a delectable and special flavor.

STEAMED WHITE RICE

*M*easure 1 cup white long- or medium-grain rice, 2 cups water, and 1 teaspoon salt into a heavy saucepan. Place over high heat and when the water boils vigorously, stir several times and cover with a tight-fitting lid. Turn the heat *very* low and cook 14 minutes.

Turn off the heat, fluff the grains with a fork, replace the cover and allow the rice to steam. The water should be completely absorbed and the grains separate, flaky, and tender, but with some firmness, 4 to 5 minutes.

For extra-tender rice, start with ⅓ cup more water and increase the cooking time by 4 to 5 minutes.

Serves 4

GREEN RICE

*T*his is an old idea for rice but still a good one if the flavors are compatible with the entrée. The watercress and tarragon are very pleasant with seafood.

Rice being hulled in Georgia at the beginning of this century.

2 quarts water
3 teaspoons salt
1 cup top-quality long-grain rice
4 tablespoons (½ stick) butter
1 cup chopped fresh parsley

½ cup chopped watercress
2 tablespoons chives, or more to taste (optional)
2 tablespoons chopped fresh tarragon, if available (do not use dried)

1. Bring the water and salt to a boil, and add the rice gradually, so the water keeps boiling. Continue to boil until the rice is tender, 15 to 18 minutes. Keep the pan uncovered and be sure not to overcook the rice. Taste the rice after 12 to 14 minutes. Continue to taste until the rice is tender.

2. Drain at once and fluff with a fork. Add the butter, parsley, watercress, chives, and tarragon. Mix well and serve.

Serves 4

Herbs cannot be added to the rice ahead of time as they will turn black if held very long.

OVERCOOKED RICE IS SOGGY RICE

*B*oiled rice must be drained immediately after removing it from the heat. Fluff it with a fork, not a spoon.

If you prefer rice that is somewhat sticky, choose medium fat-grain rice. If you prefer every grain to stand apart, choose long-grain rice.

DEEP SOUTH RED BEANS AND RICE

*M*any recipes for Red Beans and Rice call for dried kidney beans, but the dried dark-red round bean is the authentic bean.

1 pound dried red beans
3 quarts water, or more as needed
¼-pound slice uncooked ham or ½ small ham
*   hock*
1 medium onion
2 ribs celery, cut in half
2 bay leaves
2 sprigs fresh thyme or ½ teaspoon dried
¼ small fresh or dried red chile pepper, or more
*   to taste*
Salt and freshly ground black pepper to taste
2 cups freshly cooked white rice
Chopped fresh parsley, for garnish

1. Wash the beans thoroughly. Bring 1½ quarts of the water to a boil in a large pot, add the beans, and boil 5 minutes.

2. Remove the pot from the heat and allow the beans to soak 1 hour.

3. Drain the beans and set them aside.

4. Add 1½ quarts of fresh water to the pot. Add the ham, onion, celery, bay leaves, thyme, and chile pepper. Bring to a boil and cook 20 minutes. (This seasons the stock.) Add the red beans and simmer until they are tender but not mushy, about 1 hour.

5. Discard the meat, onion, celery, and bay leaves. Add salt and pepper to taste. There should be a little sauce but the beans must not be soupy. If there is too

Sacks of rice being loaded aboard a paddlewheeler in Louisiana in the 1870s.

much sauce, reduce it quickly over high heat.

6. Serve the beans over the rice. Sprinkle with the parsley.

Serves 6 to 8

TO COOK RICE IN ADVANCE

Steam or boil the rice, drain it well if it was boiled, and fluff it with a fork. Taste for salt. Allow the rice to get cold, then put it in a shallow ovenproof dish. Cover with foil, and refrigerate. (The rice must be cold before it is covered with foil or it will steam and become soggy.)

When you are ready to serve the rice, transfer it, leaving the foil intact, to a preheated 325°F oven and bake for about 30 minutes. Remove the foil, fluff the rice with a fork, add butter and seasonings, and serve.

BAKED BROWN RICE WITH ALMONDS

*T*he unique flavor of pine nuts and the crunchy texture as well as the compatible flavor of almonds are most pertinent to brown rice. Either variation is delicious with the Lamb and Limestone or the Warm Chicken and Sweetbread entrée salad.

3 tablespoons unsalted butter
1 cup brown rice
1½ cups Rich Chicken Stock (see Index)
1 bay leaf
2 sprigs fresh thyme, if available (don't use

*   dried thyme)*
Salt and freshly ground white pepper to taste
⅓ cup freshly buttered and toasted slivered
*   almonds or pine nuts (see box, page 268)*

1. Preheat the oven to 350°F.

2. Heat 1½ tablespoons of the butter in a heavy ovenproof saucepan. Add the rice, and stir until the grains are coated with butter. Add the stock, bay leaf, and thyme. Season to taste with salt and white pepper.

3. Cover the saucepan with a tight-fitting lid, and place it on the middle shelf of the oven. Cook 1 to 1½ hours. (Brown rice takes longer to cook than white rice.) Taste the rice. It should be tender but not mushy.

4. Remove the pan from the oven, and discard the bay leaf, and thyme if used. Stir in the remaining butter and the nuts with a cooking fork (to fluff the rice).

Serves 4

TO TOAST NUTS

*I*n a skillet: Toast almonds, whole, sliced, or slivered in 1 tablespoon of melted butter for each cup of nuts over the lowest possible heat. Toss continuously to prevent burning. Depending on the size of the pieces, almonds will take anywhere from 30 to 35 minutes to toast.

Pine nuts come raw and must always be toasted. Use 1 tablespoon melted butter for each cup of pine nuts. Toast over the lowest possible heat, tossing continuously for 5 minutes. (Pine nuts toast much quicker than almonds.)

In the oven: Preheat the oven to 300°F. Toast the nuts on a baking sheet until nicely browned. Almonds may take as long as 1 hour; check the pine nuts after 30 minutes.

CAROLINA GRITS SOUFFLE

*V*ery light and delicate!

2½ cups water
¾ teaspoon salt, or to taste
½ cup hominy grits (not instant)
4 tablespoons (½ stick) butter
¼ cup shredded sharp Cheddar cheese
Cayenne pepper to taste
3 eggs, separated

1. Preheat the oven to 375°F.

2. Bring the water with the salt to a boil in a large heavy saucepan, and pour in the grits. Simmer, stirring constantly, over medium heat until the grits taste done and are thick and perfectly smooth, 20 minutes. Add the butter, stir, and remove from the heat. Add the cheese, cayenne pepper, and egg yolks. Blend well and set aside, covered, to thicken, but keep warm.

3. Beat the egg whites until they are stiff but not dry and grainy, and fold them into the grits mixture, leaving large pieces of egg white showing.

4. Pour the mixture into a 1-quart buttered casserole or soufflé dish. Bake until golden brown and firm in the middle, 35 to 40 minutes. Serve at once.

Serves 6

FRIED GRITS

*F*ried grits is a beloved dish of the South—it is a part of our heritage. We like it with broiled ham, or bacon and eggs, or with game and fish. Cooked to a crisp, golden brown in an iron skillet over a campfire in October with spitted quail—or for breakfast in a warm kitchen on a snowy day—this is what good living is all about.

5 cups water
Salt to taste
1 cup hominy grits (not instant)
½ cup all-purpose flour
Lard, solid vegetable shortening, or oil for
  frying (see step 4)

1. Bring the water and salt to a boil in a large heavy saucepan. Add the grits and simmer, stirring constantly, over medium heat until the grits taste done and are thick like mush, 20 minutes. (You may have to add a little more boiling water.)

2. Pour the hot grits onto a meat platter or large plate to make a layer ¾ inch deep. Cover and set aside to cool, then refrigerate to chill.

3. When the grits are cold, cut them into rectangular pieces. Dredge the pieces with flour (not cornmeal). Shake off any excess flour.

4. Heat the lard or oil to a depth of ½ inch in an iron skillet. Fry the grits until golden brown, 2 minutes. Turn, and when both sides are golden brown, drain on paper towels and sprinkle with salt. Serve piping hot.

Serves 4

A CASSEROLE OF GRITS

*T*he cooking time depends upon the kind of grits. The old-fashioned long-cooking grits have more flavor than precooked grits. Serve this with broiled ham or chicken, sautéed quail, or pheasant.

4 cups water
1 teaspoon salt
¾ cup hominy grits
5½ tablespoons butter
3 or 4 eggs, beaten (see Owl)
Salt to taste
Cayenne pepper to taste

1. Bring the water and salt to a boil, add the grits, and simmer, stirring constantly, over medium heat until the grits taste done and are thick and perfectly smooth, about 20 minutes.

2. Preheat the oven to 350°F.

3. When the grits are done, add 4 tablespoons of the butter, the eggs, salt, and cayenne. Stir well. Pour the mixture into a buttered shallow casserole, and dot with the remaining butter.

4. Bake until the grits are golden brown, 25 to 30 minutes.

Serves 6

When boiling grits, 5 parts water to 1 part grits is about perfect. Using 3 eggs makes a nice casserole, but 4 eggs makes it richer and gives it greater volume.

HOMEMADE NOODLES

*T*here are few dishes that are more fun for a good cook than homemade noodles, especially if you have a pasta machine. Lacking that happy gadget, you can make these noodles by hand. The egg-rich dough is rolled out like a pie crust, allowed to dry, then rolled up like a jelly roll and sliced. Pop them into boiling salted water, and in a matter of minutes you have the best noodles in the world.

2¼ cups all-purpose flour
1 teaspoon salt
1 tablespoon vegetable or olive oil
3 eggs
1 tablespoon water, or more if needed

1. *To Make Dough by Hand:* Sift the flour into a large bowl. Make a well in the center, and add the salt, oil, eggs, and water. Gradually stir the flour into the eggs, then knead until you have a firm ball of dough, adding more water, a spoonful at a time, if needed, 4 minutes. Cover the dough and allow it to rest in the refrigerator for 1 hour before rolling.

2. *To Make Dough in a Processor:* Combine the sifted flour, salt, oil, eggs, and water in a processor. Twirl until a dough is formed, a few seconds or less. (Do not overbeat the dough, which makes it tough.) Toss the dough onto a lightly floured board and knead in enough extra flour to keep it from being sticky. Wrap in foil and refrigerate for 30 minutes.

Makes about 1 pound

ROLLING NOODLES BY HAND

1. Knead the noodle dough on a lightly floured board until it is smooth and satiny.

2. Roll out the dough to a rectangle about 12 x 30 inches. The dough should be thin and will probably hang over the edge of the board.

3. Place the dough on a clean towel and allow it to dry for about 20 minutes.

4. Roll up the dough from the short side like a jelly roll. Cut across the roll with a sharp knife, making noodles ¼ inch wide.

5. Separate the coils of noodles. Spread them out on a rack or a floured board or baking sheet and allow them to dry.

PASTA MACHINES

*A*ll the doughs included here are easy to roll in a pasta machine. If you are lucky enough to own one, follow the directions included with your machine for uniformly cut noodles. If you are using a pasta machine, dust the dough generously with flour as needed to prevent it from sticking. It will not toughen the noodles.

WATERCRESS NOODLES WITH WALNUTS

*W*atercress noodles are a most elegant and appetizing shade of green and are far superior to spinach noodles. They are rich but do not have an assertive watercress flavor. Serve these beautiful watercress noodles with walnuts as a light entrée or with a veal chop, broiled ham or chicken, sautéed rabbit, chicken, or sweetbreads. The veal chop is especially delicious.

1 teaspoon butter
⅓ cup walnut pieces
½ pound Watercress Noodles (recipe follows)
6 tablespoons walnut oil or unsalted butter, warmed
Salt and freshly ground white pepper to taste
2 tablespoons chopped fresh parsley
Lemon juice to taste

1. Bring a large kettle of salted water to a boil.

2. Meanwhile melt the butter in a skillet over low heat. Add the walnuts and toss continuously until they are a bit crisper. Do not allow them to brown. Set aside.

3. Drop the noodles into the boiling water and cook until tender, 4 minutes. Drain thoroughly.

4. Toss the hot noodles into a warm large bowl. Add the warmed walnut oil or butter and stir well. Add the walnuts, salt, white pepper, parsley, and lemon juice. Serve at once.

Serves 4

WATERCRESS NOODLES

½ pound watercress (2 large bunches)
2 cups all-purpose flour, sifted
2 eggs
1 egg yolk
2 teaspoons good-quality olive or vegetable oil
1 teaspoon salt

---

1. Remove the coarsest stems from the watercress, leaving the tender stems intact. Drop the watercress into lightly salted boiling water and boil until the stems are tender, 3 to 4 minutes. The watercress must retain its bright color. Drain at once.

2. Purée the watercress in a processor or blender until the mixture is perfectly fine and no stem pieces are showing.

3. Spread the watercress out on several thicknesses of paper towels. Cover with more paper towels and pat heavily so the towels will absorb the water. Repeat this process several times, until the watercress is like a dried green curd. You should have 3 to 4 tablespoons.

4. *To prepare the noodles by hand:* Sift the flour into a large wooden bowl or onto a clean flat surface. Make a well in the center of the flour. In a bowl, combine the eggs, yolk, oil, salt, and watercress curd. Blend thoroughly, and pour into the center of the flour. With a fork, blend the flour little by little into the watercress mixture, using more flour as needed. Knead for about 4 minutes. The dough should be soft, pliable, and not the least bit sticky. Cover the dough and allow it to rest 1 hour in the refrigerator before rolling.

5. *To prepare the noodles in a processor:* Combine the eggs, yolk, oil, salt, and watercress curd in a processor. Blend. Add the flour to the watercress mixture quickly while the processor is running. Process just a few seconds. Toss the dough onto a lightly floured surface and knead until it is soft, pliable, and not sticky, adding a little sifted flour as needed, 4 minutes. Cover the dough and allow it to rest 1 hour in the refrigerator before rolling.

6. Roll the dough out by hand until it is ¹/₁₆ to ⅛ inch thick, and cut into noodles; or roll and cut on a pasta machine, following the manufacturer's directions.

Makes about 1 pound

Watercress noodle dough will freeze well either in a flat cake, to thaw and roll out later, or cut into noodles.

MOTHER'S DAY DINNER

Veal Fricassee

Garden Fresh Peas

Watercress Noodles with Walnuts

◆

The Ultimate Vanilla Ice Cream with Fresh Strawberries

Coffee   Tea

NOODLES WITH HAM AND MUSHROOMS

*W*atercress noodles are such a gorgeous color, but any fresh pasta will be fine in this recipe. Serve with a crisp Bibb salad, crunchy bread, and cold chocolate soufflé for dessert.

½ pound fresh noodles (Homemade or
   Watercress; see page 269)
3 tablespoons unsalted butter
½ pound mushrooms, sliced
¼ pound baked country ham, prosciutto, or
   any good baked ham, slivered
3 tablespoons chopped fresh parsley or fresh
   chervil
1 tablespoon chopped fresh marjoram or
   tarragon or ½ teaspoon dried
1 cup heavy or whipping cream
Salt and freshly ground white pepper to taste
1 cup freshly grated Parmesan cheese

1. Drop the noodles into a large pot of boiling salted water and cook until tender, 4 minutes. (Tasting is the best test.)

2. In the meantime, melt the butter in a medium skillet, add the mushrooms, and sauté over medium-high heat about 3 minutes. They should remain crisp.

3. Drain the noodles well, and combine them with the mushrooms, ham, herbs, and cream. Blend, and add salt and white pepper to taste.

4. Serve with Parmesan cheese.

Serves 4

WHOLE-WHEAT NOODLES

Whole-wheat noodles are made exactly like Homemade Noodles, substituting whole-wheat for half the white flour. Whole-wheat noodles are not compatible with all sauces, nor are they for every day, but they are flavorful with walnuts or pecans and prosciutto or baked country ham.

Whole-wheat noodles take a little longer to cook than white flour noodles: 5 to 6 minutes for fresh, 10 for dry.

MUSHROOM SAUCE FOR NOODLES

A bouquet of fresh herbs in season may be added to this sauce, but it is mainly a pleasant winter dish served as is with good noodles and a little salad or with a light meat—and with a crunchy bread.

3 ounces dried mushrooms
1 pound fresh mushrooms
¾ cup (1½ sticks) unsalted butter
1 pound fresh noodles (see page 269)
½ cup chopped fresh parsley
Salt and freshly ground black pepper to taste

1. Cover the dried mushrooms with water and allow them to stand at least 30 minutes—longer is better.

2. In the meantime, slice the fresh mushrooms and set aside.

3. Drain the dried mushrooms, reserving the mushroom water in a small saucepan. Mince these mushrooms fine.

4. Melt the butter in a heavy skillet (not black iron as it darkens mushrooms). Add the sliced and the minced mushrooms, and sauté over medium heat 3 minutes. They should remain crisp.

MID-WINTER NIGHT'S DINNER

Old-Fashioned Pot Roast

A Very Special Mushroom Sauce with Homemade Noodles

Romaine and Cherry Tomato Salad

Red and Green Table Grapes

5. In the meantime, reduce the reserved mushroom broth to 1 to 2 tablespoons, and add this to the mushrooms. Keep warm.

6. Cook the noodles in a large pot of boiling salted water until tender but still firm to the bite, 4 to 6 minutes (depending on the noodles). Drain well, and toss with the mushroom sauce, parsley, and salt and pepper.

Serves 4

PERFECT GARDEN TOMATO AND BASIL SAUCE FOR NOODLES

◆◆◆

*T*his is a glorious sauce when summer tomatoes are at their peak. It is almost uncooked, so the exquisite freshness comes right through. Serve with poppy seed rolls and a simple green salad dressed with excellent olive oil and vinegar. There may be a light summer meal to surpass this, but I cannot think of it at the moment.

◆

3 to 3½ pounds ripe tomatoes
10 tablespoons (1¼ sticks) unsalted butter, at
     room temperature
12 scallions (green onions), white part only,
     thinly sliced
½ cup water
¼ cup chopped fresh parsley
¼ cup chopped fresh basil
Salt to taste
1½ pounds fresh noodles (see page 269)
Chopped fresh parsley, for garnish
Chopped fresh basil, for garnish
Freshly grated Parmesan cheese

◆

1. Put the tomatoes in a large saucepan and pour in rapidly boiling water to cover. Leave them for 5 to 10 seconds, depending upon the size of the tomatoes, and then drain.

2. Peel the skins from the tomatoes and discard. Cut the tomatoes in half and squeeze each half to remove the seeds. Finely chop the tomatoes.

3. Combine 6 tablespoons of the butter, the scallions, and the water in a saucepan. Bring to a boil, reduce the heat, and cook slowly until the scallions are limp and

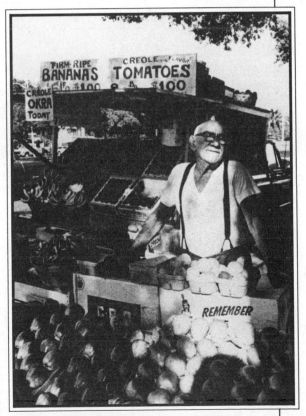

This New Orleans produce vendor has everything you need for your Creole recipe.

the water has boiled away, 2 minutes. Do not allow the butter or scallions to sizzle (this changes the flavor). Add the parsley, basil, and tomatoes. Cook 8 to 10 seconds, no longer. Add salt to taste (no pepper when using this much basil).

4. In the meantime, cook the noodles in boiling salted water until tender but still firm to the bite, 4 to 6 minutes (depending on the noodles.) Drain at once and toss with the remaining butter.

5. Serve the pasta in warm soup plates with a generous amount of sauce in the center. Garnish each serving with a sprinkling of chopped parsley and basil. Pass the Parmesan cheese.

Serves 6

VARIATION: Plum tomatoes may be used; the flavor will not be as delicate, but it will be good.

Don't use olive oil or garlic in the sauce, as that would rob it of its exquisite light character. There is a time and place for everything.

CHAPTER NINE
◆◆◆

BREADS

BREAD WINNERS

◆◆◆

*O*ur homemade Southern breads and rolls, we are told, have a character all their own. Our cornbreads and muffins, of course, are native to our cuisine and they do have, just as they should, a great affinity for many of our favorite Southern dishes. Heavy, coarse cornmeals are praised by some, but elegant, feathery-light cornbreads are made with finely ground white (not yellow) cornmeal, and never corn flour.

Our yeast rolls and biscuits have, I believe, remained somewhat unique. In fact, hot homemade breads of all kinds have been a cornerstone of our menus. For breakfast or lunch, for tea in the afternoon, or for dinner, we have repertoire of delicious breads to choose from.

For those who like to bake, and Southern cooks are bakers, it is a rich heritage, and one that we like to share with others.

————— ◆◆◆ —————

HOMEMADE BREAD

◆◆

*I*f I were asked which loaf of bread has the definitive traditional flavor of the South, I would say it is this bread. All vegetable shortening can be used, but lard gives the authentic flavor and it does make a delicious crisp crust.

◆

1 package dry yeast
¼ cup lukewarm water
6 cups all-purpose flour, sifted
¼ cup sugar
¼ teaspoon baking soda
1 ¼ teaspoons salt
½ cup lard or solid vegetable shortening, or ¼
*   cup lard and ¼ cup shortening*
2 cups buttermilk, or more as needed

◆

1. Dissolve the yeast in the water.
2. Sift 5 cups of the flour with the sugar, baking soda, and salt into a large bowl, or the bowl of an electric mixer or food processor.
3. Cut the lard or shortening into the flour, using a pastry blender or a fork, until it resembles fine meal.
4. Add the dissolved yeast and the buttermilk. (The amount of buttermilk needed will vary—the dough will be sticky but should not be wet.) Blend well.
5. Lift the dough onto a lightly floured surface and knead it heavily, adding enough extra flour to make a firm dough. Knead the dough until the imprint of your fingers pressed hard into the dough remains a few seconds, about 5 minutes.
6. Put the dough in a greased bowl, turning it to coat the surface. Cover the bowl with plastic wrap and leave it in a warm spot until the dough has doubled in bulk, 1½ hours.
7. Again place the dough on a lightly floured surface and knead it well for 2 minutes.
8. Divide the dough in half. Roll out each half to rid it of air bubbles. Roll up each piece of dough as you would a jelly roll, tucking the ends under. Place the loaves into greased standard (9½ x 4½ x 3-inch) loaf pans.
9. Place the pans in a warm spot,

cover them with plastic wrap, and leave them until the dough has again doubled in bulk, 1 hour.
10. Preheat the oven to 425°F.
11. Bake the loaves for 15 minutes. Reduce the heat to 375°F and bake 30 minutes longer. Rap the bread with your knuckle. If it sounds hollow, it is done.
12. Turn the loaves out onto a rack, turning them several times during the cooling process (to keep them crisp).

Makes 2 loaves

🦉 To freeze the dough before baking: Allow the dough to rise one time (step 6). Punch it down, and knead it for 2 minutes. Roll it out, roll up the dough, and place it in the loaf pans. Cover the pans tightly with foil, and freeze them. When you are ready to use the dough, remove the pans from the freezer, uncover, and allow the dough to thaw. When thawed, cover loosely with plastic wrap and let it rise until doubled in bulk. Bake as directed. (It usually takes 7 to 8 hours to thaw and rise. I often transfer the frozen loaves to the refrigerator the night before baking. Then it takes about 2 hours at room temperature the next day for the loaves to be ready to bake.)

TRAPPIST BREAD

I have been told by many that this is one of the best whole-wheat breads they ever tasted. There is, however, a great difference in the flavor of whole-wheat flours, so shop around. I named this loaf after the writer, Thomas Merton, a Trappist monk who lived at Gethsemane in Bardstown, Kentucky.

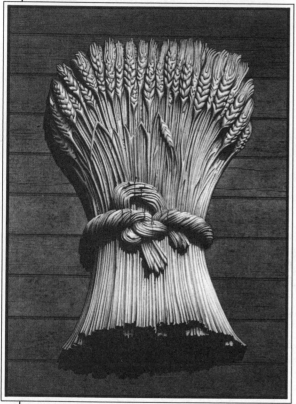

A bakery sign from around 1900 depicts a sheaf of wheat.

---

1 package dry yeast
¾ cup lukewarm water
1 cup Classic Sourdough Starter (recipe follows)
2 tablespoons honey
3 tablespoons butter, melted
1 tablespoon salt
3½ cups unsifted whole-wheat flour

---

1. Dissolve the yeast in ¼ cup of the water.

2. Mix the starter well. Put the starter and the remaining water in a large bowl, or in the bowl of an electric mixer or food processor. Add the honey, butter, dissolved yeast, and salt, and mix well. Add 3 cups of the flour, 1½ cups at a time, and beat thoroughly until the dough is free of lumps.

3. Place the dough on a lightly floured surface and knead it 5 to 6 minutes. Add just enough extra flour to keep the dough from being sticky.

4. Place the dough in a greased bowl, turning it to coat the surface. Cover the bowl with plastic wrap and leave it in a warm spot, free of drafts, until the dough has doubled in bulk, about 1½ hours.

5. Punch the dough down, and divide it in half. Roll each half out 1¼ inches thick on a lightly floured surface to rid it of air bubbles. Roll up each half as you would a jelly roll and place them, tucking the ends under, in 2 greased small (7 x 4 x 2-inch) loaf pans. Cover the pans with plastic wrap and leave them in a warm spot, free of drafts, until the dough has again doubled in bulk, 1 to 1¼ hours.

6. Preheat the oven to 400°F.

7. Bake the loaves for 15 minutes. Reduce the heat to 375°F and bake until the bread sounds hollow when rapped with your knuckle, 20 to 25 minutes longer. Remove the loaves from the pans at once and cool them on a rack. Turn the bread so that it cools evenly.

Makes 2 small loaves

VARIATIONS: *Trappist Bread with Prunes:* Add ¾ cup pitted prunes, plumped and cut in half, to this bread after it has risen once (at the beginning of step 5). This is not a sweet bread, but the addition of the prunes is utterly delicious. Nice for a family meal with broiled ham or sausage. A favorite.

Trappist Bread with Nuts: Add 1 cup coarsely chopped walnuts or pecans to the bread dough after it has risen once (at the beginning of step 5).

CLASSIC SOURDOUGH STARTER

1 package dry yeast
2 cups bottled spring water, lukewarm
2 cups all-purpose flour

1. Dissolve the yeast in the spring water in a plastic, ceramic, or glass container. When it is dissolved, add the flour. Mix well. (The entire dissolving and mixing process can be done in a food processor, then the mixture transferred to a container.)

2. Cover the container lightly and let it stand at room temperature for about 2 days. It should then be bubbly and "working," with a pleasant fermented odor. Refrigerate for another 24 hours.

3. When slightly yellowish clear liquid has formed on top of the starter, it is ready. Mix well and use as directed.

To renew starter: Each time you use 1 cup of starter, replenish the remainder with 1 cup of warm bottled spring water and 1 cup of flour. Mix thoroughly until free of lumps. Allow it to stand at room temperature overnight, then refrigerate. When the liquid has risen to the top of the starter, it is ready to be used again.

Important: When the starter is 10 days to 2 weeks old and you are not ready to use it, the starter must be fed. Mix the starter well, then remove 1 cup of the mixture and discard it. Add 1 cup of warm spring water and 1 cup of flour to the remaining starter. Let it stand at room temperature overnight, then refrigerate for another day. When the liquid has come to the top, the starter is ready to be used again.

SOURDOUGH STARTER POINTERS

*B*ottled spring water is free of added chemicals and makes a better starter than tap water.

Water that was used to boil potatoes makes a good starter, but not a long-lived starter. Ginger beer makes a good starter, and a tiny pinch of dried ginger added to any starter is a splendid idea.

If the starter does not ferment and bubble, the yeast may have been out of date or bad.

If the starter is used and fed more than once a week, it may become too weak to be effective. More yeast (½ package) can be added to get the starter going again, or you can make a new starter. I prefer to make a new starter.

The odor of the starter will vary according to the fermentation that has taken place, but at all times a sound starter will smell pleasant and a bit sour. Always mix the starter well before using it.

If the liquid on top of the starter at any time turns a blackish green, the starter has gone bad. Discard it.

SOUTHERN HERITAGE POTATO BREAD

*T*his rich potato bread is exquisitely moist and delicious. It is also redolent of our early breads, as the sponge is made up and allowed to rise and ferment to a small degree the night before baking.

1 package dry yeast
¼ cup lukewarm water
1 large mealy potato (about 12 ounces)
⅔ cup sugar
4 eggs, beaten
1 cup (2 sticks) unsalted butter,

at room temperature
2 teaspoons salt
6½ to 7 cups sifted all-purpose flour
1½ teaspoons butter, melted

1. Dissolve the yeast in the water.

2. Peel and coarsely chop the potato. Place it in a small saucepan, cover with water, and cook over medium heat until soft, 20 to 25 minutes. Drain the potato, but reserve ¾ cup of the cooking water and keep it warm. Sieve or rice the warm potato into a large mixing bowl, and add the reserved potato water, the dissolved yeast, and the sugar. Mix well. Cover with foil and leave to rise overnight at room temperature.

3. The next morning, add the eggs, butter, and salt. (This is done easily in a heavy-duty electric mixer.) Blend thoroughly. Add the flour, 2 cups at a time, beating hard. When 6 cups of flour have been added, turn the dough onto a lightly floured surface. Knead the dough while adding extra flour until the dough is velvety and soft but not sticky, 4 minutes.

4. Place the dough in a greased large bowl, and turn it to coat the surface. Cover the bowl with plastic wrap and leave it in a warm, draft-free spot until the dough has doubled in bulk, about 1½ hours.

5. Punch the dough down, cut it in half, and roll each half out ½ inch thick on a lightly floured surface to rid it of air bubbles. Roll up each half as you would a jelly roll and place the loaves, tucking the ends under, in 2 greased standard (9½ x 4½ x 3-inch) loaf pans. Brush the tops with melted butter. Cover the pans with plastic wrap and allow the dough to double in bulk again, 2 hours or more. (Do not place this dough in an overly warm place. If the large amount of butter melts before baking, the texture will be grainy.)

6. Preheat the oven to 375°F.

7. Bake the bread on the middle shelf of the oven until it is golden brown and sounds hollow when rapped with your knuckle, about 45 minutes. Watch it carefully—don't overbake.

8. Turn the loaves out onto a rack to cool, turning them several times during the cooling process.

Makes 2 loaves

VARIATION: *Southern Heritage Potato Rolls:* Prepare the dough as directed, forming it into small rounds with a floured biscuit cutter in step 5. (The rolls may be brushed generously with butter, covered with plastic wrap, and refrigerated for 1 day or overnight. Remove from the refrigerator and allow to rise until doubled in bulk, about 3 hours.) Bake them in a preheated 375°F oven for 10 to 12 minutes. Makes about 45 rolls.

ELIZABETH CHOWNING'S DIVINE BREAD

*T*his is one of the most divine of Southern breads—so much so it named itself. It ages better than most breads, it freezes well, and it has an exquisite flavor. The variations are endless: the glazed pear, apricot, or yellow plum bread makes you want to live and live—bake and bake.

2 packages dry yeast
1½ cups lukewarm water
½ cup sugar
1 tablespoon salt
4 tablespoons (½ stick) unsalted butter, melted
4 large eggs

7 cups sifted all-purpose flour
1 egg yolk, beaten
2 tablespoons heavy or whipping cream, or
    more to taste
Poppy seeds, for garnish

1. Dissolve the yeast in the water in a large bowl, or in the bowl of an electric mixer or food processor.

2. Add the sugar, salt, butter, and eggs and mix thoroughly. Add about 6½ cups flour, 1 cup at a time, mixing well.

3. Turn out the dough onto a lightly floured surface and knead it for 3 minutes. Add just enough of the remaining flour to keep it from being sticky. (Too much flour makes this bread heavy.)

4. Put the dough in a greased large bowl and turn it to coat the surface. Cover the bowl with plastic wrap and leave it in a warm place until the dough has doubled in bulk, 1 to 1¼ hours. (If after the rising the dough still seems too sticky to work with, chill it thoroughly. Cold dough is always easier to manage.)

5. Punch the dough down, and roll it out on a lightly floured surface to rid it of air bubbles. Make 2 free-form loaves.

6. Place the loaves on a lightly greased or non-stick baking sheet. Cover with plastic wrap and leave in a warm spot until the dough has doubled in bulk again, about 1¼ hours. The dough should feel light and springy.

7. Preheat the oven to 350°F.

8. Mix the egg yolk thoroughly with the cream and brush the glaze on the tops of the loaves. Sprinkle with poppy seeds.

9. Place the baking sheet on the middle shelf of the oven and bake until the bread is golden brown and sounds hollow when rapped with your knuckle, 45 to 50 minutes.

10. Turn the loaves out onto a rack, turning them several times during the cooling process.

Makes 2 loaves

VARIATIONS: *Divine Braids:* Prepare the dough through step 5, dividing the dough in half. Cut each half into 3 even strips. Braid the strips into 2 loaves, pinching the ends under. Proceed with step 6.

Divine Mink Stoles: Make up the dough through step 4. Punch the dough down and roll it out ½ inch thick and 6 inches wide on a lightly floured surface. Cut into strips 1 inch wide.

Man, mule, and machine threshing wheat.

Fold each strip in the shape of a mink stole crossed over your shoulders. Place the stoles about 3 inches apart on a lightly greased or non-stick baking sheet.

Cover loosely with plastic wrap and allow the rolls to rise until light and springy, 45 minutes to 1 hour. Brush them with the mixture of egg yolk and cream, and sprinkle them with poppy seeds. Bake on the middle shelf of a preheated 375°F oven until golden brown, 20 to 25 minutes. Serve warm or cold.

GLAZED PEAR, APRICOT, OR PLUM BREAD

1 recipe Chowning's Divine Bread
1½ cups chopped glazed pears, apricots, or
*   yellow plums*

1. Prepare Chowning's Divine Bread through step 4. Knead the chopped fruit into the dough.

2. Roll out the dough and follow the directions for Divine Braids. Place the loaves on a lightly greased or non-stick baking sheet. Cover them with plastic wrap and leave in a warm spot until the dough has doubled in bulk and become light and springy, about 1 hour.

3. Preheat the oven to 350°F.

4. Brush the loaves with the mixture of egg yolk and cream (omit the poppy seeds), and bake for 35 to 40 minutes.

Glazed pears, apricots, and plums are found in gourmet shops. The finest ones come from Australia, Oregon, and

California. The plums are the hardest to find, but they are luscious. Lacking glazed fruits, you can substitute good-quality dried fruits, but you will have a different product.

DIVINE ROLLED KUCHEN WITH PRUNE AND WALNUT FILLING

1 recipe Chowning's Divine Bread
1 cup packed ready-to-eat prunes, coarsely chopped
½ cup chopped walnuts

1. Prepare Chowning's Divine Bread through step 4. While the bread is rising, mix together the prunes and walnuts in a small bowl and set aside until ready to use.

2. Knead the dough lightly and divide it in half. Roll out each half into a rectangle ½ inch thick. Cover each half with half the filling. Press the filling well into the dough, then roll up tightly as you would a jelly roll. Tuck the ends under and place on a lightly greased or non-stick baking sheet.

3. Cover the loaves with plastic wrap and leave them in a warm spot, free of drafts, until the dough has doubled in bulk and is light and springy, 1 to 1¼ hours. Brush the tops with the mixture of egg yolk and 2 tablespoons cream (don't add the poppy seeds).

4. Preheat the oven to 350°F.

5. Place the baking sheet on the middle shelf of the oven and bake until the loaves are golden brown and sound hollow when rapped with your knuckle, 30 to 45 minutes.

6. Remove the loaves to a rack and allow to cool. Slice and serve.

Makes 2 loaves

These loaves freeze well. Allow them to cool first.

DARK SOURDOUGH RYE BREAD WITH CARAWAY SEEDS

*T*his is a dark rye bread with a more pronounced rye flavor. It has been a favorite bread among my students. Great for sandwiches.

1 package dry yeast
1½ cups lukewarm water
1 cup Classic Sourdough Starter (see page 279)
1 tablespoon salt
2 tablespoons light molasses
2 tablespoons butter, at room temperature, or solid vegetable shortening
7 tablespoons caraway seeds
4 cups regular ground rye flour (don't sift)
3 cups all-purpose flour, sifted, plus more as needed
1 egg white, lightly beaten

1. Dissolve the yeast in the water in a large mixing bowl or food processor. Add the starter and mix thoroughly.

2. Add the salt, molasses, butter or shortening, 2 tablespoons of the caraway seeds, and the flours, 2 cups at a time, beating hard after each addition until both rye and white flours have been incorporated.

3. Place the dough on a lightly floured surface and knead it thoroughly 8 to 10 minutes. Add a little extra of either flour as needed. The dough must not be the least bit sticky.

4. Put the dough in a greased bowl, and turn it to coat the surface. Cover the bowl with plastic wrap and leave it in a warm spot, free of drafts, until the dough has doubled in bulk, 1½ to 2 hours.

5. Punch the dough down and knead it for a few minutes to expel the air bubbles.

Divide the dough in half, and shape each half with your hands into a smooth, round ball. Place the halves in 2 greased round 9-inch glass baking dishes. Cover the dishes with plastic wrap and leave them in a warm place until the dough has doubled in bulk again, about 1 hour.

6. Preheat the oven to 375°F.

7. Brush the tops of the dough with the egg white, and sprinkle with the remaining caraway seeds. Bake until the loaves sound hollow when rapped with your knuckle, 45 to 50 minutes.

8. Cool the loaves on a rack, turning them several times as they cool.

Makes 2 loaves

VARIATIONS: Substitute ½ cup coarsely ground rye flour for ½ cup regular ground rye if a rough texture is desired.

For a bread with a sharper bite, mix the dissolved yeast, starter, and 2 cups of the rye flour in a bowl and leave it, covered with foil or waxed paper (not plastic wrap), at room temperature overnight. Add the salt and the remaining ingredients the next day, and proceed with the recipe.

DARK SOURDOUGH RYE ROLLS

1 recipe Dark Rye Bread with Caraway Seeds

---

1. Follow the directions for making Dark Sourdough Rye Bread through step 4.

2. Punch the dough down and knead it for a few minutes. Roll it out on a lightly floured surface to rid it of air bubbles. Pinch off ½-cup pieces. Using the palms of your hands, form each into a round or oval-shaped roll. Place the rolls on greased baking sheets about 2 inches apart. Cover with plastic wrap and allow to rise in a warm spot until tripled in bulk, 1 hour.

3. Preheat the oven to 425°F.

4. Brush the tops of each roll with the egg white and sprinkle with caraway seeds. Place the rolls on the middle shelf of the oven and bake until golden brown, about 25 minutes.

Makes 20 rolls

TESTING FOR DONENESS

*B*reads can be tested for doneness by inserting a cake tester, skewer, or thin knife in the center of the loaf. If it comes out clean, with no crumbs attached, the bread is done.

You can also test a bread by rapping it with your knuckle. If the bread sounds hollow, it is most likely done.

Tea breads can be tested by pressing down lightly on the center with your fingers. If the bread springs back quickly, it is done.

KENTUCKY CORNMEAL MELBA BREAD

I created this bread to be served with menus that need the crunchiness of cornbread. Serve it plain when it is first baked; after that, slice it thin, butter it, and toast it. The toast keeps for several days crisp as can be. It freezes well before slicing or after toasting. Wonderful spread with Country Ham Butter.

1 package dry yeast
¼ teaspoon plus 1 tablespoon sugar
¼ cup lukewarm water
1 cup sour cream
¾ cup milk or water
4 tablespoons (½ stick) butter, melted

3 large eggs
2 cups fine white cornmeal, plus more as needed
3½ cups all-purpose flour, plus more as needed
1¼ teaspoons salt

1. Dissolve the yeast and ¼ teaspoon sugar in the water.

2. Combine the sour cream, milk, butter, and eggs in the large bowl of an electric mixer or in a food processor. Beat until thoroughly mixed. Add the dissolved yeast and the cornmeal. Mix.

3. Sift the flour with the salt and 1 tablespoon sugar. Add the flour mixture to the ingredients in the bowl, and mix well. Add up to 2 tablespoons additional water if the dough seems overly stiff.

4. Place the dough onto a floured surface and knead it thoroughly for 2 to 3 minutes. Add a little flour or cornmeal as needed to make a pliable dough but one that is not sticky. (Your fingerprints should not pop back at once when pressed into the dough.)

5. Place the dough in a well-greased roomy bowl and turn it to coat the surface. Cover the bowl with plastic wrap and leave it in a fairly warm spot, free of drafts, until the dough has doubled in bulk, about 1¼ hours.

6. Punch the dough down and knead it again to rid it of air pockets. Roll out the dough about 1 inch thick, and divide it into thirds. Form each third into a loaf and place each in a greased small loaf pan (7 x 4 x 2 inches); or divide the dough in half and use two standard (9½ x 4½ x 3-inch) loaf pans. Press the dough firmly into the pans. Cover each pan with plastic wrap.

7. Leave the pans in a warm, draft-free spot until the dough has doubled in bulk again, about 1 hour.

8. Preheat the oven to 375°F.

9. Bake the small loaves for 25 to 30 minutes and the larger loaves for 35 to 40

minutes. Insert a skewer in the center of the bread; if it comes out clean, the loaves are done.

10. Turn the breads out and serve cut in generous slices with unsalted butter for lunch or dinner. Allow the second bread to cool on a rack, then wrap it well to refrigerate or to freeze, to be made into Cornmeal Melba Toast (see below).

Makes 3 small loaves

Cornmeal breads are wicked the way they dry out so quickly. This bread is delectable eaten fresh from the oven, but it does not hold well. However, this was designed to be made into melba toast—a superlative crunchy toast that holds its crispness well.

CORNMEAL MELBA TOAST

Preheat the oven to 300°F. Slice the bread as thin as possible. Brush one side of each slice with melted butter. Place the slices, butter side up, on a baking sheet and bake until golden brown, about 30 minutes. Store in a tight tin, or freeze. It is best, of course, when freshly toasted.

GREASING THE BOWL

*B*reads should be left to rise in bowls that have been greased with either solid vegetable shortening or butter. Never use oil—it will soak into the dough—or margarine—it can cause the bread to burn in the baking.

Always turn the dough to coat it with the shortening used to grease the bowl. This will prevent the outer layer of dough from drying out.

MONTICELLO ROLLS

*T*his is a lovely, velvety dough and is typical of the fine hot breads that are made in the South. Yeast doughs rich in eggs and butter are not kneaded as heavily as lean doughs (flour, yeast, shortening, and water), and they keep longer better before baking.

1 package dry yeast
¼ cup lukewarm water
1 large mealy potato
4 tablespoons (½ stick) butter, cut into pieces
2 tablespoons sugar
2 eggs
1½ teaspoons salt
3½ cups all-purpose flour, sifted
6 tablespoons (¾ stick) butter, melted

1. Dissolve the yeast in the water.

2. Peel and coarsely chop the potato. Place it in a small saucepan, cover with water, and cook over medium heat until soft, 20 to 25 minutes. Drain the potato but reserve the cooking water; keep it warm.

3. While it is still hot, sieve or rice the potato into a large bowl (not a food processor—it will turn the potato gummy). Add 4 tablespoons butter and ¼ cup of the warm potato water. Mix by hand or with an electric mixer until the butter has melted.

4. Add the sugar and eggs and mix well. Add the dissolved yeast and the salt. Beat in 3 cups of the flour, 1 cup at a time, until you have a malleable dough.

5. Lift the dough onto a lightly floured surface. Knead it lightly, adding enough extra flour to keep the dough from being overly sticky, about 2 minutes. This is a soft dough and too much flour will make the rolls dry instead of light and moist.

6. Put the dough in a greased bowl and turn it to coat the surface. Cover the bowl with plastic wrap, and leave it in a warm spot until the dough has doubled in bulk, about 1 hour. (After it has doubled, the dough can be punched down, covered, and refrigerated until well chilled, or overnight if desired, before forming it into rolls.)

7. Place the dough on a lightly floured surface. Knead it gently for 1 minute. Roll out the dough ¼ inch thick. Cut it into circles with a 2½-inch biscuit cutter.

8. Brush the tops with the melted butter. With the dull edge of a knife, press a crease just off-center in each round. Fold the dough over, so that the larger part overlaps the smaller.

The west facade of Monticello, the classic revival home Thomas Jefferson designed and built near Charlottesville, Virginia, in 1770. Jefferson lived in his beloved house for 56 years.

9. Place the folded rolls, barely touching each other, on a non-stick or lightly greased baking sheet, and put it in a warm spot free of drafts. Cover with plastic wrap and allow the dough to double in bulk again. It should spring back at once when lightly touched, about 45 minutes.

10. Preheat the oven to 375°F.

11. Place the baking sheet on the middle shelf of the oven and bake until the rolls are golden brown, and a skewer inserted in the center of a roll comes out clean, 15 to 20 minutes. Brush immediately with more melted butter. Serve piping hot.

Makes 36 rolls

🦉 If the rolls do not touch, they are likely to spring open when rising or baking.

A PICNIC UNDER THE WILLOWS

Country Ham Butter with Cornmeal Melba Toast

Southern Fried Chicken

Elizabeth Chowning's Divine Bread

Fayette County Chow-Chow

Honeydew and Ginger Pickle

♦

South Carolina Country Jam Cake

Amber Iced Tea

TIDEWATER FEATHER ROLLS

◆◆◆

*T*hese are light and feathery rolls, just as the name implies. We made them day after day in Virginia and served them for dinner with all kinds of meats, and they were always welcome.

Biscuits on the production line in 1932. They look good, but homemade are not difficult and are always the best.

◆

1 package dry yeast
¼ cup lukewarm water
2 cups milk
8 tablespoons (1 stick) butter, cut into pieces
¼ cup sugar
2 eggs
¾ teaspoon salt
5 cups sifted all-purpose flour
4 tablespoons (½ stick) butter, melted

◆

1. Dissolve the yeast in the water.

2. Scald the milk, but do not let it boil, and pour it into a large mixing bowl. Add 1 stick butter and the sugar, and stir until the butter has melted. Add the eggs and beat well. When the mixture has cooled to lukewarm, add the dissolved yeast. Stir thoroughly.

3. Add the salt and the flour, 1 cup at a time, beating thoroughly. When all the flour has been added, put the dough on a lightly floured surface and knead until it is smooth and elastic, 3 minutes.

4. Place the dough in a greased bowl and turn it to coat the surface. Cover the bowl with plastic wrap and leave it in a warm spot until the dough has doubled in bulk, 1¼ hours.

5. Punch the dough down and knead it on a lightly floured surface, 3 minutes.

6. Roll the dough out ½ inch thick. Cut it into rounds with a 2½-inch cutter. Brush the tops lightly with the melted butter. Score the rounds slightly off-center, and fold so that the larger half overlaps.

7. Place the rolls, barely touching each other, on a greased baking sheet. Cover with plastic wrap and leave in a warm spot until the rolls have doubled in bulk, about 45 minutes.

8. Preheat the oven to 375°F.

9. Bake the rolls until golden brown and a skewer inserted in the center of a roll comes out clean, 20 to 25 minutes. Brush the tops with more melted butter while the rolls are piping hot. Serve.

Makes 36 rolls

To freeze: Allow the rolls to cool completely. Place them in plastic bags and freeze. To serve, thaw, and brush the tops again with melted butter. Bake in a preheated 325°F oven for about 15 minutes.

POPPY SEED BOWKNOTS

◆◆◆

*T*hese rolls are a real boon for a party, as they can be made ahead and frozen. Place the frozen rolls in a preheated 350°F oven and heat thoroughly, about 15 minutes. They will become crisp again as they cool. A favorite served cold.

1 package dry yeast
¼ cup lukewarm water
4 tablespoons (½ stick) unsalted butter
4½ cups all-purpose flour
1 tablespoon sugar
1 tablespoon salt
1½ cups buttermilk, at room temperature
1 egg white, lightly beaten
2 tablespoons poppy seeds, or more to taste

1. Dissolve the yeast in the water.

2. Melt the butter and allow it to cool.

3. Sift the flour with the sugar and salt.

4. Pour the buttermilk into a large bowl, or the bowl of an electric mixer or food processor. Add the dissolved yeast and the butter. Mix thoroughly. Add 4 cups of the flour and mix thoroughly.

5. Lift the dough onto a lightly floured surface and knead it heavily, 3 minutes. Add just enough extra flour to keep the dough from being too sticky. It should be a soft and malleable dough—softer than a bread dough but not sticky.

6. Put the dough in a greased bowl and turn it to coat the surface. Cover the bowl with plastic wrap and leave it in a warm spot until the dough has doubled in bulk, 1 hour.

7. Lift the dough again onto a lightly floured surface. Knead it thoroughly, 2 minutes. Roll the dough out into a rectangle ½ inch thick and 6 inches wide. Cut the dough into strips 1 inch wide. Pulling each strip gently, tie it into a simple knot by slipping one end over, then under, then back over the other. Place the rolls about 2 inches apart on a non-stick or lightly greased baking sheet. Cover with plastic wrap and leave in a warm spot until the rolls have doubled in bulk again, 45 minutes to 1 hour.

8. Preheat the oven to 375°F.

9. Brush the tops with the egg white and sprinkle with poppy seeds. Bake the rolls on the middle shelf of the oven until golden brown and a skewer inserted in a bowknot comes out clean, 20 to 25 minutes. Cool on the baking sheet and serve.

Makes 24 rolls

POPPY SEED BRAIDED BREAD

1. Follow the directions for making Poppy Seed Bowknots, but roll the dough out into a rectangle the same size as the bowknots and cut it into 3 lengthwise strips for 1 large loaf. For 2 small loaves, cut the strips in half horizontally to make 6 strips. Braid the dough and place it in a greased 13 x 4½ x 2¼-inch loaf pan or into 2 smaller loaf pans.

2. Leave the loaves in a warm spot until the dough has doubled in bulk, about 1¼ hours. Brush the tops with the egg white and sprinkle with poppy seeds.

3. Preheat the oven to 425°F.

4. Bake the loaves for 15 minutes. Reduce the heat to 375°F, and depending upon the size of the pan, bake 20 to 30 minutes longer. Rap the bread with your knuckle. If it sounds hollow, the loaves are done.

5. Remove the braids from the pans and cool them on racks, turning the loaves several times during the cooling process to keep them crisp.

Makes 2 loaves

This is a delicious bread with unsalted butter or for sandwiches. It also makes wonderful Toast Charlotte, as it is not the least bit sweet.

CORNMEAL CROISSANTS

*T*hese cornmeal croissants were designed to be a sandwich croissant. Delicious with sliced white meat of chicken or turkey, chicken salad, baked ham—but not beef or any heavy meat. Charming cocktail sandwiches when made rather small.

Harvest time in Kentucky.

---

1 package dry yeast
½ teaspoon sugar
¼ cup lukewarm water
2¼ cups sifted all-purpose flour
2 tablespoons milk
½ teaspoon salt
6 tablespoons white cornmeal
1¾ sticks (14 tablespoons) unsalted butter,
    cold, cut into pieces
½ cup cold milk, or more as needed

---

1. Dissolve the yeast and the sugar in the water.

2. In a small bowl, blend ½ cup of the flour with the dissolved yeast mixture and 2 tablespoons milk. Cover with plastic wrap and set aside until the sponge is light and bubbly, about 30 minutes.

3. In the meantime, combine 1½ cups of the flour with the salt and cornmeal, and mix thoroughly. Using a pastry blender, cut 2 tablespoons of the butter into the mixture until it looks like coarse meal. Add the yeast sponge and mix thoroughly. Add the cold milk to form a soft, malleable dough. It should look like biscuit dough. Cover the dough with foil or wax paper and refrigerate 15 to 20 minutes.

4. Blend the remaining ¼ cup flour into the remaining butter until the mixture is smooth. Keep the butter cold and firm. Form the butter into a 4-inch square. Wrap it in foil or wax paper and chill in the refrigerator, 20 to 25 minutes.

5. Roll the dough out into a 12-inch square (approximately). Place the chilled butter patty in the center. (The dough and the butter should have about the same texture and be at the same temperature.) Fold one-third of the dough over the center third. Then fold the remaining third on top to make 3 layers. Turn the folded dough so that an open end faces you.

6. Roll the dough out on a lightly floured surface into a 12 x 8-inch rectangle and fold it over again as before, keeping an open end facing you.

7. Roll the dough into a rectangle again and fold it over again into 3 layers. This makes 2 turns.

8. Wrap the dough well and refrigerate it until it is thoroughly chilled, a minimum of 20 minutes or as long as overnight.

9. Roll the dough out on a lightly floured surface, repeating the process of folding and rolling 2 more times. This makes 4 turns in all.

10. Wrap the dough again, and refrigerate 20 to 30 minutes.

11. Roll the dough out into a 20 x 8-inch rectangle (approximately). Cut the dough in half. Cut each half into 4 triangles or wedges. Roll up each triangle beginning with the wide end, and turn the ends toward each other to form a crescent, with the pointed tip on top.

12. Place the croissants 3 inches apart on a foil-lined baking sheet. Cover with plastic wrap and leave at room temperature until the dough has doubled in bulk and feels light and springy, 45 to 60 minutes.

13. Preheat the oven to 400°F.

14. Bake the croissants for 5 to 6 minutes. Reduce the heat to 375°F and bake until golden brown, 20 to 25 minutes longer. Serve, or cool and freeze.

Makes 8 large croissants

Croissant dough, like puff-paste dough, must be kept cool at all times. If the temperature is over 72°F in the room where the croissants are rising, the butter will melt and they will not be flaky.

Cocktail croissants are simply cut smaller and require less time in baking. This amount of dough will make 16. They will bake in 15 to 16 minutes.

SOUTHERN BUTTERMILK BISCUITS

This is the true Southern biscuit—made with buttermilk, rolled not too thick, and baked until golden brown. We like them with sausage and grits for a leisurely breakfast or with fried chicken anytime. They are a perennial favorite for cocktail parties and receptions when cut small and served piping hot, filled with sliced baked country ham. Now can you think of anything better? I don't believe you can.

2 cups all-purpose flour, plus more as needed
¼ teaspoon baking soda
1 tablespoon baking powder
1 teaspoon salt
6 tablespoons lard or solid vegetable shortening
¾ cup buttermilk

1. Sift the dry ingredients into a roomy bowl. Cut in the shortening with a pastry blender or a fork until the mixture has the texture of coarse meal. Add the buttermilk and mix with your hand, lightly but thoroughly. Add a little more flour if the dough is too sticky. Knead for 1 minute. Wrap in wax paper or foil and refrigerate until well chilled, at least 20 minutes.

2. Preheat the oven to 450°F.

3. Roll the dough out ½ inch thick on a lightly floured surface or pastry cloth. (Always roll from the center out for tender, crisp biscuits.) Cut the dough into the desired size biscuits.

4. Place the biscuits on a dark baking sheet and bake until golden brown, 10 to 12 minutes.

Makes 25 to 30 biscuits

VARIATIONS: *Cheese Biscuits:* Work ¼ to ½ cup freshly grated sharp natural Cheddar or Parmesan cheese into the dough before rolling it out ⅜ inch thick. Cut into small biscuits and bake in a preheated 375° to 400°F oven. Serve with salad for luncheons, or for cocktails.

Rosemary Biscuits: A favorite. Work ½ to 1 teaspoon crushed dried rosemary into the dough before rolling it out ½ inch thick. Cut into 2- to 2¼-inch biscuits. Serve with sausage, pork, or lamb. Especially delicious

This belle could easily have graced a soap label. What a surprise to find her on baking powder! Perhaps she did bring bakers luck.

as small biscuits served with smoked country sausage for a wintertime hors d'oeuvre or a Sunday brunch.

Watercress Biscuits: Work ½ cup chopped watercress lightly into the dough before rolling the dough very thin. Cut into 2-inch rounds. Make sandwiches of the rounds, using more whole watercress leaves as the filling. Press the biscuit halves together firmly to form a whole biscuit with an inner layer of watercress. Bake in a preheated 450°F oven. If the biscuits are baked at once, the watercress will remain bright and green. My students' favorite—mine, too. Delicious with chicken or seafood salads, ham, veal, baked or broiled chicken, pheasant or quail.

Hearty Biscuits: Use 5 teaspoons baking powder. Roll the dough out ½ inch or thicker, and bake in a preheated 450°F oven. This ultimate tender and crisp biscuit is at its best when served with broiled or fried chicken, broiled or sautéed ham, country ham, or chicken salad.

If some dough is left over, it is wiser to bake the biscuits and freeze them, as the buttermilk dough will not keep over 10 to 12 hours.

THE ULTIMATE EXTRA-FLAKY BISCUIT

1 recipe Southern Buttermilk Biscuit dough
6 tablespoons (¾ stick) unsalted butter, chilled

1. Make up the Southern Buttermilk Biscuit dough. Cover with wax paper or foil, and refrigerate until well chilled, at least 20 minutes.
2. Roll the dough out into a rectangle

MAKING BISCUITS

*L*ard makes a crisper biscuit than vegetable shortening.

To make biscuits with a smooth top, the dough must be covered and thoroughly chilled, then kneaded lightly but well.

Overkneading biscuit dough brings out the gluten and toughens them.

Too much flour on the pastry board will toughen the biscuits. A pastry cloth helps prevent the need for extra flour.

Biscuits must be baked in a very hot oven or they will toughen.

½ inch thick on a lightly floured surface. Dot with the cold butter.

3. Fold one-third of the dough over the center. Then fold the remaining third over the top to make 3 layers.

4. Roll out the dough ½ inch thick. (The butter will smear some. Do not worry, but be careful to keep the dough and the butter cold.)

5. Preheat the oven to 450°F.

6. Cut the dough into biscuits. Place them on a dark baking sheet and bake until golden brown, 10 to 12 minutes.

Makes 25 to 30 biscuits

Biscuits bake faster and browner on a dark baking sheet.

If the butter leaks from the biscuit during baking, it was not kept sufficiently cold throughout the process.

POTATO YEAST BISCUITS

*T*his old-fashioned biscuit has a lovely flavor and freezes unusually well. Divine with thinly sliced Virginia or Kentucky baked country ham, or any good baked ham. Delicious with fried chicken or sausage, or all on its own with butter, for heaven's sake.

½ package dry yeast
¼ cup lukewarm water
1 small mealy potato
½ cup milk
6 tablespoons (¾ stick) butter, cut into pieces

1 tablespoon sugar
2½ cups all-purpose flour, plus more as needed
⅔ teaspoon salt
¼ cup butter, melted

1. Dissolve the yeast in the water.

2. Peel and coarsely chop the potato. Place it in a small saucepan, cover with water, and cook over medium heat until soft, 20 to 25 minutes. Drain the potato and put it through a ricer or a sieve. Measure out ½ cup.

3. Combine the milk and butter in a small saucepan and heat gently until the butter has melted.

4. Spoon the potato pulp into a mixing bowl. Add the sugar and the warm milk mixture. Mix. Add the dissolved yeast.

5. Sift the flour and salt together and add it to the yeast mixture, beating thoroughly. Knead the dough well on a lightly floured surface, 4 minutes. Add enough extra flour to make a medium-stiff dough.

6. Place the dough in a greased bowl, turning it to coat the surface. Cover the bowl with plastic wrap and leave it in a warm spot, free of drafts, until the dough has doubled in bulk, about 1¼ hours.

7. Lift the dough onto a lightly floured surface. Knead for 1 minute.

8. Roll the dough out ½ inch thick. Cut it with a 2-inch biscuit cutter. Dip each biscuit completely in the melted butter and lay them on a baking sheet. Lightly cover with plastic wrap and leave in a warm place until tripled in bulk, 1 to 1¼ hours.

9. Preheat the oven to 375°F.

10. Bake the biscuits until golden brown, 10 to 15 minutes. Serve at once.

Makes 24 biscuits

LEXINGTON SPOONBREAD

❖❖

*T*his is a rather substantial spoonbread. It is a versatile starch used instead of potatoes or rice and utterly delightful with most chicken and ham dishes.

1 cup sifted fine white cornmeal
4 cups milk
3 tablespoons butter
1½ teaspoons salt
4 eggs, separated

1. Preheat the oven to 350°F.

2. Combine the cornmeal and 1 cup of the milk in a heavy saucepan. Blend, then add the remaining milk and cook over medium heat, stirring constantly, until the mixture is thick and smooth, about 5 minutes. Remove from the heat and add the butter and salt. Beat in the egg yolks.

3. Beat the egg whites until they are stiff but not dry and grainy. Fold them into the cornmeal mixture.

4. Spoon the batter into 2 buttered 1-quart soufflé dishes or shallow baking dishes. Bake until lightly browned. Depending on the size and depth of the dish, this will take 35 to 50 minutes. Serve at once.

Serves 6 to 8

Leverage—not electricity—is the key to this grinder.

CORNMEAL SPOONBREAD SOUFFLE

◆◆

*T*his Southern heritage spoonbread is so light and delectable—it had to be called a soufflé. It is delicious with all kinds of chicken and ham dishes, and especially veal and rabbit stews.

2 cups milk
5 tablespoons fine white cornmeal
2 tablespoons butter
1 teaspoon salt
3 eggs, separated
1½ teaspoons baking powder

1. Preheat the oven to 350°F.
2. Scald the milk in a heavy saucepan, but do not allow it to boil. Add the cornmeal and cook over medium heat, whisking constantly, until the mixture is like thick mush, about 5 minutes. Add the butter and salt. When the butter has melted, add the egg yolks and baking powder.
3. Beat the egg whites until they are stiff but not dry and grainy. Fold them into the cornmeal mixture.
4. Pour the batter into a buttered 1-quart soufflé dish or a 1½-quart shallow baking dish. Bake until lightly browned. Depending on the type of dish, this will take 30 to 40 minutes. Serve at once.

Serves 4

HUSH PUPPIES

◆◆

*T*he story goes that in Georgia at the fish fries, the barking, playful hounds would be quieted by the cook's making up quick cakes of cornmeal and water, and frying them in the black skillets used for the fish—then throwing these crunchy morsels to the dogs with the accompanying warning, "Now, hush, puppy!" Well, anyway, that is the way the story goes.

A good-time picnic made even better by fresh corn sticks.

2 cups white cornmeal
1 teaspoon salt
2 tablespoons chopped scallions (green onions)
1 cup milk, or more as needed
2 eggs
¼ cup lard or vegetable shortening, melted
Oil for deep-frying

1. Combine the cornmeal, salt, and scallions in a medium bowl. Mix well, then add the milk, eggs, and melted shortening, and mix again. The mixture must not be crumbly. Add more milk if necessary.

2. Heat the oil in a deep-fat fryer to 375°F.

3. Form the batter into 1½-inch balls and fry them a few at a time until they are light golden brown, 2 to 3 minutes. Drain on paper towels and serve at once.

Serves 4

🦉 Lard makes a crisper hush puppy than does vegetable shortening.

HOE CAKES

◆◆◆

*W*e do not know the lineage of the name "hoe cake." It was a favorite bread of country people in the South but it was not baked on a hoe. That would have been impossible. If you enjoy cornmeal and you like the texture of hot, crisp bread, you will love hoe cakes when they are served with the right menu. They are delicious with an all vegetable meal, or with hearty bean and vegetable soups. Marvelous with a wilted lettuce or spinach salad.

◆

1 cup fine white cornmeal
1 teaspoon salt
1 tablespoon lard or solid vegetable shortening
¾ cup boiling water, or as needed
Lard or solid vegetable shortening (see step 3)

◆

1. Combine the cornmeal, salt, and lard or shortening. Mix well.

2. Slowly add water that is boiling hard to the meal, mixing thoroughly and quickly. When the mixture is soft but not too wet, form it into thin 2½-inch cakes.

3. Melt enough lard or shortening on a heavy black iron griddle to form a thick coating. When it is very hot, but not smoking, add the hoe cakes, a few at a time, and fry until one side is golden brown, 2 to 3 minutes. Turn and brown the second side. Drain on paper towels and serve at once.

Makes 6 to 8 cakes

🦉 If the imprint of your fingers will not stay in the hoe cakes when they are formed, you have used too much water.

CLASSIC ENGLISH MUFFINS

◆◆◆

*T*his is a fine-textured English muffin (which I prefer). The proportions of salt and sugar are perfect—don't change them. Salt makes yeast bread "pully" and that is the correct texture of a good English muffin. The secret to a fine "crumpet," as the English call them, is sautéing them carefully. They do absorb loads of butter but they are utterly delectable. They freeze well, but few breads can compare to these muffins when they are freshly made and broiled with butter. You'll see.

◆

1 package dry yeast
2 tablespoons lukewarm water
½ cup milk
7 tablespoons unsalted butter, or more as needed
1 tablespoon sugar

1 cup water
1 tablespoon salt
4½ cups all-purpose flour, sifted
¼ cup white cornmeal

◆

1. Dissolve the yeast in the luke-warm water.

2. Scald the milk in a small saucepan, but do not allow it to boil. Melt in it 3 tablespoons of the butter. Pour the milk into a large bowl, or the bowl of an electric mixer or food processor. Add the sugar, water, and dissolved yeast. Mix thoroughly.

3. Add the salt and 4 cups of the flour, 1 cup at a time, and beat well to activate the gluten.

4. Lift the dough onto a lightly floured surface. Knead it thoroughly 7 to 8 minutes. Add just enough extra flour to make a firm dough.

5. Put the dough in a greased bowl and turn it to coat the surface. Place the bowl in a warm spot, free of drafts. Cover it with plastic wrap and leave until the dough has doubled in bulk, about 1¼ hours. (After it has doubled, the dough can be formed

*T*he basic elements of corn are the hull, the germ, and the endosperm. Corn is steamed first, to loosen the hull. Then the grains are split and the hull and the germ removed. What remains is the endosperm, the part that is made into grits and cornmeal. The endosperm is passed through heavy steel rollers that break it into granules. The largest of these granules become grits, the medium ones become cornmeal, and the finest are corn flour.

into muffins, or it can be covered and refrigerated until the next day.)

6. When you are ready to make the muffins, put the dough again on a lightly floured surface and knead it lightly to rid it of air bubbles.

7. Roll out the dough ½ inch thick. Cut it into 3½-inch rounds, and dip the bottom of each muffin in cornmeal. Place the muffins on a baking sheet, that has been sprinkled with cornmeal, cover them with plastic wrap, and leave them in a warm spot until the dough has doubled in bulk again, 30 to 40 minutes.

8. Melt 2 tablespoons of the butter over medium heat in a black iron skillet or electric griddle. Turn the heat down. Cook the muffins over rather low heat, turning them several times to keep them from becoming too brown, about 20 minutes in all. Add butter from time to time to keep the griddle well greased. Shake the griddle often so the muffins move about and cook and brown evenly.

9. When they are done, allow the muffins to cool just until they can be handled. (A rack is unnecessary.)

10. To serve, split the muffins, butter the cut side, and toast under the broiler.
Makes 12 muffins

The cornmeal is used on the bottom of the muffins so they will not stick to the griddle.

SOUR CREAM CORN MUFFINS

*T*his is the finest corn muffin of all. The sizzling-hot iron muffin pan is traditional and does give the bread a lovely crunch. But lacking the pan, try another way—don't miss this muffin. Freeze, split, butter, and broil.

⅞ cup fine white cornmeal
1 cup sour cream
1 egg
⅔ teaspoon salt
⅛ teaspoon baking soda

1½ teaspoons baking powder
1 teaspoon sugar
2 tablespoons butter, melted
4 teaspoons solid vegetable shortening or lard

1. Place an iron muffin pan (8 muffins or sticks) in the oven and heat the oven to 450°F.

2. While the pan is heating up, measure the cornmeal into a roomy bowl. Add the sour cream and egg, and beat thoroughly. Add the salt, baking soda, baking powder, sugar, and melted butter. Beat again.

3. Remove the pan from the oven and put ½ teaspoon of the shortening or lard in each mold. Spoon cornmeal batter into the molds, filling them two-thirds full. The pan should be so hot that the grease sizzles when you add the batter.

4. Bake until golden brown and a skewer inserted in the center of a muffin comes out clean, about 20 minutes. Serve at once.

Makes 8 muffins

VARIATION: Use 2 eggs for really light muffins.

The muffins can be made in aluminum or non-stick muffin pans.

◆

SOUR CREAM CORNMEAL BATTER CAKES

1. Make the batter for Sour Cream Corn Muffins.

2. Heat a flat iron griddle (sometimes called a "spider") or an electric griddle and add a good coating of solid vegetable shortening or lard, about 2 tablespoons. When the fat is hot, drop the batter onto the griddle in spoonfuls. Allow one side to

A landslide of corn, delivered to Baltimore harbor, is cleaned by hand in the 1930s.

brown before turning with a spatula to the other side.

Makes 10

Always be sure to use enough fat on the griddle so the cakes do not stick. Do not use butter or margarine, as it will burn.

STOLLEN

◆◆◆

Our German bakeries always had stollen at Christmas and many of them were dry and heavy. No proper stollen is light, but this one is the best example I have found. Mace is a more delicate flavoring than nutmeg—at least more intriguing. If you do use nutmeg, it must be freshly grated.

2 packages dry yeast
½ cup lukewarm water
1 lemon
½ navel orange
1 cup sugar
1 cup milk
1 cup (2 sticks) plus 1 ½ tablespoons butter, at room temperature
1 teaspoon ground mace or freshly grated nutmeg
3 eggs
2 teaspoons salt
8 cups sifted all-purpose flour
1 ½ cups chopped blanched almonds
1 ¼ cups (7 to 8 ounces) chopped citron
1 cup golden raisins

FROSTING

1 ½ cups sifted confectioners' sugar
2 tablespoons milk, or more as needed
1 teaspoon vanilla extract or cognac vanilla (see Index), or 1 tablespoon white Jamaica rum

1. Dissolve the yeast in the water.

2. If you are using a food processor, cut the colored part of the peel from the lemon and orange, and sliver it. Combine the slivered peel with the sugar and twirl until the peel is finely grated. Or, if you prefer, grate the lemon and orange peel by hand and mix it with the sugar. Set it aside.

3. Scald the milk, but do not allow it to boil, and pour it into a large mixing bowl, or the bowl of an electric mixer or a large processor. Add the sugar, 1 cup of the butter, and the mace or nutmeg. Stir until the butter has melted. Add the eggs and the dissolved yeast. Mix thoroughly.

4. Add the salt and 7 cups of the flour, 1 cup at a time, beating it in well.

5. Lift the dough onto a lightly floured surface and knead 3 to 4 minutes. Add just enough extra flour to make a soft, pliable dough.

6. Measure out ½ cup of the almonds and ¼ cup of the citron, and set them aside.

7. Add the remaining almonds and citron and the raisins to the dough and knead them in thoroughly. Form the dough into a large ball.

8. Put the dough in a large greased bowl and turn it to coat the surface. Cover the bowl with plastic wrap and leave it in a warm spot until the dough has doubled in bulk, 1½ hours. (This dough will not rise as high as doughs not laden with nuts and fruits, and it will rise more slowly.)

9. After the first rising, cover the dough and refrigerate until the next day.

10. Lift the dough onto a lightly floured surface and knead it lightly, 3 minutes. Divide the dough in half. Form each half into an oval about 12 inches long and 1 to 1¼ inches thick. Flatten one side of each oval to ½ inch in thickness. Turn the unflattened half over the flattened half. Dampen the inside edges of the dough with water and lightly press the edges together. Press the fold side down rather firmly also.

11. Place the loaves on separate lightly greased or non-stick baking sheets. Brush the tops with the remaining butter. Cover the loaves with plastic wrap and leave them in a warm spot, free of drafts, until the dough has doubled in bulk again, 1 hour.

12. Preheat the oven to 350°F.

13. Bake the stollen on the middle shelf of the oven until it is golden brown and the bread sounds hollow when rapped with your knuckle, 30 to 35 minutes. (You may have to bake them separately if your oven is not large enough to hold both sheets on the middle shelf.)

14. Blend the frosting ingredients. Place the loaves on racks and brush them, while still hot, with the frosting. Sprinkle with the reserved almonds and citron before the frosting sets.

Makes 2 loaves

VARIATIONS: Add ⅓ to ½ cup chopped pistachio nuts to the dough with the almonds, and sprinkle some on top of the stollen—delicious and very beautiful.

Crystallized cherries are traditional in stollen, but it is so difficult to find really delicious ones that I usually omit them. Any fine-quality crystallized or glazed fruit works well in stollen.

RICH AND WONDERFUL KUCHEN

*K*uchen is the German word for "yeast cake," and it has always been one of the most beloved bakery sweets in Louisville because of the town's German heritage. This yeast cake is not low in calories, but it is the most delicious one I have ever tasted. It keeps well, freezes well, and you will love it.

1 package dry yeast
2 tablespoons lukewarm water
1 cup milk
1 cup (2 sticks) butter, at room temperature
½ cup sugar
2 whole eggs
1 egg yolk
1 teaspoon salt
4 ½ cups sifted all-purpose flour

NUT FILLING

2 tablespoons butter, at room temperature
2 teaspoons ground cinnamon
½ cup sugar
½ cup chopped walnuts, pecans, hickory nuts, or hazelnuts
1 cup golden raisins

1. Dissolve the yeast in the water.

2. Scald the milk, and pour it into a large mixing bowl. Add the butter and sugar, and stir until the butter has melted. Beat in the eggs and yolk. When the mixture has cooled to lukewarm, add the dissolved yeast. Mix in the salt and 4 cups of the flour, 2 cups at a time.

3. Turn the dough out on a lightly floured surface and knead, adding a little extra flour if needed if the dough feels too sticky. Continue to knead until the dough is soft, smooth, and elastic, 2 minutes.

4. Put the dough in a greased bowl, turning it to coat the surface. (This prevents the top from crusting over.) Cover the bowl with plastic wrap, place it in a warm spot, and leave it until the dough has doubled in bulk, 1 ¼ hours.

5. When the dough has risen, it may be punched down and completed, or it may be covered and set in the refrigerator for several hours or overnight. (It is easier to work with a cold dough.)

6. When you are ready to make the kuchen, remove the dough from the refrigerator and turn it out onto a lightly floured surface. Knead it for a second or two, then divide it in half. Roll each half into a rectangle 1 inch thick.

7. Fill the kuchen: Brush the dough with the butter. Stir together the cinnamon and sugar, and sprinkle the dough with the nuts, raisins, and cinnamon sugar. Press the fruit and nuts well into the dough.

8. Roll each rectangle up tightly like a jelly roll, tuck the ends under, and place them in 2 greased standard (9½ x 4½ x 3-inch) loaf pans. Cover the pans with plastic wrap and leave them in a warm spot until the dough has doubled and springs back at once when lightly touched, 1 to 1¼ hours.

9. Preheat the oven to 350°F.

10. Bake the loaves until golden and the bread sounds hollow when rapped with your knuckle, about 45 minutes. Turn the loaves out onto a rack and allow them to cool before serving.

Makes 2 loaves

A GARDEN CLUB TEA

Rich and Wonderful Kuchen

Williamsburg Tea Bread

Queen Anne's Cake

Rosemaries

Carolina Moravian Ginger Thins

Coffee   Spiced Tea

NORTH CAROLINA MORAVIAN SUGAR CAKE

◆◆

Speak of Moravian Sugar Cake to someone from North Carolina and their face lights up. It is not really a cake, but it is a cake, too—light, sweet, and delicious. The Moravians created this yeast cake to be eaten on Sunday when they came back from church. The dough can be made up the day before (or two days ahead if desired), allowed to rise, then covered and refrigerated. The night before baking, it can be formed into cakes, covered, and refrigerated. Early next morning place the cakes in a warm spot and allow them to double in bulk. Bake and eat—eat—eat.

◆

1 package dry yeast
¼ cup lukewarm water
1 large mealy baking potato
1 cup milk or potato water (see step 2; milk is best)
¾ cup (1½ sticks) butter, cut into pieces
⅔ cup sugar
2 eggs
1½ teaspoons salt
6 cups sifted all-purpose flour, plus more as needed

TOPPING

⅔ cup light brown sugar
⅔ cup granulated sugar
Pinch of salt
½ teaspoon ground cinnamon
6 tablespoons heavy or whipping cream
8 tablespoons (1 stick) butter

◆

1. Dissolve the yeast in the water.

2. Peel and coarsely chop the potato. Place it in a small saucepan, cover with water, and cook over medium heat until soft, 20 to 25 minutes. Drain the potato, but reserve the cooking water if you are planning to use it, and keep it warm. (Or warm the milk over low heat.)

3. Rice or sieve the potato into a large bowl or the bowl of an electric mixer (not a food processor). You will need 1 cup of mashed potato.

4. Add the milk or potato water and the yeast to the mashed potato. Stir in the butter and allow it to melt.

5. Add the sugar and the eggs. Mix thoroughly. Add the salt and the flour, mixing thoroughly until the dough is well blended.

6. Lift the dough onto a lightly floured surface. Knead it thoroughly, 3 minutes. Add just enough extra flour to keep the dough from being sticky. This is a soft and malleable dough, but it is easy to handle.

7. Place the dough in a large greased bowl, and turn it to coat the surface. Place the bowl in a warm spot, free of drafts. Cover it with plastic wrap and leave until the dough has doubled in bulk, about 1¼ hours.

8. The dough can be formed into a cake or rolls at this point, but it is easier to handle if you can refrigerate it for at least 1 hour, or as long as overnight. When you are ready to form the dough, lift it again onto a lightly floured surface. Knead thoroughly to rid it of air bubbles.

9. Divide the dough into thirds, and roll each piece out about ¼ inch thick. With the palms of your hands, form the pieces of dough into ropes about 9 inches long. Coil the ropes of dough into the center of three 9- or 10-inch greased or buttered round or square cake pans, starting at the center. (Of course you can design the ropes to suit your fancy, but leave some spaces in the top to hold the topping.)

10. Place the pans of dough in a warm spot, free of drafts. Cover them with plastic wrap and leave until the dough has doubled in bulk again and is light and springy to the

touch, 45 minutes to 1 hour.

11. In the meantime, combine the topping ingredients in a heavy saucepan. Bring them to a boil and simmer until well mixed, about 1 minute. Set aside to cool.

12. Preheat the oven to 350°F.

13. When the cakes have risen, brush them rather generously with the topping, putting most of the topping in between the creases.

14. Place the pans on the middle shelf of the oven and bake until the cakes are golden brown and the topping has formed a lovely glistening glaze, 20 to 25 minutes. The ropes of dough will have separated just enough to be attractive.

15. Cool the loaves in the pans and serve.

Makes 3 small cakes

VARIATION: The dough can be rolled into 9-inch circles, ½ inch thick, and placed in round cake pans. Allow the dough to rise until it is light and springy. Then brush it with the topping and punch small holes in the dough here and there, filling them with some of the topping.

🦉 Potato doughs should not be mixed in a processor as it makes the potatoes gummy.

ST. AUGUSTINE ORANGE ROLLS

◆◆

*T*his is the quintessential orange roll—the one I taught in all my bread classes. Wonderful for breakfast, brunch, or a picnic. Just do not make them too far ahead— they are at their best the day they are baked.

◆

2 packages dry yeast
¼ cup lukewarm water
1 cup milk
8 tablespoons (1 stick) butter, cut into pieces
½ cup sugar
¼ cup fresh orange juice
1½ tablespoons grated navel orange peel
1 teaspoon grated lemon peel
2 eggs
1 egg yolk
1½ teaspoons salt
5½ cups all-purpose flour, sifted

GLAZE

1 cup sifted confectioners' sugar
2 tablespoons grated navel orange peel
½ cup fresh orange juice

◆

1. Dissolve the yeast in the water.

2. Scald the milk, but do not allow it to boil. Pour it into a large bowl, or into the bowl of an electric mixer or food processor.

Add the butter, sugar, orange juice, orange peel, and lemon peel. Mix well until the butter has melted. Add the eggs, yolk, and dissolved yeast, and beat thoroughly.

A cigar box label from the 1880s.

3. Add the salt, and beat in 4 cups of the flour, 2 cups at a time, until the dough is smooth.

4. Place the dough on a lightly floured surface and knead it thoroughly, 2 minutes. Add just enough flour to keep it from being too sticky. The dough should feel elastic and satiny.

5. Place the dough in a well-greased bowl, turning it to coat the surface. Set the bowl in a warm place, free from drafts. Cover it with plastic wrap and allow the dough to rise until doubled in bulk. It should spring back at once when lightly touched, 1½ hours. (At this stage the dough may be punched down, covered with foil, and placed in the refrigerator for a few hours or overnight—no longer. Cold dough is easier to handle than warm dough, and this is a sticky dough.)

6. When you are ready to use the dough, place it again on a lightly floured surface and knead for 3 minutes. Divide the dough in half and roll each piece into a rectangle ½ inch thick and 6 inches wide. Cut each rectangle into strips 1 inch wide.

7. Take each strip and pull it a bit, then tie it into a simple knot by slipping one end over, then under, then back over the other. Arrange the knots 1½ inches apart on non-stick or lightly greased baking sheets. Place them in a warm spot, cover with plastic wrap, and allow the rolls to become light and springy, and almost tripled in bulk, 1¼ hours.

8. Preheat the oven to 350°F.

9. Place the baking sheets on the middle shelf of the oven, and bake only until golden brown and a skewer inserted in the center of a roll comes out clean, 15 to 18 minutes. To ensure moist rolls, do not overbake.

10. While the rolls are baking, blend together the frosting ingredients. Brush the baked rolls generously with the frosting while they are still hot.

Makes 36 rolls

VARIATION: Sprinkle the frosted rolls with extra grated orange peel or with grated blanched almonds. Most attractive, indeed.

COUNTRY INN SWEET ROLLS

*T*his is a moist and velvety dough, lovely for tea rings and fancy shapes and sizes. It is a valuable breakfast bread as the rolls can be formed, then (without allowing them to rise) covered, and refrigerated overnight. Remove them from the refrigerator several hours before breakfast, brunch, or going to church. Put them in a warm place to rise. Bake, and serve fresh from the oven.

1 package dry yeast
¼ cup lukewarm water
3½ cups sifted all-purpose flour
8 tablespoons (1 stick) butter, chilled
1 cup granulated sugar
1½ teaspoons salt
2 eggs
1 cup sour cream
1½ tablespoons butter, at room temperature

2 teaspoons ground cinnamon
½ cup chopped pecans (optional)
1½ tablespoons milk or fresh orange juice
½ cup confectioners' sugar

1. Dissolve the yeast in the water.
2. Sift the flour, again, into a large bowl. Cut the chilled butter into the flour

with a pastry blender until the mixture looks like coarse meal.

3. Add ½ cup of the sugar, the salt, dissolved yeast, eggs, and sour cream. Mix thoroughly. Knead the dough in the bowl. This is a sticky dough that really does not knead. If it feels too wet to the touch, add a bit more flour to make the dough stiff enough to handle.

4. Put the dough in a greased bowl, cover, and refrigerate it overnight before the first rising. In the morning, put the bowl in a warm spot and allow the dough to rise until it has doubled in bulk, 2 to 2½ hours.

5. Punch the dough down, cover it, and return it to the refrigerator to firm up and chill, 30 minutes. (This dough is easier to work with when cold.)

6. When you are ready to form the dough into rolls, put it on a lightly floured surface. Knead it lightly and roll it out into a rectangle. Brush the dough with the softened butter.

7. Mix the remaining sugar and the cinnamon and sprinkle this over the buttered dough. Sprinkle with pecans if desired.

8. Roll up the dough lengthwise, as if you were forming a jelly roll. Slice the dough into 2 inch rounds. Place the rolls close together in a lightly greased 9- or 10-inch shallow cake pan. Cover with plastic wrap and leave in a warm place until the rolls have doubled in bulk, 1½ hours.

9. Preheat the oven to 350°F.

10. Bake the rolls for 20 to 25 minutes.

11. Meanwhile, prepare the glaze. In a small bowl, combine the milk or orange juice with the confectioners' sugar. The mixture should be smooth and an easy spreading consistency. You want just a thin sparkling film on the sweet rolls.

12. Remove the rolls from the oven and spread with the glaze while they are still hot.

Makes 8 to 10 sweet rolls

HOT CROSS BUNS

*E*aster wouldn't be Easter without the traditional English Good Friday rolls called Hot Cross Buns. The spiced rolls were first made in pagan England, and the early Christians added the cross. Later the English colonizers brought this custom to us and we have adopted it almost as our own. The touch of refreshing lemon on these rolls is one of their greatest charms.

1 package dry yeast
¼ cup lukewarm water
1 cup milk
½ cup sugar
8 tablespoons (1 stick) butter, cut into pieces
2 large eggs
1½ teaspoons ground cinnamon
½ teaspoon ground allspice
¼ teaspoon ground mace or freshly grated nutmeg
1 teaspoon salt
5½ cups sifted all-purpose flour
1 cup currants, or more to taste
1 egg yolk
2 tablespoons heavy or whipping cream or water (cream is best)
1 cup sifted confectioners' sugar
1 tablespoon fresh lemon juice, plus more as needed
½ teaspoon grated lemon peel

1. Dissolve the yeast in the water.

2. Scald the milk, but do not allow it to boil, and pour it into a large mixing bowl, or the bowl of an electric mixer or food processor. Add the sugar and butter and stir until the butter melts. Add the eggs and beat thoroughly.

3. Combine the spices and salt and

sift them with the flour.

4. Add the dissolved yeast to the butter and egg mixture. Beat. Add 5 cups of the flour mixture, 2 cups at a time, mixing thoroughly. Do not overbeat.

5. Lift the dough onto a lightly floured surface and knead for 3 minutes. Add just enough extra flour to keep the dough from being too sticky.

6. Put the dough in a greased bowl and turn it to coat the surface. Cover the bowl with plastic wrap and leave it in a warm spot until the dough has doubled in bulk and feels light and springy, 1½ hours.

7. Lift the dough onto a lightly floured surface again and knead in the currants. At this point, you can cover and refrigerate the dough overnight, or you can allow it to rise again in a bowl, covered loosely with plastic wrap. If you refrigerate overnight, the dough will rise the next morning in 2 to 2½ hours; if you are allowing the dough to rise right after kneading in the currants, put in a warm spot until it doubles in bulk, about 1 hour. Then form into rolls.

8. Pinch off small pieces of the dough and form them into rounded balls 1¼

inches in diameter. Place them 2 inches apart on a non-stick or lightly greased baking sheet or close together in greased cake pans.

9. Blend the egg yolk and the cream or water, and brush about half of this mixture over the rolls. Cover the rolls and leave them in a warm place until they have doubled in bulk and spring back at once when lightly touched, 40 minutes.

10. Preheat the oven to 350°F.

11. Brush the rolls all over with the remaining egg yolk mixture. Place the pans on the middle shelf of the oven and bake until the buns are light brown, 20 to 25 minutes.

12. Blend the confectioners' sugar with the lemon juice. Dilute a small amount of this mixture with more lemon juice or water to make a thin glaze. While the buns are still hot, brush them lightly with the diluted frosting, and sprinkle with grated lemon peel. Allow buns to cool in the pan.

13. After the rolls have cooled, frost with the remaining icing, using an icing tube to form a cross on each bun.

Makes 36 buns

ST. PETERSBURG ORANGE AND APRICOT BREAD

◆◆◆

A fine cook from St. Petersburg gave me this bread years ago and it has been a favorite ever since. Wonderful for tea, breakfast, lunch, or just when you want to taste something simply delicious.

◆

1 package (7 ounces) dried apricots
1 egg
1 cup sugar
2 tablespoons butter, melted and cooled
2 cups all-purpose flour
¾ teaspoon salt
¾ cup fresh orange juice
1 teaspoon grated orange peel
1 tablespoon baking powder

◆

1. Soak the apricots in warm water to cover for 30 minutes.

2. Preheat the oven to 325°F.

3. Drain the apricots thoroughly, setting a few of them aside to be added to the batter whole. Mash the remaining apricots with a fork. Do not purée.

4. Combine the egg and sugar in a large bowl and beat with an electric mixer until the mixture drops from a spoon in ribbons. Beat in the melted butter.

5. Sift the flour with the salt. Add it to the egg mixture alternately with the orange juice and grated peel. Add the baking powder and mix it in quickly. Add the mashed apricots and mix thoroughly. Fold in the whole pieces of apricot by hand.

6. Spoon the batter into 2 small (7 x 4 x 2-inch) foil-lined pans. Set the pans on the middle shelf of the oven and bake until the batter springs back at once when lightly touched, about 1 hour.

7. Allow the bread to stand for 5 minutes before removing it from the pan. Turn the bread out onto a cake rack, remove the foil, and let it cool thoroughly before slicing it thin.

Makes 2 small loaves

Drain the apricots well or there will be too much moisture and the bread will be heavy. The oven temperature must be kept low, as this loaf burns easily. The whole

Oranges grow in states other than Florida. This bread is wonderful made with any of them.

apricots will show up in an attractive pattern when the bread is sliced.

RUTHERFORD WYND PUMPKIN BREAD

*W*hen the leaves turn yellow and orange and a flaming red, it's time to get a can of pumpkin and make this bread. Lovely to share—lovely to be alone with.

8 tablespoons (1 stick) butter, at room
    temperature
1½ cups sugar
2 eggs
1¾ cups sifted all-purpose flour
⅛ teaspoon baking soda
1¼ teaspoons baking powder
½ teaspoon ground cinnamon
¾ teaspoon salt
½ teaspoon freshly grated nutmeg
1 cup canned pumpkin
¼ cup water, or more as needed
½ cup coarsely chopped pecans or walnuts

1. Preheat the oven to 350°F.

2. Cream the butter and sugar thoroughly in the large bowl of an electric mixer or in a food processor. Add the eggs and continue to beat until the mixture becomes thick and smooth.

3. Resift the flour with the baking soda, baking powder, cinnamon, salt, and nutmeg. Add the flour, pumpkin, and water alternately to the creamed butter and eggs. Do not overbeat. Fold in the nuts with a spatula.

4. Spoon the batter into a lightly greased or foil-lined standard (9½ x 4½ x 3-inch) loaf pan. Place the pan on the middle shelf of the oven and bake for about 1 hour. When a skewer inserted into the center comes out dry, the bread is done.

5. Remove the pan from the oven and allow the bread to stand 5 minutes, then turn it out onto a rack. Cool the bread thoroughly before slicing.

Makes 1 loaf

SPICED PRUNE AND WALNUT BREAD

◆◆◆

*T*his is the bread for a gloomy day. Sit in a soft, comfortable chair in front of an open fire with a cup of tea—and slice after slice of this soothing bread. Your troubles will fade away.

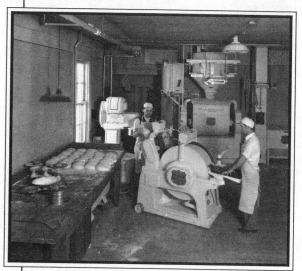

Readying the loaves for the oven using the latest equipment, 1932.

◆

4 cups boiling water
2 cups dried prunes
1 cup sugar
Slivers of peel from 1 small navel orange
Slivers of peel from ½ lemon
3 tablespoons butter, at room temperature
2 eggs
½ teaspoon ground cloves
1½ teaspoons ground cinnamon
½ teaspoon salt
2 teaspoons baking powder
2 cups sifted all-purpose flour
½ cup fresh orange or prune juice (see Owl), or
    more as needed
½ cup chopped walnuts

◆

1. Preheat the oven to 325°F.
2. In a medium bowl, pour the boiling water over the prunes and let them soak until plumped, 20 minutes. Drain well, reserving the water, and chop. You should have 1½ cups.

3. Grease and dust with flour a large (13 x 4½ x 2¼-inch) loaf pan or 2 standard (9½ x 4½ x 3-inch) loaf pans. Set aside.
4. Put the sugar and slivers of orange and lemon peels in a food processor. Turn on and process until the citrus peel is very finely grated and thoroughly blended with the sugar.
5. Using an electric mixer, cream the sugar mixture and the butter thoroughly. Add the eggs and beat until the batter falls in ribbons from a spoon.
6. Add the spices, salt, and baking powder to the sifted flour, and toss together. Add this to the sugar mixture alternately with the orange or prune juice. When the batter is smooth, fold in the chopped prunes and nuts by hand with a rubber spatula. (An electric mixer would pulverize the prunes too much.)
7. Spoon the batter into the prepared pan and place it on the middle shelf of the oven. Bake, depending upon the size of the pan, 1 to 1¼ hours. When it is done, the loaf will spring back at once when touched, and a skewer inserted in the center will come out clean.
8. Cool the bread in the pan for 5 minutes, then loosen it with a sharp, thin knife and turn it out onto a rack. Cool the bread thoroughly before slicing. The bread will ripen and have even more flavor the next day.

Makes 1 large loaf or 2 standard loaves

🦉 For prune juice, use the soaking water from the prunes. The amount of liquid needed will vary with the moisture from the prunes.

WILLIAMSBURG TEA BREAD

*T*his date and pecan bread has a character all its own. It is best when made in the late fall, when the fresh-packed dates and pecans are in. It is good almost anytime but is especially wonderful for receptions, teas, and luncheons—and it freezes well.

This recipe was originally given to me by Marion Flexner, a famous Southern cook and author.

½ pound pitted dates
½ pound pecans
2 eggs
¾ cup sugar
¾ cup sifted all-purpose flour
Pinch of salt
½ teaspoon baking powder
½ teaspoon vanilla extract or cognac vanilla
   (see Index)

1. Preheat the oven to 300°F.
2. Cut the dates in half. Chop the pecans very coarsely, and only if they are very large. Set the dates and pecans aside.
3. Beat the eggs in an electric mixer or a food processor. Add the sugar, and beat until the mixture is thick and smooth.
4. Add the flour, salt, and baking powder and mix thoroughly.
5. Stir in the dates, pecans, and vanilla with a wooden spoon or rubber spatula and mix thoroughly. (Don't process—the dates and pecans should remain chunky.)
6. Spoon the batter into a greased, foil-lined standard loaf pan (9½ x 4½ x 3 inches) or in a long loaf pan (13 x 4½ x 2¼ inches). Cover the pan with foil, and bake on the middle shelf of the oven for 1½ hours.

The Dakin family enjoys tea under the oaks on Racimo Plantation, Louisiana, in the 1880s.

7. Increase the heat to 325°F and remove the foil. Continue to bake until the loaf is light brown and a skewer inserted into the center of the loaf comes out clean, another 15 to 30 minutes. Turn the bread out onto a rack and cool it completely before slicing.

Makes 1 loaf

VARIATION: For an especially moist, fruitcake-like texture, mash a portion of the dates.

This method of baking creates a loaf that has a fairly crisp crust and moist inside. If you prefer a softer texture throughout, omit the foil covering and cook the loaf at 300°F for 1¾ to 2 hours.

OLD PINEY NUT BREAD

*M*other was such a wonderful cook in many ways, but I liked nothing better than her nut bread, which she made with hickory nuts, the wild pecan that is native to Kentucky. The flavor of the cultivated Southern pecan is redolent of the wild species, although considerably milder.

This bread freezes well, slices thin, and is altogether exquisite. One of the most successful ways of serving nut bread is on the buffet with the coffee urn, to be eaten at random after cocktails and hors d'oeuvres. But then, it is just as wonderful for teas and receptions.

◆

*4 tablespoons (½ stick) butter, at room
    temperature*
¾ cup sugar
2 eggs
2 cups sifted all-purpose flour
1½ teaspoons baking powder
½ teaspoon salt
¾ cup milk
*1½ cups chopped hickory nuts, pecans, or
    walnuts*

◆

1. Preheat the oven to 325°F.

2. Cream the butter thoroughly with the sugar in the large bowl of an electric mixer. Add the eggs and continue to beat until the mixture is thickened and smooth.

3. Sift the flour with the baking powder and salt. Add this to the creamed mixture alternately with the milk, at a very low speed (or by hand, which is best), until well blended. Add the nuts and mix them in thoroughly.

4. Grease a standard (9½ x 4½ x 3-inch) loaf pan and line it with greased foil. Spoon in the batter, and place the pan on the middle shelf of the oven. Bake until the loaf is golden brown, feels fairly firm to the touch, and a skewer inserted into the center of the loaf comes out clean, 60 to 70 minutes. If the bread springs back at once when lightly touched, the bread is done. Turn the bread out onto a rack, remove the foil, and allow it to cool completely before slicing. (It will slice better the day after baking.)

Makes 1 loaf

Careful: This will dry out if overbaked. Freezes beautifully.

CHAPTER TEN

PICKLES
AND
PRESERVES

SUMMER'S BOUNTY
FOR WINTER'S TABLE

◆◆◆

Making relishes, chutneys, preserves, and marmalades may come close to a science but it is also an art—a row of these preserved fruits is a beautiful thing.

The late autumn garden is a Southern cook's paradise. It is "pickling" time. The pepper plants are weighted down with colorful peppers of every size and color. The tiny red ones are the cayenne—hot as ___! We put them in green tomato relishes of every kind and we dry them for cooking in the winter. The dried ones are the hottest.

The bell peppers—sweet red, green, and yellow—and the true Georgia pimento are abundant, and we can't preserve them fast enough. They make our pot roasts sing. The Southern watermelons bear late into the autumn. They are not as sweet as the summer melons, but they are divine for watermelon pickles. In October and November the Jerusalem artichokes are ready to be dug, and nothing is better than pickled artichoke with a sweet and tender pork roast or a white meat turkey sandwich.

All winter long you will reap the summer's bounty and you will be proud. You will have relishes and chutneys for your meat. You will have English muffins, pancakes, and toast with garlands of your finest preserves. Put a bottle of Aunt Nettie's Major Grey Mango Chutney or Fabulous Spiced Green Seedless Grapes under my Christmas tree anytime. They are precious gems. This chapter is full of gems—read on.

◆◆◆

AUNT NETTIE'S MAJOR GREY MANGO CHUTNEY

*T*his is a true Madras Indian chutney from Aunt Nettie's collection. Aunt Nettie lived and cooked all over the world, and this is her prize recipe. In the world of mango chutneys it has no peer. It must be made with mangoes, and it keeps best when frozen; however, when properly processed, it will keep well on the shelf. The recipe can be cut in half successfully.

10 pounds underripe mangoes
1 pound fresh ginger, peeled and finely chopped, or 1 pound crystallized ginger, finely chopped
1 pound seedless raisins, ground
1 pound currants
2 heads garlic, cloves separated, peeled, and cut in half
5 large red bell or pimento peppers, cored, seeded, and slivered
6 cinnamon sticks
2 quarts cider vinegar
¼ cup ground ginger
¼ cup cayenne pepper
¼ cup uniodized salt
8 pounds sugar

1. Peel the mangoes, slice the flesh from the pits, and cut the flesh into rather thick slices. (The fruit must be underripe.)

2. Put all the ingredients except the sugar into a heavy 8-quart preserving pan.

3. Caramelize the sugar slightly: Put half the sugar in a large heavy iron skillet over medium heat. When the sugar starts to melt, start stirring. Stir constantly until the sugar has turned a very light amber. Remove from the stove.

4. Add all the sugar to the mango mixture and stir thoroughly to dissolve it. Bring the mixture to a low boil, stirring frequently. This mixture sticks and burns easily—watch it carefully. Place it over a "flame-tamer" if the pan is not a very heavy one.

5. Cook until the mixture has cooked

Trees in Florida lush with mangoes, ready for picking.

low and the flavors have blended, 2½ to 3 hours. Remove the cinnamon sticks. Pour the chutney into hot sterilized jars (see page 311) to ¼ inch from the top of each jar. Seal at once. Process in a boiling water bath (see page 315) for 5 minutes.

Makes 16 pints

VARIATION: Add 1 to 2 pounds blanched whole almonds to the chutney 3 minutes or so before removing from the heat (step 5).

If the chutney is kept refrigerated or frozen, the processing is unnecessary; but if the chutney is stored on the shelf, the processing is necessary.

PICKLED PEACHES

◆◆◆

Clingstone peaches are the best for pickling, but freestones can be used. The quality of the peaches is the important thing: They should be firm and perfect, with no brown or soft spots. The sugar is added in small amounts to prevent the fruit from hardening and shriveling. Pickled Peaches are one of the great favorites of the South.

This crew is packing peaches—and they look like they would rather be eating them!

◆

4 quarts (about 24) firm, barely ripe peaches
3 pieces dried ginger, or about 2 ounces peeled fresh ginger
2 cinnamon sticks
1 tablespoon whole allspice
1 tablespoon whole cloves
6 cups sugar
2 cups water
3 cups cider vinegar

◆

1. Dip the peaches in boiling water for 1 to 2 minutes and then slip off the skins.
2. Tie the ginger, cinnamon, allspice, and cloves in a cheesecloth bag.
3. Combine 2 cups of the sugar, the water, vinegar, and spice bag in a large stainless steel or enamel pan. Bring the spice mixture to a boil and simmer about 5 minutes.

4. Add the peaches, a few at a time, to the boiling marinade and allow them to cook until they are tender, about 5 minutes. Remove each batch with a slotted spoon and place them in a large bowl.
5. When all the peaches have been cooked, pour the boiling syrup, with the spice bag, over them. Cover the bowl and allow the peaches to stand in a cool place overnight.
6. The next day, using a slotted spoon, transfer the peaches to hot sterilized jars (see box, opposite).
7. Pour the syrup with the spice bag into a saucepan, add the remaining sugar, and boil until the sugar has dissolved, about 5 minutes. Discard the spice bag and pour the hot syrup over the peaches to ¼ inch from the top of each jar. They must be completely covered with the syrup or the fruit will become discolored. Seal at once. Process in a boiling water bath (page 315) for 10 minutes. Store in a cool, dark place.

Makes 6 pints

🦉 If the syrup has boiled away too rapidly and there is not enough to cover the peaches, make up half of the recipe of sugar, water, spices, and vinegar. Boil until slightly thickened, 5 to 8 minutes, and pour over the peaches.

CHUNKY PEACH AND PLUM SAUCE

◆◆◆

Serve with broiled chicken, game, ham, or on a relish tray, or with Chinese dishes. A great favorite of mine as well as of my students.

2 pounds large deep-red plums, not too ripe
4 large green or red bell peppers (red is best)
1 fresh red chile pepper, or more to taste
3 pounds unripe peaches or mangoes
5 cups cider vinegar
2½ cups water
2 cups granulated sugar
1½ cups loosely packed light brown sugar
2 cinnamon sticks, broken in half
1 large onion, chopped

½ cup finely grated peeled fresh ginger (or minced very fine in a processor)
¼ cup mustard seeds
6 cloves garlic, minced

1. Cut the plums into quarters and discard the pits.
2. Core, seed, and sliver the bell peppers.
3. Seed and sliver the chile pepper

(continued on following page)

◆◆ STERILIZING JARS AND EQUIPMENT

To sterilize jars for preserves, pickles, jams, and relishes:

1. Check jars for nicks or cracks. If using screw bands, make sure they are not bent. Assemble enough new lids for all the jars.
2. Wash the jars, lids, and screw bands thoroughly with soap and warm water. Rinse them well.
3. Place the jars in a pan made for the purpose or in a large, deep pan. Place the jars on a rack, if available, to hold them upright.
4. Cover the jars with water, and cover the pan. Bring to a boil and boil hard for 15 minutes. Leave the jars in this water until you are ready to use them.
5. In another covered pan, simmer every instrument that will come in contact with the food, such as a large stainless steel spoon, large- or small-mouth funnels, new lids for the jars, screw bands, a "grip-tight" lifter, a stainless cup to pour the food into the jars, and any other piece of equipment you find useful. Simmer them 15 minutes to sterilize them. Lift them out of the water only with sterile tongs. As the water in the pan boils down, keep replenishing it with boiling water.
6. Never touch the jars or lids or food with your hands. Use the sterile instruments only.
7. Sterilize an aluminum or stainless steel tray by heating it for 20 minutes in a 425°F oven.
8. Lift the sterile jars out of the water a few at a time, drain them, and place them on the sterile tray.
9. Fill the jars with the boiling-hot mixture, leaving the amount of head space noted in the recipe. Work fast so the jars and the contents will not cool off.
10. Wipe the mouth of each jar with a clean wet cloth. Place the lids on the jars, and then the screw bands. Preserves, conserves, marmalades, and jellies can be sealed with paraffin. Not so relishes, vegetables, and fruit butters.
11. Do not set the hot jars on a cold surface, as they might crack.
12. Jellies, jams, and relishes do not have to be processed further, if every sanitization rule is carefully followed.
13. When the jars have cooled completely, rinse them with warm water to remove any food that spilled. Store in a dark cool place.
14. If the food is to be frozen, heavy freezer jars must be used. Sterilize the jars, but leave 1-inch head space when you fill them (see page 321 for more information).

If the food is contaminated while transferring it to the jars, spoilage will result. If the food has been contaminated, sealing the jars will not prevent spoilage.

One can often hear the lids on the jars snap as they seal. If the lid is curved down in the center, it has sealed. The screw bands can then be removed, if you desire.

4. Peel the peaches or mangoes, and coarsely chop the flesh. Discard the pits.

5. Combine the vinegar, water, and both sugars in an extra-heavy stainless steel or enamel saucepan. Stir thoroughly to dissolve the sugars as much as possible. Bring to a boil, add the cinnamon sticks, and boil 3 minutes.

6. Add the fruit, bell and chile peppers, onion, ginger, mustard seeds, and garlic. Bring the mixture back to a boil, reduce the heat, and simmer gently for at least 1 hour. The mixture burns easily, so use a "flame-tamer" under the pan. Stir frequently. The sauce should cook low and be thick.

7. Discard the cinnamon sticks, and spoon the boiling sauce into hot sterilized jars (see page 311) to ¼ inch from the top of each jar. Seal at once. Process in a boiling water bath (see page 315) for 5 minutes. Or spoon the sauce into prepared freezer jars (see page 321), leaving 1-inch head space. Cool and freeze.

Makes 4 pints

VARIATION: To make a smooth sauce: About 25 minutes before the sauce is done, press it through a food mill or twirl it in a processor until smooth. Return it to the heat and continue cooking.

PRESERVED KUMQUATS

T*he* season for Florida kumquats is short, so preserve them while you can. They are wonderful with game dishes and make very special gifts.

2 pounds kumquats
4 cups sugar
¼ cup light corn syrup
1 teaspoon fresh lemon juice
1 quart water

1. Wash and stem the kumquats. Prick each one several times with a large needle so they will absorb the syrup thoroughly.

2. Place the kumquats in a large saucepan and cover well with water. Bring to a boil, reduce the heat, and simmer until tender, 8 minutes. Drain.

3. Combine the sugar, corn syrup, lemon juice, and 1 quart water in a large saucepan and bring to a boil. Boil a few seconds, then add the kumquats and cook, holding the syrup at 218°F on a candy thermometer, until the kumquats are transparent, another 10 minutes. If the syrup boils too low, add a little boiling water.

4. Set the pan aside and allow the kumquats to cool, then stand in the syrup at room temperature, loosely covered, overnight or longer. Keep them submerged by weighting them down with a heavy bowl or plate.

5. Bring the mixture to a boil again and cook until the syrup becomes a jelly and registers 222°F on a candy thermometer, 5 to 6 minutes. Spoon the fruit into hot sterilized jars (see page 311), pour in syrup to within ¼ inch of the top of each jar, and refrigerate.

Makes 1 pint

A "model" kitchen in Alabama in the 1920s with its Hoosier cabinet prominently displayed—a valuable antique today.

INDIAN RIVER HOT MANGO SLICES

◆◆◆

*T*his is a fascinating, beautiful, and delicious fruit side dish for curry. The hot peppers will, of course, have to be adjusted to your taste, as they can be terribly hot, but don't discount their flavor.

◆

2 ripe mangoes
1 yellow chile pepper, seeded and sliced in thin
    rounds
1 red chile pepper, seeded and sliced in thin
    rounds
¼ cup lime juice
Salt to taste

◆

1. Peel the mangoes and slice them in thin pieces into a bowl. Add the chile peppers, lime juice, and salt to taste. Toss, and let marinate 30 minutes.

2. Taste the mangoes. If they are overly hot, cover the mixture with ice water and set it aside for 1 hour.

3. Drain the mixture. Taste, and add more lime juice if desired. Serve the mangoes with the peppers as garnish. Or refrigerate to use at another time.

Makes 1½ pints

FLORIDA SPICED ORANGES

◆◆◆

*D*elightful served with duck, roast turkey, quail, baked ham, or on the holiday relish tray.

◆

6 navel oranges or tangelos
1 cup cider vinegar
4 cups sugar
½ cup water
1½ teaspoons whole cloves
3 cinnamon sticks, broken in thirds

◆

1. Wash the oranges or tangelos thoroughly. Slice them into thin rounds and discard the seeds.

2. Put the fruit in a heavy saucepan and cover well with water. Bring to a boil, reduce the heat, and simmer, uncovered, until tender, about 45 minutes. Drain.

3. Combine the vinegar, sugar, ½ cup water, and the spices in a large saucepan. Bring to a boil, and boil 5 minutes. Add the orange slices and boil gently until the slices are clear and well glazed, about 8 minutes.

4. Using a slotted spoon, transfer the orange slices to hot sterilized jars (see page

Working on young citrus trees in Florida in the 1920s. They're probably bearing well today.

311). Pour the boiling hot syrup over them, covering them well, to ¼ inch from the top of each jar. Seal at once, or cool and refrigerate. Or fill prepared freezer jars, leaving 1-inch head space. Cool and freeze.

Makes 2½ pints

SLIVERED AND SPICED CUCUMBER AND PEPPER RELISH

*T*his relish should have a fabulous name—it is just that delicious—but I cannot think of one just now. In the late summer I like to add yellow bell peppers—very beautiful. And, oh, how good this relish is all winter long with roast beef, brisket or pork roasts, and on and on. You'll love it.

Shelves of home-canned pickles and preserves fill the cook with pride and security.

4 quarts firm small cucumbers
½ cup plus 3 tablespoons uniodized salt
1 cup slivered firm red bell pepper
1 cup slivered firm green bell pepper
4 cups cider vinegar
1¼ cups sugar
¼ fresh red or yellow chile pepper, seeded and slivered, or more to taste (optional)
3 tablespoons mustard seeds
1 teaspoon celery seeds
1½ teaspoons turmeric
1¼ cups slivered sweet white onions

1. Wash the cucumbers thoroughly, put them in a large bowl, and cover with cold water and ½ cup of the salt. Marinate, covered, in the refrigerator 3 to 4 hours or overnight.

2. Drain and rinse the cucumbers. Cut them into ¼- to ½-inch slices and then into slivers to match the peppers. Set aside.

3. Combine the vinegar, sugar, chile pepper, mustard and celery seeds, turmeric, and the remaining salt in a heavy stainless steel or enamel pan. Bring the mixture to a boil and cook 2 minutes. Set it aside to cool to room temperature. Taste for salt; if needed, add up to ¾ teaspoon.

4. Bring the pickling solution back to a hard boil. Add the bell peppers, onions, and cucumbers, and stir well. Allow the mixture to come barely to the boiling point; the vegetables should just heat through. Do not allow them to cook or they will become limp.

5. Spoon the boiling mixture into hot sterilized jars (see page 311) to ¼ inch from the top of each jar. Seal at once.

Makes 6 pints

VARIATION: *Chopped Cucumber and Pepper Relish:* Chop all the vegetables, coarse or fine, as desired.

BEST VARIATION OF ALL: Substitute Jerusalem artichokes, slivered or chopped, for half the cucumbers. But—the Jerusalem artichokes must not be heated at all or they will go limp.

The amount of sugar can be varied. Some like a sweet relish. I prefer it not overly sweet.

LATE SUMMER RELISH

*W*hen the late green tomatoes in the garden begin to turn whitish, they will not be as pretty when canned as the deep green ones. Serve this relish with beef or pork roast, short ribs, beef stews, and dried beans.

4 cups thinly sliced green tomatoes
2 cups thinly sliced red bell or pimento peppers
2 cups thinly sliced green bell peppers
1 cup thinly sliced onions
¼ cup uniodized salt
4 cups distilled white vinegar
1 cup sugar
2 teaspoons mustard seeds
2 teaspoons celery seeds
1 teaspoon freshly ground white pepper or ½ fresh small chile pepper, seeded and slivered

Wagons laden with baskets of Virginia tomatoes.

1. Mix the vegetables with the salt in a large bowl. Allow them to stand overnight, covered, in a cool place. The refrigerator is best.

2. The next morning, drain the vegetables thoroughly, pressing them down hard to extract as much juice as possible.

3. Pour the vinegar into a large saucepan and add the sugar and spices. Bring to the boiling point, and add the vegetables. Bring to a hard boil and allow the vegetables just to heat through but not to cook. (You want to retain the color and crispness of the vegetables.)

4. Spoon the hot mixture into hot sterilized jars (see page 311), covering the vegetables with the liquid to ¼ inch from the top of each jar. Seal at once.

Makes 4 pints

VARIATION: The ingredients may be coarsely chopped or minced instead of sliced.

🦉 A small amount of extra vinegar may be added if needed to cover the vegetables in the jars.

PROCESSING SEALED JARS

*I*f you are planning to keep the food you can on a shelf rather than in the freezer or refrigerator, it is very important that everything that touches the food is sterilized and remains sterilized during the entire process. If you feel one of the implements has lost its sterile quality or you want to take extra precautions, you must process the jars, once they are sealed, in a boiling water bath.

Place the jars in a processing rack and immerse the rack in a large pot of rapidly boiling water to cover by 2 inches. If you don't have a rack, place a folded towel on the bottom of the pot. Gently lower the jars onto the towel. The towel will keep the jars from knocking into each other and possibly cracking. Maintain a rapid boil for 10 minutes or whatever the recipe suggests. The jar should be completely submerged at all times.

OLD-FASHIONED INDIA RELISH

◆◆◆

*W*hat magic the food processor makes of this relish, so good to serve in the winter with all kinds of beans, roasts, and on the relish tray.

◆

3 pounds cucumbers
3 tablespoons uniodized salt
3 pounds green tomatoes
1 cup finely chopped cabbage
1 ½ cups finely chopped onions
1 cup finely chopped red bell peppers
1 cup finely chopped green bell peppers
2 fresh red chile peppers, seeded, deveined, and finely chopped, or more to taste
3 cups cider vinegar
2½ cups sugar
⅓ cup mustard seeds
1 tablespoon celery seeds
½ teaspoon ground cinnamon
¾ teaspoon turmeric
¼ teaspoon ground mace

◆

1. Peel the cucumbers and chop them fine. Put them into a bowl with 1½ tablespoons of the salt.

2. Remove a thin slice from the top and bottom of the tomatoes. (Do not peel.) Chop them very fine, and put them in a separate bowl with the remaining salt.

3. Cover the cucumbers and tomatoes with plates and weight each down with a heavy object. (This is to help draw the juice out of the vegetables.) Allow to stand overnight in a cool place, or refrigerate if possible.

4. The next morning, turn them into a colander and press down firmly to force out as much of the liquid as possible.

5. Put the cucumbers and tomatoes in a large pan. Add the cabbage, onions, and bell and chile peppers, and mix well.

6. Add 1 cup of the vinegar to the vegetables and heat only to a low boil. Add the remaining vinegar, the sugar, mustard and celery seeds, cinnamon, turmeric, and mace. Mix thoroughly and heat just to the boiling point. Do not cook.

7. Ladle the relish into hot sterilized jars (see page 311) to ¼ inch from the top of each jar. Seal at once.

Makes 6 pints

CAROLINA CHIPS

◆◆◆

*T*his is the easiest of all homemade sweet pickles, very crisp and delicious. The tedious process of brining has been done for you, so the rest is just fun and flavor. They make wonderful gifts from your kitchen.

◆

4 quarts large sour or dill pickles (without garlic)
1 quart cider vinegar
2 tablespoons whole allspice
2 tablespoons whole cloves
2 tablespoons celery seeds
2 tablespoons mustard seeds
2 cinnamon sticks, each broken into 3 pieces

1 tablespoon black or white peppercorns
10 cups sugar
3 cloves garlic
2 hot red chile peppers, dried or fresh, cut in pieces
2 pieces dried or fresh ginger
2 bay leaves

◆

1. Drain the pickles, then cut them into thick slices or chunks.

2. Combine the vinegar with the spices and sugar in a heavy stainless steel or enamel pan. Bring the mixture to a boil, reduce the heat, and simmer 5 to 6 minutes. Remove the pan from the heat and add the pickles, garlic, chile peppers, ginger, and bay leaves. Mix well.

3. Cover the pan and allow the mixture to ripen at room temperature for 2 to 3 days or more before canning. Stir every so often.

4. Spoon the pickles into hot sterilized jars (see page 311) and be sure they are submerged in the liquid. The liquid should come to ¼ inch from the top of each jar. Seal at once.

Makes 4 quarts

I do not process these pickles, but if they are to have a long shelf life or are made commercially, they should be.

If the pickles are allowed to drain overnight, the finished pickle will be sweeter. By draining the pickles quickly, a great deal of the original vinegar is left in the pickle. Thus they are not quite so sweet.

A trade card from 1885 featured Cupid holding a "love-conquered" pickle.

CHECK POINTS FOR PICKLING

1. Always use uniodized salt.

2. Pickling or canning salt is best as even uniodized salt has added chemicals that will cloud and discolor the pickles, especially the fruits.

3. Always sterilize jars by boiling 15 minutes even when the product is to be stored in the refrigerator.

4. It is not satisfactory to freeze pickles or relishes.

5. Small pickling cucumbers are best in making relishes and pickles. They must be completely firm and used not later than 1 day after harvesting. One can get by with larger and very firm cucumbers when the relish is combined with other vegetables.

6. Store all home-packed relishes and pickles in a dark, cool place. Light-sensitive fruits will darken gradually.

7. Pack food as solidly as possible to avoid air pockets. Most pickled relishes and fruits should have only ¼-inch head space to prevent air pockets that turn the fruit dark. Some products can tolerate ½-inch head space.

8. When foods darken at the top of the jar either the air space was too great or the liquid did not cover the food. Cloudy liquids are caused by minerals in the water or fillers in the table salt.

9. The tops of the jars must be wiped with clean paper towels before sealing.

Water processing or freezing any of the pickles and relishes included in this book will cause them to lose their crispness and much of their special flavor. Because of this, you must take extra precautions to make sure that all the equipment you use remains sterile during the preserving process. If you think something that wasn't sterile has come in contact with the food to be preserved, refrigerate the questionable jars and eat those pickles first.

STATE FAIR BREAD AND BUTTER PICKLES

*T*his is a blue ribbon winner at the state fair. The secret is truly fresh cucumbers, as in most pickle recipes—and the proportions are excellent.

Leon County in Florida took first prize at this 1915 fair.

8 medium firm, fresh garden cucumbers (not waxed)
2 cups sliced onions
2 red bell peppers, cored, seeded, and chopped
½ green bell pepper, cored, seeded, and chopped
¼ cup uniodized salt
2 quarts crushed ice
2½ cups sugar
2½ cups cider vinegar
1 tablespoon plus 1 teaspoon mustard seeds
1¼ teaspoons celery seeds
¾ teaspoon turmeric
¼ teaspoon ground cloves

1. Wash the cucumbers and slice them thin.

2. In a large bowl, combine the cucumber slices, onions, and peppers with the salt and ice. Mix thoroughly. Add enough water to cover, and refrigerate, loosely covered, overnight.

3. The next day, drain and rinse the pickle mixture.

4. Combine the remaining pickling ingredients in a large saucepan and bring to a boil. Boil a few seconds just to blend. Add the vegetables and bring back just to a boil. Taste quickly for salt. Do not allow the cucumbers to cook.

5. Remove the pan from the heat at once. Stir thoroughly. (The vegetables will have changed color a bit.)

6. Fill hot sterilized jars (see page 311) immediately with the pickles. Bring the cooking liquid back to a boil and pour it over the pickles to ½ inch of the top of each jar. The pickles must be completely covered with the liquid. Seal at once.

Makes 5 pints

If the cucumbers are allowed to cook or boil, the pickles will not be crisp.

OLD PINEY PICKLED WATERMELON RIND

*O*ne large watermelon usually makes about 5 pounds of rind. Choose a watermelon that is not quite ripe, as the rind will be thicker. This rind is a beautiful color, and delicious with rare roast beef, turkey, broiled chicken, pheasant, quail, or a fine country ham.

1 large watermelon
2 tablespoons pickling lime
6 cups cold water
6 cups granulated sugar
2 cups packed light brown sugar
1 quart cider vinegar
3 pieces dried ginger (see Owl)
3 cinnamon sticks, broken
1 tablespoon whole cloves
1 tablespoon whole allspice
1 lemon, seeded and thinly sliced

Boatloads of watermelons in Baltimore harbor, 1931.

1. Wash the watermelon and remove the green skin and all of the pink flesh. (Use the flesh to make Watermelon and Raspberry Sherbet, see Index.) Cut the rind into uniform pieces about 1 inch wide. Put them in a large bowl.

2. Dissolve the lime in 2 cups of the water. (This is easily done in a blender or processor.) Pour the lime water over the watermelon rind and add enough extra water to completely cover the rind. Refrigerate, covered, overnight.

3. The next day, drain the rind and rinse it thoroughly. Cover it again with cold water and allow to stand 1 hour. Drain again.

4. In a large pan, cover the rind again with cold water and bring it to a boil. Cook, uncovered, over medium heat until the rind is tender and can be easily pierced with a toothpick. This usually takes about 2 hours. Drain again thoroughly.

5. Return the rind to the pan. Add the sugars, vinegar, 4 cups water, ginger, spices, and lemon slices. Mix thoroughly. Bring the mixture to a low boil and simmer until the rind is transparent, 1½ hours or more. Remove the pan from the heat, cover, and allow to stand at room temperature overnight.

6. Next day, bring the mixture to a hard boil again. Then ladle the rind into hot sterilized jars (see page 311), covering the pickles well with the hot syrup and spices to ¼ inch of the top of each jar. Seal at once.

Makes 6 pints

If the syrup boiled so low that there is not enough to cover the pickles in the jars, make up an extra batch of syrup using 1½ cups sugar, 1 cup vinegar, and 1 cup water, and allow it to boil until it has formed a syrup. Pour it, boiling hot, over the hot watermelon rind pickles.

If the dried ginger is in large pieces, use 3 and discard them before bottling the pickles. If the ginger is in small cracked pieces, use 1 tablespoon tied in a cheesecloth bag so it can be easily removed and discarded.

HONEYDEW AND GINGER PICKLE

*T*his is one of the most charming and delicate of relishes but not as versatile as some. It is delectable with chicken salad, or turkey or breast of chicken sandwiches. I usually make only one batch, as it does lose its lovely fresh green color after a month or so. Then I make another.

Canning Club at Work

Many hands made the work go quickly in Tupelo, Mississippi, in 1919.

♦

1 hard green medium honeydew melon
2 cups sugar
⅛ teaspoon salt
¾ cup white wine vinegar
½ cup water
1 cup fresh lime juice (about 8 large limes)
3 tablespoons finely chopped peeled fresh ginger
1 teaspoon white peppercorns
2 teaspoons coriander seeds
6 whole cloves

4 small cinnamon sticks

♦

1. Select a honeydew that is not the least bit ripe. Halve it, remove the seeds, and cut the flesh into cubes.

2. Combine the sugar, salt, vinegar, water, lime juice, and ginger in a large saucepan. Bring to a boil and cook over high heat for a few minutes to dissolve the sugar and to blend the ingredients.

3. Add the honeydew cubes to the pickling solution and allow them to heat through but not to cook. Remove the pan from the heat.

4. With a slotted spoon, divide the pieces of honeydew among 4 or 5 hot sterilized half-pint jars. Divide the peppercorns, coriander seeds, cloves, and cinnamon among the jars.

5. Taste the pickling solution. Add more lime juice or sugar if needed. Bring the liquid to a boil and pour it over the honeydew and spices. The pickles must be completely covered with liquid. Cool and refrigerate. Enjoy . . . enjoy!

Makes about 2 pints

FABULOUS SPICED GREEN SEEDLESS GRAPES

♦♦♦

*T*his is one of the stars in my collection of relishes. It evolved over years of working with fruits for preserving. The grapes turn a gorgeous deep amber color and they are heaven with baked fowl, quail, pheasant, ham, chicken salad, or sliced white meat of turkey sandwiches. Unexcelled for the holidays.

♦

5 pounds firm seedless green grapes (small size, thin skinned, unripe)
6 cups sugar
1 cup cider vinegar
½ cup water
2 thin lemon slices, seeded
1 tablespoon broken cinnamon stick
1 tablespoon whole cloves

♦

1. Wash the grapes, pull them from the stems, and cut each grape in half length-

wise. Discard any soft grapes.

2. Place the grapes in a heavy stainless steel or enamel pan. Add the sugar, vinegar, water, lemon, and spices. Stir well with a wooden spoon and bring to a boil. Reduce the heat and simmer until the grapes have turned a beautiful deep amber and are transparent, 60 to 80 minutes. (When cold, the syrup should be slightly runny, not solid like jelly.)

3. Ladle the boiling hot grapes with

their syrup into hot sterilized jars (see page 311) to ¼ inch from the top of each jar. Seal at once. Or cool and refrigerate. Or ladle the grapes into prepared freezer jars (see box, below), leaving 1-inch head space, cool, and freeze.

Makes 5 pints

🦉 Use the Thompson green seedless grape—the smaller the better. Do not use the late-harvest large green seedless grapes that have tough skins. The grapes should not have ripened the least bit.

Before you harvest the grapes, you have to put together the baskets.

❖ CHECK POINTS FOR FREEZING

1. Sterilize freezer jars, screw bands, if using, new lids, and all equipment that will come in contact with the foods or jars (see page 311).

2. Pack the food into the jars as solidly as possible. Leave enough head space (check recipes) for the food to expand upon freezing.

3. When the jars have cooled, freeze as quickly as possible.

4. Because frozen food gradually deteriorates (the lower the freezing temperature, the slower the deterioration), freeze only what you can use in a reasonable amount of time.

5. The optimum method for thawing frozen food is to let it thaw slowly in the refrigerator overnight.

OLD PINEY PICKLED PEARS

❖❖

*S*erve with chicken salad or sandwiches, roast turkey, ham, grouse, quail, capon, or pork roast. Notable on the relish tray.

◆

5 pounds firm pears, not quite ripe
Juice of ½ lemon
4 cups sugar
3 cups cider vinegar
5 cups water
2 medium pieces dried ginger
1 tablespoon whole cloves
1 tablespoon whole allspice
3 thin lemon slices
3 cinnamon sticks, broken in half

◆

1. Peel the pears. Leave them whole if they are very small; cut in half and core if they are medium-size; cut in fourths or eighths if the pears are large. Keep them in a bowl, covered with cold water mixed with the lemon juice, until ready to cook.

2. Combine the sugar, vinegar, and 5 cups water in a large heavy stainless steel or enamel kettle. Tie the ginger, cloves, and allspice in a cheesecloth bag, and add it to the mixture. Bring the mixture to a boil,

A celebration of pears and other fruit in a 19th-century painting by C. V. Bond.

and add the pears and the lemon slices. Boil gently until the pears are transparent and the syrup registers 222°F on a candy thermometer, about 30 minutes.

3. Remove the kettle from the heat

and allow the ingredients to stand at room temperature, lightly covered, overnight for the fruit to plump.

4. The next day, bring the pears again to a boil. Discard the spice bag, and, using a slotted spoon, pack the fruit into hot sterilized jars (see page 311). Put 1 piece of cinnamon in each jar. When the syrup reaches 222°F on a candy thermometer, pour it over the pears. It must cover the pears well and be ¼ inch from the top of each jar. Seal at once.

Makes 4 pints

OCTOBER PICKLED SECKEL PEARS

*T*he charming little Seckel pear that comes to market in early fall is our very favorite.

1 recipe Old Piney Pickled Pears, substituting 4 pounds hard small Seckel pears with stems

Peel the pears, leaving them whole and taking great pains to leave the stems on, as they are more attractive that way. Follow the directions for Old Piney Pickled Pears.

PICKLED ZUCCHINI OR CUCUMBERS WITH PEPPERS AND DILL

*F*or these pickles, use the beautiful fresh green dill heads that have developed seeds but have not turned brown. This lovely fresh green with the streaks of red or yellow peppers in the jars is charming indeed. Add some chopped dill if you like.

3¾ pounds small, firm, perfect zucchini or garden cucumbers
4 cups sliced sweet white onions (1¼ pounds)
4 cups distilled white vinegar
¼ cup water
1 cup sugar
¼ cup uniodized salt
2 teaspoons yellow mustard seeds

1 teaspoon dry mustard
3 large red, yellow, or green bell peppers, cored, seeded, and slivered
8 beautiful seed heads of dill, washed and dried

1. Slice the zucchini or cucumbers and the onions ⅜ inch thick, cover with ice

water, and refrigerate, loosely covered, 3 to 4 hours. Drain thoroughly.

2. Combine the vinegar, water, sugar, salt, mustard seeds, and dry mustard in a large stainless steel or enamel pan and bring to a boil. Add the zucchini or cucumber and onions. Bring the mixture back to a hard boil and cook just 2 to 3 minutes. At the last minute stir in the bell peppers.

3. Spoon the mixture into hot sterilized jars (see page 311) to ¼ inch from the top of each jar. The pickles must be completely covered with the syrup. Working fast, put 2 or 3 dill heads in each jar. Seal at once, or cool and refrigerate.

Makes 4 pints

FAYETTE COUNTY CHOW-CHOW

This is a recipe given to me years ago by a good friend and excellent cook in Lexington. It is a favorite Kentucky chow-chow, a bit sweeter than most. We like it with warm ham, and roasts, and chicken sandwiches—and with all kinds of beans. In Mississippi they say one has to have chow-chow with black-eyed peas.

3 pounds tiny gherkin cucumbers
3 pounds tiny pickling onions
1½ heads cauliflower, cut into flowerets
2¼ cups uniodized salt
24 small onions
8 large red bell peppers, cored and seeded
12 medium cucumbers
8 cups sugar
2 quarts cider vinegar
1 cup all-purpose flour
½ cup dry mustard
3 tablespoons turmeric
1 tablespoon celery seeds
1 tablespoon mustard seeds

1. Put the gherkins, pickling onions, and cauliflower in separate bowls. Add ¼ cup of the salt to each bowl, and pour in ice water to cover. Leave, loosely covered, in a cool place, preferably the refrigerator, all day or overnight.

2. Chop the small onions, peppers, and cucumbers separately, and put them in separate bowls. Add ½ cup salt to each, and cover with ice water. Leave, loosely covered, in a cool place, preferably the refrigerator, all day or overnight.

3. When you are ready to make the pickles, drain the gherkins, pickling onions, and cauliflower thoroughly. Drain the chopped vegetables.

4. In a heavy stainless steel or enamel kettle, combine 6 cups of the sugar with 6 cups of the vinegar. Bring to a boil and stir in all of the vegetables, mixing them well.

5. Quickly mix the flour, mustard, and turmeric with the remaining 2 cups of vinegar until it is very smooth. Stir the paste, along with the celery and mustard seeds, into the vegetables and cook until the sauce has thickened and the flour does not taste raw, 3 to 4 minutes. Taste for sweetness. Add up to 2 cups more sugar if desired, but cook it long enough to dissolve it well.

6. Spoon into hot sterilized jars (see page 311) to ¼ inch from the top of each jar. Seal at once or cool and refrigerate.

Makes about 8 pints

🦉 The gherkins should be sliced in half lengthwise if they are not really tiny.

SOUTH CAROLINA ARTICHOKE CHOW-CHOW

*I*f there is a relish that says "Carolina" above all others, it is Jerusalem artichoke pickles and relishes. Jerusalem artichokes are delightfully crisp, but they go limp when cooked; thus the need to pickle them without cooking or heating.

1 gallon Jerusalem artichokes
1 cup uniodized salt
1 quart green tomatoes (4 large), coarsely chopped
1 quart onions (8 medium), coarsely chopped
6 large red bell peppers, cored, seeded, and chopped
6 large green or yellow bell peppers, cored, seeded, and chopped
1 large rib pale celery, coarsely chopped
2 quarts cider vinegar
½ cup all-purpose flour
½ cup dry mustard
3 tablespoons turmeric
6 cups sugar
5 tablespoons mustard seeds
2 tablespoons celery seeds

1. Select very firm, freshly dug Jerusalem artichokes. Scrub them with a very stiff brush and cut off any discolored spots. Cover them with cold water and ¼ cup of the salt, and refrigerate, loosely covered, overnight.

2. Combine the tomatoes, onions, bell peppers, and celery in a large bowl. Add the remaining salt and cover with cold water.

Keep in a cool place (the refrigerator if possible), loosely covered, overnight.

3. The next day, drain the artichokes and rinse them in cold water. Chop them coarsely and set aside.

4. Drain the tomatoes, onions, peppers, and celery, reserving the liquid. Do not rinse the vegetables.

5. Pour the vinegar into a large heavy stainless steel or enamel pan.

6. Combine the flour, dry mustard, turmeric, and sugar and mix thoroughly. Add this to the vinegar and beat it hard with a whisk before heating it. Add the mustard and celery seeds. Bring the mixture to a boil.

7. Add all the vegetables except the artichokes. Bring to a boil, stirring constantly. (This is where the heavy pan is needed, as the mixture sticks easily.) Allow to cook not over 1 minute. Quickly stir in the artichokes. Do not allow them to cook. If you are short of liquid, add the reserved liquid from the vegetables. Taste for salt.

8. Spoon into hot sterilized jars (see page 311) to ¼ inch from the top of each jar. Seal at once.

Makes 12 pints

MOUNT PLEASANT JERUSALEM ARTICHOKE PICKLE

*T*his recipe from the Robertson family in South Carolina is over 100 years old—a valuable heirloom as well as an edible treasure. Use the artichokes as you would any delicious pickle. They make divine hors d'oeuvres.

1 peck (8 quarts) Jerusalem artichokes
Uniodized salt (see step 1)
1 small lump or 2 tablespoons alum
¼ cup yellow mustard seeds
1 gallon cider vinegar
1 cup packed light brown sugar
1 can (4 ounces) dry mustard
2 cups water
2 tablespoons celery seeds
2 tablespoons whole allspice
1 tablespoon whole cloves

Jerusalem artichokes really do look a lot like fresh ginger.

1. Select firm Jerusalem artichokes with no soft spots. Scrub them thoroughly with a stiff brush. Cover them with cold water and salt, measuring 1 tablespoon salt per quart of water. Allow to stand in the refrigerator, if possible, overnight.

2. The next day, drain and rinse the artichokes well. Cover them again with cold water and add the alum. Marinate the artichokes in the alum water overnight or at least 8 hours.

3. Add the mustard seeds to 1 cup of the vinegar and marinate overnight.

4. The next day, drain the artichokes well and rinse them thoroughly in several changes of water. (This thorough rinsing is very important.) Set aside.

5. Mix the brown sugar and dry mustard together and dissolve in 2 cups water.

Combine in a pan with the marinated mustard seeds and its vinegar, the remaining vinegar, celery seeds, allspice, and cloves. Bring to a boil and boil 15 minutes. Allow to cool.

6. Put the artichokes in a hot clean large crock or jar. Pour the cooled marinade over the artichokes. Cool, and refrigerate. Allow the artichokes to stand a week or longer before using. Taste again for salt.

Makes 2 gallons

If the artichokes are very large, they can be cut in half. When the artichokes have been eaten, more artichokes can be added to the same liquid. This liquid will serve 2 or 3 batches of artichokes—then you will have to start anew.

ORANGE AND FRESH PEACH MARMALADE

*T*his marmalade is boiled 5 minutes, then allowed to stand for several hours for the peaches to absorb the sugar slowly. This method keeps the peaches soft and mellow.

12 perfect peaches (not too ripe)
3 large oranges
½ lemon
¼ cup sugar plus ¾ cup for each cup of
     prepared fruit
1½ tablespoons fresh lemon juice, or to taste

1. Peel and chop the peaches. Using a vegetable peeler or a sharp knife, cut the peel from 1 orange and ½ lemon in a very thin layer. Reserve these peels. Cut all 3 oranges into wedges, and remove the peel, white pith, and seeds. (This peel is not needed for this marmalade.)

2. In a food processor, combine the reserved peels with ⅛ cup of the sugar and the orange sections. Twirl until chopped, but not too fine.

3. Stir together the peaches, processed mixture, lemon juice, and the remaining ⅛ cup sugar.

4. Measure the fruit mixture into a heavy stainless steel or enamel kettle, and add ¾ cup sugar for every 1 cup fruit. Boil rapidly 5 minutes. Remove the kettle from the heat and allow the mixture to stand, loosely covered, several hours or overnight at room temperature.

5. Return the mixture to the heat and boil again until the marmalade is thick and registers 222°F on a candy thermometer, 20 minutes. The marmalade must boil until thick, but watch it carefully to prevent sticking as it cooks low. Stir constantly with a wooden spoon and put a "flame-tamer" under the kettle.

6. Spoon the marmalade into hot sterilized jars (see page 311) to ¼ inch from the top of each jar. Cool and refrigerate. Or spoon the marmalade into prepared freezer jars (see page 321), leaving 1-inch head space. Cool and freeze.

Makes 1½ pints

VARIATIONS: *Grand Marnier Marmalade:* Put ¾ tablespoon of Grand Marnier, or more to taste, in each half-pint jar after adding the marmalade. Stir to blend. An elegant present for a friend or to save for exquisite Christmas gifts.

Peach Brandy Marmalade: Spoon peach brandy or Cognac into the jars after adding the marmalade. Stir to blend.

A VERY SPECIAL PEAR MARMALADE

◆◆◆

My grandmother McGregor said marmalade for breakfast was a great digestive. I needed that, because at her house I also had fried country ham and hot biscuits for breakfast. Her house in the country was my favorite place to stay "all night." The pear tree was huge and near the kitchen, and the pears were hard as rocks. No matter—they made the best of all marmalades.

If your kettle's too big for the stove, cook the marmalade outdoors—that's what this couple is doing!

◆

4 pounds hard unripe pears, peeled, cored, and cut into small, even dice
5½ cups sugar
Juice of 3 lemons
8 ounces preserved ginger in syrup

◆

1. Put the pears in a heavy stainless steel or enamel pan—the heavier the better. Add the sugar and the lemon juice. Bring to a boil and stir until the sugar has dissolved, 5 minutes.

2. Dice the pieces of preserved ginger to match the pear pieces as nearly as you can. Add all the syrup and the diced ginger to the pears.

3. Simmer until the pears become transparent and turn the color of the ginger, 20 to 25 minutes. Do not take the marmalade higher than 220°F on a candy thermometer; it will thicken more as it cools.

4. Spoon into hot sterilized glasses or small jars (see page 311). Cool, and refrigerate. Or spoon the marmalade into prepared freezer jars (see page 321), leaving 1-inch head space. Cool, and freeze.

Makes 3 pints

🦉 The pears and ginger don't have to be cut so precisely, but it does make them more attractive.

Select hard pears such as Kieffer, or Seckel.

FABULOUS LEMON MARMALADE

◆◆◆

*T*his is the lemon marmalade to serve with English muffins, with your best homemade bread, buttered and toasted, and with banana fritters! You will think you are in heaven.

◆

4 to 5 perfect lemons
1⅓ cups cold water
Sugar (see step 3)

◆

1. Peel 3 of the lemons with fine fresh skin, removing just the yellow part of the peel. Cut the peel into the thinnest possible slivers. (Long, sharp scissors are excellent for this.)

2. Slice the lemon pulp very thin and discard the seeds. (Keep the white pith; it has valuable pectin.) Combine the pulp, the slivered peel, and enough juice from the remaining lemons to make 1 cup of prepared lemon. Put it in a mixing bowl, add the cold water, and allow to stand, loosely covered, at room temperature for 3 hours at least.

3. Measure all the lemon mixture by cupfuls into a saucepan and add an equal amount of sugar. Bring to a boil, reduce the heat, and simmer until the marmalade jells (see page 330), 25 to 30 minutes.

4. Allow the marmalade, loosely covered, to stand overnight.

5. The next day, stir the marmalade gently but thoroughly to distribute the rind and bits of pulp. Spoon it into hot sterilized jars (see page 311). Let the jars cool, then refrigerate. Or spoon the marmalade into prepared freezer jars (see page 321), leaving 1-inch head space. Cool, and freeze.

Makes 1½ pints

NORTH CAROLINA PEACH MARMALADE

◆◆◆

*Y*ou will have a finer marmalade if you wait for local peaches to arrive. Shipped fruit is usually picked green and never develops the exquisite flavor of tree-ripened fruit.

A beautifully ripe peach ready for marmalade.

6 ripe but firm large peaches
2 navel oranges
½ lemon
Sugar (see step 5)

1. Peel the peaches. Cut them in half and discard the pits.
2. Slice the oranges and discard the seeds. (Do not peel.)
3. Slice the lemon and discard the seeds. (Do not peel.)
4. Chop the fruit in a food processor or by hand.
5. Measure the chopped fruit by cupfuls into a bowl and add an equal amount of sugar. Mix thoroughly, cover loosely, and allow to stand overnight.
6. Next morning, bring the mixture to a boil in a saucepan and cook, uncovered, for 20 minutes. Pour into hot sterilized jelly glasses (see page 311) to ⅛ inch from the top of each glass. Cool, and refrigerate. Or spoon the marmalade into prepared freezer jars (see page 321), leaving 1-inch head space. Cool, and freeze.
Makes 1 pint

SPICY PLUM BUTTER

*T*o serve as a spicy sweet relish with ham or fresh pork, but best for breakfast with muffins or hot buttered toast. A favorite.

2 pounds fresh purple prune plums
1 scant cup sugar
1 teaspoon ground cinnamon
1 teaspoon ground allspice
½ teaspoon ground cloves

1. Wash the plums and put them in a heavy saucepan. Barely cover with water. Bring to a boil and cook until the pits can be easily removed from the plums, 15 minutes. Do not discard the skins.
2. Add the sugar and spices to the pitted fruit. Boil, adding a little water if necessary and stirring often, until the butter is the consistency of jam, 30 to 40 minutes.
3. Spoon into hot sterilized jars (see page 311). Cool, and refrigerate. Or spoon into prepared freezer jars (see page 321), leaving 1-inch head space. Cool, and freeze.

Makes 2 pints

*C*ooking and preserving in small batches is a wise procedure. Preserves and jellies cook much better in small lots, and you can learn the ways and flavors of the different fruits before it is too late and your sugar bill has gone out of bounds. Easy does it.

Because water processing ruins the flavor and texture of many fruit preserves, cooking in small batches permits you the choice of storing the extra pint or two in the freezer while you enjoy the first. Freezing will keep the preserves safe from bacterial growth, and tasty, too.

If you give any of the frozen or refrigerated preserves to your friends or relatives as gifts, be sure to write on the label that it must be refrigerated immediately to ensure safe eating.

WINTERTIME PERFECT PRUNE BUTTER

◆◆◆

Serve with buttered and broiled English muffins or whole-wheat toast, or with hot biscuits, Kuchen, or freshly baked Divine Bread. Also nice on the relish tray for turkey, pork, or ham.

◆

1 pound large ready-to-eat prunes, pitted
1 cup sugar
½ cup cider vinegar
½ teaspoon ground cinnamon
½ teaspoon ground allspice
¼ teaspoon ground cloves

◆

1. Put the prunes in a saucepan and cover well with water. Bring to a boil, reduce the heat, and cook at a low boil until soft, adding water if necessary, 20 to 25 minutes. The prunes must be cooked until they are very tender and the juices have boiled low. (This intensifies the flavor.)

2. Add the sugar, vinegar, and spices and simmer 6 to 7 minutes.

3. Spoon into hot sterilized jars (see page 311) to ⅛ inch from the top of each jar. Cool, and refrigerate. Or spoon the butter into prepared freezer jars (see page 321), leaving 1-inch head space. Cool, and freeze.

Makes 1½ pints

VARIATION: *Spiced Prune and Walnut Butter:* Add ⅓ to ½ cup coarsely chopped walnuts (or unblanched almonds) to the prune butter just before spooning it into the jars, or just before serving it. This just might turn out to be one of your favorites—it is mine.

RHUBARB STRAWBERRY PRESERVES

◆◆◆

This method of testing the sweetness before the preserves are finished helps in not overloading with sugar. Older recipes often had too much sugar, which robs preserves of their fresh taste. Seven cups of sugar here should be about right for good, sweet fruit—but the fruit flavors do vary, and rhubarb is very tart.

◆

5 medium stalks rhubarb
1 quart perfect strawberries
7 cups sugar, or more to taste

◆

1. Rinse the rhubarb stalks and cut them into ½-inch pieces. Rinse and hull the strawberries.

2. Combine the fruits and the sugar in a large saucepan and allow the mixture to stand for 3 to 4 hours. Then bring the mixture to a boil and cook until the preserves begin to thicken, 25 minutes.

3. Remove the pan from the heat. Put a small spoonful of the preserves on a plate and chill it in the freezer for a few minutes. When it is cool, taste for sweetness. If it is not sweet enough, put ½ to 1 cup of sugar in a small saucepan. Add ⅓ cup water, bring to a boil, reduce the heat, and simmer

until it is a clear syrup, 3 minutes. Stir this into the preserves.

4. If you add more sugar, continue cooking until the preserves are thick, 8 to 10 minutes.

5. Spoon into hot sterilized jars (see page 311) to 1 inch from the top of each jar. Cool, and refrigerate. Or spoon into prepared freezer jars (see page 321), leaving ¼-inch head space. Cool, and freeze.

Makes 1½ pints

◆◆◆
TO TEST THE JELLYING POINT

*L*ift out a metal spoonful of the boiling syrup. Tilt the spoon until the syrup runs back into the pan. When the jellying point is reached, the last two drops will run together and flake, or sheet, from the spoon. The jelly should register 220°F on a candy thermometer. Remove from the heat at once.

ELINOR'S STRAWBERRY PRESERVES

◆◆◆

*T*his recipe for strawberry preserves has been in my friend Elinor's family for 125 years. The only change is that we now know freezing is the best way to preserve its freshness. The berries are picked early in the morning while still fresh with dew, and by 10 o'clock Elinor has the first quart bubbling away. Fabulous preserves.

---

1 pound strawberries (see Owl)
2 cups sugar

---

1. Rinse and hull the strawberries. Drain them well.

2. Put the strawberries in a heavy shallow pan. Gently stir 1 cup of the sugar into the berries and allow them to marinate to absorb some of the sugar, 5 minutes.

3. Bring the berries gradually to a rolling boil. Cook, skimming off the foam that rises to the top, 5 minutes.

4. Add the second cup of sugar gradually, sprinkling it into the preserves. Continue to boil rather fast until the syrup jells

(see box, above), 220°F on a candy thermometer. Skim again.

5. Remove the pan from the heat and pour the preserves into an earthenware bowl. Let them stand, loosely covered, overnight.

6. The next day, pour the preserves into hot sterilized jars (see page 311) to ¼ inch from the top of each jar. Seal at once. Or pour the preserves into prepared freezer jars (see page 321), leaving ¼-inch head space. Cool, and freeze.

Makes 1 pint

VARIATION: *Raspberry Preserves:* Follow the recipe for Elinor's Strawberry Preserves, substituting raspberries, and adding 2 to 3 teaspoons of lemon juice with the second cup of sugar.

🦉 It is imperative to make these preserves 1 batch at a time to maintain the short cooking period so vital to fine preserves. However, several batches can be cooked separately, then poured into the same earthenware bowl to ripen overnight.

One pound of strawberries is a little over a quart. It will vary some.

When setting out to pick strawberries, remember to wear your bonnet out in that hot sun!

OLD SEELBACH HOUSE PEACH AND ALMOND PRESERVES

◆◆◆

*P*eaches and almonds have great affinity for each other. This is an heirloom preserve we enjoy with hot rolls or pound cake for dessert.

---

3 pounds firm and barely ripe peaches
4 cups sugar, or more to taste
3 cups water
¼ cup slivered crystallized ginger
½ cup blanched whole almonds

---

1. Dip the peaches in boiling water to cover. Allow to stand 1½ to 2 minutes. Drain at once, and remove the peels. Cut the fruit in half, and discard the pits. Cut the halves into thirds.

2. Combine the sugar and water in a heavy stainless steel or enamel pan. Bring to a boil, stirring to dissolve the sugar, and boil 2 minutes.

3. Add the peaches and cook until the fruit is tender and transparent, depending upon the ripeness of the peaches, 4 to 5 minutes.

4. Allow the peaches to stand, loosely covered, in the syrup for several hours or overnight at room temperature.

5. Bring the fruit again to a boil. Add the ginger and almonds and mix thoroughly. Remove the mixture from the stove.

6. Using a slotted spoon, pack the fruit into hot sterilized jars (see page 311), leaving room for the syrup.

7. Boil the syrup until it reaches 222°F on a candy thermometer. Pour the boiling syrup over the fruit, filling the jars to ¼ inch from the top of each jar. Cool, and refrigerate. Or spoon the preserves into prepared freezer jars (see page 321), leaving 1-inch head space. Cool, and freeze.

Makes 2½ pints

The original Seelbach Hotel in Louisville is one of the South's most famous old hotels.

◆◆◆

*J*ellies are strained fruit juices and sugar boiled to the jellying point, generally 220° on a candy thermometer. At sea level the jellying point is 222°F.

Marmalades are very much like jellies except they always include the fruit skin and pulp.

Preserves are made from crushed fruit and sugar boiled until they become thick.

Jams are usually made of fruit juice and pulp but without seeds. They are boiled until they become thick like preserves but are smooth.

Conserves are made like preserves but they contain two or more fruits and often include nuts and spices.

Fruit Butters are made of fruits that are puréed before cooking. Sugar is added and they are boiled until thick and have a texture that resembles butter.

1 pound juicy fruit will usually yield 1 cup juice.

1 cup juice plus ¾ cup sugar will yield 1 cup jelly.

BING CHERRY AND ORANGE PRESERVES

*T*he combination of black Bing cherries and oranges makes a most pleasing and rather unusual preserve—delicious when it is first made, and again all winter long with hot rolls for dessert on snowy nights or for breakfast with English muffins or toast.

2 oranges
1¾ cups sugar
3 cups pitted sweet Bing cherries, firmly packed
3 tablespoons fresh lemon juice, or more to taste

1. Wash the oranges. Using a sharp knife, cut off the peel (with a little of the pith). Cut the peel into thin slivers, cover it with cold water in a saucepan, and boil until tender, 15 minutes. Drain, and cool.

2. Remove all the white pith from the outside of the oranges. Cut the oranges into sections, removing the seeds.

3. In a processor, combine 1 cup of the sugar with the orange peel and process until the peel is finely grated. Add the pitted cherries and process just a second— no more or the cherries will be puréed. Combine this mixture in a large glass or ceramic bowl with the remaining ¾ cup sugar, the orange sections, and the lemon juice. Mix thoroughly, cover loosely, and allow to marinate for several hours or over-

night at room temperature.

4. Pour the cherry mixture into a shallow heavy pan (the heaviness is important). Bring it to a boil and cook over medium-high heat until the syrup jells (see page 330) and registers 220°F on a candy thermometer, about 25 minutes. Remove from the heat at once. Allow the mixture to stand, loosely covered, overnight.

5. Next day, fill hot sterilized jars (see page 311) with the preserves to ¼ inch from the top of each jar. Cool, and refrigerate. Or spoon the preserves into prepared freezer jars (see page 321), leaving 1-inch head space. Cool, and freeze. (The flavor remains much fresher if frozen.)

Makes 1½ pints

The amount of lemon juice is determined by the sweetness and ripeness of the cherries. Just before the mixture jells, put a spoonful of it in the freezer to cool, then taste it. If it needs extra acid, add another tablespoon of lemon juice.

GOOSEBERRY PRESERVES

A road through bluegrass country. Maybe there are some berries in that distant hedge.

4 cups gooseberries
1 cup cold water
3 cups sugar

1. Wash, stem, and remove the blossom ends from the gooseberries.

2. Put the berries in a heavy shallow pan and add the water. Bring to a boil, reduce the heat, and simmer 5 minutes.

Add 1½ cups of the sugar and simmer another 5 minutes. Add the remaining sugar and boil rapidly 5 minutes. Remove from the heat and allow the preserves to stand until cold.

3. Skim out the berries and put them in hot sterilized jars (see page 311).

4. Bring the syrup to a boil and cook until it reaches the jellying point (see page 330), or reaches 220°F on a candy thermometer. Pour the hot syrup over the berries to ¼ inch from the top of each jar. Cool, and refrigerate. Or spoon the preserves into prepared freezer jars (see page 321), leaving 1-inch head space. Cool, and freeze.

Makes 1½ pints

This recipe may be cut in half. Gooseberries may be mixed as desired with red currants. A favorite.

INDIAN RIVER KUMQUAT PRESERVES

Serve with roast duck, crown roast of pork, or on the holiday relish tray.

2 pounds kumquats
4 cups sugar
2 thin lemon slices
1 quart water

1. Scrub the kumquats thoroughly. Prick each kumquat several times with a large needle. Put them in a large saucepan, cover well with boiling water, and simmer, uncovered, until the fruit is tender, 25 to 30 minutes. Drain.

2. Combine the sugar, lemon slices, and 1 quart water in a large saucepan. Bring to a boil and boil 5 minutes. Add the kumquats and boil gently until the fruit is transparent, 25 minutes. Remove from the heat and allow to stand, covered loosely, overnight for the fruit to plump.

3. Discard the lemon slices, and bring the mixture again to a boil. Skim the kumquats from the syrup with a slotted spoon, and put them in hot sterilized half-pint jars (see page 311). Continue to boil the syrup until it reaches 220°F on a candy thermometer, 8 to 10 minutes. Pour the boiling syrup over the kumquats, covering them well, to ¼ inch from the top of each jar. Seal at once, and refrigerate. Or fill prepared freezer jars (see page 321), leaving 1-inch head space. Cool, and freeze.

Makes 2 to 3 pints

VARIATION: *Kumquat and Ginger Preserves:* Add 1 small piece of fresh ginger to each jar of kumquat preserves before sealing. Delicious with cream cheese.

A roadside fruit stand in Florida featured a one-cent sale, making it a "must" stop for customers in 1922.

APRICOT AND ALMOND CONSERVE

◆◆◆

Serve with roast pork, ham, fowl, or game.

◆

1 pound dried apricots
⅓ cup sugar
½ cup slivered blanched almonds

◆

Put the apricots in a saucepan with water to cover and bring to a boil. Reduce the heat and simmer until tender, 10 to 12 minutes. Add the sugar and cook until a light syrup has formed, a few minutes more. Stir in the almonds. Spoon into a hot sterilized jar (see page 311) to ¼ inch from the top of the jar. Cool and refrigerate.

Makes 1 pint

STUFFED PRUNES IN SHERRY

◆◆◆

Serve as a conserve with chicken salad, ham, or turkey—or for a bite of something delicious anytime. Especially nice on the tea table or served as a dessert garnished with whipped cream. An exquisite gift idea.

◆

1 pound ready-to-eat pitted prunes
1 ½ cups walnut halves or blanched whole
    almonds
1 ½ cups sherry or Madeira

◆

Stuff each prune with a walnut or almond. Put the prunes in a jar and cover with sherry or Madeira—several days in advance of serving, if possible. Refrigerate until ready to serve.

Makes 1¼ pints

🦉 The prunes keep indefinitely when refrigerated and kept covered with the wine.

RASPBERRY, CURRANT, AND RHUBARB CONSERVE

◆◆◆

The fruits in this conserve can be changed about as desired. If you have a wealth of raspberries, for instance, use a larger quantity of them; just be careful to weigh the fruit and sugar. And take into account the natural acidity and sweetness of the fruits you combine.

3 cups raspberries
3 cups ripe red currants, stems removed
2 cups sliced deep red rhubarb
Sugar (¾ pound for each pound of fruit)
2 navel oranges
2 medium lemons
¼ cup coarsely chopped walnuts

1. Combine the raspberries, currants, and rhubarb, and weigh them. Put them in a heavy stainless steel or enamel kettle with ¾ pound of sugar for every pound of fruit.

2. Slice the oranges and lemons thin. Discard the seeds. Chop the slices rather fine in a food processor, or grind in a mill.

3. Stir the raspberry mixture to help dissolve the sugar. Add the orange and lemon mixture and stir again. Bring the fruit to a boil, reduce the heat, and simmer, stirring often, until the conserve is thick and clear and registers 222°F on a candy thermometer, 25 minutes. A spoonful of conserve poured on a plate should jell in a few minutes in the refrigerator.

4. Add the walnuts and heat thoroughly.

Black raspberries—juicy and sweet.

5. Spoon into hot sterilized half-pint jars (see page 311) to ¼ inch from the top of each jar. Cool, and refrigerate. Or spoon the conserve into prepared freezer jars (see page 321), leaving 1-inch head space. Cool, and freeze.

Makes 2 pints

PEAR AND GINGER CONSERVE

*T*he culinary use of ginger came to the South from different sources: to South Carolina from the Orient, to Virginia from England. Thus we have appreciated and used this amazing spice in many ways for a long time. In preserving if there is such a thing as "edible soul mates" (and I think there is), it is ginger and pears.

5 pounds unripe Kieffer, Bosc, or Anjou pears
⅓ cup water
10 cups sugar
3 navel oranges
2 lemons
⅓ cup finely slivered preserved ginger or
    crystallized ginger
¼ cup coarsely chopped walnuts

1. Peel, core, and coarsely chop the pears. Put them in a heavy kettle with the water and 5 cups of the sugar. Mix well, and bring to a boil. Reduce the heat and simmer 3 minutes. Allow to stand, loosely covered, overnight at room temperature for the pears to absorb the sugar.

2. Grate the peel of 1 orange and 1 lemon in a food processor with a little of the

remaining sugar, or grate them by hand. Add the peel to the pears. Add the juice from the 3 oranges and 2 lemons, and the remaining sugar. Add the ginger and mix thoroughly.

3. Bring the mixture again to a boil and cook over medium heat until the conserve is clear and the syrup is thick and registers 222°F on a candy thermometer, 25 to 30 minutes. It should jell when put on a cool plate and placed in the refrigerator. Add the nuts and heat thoroughly.

4. Spoon into hot sterilized half-pint jars (see page 311) to ¼ inch from the top of each jar, and seal at once. Cool, and refrigerate. Or spoon the conserve into prepared freezer jars (see page 321), leaving 1-inch head space. Cool, and freeze.

Makes 5 pints

ORANGE AND APPLE MINCEMEAT

◆◆◆

*T*raditionally, mincemeat was made with meat—beef, or calf or beef tongue—and an addition of fruits and spices. However, it can be all fruit. Mincemeats that omit meat are delicious and are superb in cookies, cakes, and tarts for the holiday season.

◆

3 cups chopped cored peeled tart apples (3 large apples)
1 cup golden raisins
1 cup sugar
½ cup fresh orange juice
¼ cup orange or lemon marmalade
2 teaspoons ground cinnamon
1 teaspoon ground cloves
1 tablespoon finely chopped fresh ginger, or 1 teaspoon ground ginger
½ teaspoon salt
½ cup chopped walnuts
2 tablespoons brandy or aged bourbon whiskey

◆

1. Combine all the ingredients except the walnuts and brandy or bourbon in a heavy saucepan.
2. Cook on a "flame-tamer" over medium-low heat, stirring frequently, until the ingredients are well blended, 30 to 40 minutes.
3. Add the walnuts and liquor, stir, and pour into hot sterilized jars (see page 311). Seal at once.
4. If possible, allow to ripen for 1 week before using.

Makes 1 quart

VARIATION: For mincemeat cookies or cake, add ½ to 1 cup chopped cooked pitted prunes to 1 cup of this mincemeat.

Fresh ginger is preferred to the ground ginger here. This is a delicious mincemeat and is worthy of the added expense and trouble of fresh ginger.

PEAR MINCEMEAT

◆◆◆

*U*se this for mincemeat pies, tarts, cookies, and cakes.

2 quarts firm underripe pears
3 large apples
2½ cups (1 pound) dark raisins
⅓ pound beef suet, chopped
Grated peel of 3 lemons
Juice of 3 lemons
2 cups packed light brown sugar
2 cups granulated sugar
1 pound currants
1 cup finely chopped candied orange peel
2 teaspoons ground cinnamon
2 teaspoons ground cloves
2 teaspoons ground allspice
1 teaspoon freshly grated nutmeg
1 teaspoon ground mace
1 tablespoon finely chopped fresh ginger, or
    1 teaspoon ground ginger
2 cups fresh orange juice

A 19th-century tinsel painting features a still life of almost a dozen varieties of fruit.

1. Peel, core, and chop the pears and apples. In a large pan or kettle, combine all the ingredients. Cook over medium heat until the fruit is tender and well blended, about 45 minutes. Pack in hot sterilized jars (see page 311) and seal at once.

2. Process in a water bath for 5 minutes (see page 315); or allow to cool, and freeze.

Makes 3 quarts

VARIATION: Just before using the mincemeat in baking, add ⅓ cup brandy or aged bourbon or 3 tablespoons Jamaican rum to every 3 cups mincemeat. (Or add more to taste.)

COLONIAL VIRGINIA MINCEMEAT

*M*incemeat for holiday cookies and pies—and all homemade! Yum-yum. Wonderful Christmas gifts from your kitchen. If the yield is too much for your needs, you may cut the recipe in half.

1 pound light brown sugar
2 pounds granulated sugar
2 pounds beef kidney suet (see Owl), ground
2 large lemons
2 large navel oranges
½ pound candied citron
¼ pound candied lemon peel
¼ pound candied orange peel
3 pounds seeded raisins
1 pound seedless raisins
3 pounds currants
1½ teaspoons uniodized salt
1 tablespoon ground cinnamon

1 tablespoon freshly grated nutmeg
1½ teaspoons ground mace
1 teaspoon ground ginger
½ teaspoon ground cloves
3 pounds tart apples, peeled, cored, and
    chopped
4 cups brandy
1 cup aged bourbon whiskey

1. In a large kettle, combine the brown sugar, all but 1 cup of the granulated sugar, and the suet.

2. Cut the colored peel from the lemons and oranges and grind it with 1 cup sugar in a food processor until finely grated. (Or if desired, grate the lemons and oranges by hand.) Add the peel and sugar to the suet.

3. Squeeze the juice from the lemons and oranges. Strain and add the juice to the suet.

4. Chop the citron, candied lemon peel, and candied orange peel in a processor or by hand, and add them to the suet.

5. Add both raisins and the currants, salt, spices, and apples.

6. Add the brandy and bourbon, and mix thoroughly. Do not cook.

7. Spoon the mincemeat into hot sterilized large jars (see page 311) and seal. The mincemeat will age better when stored in large amounts.

Makes 8 quarts

Ask your butcher for the suet from around the beef kidney, as free of meat as possible. Chill it and then grind it.

CHAPTER ELEVEN

CAKES, COOKIES, AND PIES

SWEET TEMPTATIONS

◆◆◆

"*T*o take the cake" is an expression that grew out of the very old Southern custom of presenting a cake to the winner of the "cake walk" dance contests. These contests were often an important part of the entertainment for big barbecues, political rallies, and social gatherings in the Deep South of long ago. It was certainly a fun dance, and gradually the name "cake walk" evolved until it became an expression for anything that was fun and easy to do. (I have named a confection in this book "Chocolate Cakewalk" because it is so easy to make and it is fun. Don't miss it.)

Considering all the wonderful things we make in our home kitchens, cookies, cakes, and pies are possibly the most amazing as we start with such simple ingredients: butter, sugar, flour, eggs, milk, and flavorings. In an hour or so they are transformed into a gorgeous two-layered cake, soft and yummy, or maybe cookies so crisp and good they could be called melt-aways because they vanish so fast.

◆◆◆

CAMILLE'S GOLDEN COINTREAU CAKE

*T*his is the cake I created when as a young woman I catered debutante parties and weddings in Louisville. It has never been published before. This cake holds a secret all to itself—it is a magical formula that will fool you. The list of ingredients at first glance seems not unlike most good sponge cakes, but there is a difference. The texture is unusually moist, tender, and diaphanous. This delicacy in contrast to the elusive, rich frosting sets the cake apart. It is a gala occasion cake. In fact, if the occasion is not gala, the cake will make it so. You'll see.

8 large eggs
1½ cups sugar
⅓ cup fresh orange juice
1 cup all-purpose flour
1½ teaspoons Cointreau
½ teaspoon vanilla extract or cognac vanilla
    (see Index)
¼ teaspoon salt
½ teaspoon cream of tartar
Cointreau Frosting or Classic Buttercream with
    Cointreau (recipes follow)

This bridal shower around 1910 is missing nothing except the perfect cake. Need I say more?

1. Preheat the oven to 325°F.
2. Separate the eggs. Put the yolks in one large mixing bowl and the whites in another large mixing bowl.
3. Beat the egg yolks with an electric mixer until they have thickened and are smooth. Beat in the sugar slowly, then continue beating until the mixture turns a lighter shade of yellow and is smooth. Add the orange juice and blend thoroughly.
4. Measure the flour, then sift it twice. Sprinkle the sifted flour over the egg yolk mixture and gently fold it in by hand with a whisk or a rubber spatula, or with the electric mixer on a very low speed. Fold in the Cointreau and vanilla.
5. Add the salt to the egg whites and beat until they begin to turn white and foamy. Add the cream of tartar, and continue to beat until the egg whites hold a stiff peak but are not dry and grainy, about 4 minutes more.
6. Fold a few spoonfuls of the egg whites into the batter to lighten it. Then add the remaining egg whites to the batter, gently folding them in.
7. Spoon the batter into a 10 x 4½-inch ungreased angel food cake pan (a tube pan with a removable bottom). The pan should be no more than three quarters full. Place the cake pan on the middle shelf of the oven and bake until a cake tester inserted into the center of the cake comes out clean, or until the cake springs back at once when lightly touched, about 1¼ hours.
8. Remove the cake from the oven, turn it upside down on the tube pan legs, and allow it to rest overnight before frosting.
9. Loosen the cake with a thin sharp knife, and unmold it. Put the cake on a plate or on a flat surface covered with wax paper or foil. Spread the frosting over the cake.

Serves 12 to 14

This cake keeps for weeks in the wintertime, and freezes beautifully any time. Even the frosting does amazingly well in the freezer, and the frozen slices are quite good served as is with coffee.

COINTREAU FROSTING

8 tablespoons (1 stick) unsalted butter, cut into pieces
3¾ cups confectioners' sugar, sifted
⅛ teaspoon salt
1 large egg yolk
6 to 8 tablespoons Cointreau, or more as needed

1. Put the butter in a large mixing bowl. Add the confectioners' sugar and salt. Beat well with an electric mixer. Add the egg yolk, then slowly add 6 tablespoons of the Cointreau. Continue to beat the frosting until it is smooth, thick, and pliable, 3 minutes. Add more Cointreau as needed; it usually takes at least 8 tablespoons. This frosting must be thick.
2. Frost the cake generously in a swirl design. Allow the frosting to firm for 30 minutes, then lift the cake to a serving platter.

CLASSIC BUTTERCREAM WITH COINTREAU

1 cup (2 sticks) unsalted butter, cut into pieces
5 large egg yolks
⅔ cup sugar
¼ teaspoon cream of tartar
⅛ teaspoon salt, or to taste
5 tablespoons cold water
3 tablespoons Cointreau

1. Cream the butter until it is light and smooth. Set aside.
2. Beat the egg yolks with an electric mixer until they have doubled in bulk, 3 minutes.
3. Combine the sugar, cream of tartar, salt, and water in a heavy saucepan, bring to a boil, and cook over medium heat until the syrup spins a thread when it falls from a wooden spoon or until a candy thermometer registers 235° to 236°F. (If the syrup is not cooked to this point, the buttercream will never firm up.)
4. Immediately pour the hot syrup in a steady stream into the egg yolks, beating constantly. Continue to beat until the mixture has cooled, 15 to 20 minutes.
5. Add the butter to the yolk mixture a tablespoonful at a time. If the frosting should look curdled while you are adding the butter, place the frosting over hot (not boiling) water and beat vigorously until it is smooth again. Add the Cointreau and mix thoroughly. If necessary, chill the frosting until it has a good spreading consistency, 35 to 45 minutes.
6. Frost the cake generously in a beautiful swirling design, and then keep the cake refrigerated.

SOUTH CAROLINA COUNTRY JAM CAKE

This jam cake is a good traveler anytime, as it keeps well and is firm enough to transport. It is a great "woodsy" cake—"woodsy" being the name of our picnic basket. Oh, how I love to cook food for the "woodsy"—picnics in the woods, picnics on a boat, picnics by the side of the road.

3⅓ cups sifted all-purpose flour
¼ teaspoon baking soda
2½ teaspoons baking powder
1 teaspoon salt
1½ teaspoons ground cinnamon
¾ teaspoon ground cloves
1 teaspoon ground allspice
1 teaspoon freshly grated nutmeg
1 cup (2 sticks) butter, cut into pieces
2 cups sugar
4 large eggs
1 cup buttermilk or sour cream
1 cup raspberry or blackberry preserves
1 cup chopped pecans or walnuts
Creamy Caramel Frosting (recipe follows)

The perfect picnic spot for a jam cake—it's got woods and water.

1. Preheat the oven to 350°F.
2. Combine the sifted flour with the baking soda, baking powder, salt, and spices in a large bowl, and sift again. Set aside.
3. Cream the butter and sugar thoroughly with an electric mixer. Add the eggs, and beat until the mixture falls in ribbons from a spoon. It should be smooth and silky looking like mayonnaise.
4. Add the flour mixture in batches, alternating with the buttermilk or sour cream, beating it in by hand with a rubber spatula or a whisk. Blend in the jam and nuts and mix thoroughly.
5. Spoon the batter into 2 greased and lightly floured 9-inch cake pans. The pans should be no more than three quarters full. Place the pans on the middle shelf of the oven and bake until a skewer or cake tester inserted into the center of the cake comes out clean, 35 minutes.
6. Run a thin knife around the edges of the pans to loosen the cake. Turn it out onto a cake rack, and allow it to cool before you frost it.
7. Spread the top of 1 cake layer with warm Creamy Caramel Frosting. Center the second layer on top of the first. Frost the top and sides of the cake with the remaining frosting.

Serves 12 to 16

This cake was usually made in country kitchens with blackberry jam—the kind with the seeds. The nuts, of course, can be omitted.

CREAMY CARAMEL FROSTING

2¾ cups light brown sugar
1 cup heavy or whipping cream
1 tablespoon light corn syrup
Pinch of salt
4 tablespoons (½ stick) butter
2 teaspoons vanilla extract or cognac vanilla (see Index)

Combine the sugar, cream, corn syrup, and salt in a heavy saucepan. Stir until smooth and well mixed. Add the butter. Bring to a boil and cook over low heat until the mixture reaches 234°F on a candy thermometer for a soft frosting or 236°F for a firmer frosting, or the syrup forms a soft ball when dropped into cold water, 20 to 30 minutes. Remove from the heat and stir in the vanilla. Beat until creamy, 10 minutes.

Watch the frosting carefully as you beat it, and use it before it loses all of its gloss. If it should turn dull and harden too much to spread, add a bit of cream or boiling water and mix quickly.

QUEEN ANNE'S CAKE

*T*he flower we call Queen Anne's Lace, which grows along the roadside in the summer, is wild carrot. Cultivated garden carrots have been a time-honored ingredient in cakes for many decades. They make a moist cake, and they blend beautifully with spices. Strange as it may seem, a light touch of spice is delightful in hot weather and is most pleasant with summer fruit or a tall glass of iced tea. Queen Anne's Cake is also a boon for weddings, as it is firm enough to withstand garlands of frosting and can be made ahead.

---

1 cup (2 sticks) butter, cut into pieces
2 cups sugar
4 large eggs
2 cups grated carrots (about 6 carrots grated in a food processor)
2 cups sifted all-purpose flour
2 teaspoons ground cinnamon
¼ teaspoon ground ginger
1 teaspoon baking soda
1 teaspoon salt
1 teaspoon vanilla extract or cognac vanilla (see Index)
Queen Anne's Frosting (recipe follows)

---

1. Preheat the oven to 350°F.

2. Cream the butter and sugar thoroughly with an electric mixer. Add the eggs, and beat until the mixture is smooth and silky looking like mayonnaise and falls in ribbons from the spoon. Beat in the grated carrots.

3. Combine the flour with the cinnamon, ginger, baking soda, and salt. Sift again, and fold into the carrot mixture by hand with a rubber spatula or a whisk. Add the vanilla and mix well.

4. Spoon the batter into 2 greased and lightly floured 9-inch cake pans. The pans should be no more than three quarters full. Place the pans on the middle shelf of the oven and bake until the cake springs back at once when lightly touched, 30 to 35 minutes.

5. Cool the cake for about 5 minutes, then unmold it onto a cake rack and let it cool completely. Cakes containing ginger often split if they are removed from the pan while steaming hot.

6. Spread the top of 1 cake layer with the Queen Anne's Frosting. Center the second layer over the first. Frost the top and sides of the cake with the remaining frosting.

Serves 16

VARIATIONS: *Queen Anne's Spiced Cake:* Add ½ teaspoon ground allspice, ½ teaspoon ground mace or freshly grated nutmeg, and ¼ teaspoon ground cloves. Omit the ginger. Frost with Queen Anne's Frosting.

Use up to 1½ teaspoons ground ginger and 1 tablespoon brandy in the batter for a superb ginger cake. Serve with whipped cream.

QUEEN ANNE'S FROSTING

8 tablespoons (1 stick) butter, at room temperature
8 ounces cream cheese, at room temperature
2¾ cups sifted confectioners' sugar
Tiny pinch of salt
1 teaspoon vanilla extract or cognac vanilla (see Index)

---

1. Put the butter and cheese in the bowl of a food processor or electric mixer. Process until the mixture is smooth and free of lumps. Add the confectioners' sugar, salt, and vanilla. Process until smooth.

2. Chill until the frosting has a good spreading consistency, about 1 hour.

VARIATION: A little lemon juice may be added to the frosting if desired.

WHITE TRILLIUM CAKE

❖❖❖

*T*his cake was known in Louisville as Jenny Benedict's Soufflé Cake. Jenny Benedict was famous for the sandwiches, cakes, and ice creams that she served at her restaurant and in catering debutante parties and weddings in the early days of the twentieth century. We are told that Miss Benedict was very partial to flavoring her cakes with rum.

❖

3 cups sifted all-purpose flour
2½ teaspoons baking powder
½ teaspoon salt
1 cup (2 sticks) butter, cut into pieces
2 cups sugar
1 tablespoon milk
1 cup water
1 teaspoon vanilla extract
6 large egg whites
Butter Frosting (recipe follows)

❖

1. Preheat the oven to 350°F.
2. Combine the sifted flour with the baking powder and salt, and sift again. Set aside.
3. Cream the butter and sugar thoroughly with an electric mixer. Add the milk and beat hard. (The mixture will become smoother.)
4. Add the flour mixture to the butter and sugar in batches, alternating with the water, beating it in by hand with a rubber spatula or a whisk. Add the vanilla and mix well.
5. Beat the egg whites until they hold a stiff peak but are not dry and grainy. Gently fold them into the batter.
6. Spoon the batter into 2 greased and lightly floured or wax-paper-lined 9-inch cake pans. Place the pans on the middle shelf of the oven and bake until the layers spring back at once when lightly touched, 30 to 35 minutes.
7. Remove the pans from the oven and allow them to rest a few minutes. Then turn them out onto cake racks and let them cool completely.
8. Spread the top of 1 cake layer with Butter Frosting. Center the second layer on top of the first. Frost the top and sides of the cake with the remaining frosting. Allow

The bride cuts the cake, but where's the groom? He must take the first bite!

the cake to mellow a few hours before serving.

Serves 8 to 10

🦉 The water in the cake may surprise you, but water makes a lighter white cake than milk.

❖

BUTTER FROSTING

❖

¾ cup (1½ sticks) butter, cut into pieces
2¾ cups confectioners' sugar, sifted
1 to 2½ tablespoons heavy or whipping cream,
*   warmed*
1½ teaspoons vanilla extract, cognac vanilla
*   (see Index), or rum*

❖

Cream the butter and sugar together in a processsor or with an electric mixer. Add the cream gradually, stirring until the frosting has a good spreading consistency. Stir in your choice of flavoring.

SOUTHERN HEIRLOOM CAKE

◆◆

*T*his yellow butter cake is one of the finest of our Southern cakes. It has a smooth, close-grained texture and an exquisite flavor. The flavor, of course, will vary with the liquid that is chosen, but this is what makes baking interesting. One can make this cake quite plain or very fancy—the variations are endless. Fresh coconut with orange filling is a happy Christmas choice.

The Brent family celebrates Christmas in Pensacola, Florida, around 1900. On the table there appear to be the remnants of a layer cake not unlike the Heirloom Cake featured here. I'm surprised there's any left at all.

◆

1 cup (2 sticks) butter, cut into pieces
2 cups sugar
4 large eggs, separated
2⅔ cups sifted all-purpose flour
2 teaspoons baking powder
½ teaspoon salt
1 cup milk, heavy or whipping cream, or sour
    cream
2 teaspoons vanilla extract or cognac vanilla
    (see Index)
Orange Filling (for layers; recipe follows)
Rich Chocolate Frosting (see page 348) or
    Seven-Minute Frosting (recipe follows)
2 cups freshly grated coconut (2 whole
    coconuts), if using the Seven-Minute
    Frosting
2 oranges, for garnish

◆

1. Preheat the oven to 350°F.
2. Grease and dust with flour then line with wax paper 2 round or square 9-inch cake pans, or one 8-inch springform pan, or an 8 x 12-inch rectangular pan.
3. Cream the butter and sugar thoroughly with an electric mixer. Add the egg yolks, and beat hard until the mixture is smooth and looks like mayonnaise. The sugar crystals should be almost dissolved.
4. Combine the sifted flour with the baking powder and salt, and sift again. Add this to the egg mixture alternately with the milk or cream, folding it in by hand.
5. Beat the egg whites until they are stiff but not dry and grainy. Fold them into the batter. Add the vanilla, and give the batter several hard strokes with a rubber spatula to rid it of air bubbles.
6. Fill the pan(s) not more than three-quarters full with the batter. Place the pan(s) on the middle shelf of the oven and bake until the cake springs back at once when lightly touched, about 35 minutes. The timing varies with the size of the pan.
7. Let the cake sit for 5 minutes, then remove it from the pan(s) and cool thoroughly on a wire rack.
8. If you are making a layer cake, spread the top of 1 cake layer with the Orange Filling. Center the second layer on top of the first. Frost the top and sides of either version of the cake with Rich Chocolate or Seven-Minute Frosting. Press coconut generously into the Seven-Minute frosting. To serve, place the cake on a cake stand and garnish around the bottom with orange sections.
Serves 16

🦉 For freshly grated coconut, crack a coconut and with a sharp knife peel off the brown skin from the meat. Grate the coconut meat in a food processor. Refrigerate for no more than 2 days.

ORANGE FILLING

2 tablespoons cornstarch
½ cup sugar
Tiny pinch of salt
½ cup fresh orange juice
1 tablespoon fresh lemon juice
1 tablespoon grated orange peel
2 large egg yolks
3 tablespoons butter

1. Mix the cornstarch, sugar, and salt in a heavy saucepan or in the top of a double boiler. Add the orange and lemon juices and the orange peel. Bring slowly to a boil, stirring with a whisk to keep the sauce from lumping, until the mixture has thickened and is clear, 3 to 4 minutes. Remove the pan from the heat and let it stand a few minutes.

2. Stir in the egg yolks and place the pan in the bottom of the double boiler over hot water. Cook gently until thick. Remove the pan from the heat and stir in the butter. Cool, then refrigerate until cold.

3. Spread the filling between layers of cake.

SEVEN-MINUTE FROSTING

3 large egg whites
⅔ cup superfine sugar
⅛ teaspoon salt
5 tablespoons light corn syrup
1 teaspoon vanilla extract or cognac vanilla (see Index)

In a stainless steel pan set in a larger pan of hot water, or in the top of a double boiler, combine the egg whites, sugar, salt, and corn syrup. Beat the mixture constantly over the quietly boiling water with an electric mixer or a rotary beater until the whites hold a stiff peak. Remove from the heat and beat in the vanilla.

LUSCIOUS CHOCOLATE CAKE

*T*here could be only one name for this cake and that is luscious. It is a lovely chocolate sponge cake, and one of the best of its genre. The texture is so soft and moist, one would think it was made with butter. I wish I had a recording of the many telephone calls I have received about this cake. One letter writer said, "I ate all I could, but I did not want to leave it, so I just sat down beside it."

Although this cake has always been wonderful, it was made truly luscious the day I added a thin layer of apricot preserves under the frosting.

4 ounces unsweetened chocolate
1 cup milk
5 large eggs, separated
2 cups sugar
1 cup all-purpose flour, sifted
1 teaspoon baking powder
Tiny pinch of salt
1½ teaspoons cognac vanilla (see Index)

⅓ cup apricot preserves
Rich Chocolate Frosting (recipe follows)

1. Preheat the oven to 350°F.
2. Grease and dust with flour or line with foil two 9-inch round cake pans.
3. Combine the chocolate and the

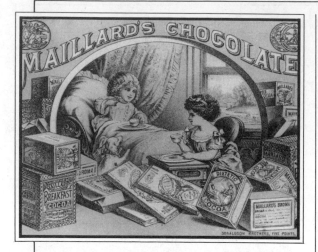

milk in the top of a double boiler, and heat over hot water until the chocolate has melted. Beat until smooth. Remove from the heat and allow to cool down just a bit.

4. While the chocolate mixture is cooling, beat the egg yolks and sugar thoroughly with an electric mixer. (The sugar will remain granular.) Add the chocolate mixture and beat very hard until the sugar is no longer granular. Fold the flour, baking powder, salt, and vanilla into the chocolate mixture by hand.

5. Beat the egg whites until they are stiff but not dry and grainy. Fold them into the chocolate batter.

6. Spoon the batter into the prepared pans. The pans should be no more than three quarters full. Bake until the cake springs back at once when lightly touched, about 35 minutes.

7. Invert the cakes onto racks or onto a wooden board covered with wax paper. Allow the cakes to cool completely before frosting.

8. Spread 1 cake layer with the apricot preserves. Cover the preserves with a coating of the chocolate frosting. Center the second layer on top of the first. Frost the top and sides of the cake lavishly with the remaining frosting. The frosting must be thick.

Serves 16

VARIATIONS: This makes 2 cakes from 1 recipe of Luscious Chocolate Cake: Bake the cake in two 8-inch springform pans. Make a double batch of Rich Chocolate Frosting. When the cakes have cooled, place them on large sheets of wax paper or foil on a flat surface. Slice the cakes in half horizontally with a long, sharp knife. Spread half of the apricot preserves on the bottom layer of each cake. Cover each cake with the second layer and frost them heavily in a swirl design. Place the cakes on platters, and garnish with glazed apricots. Each cake serves 8.

Luscious Chocolate Rum Cake: Bake the cake layers. Make the Rich Chocolate Frosting, adding ¼ cup Jamaican rum. Blend it in thoroughly, then add boiling water a scant tablespoon at a time until the frosting is of good spreading consistency. Spread one cake layer with the apricot preserves. Spread some of the frosting over the preserves. Put the second layer on top, and frost the sides and top of the cake. Garnish the top of the cake with thin slivers of glazed apricots if they are available. Very attractive, indeed, and apricots are delicious with chocolate and rum. You'll see.

RICH CHOCOLATE FROSTING

4 ounces unsweetened chocolate
8 tablespoons (1 stick) butter
2¾ cups confectioners' sugar
Tiny pinch of salt
1 teaspoon vanilla extract or cognac vanilla (see Index), or more to taste
5 tablespoons boiling water, or as needed

Melt the chocolate and the butter in a double boiler over hot water. Sift the powdered sugar with the salt into a large mixing bowl. Blend in the chocolate mixture and the vanilla. Add boiling water a tablespoon at a time, beating constantly, until the frosting is smooth, pliable, but still very thick. Cool a bit before frosting the cake.

If necessary, thin the frosting a bit with boiling water.

If the frosting becomes dull looking, a little boiling water will restore its sheen.

If the frosting is too thin, beat it extremely hard with an electric mixer—it will thicken up.

THE CHOCOLATE FINALE CAKE

*O*nce you have made this little chocolate cake, you will be able to turn it out with the greatest ease. It is incredibly rich, but served in small wedges with a bit of whipped cream, it is incredibly delicious.

A thin slice is especially good with raspberry or apricot sherbet, or with fresh strawberries or raspberries.

¾ cup sugar
4 large eggs, separated
6 ounces German sweet chocolate
¾ cup (1½ sticks) butter
5 level tablespoons all-purpose or cake flour, sifted
6 tablespoons finely grated almonds, pecans, or hazelnuts
Tiny pinch of salt
1 teaspoon vanilla extract or cognac vanilla (see Index)
The Chocolate Finale Frosting (recipe follows)
Slivered or grated almonds, for garnish (optional)

1. Preheat the oven to 350°F.
2. Beat the sugar and the egg yolks with an electric mixer until they are creamy yellow.
3. Melt the chocolate and butter in a double boiler over simmering water. Remove from the heat and stir until smooth but still warm. Add to the egg yolk mixture and beat well.
4. Fold the flour and grated nuts into the batter by hand.
5. Beat the egg whites until they are stiff but not dry and grainy. Fold them into the batter, and add the salt and vanilla.
6. Spoon the batter into an 8-inch springform pan that has been greased and dusted with flour and lined with foil. The pan should be no more than three quarters full. Bake until the outside is solid and the center still a bit creamy when tested with a knife, about 35 minutes.
7. Allow the cake to cool before turning it out onto a rack.

In 1927, when you couldn't do the baking yourself, you could get commercially baked goods delivered right to your door.

8. Spread the frosting over the cake, covering the top and sides well. Sprinkle on the nuts. Place the cake in the refrigerator so the frosting can stiffen, 1 hour, if you can wait that long.
Serves 6

The cake will fall a bit as it cools, and the center should remain a bit creamy.

THE CHOCOLATE FINALE FROSTING

5 ounces dark sweet or semisweet chocolate
2 tablespoons heavy or whipping cream
3 tablespoons butter
1 teaspoon cognac vanilla (see Index) or vanilla extract

Heat the chocolate and cream in a double boiler and mix gently until smooth. Remove from the heat and stir in the butter and vanilla.

CLASSIC CHOCOLATE BUTTER CAKE

*T*his just may be the best and most straightforward chocolate butter layer cake I know. The batter holds amazingly well. If for some reason you want to bake only half the cake, or if you are delayed in baking it, cover the batter well with plastic wrap, refrigerate, and bake the next day.

4 ounces unsweetened chocolate
2 cups sifted all-purpose flour
2 teaspoons baking powder
½ teaspoon salt
8 tablespoons (1 stick) butter, cut into pieces
2 cups sugar
2 extra-large eggs or 3 medium eggs, separated
1¼ cups milk
1 teaspoon vanilla extract or cognac vanilla (see Index)
Double recipe The Chocolate Finale Frosting (see page 349)

1. Preheat the oven to 350°F.
2. Melt the chocolate in a double boiler over simmering water. Set aside but keep warm.
3. Combine the sifted flour with the baking powder and salt, and sift again. Set aside.
4. Cream the butter and sugar thoroughly with an electric mixer. Add the egg yolks, and beat until the mixture falls in ribbons from a spoon. It should be smooth and silky looking like mayonnaise. Add the melted chocolate and blend thoroughly.
5. Add the flour mixture in batches, alternating with the milk. Beat it in by hand with a rubber spatula or a whisk. Blend in the vanilla.
6. Beat the egg whites until they hold a stiff peak but are not dry and grainy. Gently fold them into the chocolate batter.
7. Spoon the batter into 2 greased and lightly floured or wax-paper-lined 9-inch cake pans. The pans should be no more than three quarters full. Place the pans on the middle shelf of the oven and bake until the cake springs back at once when lightly touched, 30 to 35 minutes. A cake tester or small skewer inserted in the middle should come out clean.
8. Remove the cakes from the oven and allow them to cool about 3 minutes. Run a thin knife around the edges of the pans to loosen the cakes, and turn them out onto a cake rack. Cool completely before frosting.

Serves 14

🦉 A lighter-textured cake will be achieved if the flour is folded in by hand. In making larger cakes by machine, take care to not overbeat when adding the flour.

CHOCOLATE CAKEWALK

*T*his moist cake has a rich chocolate flavor seldom surpassed—the proportions must be a magic blend. It is an elegant dessert very much like a baked chocolate mousse. It is easy to prepare and can be made 4 to 6 days ahead and kept (unfrosted) under refrigeration, covered with foil.

4 ounces dark sweet chocolate
½ cup sugar
8 tablespoons (1 stick) butter
¼ cup water
2 large eggs
1 teaspoon cognac vanilla (see Index) or
     vanilla extract, or 2 teaspoons brandy or
     cognac
2 tablespoons grated walnuts, pecans, or
     hazelnuts (optional)
Cakewalk Frosting (recipe follows)

1. Preheat the oven to 350°F.

2. Combine the chocolate, sugar, butter, and water in a double boiler and heat over hot water. Stir gently until the sugar has almost dissolved. Remove the pan from the heat and beat in the eggs with an electric mixer. Add the vanilla or brandy, and nuts if desired. Mix well.

3. Spoon the mixture into a 6-inch springform pan that has been greased and dusted with flour or lined with foil, or a 1-quart charlotte mold that has been greased and lined with foil. The pan or mold should be no more than three quarters full. Place the pan on the middle shelf of the oven and bake 30 to 35 minutes. The cake will crack on the top when it is done, but it will be soft in the center.

4. Cool the cake for 1 hour. Cover it with foil and refrigerate, unfrosted, for 24 hours before eating. (It will keep up to 1 week.) Coat the top and sides with Cakewalk Frosting. This cake is very rich, so it should be cut and served in small pieces.

Serves 6

VARIATIONS: Frost the cake with 1 cup heavy or whipping cream that has been whipped and flavored to taste with cognac or vanilla. Garnish with chocolate shavings.

Spread the top of the cake with 2 tablespoons raspberry preserves before frosting with whipped cream.

Or serve the cake as is in wedges with a spoonful of whipped cream.

CAKEWALK FROSTING

6 ounces dark sweet chocolate
5 tablespoons heavy or whipping cream
1½ teaspoons cognac vanilla (see Index) or
     vanilla extract

Heat the chocolate and cream in a double boiler over simmering water. When the chocolate has melted, blend until smooth. Remove the pan from the heat and add the vanilla. Blend thoroughly. Place the frosting in the refrigerator to thicken, 30 minutes. When the frosting has cooled, beat it thoroughly.

AN ESPECIALLY GOOD CHOCOLATE POUND CAKE

*T*his is by far the best chocolate pound cake I have ever tasted, and it keeps for days and days when enclosed in an airtight plastic or tin box.

3 cups sifted all-purpose flour
1½ teaspoons baking powder
½ teaspoon salt
4 ounces unsweetened chocolate
¼ cup strong coffee
1 cup (2 sticks) butter, cut into pieces
3 cups sugar
5 large eggs

⅔ cup heavy or whipping cream
1½ teaspoons vanilla extract or cognac vanilla
     (see Index)
2 tablespoons brandy or cognac

1. Preheat the oven to 300°F.
2. Combine the sifted flour with the

baking powder and salt, and sift again. Set aside.

3. Heat the chocolate and coffee in a double boiler over simmering water. As the chocolate melts, stir until it is smooth. Set it aside to cool.

4. Cream the butter and sugar thoroughly with an electric mixer. The mixture will remain somewhat grainy. Add the eggs, and beat hard until the mixture falls in ribbons from a spoon. It should be smooth and silky looking like mayonnaise.

5. Add the flour in batches, alternating with the chocolate and the cream. Blend in the vanilla and brandy or cognac. If the batter should look a little curdled, blend in 2 or 3 tablespoons extra flour.

6. Spoon the batter into 2 greased and lightly floured 8 x 4 x 3-inch loaf pans or one 10-inch tube pan lined with foil and lightly buttered, filling the pans not more than three-quarters full. Place the pans on the middle shelf of the oven and bake until the cake springs back at once when lightly touched, 1½ to 1¾ hours.

7. Remove the cake from the oven and allow it to rest in the pan before unmolding 20 to 30 minutes. Cool the cake thoroughly before slicing. Store in an airtight plastic or tin box, or wrap in foil and freeze.

Serves 10 to 12

If at any time the cake seems to be getting too brown while baking, cover it loosely with foil and reduce the heat. This means your oven temperature is over 300°F.

DELECTABLE SOUR CREAM POUND CAKE

*T*his is a soft, velvety pound cake that keeps better than any pound cake I know. It has a delicious crunchy top that comes from being baked in low heat—not from an overload of sugar. This cake is just as delicious when the sugar is cut to 2¾ cups, which makes it especially delightful for breakfast or tea with a dish of strawberries. Bake it both ways. You will love this cake.

3 cups sifted all-purpose flour
¼ teaspoon baking soda
¼ teaspoon salt

1 cup (2 sticks) butter, cut into pieces
3 cups sugar (2¾ cups for cakes to be served with fruit)
6 large eggs, separated
1 cup sour cream
1½ teaspoons vanilla extract or cognac vanilla (see Index), or ⅔ teaspoon ground mace

1. Preheat the oven to 325°F.

2. Combine the sifted flour with the baking soda and salt, and sift again. Set aside.

3. Cream the butter and sugar thoroughly with an electric mixer. Add the egg yolks, and beat hard until you have a fairly smooth mixture. This will not "ribbon" with just the yolks.

Coffee cakes proudly displayed in 1922 show the successful results of cooking in the Louisville Gas & Electric Company's new ovens.

4. Add the flour mixture in batches, alternating with the sour cream, blending by hand with a rubber spatula or a whisk. Blend in the vanilla or mace.

5. Beat the egg whites until they hold a stiff peak but are not dry and grainy. Gently fold them into the cake batter.

6. Spoon the batter into a greased and lightly floured heavy 9- or 10-inch tube pan, or two 8 x 4 x 3-inch loaf pans, filling the pans not more than three-quarters full. Bake until the cake springs back at once when lightly touched, about 1 hour and 15 to 20 minutes (this will vary with the pans used). A cake tester or skewer inserted into the cake should come out clean. Remove the cake from the oven and allow it to rest 5 minutes.

7. Run a thin knife around the edges of the pan to loosen the cake, and unmold it onto a rack. Turn the cake right side up to cool. Store in a tightly closed plastic or tin box.

Serves 10 to 15

OLD-FASHIONED YELLOW PUDDING CAKE

*T*his is an old-fashioned pudding cake that should never be allowed to go out-of-date. It is easy to prepare with an electric mixer.

My mother served it during the cold days of winter with sliced bananas and rich Old Seelbach House Lemon Sauce. In the summer, green seedless grapes should be added to the bananas. These are family desserts of which happy memories are made.

8 tablespoons (1 stick) butter, cut into pieces
1 cup sugar
2 large eggs, at room temperature
1 ¾ cups sifted all-purpose flour
1 ¾ teaspoons baking powder
¼ teaspoon salt
½ cup milk
1 teaspoon vanilla extract or cognac vanilla
(see Index)
Old Seelbach House Lemon Sauce (recipe
follows)

1. Preheat the oven to 350°F.

2. Cream the butter and sugar thoroughly with an electric mixer. Add the eggs, and beat until the mixture falls in ribbons from a wooden spoon. It should be smooth and silky looking like mayonnaise.

3. Combine the sifted flour with the baking powder and salt. Add this to the egg mixture in batches, alternating with the milk. A mixer should be on a very low speed. Or blend it in by hand with a whisk (which is best). Stir in the vanilla.

4. Spoon the batter into an 8- or 9-inch springform pan or a 1½-quart round pudding pan that has been greased and dusted with flour. Place the pan on the middle shelf of the oven, and bake until the cake springs back at once when lightly touched, about 35 minutes.

5. Cut into wedges and serve warm with lemon sauce.

Serves 6

OLD SEELBACH HOUSE LEMON SAUCE

½ cup sugar
Slivered peel from ½ lemon
1 tablespoon cornstarch or arrowroot
¼ teaspoon salt
1 cup water
2 large egg yolks
3 tablespoons fresh lemon juice, or as needed
2 tablespoons butter

The ingredients and recipe for a gold cake as taught in the home economics class at the Rabun Gap Industrial School, Georgia, 1903, don't seem to take into account the need for the baking pan size or the oven heat.

1. Combine the sugar and slivered lemon peel in a food processor and twirl until the lemon peel is grated fine. Add the cornstarch or arrowroot and salt and process a second or two more. Add the water and process another 20 seconds.

2. Pour the mixture into an enamel or stainless steel very heavy saucepan. Boil over medium heat until the sauce is clear and thick enough to coat a wooden spoon, about 5 to 6 minutes. Remove the pan from the heat and allow the sauce to cool down slightly.

3. Whisk the egg yolks and lemon juice into the sauce. Return it to the stove and cook over medium heat while continuing to whisk until the yolks have thickened the sauce a little, 3 minutes.

4. Add the butter to the sauce. Blend it in by whisking in 1 direction. Taste and add more lemon if desired.

Makes about 1¼ cups sauce

◆

PINEAPPLE UPSIDE-DOWN CAKE

Old-Fashioned Yellow Pudding Cake batter
5 tablespoons butter, melted
1 cup packed light brown sugar
1 can (8 ounces) unsweetened pineapple slices,
     drained
9 cooked pitted prunes (optional)

◆

1. Preheat the oven to 350°F.

2. Prepare the cake batter through step 3, and set it aside.

3. Butter a 9-inch square cake pan, and then pour the melted butter into the pan. Sprinkle the brown sugar evenly over the melted butter. Fit the pineapple slices in an attractive pattern over the brown sugar. If you like, fill each pineapple ring with a prune.

4. Carefully pour the cake batter over the fruit. The pan should be no more than three quarters full. Place the pan on the middle shelf of the oven, and bake until the cake springs back at once when lightly touched, about 45 minutes.

5. Remove the cake from the oven and let it rest for 5 minutes. Then loosen the edges with a sharp knife, put a plate over the cake pan, and invert the cake onto the plate.

6. Serve warm, cut into wedges with lemon sauce spooned over.

Serves 6

UPSIDE-DOWN FRUIT PUDDING

◆◆◆

*T*his fruit tart is the original of the upside-down Southern puddings we love for informal meals. This is a beautiful batter, moist and flavorful, and you can have many variations using the different fruits appropriate to each season of the year.

CARAMEL AND FRUIT

1 cup sugar
¼ teaspoon cream of tartar
⅓ cup water
3 tablespoons butter
1 pound fruit, such as apples, pears, peaches,
    plums, fresh apricots, cooked prunes,
    cooked dried apricots, or fresh or canned
    pineapple

BATTER

8 tablespoons (1 stick) butter, cut into pieces
½ cup sugar
2 large eggs
1 teaspoon vanilla extract or cognac vanilla
    (see Index)
¾ cup minus 1 tablespoon (11 tablespoons)
    sifted all-purpose flour
½ teaspoon baking powder

1. Preheat the oven to 350°F.
2. Prepare the caramel: Combine the sugar, cream of tartar, and water in a skillet and cook over medium-high heat until it turns to a light caramel, 2 to 3 minutes. Pour at once into a 9-inch enameled iron skillet or a warmed 1½-quart glass baking dish. Tilt the skillet or dish to distribute the caramel evenly over the bottom. Dot the caramel with the butter.
3. Slice the chosen fruit and place it attractively over the butter and caramel

The best fruit puddings start with the freshest fruit.

coating. Set aside.
4. Prepare the batter: Cream the butter and sugar together with an electric mixer. Add the eggs one at a time, beating hard after each addition and continuing to beat until the mixture falls in ribbons from a wooden spoon. It should be smooth and silky looking like mayonnaise. Add the vanilla.
5. Sift the flour with the baking powder. Gently fold the flour into the egg mixture with a rubber spatula or a whisk. Spoon the batter over the fruit in the prepared pan. The pan should be no more than three quarters full. Place the pan on the middle shelf of the oven and bake 5 minutes. Lower the heat to 325°F and bake until the batter springs back at once when lightly touched, about 30 minutes.
6. To unmold, cover the pan with a serving plate, and invert. Serve warm.
Serves 4 to 6

YELLOW SPONGE CAKE ROLL

*O*f all the batters for sponge rolls, this one is special. It is very versatile and can be an excellent breakfast roll with jelly, or a fancy dessert. It must be made with soft wheat flour for the texture to be close-grained and soft.

6 large eggs, at room temperature
¾ cup sugar
1 cup twice-sifted soft wheat or cake flour
¼ teaspoon salt
Grated peel of ½ lemon

½ teaspoon vanilla extract or cognac vanilla
    (see Index)
Lemon Buttercream (recipe follows)
Confectioners' sugar, for garnish

Haussner's Restaurant in Baltimore, Maryland, 1949, where the variety of cakes can be matched only by the variety of artwork.

1. Preheat the oven to 375°F.

2. Line a 10½ x 15½ x 1-inch baking sheet with foil. Grease it very lightly, and set aside.

3. Combine the eggs and sugar and beat with an electric mixer until the mixture falls in ribbons from a spoon. It should be smooth and silky looking like mayonnaise.

4. Combine the flour, salt, lemon peel, and vanilla in a small bowl. Gently but thoroughly fold this into the egg mixture by hand.

5. Pour the batter into the prepared pan in an even layer. The pan should be no more than three quarters full. Place the pan on the middle shelf of the oven. Prop the oven door slightly open with a knife during the entire baking period of 15 minutes. When a cake tester or skewer inserted into the cake comes out clean, the roll is done.

6. Immediately cover the cake with a clean cloth or waxed paper. Invert it and lay the cake on a flat surface. Cut off the brown edges, as they will keep the cake from rolling well. Use the towel or waxed paper to help roll up the cake, starting from the short side of the cake, and set it aside to cool.

7. When the cake is thoroughly cooled, unroll it and spread one side with Lemon Buttercream. Roll it up again, put it seam side down on a serving plate, and sprinkle the top of the roll with sifted confectioners' sugar.

Serves 6 to 8

This sponge roll may be cut into strips and used as you would ladyfingers.

Lemon peel may be grated in a food processor with the sugar in any recipe that calls for both.

LEMON BUTTERCREAM

½ cup plus 2 tablespoons sugar
¼ cup water
⅛ teaspoon cream of tartar
5 large egg yolks
1 cup (2 sticks) butter, cut into pieces
3 tablespoons fresh lemon juice

1. Combine the sugar, water, and cream of tartar in a heavy saucepan. Bring to a boil and cook over medium-high heat until it reaches 238°F on a candy thermometer, or until the syrup spins a thread when lifted with a spoon, about 8 minutes.

2. Meanwhile, beat the egg yolks with an electric mixer until they are light and have changed to a paler yellow.

3. Pour the sugar syrup into the egg yolks, beating constantly. Continue beating until the mixture has cooled, 15 minutes.

4. Cream the butter and blend it thoroughly with the egg yolk mixture. Add the lemon juice, and mix well.

VARIATIONS FOR FILLING: *Apricot Preserves and Almonds:* Spread the sponge roll with apricot preserves. Sprinkle with a few slivered blanched almonds. Roll as directed.

Seasoned Whipped Cream and Fresh Fruit: Spread the sponge roll with sweetened whipped cream and cover with strawberries, raspberries, sliced nectarines and kiwi fruit, or sliced fresh peaches. Roll as directed.

Old-Fashioned Jelly Roll: Spread the sponge roll with currant, apple, raspberry, or strawberry jelly. Roll as directed. Great for breakfast, lunch, or supper. A divine jelly roll is always welcome at a tailgate party, in the picnic basket, or for an after-the-concert party.

WINTER NUT CAKE

❖❖

*F*or this heirloom cake we use hickory nuts—a nut indigenous to the Southern states, with an exceptionally delicious and unique flavor. Hickory nuts are wild pecans, so the cultivated pecans are closest to that flavor, but walnuts work fine too. The cake is usually made with a caramel frosting, but it can also be made in loaf pans and sprinkled with confectioners' sugar before serving.

2½ cups all-purpose flour
2 teaspoons baking powder
¼ teaspoon salt
1 cup (2 sticks) butter, cut into pieces
2 cups sugar
4 large eggs, separated
¾ cup milk
1½ cups chopped hickory nuts, pecans, or
*   walnuts*
1 teaspoon vanilla extract or cognac vanilla
*   (see Index)*
Creamy Caramel Frosting (see page 343)

1. Preheat the oven to 350°F.
2. Measure the flour and sift it into a bowl. Add the baking powder and salt, and sift again. Set aside.
3. Cream the butter and sugar thoroughly with an electric mixer. Add the egg yolks, and beat hard until the mixture turns a lighter shade of yellow and is smooth.
4. Add the flour in batches, alternating with the milk, beating it in by hand with a rubber spatula or a whisk. Fold in the nuts and vanilla.

5. Beat the egg whites until they hold a stiff peak but are not dry and grainy. Fold a few spoonfuls into the batter to lighten it, then add the remaining egg whites.
6. Spoon the batter into 2 lightly greased and floured or wax-paper-lined 9-inch cake pans or two 8 x 4 x 3-inch loaf pans. The pans should be no more than three quarters full. Place the pans on the middle shelf of the oven and bake until the cake springs back at once when lightly touched, 35 minutes for the cake pans or 45 to 60 minutes for the loaf pans. A cake tester or skewer inserted into the center of the cake will come out clean when the cake is done. Allow the cakes to rest 3 minutes before unmolding.
7. Run a thin sharp knife around the edges of the pans to loosen the cake. Unmold them onto a rack, and cool completely before slicing or frosting. (If you have baked this cake in two 9-inch pans, frost as for a layer cake. Frost the loaf pan cakes as individual cakes.)
Serves 14 to 16

THE ULTIMATE SOUTHERN PECAN CAKE

❖❖

*T*he finely chopped pecans in this cake are used instead of flour. This makes a very tender and wonderful cake, redolent with the unique flavor of our very special nut.

As with any other ingredient, the freshest pecans should be used to ensure the best baking results.

---

2 cups pecans
5 large eggs, separated
⅔ cup sugar
1 teaspoon vanilla extract or cognac vanilla
   (see Index), or 1 tablespoon cognac
Dark Sweet Chocolate Frosting or Whipped
   Cream Frosting (recipes follow)

---

1. Preheat the oven to 325°F.

2. Roughly chop ½ cup of the pecans in a food processor. Set them aside. Finely chop the remaining pecans in the processor. Add them to the chopped nuts.

3. Beat the egg yolks in a large bowl with an electric mixer until they are fluffed up a bit. Add the sugar, and beat hard until the mixture turns a lighter shade of yellow and is smooth. Gently fold in the nuts with a rubber spatula. Add the vanilla or cognac, and mix well.

4. Beat the egg whites until they hold a stiff peak but are not dry and grainy. Using a rubber spatula, gently fold a third of the egg whites into the nut mixture to lighten it. Then fold in the remaining whites.

5. Grease and dust with flour or line with foil (the foil is best here) an 8-inch springform pan.

6. Spoon the batter into the prepared pan. The pan should be no more than three quarters full. Place the pan on the middle shelf of the oven and bake until the cake springs back when lightly touched, 50 to 60 minutes.

7. Allow the cake to cool about 5 minutes. Then run a thin knife around the sides to loosen the cake, and unclamp the pan, but let the cake cool completely before removing it from the bottom of the pan.

8. Coat the top and sides with the frosting.

   Serves 6 to 8

VARIATION: Substitute walnuts or hazelnuts (filberts) for the pecans.

DARK SWEET CHOCOLATE FROSTING

---

8 ounces dark sweet chocolate
1 cup heavy or whipping cream

---

1. Break the chocolate into coarse pieces, and place them in a double boiler over barely simmering water. When the chocolate has melted, add the cream. Stir until smooth. Remove the pan from the heat and beat hard. Place it in the refrigerator for the frosting to firm up, about 30 minutes.

2. Frost the cake in a swirl design.

If possible, use Tobler, Lindt, or Callebaut chocolate. Merken's coating chocolate is available at candy supply stores and is excellent. If any of these chocolates is used, vanilla is not needed. If a supermarket chocolate (such as Baker's) is used, add 1 teaspoon vanilla.

WHIPPED CREAM FROSTING

1½ cups heavy or whipping cream, cold
1 tablespoon confectioners' sugar
Vanilla extract to taste, or 1 tablespoon kirsch,
   rum, Cointreau, or cognac

---

1. Combine the cream, sugar, and flavoring and whip, slowly at first and picking up momentum as you go (this stabilizes the cream; too much sugar and flavoring will break it down).

2. Cover the cake with the flavored whipped cream, and refrigerate.

LATE HARVEST GINGERCAKE

*A*n October luncheon on Gingercake Mountain in North Carolina: Chicken salad with slivers of country ham, potato rolls, pickled peaches, Late Harvest Gingercake with whipped cream, and coffee or chilled cider.

1⅔ cups sifted all-purpose flour
¾ teaspoon salt
¼ teaspoon baking soda
1½ teaspoons baking powder
2 teaspoons ground ginger
½ teaspoon ground cinnamon
½ teaspoon freshly grated nutmeg
¼ teaspoon ground cloves
8 tablespoons (1 stick) butter, cut into pieces
1½ cups sugar
2 large eggs
1 cup canned pumpkin
⅓ cup water
½ cup coarsely chopped walnuts or pecans

1. Preheat the oven to 350°F.

2. Combine the sifted flour, salt, baking soda, baking powder, and spices, and sift again. Set aside.

3. Cream the butter and sugar thoroughly with an electric mixer. Add the eggs, and beat until the mixture falls in ribbons from a spoon. It should be smooth and silky looking like mayonnaise.

4. Add the flour mixture in batches, alternating with the pumpkin and water, blending it in by hand with a rubber spatula or a whisk. (This can be done on the lowest speed of a mixer if desired.) Fold the nuts into the batter thoroughly by hand.

5. Spoon the batter into a greased and lightly floured or foil-lined 9 x 5 x 3-inch loaf pan. The pan should be no more than three quarters full. Place the pan on the middle shelf of the oven and bake until the cake springs back at once when lightly touched, 60 to 70 minutes. A cake tester or skewer inserted into the center of the cake will come out clean. Remove the cake from the oven, but do not unmold it for 15 minutes or so.

6. Run a thin sharp knife around the edges of the pan to loosen the cake. Unmold it onto a rack and cool thoroughly before slicing.

Serves 8 to 10

Gingerbreads and gingercakes have a tendency to break if turned out of the pan while still hot.

The water content of fresh pumpkin varies so much that it is difficult to control. Use a good-quality brand of canned pumpkin because it is consistent.

MISTY VALLEY NUT LOAF

*I*f you have ever spent a day or even just an hour where Thomas Jefferson spent his lifetime—the Blue Ridge Mountains—you will understand why I named this Old Virginia cake the Misty Valley Nut Loaf. The beauty of the blue haze that rises from those mountains stays with you forever.

Enjoy this delightful loaf any time, served with sweet cream butter for tea, or for brunch with coffee, or a little Sunday night supper.

A breathtaking view of the Blue Ridge Mountains at Sharptop near the Peaks of Otter Lodge.

❖

1½ cups sifted all-purpose flour
⅛ teaspoon salt
2 teaspoons baking powder
8 tablespoons (1 stick) butter, cut into pieces
1 cup sugar
2 large eggs
½ cup milk
1 teaspoon vanilla extract or cognac vanilla
   (see Index)
1¼ cups chopped pecans

❖

1. Preheat the oven to 350°F.
2. Combine the sifted flour with the salt and baking powder, and sift again. Set aside.
3. Cream the butter and sugar thoroughly with an electric mixer. Add the eggs, and beat until the mixture is smooth.
4. Add the flour in batches, alternating with the milk. Blend it in with a rubber spatula. Stir in the vanilla and pecans.
5. Spoon the batter into a greased and lightly floured or wax-paper-lined 8 x 4 x 3-inch loaf pan. The pan should be no more than three quarters full. Place the pan on the middle shelf of the oven and bake until the cake springs back at once when lightly touched, 45 to 50 minutes. (Watch it carefully: An overbaked nut cake will be dry.) Remove the cake from the oven and allow it to rest 3 minutes before unmolding.
6. Run a thin sharp knife around the edge of the pan to loosen the cake. Unmold it onto a rack and cool before slicing.

Serves 8 to 10

🦉 When the cake cools, wrap it in foil and refrigerate or freeze overnight before cutting.

CAM'S PRUNE AND SPICE CAKE

◆◆◆

*T*his is a family heirloom cake which I named after my daughter because she loved it so. Everyone does. It travels well and stays moist and delicious to the last crumb.

❖

2 cups sifted all-purpose flour
1 teaspoon salt
1 scant teaspoon baking soda
1 teaspoon baking powder
1 teaspoon ground cinnamon
1 teaspoon ground allspice
1 teaspoon freshly grated nutmeg
½ teaspoon ground cloves
1 cup (2 sticks) butter, cut into pieces
1½ cups sugar
3 large eggs

1 cup buttermilk or sour cream
½ cup very lightly chopped cooked pitted prunes
1 cup chopped cooked pitted prunes (not puréed)
1½ teaspoons vanilla extract or cognac vanilla
   (see Index)
Caramel Buttermilk Frosting (optional; recipe follows)

◆

1. Preheat the oven to 350°F.

2. Combine the flour, salt, baking soda, baking powder, and spices, and sift again. Set aside.

3. Cream the butter and sugar thoroughly with an electric mixer. Add the eggs, and beat hard until the mixture falls in ribbons from a spoon. It should be smooth and silky looking like mayonnaise.

4. Add the flour mixture in batches, alternating with the buttermilk, folding it in by hand with a rubber spatula or a whisk. This can be done on the lowest speed of the mixer, but the texture of the cake is better when the flour is folded in by hand.

5. Fold in all the prunes, and stir in the vanilla.

6. Spoon the batter into a greased and lightly floured 9- or 10-inch tube pan, or 2 loaf pans. The pan(s) should not be more than three quarters full. Place the pan(s) on the middle shelf of the oven and bake until the cake springs back at once when lightly touched, about 50 minutes. A cake tester or skewer inserted into the middle should come out clean. Allow the cake to rest 3 minutes before unmolding.

7. Unmold the cake onto a rack and cool it thoroughly before frosting.

8. Spread hot Caramel Buttermilk Frosting over the top of the cake and allow it to drip down the sides.

Serves 10 to 12

This cake is delicious served without frosting, if desired.

The prunes may vary in the amount of moisture they give to the batter, so if the batter looks a little loose or curdled after adding the prunes, add a tablespoon or so of flour.

CARAMEL BUTTERMILK FROSTING

---

1 cup sugar
½ cup buttermilk
1 teaspoon baking soda
1 tablespoon light corn syrup
4 tablespoons (½ stick) butter
½ teaspoon vanilla extract or cognac vanilla
(see Index)

1. Combine all the ingredients except the vanilla in a heavy saucepan. Bring to a boil and cook over medium-high heat, stirring occasionally, until the syrup reaches 236°F on a candy thermometer or a spoonful of the syrup dropped in cold water immediately forms a soft ball, 12 to 15 minutes.

2. Remove the pan from the heat and stir in the vanilla.

This very pale caramel frosting is a bit sticky, but it has an exquisite flavor.

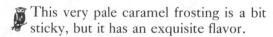

SERVING GUIDELINES

*I*t is impossible to chart the exact number of people a cake will serve, as the human element varies so. A generous person will be inclined to get only 12 slices from a 9-inch cake, where another will cut thinner pieces and serve maybe 16.

A very rich cake should be cut into small servings. Cake that is to be served with ice cream should be cut small. Pudding cake with a sauce should be rather bountiful.

CHARLOTTESVILLE FRUIT AND SPICE CAKE

*T*he almond filling in this heavily scented Old World cake sets it apart from most fruitcakes. Beautiful on the tea table or on the buffet to be enjoyed with coffee during the winter holidays. An exceptionally good keeper.

1¼ teaspoons baking powder
½ teaspoon salt
½ teaspoon ground mace or freshly grated
    nutmeg
¼ teaspoon ground allspice
¼ teaspoon ground cloves
⅔ teaspoon ground cinnamon
2 cups twice-sifted all-purpose flour
¾ cup (1½ sticks) butter, cut into pieces
1⅛ cups sugar
4 large eggs
1 cup golden raisins
½ cup chopped seeded raisins
⅓ cup candied citron, finely chopped
⅓ cup candied orange peel, finely chopped
⅓ cup candied lemon peel, finely chopped
¼ cup grated blanched almonds (see Owl)
½ cup chopped unblanched almonds
2 teaspoons vanilla extract or cognac vanilla
    (see Index)
¼ cup brandy or aged bourbon whiskey
Brandy, for glazing

ALMOND FILLING

1 cup grated blanched almonds
1 large egg
½ cup sugar
⅓ teaspoon almond extract

1. Preheat the oven to 300°F.
2. Combine the baking powder, salt, spices, and flour. Stir, and set aside.
3. In a large bowl, cream the butter and sugar thoroughly with an electric mixer. Add the eggs, and beat until the mixture falls in ribbons from a spoon. It should be smooth and silky looking like mayonnaise. Add the flour to the egg mixture, beating it in by hand with a rubber spatula or whisk. (This can be done with an electric mixer on a very slow speed, but blending it in by hand makes a lighter cake.)
4. In another bowl, toss the fruits with the grated almonds and the chopped almonds. Add this to the batter and mix well by hand. Stir in the vanilla and brandy or bourbon. Set aside.
5. Mix the filling ingredients together in a food processor or with a mixer.
6. Spoon half the batter into a greased and foil-lined 10-inch tube pan. Completely cover the batter, as best you can, with spoonfuls of the filling. Cover the filling with the remaining batter. The pan should be no more than three quarters full.
7. Bake until the cake springs back at once when lightly touched, 1¾ hours. Remove the cake from the oven and brush the top with brandy. Allow the cake to cool 5 minutes before unmolding.
8. Run a thin sharp knife around the edge of the pan to loosen the cake, then unmold it and set it on a rack to cool. Do not slice this cake for several hours. Store in a tight tin box with a piece of apple to keep it moist or wrap in foil and freeze.

Serves 12 to 16

🦉 Almonds should be grated in a Mouli or other rotary grater, not in a food processor. Done in a processor, nuts are likely to become oily. The grated almonds should be very dry.

*S*eeded raisins (the sticky kind) are made from grapes that have seeds. The seeds are extracted.
    Seedless raisins are made from seedless Thompson grapes. They are the raisins that do not stick together and rattle around in the box.

THE JEWEL BOX CAKE

*I*f I had to choose only one fruitcake in all the world, it would be this one. It is as delicious as it is beautiful—what more could one ask? And it is lighter than most holiday cakes. For teas or receptions, it is lovely served with or without the frosting.

1 cup golden raisins
1 ¼ cups finely slivered glazed or dried apricots
½ cup candied orange peel, finely chopped
½ cup candied lemon peel, finely chopped
1 cup candied pineapple (4 rings), diced
½ cup plus 1 ½ tablespoons brandy or aged
    bourbon whiskey, plus more as needed
2 ⅔ cups sifted all-purpose flour
¼ teaspoon salt
2 teaspoons baking powder
1 cup (2 sticks) unsalted butter, cut into pieces
1 ½ cups sugar
6 large eggs, separated
¼ cup heavy or whipping cream
½ cup shredded tart apple (1 small apple)
¼ cup grated blanched almonds
¼ cup chopped blanched almonds
¼ cup blanched pistachios or chopped citron
1 ½ teaspoons vanilla extract or cognac vanilla
    (see Index)
*Luscious Lemon Frosting (optional; recipe
    follows)*

1. An hour or so before baking the cake, marinate the raisins, apricots, orange and lemon peels, and pineapple in ½ cup liquor in a closed jar. Shake it several times.

2. Preheat the oven to 275°F.

3. Combine the sifted flour with the salt and baking powder, and sift again.

4. Cream the butter and 1 cup of the sugar thoroughly with an electric mixer. Add the egg yolks, and beat until the mixture is smooth.

5. Add the flour mixture in batches, alternating with the cream. Beat it in by hand with a rubber spatula or with an electric mixer at very low speed.

6. Fold in the marinated fruit and liquor. If the fruit absorbed all of the liquor, add an additional 2 tablespoons of liquor to the cake batter. Fold in the apple, almonds, pistachios or citron, and vanilla.

7. Beat the egg whites until they hold a soft peak. Add the remaining sugar and beat until they hold a stiff peak but are not dry and grainy. Fold a few spoonfuls into the batter by hand with a rubber spatula, then fold in the rest. If the batter looks the least bit curdled, fold in 2 or 3 extra tablespoons of sifted flour.

8. Spoon the batter into a 10-inch tube pan that has been greased and lined with foil. The pan should be no more than three quarters full. Bake until the cake springs back at once when lightly touched, 2 to 2 ½ hours. A skewer or cake tester inserted into the center of the cake should come out clean. Remove the cake from the oven and brush the top with 1 ½ tablespoons brandy or bourbon.

9. Run a thin sharp knife around the edge of the pan to loosen the cake, and unmold it onto a rack to cool.

10. Serve the cake as is, or when cool frost the top and sides with Luscious Lemon Frosting in a swirling design.

Serves 12 to 16

Frosting protects a cake to a certain extent, but fruitcakes keep best when stored in a tight tin box with a piece of apple.

Grate the almonds in a rotary grater, not in a food processor.

The shredded apple helps to preserve the moistness of the cake.

LUSCIOUS LEMON FROSTING

Peel of 1 lemon
2 ¾ cups confectioners' sugar, sifted
8 tablespoons (1 stick) butter
1 large egg yolk
Pinch of salt
2 tablespoons lemon juice, or more to taste

1. Sliver the lemon peel and combine it with about 1 cup of the sugar in a food processor. Twirl until the lemon peel is finely grated. (You can, if you prefer, grate the lemon peel by hand and add it to the sugar.)

2. Add the butter to the sugar mixture and blend until the mixture is smooth.

3. Add the egg yolk, salt, remaining sugar, and lemon juice. Blend until the frosting is perfectly smooth. Taste, and add another tablespoon of lemon juice if desired.

🦉 This frosting will keep in a covered jar in the refrigerator for several days.

IMPERIAL CHEESECAKE

❖❖❖

When this cheesecake is garnished with luscious strawberries, it leaves nothing to be desired.

◆

2 cups ground vanilla wafers (about 60 wafers)
8 tablespoons (1 stick) unsalted butter, melted
2½ pounds cream cheese, at room temperature
1¾ cups sugar
Grated peel of 1 lemon
Grated peel of ½ navel orange
3 tablespoons all-purpose flour
¼ teaspoon salt
5 large eggs
2 large egg yolks
¼ cup heavy or whipping cream
1 teaspoon vanilla extract or cognac vanilla (see Index)
½ to ⅔ cup pure strawberry jelly or sieved apricot preserves, warmed (optional)
1½ quarts perfect strawberries (optional)
Whole mint or gardenia leaves (optional)

◆

1. Preheat the oven to 300°F.
2. Combine the vanilla wafer crumbs and melted butter. Blend well.
3. Generously butter a 9-inch springform pan on the sides and bottom. Press the crumbs onto the sides and bottom, making a thin layer. Reserve some crumbs for the top if you are not using strawberries. Chill the crust for at least 10 minutes but it can be made way ahead of time.

4. Beat the cheese until it is perfectly smooth. Combine the sugar, lemon peel, orange peel, flour, and salt. Add this to the cheese. Add the eggs and egg yolks, one at a time, beating well. Add the cream and vanilla. Mix thoroughly.

5. Spoon the mixture into the prepared pan. The pan should be no more than three quarters full. Sprinkle the reserved crumbs on top if you are not using the strawberries. Bake on the middle shelf of the oven for 1 hour. Turn off the heat and leave the cake in the oven with the door open 15 to 20 minutes longer. Remove the cake from the pan and allow it to cool thoroughly. Then refrigerate it.

6. If you are garnishing the cake with strawberries, brush the top of the cake with warm strawberry jelly or sieved apricot preserves. Garnish lavishly both the top and around the bottom of the cake with whole strawberries. Tuck a cluster of mint or gardenia leaves, if available, at the bottom of the cake.

Serves 15 to 18

🦉 This recipe may be cut in half, using 3 whole eggs and 1 egg yolk, to fill one 9 x 2-inch round glass baking dish.

CHARLESTON SHORTBREAD COOKIES

A beautiful teapot full of good English tea and a silver tray of these cookies will take you right back to South Carolina, I promise.

30 blanched whole almonds
8 tablespoons (1 stick) butter, cut into pieces
4 tablespoons sugar
1 cup sifted all-purpose flour
⅛ teaspoon salt
½ teaspoon vanilla extract or cognac vanilla (see Index)

1. Preheat the oven to 325°F.

2. Place the almonds on a baking sheet and bake for 30 minutes. Set them aside, and leave the oven on.

3. Cream the butter and sugar thoroughly with an electric mixer until fluffy. Add the flour and salt, and mix well. Blend in the vanilla.

4. Roll the dough into small balls and place them on a lightly greased or nonstick baking sheet. Flatten each one with your fingertip, and place an almond in the center.

5. Bake the cookies on the middle shelf of the oven until they take on just a bit of color, 20 to 25 minutes.

6. Cool them on a rack, and then store in an airtight tin (these keep superbly).

Makes 25 to 30 cookies

VARIATIONS: Add ⅓ cup sliced almonds to the dough: Toast ⅓ cup slivered almonds

Hampton Plantation, Charleston County, South Carolina.

in 1½ teaspoons butter in a heavy skillet until the almonds are crisp and have taken on a bit of color. Do not allow the almonds to get very dark, however. Add them to the dough and omit the whole almonds.

Omit the almonds and add 1 tablespoon brandy.

WINTER APPLE COOKIES

T his is an "old time" moist, spicy cookie for a wintry day's nibbling with a cup of tea, or for the lunch box or for after supper by the fireside. It can also be baked in tiny marionette pans.

8 tablespoons (1 stick) butter, cut into pieces
1⅓ cups light brown sugar, not too firmly
    packed
1 large egg
½ teaspoon salt
½ teaspoon baking soda
1 teaspoon ground cinnamon
½ teaspoon ground cloves
½ teaspoon ground mace
2 cups sifted all-purpose flour
¼ cup milk or apple juice
1 cup golden raisins
1 cup chopped walnuts
1 cup coarsely chopped peeled apple
1 cup confectioners' sugar
3 tablespoons apple cider, apple juice, milk, or
    brandy for glaze

1. Preheat the oven to 350°F.
2. Cream the butter and brown sugar thoroughly with an electric mixer until fluffy. Add the egg and beat again.
3. Sift the salt, baking soda, and spices with the flour. Add the flour to the creamed mixture alternately with the milk or apple juice. Stir in the raisins, walnuts, and apple by hand. Work fast with the apple so it will not turn dark.
4. Drop the dough by spoonfuls onto a lightly greased or nonstick baking sheet, placing the cookies 2 inches apart (1½ tablespoons of dough makes a nice-size cookie). Don't flatten—this is not a thin, crisp cookie.
5. Bake on the middle shelf of the oven until the cookies spring back when touched and are light brown all over, 15 to 20 minutes.
6. Meanwhile, blend the confectioners' sugar with the cider or other liquid for the glaze. While the cookies are still hot, brush them with the glaze. Remove the cookies to a rack and cool.

Makes about 30 cookies

🦉 Golden Delicious apples are excellent in cookies and cakes, as they don't darken as quickly as other apples.

COLONIAL VIRGINIA MINCEMEAT COOKIE

*O*ur English heritage shines through very clearly in this Virginia cookie. Rum is the favorite flavor in the glaze, but apple juice or cider is delicious too.

2 cups mincemeat, homemade if possible (see
    Index)
2 tablespoons finely chopped crystallized orange
    peel
2 tablespoons finely chopped crystallized lemon
    peel
2 tablespoons finely chopped citron
¼ cup brandy or rum, if using commercial
    mincemeat; less or to taste for homemade
    mincemeat
1 cup (2 sticks) butter, cut into pieces
2 cups sugar
3 large eggs
4 cups sifted all-purpose flour

½ teaspoon salt
1 teaspoon baking soda
½ teaspoon ground ginger
1 teaspoon ground cloves
1 teaspoon freshly grated nutmeg
½ cup finely diced peeled apple
½ cup chopped pecans or walnuts, or more to
    taste
1½ teaspoons vanilla extract

GLAZE

2 cups confectioners' sugar
½ cup brandy, rum, apple juice, or cider

1. In a mixing bowl, combine the mincemeat, orange peel, lemon peel, citron, and brandy or rum. Allow to stand 1 hour, or longer if possible.

2. Preheat the oven to 350°F.

3. Cream the butter and sugar thoroughly with an electric mixer until fluffly. Add the eggs and beat again.

4. Sift the flour with the salt, baking soda, and spices. Add it to the egg mixture and mix thoroughly. By hand, stir in the mincemeat mixture, apple, nuts, and vanilla.

5. Drop by teaspoons, 2 inches apart, onto a lightly greased or nonstick baking sheet. Bake until the cookies are light brown, 20 to 25 minutes.

6. While the cookies are baking, blend the confectioners' sugar and brandy or other liquid for the glaze. While the baked cookies are still hot, brush the tops lightly with the glaze. Remove to a rack, and cool.

Makes 90 cookies

SHINY GLAZE

*U*se this for apple, mincemeat, or any cookie or cake that needs a shiny glaze rather than a frosting.

1½ cups confectioners' sugar
1 tablespoon butter, at room temperature
⅛ teaspoon salt
¼ teaspoon vanilla extract or cognac vanilla (see Index)
3½ tablespoons (approximately) milk, cream, apple juice, apple cider, or Calvados

Cream thoroughly all the ingredients with an electric mixer until soft and free of lumps. Add enough additional liquid to make a good spreading consistency. Spread this over cookies or cake with a brush while they are still hot, so the glaze will shine.

Makes enough for one 9- or 10-inch tube cake, 24 sweet rolls, or 90 cookies

Calvados is French apple brandy, by far the most delicious choice for this glaze.

CHECK POINTS FOR COOKIES

*O*ver-baking and over-browning are pitfalls in baking fine cookies. Many cookies should be dried out in the last quarter of baking rather than cooking them further: Cut off the heat, and leave the cookies to finish cooking or to dry out with only the heat of the pilot light or the oven light.

The same care should be used in mixing cookie dough as in making cakes—creaming the butter and sugar well, for instance, and folding in nuts and fruits by hand so they will be well distributed through the dough and not be pulverized. Using lightly salted butter helps distribute the salt in the cookie dough evenly.

Use only top-quality ingredients. Butter is the only shortening for baking; it deepens the fine flavor in cookies and cakes as they ripen. Vanilla extract must be the real thing, not "flavoring."

Grease baking sheets lightly with solid vegetable shortening or butter. Margarine will burn.

Use only flat baking sheets with no sides or very low sides. High-sided pans, such as cake pans, prevent proper browning of cookies.

Use only shiny baking sheets (they reflect the heat), or white or gray nonstick pastry sheets. Dark or discolored sheets cause the cookies to burn on the bottom and to brown unevenly. (Dark sheets absorb the heat.)

Baking sheets lined with heavy foil are excellent for cookies that should not brown very much.

If baking sheets are greased too heavily, the cookies will spread too much. If the cookie dough is warm, the cookies will spread. Work with cold dough.

Bake only 1 sheet of cookies (on the middle shelf) at a time. Place the sheet 2 inches away from the sides of the oven for good circulation and even baking.

If the cookies with an appreciable amount of sugar tend to stick to the pan, return them to the oven to warm up slightly, then remove them with a spatula.

CHOCOLATE APRICOT BROWNIES

❖❖

*T*his is the ultimate brownie. After they cool, cut them with a round 2¼-inch cutter. Serve on your very best dessert plates with a garnish of whipped cream— then sit back and enjoy the party.

◆

3 glazed apricots
3 ounces unsweetened baking chocolate
8 tablespoons (1 stick) butter
1 cup sugar
2 large eggs
½ cup sifted all-purpose flour
1½ teaspoons vanilla extract or cognac vanilla
    (see Index)
Tiny pinch of salt

◆

1. Preheat the oven to 350°F.
2. Cut the apricots into ⅛-inch slivers with sharp kitchen shears, and set aside.
3. Combine the chocolate, butter, and sugar in the top of a roomy double boiler over simmering water. When the chocolate has melted, remove the pan from the heat and stir the mixture until it is smooth.
4. Beat in the eggs and flour and blend thoroughly. Stir in the vanilla and apricots.
5. Spoon the batter into a lightly greased or nonstick 9-inch square cake pan, and bake 20 minutes. Allow the brownies to cool completely before cutting them into squares.

Makes nine 3 x 3-inch brownies

🦉 This recipe can be doubled and baked in 2 cake pans. The brownies freeze well, although nothing surpasses the flavor of oven fresh.

LISA'S BUTTER LEAF COOKIES

❖❖

*T*his is one of the most delicate of sugar cookies—exquisitely so—but keep the dough cold while rolling, and don't reroll any more than absolutely necessary. My daughter Lisa liked to make these when she was a little girl. We used a leaf-shaped cookie cutter and traced the veins of the leaf very gently with a knife. Pretty.

Housewives in Florida, around 1915, churned their own butter. Their cookies must have been truly aromatic.

◆

1 cup (2 sticks) butter, cut into pieces
1 cup sugar
2 large eggs
3 cups sifted all-purpose flour
1 teaspoon baking powder
¼ teaspoon salt
1 teaspoon vanilla extract or cognac vanilla
    (see Index)
Coarse or regular granulated sugar

◆

1. Cream the butter and sugar thoroughly with an electric mixer until fluffy. Add the eggs, and beat again.

2. Sift the flour with the dry ingredients, and add it to the creamed mixture. Stir in the vanilla.

3. Form the dough into a ball, wrap it in foil, and refrigerate 1 hour.

4. Preheat the oven to 350°F.

5. When the dough is firm, pinch off a small piece at a time, leaving the rest in the refrigerator. Roll each batch out quite thin on a floured pastry cloth, and cut into desired shapes. Sprinkle the cookies with the coarse sugar, and bake on a lightly greased or nonstick baking sheet until pale gold, 8 to 10 minutes. Cool them on a rack.

Makes about sixty 3-inch cookies

If dough is too soft to handle, add a little sifted flour. Too much flour, however, will make the cookies tough and dry.

These cookies should be very thin and crisp with an all over pale golden hue. If the edges brown while the center remains white and undone, your oven is too hot.

These cookies can be made in a food processor, but adding the flour by hand or with a less powerful type of mixer makes a flakier cookie.

MONTICELLO CHOCOLATE SNAPS

*A*n exquisitely thin, crisp cookie in the European tradition. They are utterly delectable eaten plain or coated with chocolate—and this cookie is worthy of the best chocolate money can buy.

⅓ cup whole unblanched almonds
5 tablespoons butter, cut into pieces
1¼ cups light brown sugar, firmly packed
1 cup sifted all-purpose flour
1½ teaspoons ground cinnamon
⅛ teaspoon ground cloves
⅔ teaspoon salt
¼ cup water (approximately)
12 ounces German sweet chocolate or your favorite semisweet coating chocolate (optional)

1. Preheat the oven to 325°F.

2. Place the almonds on a baking sheet and bake for about 30 minutes to allow them to dry out. Set them aside to cool.

3. Grind or finely chop two thirds of the almonds (you should have under ⅓ cup). Set aside.

4. Coarsely chop the remaining almonds (you should have about ⅓ cup). Set aside.

5. Cream the butter and brown sugar thoroughly with an electric mixer until fluffy.

6. Combine the sifted flour with the cinnamon, cloves, and salt. Add the flour mixture to the butter and sugar. Mix thoroughly.

7. Fold in both batches of nuts by hand. Add enough water to form a stiff dough.

Cooking class at Monsarret Departmental School in Louisville, 1927.

8. Wrap the dough in foil and refrigerate for 30 minutes.

9. Preheat the oven to 300°F.

10. Form the dough into small or medium balls. Place them on nonstick baking sheets about 2 inches apart. Flatten the cookies with your fingers. They must be thin.

11. Bake until the cookies feel rather firm in the center, 20 to 25 minutes. They will turn a golden hue all over but they must not brown on the edges.

12. In the meantime, if you want to glaze the cookies, melt the chocolate in the top of a double boiler over simmering water. While the cookies are still hot, brush the tops of them completely with the chocolate. Remove to a rack, and cool.

Makes 48 cookies

🦉 In damp weather this cookie may become a bit chewy. To help prevent this, place the cookies in a tight tin box as soon as they have cooled.

ROSEMARIES

◆◆

*T*his is one of the most elegant of all cookies, and the homemade candied pineapple makes them very special. If you don't have time to prepare it, use pineapple preserves rather than store-bought candied pineapple. Rosemaries are at their best the day they are baked, but they can be frozen unbaked, and then baked as you need them. Oh, the flavor of freshly baked cookies!

◆

3 tablespoons pineapple preserves or small chunks of homemade candied pineapple (recipe follows)
8 tablespoons (1 stick) butter, cut into pieces
⅓ cup sugar
1 large egg yolk
1 cup sifted all-purpose flour
1 teaspoon vanilla extract or cognac vanilla (see Index)

◆

1. At least 3 days ahead, prepare the homemade candied pineapple if you are using it.

2. Cream the butter and sugar thoroughly with an electric mixer until fluffy. Add the egg yolk and beat again. Add the flour and vanilla, and blend well.

3. Wrap the dough in foil and refrigerate to allow it to firm up, at least 20 minutes.

4. Preheat the oven to 325°F.

5. Pinch off small balls of dough, about 1 scant teaspoon each. Place them on a lightly greased or nonstick baking sheet 2 inches apart and press each ball slightly to flatten it. Make a small indentation in the center of each cookie, and spoon in ½ teaspoon pineapple preserves or press on a small chunk of candied pineapple.

6. Place the cookies on the middle shelf of the oven and bake only until light golden brown, 20 to 25 minutes. They must not be allowed to get very brown. Cool the cookies on a rack.

Makes 15 to 18 cookies

🦉 If you wish to prepare Rosemaries ahead, make them up through step 5 and freeze them in the pans. Then bake them the day of the party. If baked frozen, they will, of course, require a longer baking period. Allow 25 to 30 minutes.

◆

CANDIED PINEAPPLE

1 can (4 ounces) pineapple rings or chunks
3 tablespoons light corn syrup

◆

1. Drain the pineapple thoroughly, reserving the juice. Cut the pineapple into small pieces.

2. Combine the corn syrup and ½ cup of the pineapple juice in a medium very heavy stainless steel or enamel saucepan. Bring to a boil and cook until the syrup spins a thread, 5 minutes. Add the pineapple and simmer until the fruit is transparent, 35 to 40 minutes.

3. Remove the pan from the heat, cover it loosely with foil, and allow the pineapple to stand overnight.

4. Return the pineapple and syrup to a boil and cook, spooning the syrup over the pineapple, 2 minutes.

5. Place a clean piece of muslin or cheesecloth over a cake rack in a warm, sunny room. Remove the pieces of pineapple with a slotted spoon and place them on the cloth. Leave them there until they are almost dry, 1½ to 2 days.

6. Remove the pineapple pieces from the cloth and place them on a piece of heavy foil. Allow them to complete drying at least 1 day. Store between layers of wax paper or foil in a plastic container. It will keep 4 to 6 weeks at room temperature.

Makes about 1½ cups

CAROLINA MORAVIAN GINGER THINS

*Y*ou know those very thin, thin ginger cookies that come in an expensive tin and that everyone loves—well, here they are.

5 tablespoons light molasses
⅓ cup water
½ cup granulated sugar
⅔ cup light brown sugar, not too firmly packed
⅔ cup butter
½ teaspoon salt
2 teaspoons ground cinnamon
¼ teaspoon ground allspice or cloves
1½ teaspoons ground ginger
1½ teaspoons baking powder
2¾ cups sifted all-purpose flour

1. Combine the molasses, water, and granulated and brown sugars in a saucepan. Bring to a boil over medium heat and add the butter. Allow the butter to melt while stirring the mixture, then remove the pan from the heat and set it aside to cool.

2. When the mixture is cool, pour it into the bowl of an electric mixer. Add the salt, spices, and baking powder. Blend well. Add the flour and mix thoroughly, but do not overbeat. Cover the dough and refrigerate until it is easy to handle, several hours.

3. Preheat the oven to 300°F.

4. Place the dough on a lightly floured surface and knead it for about 2 minutes. Then roll it out ⅛ inch thick (this makes a thin, crisp cookie). Using a plain or scalloped 2-inch cutter, cut the cookies out and place them on a white or light gray nonstick baking sheet.

5. Bake for 10 to 12 minutes. They must not brown the least bit. Leave the cookies in the oven to dry out, 10 to 15 minutes. Then cool them on racks, and store in a tight tin.

Makes 80 cookies

A company that thought very highly of the quality of their spices.

CRACKLY-TOP SPICE COOKIES

O ld-fashioned crackly tops! While Daddy reads you a good story, have a glass of cold milk and a crackly top that Mother baked—then off to bed, with one last cookie in your hand.

Can you imagine the size of their smiles if one hand held a Crackly-Top Spice Cookie?

¾ cup (1½ sticks) butter, cut into pieces
1 cup light brown sugar, not too firmly packed
1 large egg
¼ cup molasses
2¼ cups sifted all-purpose flour
½ teaspoon salt
1 teaspoon ground ginger
1½ teaspoons ground cinnamon
¼ teaspoon ground cloves
¼ teaspoon baking soda
1½ teaspoons baking powder
½ cup granulated sugar

1. Cream the butter and brown sugar thoroughly with an electric mixer until fluffy. Add the egg and molasses, and mix again.
2. In a separate bowl, sift the flour with the salt, ginger, cinnamon, cloves, baking soda, and baking powder. Add the dry ingredients to the butter mixture. Mix thoroughly but do not overbeat.
3. Wrap the dough in foil and refrigerate it until it is firm enough to handle easily, about 1 hour.
4. Preheat the oven to 375°F.
5. Form the dough into about 60 medium balls. Toss the balls in the granulated sugar, place them on a lightly greased or nonstick baking sheet, and flatten each one a bit. Sprinkle one drop of water in the center of each cookie.
6. Bake until delicately browned, 10 to 12 minutes. Cool the cookies on racks.
   Makes 60 cookies

This is a good traveler.

CHOCK-FULL-OF-CHOCOLATE COOKIES

T his is a wonderful cookie and my variation of chocolate chip—it's not too sweet. The better the chocolate, the better the cookie.

◆

8 tablespoons (1 stick) unsalted or lightly salted
    butter, cut into pieces
½ cup sugar
1 large egg
½ teaspoon salt
1 cup sifted all-purpose flour
1 teaspoon vanilla extract or cognac vanilla
    (see Index)
12 ounces semisweet or dark baking chocolate or
    German sweet chocolate

◆

*Camping out at Eagle Lake in Florida during the
1880s. Hope the children reminded the adults to pack
the cookies.*

1. Preheat the oven to 350°F.

2. Cream the butter and sugar thoroughly with an electric mixer until fluffy. Beat in the egg, salt, flour, and vanilla until just mixed.

3. Use a mallet to break the chocolate bars into about ½-inch pieces (some of the chocolate will shatter, but include it all). Stir the chocolate pieces into the dough by hand.

4. Place the dough by spoonfuls (about 1¼ tablespoons for a generous cookie) 2 inches apart on a lightly greased or nonstick baking sheet. Flatten them a bit with a spoon if you want them to be thin and crisp. If you want a chewy cookie, make them a bit thicker.

5. Bake on the middle shelf of the oven until the cookies are very light brown, about 20 minutes. Watch them carefully or the chocolate that sinks to the bottom of the cookie will burn. Cool the cookies on a rack.

Makes 24 cookies

VARIATION: If you prefer a caramel flavor, use half light brown sugar.

🦉 This dough keeps well in the refrigerator for a week, so these cookies can be baked in batches as needed. Wrap it in foil or put it in a plastic container.

CHOCOLATE WHISPERS

◆◆◆

*F*or years I searched for the secret to a very delicate cookie with just a whisper of chocolate to enjoy with coffee or ice cream. Here it is. Store-bought superfine sugar is not as fine as home-processed, but it will work if you don't own a food processor. The measurements remain the same.

◆

½ cup sugar
Peel from ⅓ lemon
8 tablespoons (1 stick) butter, cut into pieces
Pinch of salt
2 large egg whites
⅓ cup sifted all-purpose flour
8 ounces semisweet baking chocolate (Lindt,
    Tobler, or Callebaut if possible) or German
    sweet chocolate

◆

1. Put the sugar in a food processor and process until very fine, 3 to 4 minutes or more. Sliver the lemon peel and add it to the sugar. Process until finely grated.

2. Add the butter and salt and process until creamy. Add the egg whites one at a time, and beat them in very quickly, using an on-off action 1 or 2 times. Don't overbeat. Add the flour and process it into the mixture quickly.

3. With a rubber spatula, transfer the dough to a bowl. Cover it, and allow it to rest in the refrigerator 1 hour or longer, until the dough is firm and easy to handle.

4. Preheat the oven to 350°F.

5. Lightly grease a nonstick baking sheet with vegetable shortening and dust it with flour. Drop the dough by teaspoons about 2 inches apart onto the sheet or roll it into small balls. Flatten them with your fingertips.

6. Bake the cookies on the middle shelf of the oven for 10 to 12 minutes. Watch carefully so they won't brown too much.

7. In the meantime, melt the chocolate in the top of a double boiler over simmering water.

8. Remove the cookies from the oven. Allow them to cool slightly, then brush the tops lightly with the chocolate, covering them well. Transfer the cookies to a rack to cool completely. Put the finished cookies in airtight tin boxes as soon as the chocolate has set.

Makes 24 cookies

🦉 If the dough runs too much on the baking sheet, add a little more flour or a tablespoon of grated blanched almonds. (The almond dust can be added in any case if desired. It lends a slightly crunchy texture—very nice.)

A nonstick baking sheet will help, as the cookies are so delicate, but the sheet should not be dark, because this causes the cookies to brown excessively. T-Fal nonstick baking sheets are not cheap, but they are excellent.

CHOCOLATE PARFAIT WACHERS

*T*his is the wafer that you have dreamed of. Notebook-paper thin, crisp, and with just the right amount of sweetness to serve with sherbets, ice cream, summer fruits, a cup of coffee—or to quiet a nagging sweet tooth.

⅔ cup sugar
7 tablespoons butter, cut into pieces
Pinch of salt
⅔ cup (4 or 5 large) egg whites
1 cup minus 2 tablespoons sifted all-purpose
    flour
2 tablespoons unsweetened cocoa powder
    (premium quality)
1½ teaspoons vanilla extract or cognac vanilla
    (see Index)
Confectioners' sugar, for dusting

1. Preheat the oven to 350°F.

2. Put the sugar in a food processor and process it 3 to 4 minutes. This will make superfine sugar to perfection.

3. Cream the sugar, butter, and salt thoroughly in the processor or with an electric mixer until fluffy. Add the egg whites a little at a time, beating constantly until the mixture looks like meringue. In a processor, this goes very fast.

4. Toss the flour and cocoa together in a bowl and add it to the egg white mixture, along with the vanilla. Blend quickly until just mixed.

5. Lightly butter and flour 2 gray or white nonstick baking sheets. Drop the batter onto them, 1 tablespoon at a time. Spread the wafers out thin with the back of a teaspoon, leaving 2 to 3 inches between them for spreading.

6. Bake on the middle shelf of the oven for 10 to 12 minutes. If the wafers still feel soft in the center, cut off the heat and leave them in the oven to dry out for 20 minutes or more.

7. When the wafers are done, cool them on a rack. Then put them in a tightly closed tin right away to keep them crisp. Just before serving, sprinkle the cookies with sieved confectioners' sugar.

Makes 50 cookies

VARIATION: *Vanilla Parfait Wafers:* Process and add 1 teaspoon grated lemon peel after processing the sugar (sugar can remain in the bowl), omit the cocoa, and use 1 cup sifted flour.

🦉 Treat this wafer like a meringue, as in a way it is. It certainly absorbs moisture and goes chewy like a meringue. If you use dark bitter cocoa, you may want to add 2 tablespoons sugar. I use Droste's cocoa.

It must have been hard to hold still for this birthday photo in 1922 with all those tempting treats on the table.

ALMOND MARIONETTES

*T*hese Almond Marionettes are very special little cookies. They are half-cake, half-tart, and every bite is tantalizing and calls for another. They are delicate, crisp, and exquisitely sinful. I serve them often for large parties and receptions, and they make a lovely sweet with coffee after a cocktail or buffet supper. They are perfect to have in the freezer to bake on short notice for unexpected company, too, or just for yourself on a "blue" day.

8 tablespoons (1 stick) butter, cut into pieces
¼ cup sugar
1 large egg yolk
1 cup sifted all-purpose flour
¼ teaspoon salt
1 teaspoon vanilla extract or cognac vanilla
　　(see Index)
Almond Filling (recipe follows)
Confectioners' sugar for dusting

1. Cream the butter and sugar thoroughly with an electric mixer until fluffy. Add the egg yolk, and beat again. Blend in the flour, salt, and vanilla. Wrap in foil and place in the refrigerator to firm up, 30 minutes.

2. Preheat the oven to 350°F.

3. Press the dough into tiny (2-inch) tart pans with the tip of your thumb. The dough should be thin around the sides of the little cakes but thick enough in the center to hold a filling. Put 1 to 2 teaspoons filling in the center of each cookie.

4. Bake until a very light golden color, 20 to 25 minutes. Cool in the tart pans. Dust with sieved confectioners' sugar just before serving.

Makes 15 to 18 cookies

VARIATIONS: After baking and before the cookies have cooled, brush the almond

TO STORE COOKIES

*C*ool all cookies before storing them.

Put soft, chewy cookies in tight tins or in airtight plastic containers by themselves.

Store crisp, thin cookies in airtight tins by themselves.

filling with apricot preserves seasoned with dark rum.

Put pineapple preserves instead of almond filling in the center of the marionettes. A favorite.

These freeze well before baking; and if the little tart pans are filled and placed on baking sheets, then frozen, they can be ready to eat in 25 to 30 minutes by placing them while still frozen in a preheated 350°F oven. Both the almond and the pineapple fillings freeze well.

These cookies can be baked early in the morning before a party, but they lose their delightful crispness if kept over a day. Don't let this deter you from making them. They are utterly delectable!

ALMOND FILLING

½ cup sugar
5⅓ tablespoons butter, cut into pieces
⅔ cup grated blanched almonds
1 large egg
½ teaspoon almond extract

Cream the sugar and butter thoroughly until fluffy. Add the remaining ingredients and mix well. Covered and refrigerated, the filling will keep for several weeks.

FREEZING COOKIES

*F*reshly baked cookies have a charm far superior to those that have been stored in a tin. Most cookies can be formed unbaked on sheets of heavy foil and frozen, then baked as needed. This gives a fresher flavor than freezing prebaked cookies.

Frosted cookies do not freeze well.

Unbaked cookies in tiny foil or tart pans may be placed on baking sheets and frozen.

Do not freeze doughs with large amounts of egg white, such as meringues.

If you do freeze baked cookies, wrap them (after they have cooled) in moisture- and vapor-proof bags before freezing. To freshen thawed cookies, place them in a preheated 325°F oven for 5 minutes or just until heated through, then allow them to cool. They will crisp up.

FLAKY BUTTER PASTRY

*T*his Flaky Butter Pastry is the quintessential butter pastry of all so-called pie crusts. It does not rank second to puff paste. It stands alone. It has a versatility very few crusts have. It is by far the easiest of all crusts to blend and to roll, and the flavor is unsurpassed. This is the pastry I teach first to a new student, and it always remains a favorite. It flakes, and it melts in one's mouth. A most divine crust for apple, rhubarb, peach, or strawberry pie.

The recipe makes enough for a 2-crust pie. See the Variation for the amounts needed to make just 1 crust.

2¼ cups (11 ounces) sifted all-purpose flour
¾ teaspoon salt
14 tablespoons (1¾ sticks) butter, chilled and
  cut into pieces
⅓ cup ice water, or as needed

1. Sift the flour and salt into a mixing bowl. Cut the butter into the flour with a pastry blender until the mixture resembles coarse meal.

2. Sprinkle on the ice water a little at a time, blending it quickly into the dough by gathering up the mixture, working it lightly with your fingers, then squeezing it together. (Work fast, as the mixture must

stay cold.) The dough should be soft enough to easily form into a ball. If it is not, add a little more water.

3. Form the dough into a ball. Cut it in half, and roll each half out at once on a lightly floured surface or pastry cloth. (Or cover with foil and refrigerate until ready to use.)

4. As soon as it has been rolled out, fit the bottom crust into the pie pan. Then it can be covered and refrigerated or frozen until ready to use. Roll out the top crust, place it on a wax-paper-lined baking sheet, cover with foil, and refrigerate. or freeze until ready to use.

Makes 2 crusts

VARIATION: For a 1-crust pie: Use 1 cup plus 2 tablespoons (5½ ounces) flour, a pinch of salt, 7 tablespoons butter, and about ¼ cup ice water. This will give you a little extra pastry dough, but don't try to change the proportions. Use the extra to make turnovers or toast fingers.

❖❖ PIES

*I*t has been said that to make a good pie one must have a "warm" heart and a cold hand. If you enjoy cooking, chances are you have a warm heart. Few cook just for themselves.

The charm and goodness of any pie, as all of us know, is largely dependent upon the excellence of the crust; it must be tender and flaky.

The dough for any kind of pastry must be made quickly to achieve this and it must be kept cold throughout the process. If the butter or shortening melts or becomes too soft, it will be absorbed by the flour and then the pastry will be heavy and tough.

Pastry made with butter is the easiest of all to blend, which makes it the best "learning" pastry, and it has, of course, a delicious flavor that is especially pleasing with fruit, but a bland crust made of vegetable shortening is better with rich fillings such as chess or chocolate.

In any case, choose a few pies whose flavor you enjoy the most and practice. Make them over and over again. Kitchen experience is the best teacher of all. Pastry making is a craft that once you have mastered you will be very proud of and it will be amazingly useful to you.

There may be someone who doesn't like a delectable golden brown crust with a yummy filling—but I have never met them.

FRENCH PASTRY

❖❖

*T*his is a classic French pastry that I have taught for many years. It makes a fine pastry crust and is wonderfully versatile. Because it has some vegetable shortening, it is not quite as rich as the Flaky Butter Pastry, nor is it quite as easy to blend or to roll, but it is very versatile and can be used for all pies.

◆

2 cups sifted all-purpose flour
¾ teaspoon salt
7 tablespoons butter, chilled and cut into pieces
¼ cup solid vegetable shortening, chilled
6 to 8 tablespoons ice water

◆

1. Sift the flour and salt together in a mixing bowl. Fluff it up with a pastry blender.

2. Cut the butter and shortening into the flour with a pastry blender until the mixture resembles coarse meal.

3. Sprinkle on the ice water a little at a time, blending it quickly into the dough by gathering up the mixture, working it lightly with your fingers, then squeezing it together. Divide the dough in half and roll out the bottom crust at once on a lightly floured

surface or pastry cloth. (Or, if desired, wrap the dough in foil and refrigerate it until you are ready to use it; but rolling it out at once is easier.)

4. As soon as it has been rolled out, fit the bottom crust into the pie pan. Then it can be covered and refrigerated or frozen. Roll out the top crust, place it on a wax-paper-lined baking sheet, cover with foil, and refrigerate or freeze until ready to use.

Makes 2 crusts

STANDARD PASTRY

◆◆

*T*his is the classic American pie crust. It is made with vegetable shortening, which is a hard fat, so it is not as easy to blend or to roll as a butter pastry, but it is more economical and not as rich. There are certain times when this is the perfect pastry for that very reason. For instance, pecan pie and several Southern pies that are on the sweet side need the blandness of the vegetable shortening crust. (Lard, which has been used in the South for pastry for several hundred years, does make a lovely, crisp crust, but vegetable shortening is excellent and more in favor today.)

This recipe is for a 2-crust pie. See the Variation for the amounts needed to make a 1-crust pie.

◆

2 cups sifted all-purpose flour
1 teaspoon salt
⅔ cup solid vegetable shortening, chilled
6 to 8 tablespoons ice water

◆

1. Sift the flour and salt together in a mixing bowl. Cut the vegetable shortening into the flour with a pastry blender until the mixture resembles coarse meal.

2. Sprinkle on the ice water a little at a time, blending it quickly into the dough by gathering up the mixture, working it lightly with your fingers, then squeezing it together. Form the dough into a ball. Cut it in half and roll out the bottom crust at once on a lightly floured surface or pastry cloth. (Or, if desired, wrap the dough in foil and refrigerate it until you are ready to use it; but rolling it out at once is easier.)

3. As soon as it has been rolled out, fit the bottom crust into the pie pan. Then it can be covered and refrigerated or frozen. Roll out the top crust, place it on a wax-paper-lined baking sheet, cover with foil, and refrigerate or freeze until ready to use.

Makes 2 crusts

VARIATION: For a 1-crust pie: Use 1½ cups flour, ¾ teaspoon salt, ½ cup chilled vegetable shortening, and 3 to 6 tablespoons ice water.

🦉 If the pastry feels hard and is difficult to roll, you didn't use enough water. If the pastry is as soft as biscuit dough and is tough when baked, you used too much.

Pastry dough must be kept cold or it will not be flaky.

◆◆

PIE PANS

*T*he advantages of baking 9- or 10-inch pies in heatproof glass pans are twofold: First, you can see through the glass and accurately judge when the crust has browned sufficiently. Second, pie crusts this size bake best in heavy pans. The heat penetrates the crusts more thoroughly, and at the same time the heavier pans hold the heat, resulting in a drier, crisper crust.

Shiny white ceramic pans reflect the heat instead of absorbing it. They are attractive, but they do not bake as efficiently as glass.

WINDFALL APPLE PIE

Keep a 9-inch skillet or baking dish handy for this fabulously delicious and easy one-crust pie. I called it the Windfall Apple Pie because I make it in the summer with the less-than-perfect apples that fall from the trees in my backyard—the misshapen ones. In the winter I use Granny Smiths, Winesaps, or Golden Delicious from the grocery. In any season, this pie is a glorious windfall.

HOW TO ROLL OUT PASTRY

1. Make up the dough for a 2-crust pie and divide it in half. Wrap one half in foil and refrigerate it.

2. Place the other half of the dough on a lightly floured surface. Flatten it a bit with a rolling pin. Then roll lightly from the center to the edge, lifting the rolling pin on each stroke as it nears the edge. Always roll from the center out, forming a circle large enough to extend 1 inch over the edge of the pie pan. Roll the pastry thin—never over ⅛ inch thick. The bottom crust should be even less than ⅛ inch thick, if possible.

3. Roll the pastry up on the rolling pin. Lift it over the center of the pie pan, and unroll. With your fingers, fit the pastry loosely into the pie pan. (This helps keep the dough from shrinking below the edge of the pan.)

4. Fill the pastry as desired.

5. Roll the second half of the dough exactly as you did the first. Roll it up loosely on the rolling pin, center it over the pie, and unroll.

6. Moisten the bottom edge of the pie crust with water, then press the top and bottom edges together. Trim off the excess dough with scissors. Fold the edges of the crusts under the rim of the pie plate, pressing them together firmly.

7. Make a few slits in the top crust with a sharp knife to allow the steam to escape.

8. Press the edges down around the rim of the pie plate with the tines of a fork, or flute. Bake as directed.

To Flute: Place your right index finger on the inside rim of the pastry, your left index finger and thumb outside. Press together, and work around the rim to form a fluted rim. The fluted edge has a greater tendency to overbrown than pastry edges that are pressed flat with the tines of a fork.

A bumper crop of apples from Rappahannock County, Virginia.

2 pounds tart apples, peeled and cored
7 tablespoons butter
½ cup plus 1 tablespoon sugar
2 tablespoons apple juice, Calvados, brandy, or cider
Flaky Butter Pastry for 1-crust pie (see page 376)
2 tablespoons heavy or whipping cream

1. Preheat the oven to 425°F.

2. Slice the apples thin. Arrange them in a 9-inch skillet or pan (not black iron). Dot them with the butter, and sprinkle with ½ cup of the sugar and the chosen liquid.

3. Roll out the pastry, and cut it to fit just inside the rim of the pan. Place the pastry over the apples, leaving a small space between it and the edge of the pan.

4. Prick the pastry to allow the steam to escape. Brush it with the cream, and sprinkle it with the tablespoon of sugar (so it will glaze).

5. Bake until the apples are cooked and the crust is golden brown, 30 to 35 minutes.

Makes 1 pie

Calvados is very delicious in this pie.

MARYLAND'S CHESS AND APPLE TART

*T*his tart is typical of the very rich but superb desserts that were served in the majestic homes in Maryland in the early 19th century. Make no mistake about it, this tart is just as delicious today. Serve it in small wedges with coffee. Divine.

Bel Air in Maryland is a Palladian-style mansion built at the turn of the century as a summer home.

Standard or French Pastry for 1-crust pie (see pages 378 and 377)
1 cup (2 sticks) butter, cut into pieces
1½ cups sugar
4 large eggs
Pinch of salt
½ teaspoon vanilla extract or cognac vanilla (see Index)
½ teaspoon freshly grated nutmeg
3½ cups peeled, cored, and chopped tart apples (3 large apples)

1. Preheat the oven to 400°F.
2. Roll out and line a 10-inch pie pan with the pastry. Trim the edge even with the rim of the pan. Cover with foil, and weight it down with dried beans. Place the pie pan on the bottom rack of the oven and bake about 10 minutes.
3. Remove the beans and the foil, and set the partially baked crust aside to cool.
4. Reduce the oven temperature to 325°F.
5. While the crust is cooling, cream the butter and sugar thoroughly with an electric mixer until fluffy. Add the eggs, salt, vanilla, and nutmeg, and mix well.
6. Fold the chopped apples into the egg mixture by hand.
7. Pour the egg and apple mixture into the cooled pie shell. Place the pie pan on the lower rack of the oven, and bake until the apples are tender and the blade of a knife inserted into the custard comes out clean, 45 to 60 minutes. Serve warm or cold.

Makes 1 pie

🦉 If the edges of the crust brown too quickly, cover them with a strip of foil until the pie is done.

If the pie is cooked at too high a temperature or cooked too long, the filling will "whey," just as in cooking any custard.

HOLIDAY MINCEMEAT PIE

Standard Pastry for 2-crust pie (see page 378)
3 cups mincemeat (see Index)

1. Preheat the oven to 400°F.
2. Roll out and line a 9-inch pie pan with the bottom crust. Trim away the

extra, leaving ½-inch overhang.

3. Put your chosen mincemeat in the pie shell. Roll out the remaining pastry and place it carefully over the filled pie shell. Pinch the edges of the crusts together with the tines of a fork and trim the pastry even with the edges of the pan. Cut a few thin slits in the top crust.

4. Place the pie on the bottom rack of the oven and bake for 20 minutes. Reduce the heat to 375°F and continue baking until the crust is golden brown, another 25 minutes.

Makes 1 pie

Young people's Christmas party in Hanover, North Carolina, around 1900.

STRAWBERRY, APRICOT, AND PINEAPPLE PIE

❖❖❖

*T*his is a light and refreshing early summer fruit pie. You can mix the fruits in the proportions that suit your fancy.

◆

Flaky Butter or French Pastry for 2-crust pie (see pages 376 and 377)
1 can (1 pound) apricots, well drained
1 cup canned crushed unsweetened pineapple, well drained
1½ cups halved strawberries
⅔ cup sugar, or more as needed
3 tablespoons all-purpose flour
Tiny pinch of salt
3 tablespoons butter
1½ tablespoons heavy or whipping cream
Sugar, for garnish (coarse is best)

◆

1. Roll out and line a 9-inch pie pan with the bottom crust. Trim leaving a ½-inch overhang. Wrap the remaining dough in foil and refrigerate.

2. Preheat the oven to 425°F.

3. Put the apricots, pineapple, and strawberries in the pie shell.

4. Toss the sugar, flour, and salt together, then sprinkle it over the fruit. Dot with the butter.

5. Roll out the remaining pastry and cut it into 1-inch strips. Cover the pie with the pastry strips, crisscross fashion. Crimp the strips to the edge of the pastry with the tines of a fork. Trim the pastry even with the rim of the pan.

6. Brush the pastry strips with the cream and sprinkle with sugar—the coarser the better.

7. Place the pie pan on the lower shelf of the oven and bake 15 minutes. Then lower the heat to 375°F and bake until the crust is golden brown, another 35 to 45 minutes. Before the pie is done, taste a little of the juice for sweetness. Add a sprinkling of sugar in between the strips of pastry if desired. (It is difficult to control the sweetness of the mixed fruits except by using this

Imagine the remarkable variety of fruit pies that could come out of this market in New Orleans.

method. If the fruit were cooked before adding it to the pie, it would become over-cooked and dull.) Serve warm or at room temperature.

Makes 1 pie

🦉 If at any time the top crust browns too soon or too much, cover it loosely with foil. If the bottom crust starts to brown too much, lower the heat. This means your oven is overheating.

RHUBARB CREAM PIE

I have seen this rhubarb pie attract a loyal following from otherwise rhubarb dissenters. Rhubarb can be very tart, but the creamy custard quiets all that and the counterpoint of flavors is lovely indeed.

Flaky Butter Pastry for 1-crust pie (see page 376)
3 large eggs
3 tablespoons milk
2 cups sugar
Tiny pinch of salt
¼ cup sifted all-purpose flour
1 teaspoon fresh lemon juice
1 pound rhubarb (4 cups of 1-inch pieces)
2 tablespoons butter

1. Preheat the oven to 425°F.
2. Roll out the dough to ⅛ inch thick and large enough to fit a 9-inch pie pan. Trim the edge even with the rim of the pan. Line the shell with foil so that it covers the edges of the crust, and fill it with dried beans.
3. Place the pan on the lower shelf of the oven and bake until it has barely begun to brown, 15 minutes. Remove the beans and the foil. Continue to bake 5 minutes longer. The crust should be well set but not very brown. Remove the crust from the oven and set it aside to cool.
4. Reduce the oven temperature to 400°F.
5. Combine the eggs, milk, sugar, salt, flour, and lemon juice in a blender or food processor. Blend, and set aside.
6. Put the rhubarb in the cooled shell. Dot it with the butter. Then pour the egg mixture over the rhubarb.
7. Place the pie pan on the lower shelf of the oven, and reduce the heat at once to 350°F. Bake until a knife inserted into the center of the custard comes out clean, 45 to 50 minutes.

Makes 1 pie

🦉 If the rim of the pie browns too much or too soon, the oven is too hot. Cover the rim with a strip of foil.

Cooking too long or at too high a temperature will cause the custard to curdle or "whey."

JUPITER ISLAND LIME MERINGUE PIE

◆◆◆

Jupiter Island is a small and beautiful spot on the Indian River in Florida, where I learned of this pie—a great favorite. I think it has a clearer flavor than Key Lime Pie.

◆

Standard Pastry for 1-crust pie (see page 378)
3 tablespoons all-purpose flour
¼ cup cornstarch
¼ teaspoon salt
1⅔ cups sugar
2 cups water
5 large egg yolks
⅔ cup fresh lime juice (5 or 6 limes)
2 teaspoons grated lemon peel (see Owl)
Green food coloring (optional)

MERINGUE

5 large egg whites
Tiny pinch of salt
10 tablespoons sugar

◆

1. Preheat the oven to 400°F.
2. Roll out and line a 9-inch pie pan with the pastry. Trim the edge even with the rim of the pan. Cover with foil, and weight it down with dried beans. Place the pie pan on the bottom rack of the oven and bake about 10 minutes.
3. Remove the beans and the foil, and set the partially baked crust aside to cool.
4. Reduce the oven temperature to 350°F.
5. Mix the flour, cornstarch, and salt with half the sugar in a heavy stainless steel or enamel saucepan. Add the water, and mix well. Bring to a boil and beat constantly with a whisk until the mixture is fairly thick, 3 minutes. Remove from the heat.
6. Beat the egg yolks with the remaining sugar until well mixed. Mix a little of the hot cornstarch mixture into the yolks to temper them. Then add the egg yolk mixture to the remaining cornstarch and sugar. Blend thoroughly. Cook (over direct heat if using enameled iron; if not, over simmering water), stirring constantly, until the filling is quite thick, 3 to 5 minutes. Do not allow it

The lighthouse on Jupiter Island in Florida.

to boil hard. Remove from the heat.

7. Gently blend in the lime juice, lemon peel, and 2 or 3 drops of green food coloring, if desired. Put the filling in the refrigerator to cool and firm up, 6 minutes.
8. Make the meringue: Beat the egg whites with the salt until they form a soft peak. Add the sugar gradually, beating until the whites hold a stiff peak.
9. Spoon the lime filling into the pie shell. Cover it with the meringue, making sure the meringue covers the filling and seals the edge of the crust (to prevent shrinking and weeping).
10. Place the pie on the middle shelf of the oven and bake until the meringue is light golden brown, 15 to 18 minutes. Watch it carefully.

Makes 1 pie

🦉 When stirring the filling as it cooks, go around the sides and bottom of the pan continually, lifting the filling so it will not overcook in spots.

Do not use lime peel in this pie as it is bitter.

BARBARA FRITCHIE PIE

◆◆◆

Barbara Fritchie lived in Frederick, Maryland, during the Civil War. Legend has it that in 1862 she waved a Union flag defiantly at Stonewall Jackson and his troops as they passed by her home. Jackson ordered the troops to fire, and they did. Poor Barbara Fritchie! No one seems to know how the pie came into the scheme of things, but this I do know—it is one of the best chess pies on earth.

◆

Standard Pastry for 1-crust pie (see page 378)
¾ cup light brown sugar
¾ cup granulated sugar
4 tablespoons (½ stick) butter, cut into pieces
2 large eggs, separated
½ cup heavy or whipping cream
Pinch of salt
1 teaspoon vanilla extract or cognac vanilla
    (see Index)

◆

1. Preheat the oven to 425°F.
2. Roll out and line a 9-inch pie pan with the pastry. Trim the edge even with the rim of the pan. Cover with plastic wrap or foil, and refrigerate until ready to use.
3. Cream both sugars with the butter thoroughly in the large bowl of an electric mixer until well blended. Add the egg yolks and continue beating until the mixture turns a bit lighter and is smooth.
4. Add the cream, salt, and vanilla, and mix with a spoon or spatula. (The cream must not be whipped.)
5. Beat the egg whites until they are stiff but not dry and grainy. Gently fold them into the sugar and yolk mixture.
6. Spoon the filling into the pie shell, place it on the lower shelf of the oven, and bake for 15 minutes.
7. Lower the heat to 375°F and bake until a knife inserted into the filling comes out clean, 20 to 25 minutes longer. Cool before serving.
    Makes 1 pie

The pie will signal when it is done by rising a bit in the center.

OLD-FASHIONED
BRANDIED PUMPKIN PIE

◆◆◆

Otto Seelbach, a member of the Louisville Seelbach Hotel family who knew good food and food chemistry, told me years ago that a pumpkin pie should "cry." That is, small teardrops of moisture should rise to the top after the pie rests for a while. In other words, a delicious pumpkin pie must be moist and luscious. This is *the* pumpkin pie that cries.

◆

Standard Pastry for 1-crust pie (see page 378)
1 cup canned pumpkin
1 cup heavy or whipping cream or evaporated
    milk
3 large eggs
1 cup light brown sugar
1 teaspoon ground cinnamon

½ teaspoon ground ginger
¼ teaspoon ground cloves
½ teaspoon freshly grated nutmeg
¼ cup brandy
Whipped cream

◆

1. Preheat the oven to 400°F.
2. Roll out and line a 9-inch pie pan with the dough. Trim the edge even with the rim of the pan. Cover with foil, and weight it down with dried beans. Place the pie pan on the bottom rack of the oven and bake about 15 minutes.
3. Remove the beans and the foil, and set the partially baked crust aside to cool.
4. Measure the pumpkin into a roomy bowl. Add the heavy cream or evaporated milk and the eggs, and beat thoroughly with a whisk.
5. Combine the sugar with the spices. Toss them together well, then beat them into the pumpkin mixture. Add the brandy, and mix thoroughly.
6. Spoon the filling into the partially baked crust.
7. Place the pie on the lower shelf of the oven and bake 8 minutes. Reduce the heat to 350°F and continue to bake until a knife inserted in the middle comes out clean, another 35 to 40 minutes. Serve

warm or cold, with whipped cream.
Makes 1 pie

🦉 Evaporated milk works quite well in a spicy pie like pumpkin.

FLORIDA EVERGLADES COCONUT PIE

*I*t probably goes without saying that this is one of Florida's favorite pies. And it has a devoted following all through the South.

Standard Pastry for 1-crust pie (see page 378)
½ cup sugar
3 tablespoons cornstarch
4 large egg yolks
1¾ cups milk, warmed
½ teaspoon salt
1 cup well-drained freshly grated, or 1 cup
    packaged coconut
1 teaspoon fresh lemon or lime juice
1½ tablespoons butter
1 teaspoon vanilla extract

MERINGUE

4 large egg whites

Tiny pinch of salt
½ cup sugar

1. Preheat the oven to 400°F.
2. Roll out and line a 9-inch pie pan with the dough. Trim the edge even with the rim of the pan. Cover with foil, and weight it down with dried beans. Place the pie pan on the bottom rack of the oven and bake about 15 minutes.
3. Remove the beans and the foil, and set the partially baked crust aside to cool.
4. Reduce the oven temperature to 350°F.

Harvesting coconuts in Florida, 1891.

5. Combine the sugar and the cornstarch in a mixing bowl. Add the egg yolks, and beat hard with a whisk or an electric mixer.

6. Add the warm milk, and transfer the mixture to the top of a double boiler. Cook over simmering water until the mixture thickens and is smooth, 8 minutes.

7. Remove from the heat. Add the salt, coconut, lemon or lime juice, butter, and vanilla. Allow to cool slightly.

8. Make the meringue: Beat the egg whites with the salt until they hold a soft peak. Slowly add the sugar, beating until the whites hold a stiff peak.

9. Spoon the cooled filling into the pie shell, and cover it with the meringue, making sure the meringue covers the filling and seals the edge of the pie crust (this helps prevent shrinking and "weeping").

10. Place the pie pan on the middle shelf of the oven and bake until the meringue is light golden brown, about 15 minutes.

Makes 1 pie

If a cornstarch mixture is beaten hard after it has thickened, it will thin out. Watch it carefully.

OLD PINEY CHOCOLATE PIE

❖❖❖

A perfect cream pie filling is never stiff and gummy. It must be soft, and it should run just a little when cut. This is that kind of pie—chocolaty and smooth, with a crisp crust—a luscious combination.

Standard Pastry for 1-crust pie (see page 378)
3 ounces unsweetened chocolate
1¾ cups milk
1 cup sugar
½ teaspoon salt
5 tablespoons all-purpose flour
4 large egg yolks
2 tablespoons butter
1½ teaspoons vanilla extract or cognac vanilla
   (see Index)
4 large egg whites
½ cup sugar

1. Preheat the oven to 400°F.

2. Roll out and line a 9-inch pie pan with the dough. Trim the edge even with the rim of the pan. Cover with foil, and weight it down with dried beans. Place the pie pan on the bottom rack of the oven and bake about 15 minutes.

3. Remove the beans and the foil, and set the partially baked crust aside to cool.

4. Reduce the oven temperature to 350°F.

5. Combine the chocolate and the milk in the top of a double boiler and heat over simmering water. Beat until the chocolate has melted and the mixture is smooth.

6. Combine the sugar, salt, and flour, and mix well. Add to the chocolate and milk. Beat thoroughly.

7. Pour a small amount of the chocolate mixture into the egg yolks to temper them, and mix well. Add the yolks to the remaining chocolate mixture, and blend thoroughly.

8. Cook over simmering water, stirring constantly, until the mixture has thickened, 8 minutes. Add the butter, and blend. Remove from the heat, and add the vanilla. Spoon the filling into the partially baked pie shell.

9. Make the meringue: Beat the egg whites with a tiny pinch of salt until they hold a soft peak. Slowly add the sugar, beating until the whites hold a stiff peak.

10. Cover the warm filling with the meringue, making sure the meringue covers the filling and seals the edge of the crust (this helps prevent shrinking and "weeping").

11. Place the pie on the middle shelf of the oven and bake until the meringue is lightly browned, 10 to 15 minutes. Cool before serving.

Makes 1 pie

DEEP SOUTH PECAN PIE

*P*ecan pie is not a difficult pie to make, but it is rich and rather sweet—so much so that it is at its best when served after a very light meal.

Standard Pastry for 1-crust pie (see page 378)
3 large eggs
½ cup sugar
½ teaspoon salt
6 tablespoons (¾ stick) butter, melted
1 cup dark corn syrup
1 teaspoon vanilla extract or cognac vanilla
  (see Index)
1 cup pecan halves

1. Preheat the oven to 375°F.

2. Roll out and line a 9-inch pie pan with the pastry. Trim the edge even with the rim of the pan.

3. Combine the eggs, sugar, salt, butter, corn syrup, and vanilla. Mix thoroughly, and fold in the pecans.

4. Spoon the filling into the pie shell.

5. Place the pie pan on the lower shelf of the oven and bake until the bottom crust is golden brown and the center of the pie seems well set when the pie is shaken, 45 to 50 minutes. The pie will rise a bit in the

The pie class of 1911, Kentucky State Normal School.

center when it is done. Cool, and serve.

Makes 1 pie

🦉 Overcooking can make a pecan pie gummy. Time it carefully.

JEFF DAVIS PIE

❖❖❖

*T*his is one of Kentucky's most famous pies. There have been many versions, but I am partial to this one, given by Marion Flexner in *Dixie Dishes*.

◆

Standard Pastry for 1-crust pie (see page 378)
1 cup sugar
2 tablespoons all-purpose flour
4 tablespoons (½ stick) unsalted butter, cut into pieces
¼ teaspoon salt
4 large eggs
1 cup heavy or whipping cream
½ teaspoon freshly grated nutmeg
1 teaspoon vanilla extract or cognac vanilla (see Index)

◆

1. Preheat the oven to 425°F.

2. Roll out and line a 9-inch pie pan with the dough. Trim the edge even with the rim of the pan. Cover with foil, and weight it down with dried beans. Place the pie pan on the bottom rack of the oven and bake 15 minutes.

3. Cream the sugar and the flour with the butter thoroughly until smooth, using an electric mixer.

4. Add the salt and the eggs, and beat thoroughly. Add the cream, nutmeg, and vanilla, and mix well by hand (the cream must not be whipped). Spoon the filling into the prepared shell.

5. Place the pie pan on the bottom shelf of the oven and bake for 15 minutes. Reduce the heat to 350°F and bake until a knife inserted into the custard comes out clean, another 30 minutes. Cool slightly and serve.

Makes 1 pie

CHAPTER TWELVE

DESSERTS AND CANDIES

FABULOUS FINALES

Southerners really do have a sweet tooth, and I am among the most guilty. I adore desserts—ice creams, sherbets, pies, puddings, cookies, cakes, and candies—the entire collection.

Grandfather William Irvin Hamby, who was known as Colonel Hamby, said that ice cream was *the* perfect dessert. If Grandfather were living today he would be known as a gourmet because he was always planning delicious food. Grandfather had been an aide-de-camp of General Nathan Bedford Forrest during the Civil War. He kept the visitors to his spa and all of his family glued to his side for hours on end listening to stories of the war—always with a very sly account of "his" bravery.

But back to the ice cream. During the hot summer days the hand-cranked ice cream freezers were turning all the time for the hotel and the soda fountain. Vanilla was the leader, pure, rich, and wonderful. Janet Appelgate, my assistant teacher, and I worked for many months to re-create those sherbets and ice creams, to bring them to you as marvelous as they were then. The vanilla can be seasoned with fresh peaches, strawberries, pineapple, or to your fancy. My favorite is the apricot ice cream. The ices are sheer nectar and are unbelievably easy—with our deep-freezers today, we can just mix and freeze. In this same category are the most glamorous frozen soufflés, and they too are deceptively easy.

During the long cold days of winter at the hotel we had glorious puddings or some kind of pie every day—Mother's rice pudding with currant jelly under the meringue, or The Prince of Puddings with bourbon or nutmeg sauce, or Barbara Fritchie Pie. But, I have to agree with Grandfather, ice cream is a perfect dessert.

APPLE AND ALMOND MACAROON PUDDING

*M*any students have said this pudding is "the apple's finest hour." Use a tart apple such as the Granny Smith. It is good even without using any brandy, as the almond macaroons and apples are so compatible, but the Calvados does make it special.

6 tablespoons (¾ stick) butter
3 tablespoons all-purpose flour
1 cup milk
¾ cup sugar
3 large egg yolks
1½ teaspoons vanilla extract or cognac vanilla
   (see page 396)
1½ tablespoons Calvados or brandy
4 large tart apples, peeled, cored, and thinly
   sliced
5 large egg whites
Pinch of salt
4 almond macaroons, dried and crumbled
Calvados Sauce or Vanilla Sauce (recipes
   follow)

There are so many delicious ways to prepare apples, I know not one of these went to waste in 1920.

1. Preheat the oven to 375°F.

2. Melt 3 tablespoons of the butter in a heavy saucepan. Add the flour and blend it well until smooth. Slowly add the milk, stirring constantly with a whisk, over medium heat; cook until the mixture thickens, 1 minute. Add ½ cup of the sugar and beat hard. Add the egg yolks, and blend them in. Remove the pan from the heat, and add the vanilla and the Calvados or brandy. Set aside but keep warm.

3. Melt the remaining butter in a skillet. Add the sliced apples, sprinkle them with the remaining sugar, and gently sauté until tender, about 7 minutes.

4. Beat the egg whites with the salt until they hold a stiff peak. Fold a small amount into the egg yolk mixture to lighten it, then fold in the remaining egg whites.

5. Place half of the apples in a buttered shallow 1½-quart baking dish. Cover them with half of the egg mixture. Add the remaining apples, and sprinkle them with the macaroon crumbs. Cover the apples and macaroons with the remaining egg mixture, filling the dish almost to the rim.

6. Bake until the top is golden brown and the pudding is fairly firm, 25 to 30 minutes. Serve at once with warm Calvados or Vanilla Sauce.

Serves 8

CALVADOS SAUCE

1 cup sugar
8 teaspoons cornstarch or arrowroot
½ teaspoon salt
4 slivers lemon peel
2 cups water
4 tablespoons (½ stick) butter
¼ cup Calvados, or more to taste

Combine the sugar, cornstarch or arrowroot, salt, and lemon peel in a heavy saucepan. Mix well. Add the water, and cook over medium heat until the sauce has thickened, 5 minutes. Add the butter and cook a few minutes longer. Remove the pan from the heat, sieve out the lemon peel, and add the Calvados.

Makes 2 cups

--- ◆ ---
VANILLA SAUCE
--- ◆ ---

½ cup sugar
1½ tablespoons cornstarch
Pinch of salt
1 sliver lemon peel
1 cup water
3 tablespoons butter

1 teaspoon vanilla extract or cognac vanilla
(see page 396)

--- ◆ ---

Combine the sugar and cornstarch in a saucepan and mix thoroughly. Add the salt, lemon peel, and water. Bring to a boil and cook over medium-high heat until the sauce is clear, 5 to 7 minutes. Discard the lemon peel, and add the butter. Remove the pan from the heat, and stir in the vanilla.

Makes 2 cups

VARIATION: For a creamier sauce, add 1 tablespoon heavy or whipping cream.

THE PRINCE OF PUDDINGS

--- ◆◆ ---

*B*read pudding is for cold winter nights when it is good to be by the fireside. These puddings, made with care, are warm and comforting. They fill up our tummies with goodness and they stick to the ribs. This one is especially wonderful.

Serve it warm with your favorite sauce, or quite simply with your best homemade jelly or preserves. (They should be tart, such as currant, apricot, raspberry, plum, rhubarb and strawberry jelly, or strawberry preserves.) Or use a fresh fruit sauce.

--- ◆ ---

½ cup sugar
Peel of 1 lemon, slivered
2½ cups soft bread crumbs (about 6 slices)
2 cups milk
4 tablespoons (½ stick) butter, melted
2 whole large eggs
3 large eggs, separated
1 teaspoon baking powder
½ teaspoon vanilla extract or cognac vanilla
(see page 396)
Kentucky Bourbon Sauce (see page 394)

1. Preheat the oven to 350°F.

2. Put the sugar and lemon peel in a food processor and process until the lemon peel is finely grated or finely grate the peel by hand. Add the bread crumbs, milk, and butter. "Pulse" just enough to blend well. Add the whole eggs and 3 egg yolks, and pulse again, only until the mixture is well mixed. (If you are using an electric mixer, add the ingredients in the same order.) Pour the bread mixture into a bowl. Stir in the baking powder.

3. Beat the egg whites until they hold a stiff peak but are not dry and grainy, then fold them into the mixture. Stir in the vanilla.

4. Pour the mixture (it will be liquid like a custard) into a buttered shallow 2-quart baking dish. Place the dish in a pan of hot water, and bake until a knife stuck into the center comes out clean, about 1 hour.

5. Serve at once with Kentucky Bourbon Sauce.

Serves 8

DATE-AND-NUT STEAMED PUDDING

A wintry pudding for those who love dates. This is a moist pudding that improves in flavor when made a few days ahead. Serve hot, with Kentucky Bourbon Sauce.

1 cup loosely packed light brown sugar
Slivered peel of 1 navel orange
1 pound pitted dates
2 large tart apples, peeled and cored
1 large potato, peeled
2 large eggs
1 large egg white
2 tablespoons fresh orange juice
1 cup sifted all-purpose flour
½ cup soft bread crumbs
1 teaspoon ground cinnamon
½ teaspoon ground cloves
¼ teaspoon salt
1½ teaspoons vanilla extract or cognac vanilla (see page 396)
2½ teaspoons baking powder
3 tablespoons butter, melted
½ cup coarsely chopped pecans
Kentucky Bourbon Sauce (recipe follows)

1. Combine the brown sugar and orange peel in a food processor. Twirl until the peel is finely grated, about 2 minutes. Transfer to a large mixing bowl.

2. Chop ½ pound of the dates in the processor, and add them to the sugar mixture.

3. Purée the remaining dates in the processor, and add this to the mixture.

4. Using the processor shredder blade, shred the apples and potato (you should have 1 cup of each). Add this to the mixture in the bowl, and beat thoroughly with an electric mixer. (A processor would purée the mixture.)

5. Add the eggs, egg white, and orange juice, and mix again. Add the flour, bread crumbs, spices, salt, vanilla, baking powder, and melted butter. Mix thoroughly. Fold in the pecans by hand.

6. Spoon the mixture into a greased heavy 9-inch tube or bundt pan. Cover it with foil. Place the pan in a large pan or roaster that has a cover. Pour in enough hot water to come two-thirds of the way up the side of the pudding pan. Cover the large pan and place it over high heat. Bring the water to a boil, reduce the heat, and simmer for 3½ hours, adding hot water as needed to maintain the water level.

PUDDINGS

*G*lamorous desserts dazzle our taste buds, but we respond to puddings with love. They touch our emotions with their homey, cozy goodness and luscious sauces. Puddings are nostalgic and charming to the old, but they are exciting to the young, with that eager sweet tooth always at hand.

We can now make a pudding with our electric gadgets in a flash, but they are worth the little extra effort that it takes to cook from scratch. These warm, comforting desserts do more than fill our tummies—they touch our hearts.

7. When the pudding is done, a knife inserted in the center will come out nearly clean. Loosen the pudding from the pan with a sharp knife. To unmold, place a flat pan or plate over the pudding pan and invert them both. Cool, wrap in foil, and allow to age a few days before serving.

8. To serve, place the wrapped pudding in a preheated 325°F oven until just heated through, 20 minutes. Serve with room temperature Kentucky Bourbon Sauce.

Serves 15

KENTUCKY BOURBON SAUCE

⅔ cup sugar
1 large egg
8 tablespoons (1 stick) butter, melted
1 tablespoon fresh lemon juice
Freshly grated nutmeg to taste
⅓ cup best bourbon whiskey

1. Combine the sugar and egg in a small bowl and beat with an electric mixer until well blended.

2. Stir the melted butter into the egg mixture. Cook in the top of a double boiler over simmering water, whisking constantly, until the sugar has dissolved and the sauce has thickened a bit, about 5 minutes.

3. Remove the pan from the heat and add the lemon juice, nutmeg, and bourbon.

Makes 1½ cups

VARIATION: Some recipes in the South omit the bourbon and substitute vanilla extract to taste. This makes a versatile sauce for rice pudding, yellow pudding cake, and old-fashioned jam pudding. All are served warm with the warm sauce.

NEW ORLEANS BURNT CREAM

*I*n New Orleans this dessert is called "Burnt Cream." It is the Crème Brûlée I learned when I was studying at the Cordon Bleu years ago. I have never tasted a better one. Crème Brûlée should be served only after a very light meal, and never when there is another creamed dish on the menu. It is such a luscious dessert that it should not be forgotten.

2 cups heavy or whipping cream
4 large egg yolks
3 tablespoons granulated sugar
⅛ teaspoon salt
1 teaspoon vanilla extract or cognac vanilla
    (see page 396)
½ cup light brown sugar

1. Preheat the oven to 350°F.

2. Scald the cream (do not allow it to boil). Beat the egg yolks with an electric mixer or a whisk until they are light and creamy. Beat in the granulated sugar and salt. Add a little of the cream to the egg yolks to warm them. Then continue to add the rest of the cream, pouring slowly. Blend well, and add the vanilla.

3. Pour the mixture into a shallow 1½-quart baking dish. Put the baking dish in a roasting pan, and add enough warm water to come two-thirds up the side of the baking dish. Bake until a knife inserted into the custard 1 inch from the edge comes out clean, about 1 hour. Remove the dish from the oven, and refrigerate the custard at once to stop the cooking.

4. To finish the crème brûlée, sift a layer of brown sugar to a depth of ⅓ inch over the cold custard. Put the baking pan in a pan of crushed ice and place it under the broiler long enough for the brown sugar to melt and form a crunchy crust. This takes a very few minutes. Either serve as is or allow the dish to chill again.

Serves 6 to 8

CLOUDS IN CHOCOLATE CREAM

*T*his dessert has many names. It is called Chocolate Floating Island, Bowls on Chocolate, or Clouds in Chocolate Cream, but what's in a name? It is a delicious chocolate custard that you can make just any time, and then if it is your fancy to dress it up, add the clouds. They are as attractive as they are good.

4 large egg yolks
⅔ cup sugar
⅛ teaspoon salt
2 cups milk
¼ cup heavy or whipping cream
2 ounces semisweet chocolate, melted
1½ teaspoons vanilla extract or cognac vanilla
*   (see page 396)*
Clouds (recipe follows)
Chocolate shavings, for garnish
Dutch Chocolate Sauce (recipe follows)

1. With an electric mixer, beat the egg yolks with the sugar and salt until they are almost creamy. Stir in the milk and the cream.

2. Pour the mixture into a heavy saucepan or the top of a double boiler placed over simmering water and cook gently, stirring constantly with a rubber spatula or wooden spoon, until the custard begins to coat the spoon, about 5 to 8 minutes. Add the melted chocolate, blend it in thoroughly, and pour the custard at once into a cool bowl. Blend in the vanilla. Cover, and refrigerate for a minimum of 30 minutes.

3. When you are ready to serve the dessert, spoon the chilled chocolate cream into a crystal bowl. Arrange the clouds in pyramid fashion on top of the cream. Sprinkle shaved chocolate on top. Pass a sauceboat of Dutch Chocolate Sauce if desired.

Serves 4 to 5

CLOUDS

4 large egg whites
¾ cup sugar

1. Beat the egg whites until they hold a soft peak. Gradually add the sugar, beating constantly, and continue beating until the egg whites form a stiff meringue.

2. Using a wet spoon, dip into the meringue and scoop up large egg-shaped clouds. Slip them from the spoon into a large shallow pan of simmering water. Allow the clouds to poach 1 to 2 minutes on one side, then turn them and poach on the other side.

3. Lift the clouds from the water with a slotted spoon and put them on paper towels to drain. Repeat the process until you have made all the clouds.

If the poaching water for the clouds heats beyond simmering, the egg whites will disintegrate. If the clouds start to puff a lot, they have cooked too long and will disintegrate. The poaching is not difficult to do; it is just a matter of timing.

DUTCH CHOCOLATE SAUCE

*I*f you want a light chocolate sauce that has the full, delicious flavor of chocolate without being the least bit "fudgy," this is your sauce. It must be made with Droste's or an equally fine imported cocoa. When made this way, the sauce does not need vanilla or any liqueur to enhance the flavor. A favorite with vanilla ice cream, too.

7 tablespoons unsweetened Dutch cocoa
¾ cup sugar

1 cup cold water
4 tablespoons (½ stick) unsalted butter
Tiny pinch of salt (if desired)

1. Combine the cocoa and sugar in a heavy saucepan. Mix well and add the water, beating hard with a whisk. Bring the mixture to a boil, continuing to beat, then lower the heat and simmer 3 to 4 minutes. Add the butter, and simmer, stirring the sauce so it won't stick to the bottom of the pan, for about 5 minutes more. Add the salt if desired.

2. The sauce should be thick enough to coat a wooden spoon. If you want a thicker sauce, cook it a bit longer over very low heat while continuing to stir. Serve the sauce hot.

Makes 1 cup

HOW TO MAKE COGNAC VANILLA

*T*he best and purest vanilla extract in the world is the one you make yourself. It is not cheap, but few things of quality are; and ounce for ounce, the extract made from the vanilla bean using an alcohol base is not as expensive as the small bottles of vanilla that are mislabeled "pure" in supermarkets and gourmet shops.

When I was young, the vanilla beans (still in their outer brownish shells) were so cheap they were shipped in burlap sacks from Mexico. My father had the outer coat shelled from the beans, and then the black, moist bean itself was cut and marinated in grain alcohol. It was stored in chemical bottles (I can see them now) to be used in making ice creams and chocolate and fruit syrups for the soda fountain—Dawson Springs Salts and Water Company—next to our hotel. They knew no other way and little did they realize the superiority of their product.

Nothing can be easier to make than pure vanilla extract. The cheapest one using pure grain alcohol is better than any vanilla you can buy. Brandy also makes a fine vanilla, but cognac makes the world's best.

Cognac and brandy were used in cakes and sweets hundreds of years before vanilla was discovered, because in addition to adding flavor, they have a leavening power which makes the product lighter.

Any French-type brandy made from grapes produces an excellent vanilla. Cognac has more depth of flavor and makes a superior extract, but either cognac or brandy is an elixir of great flavor, and in cooking, "flavor is everything."

Cut a vanilla bean lengthwise and then crosswise into small pieces, thus exposing the hundreds of black shiny seeds, which are the source of the vanilla flavor. Place these cut pieces in a bottle that can be closed airtight. Cover with cognac, brandy, or grain alcohol (2½ ounces for 1 vanilla bean), close tightly, and store at room temperature. Shake the bottle well every few days. It will take 2 to 3 weeks for the vanilla to reach its maximum flavor. This extract will always have the bouquet of cognac or brandy. (It will never smell like the vanilla extract from the grocery, which is often vanillin, an imitation vanilla.) The pure extract made this way has a more delicate and exquisite aroma and flavor, and is vastly superior. The true vanilla essence comes out in baking.

Fresh cognac or brandy may be added to the vanilla beans two or three times after the liquid has been used up. After that, new beans should be used, as the flavor from the old beans will have been spent.

A VERY SPECIAL CUSTARD

❖❖

*V*anilla pot de crème is a perfect custard—light, exceptionally easy to make, and a lovely last touch for a thousand menus. It is not so rich that it is cloying, but the flavor is so exquisite that it is very satisfying. It is at its most charming served with a cluster of seedless green grapes by its side on the dessert plate.

Pot de crème is simply a custard served in the little cup in which it is baked.

CUSTARDS

*T*he delicate and delicious dessert we call custard is often erroneously attributed to the French. Actually, it is an English dish—so much so that the French call it *crème à l'anglaise*. That is the plain version that came to us from our British forebears as "boiled" custard. Of course, it isn't boiled at all. It better not be, or it will curdle and be an unsightly mess.

But the French, as they have been prone to do since the Italians in Catherine de Medici's time taught them many refinements in cooking, adopted the custard and developed it in glorious ways. The French perfected custards in so many ways that they have become famous for most of the great custard desserts and sauces, and there are many.

The main thing to know about custards of all types is that they cannot withstand high or prolonged heat. As soon as the custard coats a wooden spoon, it must be removed from the heat and poured into a cooler bowl or pan at once, then quickly chilled to stop the cooking.

When cooking custard dishes in the oven, place them in a pan of water, which tempers the heat.

To test the doneness of custards, plunge a stainless steel knife into the center of the custard; if it comes out just barely clean, the custard is done. Remember, a custard continues cooking for a few seconds after it has been removed from the heat. If the knife blade comes out too clean, the custard is likely to overcook.

Keeping these facts in mind, you will have at your command many enjoyable and beloved desserts, for the whole western world loves a good custard.

---

6 large egg yolks
½ cup sugar
⅛ teaspoon salt
2 cups milk
1 teaspoon vanilla extract or cognac vanilla
    (see page 396), or 1 tablepoon cognac

1. Preheat the oven to 350°F.

2. Blend the egg yolks, sugar, salt, and milk, using an electric mixer or a whisk. Add the flavoring. Pour into pot-de-crème or custard cups, filling them almost to the top.

3. Put the cups in a baking pan and add enough hot water to come halfway up the sides of the cups. Place the pan on the middle shelf of the oven and bake until a stainless steel knife inserted in the middle comes out just barely clean, 1 to 1¼ hours. (The baking time will vary with the size of the cups used.) Refrigerate at once to stop the cooking. Serve when cold.

Serves 6 to 8

The freshest milk being prepared for the delivery van of a family dairy.

TENDER COCONUT CUSTARD

Southerners are fond of coconut in almost any guise, and when blended into a custard, it is a special favorite. When there is no time to make a pie, this easy but flavorful sweet will be welcome.

This young lady with her prize papayas was photographed in Florida.

⅓ cup sugar
3 large egg yolks
2 cups milk, warmed
Tiny pinch of salt
1 teaspoon vanilla extract or cognac vanilla
    (see page 396)
⅔ cup grated fresh or canned flaked coconut
6 tablespoons apricot or peach preserves or
    currant jelly, warmed

1. Preheat the oven to 350°F.
2. Combine the sugar and the egg yolks in a mixing bowl, and beat them thoroughly with an electric mixer or a whisk. Add the warm milk, salt, and vanilla. Mix thoroughly. Add the coconut and blend it in well.
3. Pour the mixture into custard cups. Put the cups in a baking pan, and add warm water to come halfway up the sides of the cups. Place the pan on the lower shelf of the oven and bake until a stainless steel knife stuck into the custard comes out almost clean, 30 to 35 minutes. Allow the custard to cool slightly, then spread it with warmed preserves or jelly.
Serves 6

RICH CHOCOLATE MOUSSE WITH GRAND MARNIER

Of all the chocolate mousses, this is the most delectable. It is richer than Rockefeller and should be served in tiny portions.

Grand Marnier is made with a very fine cognac and flavored with orange—an exquisite liqueur for enhancing glamorous desserts.

4 large eggs, separated
¾ cup sugar
¼ cup Grand Marnier or other fine orange
    liqueur
6 ounces semisweet or dark sweet chocolate
¼ cup water
¾ cup (1½ sticks) unsalted butter, at room
    temperature
1 cup whipped cream (½ cup heavy or
    whipping cream)
Chocolate shavings, for garnish (optional)

1. Beat the egg yolks and the sugar in a large mixing bowl with an electric mixer until they change to a lighter shade of yellow and are smooth. Add the Grand Marnier, and beat thoroughly.

2. Heat the chocolate and water in the top of a double boiler over simmering water until the chocolate has melted. Remove from the heat and add the butter, a little at a time, beating constantly until the mixture is smooth. Add this to the egg yolk mixture, and mix thoroughly.

3. Beat the egg whites until they are stiff but not dry and grainy. Fold them into the chocolate mixture. Spoon the mousse into small dessert cups, or pour it into a pretty bowl. Refrigerate several hours until well set.

4. Serve garnished with whipped cream sprinkled with chocolate shavings, or with whipped cream that has been flavored with 1½ teaspoons Grand Marnier.

Serves 6 to 8

🦉 Chocolate and orange make a delightful combination in almost any guise. They have great affinity for each other.

BROWN DIAMOND MOUSSE

*T*his dessert has beauty, style, and is absolutely delicious. It does sparkle like brown diamonds. Also, it is uncooked—no small virtue.

2 large egg yolks, at room temperature
2 large eggs, at room temperature
6 tablespoons sugar, plus more for the whipped
    cream
3 tablespoons Jamaican rum
1 tablespoon fresh lemon juice
¼ cup water
1 tablespoon unflavored gelatin
2 cups heavy or whipping cream
Almond Praline powder and crystals (recipe
    follows)
1 teaspoon vanilla extract or cognac vanilla
    (see page 396)

1. Beat the egg yolks and whole eggs in a large mixing bowl with an electric mixer until they are light and fluffy. Add the sugar a little at a time, keeping the mixture airy. Stir in the rum.

2. Combine the lemon juice, water, and gelatin in a heatproof measuring cup. Stir well to dissolve the gelatin. Set the cup in a pan of boiling water (the water should not come more than two-thirds of the way up the cup) and heat it until the gelatin is clear, 1½ minutes. Remove the cup and set it aside to cool a little. Then stir the gelatin into the egg and rum mixture.

3. Whip 1 cup of the cream until it is stiff, and fold it into the egg and rum mixture. Add 3 tablespoons praline powder, and mix.

4. Pour the mousse into a 1½-quart soufflé dish or a pretty glass bowl. Refrigerate for several hours until firm. (Place the bowl in the freezer for about 30 minutes to hasten the process if necessary, but don't allow it to freeze.)

5. Whip the remaining cream, and flavor it with a little sugar and the vanilla. Cover the mousse with the whipped cream and sprinkle it with praline crystals.

Serves 6 to 8

◆ ALMOND PRALINE ◆

1 cup sugar
1 tablespoon fresh lemon juice
¾ cup toasted almonds

———— ◆ ————

1. Combine the sugar and lemon juice in a heavy skillet and place it over high heat. When the sugar has completely dissolved and turned amber, quickly remove the skillet from the heat. Toss in the almonds and stir. Pour at once onto a buttered marble slab or heavy baking sheet and allow to cool. Stores indefinitely in a jar.

2. To make praline powder, pulverize some of the praline to a powder with a mallet, or grind it in a blender or food processor.

3. To make praline crystals, beat the praline with a mallet only until well chopped. These little bits of caramel will taste crunchy and good, and sparkle like diamonds.

Makes about ¾ cup

RICE PUDDING WITH CURRANT JELLY AND LEMON SAUCE

———— ◆◆◆ ————

*E*ven for family weekday meals, Mother always used the currant jelly in this most divine of rice puddings.

Louisiana rice, ready to be harvested.

———— ◆ ————

⅔ cup long-grain rice
3 cups milk
Peel of 1 lemon
1 cup sugar
2 tablespoons fresh lemon juice
2 tablespoons butter
¾ teaspoon salt
4 eggs, separated
6 tablespoons red currant jelly, heated
Classic Lemon Sauce (recipe follows) or Old
    Seelbach House Lemon Sauce (see Index)

———— ◆ ————

1. Rinse the rice, combine it with the milk in a double boiler, and cook until the rice is barely tender, about 30 minutes.

2. In the meantime, sliver the lemon peel and put it in a food processor with ½ cup of the sugar. Twirl until the peel is finely grated. (The lemon peel can be grated by hand if desired.)

3. Preheat the oven to 350°F.

4. When the rice is ready, add the lemon peel and sugar mixture, the lemon juice, butter, salt, and egg yolks. Mix well.

5. Pour the pudding into a shallow 1½-quart baking dish and bake until the custard is not quite set, about 30 minutes. A knife stuck into the center should come out not quite clean.

6. Remove the pudding from the oven (leaving the oven on), and allow to cool for 10 to 15 minutes. Spoon the currant jelly over the top.

7. Beat the egg whites until they reach a soft peak. Gradually add the remaining ½ cup sugar, continuing to beat the whites until they hold a stiff peak. Spread them over the pudding, and return it to the oven to bake until the meringue has become a very light brown, 15 to 20 minutes. Serve warm, with lemon sauce.

Serves 6

Red currant jelly is by far the best jelly to use in this pudding; however, it may be omitted. If you omit the jelly, add ½ cup golden raisins or dried currants to the rice along with the egg yolks.

This pudding reheats very well in a preheated 325°F oven. The meringue will become quite crisp and brown, but if it was not browned too much in the first baking, it works out well.

CLASSIC LEMON SAUCE

This is a translucent sauce, simple, quick, and lemony. A wonderful sauce to have in your collection.

½ cup sugar
¼ teaspoon salt
1 tablespoon cornstarch
1 cup water
2 teaspoons grated lemon peel
3 tablespoons fresh lemon juice
3 tablespoons butter

Combine the sugar, salt, and cornstarch in an enamel or stainless steel saucepan. Stir in the water and bring to a boil. Cook over medium-high heat until the sauce is clear and thick enough to coat a wooden spoon, 5 to 6 minutes. Remove the pan from the heat. Add the lemon peel and juice. Blend in the butter.

Makes about 1¼ cups

BISHOP WOODFORDE'S PUDDING

This is a very old Southern pudding that tastes mighty good after a hearty beef stew supper when the weather is cold and everyone is hungry. It always falls a bit in the center, but don't fret—cover it with warm Nutmeg Sauce and enjoy.

8 tablespoons (1 stick) butter, at room temperature
½ cup sugar
2 large eggs, at room temperature
1½ cups all-purpose flour, sifted
½ teaspoon salt
1 teaspoon baking soda
½ cup buttermilk or sour cream
1 cup blackberry jam (with seeds)
1 teaspoon ground cinnamon
½ teaspoon freshly grated nutmeg
¼ teaspoon ground cloves
Nutmeg Sauce (recipe follows)

1. Preheat the oven to 350°F.

2. Cream the butter and the sugar thoroughly in a large bowl with an electric mixer. Add the eggs, and beat until the mixture looks like mayonnaise.

3. Combine the flour, salt, and baking soda in a mixing bowl and add this, alternating with the buttermilk or sour cream and stirring constantly, to the egg mixture. Add the jam and spices, and mix well.

4. Pour the mixture into a 1½-quart pudding pan or shallow casserole that has been greased and dusted with flour. Bake until the pudding springs back at once

when lightly touched, 35 to 40 minutes. Serve warm with Nutmeg Sauce.

   Serves 8

NUTMEG SAUCE

◆

½ cup sugar
1 rounded tablespoon cornstarch
1 cup water
¼ teaspoon salt

2 tablespoons butter
½ teaspoon vanilla extract or cognac vanilla
   (see page 396)
½ teaspoon freshly grated nutmeg, or to taste

◆

Mix the sugar and cornstarch in a saucepan, stirring well. Add the water and salt. Cook until clear and thick, about 5 minutes. Remove from the heat and blend in the butter, vanilla, and nutmeg. Keep warm.

SOUTHERN STRAWBERRY SHORTCAKE

◆◆◆

*T*he heart of a true Southern strawberry shortcake is the crisp, flaky layer of pastry—not sponge cake nor pound cake, but old-fashioned pie crust. The soul of the matter is the strawberries. I think I shall have one for lunch—and then I'll hide one to have later with tea.

◆

Standard or Flaky Butter Pastry for 2-crust pie
   (see Index)
2½ quarts strawberries, rinsed and hulled
Sugar (see step 3)
Sweetened whipped cream (see Owl)
Mint or strawberry leaves, for garnish

◆

1. Roll out the pastry ⅜ inch thick on a lightly floured surface or pastry cloth. Cut it into two 9-inch circles for a large shortcake, or into twelve 3-inch circles for individual shortcakes.

2. Place the pastry circles on a dark or nonstick baking sheet. Prick them several times with the tines of a fork so they will remain comparatively flat when baking. Chill them thoroughly before baking.

3. Slice the berries, reserving 2 cups of perfect whole berries. Sprinkle with sugar to taste and refrigerate until ready to serve.

4. Preheat the oven to 375°F.

5. Bake the pastry until golden brown, 15 to 20 minutes. Serve within a few hours or freeze.

6. Place a circle of baked pastry on a platter, or on each dessert plate if you made individual ones. Cover the pastry with the sliced strawberries. Place another pastry circle over the berries. Cover the second circle with sliced strawberries and garnish with whipped cream. Decorate the top with whole strawberries and pretty leaves such as mint, or better still, strawberry leaves.

   Serves 6

🦉 For sweetened whipped cream, whip 1 cup heavy or whipping cream with 1 tablespoon sugar until it holds soft peaks.

Strawberries by the basket, strawberries by the trayful—lots of shortcake!

WALNUT AND APPLE CRISP
WITH CORIANDER

*C*oriander is an amazing spice and appears to be more appreciated today than ever before, although it seems to have been around forever. It is especially delicious with apples.

6 tart apples
½ cup sugar, or to taste
2 teaspoons fresh lemon juice
1 teaspoon ground cinnamon
½ teaspoon ground coriander seeds
⅛ teaspoon ground cloves
½ cup coarsely chopped walnuts
3 tablespoons Calvados, cider, apple juice, or
    brandy, or more to taste

TOPPING

¾ cup sifted all-purpose flour
½ cup sugar
6 tablespoons (¾ stick) butter, chilled
Heavy or whipping cream

1. Preheat the oven to 350°F.
2. Peel, core, and slice the apples. Toss them with the sugar, lemon juice, spices, and nuts. Put the mixture in a shallow buttered casserole, and sprinkle with the Calvados, cider, apple juice, or brandy.
3. Make the topping: Mix the flour with the sugar in a roomy bowl. Cut the butter into the mixture with a pastry blender or with your fingers until the mixture is crumbly.
4. Sprinkle the topping over the apples, and bake until the apples are transparent and the topping is brown, about 40 minutes. (If the topping does not brown sufficiently, turn the oven up to 425°F for the last 5 minutes of baking.) Serve with plain heavy cream.
   Serves 4 to 6

VARIATION: Omit the ground coriander in the filling and add a sprinkling of coriander and chopped walnuts to the topping.

To obtain plain apple juice, boil the apple skins and cores, well covered with water, for about 10 minutes. Strain through a fine sieve.

ALMOND MERINGUE TORTE
WITH STRAWBERRIES

*W*hen Thomas Jefferson was our minister to France from 1785 to 1789, he became so enamored of meringues that he sent the recipe to his daughter, Mary Randolph, who was living at Monticello. And it has been recorded that meringues were first served at the White House during Jefferson's presidency (1801 to 1809).

The recipe for meringues, which originated in Switzerland, actually has remained almost the same down through the years. They are a confection that must dry out rather than bake, if they are to remain white.

This Almond Meringue Torte I believe would please Thomas Jefferson. No small boast, I admit, but it is indeed a lovely way to present delicious strawberries.

Mr. Jefferson, whom we have to thank for meringues, among other good things.

———————◆———————

¾ cup granulated sugar
1½ tablespoons cornstarch
6 large egg whites
1 cup blanched almonds, ground
1 teaspoon vanilla extract or cognac vanilla
    (see page 396)
Vanilla Buttercream (recipe follows)
3 pints perfect strawberries, rinsed and hulled
Confectioners' sugar, for garnish

———————◆———————

1. Preheat the oven to 225°F.
2. Sift together the granulated sugar and cornstarch. Set aside.
3. Beat the egg whites with an electric mixer until they begin to form soft peaks. Slowly add the sugar and cornstarch mixture, continuing to beat until the egg whites hold a stiff peak but are not dry and grainy. Fold in the almonds and vanilla.
4. Grease and flour 2 white or gray nonstick baking sheets, or if the sheets are dark, line them with foil. With a pencil, outline a 9-inch circle on each sheet as a pattern, or use two 9-inch pastry rings. Spread the meringue in the two 9-inch circles on the prepared sheets.
5. Bake until the meringues are dry and crisp, 1½ to 2 hours. If the meringue layers are not dry enough, leave them in the oven with the oven door open for several hours or overnight. If the meringue layers are made ahead, store them in a tight tin.
6. In the meantime, make the Vanilla Buttercream.
7. Thickly slice the strawberries, reserving 1 pint whole berries.
8. Place one meringue layer on a serving plate and spread half the buttercream generously over it. Cover with the sliced strawberries. Press the second meringue layer lightly on top of the strawberries, spread it generously with buttercream, and garnish with a mass of whole strawberries. You may frost the sides of the torte with buttercream and strawberries or leave them open.
9. Refrigerate for 1 to 3 hours before serving. Sprinkle the top with confectioners' sugar, and serve in small wedges. Keep refrigerated.

Serves 10

🦉 A dark baking sheet absorbs heat and will cause the meringues to brown. These meringue layers should remain white, and they will if the oven heat does not exceed 225°F.

———————◆———————

VANILLA BUTTERCREAM

◆

5 large egg yolks
⅔ cup sugar
½ cup water
⅛ teaspoon cream of tartar
¼ teaspoon salt
1 cup (2 sticks) unsalted butter, cut into pieces
1½ teaspoons vanilla extract or cognac vanilla
    (see page 396)

———————◆———————

1. Beat the egg yolks with an electric mixer, blender, or food processor until they have doubled in bulk.
2. Combine the sugar, water, cream of tartar, and salt in a heavy saucepan. Stir to dissolve the sugar a bit. Cook over high heat until a candy thermometer registers 235° to 236°F, 6 to 8 minutes. The syrup should spin a long thread when slowly poured from a wooden spoon. (If the sugar syrup is not cooked to the right temperature, the buttercream will not firm up.)

3. Immediately pour the boiling hot syrup, slowly but in a steady stream, into the egg yolks, beating constantly. Continue to beat the mixture until it has cooled to room temperature.

4. Add the butter, a little at a time, to the mixture (it must cream, not melt). Continue to beat constantly until all the butter is blended in and the buttercream is perfectly smooth. Then add the vanilla.

5. Place the buttercream in the refrigerator to firm up, 45 minutes.

Makes about 2½ cups

VARIATION: The buttercream can be flavored to your fancy with your favorite liqueur or any of the fruit brandies.

The buttercream may be made ahead, covered, and refrigerated. When ready to use, beat it thoroughly to make it pliable enough to spread.

If the buttercream curdled while you were adding the butter, the butter may have been too cold. Set the bowl of curdled buttercream over a pan of warm water (not boiling), and beat it with a whisk.

MACAROON-STUFFED PEACHES WITH RASPBERRY SAUCE

*T*his symphony of flavors—almond, peach, and raspberry—was made in heaven. Where else? The combination is too ethereal to be earthly. Of course, I am talking about the sun-ripened fruit that is all too rare these days. But let us face it—it is the touch of the sun that brings out the magical flavor.

6 ripe large peaches
12 crisp almond macaroons
1 to 2 tablespoons cognac, kirsch, or raspberry brandy
2 pints fresh raspberries
Sugar to taste

1. Dip the peaches in boiling water to cover and leave them for 2 to 3 minutes, no longer. Drain, and refrigerate without peeling.

2. Grind the macaroons in a food processor and season them to taste with your choice of liqueur, so that you have a rather soft macaroon paste.

3. One to 2 hours before serving, peel the peaches and cut them in half. Fill the cavities of the peach halves with the macaroon paste. Put the stuffed peach halves together to form whole peaches, and place them in a pretty bowl.

4. To make the sauce, put the raspberries in a blender or processor. Blend, and sweeten to taste with sugar. Spoon the sauce over the peaches, and chill before serving.

Serves 6

CAROLINA FIGS AND RASPBERRIES

*T*he season is all too short for this most elusive, and delicious, combination of fruit. To those with a sensitive palate, it is a real fascination—a connoisseur's dessert.

Serve figs and raspberries plain with a touch of lemon juice, or with cream; or serve them with good crackers and a triple crème cheese or a premium natural cream cheese.

An exquisite finale to any meal.

GLACEED STRAWBERRIES

◆◆◆

*T*hese charming strawberries for garnishing desserts are as appreciated today as they were in Queen Victoria's day—maybe more so, as we no longer take them for granted.

◆

1 quart perfect large strawberries
2 cups sugar
⅔ cup water
¼ teaspoon cream of tartar
Tiny pinch of salt
½ teaspoon vanilla extract or cognac vanilla
*   (see page 396)*

◆

1. Leave the strawberries' green hulls intact. Rinse the berries and dry them carefully on paper towels.

2. Combine the remaining ingredients in a heavy saucepan. Bring to a boil and cook without stirring until a candy ther-

mometer reaches 300°F (a little syrup dropped in cold water will thread), 15 minutes. Remove the pan from the heat and place it in a pan of cold water for a few minutes to stop the cooking. Then place the saucepan over boiling water to keep the syrup from hardening.

3. Dip each strawberry up to the hull in the hot glazing syrup. Place the berries on foil. They will cool quickly. Serve in a pretty little basket as a treat after an important meal. (The berries will not remain crisp very long, so glaze them at the last possible minute.)

Serves 6

POACHED PEACHES AND RASPBERRIES

◆◆◆

*O*ne great advantage in poaching peaches is that they can be prepared ahead. When they are done correctly, they have a marvelous flavor. The trick is not to overcook them.

Ready for partnering with peaches.

1 cup cold water
¾ cup sugar, or more to taste
2 tablespoons fresh lemon juice
6 ripe large peaches
1 pint fresh or 1 package (10 ounces) frozen
*   raspberries, thawed*

◆

1. Bring a large pan of water to a boil (in which to dip the peaches).

2. While the water is coming to a boil, in another saucepan combine the cold water, sugar, and lemon juice. Bring to a boil and cook until the syrup is clear, 5 minutes.

3. Dip the peaches one by one into the large pan of boiling water. Count to 3,

then remove the peach. Slip the skins from the peaches, cut them in half, and remove the pits. Lay the peaches in a bowl or pan and pour the hot syrup over them. Taste for sugar. Add a touch of sugar now if it's needed. Baste the peaches several times with the hot syrup, but do not cook them further. These can marinate for a while if you like.

4. Carefully lift the peaches out of the syrup with a slotted spoon. Boil the remaining syrup, whatever amount, until it becomes very thick, 6 minutes. Pour the thickened syrup over the peaches and put them in the refrigerator to chill.

5. In the meantime, purée the raspberries, fresh or frozen, in a blender or food processor, and add sugar to taste. If the peaches were not as ripe and sweet as they should be, add a touch more sugar to the raspberries to balance things out. Serve the peaches in sherbet glasses and pass the raspberry sauce.

Serves 6

STRAWBERRY SHERBET

*T*his recipe is the standard-bearer for all fine strawberry sherbets. A truly elegant and easy dessert. Unbelievable.

2 quarts fresh strawberries, rinsed and hulled
1¼ cups sugar
¾ cup water
1 tablespoon fresh lemon juice, or more to taste

1. Purée the strawberries in a blender or food processor.

2. Combine the sugar and water in a saucepan. Bring to a rolling boil and cook at a boil until clear, about 2 minutes.

3. Let the syrup cool a bit, and then add the puréed berries and the lemon juice. Taste, and add more lemon juice if needed.

4. Pour the mixture into a stainless steel bowl and cover with plastic wrap. Freeze it until almost set, 6 to 8 hours. Remove it from the freezer and whip up the mixture with an electric mixer. Freeze again until hard, overnight.

Makes 2 quarts

VARIATION: *Raspberry Sherbet:* Make exactly as you do Strawberry Sherbet, using a little less sugar and lemon juice.

This recipe may be doubled or tripled and frozen very quickly in an ice-cream freezer following manufacturer's directions.

*A*ll sherbets or ices may be poured into a large flat container and placed in the freezing unit for a quicker freezing, if time is of the essence. When frozen, transfer to a bowl for beating.

The sign in this strawberry processing plant says "No Talking," but how could you avoid discussing your favorite recipes?

ELEGANT AND EASY STRAWBERRY ICE

◆◆◆

This ruby red ice does not even have to be whipped. Spoon it into bowls or a refrigerator tray, and freeze. It is as easy as that, and as divine.

Some for today, some for tomorrow.

◆

1 quart perfect strawberries, rinsed and hulled
1 tablespoon fresh lemon juice
⅔ cup sugar, or to taste

◆

Combine the berries, lemon juice, and sugar in a blender or food processor. Blend to a purée. Pour into a refrigerator tray or small bowl, cover with plastic wrap, and freeze until frozen, at least 8 hours or overnight.

Makes 1 quart

VARIATION: *Raspberry Ice:* Substitute raspberries for strawberries, perhaps using a little less sugar.

PINK GRAPEFRUIT SHERBET

◆◆◆

Grapefruit sherbet adds an exquisitely light and zestful last touch to a good meal. Give the menu that you are planning this test: Would a cold grapefruit taste good after this meal? If so, then Pink Grapefruit Sherbet will taste even better. Choose the deepest pink or red grapefruit you can find. This sherbet will taste exactly like the grapefruit that is used—the quality comes out in the flavor. For a beautiful touch, serve it in crystal glasses garnished with ice-cold pink grapefruit sections and a sprig of mint or a tiny gardenia leaf.

◆

1¼ cups sugar
1 cup water
6 large pink grapefruit

◆

1. Combine the sugar and water in a saucepan and boil until the syrup is clear, 2 minutes. Remove the pan from the heat. Refrigerate to chill.

2. Extract the juice from the grapefruit, and strain it. (You should have almost a quart. If you are a little short, that will not matter if the grapefruit has a full, fresh flavor.)

3. Combine the cooled sugar syrup and the grapefruit juice in a good-size stainless steel bowl. Cover with plastic wrap and freeze for 8 hours or overnight.

4. When the sherbet has frozen, beat it hard with an electric mixer until it is fluffy. Return it to the freezer to firm up, another 3 to 4 hours.

Makes 1 quart

🦉 Do not make this sherbet more than 12 hours ahead. It gets icy and syrupy if kept too long.

FLORIDA MANGO SHERBET

◆◆◆

*F*lorida Mango Sherbet is a refreshing treat for the taste buds and perfect for a summer dessert. The mangoes must be allowed to ripen (they should be soft to the touch) to develop their flavor.

An attractive way to serve Florida Mango Sherbet is to put a scoop of sherbet in the center of a sherbet glass and garnish it with fresh pineapple cubes and a sprig of mint.

½ cup sugar
1 cup water
5 ripe mangoes
3 tablespoons fresh lime juice
1 teaspoon grated lemon peel

1. Combine the sugar and water in a small saucepan. Boil until the syrup is clear, 2 minutes. Refrigerate until chilled, 30 minutes.

2. Peel the mangoes, and cut the pulp away from the pits. Purée the pulp in a food processor; you should have 4 cups. Add the lime juice and grated lemon peel. Add the fruit to the chilled syrup, mix thoroughly, and taste for sweetness and lime flavor.

3. Freeze in an ice-cream freezer following manufacturer's directions. Or pour into a stainless steel bowl, cover with plastic wrap, and freeze for 8 hours or overnight. When the mixture is frozen, whip it hard with an electric mixer. Return it to the freezer for 1 to 2 hours. Whip it again 1 to 2 hours before serving.

Makes 1 quart

🦉 Mangoes vary greatly in sweetness and in flavor, so it is best to depend upon your own taste buds to bring this sherbet to perfection. To add more sugar to the sherbet, boil sugar in a small amount of water until it is clear. Allow it to cool, then add this syrup to the fruit mixture.

Mangoes ripen in the summer, just in time for ice cream season.

WATERMELON AND RASPBERRY SHERBET

*O*ne can seldom get watermelons cold enough, so watermelon sherbet is a good solution. The watermelon used for sherbet must be full-flavored or the sherbet will not be worth the effort. The counterpoint in the flavor of watermelon and raspberry is one you must not miss, as these miracles of taste don't come very often. Try filling a watermelon shell with sherbet. Very pretty—and most refreshing.

Watermelon, memorialized by Sarah Miriam Peale, a 19th-century Southern artist.

1¼ cups sugar
1⅛ cups water
3 cups watermelon purée, strained (½ large watermelon)

1 cup fresh or frozen raspberries (thawed), puréed and strained (¼ cup juice)
3 tablespoons fresh lemon juice, or more to taste

1. Combine the sugar and water in a saucepan and boil until clear, 2 minutes. Refrigerate to chill.
2. Mix the sugar syrup with the watermelon and raspberry purées and lemon juice. Cover with plastic wrap and chill thoroughly. Freeze in an ice-cream freezer following manufacturer's directions (which is best). Or place in the freezer, 8 hours or overnight; when it is frozen, beat with an electric mixer until fluffy. Freeze again until firm, another 2 to 3 hours or you can leave it overnight.

Makes 1½ quarts

HONEYDEW SHERBET

*H*oneydew melon is one of the treasures of late summer. This dessert can be as simple as plain honeydew sherbet with lime, or for a glamorous party, it can be arranged with the seedless grapes and some of the melon itself and be fantastically beautiful. Don't forget the limes. You must not use lemon juice. If you can't get limes, make something else.

1⅔ cups sugar
2 cups water
⅔ cup fresh lime juice
2 cups mashed ripe honeydew (1 medium melon)
Tiny pinch of salt
2 large egg whites, beaten

Wedges of lime, for garnish

1. Combine the sugar and water in a saucepan and boil until clear, 2 minutes. Remove the pan from the heat, add the lime juice, and cool slightly. Pour the mix-

ture into a large stainless steel bowl, cover with plastic wrap, and freeze until it is slightly frozen, 3 hours.

2. Beat in the honeydew, salt, and beaten egg whites. Freeze until hard, 8 hours or overnight.

3. Beat the sherbet well with an electric mixer and return it to the freezer, 2 hours. Serve with wedges of lime.

Makes 3 quarts

NEW ORLEANS PRALINE ICE CREAM

*P*ecan praline in any form is typical of New Orleans, and of all the Southern states where the pecan prospers. The praline technique originated in France and Italy, but they, of course, used their native nuts—almonds and hazelnuts. The pecans lend their own unique flavor to praline, and it is redolent of gay and historic New Orleans.

¾ cup sugar
1 cup water
⅛ teaspoon cream of tartar
6 large egg yolks
2 cups milk
Pecan Praline powder (recipe follows)
1 tablespoon cognac, brandy, or praline liqueur
1½ teaspoons vanilla extract or cognac vanilla (see page 396)
1 quart heavy or whipping cream

1. Combine the sugar, water, and cream of tartar in a heavy saucepan. Cook over medium heat until the syrup spins a thread or reaches 234°F on a candy thermometer, 7 to 10 minutes.

2. In the meantime, beat the egg yolks with an electric mixer until they have turned a lighter shade of yellow and are smooth.

3. Gradually pour the hot syrup into the egg yolks, beating constantly. Pour the egg yolk mixture into a large heavy saucepan. Add the milk, and cook over medium heat until the mixture forms a light custard, 8 to 10 minutes. Add the praline powder, and blend well.

4. Pour the mixture into a cool bowl, cover with plastic wrap, and refrigerate it at once, 1½ hours. Allow the mixture to become thoroughly chilled.

5. When you are ready to make the ice cream, blend the praline custard, chosen liqueur, vanilla, and cream. Freeze in an ice-cream freezer following manufacturer's directions.

6. Serve in sherbet glasses garnished with praline pecan halves.

Makes about 1 gallon

The Beauregard Keyes House in New Orleans French Quarter, named for two former owners: Confederate General P.T.G. Beauregard and author Frances Parkinson Keyes.

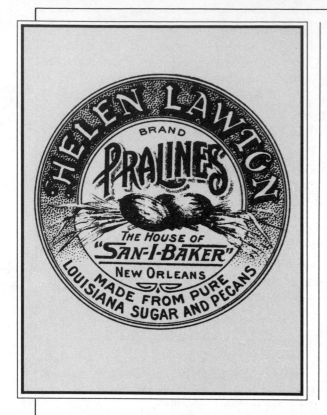

PECAN PRALINE

¾ cup sugar
⅓ cup water
¼ teaspoon cream of tartar
1 cup pecan halves

1. Combine the sugar, water, and cream of tartar in a heavy skillet. Cook over medium heat, stirring a bit, until the sugar has completely melted and has turned a rich golden brown.
2. In the meantime, butter a heavy baking sheet and scatter the pecans on it.
3. The minute the syrup is the right shade of caramel, pour it over the pecans. Cool completely.
4. When the caramel is hard, break it up with a mallet, but reserve a few of the whole pecans to use as a garnish. To make praline powder, put small pieces of praline in a food processor and grind until fine.
Makes ¾ cup

COCONUT ICE CREAM

Coconut Ice Cream makes a most pleasing dessert served with a pineapple sauce or in tandem with pineapple or orange sherbet—or alone. Especially delicious and spectacular served in a pineapple shell. For best results, use an icecream machine.

2½ cups milk
1 cup grated fresh coconut
1 cup sugar
6 large egg yolks
Juice of ½ lemon
1¼ cups heavy or whipping cream

1. Combine the milk and coconut and refrigerate for 1 to 3 hours.
2. When you are ready to make the ice cream, combine the sugar and egg yolks, and beat hard with a whisk or an electric mixer.
3. Put the sugar and egg yolk mixture in a heavy saucepan or in the top of a double boiler over boiling water. Add the milk and coconut, and cook over medium heat, stirring constantly, until the mixture lightly coats a wooden spoon, 8 to 10 minutes. Pour the custard into a stainless steel bowl, cover with plastic wrap, and refrigerate it at once, 2 to 3 hours. When the yolk and coconut mixture is perfectly chilled, add the lemon juice and blend thoroughly, then add the cream and blend again.
4. Freeze in an ice-cream freezer following manufacturer's directions.
Makes 1½ quarts

If sweetened packaged coconut is used, ¾ cup of sugar will be sufficient.

THE ULTIMATE VANILLA ICE CREAM

◆◆◆

*T*his vanilla ice cream is the master recipe for many wonderful ice creams. The custard is one secret to its goodness; when you make the custard, beat the eggs and sugar together until they are creamy. A very light custard, or one that is not allowed to thicken much, will make a delicately flavored ice cream. For an egg-rich flavor, allow the custard to coat the spoon more heavily. A prime ingredient for a very special ice cream is your own homemade cognac vanilla.

◆

6 large egg yolks
¾ cup sugar
2 cups milk, warmed
Tiny pinch of salt
2 teaspoons vanilla extract or cognac vanilla
    (see page 396)
1 quart heavy or whipping cream, chilled

◆

Sitting on the back steps, making ice cream—anticipation!

1. Combine the egg yolks and sugar in a large mixing bowl, and beat hard with an electric mixer until the mixture turns a lighter shade of yellow and is creamy. Stir the milk in with a whisk.

2. Cook the mixture in a heavy saucepan over medium heat, or in the top of a double boiler over simmering water, until the custard coats a wooden spoon nicely, 8 to 10 minutes.

3. Pour the custard into a cool bowl (stainless steel is excellent), cover with plastic wrap, and refrigerate at once. Allow it to become thoroughly chilled, about 1½ hours.

4. When you are ready to make the ice cream, add the salt and vanilla to the custard. Combine it with the cream, and blend thoroughly. Freeze in an ice-cream freezer following manufacturer's directions.

Makes about 3 quarts

SUMMERTIME PEACH ICE CREAM

◆◆◆

*F*resh peach ice cream is one of the South's favorite summer desserts, if not the favorite. Frozen or canned peaches simply will not do. Fresh ripe peaches have a sublime flavor.

Picking those glorious Georgia peaches.

◆

1 cup light cream, or ½ cup milk and ½ cup
    heavy or whipping cream
1½ cups milk
1½ cups sugar
4 large egg yolks
8 very ripe large peaches
2 teaspoons fresh lemon juice, or more to taste
¼ teaspoon salt
2 cups heavy or whipping cream, chilled

◆

1. Combine the light cream and the milk in a saucepan, and scald. Do not allow it to boil. Set aside.

2. Add ¾ cup of the sugar to the egg yolks, and mix thoroughly with a whisk or an electric mixer. Add the scalded cream and milk to the egg yolk mixture, stir well, and transfer to the top of a double boiler. Cook over simmering water until the custard lightly coats a wooden spoon, 5 minutes.

3. Remove from the heat at once, pour into a cool bowl, cover with plastic wrap, and refrigerate until the custard is cold, 35 minutes.

4. While the custard is cooling, peel and mash the peaches, leaving some lumps. You should have 4 cups. Add the lemon juice, remaining sugar, and salt. Mix. Refrigerate, covered, 1 hour.

5. When you are ready to make the ice cream, add the cream to the custard mixture and mix thoroughly.

6. Freeze in an ice-cream freezer following manufacturer's directions until the custard has turned to a soft ice cream. Stop turning, remove the cover of the container, and add the peaches. Mix them in with a long-handled spoon, and continue to freeze.

Makes about 1 gallon

The custard mixture and the peaches must be cold when freezing the ice cream; otherwise, the heavy cream will turn into buttery lumps.

APRICOT ICE CREAM

◆◆◆

*T*his is based on an eighteenth-century recipe for apricot ice cream, and it must never be changed one bit because it is perfection. It is difficult for me to say, but I think this is my favorite. It is at its best when made with canned apricots.

◆

2 cups heavy or whipping cream
¾ cup sugar
3 cans (16 ounces each) unpeeled apricot
    halves, drained and chilled
3 tablespoons fresh lemon juice
⅓ cup fresh orange juice

◆

1. Combine the cream and sugar in a saucepan and heat gently, stirring until the sugar has dissolved (do not boil). Transfer to a bowl, cover with plastic wrap, and refrigerate until chilled, 1 hour.

2. While the cream is cooling, purée the apricots in a blender or food processor.

Add the juices, and blend thoroughly.

3. Combine the apricot purée with the chilled cream mixture, and freeze in an ice-cream freezer following manufacturer's directions.

Makes about 3 quarts

This ice cream may be frozen in the freezer, whipping several times during the process with an electric mixer, but it will not be as creamy as it is when frozen in a mechanical freezer.

FLORIDA MANGO ICE CREAM

*M*ango ice cream has a unique and unusually delicate flavor. The palates that do not at first catch its evanescent flavor will call it bland. After all, some of us do not catch all of the nuances in a Beethoven symphony at first. Flavors are very much like music; one's palate must be educated, just like one's ear.

All mangoes are not full of flavor and sweetness. If the mangoes at hand are not excellent, use them for chutney, not this ice cream.

6 large egg yolks
1¼ cups sugar
2 cups milk, scalded
Pinch of salt
8 ripe large mangoes
4 cups heavy or whipping cream
1 tablespoon grated lemon peel
⅔ cup fresh lemon juice
1½ teaspoons vanilla extract or cognac vanilla (see page 396)

1. Combine the egg yolks and sugar, and beat with an electric mixer until the mixture turns a lighter shade of yellow and has increased in volume. Pour it into a heavy saucepan, or into the top of a double boiler placed over simmering water, and add the scalded milk and the salt. Stir gently with a wooden spoon, taking care to stir from the bottom each time, and cook until the mixture heavily coats the spoon, 10 minutes. Remove from the heat at once. Pour into a cool bowl, cover with plastic wrap, and refrigerate until cold, or overnight if desired.

2. Peel the mangoes and remove the pulp. You should have 7 to 8 cups of fruit. Purée it in a blender or food processor.

3. Add the mango purée, cream, lemon peel, lemon juice, and vanilla to the cold custard. Stir gently until well blended.

4. Freeze in an ice-cream freezer following manufacturer's directions. This ice cream keeps well without crystallizing.

Makes about 1 gallon

The Palace soda fountain in Tampa during the 1920s—now that's style!

PERFECT COFFEE ICE CREAM

*T*his coffee ice cream is very special. It is completely uncooked. Mix, chill, and freeze. That's it. It is delicious made plain, but the great favorite of my students is the coffee and cognac variation. We are indebted to James Beard, the dean of American cooks, for this idea.

3 tablespoons instant coffee
1 cup milk
1 cup sugar
1½ teaspoons vanilla extract or cognac vanilla
*   (see page 396)*
4½ cups heavy or whipping cream

Combine the coffee, milk, sugar, and vanilla in a blender or food processor. Mix until the sugar is dissolved, a few minutes.

Pour into a stainless steel bowl (steel chills quickly), add the cream, and mix well with a whisk. Chill thoroughly, then freeze in an ice-cream freezer following manufacturer's directions.

Makes about 3 quarts

VARIATION: *Coffee and Cognac Ice Cream:* Add ⅓ to ½ cup cognac along with the cream. Reduce the amount of cream to 4 cups.

FLORENTINE LEMON CREAM

*F*lorentine Lemon Cream becomes an instant favorite of all those who make it and all those who taste it. It is one of the easiest ice creams in the whole world to make, and it is even somewhat "creamy" without beating. It is an exquisite dessert when garnished with fresh raspberries or strawberries in the summer. In winter, a raspberry or strawberry sauce may be made by puréeing frozen berries and sugar to taste in a blender or food processor.

1 lemon
2 cups sugar
2 cups heavy or whipping cream
2 cups milk
1 cup fresh lemon juice
Lemon peel, for garnish
Mint sprigs, for garnish

1. Peel the lemon and sliver the peel. Put the sugar and lemon peel in a food processor and twirl until the peel is very finely grated. (If desired, the peel may be grated by hand.)

2. Combine the sugar with the lemon peel (if you haven't processed together) and the cream and milk in a large saucepan. Heat only until the sugar has dissolved. Do not allow the mixture to boil. Pour into a stainless steel bowl, cover with plastic wrap, and refrigerate at once. Allow the cream mixture to chill thoroughly, 1 hour.

3. Slowly add the lemon juice to the chilled mixture, stirring as it thickens. (You will be able to feel the cream become thicker as you stir it.)

4. Freeze the lemon cream for at least

4 to 5 hours (overnight is best).

5. If desired, whip with an electric mixer 1 to 2 hours before serving, or serve as is. Serve in lemon shells (see box) or sherbet glasses garnished with a curl of lemon peel or a sprig of mint.

Makes about 1½ quarts

 Don't forget, lemon juice must not be added to the milk and cream until the mixture is cold, or it will curdle.

LEMON SHELLS

*T*o make lemon shells, choose large lemons. Slice just enough off the end of each so that it will stand erect. Slice the other end off evenly and just deeply enough to easily extract the juice and pulp with a juicer, hand or electric model.

When the lemon cream has frozen hard, fill the lemon shells just as you would an ice cream cone. Put them in the freezer until serving time. Serve garnished with a small, beautiful leaf such as gardenia, mint, or rose geranium by the side of the lemon shell.

FROZEN COINTREAU SOUFFLE

*T*his Frozen Cointreau Soufflé is a glorious affair. You can use ladyfingers or your favorite yellow cake. It may be made days ahead and kept frozen. The soufflé should stand an inch or more above the rim of the soufflé dish to resemble a well-puffed cooked soufflé. The cocoa simulates the browned top.

1 cup sugar
3 tablespoons water
1 tablespoon finely grated navel orange peel
6 large egg yolks, at room temperature
½ cup Cointreau
2½ cups heavy or whipping cream
6 ladyfingers or 2 to 3 slices of your favorite
*   yellow sponge cake, cut into fingers*
Cocoa powder, for garnish

1. Combine the sugar, water, and orange peel in a saucepan, and boil 3 to 4 minutes.

2. Place the egg yolks in a small mixing bowl. Add the hot syrup in a steady stream while mixing at high speed. Continue to beat until the mixture is very thick and pale yellow. Cover, then refrigerate to cool, 45 minutes. Add ¼ cup of the Cointreau, mix thoroughly, and chill.

3. When the yolk mixture is well chilled, whip the cream until it holds stiff peaks. Fold the yolk mixture into the whipped cream with a rubber spatula.

4. Cover the bottom of a 1-quart soufflé dish with a thick layer of the soufflé mixture. Arrange the fingers of cake on top. Sprinkle the cake with some of the remaining Cointreau. Cover with more soufflé mixture, and continue alternating layers. Fill the dish right to the top, ending with a layer of soufflé mixture. (Refrigerate the remainder to use later.)

5. Tie or tape a foil collar around the dish, extending 2 to 3 inches above the rim.

6. Place the dish in the freezer and leave it until the mixture is firm, 8 hours or overnight. Then add the remainder of the mixture, return the dish to the freezer, and leave it until frozen, again 8 hours or overnight.

7. Just before serving, discard the foil collar and sprinkle the top generously with cocoa.

Serves 6 to 8

VARIATION: The soufflé mixture may be doubled (omitting the cake), then frozen in an ice cream mold.

COLD CHOCOLATE SOUFFLE

*T*his Cold Chocolate Soufflé is not overly rich or sweet. It can be served plain with whipped cream, or it can be made quite elegant when served with a sauce. Rich custard sauce served with this soufflé makes a delicious family dessert in the winter, when a custard tastes so good.

If you are pressed for time, you don't have to mold the chocolate cream in a soufflé dish: Spoon it into a bowl, refrigerate until set, and serve in sherbet glasses with the chosen sauce.

4 large egg yolks
7 tablespoons sugar
9 tablespoons cold water
Pinch of cream of tartar
1 envelope unflavored gelatin
6¼ ounces semisweet or dark sweet chocolate
1 cup heavy or whipping cream
4 large egg whites
Pinch of salt
1 tablespoon cognac, or 1 teaspoon vanilla extract or cognac vanilla (see Index)
Whipped cream and chocolate shavings for garnish, or Marron-Cognac or Rich Custard Sauce (recipes follow)

1. Beat the egg yolks with an electric mixer until they turn a lighter shade of yellow and are smooth.

2. Combine the sugar, 4 tablespoons of the water, and the cream of tartar in a heavy saucepan and cook over high heat until it reaches the soft ball stage, 236°F on a candy thermometer, 10 minutes. Pour the hot syrup in a steady stream into the egg yolks while continuing to beat.

3. Dissolve the gelatin in 3 tablespoons of the cold water in a small heatproof glass measuring cup. When the gelatin has dissolved, place the cup in a pan and pour in enough boiling water to reach halfway up the outside of the cup. Continue boiling and when the gelatin is clear and hot, pour it into the egg mixture, 5 to 6 minutes. Beat thoroughly.

4. Combine the chocolate and the remaining 2 tablespoons water in the top of a double boiler or in a small bowl set in a pan of boiling water. Heat, stirring, until perfectly smooth. Add the chocolate to the egg and gelatin mixture and beat thoroughly.

5. Whip the cream until it holds a stiff peak, and fold it into the chocolate mixture.

6. Beat the egg whites with the salt until they are stiff but not dry and grainy. Fold them into the chocolate mixture, then add the cognac or vanilla and mix well.

7. Tie or tape a greased foil collar around a 3-cup soufflé dish, extending 3 inches above the rim.

8. Spoon the mixture into the soufflé dish. It should fill the collar. Chill in the refrigerator until firmly set, 3 to 4 hours.

9. When you are ready to serve the soufflé, carefully remove the collar. Spoon whipped cream over the top, and sprinkle it with chocolate shavings. Pass extra whipped cream in a sauceboat if desired. Or serve with one of the sauces.

Serves 6

MARRON-COGNAC SAUCE

1 cup heavy or whipping cream
3 tablespoons cognac
¼ cup chopped preserved marrons (chestnuts)
3 tablespoons syrup from the preserved marrons, or to taste

Whip the cream until it forms stiff peaks, stir in the other ingredients, and serve in a sauceboat.

Makes about 2 cups

RICH CUSTARD SAUCE

6 large egg yolks
½ cup sugar
1 cup heavy or whipping cream
1 cup milk
Tiny pinch of salt
2 teaspoons vanilla extract or cognac vanilla
    (see page 396), or 1 to 2 tablespoons
    cognac, Cointreau, or sherry

1. Beat the egg yolks very thoroughly with the sugar in a heavy saucepan, using a whisk or an electric mixer. Add the cream, milk, and salt. Cook over medium heat, or over hot water, stirring the custard gently with a rubber spatula until it has thickened and heavily coats the spatula or a wooden spoon, 10 minutes.

2. Remove the pan from the heat and immediately pour the custard into a cool bowl. Flavor it as desired, cover with plastic wrap, and refrigerate as soon as possible. When thoroughly cooled, add the vanilla, stir, and serve.

Makes about 2 cups

ORANGE MARMALADE SOUFFLE

*T*his soufflé was originally called a double-boiled soufflé, and it is an old love. It is not impatient like most soufflés—it will wait for you—and it is a divine way to use up those extra egg whites.

4 tablespoons (½ stick) butter
½ cup sugar
4 large egg whites (½ cup)
¼ teaspoon cream of tartar
½ cup bitter orange marmalade
1 teaspoon vanilla extract or cognac vanilla
    (see page 396)
Cognac Sauce (recipe follows) or Rich Custard
    Sauce (see recipe above)

1. Preheat the oven to 375°F if you will be using it.
2. Use the butter to coat the inside of the top section of a 2-quart double boiler or a 2-quart casserole that has a cover. Sprinkle with ¼ cup of the sugar.
3. Beat the egg whites with the cream of tartar until they hold a stiff peak. Fold in the remaining sugar, and the marmalade and vanilla.
4. Spoon the mixture into the prepared double boiler or casserole dish. If you are using the double boiler, place the soufflé over rapidly boiling water, cover, and cook for about 1 hour. If you are using a casserole, place it in a larger pan and add enough boiling water to reach two-thirds of the way up the sides of the casserole. Cover well, and bake in the oven for 40 to 50

minutes. The boiling water will have to be replenished during the cooking period.

5. When it is done, the soufflé (cooked either way) will be fairly firm to the touch. It is ready when a knife stuck into the center comes out clean. The soufflé will hold for an hour or more in the double boiler or casserole without falling. Serve in individual dessert dishes with Cognac or Rich Custard Sauce.

Serves 6

Check the marmalade label to be sure you use a bitter orange marmalade. This is made with the Seville orange and is by far the best.

COGNAC SAUCE

2 large egg yolks
½ cup confectioners' sugar
1 cup heavy or whipping cream
3 tablespoons cognac or brandy

Beat the egg yolks with the sugar until they turn a lighter shade of yellow and are smooth, 6 minutes. Refrigerate until 30 to 40 minutes before serving. Whip the cream until it holds stiff peaks, and fold the mixture into it. Flavor with cognac or brandy, and refrigerate again until serving time.

Makes about 2 cups

ENGLISH CUSTARD SOUFFLE

*T*his is a very light and flavorful soufflé—a delight to all those who are devoted to custard. It has no fruit or nuts to weight it down and it can rise extremely high.

3 tablespoons butter
3 tablespoons all-purpose flour
1 cup milk
½ cup plus 3 tablespoons sugar
5 large egg yolks, at room temperature
6 large egg whites
1½ teaspoons vanilla extract or cognac vanilla
*   (see page 396), or 1 tablespoon cognac*
¼ teaspoon cream of tartar
Pinch of salt
Apricot-Almond Sauce, chilled (recipe follows)

1. Preheat the oven to 375°F.
2. Melt the butter over medium heat in a heavy saucepan. Blend in the flour and stir until smooth. Gradually stir in the milk; cook, stirring constantly, until a thick, smooth sauce is formed, 1 minute. Add ½ cup sugar and beat thoroughly to help dissolve it. Add the egg yolks and beat hard. Set the mixture aside but keep it warm.
3. In a large mixing bowl, combine the egg whites, vanilla or cognac, cream of tartar, and salt. Beat until the egg whites

stand in stiff peaks but are not dry and grainy. Gently fold the whites into the egg yolk mixture, leaving some particles of egg white showing.

4. Butter a 6-cup soufflé dish, sprinkle it with the 3 tablespoons of sugar, and fit it with a greased foil collar that extends 2 inches above the rim of the dish. Pour in the soufflé mixture.
5. Place the dish on the middle shelf of the oven and bake for 35 to 40 minutes. Remove the foil collar. Serve hot, with chilled Apricot-Almond Sauce.

Serves 6

APRICOT-ALMOND SAUCE

1½ cups apricot preserves
½ cup water
Tiny pinch of salt
1 tablespoon kirsch or rum, or more to taste
¼ cup slivered blanched almonds

Combine the apricot preserves, water, and salt in a saucepan. Simmer until a syrup is formed and thickens, 7 minutes. Remove

from the heat, and add the kirsch or rum and the almonds.
    Makes 1¾ cups

*T*KENTUCKY CREAM CANDY

◆◆◆

his is a very old favorite Kentucky candy. The recipe given here—the one I like—is from a 1947 cookbook by Marion Flexner, long out of print, called *Dixie Dishes*. It is a pulled candy and very creamy. The pieces of candy can be dipped in melted semisweet chocolate, allowed to harden, then stored in a tin box.

◆

3 cups superfine sugar (see step 1)
1 cup water
⅛ teaspoon baking soda or 1½ teaspoons distilled white vinegar
½ teaspoon salt
1 cup heavy or whipping cream
4 tablespoons (½ stick) unsalted butter
⅔ teaspoon vanilla extract or cognac vanilla (see page 396)
Cornstarch or unsalted butter for pulling the candy

◆

1. Twirl granulated sugar in a processor until it is superfine, about 3 to 5 minutes, or use store-bought superfine sugar.

2. Combine the sugar, water, baking soda or vinegar, and salt in a heavy 3-quart saucepan. Bring it to a boil. Remove the pan from the heat and stir until the sugar has completely dissolved.

3. Stir in the cream and bring the candy again to a boil. Cover the pan and cook to allow the sugar crystals on the side of the pan to dissolve in the steam, 2 to 3 minutes.

4. Remove the cover, add the butter, and cook until the candy reaches the hard ball stage or registers 258°F on a candy thermometer, 12 minutes.

5. Pour the candy at once onto a lightly buttered baking sheet placed on a rack, or better still, on a lightly buttered marble slab.

6. Add the vanilla and begin to cream the candy by working it with a spatula. Keep turning the outside edges to the cen-

ter. When the candy has thickened after 8 to 10 minutes, shape it into a ball.

7. Dip your fingers in cornstarch or rub them lightly with butter. Holding the candy in both hands, pull it as you would taffy, stretching it out about 6 inches to 1 foot in length. Double it over and continue pulling until it becomes white and ridges form, 30 minutes. Put more cornstarch or butter on your fingers if you need it. Then twist the candy into a rope.

8. Cut the rope into 6 equal pieces. Pull each piece out long and thin to about 1

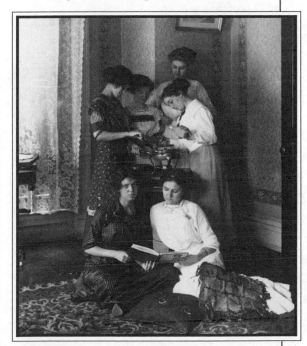

It takes two to read the recipe and four to create the dish—it must be candy.

foot in length. Butter a pair of sharp scissors and cut the rope into 1-inch pieces. Place the candy between pieces of wax paper and leave it in a cool, dry place (don't refrigerate) for 24 hours to become creamy. Store in a tight tin box.

Makes 75 pieces

VARIATIONS: *Peppermint Pink Cream Candy:* Omit the vanilla. Add 4 drops oil of peppermint and a few drops of red food coloring to the candy as you start to blend it with the spatula (step 6).

Buttercreme Wedding Mints: Add 5 drops oil of peppermint instead of the vanilla as you start to blend it with a spatula. Cut into ¾-inch pieces.

🦉 If this candy is not sufficiently pulled, it will not "cream."

SOUR CREAM FUDGE

◆◆◆

*T*here is something delightfully human about people who have a nagging sweet tooth. Have you ever noticed how they hide goodies in funny places—in dresser drawers, for instance—away from themselves, of course. Then Valentine's Day comes along and boxes of chocolate are all over the place, right out in the open. Could there ever be a better excuse for candy?

This is a delicious white fudge with a pleasing tang that tastes of lemon. It improves in flavor overnight.

◆

1 ½ cups sugar
½ cup sour cream
⅛ teaspoon salt
¾ teaspoon vanilla extract or cognac vanilla (see page 396)
1 cup coarsely chopped pecans or walnuts

◆

1. Combine the sugar, sour cream, and salt in a bowl, and mix until the sugar is well moistened. Pour the mixture into a heavy saucepan, and put it on a "flame-tamer" over medium heat. From time to time wipe the crystals from the sides of the pan with a damp pastry brush.

2. Cook until a candy thermometer reads 236°F, or a teaspoon of the syrup dropped into cold water forms a soft ball, 10 minutes. Remove the pan from the heat. Wipe any crystals again from the sides of the pan with the damp brush.

3. Cool the fudge to 110°F. Then add the vanilla, and beat with a wooden spoon until the fudge begins to lose its transparency, 5 minutes. Stir in the nuts.

4. Pour the fudge onto a buttered marble slab or a buttered baking sheet measuring about 12 x 9 inches. Cool completely, then cut into squares. Store in a tight tin box.

Makes 24 squares

A New Orleans candy wagon—another of our lost treasures.

GEORGIA'S GOLDEN BRITTLE

◆◆◆

*A*mong the Deep South brittles, this one is as easy as it is elegant. You can make it on the rainiest day. Use your own homemade vanilla and huge pecans—delectable. You'll see!

◆

1½ cups large pecans (the larger the better)
1 cup sugar
½ cup light corn syrup
⅛ teaspoon cream of tartar
⅛ cup cold water
Tiny pinch of salt
2 tablespoons unsalted butter
2 teaspoons brandy or cognac
1½ teaspoons vanilla extract or cognac vanilla
    (see page 396)

◆

1. Butter a baking sheet, a large heat-proof baking dish, or a meat platter, measuring about 13½ x 9 inches. Scatter the pecans over the butter.

2. Combine the sugar, corn syrup, cream of tartar, water, and salt in an extra-heavy 1-quart saucepan (unlined copper or enameled iron is excellent). Stir well, bring to a boil, and cook until it reaches the hard crack stage and registers 300°F on a candy thermometer, 15 minutes. Then quickly stir in the butter.

3. Remove the pan from the heat. Wait a second or two, then stir in the

brandy or cognac and the vanilla. Quickly pour the syrup over the pecans. With a wooden spoon and working fast, toss the pecans about in the syrup to cover them thoroughly, and spread the brittle out thin.

4. Allow the brittle to cool completely. Then break it into rough pieces and store it in a tin.

Makes ¾ pound brittle

KENTUCKY BOURBON TRUFFLES

◆◆◆

*B*ourbon and chocolate complement each other well and make up into a truffle that is creamy, soft, and so good. These must be kept refrigerated until serving time.

◆

12 ounces dark sweet chocolate, preferably
    imported
½ cup heavy or whipping cream

1½ tablespoons bourbon whiskey
Homemade Chocolate Coating (recipe follows)

◆

1. Make chocolate ganache: Break 8 ounces of the chocolate into small pieces. Place them in the top of a double boiler along with the cream. Heat the chocolate over simmering water, stirring often with a wooden spoon, until it melts. When the chocolate has melted, beat it with the spoon until smooth. Remove the chocolate from the heat; let it cool to room temperature.

2. When the ganache is cool, stir in the bourbon until it is well blended. Transfer the mixture to a small bowl. Refrigerate, covered with foil, overnight or up to several days to allow the ganache to ripen and harden.

3. Working with a small amount of the ganache at a time and keeping the remainder refrigerated, form it into balls about 1 inch in diameter, using about 1½ teaspoons of ganache per ball. Work with your fingertips, not the palms of your hands, to keep the mixture from becoming too soft. Place the truffles on a baking sheet lined with foil or wax paper. Continue forming truffles, in batches, placing each truffle on the baking sheet as it is formed, until the ganache is used up.

4. Refrigerate the truffles on the baking sheet, uncovered, until they are somewhat firm, about 1 hour. Cover them loosely with foil or wax paper, return them to the refrigerator, and chill until the truffles are quite firm and set, overnight or up to several days.

5. Using a paring knife, shave the remaining 4 ounces of chocolate into thin shavings. Spread them on a platter or a sheet of wax paper, and reserve.

6. Working with only 4 or 5 truffles at a time and keeping the remainder refrigerated, coat the truffles with Homemade Chocolate Coating as follows: Drop a truffle into the chocolate coating; turn it with a fork to cover it well. Gently lift the truffle out with the fork, and hold it above the pan for a few seconds to let the excess chocolate drip back into the pan. Gently scrape the bottom of the fork against the edge of the pan to remove more of the excess chocolate (this prevents the chocolate from forming "platforms" under the pieces of candy as they set). Using a spatula or knife, very gently slide the truffle off the fork and onto a foil- or wax-paper-lined baking sheet. Repeat the procedure with the remaining truffles, continuing to work with only a few at a time.

7. Using your fingertips, gently roll each truffle in the shaved chocolate to cover it well, then return it to the baking sheet. When all the truffles are coated, refrigerate them on the baking sheet, uncovered, until the coating is somewhat firm, about 1 hour. Then cover them loosely with foil or wax paper, return them to the refrigerator, and chill until the coating is quite firm and set, several hours or overnight.

8. Select a tin box or boxes large enough to hold the truffles in one layer; line it with foil or wax paper. Arrange the truffles in the box, first placing each in a tiny fluted paper cup if desired; cover tightly and refrigerate. Stored this way, truffles will keep up to 2 weeks.

Makes 24 truffles

◆

HOMEMADE CHOCOLATE COATING

◆

1 pound semisweet chocolate, such as Callebaut, Lindt, Tobler, or any good coating chocolate, broken into small pieces

◆

1. Heat the chocolate in the top of a double boiler over simmering water, stirring often with a wooden spoon, until the chocolate melts. When the chocolate has melted, stir it with the spoon until smooth. Remove the chocolate from the heat. Let it stand until it registers 90°F on an instant-reading thermometer.

2. At this point, the chocolate is ready to be used for coating. Keep the temperature of the chocolate between 86° and 90°F. If the temperature falls below 86°F and the chocolate becomes too thick, place the pan over simmering water and reheat.

Makes enough to coat twenty-four 1-ounce truffles

Do not use a microwave to melt chocolate, as it cooks from the inside out and can be burned without your knowledge.

CHAMPAGNE TRUFFLES

This is one of my stars, and it can be your star now.

6 ounces glazed apricots
1 cup dry champagne or white wine
4 tablespoons (½ stick) unsalted butter, at
    room temperature
1½ cups sifted confectioners' sugar
1 pound Homemade Chocolate Coating (recipe
    opposite)

1. Cut each apricot into ½-inch pieces. Place them in a bowl or a glass jar, and cover with the champagne. Marinate the apricots, covered, in the refrigerator for about 1 hour; the apricots should remain firm and chewy.

2. Drain the apricots well, reserving 2 tablespoons of the marinade; pat them thor-

THE STORY OF CHAMPAGNE TRUFFLES

I had never allowed myself to get into making candy until a few years ago. My daughter Lisa, who was doing public relations work in New York, happened to be assigned to the Merrill Lynch and Moët et Chandon accounts when they were sponsoring a gala celebrating the ninetieth birthday of Carnegie Hall, to raise money to save that historic building. It was to be a very elaborate affair in the Victorian style, and that it was. Isaac Stern headed the committee and Zubin Mehta and the New York Philharmonic played all through the evening. But back to the candy.

Lisa called me one afternoon and asked if I would please create a chocolate truffle made with champagne. I said very quickly, "No, I cannot," because pure chocolate will not blend with any alcohol.

"Mother, just try to think what you can do, but the candy has to be made with champagne."

Lisa had found some miniature crystal cloches at Tiffany's, made exactly like the Victorian glass bells that were used for serving mushrooms *en cloche.* "Tiffany's had to order them from France and I have bought five hundred of them. They are to be the souvenir at each place setting. I want to have a chocolate truffle in each tiny glass cloche. Mother, I'm desperate. You have to do it."

I thought it was the most charming idea. "How much time do I have?"

"Two weeks."

"*Two weeks!* Lisa, I cannot do it."

"Mother," said Lisa, "I'll give you a hundred dollars."

"I'll do it," I said, quick as a flash.

I solved the problem of the champagne and chocolate by marinating small cubes of glazed apricots in champagne, and then folding the mixture into the buttercream for the centers. When the buttercream centers had set, we coated them with imported semisweet chocolate. It is amazing what one can do when a hundred dollar bill is dangled before one's eyes.

The police roped off the street in front of Carnegie Hall very early the morning of the party. A white tent was stretched over the huge "make believe" dining room. Each small round table was covered with a silver lamé cloth, and a bouquet of lilies of the valley adorned the center of each table. Glorious Food served a lovely Victorian dinner and at each place there was a blue and silver box from Tiffany's. Inside the box was the tiny glass cloche that barely held one truffle. Glorious Food spun a nest of green sugar with a candied violet on the top of each truffle. Very Victorian. Anyway, the evening was a great success. Carnegie Hall was saved.

During the last weeks when this book was being assembled, I said to the editor, "I don't think we should have candy recipes as we have so many cakes."

"Oh, yes, we should," said Suzanne Rafer. "I want those truffles in this book."

So here they are—champagne truffles. I never did get the hundred dollars from Lisa, but the truffles are delicious.

Always keep a box of these truffles in the refrigerator. If you have company and your entrée doesn't turn out too well, serve champagne truffles in the living room with coffee. All will be forgiven. I promise.

A painting by W. A. Rogers shows the New Orleans Sugar Exchange, 1900: a busy market for a popular commodity.

oughly dry with paper towels.

3. Beat the butter in a bowl with a mixer on medium speed until it is thick and fluffy. Gradually beat the sugar in, then beat in the reserved marinade. Beat the mixture until it is very smooth and creamy, about 5 minutes. Gently fold the reserved apricots into the buttercream, first making sure they are as dry as possible. Transfer the mixture to a small bowl, cover with foil, and refrigerate overnight to allow the mixture to ripen and harden.

4. Working with a small amount of the buttercream mixture at a time and keeping the remainder refrigerated, form irregularly shaped balls about 1 inch in diameter, using about 1½ teaspoons of the mixture per truffle. Work with your fingertips, not the palms of your hands, to keep the mixture from becoming too soft. Place the truffles on a baking sheet lined with foil or wax paper. Continue forming truffles, in batches, placing each one on the baking sheet as it is formed, until the buttercream mixture is used up.

5. Refrigerate the truffles on the baking sheet, uncovered, until they are somewhat firm, about 1 hour. Then cover them loosely with foil or paper, and return them to the refrigerator. Chill until the truffles are quite firm and set, several hours or overnight.

6. Working with only 4 or 5 truffles at a time and keeping the remainder refrigerated, coat the truffles with warm Homemade Chocolate Coating as follows: Drop a truffle into the chocolate coating, and turn it with a fork to cover it well. Gently lift the truffle out with the fork, and hold it above the pan for a few seconds to let the excess chocolate drip back into the pan. Gently scrape the bottom of the fork against the edge of the pan to remove more of the excess chocolate (this prevents the chocolate from forming "platforms" under the pieces of candy as they set). Using the flat side of a spatula or knife, very gently slide the truffle off the fork and onto a foil- or wax-paper-lined baking sheet. Repeat this procedure with the remaining truffles, continuing to work with only a few at a time.

7. When all the truffles are coated, refrigerate them on the baking sheet, uncovered, until the coating is somewhat firm, about 1 hour. Then cover them loosely with foil or wax paper, and refrigerate until the coating is quite firm and set, several hours or overnight.

8. Select a tin box or boxes large enough to hold the truffles in one layer; line it with foil or wax paper. Arrange the truffles in the box, first placing each one in a tiny fluted paper cup if desired; cover tightly and refrigerate. Stored this way, truffles will keep up to 1 week, although these are at their best the first 3 days.

Makes 24 truffles

Glazed apricots are preferred for this recipe; they are available in specialty food stores and at some specialty greengrocers. If they are not available, good-quality dried apricots, simmered in water for 5 minutes and thoroughly drained, can be substituted, but they are not nearly as delicious.

CHAPTER THIRTEEN

BRUNCHES, PUNCHES, COFFEES, AND TEAS

BRUNCH IS AT ELEVEN . . .

◆◆◆

Brunch is at eleven,
Punch is at three,
Coffee is at seven,
But where's my tea?

I love brunch. One of its great charms is the time of day—eleven to twelve or thereabout. The early morning rush has subsided by then, the plans for the day are lined up, and we suddenly find ourselves very hungry. We welcome good food at that point, and the chance to enjoy it in peace, if only for a few moments.

If you are entertaining, brunch is easier than a luncheon. One main dish is enough, and it can be very special, such as Puff Paste Pocketbooks, or it can be very simple, such as fresh fruit juice, Sour Cream Pancakes with blueberries, and Piggies en Brochette—and lots of good hot coffee and tea. It can be an omelet with fresh herbs or sautéed ham, and hot biscuits with your best preserves. If you have just come from picking strawberries, have those. Call up your friend, especially if she grew up north of the Mason-Dixon line, and invite her over for brunch. Sit her down with a cup of Spiced Tea or even a Palm Beach Cooler. Then you say, "Now I will show you what a real strawberry shortcake tastes like." That will be fun.

◆◆◆

PUFF PASTE POCKETBOOKS

Chicken and Ham Filling, or Seafood and Mushroom Filling (recipes follow)
Cormeal Puff Paste (see page 430)
1½ tablespoons heavy or whipping cream

1. Prepare the filling and set it aside.
2. Roll out the puff pastry to a 21 x 10-inch rectangle, ¼ inch thick. Trim the edges to make them perfectly straight. Cut this rectangle into 14 pieces, about 3 x 5 inches each.
3. Place the pieces of pastry on a non-stick or foil-lined stainless steel baking sheet. Put the sheet in the refrigerator or freezer for a few minutes to get perfectly cold.
4. Preheat the oven to 425°F.
5. Brush the pastry with the cream, and bake until golden brown, 15 to 18 minutes. Turn off the heat and keep the pastries warm in the oven with the door ajar. (This also helps to dry out the pastries.)
6. When you are ready to serve them, heat the filling until hot. Split the pastry cases horizontally with a sharp, thin knife and spoon the filling into the bottom half. Place the top over the filled bottom piece, and serve at once.

Serves 6 to 8

CHICKEN AND HAM FILLING

10 tablespoons (1¼ sticks) unsalted butter
6 tablespoons all-purpose flour
2 cups Rich Chicken Stock (see Index)
1 cup heavy or whipping cream
3 tablespoons medium-dry Spanish sherry or Madeira, or to taste
2 cups chopped mushrooms
4 cups diced poached chicken (see Index)
1 cup slivered baked ham
2 tablespoons chopped fresh parsley

Salt and freshly ground white pepper to taste

1. Melt 6 tablespoons of the butter in a heavy saucepan. Add the flour, and blend thoroughly. Gradually add the stock, beating with a whisk, and cook over low heat until the sauce is smooth and has thickened. Add the cream and sherry or Madeira and blend well. Simmer about 5 minutes.
2. Melt the remaining butter in a skillet. Add the mushrooms and sauté them lightly, 2 to 3 minutes. Do not allow them to brown the least bit.
3. Stir the chicken, ham, mushrooms, parsley, and salt and pepper into the sauce. Allow to ripen 1 hour or so before serving.

VARIATION: *Sweetbread, Ham, and Mushroom Filling:* Use diced poached sweetbreads instead of chicken. A favorite.

🦉 If desired, extra cream sauce may be made if more is desired for Puff Paste Pocketbooks.

SEAFOOD AND MUSHROOM FILLING

¾ cup (1½ sticks) unsalted butter
4 cups sliced mushrooms
2 cups finely chopped cooked shrimp
2 cups chopped lump crabmeat or cooked spiny lobster
2 tablespoons chopped fresh parsley
Salt and freshly ground white pepper to taste
Cayenne pepper to taste
½ cup all-purpose flour
3 cups milk
1 cup heavy or whipping cream
3 tablespoons medium-dry Spanish sherry or Madeira, or to taste

1. Melt 6 tablespoons of the butter in a large heavy saucepan. Add the mushrooms and sauté them lightly for 2 to 3 minutes. Do not allow them to brown the

least bit. Add the shrimp, crabmeat or lobster, and parsley. Season with salt, white pepper, and cayenne to taste, mix well, and set aside to ripen at least 1 hour.

2. Melt the remaining butter in a heavy saucepan. Add the flour, and blend thoroughly. Gradually add the milk, beating constantly with a whisk, and cook over low heat until the sauce is smooth and has thickened, about 8 minutes.

3. Add the cream, and salt and white pepper to taste. Stir in the sherry or Madeira, and simmer until the wine has lost its raw flavor, about 5 minutes.

4. Combine the sauce with the seafood and mushrooms.

CORNMEAL PUFF PASTE

◆◆

*T*his recipe sprang from my teaching classic French puff paste and from my Southern upbringing. I love cornbread, and one day it occurred to me that I could blend the two—so I did. This paste, designed for savory pies and turnovers, flakes exactly like classic puff paste but has the added charm and flavor and crunch of cornmeal.

◆

2 cups sifted all-purpose flour
1 teaspoon salt
¼ cup fine white cornmeal
1 cup (2 sticks) unsalted butter, chilled
½ cup ice water (approximately)

◆

1. Resift the flour into a large bowl. Add the salt and mix thoroughly. Set aside 1 tablespoon of the flour.

2. Add the cornmeal to the flour and mix thoroughly.

3. Cut 1 tablespoon of the butter into the flour with a pastry blender, and work it until the mixture is like coarse meal.

4. Add the ice water to the flour mixture, working it in quickly to form a dough. The dough should be soft and pliable but not sticky. If it feels the least bit sticky, add a small sprinkling of flour. Form the dough into a ball, patting it with a little flour if it is sticky.

5. Wrap the dough in wax paper or plastic wrap and refrigerate for 15 minutes.

6. Sprinkle the reserved tablespoon of flour over the remaining butter. Using a dough scraper or the cushion of your hand, work the butter and flour together on a flat surface until the mixture is perfectly smooth and free of lumps. The butter must remain cold. Place the butter between 2 sheets of wax paper and roll or pat it into a 6-inch square.

7. Put the dough on a lightly floured surface or pastry cloth and roll it out to form a 10-inch square, about ½ inch thick. Place the butter packet in the center of the dough.

8. Fold the side pieces of dough over the butter, stretching them so they are slightly overlapping. Then fold the top and bottom pieces of dough over the side pieces, again slightly overlapping. The butter must be completely hidden. Turn the dough 90 degrees, and roll it into a rectangle about 10 x 20 inches. Fold the dough into thirds. This is called a "turn."

9. Turn the dough 90 degrees again, in the same direction as before. Roll it out again into a 10 x 20-inch rectangle. Do not roll the dough to make it wider—roll it only to make it longer. Fold the dough into thirds. Chill the dough between turns if it's warm or hard to roll out.

10. Turn the dough, roll it into a rectangle for the third time, and fold it into thirds.

11. Place the dough in a plastic bag and chill for at least 30 minutes.

12. Repeat the process of rotating, rolling, and folding until you have made 3 more "turns," covering the dough with wax

paper or plastic wrap and chilling it for 20 to 30 minutes between each turn. (After the fourth turn the dough can be wrapped well and refrigerated overnight and completed the next day, or it can be frozen and the fifth and sixth turns made after thawing.)

13. After the sixth turn the dough can be wrapped well and frozen if desired, or you can chill it thoroughly and then roll it out to use as desired for turnovers, cheese snacks, and savory pies.

Makes 14 Puff Paste Pocketbooks or 10 Roquefort Squares

To thaw puff paste, place the frozen puff paste in the refrigerator the night before using. It will be ready to roll next morning. Do not thaw puff paste at room temperature as the butter will melt.

ROLLED OMELET SOUFFLE

This rolled omelet is easier than it sounds, and it is spectacular. It will hold in a warm oven for an hour, believe it or not. And the variations are fun.

4 tablespoons (½ stick) butter
½ cup all-purpose flour
½ teaspoon salt
Cayenne pepper to taste
2 cups milk
5 large eggs, separated
Spinach and Ham Filling (recipe follows)

1. Grease a 15½ x 10½ x 1-inch jelly roll pan. Line it with wax paper, and coat the paper too. Set the pan aside.

2. Melt the butter in a heavy saucepan. Add the flour and blend until smooth. Add the salt and cayenne. Slowly pour in the milk, stirring constantly with a whisk, and cook until the mixture has thickened and is smooth again, about 5 minutes.

3. Beat the yolks and add a little of the hot sauce to temper them. Pour the yolk mixture into the sauce and cook over medium heat a minute more. Do not allow it to boil. Set the mixture aside to cool.

4. While the mixture is cooling, prepare the filling.

5. Preheat the oven to 400°F.

6. Beat the egg whites until they are stiff but not dry and grainy. Gently fold them into the cooled mixture, and spread it out in the prepared pan. Place the pan in the oven, and cook only until well puffed and brown, about 15 minutes. Invert the omelet at once onto a clean towel. Spread it with warm filling and roll it up like a jelly roll.

Serves 4 to 6

SPINACH AND HAM FILLING

4 tablespoons (½ stick) butter
2 tablespoons all-purpose flour
1 cup milk
Salt and freshly ground black pepper to taste
2 shallots, finely chopped (optional)
3 tablespoons water (optional)
½ pound mushrooms, chopped
1 cup freshly cooked chopped spinach (1 pound uncooked), well drained
½ cup slivered baked ham, or 4 slices crisp cooked bacon, chopped

1. Melt 2 tablespoons of the butter in a heavy saucepan. Add the flour and blend until smooth. Slowly add the milk, and cook, stirring constantly, until the mixture is thick and smooth, about 5 minutes. Season with salt and pepper. Keep warm.

2. Melt the remaining butter in a skillet. If using shallots, add the shallots and the water, and sauté over medium heat until the water has boiled away. Add the mushrooms and sauté until they give up their moisture, keeping them somewhat crisp, about 1 minute.

3. Combine the shallots and mushrooms, spinach, and ham with the cream sauce. Taste for seasoning, and correct if necessary. Keep warm until you are ready to fill the omelet.

VARIATIONS: Make a filling of all creamed mushrooms, or all ham, or half mushrooms and half ham.

Substitute chopped fresh asparagus for the spinach, and omit the shallots. Or use a thick, rich tomato sauce instead of the spinach mixture. Season both with fresh or dried tarragon.

ROCK RUN MILL PACAKES

*T*urn pancakes only once—flipping them back and forth toughens them. Cooking them too slowly also toughens them. These pancakes can be made with all whole-wheat flour, but then they will not be quite as light.

½ cup sifted all-purpose flour
2 tablespoons sugar
1 teaspoon salt
1 tablespoon baking powder
1 cup whole-wheat flour
1¼ cups milk
2 large eggs, separated
4 tablespoons (½ stick) butter, melted and cooled
4 tablespoons (½ stick) butter
2 tablespoons vegetable oil

1. Mix the all-purpose flour, sugar, salt, and baking powder and sift again, or mix well with a whisk.

2. Pour the milk into a large bowl. Add the flour mixture, whole-wheat flour, egg yolks, and melted butter, and mix thoroughly with an electric mixer or a whisk.

3. Beat the egg whites until they are stiff but not dry and grainy. Gently fold them into the mixture.

4. Heat the solid butter and the oil in a small saucepan, and keep warm. Heat a griddle or skillet over high heat, and brush it with the oil and butter before cooking each batch of pancakes. When the cakes bubble on top, peek under one edge, lifting it with a small spatula. If the bottom is golden, turn the pancake and brown the other side.

5. Serve with Brown Sugar, Cinnamon, and Walnut Syrup (page 440), Waffle and Pancake Syrup (page 441), or maple syrup.

Serves 4

VARIATION: These pancakes can be made with buttermilk, but the batter will not hold quite as well as when made with sweet milk.

Pancake batters will thicken somewhat upon standing. To thin, simply whisk in a few spoonfuls of milk.

The lovely Rock Run Mill in Maryland inspired these pancakes.

APPLE PANCAKES

◆◆◆

This is a delicious and hearty pancake for the weekend cook. It can be whipped up quickly and served most anytime—just great for a Saturday breakfast or Sunday brunch. Serve with good hot coffee.

◆

1 cup sour cream
½ teaspoon salt
3 tablespoons sugar
4 large eggs, separated
1 cup sifted all-purpose flour
1½ teaspoons baking powder
3 tart apples
3 tablespoons fresh lemon juice
4 tablespoons (½ stick) butter
2 tablespoons vegetable oil
Confectioners' sugar, for dusting

◆

1. Measure the sour cream into a mixing bowl. Add the salt, sugar, and egg yolks. Blend, and set aside.

2. Combine the flour with the baking powder, and set aside.

3. Peel and coarsely chop the apples (you should have 1½ cups). Toss them with the lemon juice.

4. Beat the egg whites until they are stiff but not dry and grainy.

5. Stir the flour and baking powder into the sour cream mixture. Add the apples, and then fold in the egg whites.

6. Heat the butter and oil in a small saucepan, and keep warm. Heat a skillet or griddle over high heat, and brush it with the oil and butter before cooking each batch of pancakes. When the pancakes bubble on top, peek under one edge. If the bottom is golden, turn the pancake to brown the other side. Serve with a dusting of confectioners' sugar and apricot or strawberry preserves or lemon marmalade.

Serves 4

DELICATE, DELECTABLE PANCAKES FOR TWO

◆◆◆

This is an excellent quick recipe. Children love these pancakes when they are made quite small and sprinkled with orange or lemon juice and confectioners' sugar. They are, of course, at their best served with lingonberry preserves, which are very expensive now. Cranberry jelly or preserves is a worthy substitute.

◆

1 large egg
½ cup milk
2 tablespoons cold water
2 tablespoons unsalted butter, melted
½ cup sifted all-purpose flour

2 tablespoons butter
1 tablespoon vegetable oil
Cranberry jelly, for serving

◆

1. Beat the egg hard in a mixing bowl with a whisk or electric mixer. When it is fluffy, add the milk, water, and melted butter.

2. Sift the flour lightly into the mixture while beating it. When the batter is smooth, set it aside to rest 30 minutes before using.

3. Heat the solid butter and the oil in a small saucepan, and keep warm. Heat a crêpe pan or griddle over high heat, and brush it with the butter and oil before cooking each pancake.

4. Pour 2 tablespoons batter into the prepared pan. Rotate the pan to distribute the batter evenly. Cook over high heat until golden brown on the bottom, about 40 seconds. (Lift a corner of the pancake and peek.) Turn the pancake over, and cook the second side about 15 seconds. Flip the pancake onto wax paper and keep warm.

5. Continue greasing the pan and frying the pancakes until the batter is used up. Serve a spoonful of jelly on each pancake.

Serves 2

SOUR CREAM PANCAKES

◆◆

*T*his is an all-time favorite sour cream pancake. The superb batter can be used in any number of ways with berries and fruit sauces, but blueberry pancakes are hard to beat. In the wintertime, make the Sour Cream Pancakes plain and serve them with the sauce made with frozen blueberries.

◆

1½ cups sifted all-purpose flour
Pinch of salt
2½ teaspoons baking powder
¼ teaspoon baking soda
1 teaspoon sugar
2 large eggs
6 tablespoons (¾ stick) butter, melted
⅔ cup sour cream
⅔ cup milk
1 cup blueberries, currants, or raspberries
4 tablespoons (½ stick) butter
2 tablespoons vegetable oil
Confectioners' sugar, for dusting
Blueberry Sauce (recipe follows)

◆

1. Combine the flour, salt, baking powder, baking soda, and sugar.

2. Beat the eggs in a roomy bowl until fluffy. Add the melted butter, sour cream, and milk.

3. Add the dry ingredients to the egg mixture, and beat well. Fold the berries in gently so they will not bleed.

4. Heat the solid butter and the oil in a small saucepan, and keep warm. Heat a griddle or skillet over high heat, and brush it with the oil and butter before cooking

each batch of pancakes. Pour 2 to 3 tablespoons batter for each pancake onto the griddle or skillet. When the underside is golden brown, turn the pancake.

5. To serve, sift confectioners' sugar over the top and pass the warm Blueberry Sauce.

Serves 6

🦉 This is a rather thick batter; it makes a cakelike but tender pancake. For a thinner pancake, add ¼ cup more milk.

If not serving blueberry sauce with the pancakes, increase the berries to 1½ cups.

◆

BLUEBERRY SAUCE

◆

⅔ cup sugar, or to taste
2 tablespoons cornstarch
Pinch of salt
1½ cups water
2 cups fresh blueberries
2 tablespoons butter, melted
2 tablespoons fresh lemon juice
½ teaspoon grated lemon peel

Mix the sugar and cornstarch together in a medium saucepan. Add the salt, water, berries, and melted butter. Cook, stirring often, over medium heat until the sauce has thickened and is clear, 20 to 25 minutes.

Add the lemon juice and peel, stir, and serve.

🦉 This sauce can be made with other berries, but blueberries seem to be the favorite.

INDIAN RIVER ORANGE AND LEMON PANCAKES

◆◆

*G*lorious breakfasts are full of surprises. How good to be in Florida for a while and have these orange pancakes. They blend with all kinds of yummy syrups and preserves.

◆

½ navel orange
½ lemon
3 tablespoons sugar
4 large eggs
½ teaspoon salt
1 cup heavy or whipping cream or sour cream
*   (see Owl)*
1 tablespoon lemon juice, or to taste
1 cup sifted all-purpose or cake flour
2 teaspoons baking powder
4 tablespoons (½ stick) butter
2 tablespoons vegetable oil

◆

1. Cut the peel from the orange and lemon into thin slivers. Combine the peels and sugar in a food processor, and twirl until the peels are finely grated. (Or you can grate the peels by hand and combine them with the sugar.)

2. Put 1 whole egg and 3 egg yolks (reserve the whites) in the bowl of an electric mixer or in the processor. Gradually beat in the sugar, then continue beating until the mixture falls like a ribbon when dropped from a spoon. Add the salt, heavy cream or sour cream, and lemon juice, and mix.

3. Blend in the flour and baking powder with a whisk.

4. Beat the egg whites until stiff, then fold them into the batter.

5. Heat the butter and oil in a small saucepan, and keep warm. Heat a griddle or skillet over high heat, and brush it with the oil and butter before cooking each batch of pancakes. Cook the pancakes promptly. Serve with your favorite syrup, jelly, preserves, or marmalade.

Serves 4

🦉 If you use heavy or whipping cream, beat it gently in step 2; it must not whip. If you use sour cream, you may want an extra tablespoon of sugar. The sweet cream is best.

The Sargent family of Florida, nicely outfitted in hats and gloves for the photographer—but surely not for orange picking, even in 1912.

COUNTRY BUTTERMILK PANCAKES

*O*ld-fashioned pancakes—in the country or in the city—mighty good!

The Iron Club, mustaches neatly groomed, hold their Pancake Fry. Looks like they expect to cook up many batches.

2½ cups buttermilk
2½ cups sifted all-purpose flour
3 large eggs
1 teaspoon salt
2 tablespoons sugar
1 teaspoon baking powder
2 tablespoons butter, melted
¾ teaspoon baking soda
1 tablespoon hot water
6 tablespoons solid vegetable shortening for the
   griddle

1. Mix the buttermilk with the flour until free of lumps. Cover with foil or plastic wrap, and refrigerate for 24 hours if possible.

2. When you are ready to make the batter, beat the eggs until light. Beat in the buttermilk and flour mixture a little at a time. Add the salt, sugar, baking powder, and melted butter.

3. Dissolve the baking soda in the hot water. Add this to the batter, and mix the batter well. Set it aside to rest for 30 minutes to 1 hour before using.

4. Heat the shortening in a small saucepan, and keep warm. Heat a griddle or skillet over high heat, and brush it with the shortening before cooking each batch of pancakes. When the pancakes bubble on top, check to see if the underside is golden. If it is, turn to brown the second side.

5. Serve with Spring Rhubarb Sauce (page 440) or Waffle and Pancake Syrup (page 441).

Serves 6

🦉 The flour and buttermilk mixture will ferment and take on a zesty flavor if allowed to stand in the refrigerator overnight. However, the cakes can be made immediately if desired.

A GLORIOUS PANCAKE WITH APPLES, CINNAMON, AND CORIANDER

*T*his is an oven-baked pancake, not a griddle cake—easy as pie to blend in a processor. To serve 6 to 8, double the recipe but bake it in 2 dishes. Voilà!

4 tart apples
3 tablespoons unsalted butter
4 tablespoons sugar
Juice of ½ lemon
1 cup milk
2 large eggs, separated
½ teaspoon salt
⅛ teaspoon ground coriander seeds
1 cup sifted all-purpose flour
2 teaspoons baking powder

TOPPING

¼ cup sugar
1 teaspoon ground cinnamon
¼ teaspoon ground coriander seeds

1. Peel, core, and slice the apples very thin. Combine the apple slices, butter, 2 tablespoons of the sugar, and the lemon juice in a skillet or heavy saucepan. Simmer until the apples are tender but not mushy. (If the apples are not sufficiently juicy, you may need to add 1 to 2 tablespoons water.) They must not brown. Cool in the refrigerator or freezer.

2. Stir together the topping ingredients, and set aside.

3. Preheat the oven to 400°F.

4. Combine the milk, egg yolks, remaining sugar, salt, and coriander in a roomy bowl, or in the bowl of an electric mixer or processor. Beat thoroughly.

5. Add the flour and the baking powder. Mix quickly so as not to overactivate the gluten.

6. Whip the egg whites until they are stiff but not dry and grainy. Fold them gently into the pancake batter.

7. Butter a 10-inch ovenproof skillet or a 1½-quart shallow baking dish. Arrange the apples on the bottom. Pour the batter over the apples.

8. Place the pan on the middle shelf of the oven and bake until the pancake is golden brown, 15 to 20 minutes. Five minutes before removing it from the oven, sprinkle the pancake with 1½ tablespoons of the topping.

9. Serve the pancake at once, as it falls even more quickly than a soufflé. Cut it into 4 wedges, and pass the remaining topping.

Serves 4

VARIATIONS: *Glorious Pancake with Bing Cherries:* Use 1½ cups pitted fresh Bing cherries (uncooked) instead of the apples. Omit the coriander.

Glorious Pancake with Red Plums: Use 1½ cups lightly cooked pitted red plums, sweetened to taste, instead of the apples. Omit the coriander and cinnamon.

Glorious Pancake with Peaches, Nectarines, or Apricots: Use 1½ cups thickly sliced, very lightly poached peeled peaches or nectarines or unpeeled apricots, sweetened to taste, instead of the apples.

KENTUCKY MOUNTAIN PANCAKES

Have you ever eaten a cloud? These pancakes are golden brown clouds of flour and eggs. A New York chef made them famous, but they were born in Kentucky where the peaks of the mountains seem to touch the sky.

Practice on these pancakes when the house is quiet and the children are in school. Then when you are in command of them, have a big Saturday breakfast. Or make them when you go to camp in the woods next summer. Take your black iron griddle along, a whisk, and a roomy bowl. The air will be bracing there; everyone will be hungry.

*A platter of Kentucky Mountain Pancakes
accompanied by sausage links—heaven!*

◆

2½ cups all-purpose flour
2 teaspoons sugar
1½ teaspoons salt
2 tablespoons baking powder
3 large eggs, separated
2 cups milk
7 tablespoons unsalted butter, melted and
    cooled
4 tablespoons butter
2 tablespoons vegetable oil

◆

1. Sift the flour into a bowl. Add the sugar, salt, and baking powder, and sift again. Set aside.

2. Put the egg yolks in a large bowl. Beat well by hand or with an electric mixer. Add the milk, and beat again.

3. Add the flour mixture and mix gently but thoroughly. Blend in the melted butter.

4. Beat the egg whites until they are stiff but not dry and grainy. Gently fold them into the egg mixture. Allow the batter to rest 20 to 30 minutes if you can.

5. Heat the solid butter and the oil in a small saucepan, and keep warm. Heat a black iron or electric griddle over high heat, and brush it with the oil and butter before you cook each batch of pancakes. Use 2 to 4 tablespoons batter for each pancake.

6. When the pancakes are golden brown on one side, turn them with a spatula to brown the other side. Do not turn them but once. However, shake the griddle often as the pancakes cook so they will brown more evenly. Serve at once with butter and your favorite syrup. Never keep a pancake waiting!

Serves 6

🦉 This batter can be made with an electric mixer, but it is best when prepared by hand with a whisk.

Because of the large amount of baking powder, this batter is stiffer than you might expect, but the pancakes will be very porous and tender.

WHOLE-WHEAT WAFFLES

◆◆◆

*I*f Whole-Wheat Waffles sounds too heavy, these will fool you. They are light and flavorful—and served with Brown Sugar, Cinnamon, and Walnut Syrup, they will brighten the gloomiest day.

◆

½ cup all-purpose flour
1½ cups whole-wheat flour
½ teaspoon salt
3½ teaspoons baking powder
2 large eggs, separated
1¾ cups milk or buttermilk
8 tablespoons (1 stick) butter, melted and cooled
4 tablespoons butter

2 tablespoons vegetable oil

◆

1. Sift the all-purpose flour into a bowl. Add the whole-wheat flour (unsifted), salt, and baking powder, and mix well.

2. Combine the egg yolks, milk or buttermilk, and melted butter in a roomy

bowl. Add the flour mixture a little at a time, beating thoroughly with a whisk. (This part can be done with an electric mixer or in a food processor.)

3. Beat the egg whites until they hold a stiff peak but are not dry and grainy. Gently fold them into the flour and egg mixture.

4. Heat the solid butter and the oil in a small saucepan, and keep warm. Heat a waffle iron over high heat, and brush it with oil and butter before cooking each waffle.

5. Cook until golden brown, and serve immediately with your favorite syrup.

Serves 6

🦉 This batter, stored in a covered jar, holds well overnight. It holds better when made with milk rather than buttermilk.

SOUR CREAM WAFFLES

◆◆◆

*T*his is a rather thick batter but it makes a tender, crisp waffle that has some body and good flavor.

◆

2 large eggs
1 cup sour cream
1½ cups all-purpose flour, sifted
2½ teaspoons baking powder
¾ teaspoon salt
⅓ cup butter, melted
4 tablespoons butter
2 tablespoons vegetable oil

1. Beat the eggs in a large bowl with an electric mixer or a whisk until they are fluffy. Add the sour cream.

2. Sift the flour with the baking powder and salt. Stir it into the sour cream and egg mixture. Add the melted butter, and blend.

3. Heat the solid butter and the oil in a small saucepan; keep warm. Heat a waffle iron over high heat, and brush it with the oil and butter before cooking each waffle.

4. Cook the waffles until golden brown, and serve with a delicious syrup.

Serves 4

VARIATION: *Savannah Pecan Waffles:* Add ⅓ to ½ cup chopped pecans, and cook as directed.

TENNESSEE CORNMEAL WAFFLES

◆◆◆

*T*hese waffles were served at one of the old hotels in Nashville with Chicken Hash as a special Sunday breakfast.

◆

2 cups white cornmeal
1 tablespoon all-purpose flour
1 teaspoon salt
1 teaspoon sugar
2½ teaspoons baking powder
3 large eggs, separated
½ cup sour cream

1½ cups buttermilk
4 tablespoons (½ stick) butter, melted and
    cooled
4 tablespoons (½ stick) butter
2 tablespoons vegetable oil

◆

No doubt customers always knew when Buglin' Sam the Waffle Man (right) was on the way (1920).

1. Combine the cornmeal, flour, salt, sugar, and baking powder in a large bowl, or in the bowl of an electric mixer or food processor.

2. Add the egg yolks, sour cream, buttermilk, and melted butter. Mix well but don't overbeat.

3. Beat the egg whites until they are stiff but not dry and grainy. Fold them into the batter with a whisk.

4. Heat the solid butter and the oil in a small saucepan, and keep warm. Heat a waffle iron over high heat, and brush it with the oil and butter before cooking each waffle. Cook the waffles until golden brown, and serve immediately. Pass the syrup.

Serves 6

BROWN SUGAR, CINNAMON, AND WALNUT SYRUP

❖❖❖

Serve with pancakes or waffles.

---

1 cup loosely packed light brown sugar
1 cup granulated sugar
¼ cup light corn syrup
2 cups water, or more as needed
1 cinnamon stick (2 inches)
3 tablespoons butter
1½ tablespoons finely chopped walnuts or pecans

---

1. Combine the sugars in a heavy saucepan. Add the corn syrup, water, and cinnamon stick. Simmer until a syrup has formed, 10 to 12 minutes. Add a little more water if the syrup becomes too thick.

2. Discard the cinnamon stick, and add the butter and nuts. Simmer a minute, and serve warm.

Makes 1¾ cups

VARIATION: The nuts can be omitted altogether, or chopped unblanched almonds or hazelnuts can be used instead of pecans or walnuts.

🦉 The corn syrup is used to help prevent the syrup from crystallizing. If the syrup should crystallize upon standing, add a little water and lemon juice, or a pinch of cream of tartar, and boil again for a few minutes.

SPRING RHUBARB SAUCE

❖❖❖

Serve with Sour Cream Pancakes or any delicate pancake (not whole wheat).

⅛ cup sugar, or more to taste
1 tablespoon cornstarch
1½ cups water
2 large slivers lemon peel
4 cups cubed rhubarb (deep red if possible)
Juice from ½ lemon, or to taste

1. Combine the sugar and cornstarch in a saucepan and mix well. Add the water and the lemon peel. Cook over medium heat until the mixture blends, about 8 minutes.

2. Add the rhubarb, and simmer until a sauce has formed, 15 to 18 minutes. Discard the lemon peel, and add the lemon juice. Taste for sweetness, and add a little extra sugar if desired (rhubarb varies in acidity).

Makes 2 cups

VARIATION: Add a few strawberries to the rhubarb during the last 5 minutes of cooking.

WAFFLE AND PANCAKE SYRUP

1 cup granulated sugar
½ cup loosely packed light brown sugar
1 cup cold water
4 tablespoons (½ stick) butter

Combine all the ingredients in a heavy saucepan. Bring to a boil, and boil 4 to 5 minutes for a medium-thin syrup.

Makes 1½ cups

VARIATION: Use ½ cup maple sugar instead of the light brown sugar. (Brown sugar is white sugar with molasses added.)

HOBE SOUND ORANGE SAUCE

The lemon juice heightens the flavor of the oranges. Serve this over puddings, delicate pancakes, and soufflés.

6 navel oranges or tangelos
¼ cup sugar, or more to taste
1 teaspoon lemon juice, or more to taste

1. Peel 5 of the oranges or tangelos and cut the fruit into sections, being careful to save the juice. Set aside.

2. Sliver the peel from the remaining orange, combine the peel with the sugar in a food processor, and twirl until it is finely grated; or grate the peel by hand and add it to the sugar. Section the orange and add it to the others.

3. Combine the sugar, orange sections, and orange juice in a saucepan. Taste for sweetness, and add more sugar if you like. Bring the mixture barely to a boil, remove it from the heat, and allow it to cool. Add lemon juice to taste.

Makes 2 cups

APRICOT SYRUP

*F*or waffles or pancakes—especially good with whole-wheat waffles or pancakes. This will keep for weeks in the refrigerator.

An early syrup pot with floral design.

6 ounces dried apricots
¾ cup sugar
1 lemon slice
4 whole cloves
5 cups cold water

1. In a heavy saucepan, combine the apricots with the sugar, lemon, cloves, and water. Bring to a boil, reduce the heat, and simmer until the apricots are very soft, 1 to 1¼ hours.

2. Discard the lemon slice and cloves, and purée the mixture in a blender or food processor.

Makes 2 cups

If the syrup has boiled rapidly and become too thick for your taste, add about ⅓ cup cold water and bring the syrup again to a boil. This is a thick syrup, however, so avoid adding too much water.

*I*n all baking, the greater the proportion of flour to liquid, the less the batter should be beaten in order to have a tender product. Beat only until the dry ingredients have disappeared.

PUNCHES

*T*he silver punch bowl was for many decades in the South a symbol of elegant hospitality for weddings, anniversaries, and receptions. The ceremony is still inviting but many of the old-fashioned mixtures are overly sweet for today's palate. However, I have included several of these interesting recipes, such as the Pendennis Club Wedding Punch, as a glance back into a more baroque era.

Chilled champagne will of course never go out of fashion. A correctly made eggnog is still a delicious holiday punch, but it always ignites a flow of conversation about calories. Too bad! All punches except the Wassail Cup should be served very cold or over a large block of ice. And all punches, especially those with carbonated water or champagne, must be made up one formula at a time as they are being served; otherwise the mixture will go flat and the charm of a refreshing drink will be lost.

CHAMPAGNE PUNCH

◆◆◆

A very special champagne punch for a very special small wedding.

◆

1 ounce cognac
½ ounce Cointreau
1 bottle champagne, chilled

◆

Pour the cognac and Cointreau over a block of ice in a punch bowl. Add the champagne, and serve in champagne glasses or flutes.
  Serves 6

Double or triple the recipe as needed, or make it 1 batch at a time to be sure the champagne is effervescent.

> ◆◆◆
> ### CHAMPAGNE
>
> *C*hampagne is the most festive and elegant of all drinks for weddings, anniversaries, or debut parties. But it must be served very cold.
>   Place the champagne bottles, corks up, in tubs of crushed ice at least 2 hours before the reception. The wine chills more rapidly if you use crushed ice instead of cubes.
>   Fill champagne glasses not more than three-quarters full.
>   A bottle of champagne will fill 6 glasses.

PENDENNIS CLUB
WEDDING PUNCH

◆◆◆

*M*r. Fred Crawford, the longtime manager of Louisville's Pendennis Club, gave me the recipe for this baroque punch they served at weddings and parties.

◆

2¼ cups fresh lemon juice (12 lemons)
1 quart carbonated water, chilled
½ pint Cherry Heering
½ pint Cointreau
1 pint brandy
2 bottles champagne, chilled
1 cup sugar, or to taste
Fruit in season, for garnish

◆

Just before serving, combine all the ingredients except the fruit. Pour the punch over a block of ice in a punch bowl, and garnish with strawberries, slices of orange or lemon, or other fruit.
  Serves about 40

The stately Pendennis Club of Louisville.

CHARLOTTESVILLE WEDDING PUNCH

◆◆◆

*L*ike most punches, this Deep South wedding punch is a bit on the sweet side, but it has a charming Old World flavor. But go easy—it is potent. A good time will be had by all.

◆

4 pounds fresh pineapple, cut into small cubes and chilled

6 cups fresh orange juice (about 18 oranges), chilled

4½ cups fresh lemon juice (36 lemons), chilled

5 quarts dry white wine, chilled

3 quarts carbonated water, chilled, or more to taste

1½ pints white rum

4 cups sugar, or to taste

8 bottles champagne, chilled

◆

1. Ladle the pineapple into a large bowl. Add the orange and lemon juice, white wine, carbonated water, rum, and sugar. Mix thoroughly.

2. Put blocks of ice in several punch bowls. Divide the punch evenly among the bowls. Add the champagne just before serving.

Makes 200 cups

This recipe may be divided in half. Just be sure all the ingredients are well chilled.

MAY WINE

◆◆◆

*T*his is the true *Waldmeister,* or May wine. I liked to serve this charming punch for May weddings or receptions. Sweet woodruff, with its beautiful white blossoms, grew abundantly in the gardens on the upper River Road, and I would place clusters of it around the base of the punch bowl.

Southern belle Bette Davis toasts assembled guests, who include Henry Fonda (top right) and George Brent (top left), in the 1938 film Jezebel.

◆

3 bottles chilled white wine (not too dry)

Large handful of sweet woodruff, blossoms and all

◆

Pour the wine into a large bowl. Add the sweet woodruff and marinate for 20 to 25 minutes. Sieve out the sweet woodruff or strain the wine, and pour it over a block of ice in a punch bowl. Garnish with 2 or 3 sprigs of sweet woodruff blossoms.

Serves 8 to 10

THE BEST OF MINT JULEPS

*I*t has long been debated whether the mint julep belongs to Virginia or Kentucky, but we think Kentucky has an edge on the controversy. There are myriads of recipes for this traditional Southern drink, but Henry Watterson, the famous editor of the *Courier-Journal* two generations ago, can still stand as the ultimate authority on the best of all mint juleps:

Pluck the mint gently from "its bed, just as the dew of the evening is about to form upon it. Select the choicer sprigs only, but do not rinse them. Prepare the simple syrup, and measure out a half-tumbler of aged bourbon. Pour the whiskey into a well-frosted silver cup full of ice with several sprigs of mint—just to sniff the fragrance. Throw the simple syrup away."

The Cow Horn Club, shown in 1901, was made up of Civil War veterans who blew a cow horn in order to gather and drink mint juleps. They appear to have met often!

CHAMPAGNE AND ROSE WINE PUNCH

*O*ne of the most elegant of punches.

1 bottle champagne, chilled
2 bottles rosé wine, chilled
Gardenias, for garnish

Combine the champagne and the rosé in a chilled punch bowl, silver if possible. Let 2 or 3 gardenias float on top. Very beautiful.
Serves 15 to 20

A MARYLAND SUMMER COOLER

A refreshing tall drink for an afternoon party on a hot, muggy day.

1¼ quarts perfect strawberries, rinsed
6 ripe peaches
¾ cup sugar, or more to taste
3 bottles white wine, chilled

1 quart carbonated water, chilled
Fresh mint, for garnish

1. Hull the strawberries and cut them in half. Peel the peaches and cut them up. Combine the peaches and strawberries, add the sugar, and mix well.

2. Put the fruit in a large punch bowl containing a block of ice. Add the white wine and mix thoroughly. Allow it to mellow for 5 to 10 minutes.

3. Add the carbonated water, mix thoroughly, and taste for sweetness. Place a sprig of mint in each glass, and fill with punch.

Serves 20

A WEDDING BRUNCH

Champagne

Chicken and Ham Puff Paste Pocketbooks

Warm Asparagus Salad with Mustard Dressing

◆

Florentine Lemon Cream

Chocolate Whispers

Coffee

THE PALM BEACH COOLER

A beautiful summer cooler for a luncheon or afternoon tea. A fruity California wine, not too dry, is fine here.

6 thin orange slices, seeded
6 thin lemon slices, seeded
2 cups cubed fresh pineapple
Sugar to taste
2 bottles white wine, chilled
Fresh mint, for garnish

1. Combine the orange, lemon, and pineapple in a large bowl. Add sugar to taste.

2. Add the white wine and stir well. Pour into tall glasses filled with ice, and garnish with sprigs of mint. Pass the sugar.

Serves 15

WASSAIL CUP

F or an after-the-theater party before the supper is served or for any cold night when you are resting by a glowing fire with a few friends.

1 cup sugar
2 cups water
4 sticks cinnamon
6 whole cloves
2 lemons, thinly sliced and seeded
1½ bottles red wine

spices in a saucepan and boil 4 to 5 minutes.

2. Add the lemon slices. Cut off the heat, cover, and steep 8 to 10 minutes.

3. Add the red wine and heat it, but do not allow it to boil. Strain the punch and pour it into mugs or glasses. (Put a silver spoon in each glass to absorb the heat before adding the hot wassail.)

Serves 8

1. Combine the sugar, water, and

KENTUCKY EGGNOG

*C*ookies to go with punches must not be overly sweet or rich. Chocolate Parfait Wafers (see Index), or nut cookies, balance the flavor of a good eggnog.

12 large eggs, separated
1¼ cups sugar, or to taste
1 quart milk, chilled
1 quart heavy or whipping cream, chilled
1 fifth aged bourbon
1 cup cognac or brandy
Freshly grated nutmeg, for garnish

1. Beat the egg yolks until they are light and fluffy. Add the sugar, and continue beating until the sugar has dissolved and the mixture is again light and fluffy. Chill at least 1 hour.
2. Add the milk and cream to the chilled yolks, and set over a bowl of ice. Add the bourbon and cognac or brandy very, very slowly (or the eggs will curdle).
3. Beat the egg whites until they are stiff, and fold them in. Sprinkle with freshly grated nutmeg.
   Serves 20

VARIATION: Float whipped cream flavored with Jamaican rum on top of the punch.

The quality and proof of the bourbon and cognac or brandy do matter. The

An engraving of an eggnog party held in the South at Christmastime in 1870.

flavor comes through the eggs and cream just as clearly as in any mixed drink.

When making eggnog in smaller batches, allow 1½ to 2 jiggers bourbon and 1½ tablespoons sugar to each egg.

All liqueurs and spirits containing alcohol will curdle eggs if they are not added very slowly. The mixture must be kept cold or it will separate.

OLD SEELBACH HOUSE EGGNOG

*T*he students' favorite, and mine.

12 large eggs
1 cup sugar, or to taste
2 cups heavy or whipping cream, or more to
    taste
1½ quarts milk, chilled
1 fifth brandy or cognac
Freshly grated nutmeg, for garnish

1. Separate the eggs, and refrigerate the whites.
2. Beat the yolks with the sugar until the sugar has almost dissolved. (It will finish dissolving when the cream is added.) Add the cream and mix thoroughly. Add the milk.
3. Pour the brandy or cognac very

*The interior of Seelbach's Restaurant, Louisville,
where many a delicious cup of eggnog was downed.*

slowly into the yolk mixture, stirring gently. Chill the mixture 2 or 3 hours in the refrigerator.

4. Just before serving, beat the egg whites until stiff. Fold them into the chilled mixture, and sprinkle with nutmeg.

Serves 10 to 12

VARIATION: Use half aged bourbon and half brandy.

IRISH COFFEE

Irish whiskey
Hot coffee
Sugar
Whipped cream

Pour 2 ounces of Irish whiskey into a coffee cup or Irish coffee glass. Add hot coffee to ½ inch below the rim, sweeten to taste, and spoon whipped cream on top.

COFFEE ICE

A beautiful finale to a delicious meal.

1 cup sugar
2 cups water
1 cup extra-strong brewed coffee
2 tablespoons coffee liqueur
Whipped cream, for garnish

1. Combine the sugar and water in a saucepan and cook over low heat until the sugar has dissolved. Add the coffee.

2. Freeze the mixture in an ice tray until mushy, 3 to 4 hours.

3. Serve in stemmed glasses or demitasse cups with a generous spoonful of coffee liqueur. Top with whipped cream.

Serves 6

*I*f you would start the day in good humor, what will surpass a good breakfast and a cup of hot coffee?

"This little bean is the source of happiness and wit," said Dr. William Harvey, the noted English physician, speaking of coffee in a prophetic mood in 1657. (Coffee was considered a medicine in those days and was carried in the doctor's kit.) He bequeathed 56 pounds of coffee beans (a rare gift at that time) to the London College of Physicians, directing that his friends gather once a month to drink coffee in his memory.

CHECK POINTS FOR PERFECT COFFEE

*W*hich brand of coffee is best? The brand that tastes best to you, but pick the grind that is right for your type of coffee maker. For a percolator, use regular grind; for a drip pot, drip grind; for a vacuum-style coffee maker, use drip or fine grind.

The grind is important because coffee must be fine enough for the water to circulate freely so as to extract the flavor. If coffee is too coarse, it permits water to pass through too quickly, resulting in underextraction. Good coffee is a clear, rich brown.

Whether you like a rich or mild blend of coffee, good coffee must be made full strength. Coffee cannot be "stretched."

Use fresh coffee. It will keep fresh for about a week when the container is kept tightly closed in a cool, dry place, such as the refrigerator. Try to buy coffee in amounts that can be used within a week after opening.

Water, too, should be fresh. Freshly drawn cold water is preferred for making coffee because hot water pipes often have mineral deposits which affect coffee's flavor.

For each serving of coffee, you need 1 coffee measure or 2 level measuring tablespoons of coffee and ¾ cup (6 fluid ounces) of water. This makes a strong full-bodied coffee.

When making coffee for a crowd, use ½ pound of coffee and 4 quarts of water for 20 servings; 1 pound of coffee and 8 quarts of water for 40 servings. (These proportions apply to all brewing methods, all coffee makers, automatic or not.)

When You Brew Coffee: Start with a clean coffee maker, never brewing less than three-fourths of the coffee maker's capacity. For lesser quantities, use a smaller coffeepot. If your coffee maker isn't automatic, timing is important. When using a percolator on a burner, the usual perking time for best results is from 6 to 8 minutes.

The Drip Pot: Boiling water trickles slowly through the coffee grounds and extracts the full coffee essence: Preheat the pot by rinsing it with very hot water. Measure drip-grind coffee into the filter section. Place the upper container over the filter section. Measure fresh boiling water into the upper container. Cover. When dripping is completed, remove the upper section. Stir the brew, and serve.

The Vacuum Coffee Maker: Steam from boiling water creates pressure which forces most of the water up into the top bowl, where it gently bubbles through the coffee grounds. When the lower bowl cools, a vacuum is created that pulls the brew through a filter into the lower bowl. Measure fresh cold water into the lower bowl. Place it on the heat. Place the filter in the upper bowl. Add fine or drip-grind coffee. When the water boils, reduce the heat or turn off the electricity. Insert the upper bowl with a slight twist. Let the water rise into the upper bowl.

Stir the brew well, and remove it from the heat. It should return to the lower bowl in no more than 3 minutes. When the brew has returned to the lower bowl, remove the upper bowl, and serve.

The Percolator: Water bubbles up through a tube, spraying gently over the coffee grounds. As it seeps through the grounds, the flavor is extracted. Measure fresh cold water into the percolator. Place it on the heat until the water boils. Remove it from the heat, and measure regular-grind coffee into the basket. Insert the basket into the percolator, cover, and return to gentle heat. Percolate slowly 6 to 8 minutes. (Note: The water level should always be below the bottom of the coffee basket.) Remove the coffee basket, and serve.

For Demitasse Coffee: Brew coffee by any of the three basic methods, but make it half again as strong as regular coffee. For three 4-ounce servings, you would use 3 coffee measures (6 tablespoons) of coffee to 1½ cups of water.

When You Serve Coffee: Coffee is at its peak of flavor immediately after brewing. Try to serve it then, freshly brewed and piping hot. If coffee must stand before serving, hold it at serving temperature by placing the pot (non-automatic) in a pan of hot water or over very low heat. Important: Never boil coffee after it has brewed. Boiling ruins coffee's flavor.

When You Clean Your Coffee Maker: A clean coffee maker is essential to good coffee. After each use, wash all the parts in hot water, using a light-duty detergent. Rinse thoroughly with clear water. Before using the pot again, scald it with boiling water. From time to time, disassemble all parts and scrub each thoroughly, using a narrow brush to clean hard-to-reach places.

CAFE BRULOT

---

*T*his is the coffee that became famous in New Orleans long ago, and it is still fun.

A coffee stand in New Orleans's French Market, 1883.

1½ cups cognac
12 cubes sugar
3 pieces (1 inch each) cinnamon stick

12 whole cloves
Grated peel of 1 orange
Grated peel of ½ lemon
2½ cups hot, strong brewed coffee

---

1. In the blazer of a chafing dish or in a brûlot bowl, combine the cognac, sugar, cinnamon sticks, cloves, and the orange and lemon peels. Heat the mixture gently until the cognac is warmed through. Carefully ignite the cognac and let the flame burn for a few seconds.

2. While it is still flaming, add the hot coffee. Ladle the Café Brûlot into warm demitasse cups as soon as the flame subsides.

Serves 12

VARIATION: Café Diable: Omit the cinnamon sticks.

VIRGINIA COFFEE SYLLABUB

A Colonial Virginia drink that was served at the Governor's Palace in Williamsburg.

1½ cups strong brewed coffee, chilled
1 cup heavy or whipping cream
½ cup milk
1 cup aged bourbon whiskey
¼ cup sugar, or to taste

1. Combine the coffee, cream, milk, and whiskey in a glass or china mixing bowl. Beat the mixture with a rotary beater until it is well blended. Sweeten to taste, and chill thoroughly, about 1 hour in the freezer.

2. Beat the syllabub again before pouring it into small cups or sherry glasses.

Serves 8

COFFEE PUNCH

◆◆◆

*A*favorite for weddings, anniversaries, and debut parties.

6 cups heavy or whipping cream
4 quarts fresh extra-strong brewed coffee, chilled
5 tablespoons sugar
2 quarts vanilla ice cream
1 tablespoon vanilla extract

1. Whip 2 cups of the cream.
2. Combine the coffee, sugar, remaining cream, the ice cream, and vanilla. Stir, and garnish with the whipped cream.

Serves 30

VARIATION: Add 4 to 5 tablespoons brandy or cognac.

Back in the innocent old days when coffee and children could be featured together in an advertisement.

CHILLED MOCHA COFFEE

◆◆◆

6 ounces unsweetened chocolate
1 cinnamon stick
4 cups strong hot brewed coffee
Cream and sugar to taste

1. Heat the chocolate with the cinnamon stick in a deep pan over hot water. Add the hot coffee and stir well. Strain, and discard the cinnamon.
2. Pour the coffee over ice in glasses. Pass the cream and sugar.

Serves 4

CAFE ROYALE

◆◆◆

Cognac
Hot coffee
Lumps of sugar

Float 1 tablespoon cognac on a cup of hot coffee. Put a lump of sugar in a tablespoon, fill the spoon with heated cognac, and ignite the spirit. Carefully lower the spoon with the blazing cognac into the coffee, and stir gently until the flame subsides.

ICED COFFEE

Chill fresh, extra-strong brewed coffee. Serve it over coffee ice cubes in tall glasses. Serve cream and sugar and allow each guest to season the coffee to taste.

COFFEE CUBES

*A*llow freshly made, extra-strong coffee to chill. Pour into ice cube trays and freeze. Use in coffee drinks and punches instead of plain ice.

ICED TEA CONCENTRATE

1½ quarts freshly drawn cold water
¼ pound black tea
Sugar to taste
Lemon to taste

1. Bring the water to a full boil. Remove from the heat. Add the tea, cover, and steep 5 minutes.

2. To serve, strain the concentrate into 5 quarts cold water (not ice water). Serve in ice-filled glasses with sugar and lemon if desired.

Makes 6 quarts, diluted; 30 to 35 servings

Tea for a crowd can be made a few hours ahead, but it will taste stale if brewed too far ahead.

TO MAKE PERFECT TEA

*U*se black tea. To make the best tea, use a teapot, as it helps to keep the water hot during the brewing period. This brings out the flavor of the tea.

Start with freshly drawn cold water from the tap. Never use reheated water or water from the hot water tap.

Allow the water to come to a rolling boil, then pour it over the tea at once. Do not allow the water to boil even 5 minutes.

Only boiling water extracts the finest and fullest flavor from tea leaves.

Sparkling clear, amber tea poured hot over a tall, thin glass brimful of ice is beautiful. And what could taste better on a muggy, hot day? Hot tea poured over ice is a charming and delicious way—the best way—to make iced tea, but it does require more ice.

Use up to 50 percent more tea for iced tea than for hot tea, to allow for the melting ice. Tea can always be diluted with fresh water if desired. For example: For 4 cups of hot tea, use 4 teaspoons loose tea or 4 tea bags. For iced tea, use 5 or 6 teaspoons, or 5 or 6 tea bags.

Never boil water for tea in aluminum. Use an enameled, stainless, or heatproof glass pan.

If the water has been allowed to boil even 5 minutes, it may make cloudy tea. Water must be used immediately as soon as it boils. The concentration of chemicals and minerals in the water causes tea to cloud.

Do not put warm tea in the refrigerator, as it will cloud.

SPICED TEA

❖❖❖

*T*his is an excellent spiced tea, served hot or cold.

♦

4 cups freshly drawn cold water
4 tea bags
½ cup fresh orange juice
¼ cup fresh lemon juice
½ cup sugar, or to taste
3 pieces cinnamon stick, broken
16 whole cloves
6 lemon slices, for garnish

♦

1. Bring the water to a boil, pour it over the tea bags, and steep 5 minutes. Remove the tea bags.

2. Add the fruit juices, sugar, and spices. Keep warm and allow the flavors to ripen about 20 minutes.

3. Bring almost, but not quite, to a boil, and serve, garnished with lemon slices.

Serves 6

This recipe may be tripled, but use only 1¼ cups sugar.

AMBER ICED TEA

❖❖❖

Pour freshly drawn cold water over 4 to 8 tea bags in a quart jar. Set in the refrigerator at once. Allow to sit 9 to 12 hours, according to the strength you desire. This tea will be clear. It is not as fine a brew as the one made correctly with boiling water, but some people find it easier.

HOT CHOCOLATE

❖❖❖

*T*he different brands of semisweet chocolate may vary somewhat in sweetness, so add the sugar to your taste.

♦

3 cups milk
1 cup water
6 ounces semisweet chocolate, coarsely chopped
2 teaspoons sugar
Whipped cream, for garnish

♦

Combine the milk, water, and chocolate in a heavy saucepan. (The pan must be heavy, to prevent burning; or heat the mixture over hot water or in a double boiler.) Add the sugar, and heat until piping hot. Serve garnished with whipped cream.

Serves 4

♦

THE ULTIMATE HOT CHOCOLATE

*T*he taste of orange in Grand Marnier is marvelous with chocolate.

Make Hot Chocolate, but use only 4 ounces semisweet chocolate. Add 1 tablespoon Grand Marnier to each cup chocolate. Season the whipped cream with a hint of the liqueur. Serve with hot croissants, or your favorite homemade bread, or butter cookies. Live.

INDEX
AND
CREDITS

INDEX

Stuffings:
almond, 166
autumn catch, 203–204
bread and almond, 203
bread and herb, classic,
203
crabmeat or shrimp,
Pontchartrain, 205
herb, 165
mushroom, 203
oyster, Maryland shore,
204
Pontchartrain, with
capers, 205
pork, flavorful, 139
woodland mushrooms,
ham, and olives,
149–150
see also dressings
Succotash stew, 241
Suet pastry, 113–114
Sugar:
cake, North Carolina
Moravian, 298–299
caramelizing, 102
Summer savory, 49
Sweet:
rolls, country inn,
300–301
and tender pork cream
sauce, 142
and tender pork roast,
141–142
Sweet basil, 49, 70
Sweetbread(s):
ham, and mushroom
filling, 429
preparing, 84
with tarragon chicken
salad, warm, 83–84
Sweet marjoram, 49, 70, 112
Sweet potato(es):
deep-fried, 262–263
with lemon, 264
mashed, 264–265
soufflé, 263
see also yams
Swiss chard almondine,
250–251
Syrup:
apricot, 442
brown sugar, cinnamon,
and walnut, 440
simple bar, 446
waffle and pancake, 441

T

Talmadge Farm barbecue
sauce, 138
Tangy mustard vinaigrette,
88–89
Tarragon, 112, 163
asparagus, 231
asparagus and, soufflé,
231
aspic, breast of chicken in,
82–83
calves' liver with bacon
and, 122–123
chicken liver pâté with,
25–26
chicken with sweetbread
salad, warm, 83–84
dressed eggs with, special,
26
-egg dressing, 91
French, 49, 70
fresh, shrimp with, 208
hollandaise, 229
jumbo shrimp and wild
rice with, 207–208
leek and oyster soup,
42–43
lemon, and chive sauce,
164
and mustard hollandaise,
103
potato, and artichoke
salad, 77
veal birds with, elegant,
123–124
vinegar, 89
Tartar sauce:
with capers, 192
with dill, 192
Tarts:
chess and apple,
Maryland's, 380
upside-down fruit
pudding, 354–355
Tea:
amber iced, 453
concentrate, iced, 452
spiced, 453
to make perfect, 452
Tea bread, Williamsburg,
305
Teals:
Florida blue-winged,
braised, 175–176

green-winged, roast, with
wild rice, 177
Tennessee sour cream
cornbread, 163
Thick cheese sauce, 19
Thousand Island dressing, 96
Thyme, 49, 70, 112, 172
rabbit simmered in red
wine and, 186–187
Tidewater feather rolls, 286
Toast(s):
charlotte, 69
cornmeal melba, 284
grilled buttered, 217
Toasted and buttered bread
crumbs, 251
Toasting nuts, 268
Tomato(es):
baked, perfect, 252
baked corn and, 241
baked stuffed, 251
and basil sauce for
noodles, perfect
garden, 273–274
beef, and okra soup, 35
consommé, quick, 52
green, Southern fried,
252–253
mayonnaise, shrimp salad
with, 209–210
and okra stew, Creole,
246
sauce, elegant and easy,
122
stuffed, elegant, 85–86
stuffed with seafood and
rice, 86
Tongue, corned, 114–115
Top-secret barbecue sauce,
188
Torte, almond meringue,
with strawberries, 403
Trappist bread, 278–279
with nuts, 278
with prunes, 278
Treviso, 66
Trout à la Marguery,
195–196
Truffles:
about, 424
champagne, 425
Kentucky bourbon,
423–424
Turkey, 166–172
with oysters and
mushrooms,

Y

Z

PHOTOGRAPHY CREDITS

◆◆◆

APPETIZERS

Pages 13, 28: Florida State Archives; page 15: Courtesy Antoine's Restaurant; pages 19, 27: Caufield & Shook Collection, University of Louisville Photographic Archives; page 21: Illinois Central Gulf Railroad; page 23: Courtesy Arnaud's Restaurant; page 24: The Peale Museum, Baltimore, Md.; page 26: Courtesy Georgia Department of Archives and History; page 29: The Mariners' Museum, Newport News, Va.; page 30: Maryland Historical Society, Baltimore.

SOUPS

Page 33: Florida State Archives; page 35: Maryland Historical Society, Baltimore; page 37: Ohlinger's Movie Material Store, Inc.; pages 39, 58: USDA Photo; page 40: Picture Collection, New York Public Library; pages 41, 42: Photo from C. Frank Dunn Collection, courtesy KHS Library; page 43: The Peale Museum, Baltimore, Md.; pages 46, 51: Courtesy The Historic New Orleans Collection; page 50: H. Armstrong Roberts; page 53: Alabama State Department of Archives and History; page 55: The Historical Association of Southern Florida; page 60: Standard Oil of N.J. Collection, University of Louisville Photographic Archives; page 61: Pensacola Historical Society; page 62: Caufield & Shook Collection, University of Louisville Photographic Archives.

SALADS AND SALAD DRESSINGS

Pages 63, 73: Florida State Archives; page 65: Kentucky Historical Society; pages 74, 82: The Charleston Museum, Charleston, S.C.; pages 77, 86: Caufield & Shook Collection, University of Louisville Photographic Archives; pages 79, 90: USDA Photo; page 81: Department of Travel Development, Frankfort, Ky.; page 85: The Virginia Historical Society; pages 87, 92: Courtesy The Historic New Orleans Collection; page 93: Culver Pictures; page 95: Courtesy KHS Library.

MEATS

Pages 97, 136: Special Collections, Hill Memorial Library, Louisiana State University Libraries, Baton Rouge; page 100: Culver Pictures; pages 102, 138, 143, 149: Courtesy The Historic New Orleans Collection; page 107: Kentucky Library, Western Kentucky University; page 110: R. G. Potter Collection, University of Louisville Photographic Archives; pages 112, 125, 144: Florida State Archives; page 117: Index of American Design, National Gallery of Art, Washington, D.C.; pages 120, 121, 133, 150: Caufield & Shook Collection, University of Louisville Photographic Archives; page 126: Photo from Wolff, Gretter, Cusick Collection, courtesy KHS Library; page 127: Photo Delmore A. Wenzel, The Colonial Williamsburg Foundation; page 129: Camille Glenn; page 131: Courtesy Georgia Department of Archives and History; page 140: Maryland Historical Society, Baltimore; page 146: Courtesy Seessel's, Memphis, Tenn.; page 147: Arthur Y. Ford Albums, University of Louisville Photographic Archives.

POULTRY AND GAME

Pages 151, 186: Florida State Archives; page 155: Department of Travel Development, Frankfort, Ky.; pages 158, 160: Caufield & Shook Collection, University of Louisville Photographic Archives; page 163: R. C. Ballard Thruston Collection, The Filson Club, Louisville, Ky.; page 165: Camille Glenn; page 171: Bradley Studio Collection, University of Louisville Photographic Archives; page 172: Courtesy The Historic New Orleans Collection; pages 173, 182: Picture Collection, New York Public Library; page 174: Virginia Museum of Fine Arts; page 175: South Caroliniana Library, University of South Carolina; page 178: The Mariners' Museum, Newport News, Va.; pages 179, 187: Cook Collection, Valentine Museum, Richmond, Va.; pages 185, 188: Pensacola Historical Society.

FISH AND SHELLFISH

Page 189: The Henry Morrison Flagler Museum, Palm Beach, Fla.; pages 191, 197, 200, 204, 215, 221: The Mariners' Museum, Newport News, Va.; page 193: Florida State Archives; page 194: Pensacola Historical Society; page 195: Griswold Collection, University of Louisville Photographic Archives; page 199: Photo from Wolff, Gretter, Cusick Collection, courtesy KHS Library; page 202: The Charleston Museum, Charleston, S.C.; pages 207, 210, 218, 219: Courtesy The Historic New Orleans Collection; page 211: Standard Oil of N.J. Collection, University of Louisville Photographic Archives; page 213: Courtesy New Hanover County Museum.

VEGETABLES

Page 225: The Aubrey Bodine Collection, The Peale Museum, Baltimore, Md.; pages 227, 238, 244, 251: USDA Photo; page 230: Courtesy The Historic New Orleans Collection; page 236: Elemore Morgan, The Historic New Orleans Collection; page 240: R. G. Potter Collection, University of Louisville Photographic Archives; pages 241, 248: Kit Barry, Brattleboro, Vt.; page 242: University of Louisville Photographic Archives; page 245: Thomas Jefferson Memorial Foundation, Inc./James Tkatch; page 246: South Caroliniana Library, University of South Carolina.

POTATOES, RICE, AND NOODLES

Page 255: Courtesy New Hanover County Museum; page 257: Photo from Wolff, Gretter, Cusick Collection, courtesy KHS Library; page 259: Florida State Archives; page 261: The Peale Museum, Baltimore, Md.; page 263: Maryland Historical Society, Baltimore; pages 265, 267: Courtesy The Historic New Orleans Collection; page 266: Courtesy Georgia Department of Archives and History; page 273: Josephine Sacabo, The Historic New Orleans Collection.

BREADS

Pages 275, 286, 288, 304: Caufield & Shook Collection, University of Louisville Photographic Archives; pages 277, 303: Courtesy The Historic New Orleans

Collection; page 278: Index of American Design, National Gallery of Art, Washington, D.C.; page 281: R. G. Potter Collection, University of Louisville Photographic Archives; page 285: The Thomas Jefferson Memorial Foundation, Inc./James Tkatch; page 289: Manuscript Department, William R. Perkins Library, Duke University; page 291: Arthur Y. Ford Albums, University of Louisville Photographic Archives; page 292: Griswold Collection, University of Louisville Photographic Archives; page 295: The Peale Museum, Baltimore, Md.; page 299: Kit Barry, Brattleboro, Vt.; page 305: Florida State Archives.

PICKLES AND PRESERVES
Pages 307, 321, 332: Caufield & Shook Collection, University of Louisville Photographic Archives; pages 309, 313, 318, 333: Florida State Archives; page 310: From C. Frank Dunn Collection, courtesy KHS Library; page 312: Alabama State Department of Archives and History; page 314: H. Armstrong Roberts; page 315: Virginia State Library; page 317: Kit Barry, Brattleboro, Vt.; page 319: The Peale Museum, Baltimore, Md.; page 320: Bettmann Archive; page 322: National Gallery of Art, Washington, D.C.; page 325: Rona Beame; page 326: North Carolina Department of Archives; pages 328, 335: USDA Photo; page 330: Arthur Y. Ford Albums, University of Louisville Photographic Archives; page 331: R. G. Potter Collection, University of Louisville Photographic Archives; page 337: From the collections of Henry Ford Museum & Greenfield Village.

CAKES, COOKIES, AND PIES
Pages 339, 352, 369, 375: Caufield & Shook Collection, University of Louisville Photographic Archives; pages 341, 387: From Wolff, Gretter, Cusick Collection, courtesy KHS Library; page 343: Arthur Y. Ford Albums, University of Louisville Photographic Archives; page 345: The Historical Association of Southern Florida; pages 346, 373, 386: Florida State Archives; page 348: The Charleston Museum, Charleston, S.C.; page 349: R. G. Potter Collection, University of Louisville Photographic Archives; page 354: Courtesy Georgia Department of Archives and History; pages 355, 371: Courtesy The Historic New Orleans Collection; page 356: The Peale Museum, Baltimore, Md.; pages 358, 379: USDA Photo; page 360: Virginia Division of Tourism; page 361: Kit Barry, Brattleboro, Vt.; page 365: South Caroliniana Library, University of South Carolina; page 368: Pensacola Historical Society; page 372: Special Collections Division, University of Georgia

Libraries; page 380: Maryland Department of Economic and Community Development; page 381: Courtesy New Hanover County Museum; page 382: Carl Mydans, The Historic New Orleans Collection; page 385: Florida Department of Commerce.

DESSERTS AND CANDIES
Page 389: Griswold Collection, University of Louisville Photographic Archives; page 391: Valentine Museum, Richmond, Va.; page 392: South Caroliniana Library, University of South Carolina; pages 394, 419: Kit Barry, Brattleboro, Vt.; page 397: Arthur Y. Ford Albums, University of Louisville Photographic Archives; pages 398, 407, 415: Florida State Archives; page 400: Standard Oil of N.J. Collection, University of Louisville Photographic Archives; pages 402, 411, 422, 423, 426: Courtesy The Historic New Orleans Collection; page 404: Picture Collection, New York Public Library; page 406: Paris Trail, USDA Photo; page 408: USDA Photo; page 409: Florida State News Bureau; page 410: Maryland Historical Society, Baltimore; page 412: University of New Orleans; page 413: Cooper Collection, University of Louisville Photographic Archives; page 414: Courtesy Georgia Department of Archives and History; page 421: Bradley Studio Collection, University of Louisville Photographic Archives.

BRUNCHES, PUNCHES, COFFEES, AND TEAS
Page 427: Bradley Studio Collection, University of Louisville Photographic Archives; page 432: Office of Tourist Development, Maryland Department of Economics and Community Development; pages 433, 448: The Filson Club, Louisville, Ky.; page 435: Florida State Archives; page 436: Western Kentucky University; page 438: Thomas V. Miller, Jr.; pages 440, 447, 450: Courtesy The Historic New Orleans Collection; page 442: Index of American Design, National Gallery of Art, Washington, D.C.; page 443: Caufield & Shook Collection, University of Louisville Photographic Archives; page 444: Ohlinger's Movie Material Store, Inc.; page 445: Courtesy Georgia Department of Archives and History; page 451: Kit Barry, Brattleboro, Vt.

We wish to give special thanks to the Florida State Archives, The Mariners' Museum, The Historic New Orleans Collection, and The University of Louisville Photographic Archives for their gracious help.